He was placed before the police camera to-day and was also measured by the Bertillon system. This photograph gives his profile view. He was also photographed full face.

SPORTING SPECIAL

THE WEATHER—Cloudy to-night and Wednesday; variable winds.

NEW YORK JOURNAL

14 Pages W. R. HEARST **14 Pages**

NO. 8,420—P. M. NEW YORK, TUESDAY JUNE 26, 1906. ONE CENT.

ALIENISTS DECLARE
THAW
SANE

Millionaire Assassin of Stanford White Hurried to the Tombs Where Two Noted Physicians Examine Him. Beautiful Wife of the Prisoner at the Hotel Lorraine.

Harry K. Thaw, a prisoner in the Tombs, charged with the murder of Stanford White, the famous architect, was examined by three expert alienists this afternoon and pronounced sane.

The examination was made on behalf of the State, after Thaw's lawyers had declared that the young man is mentally irresponsible, and that the shooting of White was the result of a maniacal impulse.

It is the contention of the State that Thaw deliberately and with premeditation, took the life of the architect and that jealousy and revenge for wrong done by White to his beautiful young wife, formerly Evelyn Nesbit, were the motives.

The lawyers Carlos F. McDonaId, Austin Y. Flint and Tombs Physician McGuire conducted the examination in the Tombs. There was no record, apparently reticent and restless as also she was made of the prisoner.

The experts reported that Thaw is in excellent physical as well as mental condi-

THAW IS COMMITTED
TO TOMBS WITHOUT BAIL.

Thaw was committed without bail to the Tombs to await the inquest set for Thursday. On that day the case will be presented to the Grand Jury then, and he will in the direct for murder in the first degree.

His counsel have determined that penalty will be their last of defence and William Rand, Jr. former assistant District-Attorney, who is retained to assist in the cause of the Manhattan Square Garden.

Evelyn Nesbit Thaw has been in seclusion since the tragedy last night at the roof of the Madison Square Garden.

Continued on Sixth Page.

Continued on Sixth Page.

Split Over Street Cleaning Report.
OUST WOODBURY--IVINS

Majority of Aldermen on Investigating Committee Rejects Counsel's Recommendation.

William M. Ivins accuses the Aldermanic Spans Cleaning Investigating Committee, appointed his report and findings to the Aldermen to-day and after a survey considering the recommendations were rejected by the majority of the committee, and Mr. Ivins left the committee room in disgust.

Mr. Ivins was supporting by two members of the committee, Chairman Max S. Grifenhagen and Alderman T. W. S. Brown, both Republicans. Alderman Robert F. Downing, of Brooklyn, expressed himself as favoring all the recommendations of Mr. Ivins except that in regard to the removal of the Street Cleaning Commissioner Major Woodbury, to which he took exception and he held the committee that he would present a separate report.

Urges Woodbury's Removal.
Mr. Ivins's report makes twenty-one recommendations. Among them are those Which Commissioner Woodbury be requested from office for incompetence, inefficiency, favoritism, deception, neglect of duty, waste and maladministration and reduction of the bad administration.

That the Street Cleaning Department be reorganized under a new and competent Commissioner, and that a Deputy administrator be appointed by the Borough Superintendents.

That the Mayor require the Commissioner of Street Cleaning to adopt a new and simpler system of accounting.

That the Bureau of trucks or scavengers without of the department, the offenses against its rules be amended so that these may be imposed only after trial.

That the Commissioners be required to comply with the provisions of the law that the penalties for the purchase of supplies in horses exceeding $1,000.

That the present system of more frequent be abandoned and that contracts be let on the basis of actual tonnage of dirt.

Subornate Report by Downing.
Alderman Dowling, the minority member of the committee, who says he was not admitted by the other members of the committee in the framing of their report, has subscribed to the Board of Aldermen a minority report, setting several recommendations indeed, the chief important of which are:

The appointment of Deputy commissioners to the Mayor and Brooklyn, the elimination of the chief of squads in the scavenger, which has to do with the expense of employees who are fired, and also recommends that the question of snow removal be reconsidered to be framed of the changes in the budget.

"Commissioner Woodbury," it was stated, "did not reduce, who says he was not admitted by the other members of the investigating committee. By rejecting the Woodbury's phase plan, and should not be held this afternoon. He was able to authorize called in choice this afternoon, who was not agree respect.

GERMANS TRAPPED AND MASSACRED IN AFRICA.

BERLIN, June 26.—Advices received at the War Office to-day state that the rebels in German East Africa ambushed and massacred the staff of Sergeant G. B. White, together with thirty-five native attendants and bearers in the District of Tomas on July 1.

The major of the expedition reached the governor of the District to-day.

White's body when found was terribly mutilated. The body was conspicuous only by the gold filled teeth. The bodies of five others who were also mutilated.

SUES N. Y. LIFE
FOR DIVIDENDS

A suit has been brought in the Supreme Court by Justus Ray Baum, a lawyer who holds a $10,000 life policy in the New York Life Insurance Company, against the company to make a full and proper accounting of all surplus moneys in its possession and apportion the same to policy holders similarly situated, including the plaintiff who may be entitled thereto.

The plaintiff also asks that the surplus issued by the company be reckoned so as to make these contracts in the provisions of the insurance law.

American "Want" Popularity Told in Want Ad. Gains

Still piling up—the Gains in AMERICAN Want Ads.

Last week's record reads like this:

Help Wanted—Male 47½% Gain
Help Wanted—Female 26½% Gain
Real Estate 17% Gain
Furnished Rooms to Let 21½% Gain
Business Opportunities 45% Gain

Returns and Gains Go Hand in Hand.

Sunday American Circulation Over 800,000.

Moves to Save Niagara

WASHINGTON, June 26.—The House to-day adopted the concurrent report on the bill to regulate the use of the waters of Niagara Falls in order to preserve its great beauty.

BIG TRUCK AND TROLLEY CAR IN CRASH.
6 HURT ON BRIDGE

Passengers in Panic and Women Leap from Platforms—Reserves Are Called.

Six persons were seriously injured in a collision between a huge truck and a trolley car on the Brooklyn Bridge to-day. The injured were:

ERNEST ROGERS, thirty-one, of No. 53 Fulton place, Brooklyn. Contusions of the abdomen, and abrasions of the legs and back.

LOUIS FILELLA, thirty-two, of No. 106 Lewis street, Brooklyn. A deep contusion on the right arm and face.

NATHAN HARTHA, fifty-two, of No. 289 Knickerbocker avenue. Contusions of the body and several bruises.

All the injured were taken to the Brooklyn Hospital.

A Police reserve call, crowded with firemen, was passing the head immediately beyond the Brooklyn roadway, when a huge white giant truck belonging to Joseph H. Frechter, of No. 160 Fulton street, and driven by Jacob Clauser, of No. 157 Degraw avenue, crashed and crossed into the rear of the car. For some time there was a scene of the wildest confusion. Many women jumped from the car and a panic prevailed. The driver, who arrested, the truck was completely destroyed, the trolley car proceeded on its way.

Press Time News Bulletins

MRS. EVELYN NESBIT THAW IS CALLED
TO THE DISTRICT ATTORNEY'S OFFICE.

Assistant District Attorney Nott telephoned this afternoon to Lewis Delafield, of counsel for Harry K. Thaw, requesting him to bring Mrs. Evelyn Nesbit Thaw to the District Attorney's office.

Mr. Delafield replied that he would produce young Mrs. Thaw before the District Attorney's office closed this afternoon.

WOMAN FOUND DEAD FROM STARVATION.
The body of a woman was found in High Bridge Park, opposite 174th street, to-day by Policeman Grat.

Ambulance Surgeon Bernstein, of the Washington Heights Hospital, said she had starved herself to death. She was seen half crawling into the park early to-day by Edward Burns, a newspaper man, while on his way to his place of business.

The woman was about forty years of age and wore a black waist, a black silk skirt and a white straw hat with a black band. The body was taken to the Morgue.

HOUSE PASSES THE "PORK" BILL.
Washington, June 26.—The House to-day passed without amendment the Omnibus Public Buildings Bill carrying appropriations totaling $21,051,000.

SKULL FRACTURED IN AUTO RACE.
Paris, June 26.—A message received here from the scene of the Grand Automobile Prize race says that Du Calera, who was driving an Italian machine, was thrown from the car and sustained a fractured skull.

RACING RESULTS AT SHEEPSHEAD BAY.
First—Prince Hamburg, Sr Lynnwood, Cinna.

NEWS EDITING

Second Edition

Bruce H. Westley
University of Kentucky

HOUGHTON
MIFFLIN
COMPANY
BOSTON

New York
Atlanta
Geneva, Ill.
Dallas
Palo Alto

Contents

Preface

This revision is long overdue. While the continued acceptance of the First Edition suggests that the book must have been filling a need, it has been out of date for many years. Editing skills and techniques have not changed in fundamental ways since the First Edition appeared in 1953. But the environment in which editing is done is changing rapidly, and, I believe, a new breed of editor is emerging. It is to this company of professionals and the ones who will follow them that this revision is dedicated.

How are they different from the green-eyeshade brigade of fifteen or twenty years ago? My guess is that they are younger, better educated, more aware of the research being done in their field, and, I hope, far better attuned to the great issues that threaten the stability of American society—more aware of the general need for change in it and more aware of the particular changes that will have to be made in our communication institutions if it is to survive. Among these institutions is the daily-newspaper copy desk and the way it meets its responsibility to make a significant intelligence more accessible and more meaningful to the whole population.

It won't make it any easier on the news professional to have to adapt his basic skills to the new technology that is emerging at the same time. What the editor does now with a copy pencil on a scrap of newsprint he may soon be doing with a stylus on the screen of a computerized editing console. The difficulty is that nobody can be sure what final form the technological revolution will take. Twenty years ago the process was just beginning, with the teletypesetter making its presence felt in the newsroom. At that time, some colleagues were predicting the doom of the copy desk. But automatic linecasting did not have any real effect on the role and function of the editor, at least not on newspapers that care about and can afford quality. The production revolution will probably cut deeper as it goes on, but the effect will be the same: it will change the lives of editors, but it will not replace them. In fact, it may even give them an opportunity to work toward their professional goals more effectively than before.

It is not easy for a textbook writer to be caught in the middle of such a revolution. Shall he stick to the tried and true or shall he wing off into the blue sky? What I chose to do was to attempt to convey to the student contemporary newsroom practice in all its variation while at the same time pointing to new directions and giving some indication of where technical and production change is leading us. I also attempted to represent some of the research literature that has poured forth in the last fifteen to twenty years and to apply it where it was relevant. For the new breed of desk man is professional enough to know that what he knows isn't enough.

In the acknowledgment department, I want to thank my colleagues around the country for their great patience with my procrastination, even those who sent holiday greetings in this form: "Merry Christmas, Happy New Year, and When Are You Going to Revise Your Book?" Here it is, at last.

While I, of course, take full responsibility for what is said here, I wish to express my gratitude to William B. Blankenburg and Dwight L. Teeter, two former colleagues at the University of Wisconsin School of Journalism, who gave close reading to all or part of this revision and whose advice and help were of particular value. The same may be said of Penelope Hull of the Educational Division of Houghton Mifflin, who in the course of her editing taught the author a thing or two. My wife Rosemary helped in a thousand ways, as usual.

I am particularly grateful to Mr. Joseph W. Freudenberger, editor of The Gannetteer, who helped me get illustrations from a number of newspapers in the Gannett Group, and to Mr. Emmett Dedmon, vice-president and editorial director of the Chicago Sun-Times and the Chicago Daily News, who gave permission to reprint as Appendix A (pages 361–375) the style sheet shared by those two fine newspapers.

I am also grateful for favors of one kind or another extended by the following: Harry Amon, photo editor of the Louisville Times and the Louisville Courier-Journal; Jim Ausenbaugh, Kentucky editor of the Courier-Journal; Tom Briggs, publisher of the Macon (Missouri) Chronicle Herald; Thomas P. Dolan, publisher of the Courier-News of Plainfield, New Jersey; Roy E. DuFour, manager of the research and promotion departments of the Sun-Telegraph of San Bernardino, California; J. A. Geladas, managing editor of the Telegraph-Herald of Dubuque, Iowa; George Gill, managing editor of the Louisville Courier-Journal; Larry Hale, assistant managing editor of the Binghamton (New York) Press; John P. Hamilton, assistant editor of the Rutland (Vermont) Herald; Coit Hendley, Jr., editor of the Camden Courier-Post; Stephen E. Hills, assistant promotion manager of Newsday, Garden City, Long Island; G. J. Iacomino of Fairchild Graphic Equipment; Erwin Jaffee, director of the ANPA Research Center, Easton, Pennsylvania; James H. Jesse, general manager of Gannett Florida Newspapers; Frank E. Johnson, managing editor of the Arizona Daily Star; Tom Keane, picture editor of the Evening Journal of Wilmington, Delaware; Fred Keesing, photo editor, Courier-News, Plainfield, New Jersey; Frank Leeming, director of public affairs for the St. Louis Post-Dispatch; Ted Leyte, co-publisher, The Paper, Oshkosh, Wisconsin; James C. MacDonald, who at the time was editor of the Toledo Blade; Frank Malloy, applications engineer for the Compugraphic Corporation of Wilmington, Massachusetts; Bill Moyers, at that time publisher of Newsday; Malcolm Merritt, editor, ANPA/RI Bulletin; Hamilton Mizer, publisher of the Gazette of Niagara Falls, New York; Raymond A. Moucha, editor, The Paper; George Ridge, editor, The Arizona Journalist; John H. Sengstacke, publisher, the Chicago Defender; John M. Slocum, personnel manager, the Hartford (Connecticut) Times; Howard B. Taylor, editorial consultant to the Copley newspapers, with headquarters in La Jolla, California; Margareta Tegnemark of the Swedish Information Service; and Jerry Walker, managing editor of Editor & Publisher.

1

The News Editor

In any medium of communication, someone serves as a final "gate keeper," a key decision maker who is responsible for determining what will and what will not be communicated, and sees to it that what goes out is in a finished condition.[1] The gate keepers on the daily newspaper are the news editor and the copy editors who work under his supervision. That is what this book is all about—the role and function of the newspaper's news editors in selecting and shaping the content of the newspaper press.

Newbold Noyes, editor of the Washington *Star,* put it this way: "The quality of every newspaper depends on the desk people. The desk is the heart of the newspaper. The character of a newspaper is determined by its desk."

Journalism students and perhaps the public in general have a tendency to overrate the reportorial function. That is entirely understandable, for the reporter is the newspaper representative the public *sees.* In mythology, if not in fact, he is the movie character with the fearless approach, the loud voice and manner, the porkpie hat, the dangling cigarette. Furthermore, his work frequently carries his by-line in print at the top of the story. He appears on camera and is in demand as a television interviewer. The reporter has a chance, at least, to become a public personality.

The copy-desk role is anonymous. "The man in the green eyeshade" is virtually unknown to the public, his job often underestimated in the newspaper office itself. A volunteer escort taking some visitors through

---

[1] David Manning White first applied Kurt Lewin's "gate-keeper" concept to the flow of information to and through the newspaper copy desk. See "The 'Gate-Keeper' ": A Case Study in the Selection of News," *Journalism Quarterly,* 27:383–390 (Fall 1950).

a New York newsroom hesitated at the copy desk. "This is where they write headlines and—fix things," he said.[2]

There is no intention here to underestimate the importance of the reporter. A great newspaper is an impossibility without great reporters. No newspaper, no matter how brilliantly presented, can be any better than the quality of its reporting: the way its facts are gathered, checked, and written up. That is the most important single ingredient of the press. But bad editing can nullify good reporting. And bad copy-desk management can take the edge off brilliant news gathering by constricting its presentation in both writing and typography.

Copy editing is basic to mass communications in general. Wherever language is used to communicate to a mass audience, some sort of copyreader is essential. The basic skills in newspaper editing are valuable assets to the communications technician in the fields of advertising, radio, television, magazines, trade journals, public relations, books, movies, etc. In all these areas, competence to improve the flow and meaningfulness of language, to safeguard accuracy, and to present the finished product in an attractive package is at a high premium. A good, flexible newspaper copy editor can carry his skill into any of these fields. The student, therefore, who is required to pursue a course in news editing, though primarily interested in other fields of journalism, should not let the course's newspaper orientation discourage him. If he makes the most of the opportunity, the skill he acquires will pay off in any branch of journalism.

Writers of all sorts need editors, even when they have had time to go over their own work. Much of Thomas Wolfe's greatness as a novelist he owed to his editors, and he acknowledged that fact even though he squirmed when the blue pencil went to work. The point is this: The writer doesn't exist whose work cannot be improved by the constructive vigilance of an editor who is (1) well versed in what is being written about, (2) an expert in language,

and (3) a flexible and tolerant person capable of appreciating values in the work of others.

But the newspaper has a *special* need for copyreaders. Most news writing is done at high speed. Reporters are usually under such severe pressure that they are bound to make slips and to need help in verifying and organizing their facts.

Creative, Managerial, and Police Functions

The desk by no means simply corrects the work of others. Broadly speaking, it has at least two other major functions, creative and managerial. The *creative* job largely centers around these activities: (1) The desk judges the news of the day and makes decisions about how it shall be presented. (2) It assembles single stories and "spreads" from material originating in a variety of sources. (3) It writes headlines, "cut" captions, and occasionally cutlines that are clear, vigorous, factual, and as complete a summary of the story as possible.

The *managerial* job consists of these activities: (1) The desk directs the work of compositors (typesetters) and printers, even though largely by remote control: it marks copy with the style of type the compositor is to set it in. (2) To avoid waste, it adjusts the volume of copy to the available space before the copy is sent to the composing room to be set in type. (3) It is prepared to meet emergencies, with plenty of "filler" and "time copy" on hand at all times.

Probably, though, the copydesk's chief function *is* the job of *policing* the content of the paper. (1) The desk checks copy against errors of fact and interpretation. (2) It guards the newspaper's position against being sued for libel and other legal difficulty. (3) It guards public confidence in the paper by assuring objectivity, fair play, and good taste. (4) The desk, perhaps above all, takes the kinks out of the line of communication between source and reader; it improves the flow and correctness of language in order to *clarify* the news and *make it meaningful.*

---

[2] Joseph G. Herzberg, *Late City Edition* (New York: Holt, 1947), p. 175.

The individual copy editor has many things in mind as he works on a story. He must eliminate errors of spelling, grammar, sentence structure, style, taste, fact, and organization. He must guard against unwarranted reportorial bias, verbosity, repetition, wearisome detail, overlooked facts, incongruities, advertising in disguise, libel, lottery, hoaxes, old news, ax grinding, and duplication.

Quality in Spite of Haste

The best copy desks not only perform their own duties but exert a subtle influence on the newsroom as a whole. It is a "quality-in-spite-of-haste" influence that helps keep reporters on their toes. The copy desk, in fact, can be one of the most powerful teaching influences in the office. When there is time, seasoned editors often show reporters why their copy was changed. Even if this sort of exchange is impossible, a conscientious writer can learn many of the fine points of his trade by examining the treatment his own copy gets at the desk. But it is obvious that this influence can be found only where genuine editing is the desk's chief concern. Hairsplitting and overattention to frivolous changes can have only a negative effect on the morale of the newsroom.

All this sounds like a large order, and it is. Filling it depends on a special *awareness,* a state of mind that includes alertness to all these things yet at the same time careful focus on the requirements and limitations of the reader. It is a state of mind that is attuned to minute detail—is the opera singer's name Pia Tassinari or Pio Tassarini?—yet can also deal with the *total impact* of a story on its readers. It is a mentality that can locate and correct a minor error of style but at the same time restructure an entire story to point up its more meaningful aspects while preserving the appeals that give it human interest. Mastery of copy-desk marking and the routine of "moving" copy, cuts, headlines, etc., to the composing room can give the beginner a false confidence. Learning to mark correctly is simply a matter of

learning a code. It is quite another matter to learn when and where to use the code.

"Copy Fixing?"

An anonymous writer in the *Nieman Reports* came straight to the point when he asked: "Has editing degenerated to 'copy fixing'?"[3] A great deal of editing unfortunately *is* mere "copy fixing." An editor can look pretty efficient making clear, crisp paragraph marks on the copy or assiduously laying down capitalization marks in old-style all-capital wire copy. He can even get a reputation in the composing room for clean copy that way, especially if he is very careful to pencil through X-ed out material and draw in connection lines.

But such editing will be found out. The editing profession (or craft) carries with it real responsibilities that cannot be met with mere technical skills. Perhaps they are less apparent while the editor is working on a story about the East Cupcake Kennel Club and its obedience-training classes, or the annual installation banquet of the Women of the Moose. Routine is as inescapable on the copy desk as it is in almost any occupation. But when an editor finds himself handling news of public affairs—war and peace, full employment and unemployment, surplus and deficit—he soon realizes the responsibility that rests on him. Working on a Page-One story for a paper with 50,000 circulation, he knows that he has a potential "audience" of 150,000 to 200,000 persons. Will the story be understood? Will it be read? Will the devices he uses to capture his readers' interest at the top of the story—or in the headline—actually give a wrong total impression?

The real job in editing a story is to *tell what happened,* to try to put together a clear and comprehensive report of the action from a welter of confusing and contradictory material. For example, what does the editor do with the bits and scraps of a "running" wire-service story as it is sent in piecemeal by

---

[3] "The Copy Desk," *Nieman Reports,* April 1950, p. 20.

a major wire service? First, he puts the story together as the service sent it and instructed it to be put together. A new "top" comes in every half hour or so, each putting the latest details in the lead. But the tops can be contradictory and misleading. For example, in a continuing wire-service story on a battle in Vietnam, the Allied forces could one minute be reported in resounding successes. Half an hour later the lead might carry nothing but bad news. A late-night lead based on a communiqué might be built around a further success.

Simply using what the wire services send in the suggested handling they offer might give the reader a totally false impression of what happened. *The reader would simply be at the mercy of the accident of the deadline.* If he happened to get the first edition, his total impression of the news would necessarily be drawn from the *latest* intelligence at the moment the first edition went to press. That would be at the top of the story and hence would provide the basis for the headlines. And even though the entire story is there to be found by the discriminating reader, for most readers the headline has the greatest impact.

It can be seen that the job for a news editor would be a big one in this case. For reasons that make perfectly good sense, the wire services tend to put the latest detail first, whether or not it is the most significant thing that has happened within the news cycle under consideration. Of course, the editor who fears broadcast competition welcomes this arrangement. "Just so we have later stuff than that ten-o'clock news broadcast," he reasons, "then it won't appear that the story our subscriber reads at 8:00 A.M. is old stuff— stuff he heard at ten last night." Such competitive considerations are important. But the editor's responsibility in the situation described here is to tell the story in such a way as to convey the total picture, and to tell it from the top. The details must then be dealt with carefully to show their sequence and significance. Within obvious space limits, editors have a responsibility for "full disclosure," to use the term of Sevellon Brown, late editor and publisher of the Providence *Journal.* "We cannot withhold the news," Brown goes on. And he might have said further that we cannot select the news on any other basis than *telling what*

happened and making what happened understandable to readers.

The Editor and the Reader

The reader is the editor's real employer. He doesn't make out the paycheck, but in the long run it is his dimes and nickels at the newsstand that are behind the newspaper's entire economy. Merchants will pay for advertising only in a newspaper that can clearly show that it has a great many paying readers.

What manner of man is John Q. Public? How well does he read and how much does he understand? The truth, of course, is that he ranges from a virtual illiterate at one end of the scale to a subtle and sensitive linguist at the other. There is little point in finding out about the "average" reader; writing the average reader can just understand will be all the way from extremely difficult to oversimple for many other readers.

There was a time in American journalistic history when the problem was relatively easy to solve. Before the emergence of penny papers in the 1830's, newspapers were slanted toward an élite, both in price and content, and the lower classes were presumed to get their news by word of mouth, if at all. Today, newspapers are *mass media,* and as such they must be written to reach a mass readership, not just a highly literate few.

It shouldn't be necessary to labor the point that our political institutions are based on the mass communication of ideas to people—who more or less equally share in public decisions. Long before that ideal was realized, Thomas Jefferson expressed it in his famous quote: "The basis of our governments being the opinion of the people, the very first object should be to keep that right; and were it left to me to decide whether we should have government without newspapers or newspapers without government, I should not hesitate to prefer the latter." Less often quoted is the sentence that follows: "But I should mean that every man should receive those papers *and be capable of reading them."* (Italics supplied.)

It is quite possible that Jefferson was talking about plain literacy at the time. But what he said still has great pertinence for newsworkers today. The increasing complexity of the news which readers must digest daily provides a distinct challenge to news editors. For it is the newspaper readers who really make the decisions in a democracy.

News which many readers are incapable of reading and understanding fails to fulfill the main task of the newspaper, the task for which newspapers have been given special constitutional protection. How can sound decisions be expected of an electorate which cannot understand what is being said about the facts which go into the decisions? Much of the responsibility necessarily falls on those who determine what news shall be presented in what way to the mass audience—the newsworkers. It is an awesome responsibility, indeed.

The Editor's Physical Tools

The editor works at his honorable trade with a set of tools, some of which are matters of routine, some of which he spends a lifetime improving and keeping in condition.

Equipment

First, there are the obvious *physical tools;* for example, a special copy *pencil.* It's a little bigger around than an ordinary pencil. Its lead is broad and soft. Usually the editor keeps two or three to a half a dozen of these pencils at hand, and he likes them long. He learns little tricks with that pencil, too. Because it is so very soft, its sharp point wears off rapidly. But the editor, without wasting any thought on it, keeps turning it slightly as it wears flat and uses the edge that the flatness created. He learns to produce bold strokes when they are called for, as in striking out entire lines, and then without going to the pencil sharpener finds a point which will write an inserted phrase in restricted space between lines so that it can be read instantly.

He has a soft, clean *eraser* at hand and uses it not to make the copy "pretty," but to help make it instantly clear to the man who sets it in type. *Scissors*

and *paste* are at his elbow, too. He uses them rapidly and only when necessary. There are lots of little tricks with scissors and paste that help simplify reorganizing a story.

The editor often has a *typewriter* nearby, but he uses it only when it will do the job more quickly than the other tools. Only a beginner retypes everything.

There is a *telephone* within reach, too.

Reminders

Besides these rather obvious physical tools, the editor has some *reminders* at hand. At the very minimum, these include the office style sheet and head schedule; they may also include a detailed headline count system.

The *style sheet,* showing the newspaper's preferred forms of spelling, capitalization, punctuation, and abbreviation, is usually complex enough so that even a veteran copy editor has to refer to it from time to time. It should go without saying that a desk man cannot work at peak effectiveness until he knows the style sheet thoroughly and needs to look up only occasional doubtful points. Style is more carefully considered at the copy desk than anywhere else in the newspaper office. Editors are expected to be experts on style. The beginner is expected to master the style sheet in a matter of hours.

The *head schedule* lists, shows examples of, and gives the unit count for all the headline typefaces (styles of type) ordinarily used by the newspaper. It is a device for speeding up communication between the editor and his superiors and between the desk and the composing room. For instance, rather than saying (or writing on the copy) "Give me a one-column, two-line, 24-point Bodoni boldface head in capitals and lower-case letters," the slot man (copy-desk chief) marks the headline copy "#3" and everyone understands. Needless to say, the tyro can save himself a lot of time by getting to know the head schedule in a hurry. But he may have to look up an occasional unusual item, so he has a copy of the schedule at hand.

Copy-Editing Marks

Another physical tool of the copyreader is the "shorthand" he uses to tell the compositor how he wants the original copy changed. The symbols vary from back shop to back shop, so an editor must learn the variations in each place of employment. But he can save a lot of his own time and can turn out a more legible finished product if he becomes thoroughly familiar with *and uses* the basic copyreader's marks shown here. In general, they have arisen from book printers' marks and have been adapted to the necessities of the newspaper operation. They are used to indicate a correction when the copyreader feels certain the compositor will need no other more elaborate instructions in order to understand the correction. When the copyreader doubts whether the compositor will understand, he shows the change with any means at his disposal. For example, the title "Commander" occurs relatively rarely; if it is to be abbreviated, the safe thing to do is to write the abbreviation on the copy rather than circling the word (shorthand for the instruction "abbreviate") and depending on the compositor to know that the abbreviation is "Cmdr."

Paragraphs and indentations   Editors mark all paragraphs, whether or not the conventional indentation has been made on the copy.

1. The common paragraph mark is this one:

```
Pittsburgh, Pa.--The United Mine Workers announced today
```

2. Although it is essentially a proofreader's mark, this paragraph symbol is sometimes used on copy:

```
strike was off.  The UMW said the non-gassy mines were
```

3. Where two elements are to be connected within the same paragraph, a smooth, curving, firm line is drawn from the end of the first element to the beginning of the second. Such a line should cut across, rather than tour around, deleted elements. The same mark is used to make two paragraphs one or to connect elements which have been separated by extensive deletions:

```
there would be no strike.
The UMW spokesman said the non-gassy mines were
```

4. To bring together two elements which have been separated by distance or extensive deletions but which are to remain as separate paragraphs, draw the same sort of line as above but tip it with an arrow head to indicate "new paragraph."

there would be no strike.

~~The UMW spokesman said the non-gassy mines were not involved.~~

Referring to the West Virginia fields, he said

5. To indent a line, a paragraph, or even an entire story, the same symbol is used throughout, but separate marks must be made for left and right indentations. The mark is like a bracket in reverse. To indent from the left, use this mark to the left of the copy:

(The Associated Press said the well was more than 50 feet deep.)

To indent from the right, use the reverse bracket on the right of the copy:

(The Associated Press said the well was more than 50 feet deep.)

Thus the ordinary indentation (left and right) involves a pair of marks:

(The Associated Press said the well was more than 50 feet deep.)

Indentations in body type ordinarily are standard on a given newspaper. The indent mark tells the linotype operator that he should indent "one em" if that is the standard indent on that paper. Sometimes it is "one en." (These terms are explained in Chapter 8.) But if the indent desired is other than the standard one, that fact must be noted beside the bracket:

(The Associated Press said the well was more than 50 feet deep.)

6. The same set of marks is used to indicate that a line is to be centered, as in the subhead:

] Set Free [

Capitals and small letters 7. Where the copy is already in caps and lower case, no mark need be made. However, much newspaper copy is transmitted by teletype and comes to the desk in all caps. In this case, all the letters are assumed to be "down" (lower case) except those the editor marks "up" (capitals).

The traditional mark for a capital letter is three underlines:

Washington--The Defense department today gave

Also traditionally, a double underline means small capitals and a single underline means italics. However, neither small capitals nor italics are commonly used in newspapers, so a great many copy desks allow their editors to indicate capitals with one underline.

8. Where a letter is capitalized in the copy and the editor wants a small letter instead, he simply draws a *diagonal* line through the letter from right to left:

The President said the budget

Spacing, deletions, insertions, substitutions 9. To indicate that a space is desired, draw a *vertical* line:

over the weekend

10. To indicate that no space is desired where a space appears, draw an arc above and below the space, connecting the letters to be juxtaposed:

The National League All stars

11. To delete a character, draw a bold *vertical* line through it. Then, if it appears inside a word (neither at the beginning nor at the end), "close it up" as shown above. If it appears at the beginning or end of a word, use the arc above only:

His judgement was without parallel

12-13. To delete more than one or two letters or an entire word or more, draw a firm *horizontal* line through the entire deletion, and "close it up" or not depending on whether a space is desired:

The superinten~~dinten~~dent said that he was ~~very much~~

disgusted ~~and annoyed~~ with the boys.

The purpose of the arcs shown above is to help the compositor follow the deletions speedily. They guide his eye across the copy. Hence, the arc is not ordinarily used at the end of a line; there is no point in guiding his eye into the margin or down to the next line (but see number 3, page 6).

14. Connection lines should follow the logical path of his eye to the next element he is to set:

The superintendent, ~~turned to look out the window~~

~~and~~ said he was annoyed with the boys.

The same sweeping connective mark is made to indicate that matter standing *in tabular form* is to be set *paragraph style:*

Counties which showed gains were as follows:

Grant,   5 per cent;

Sherman,   3 per cent;

Lee,   7 per cent.

15. But when such tabulations are lengthy, it is not necessary to draw dozens of these lines. The trick is to "set the style" (comma, semicolon, etc.), draw a couple of connectors, and mark in the margin the legend "run in":

Counties which showed gains were as follows:

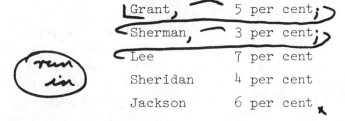

Grant,   5 per cent;

Sherman,   3 per cent;

run in   Lee   7 per cent

Sheridan   4 per cent

Jackson   6 per cent.

Note that the words "run in" are circled. *In general, all notations on copy which are not to be set as a part of the copy are circled.*

16. To substitute one letter for another, it is ordinarily enough to draw a *vertical* line through the offending letter and write the correct letter above it.

17. Where a letter is to be inserted, it is "drawn into" the line and a caret is put below the line at the exact point where the insertion is to be made. Several letters, a word, or a phrase are inserted or substituted in the same way:

```
        e                                      men
Fireman Smith and Jones reported that two police
     a matter of                         which
appeared in minutes and held back the throng who num-
bered several thousand.
```

Any element which has been deleted can be restored by marking it "stet," provided, of course, that the words are still visible under the deletion mark. When it is not clear where the passage to be restored begins and ends, a light broken line is drawn beneath it. This is a convenient device but is easily abused. When in doubt, editors prefer to erase.

Editors rarely make more than one mark in a single word, since doing so may mean the operator

will have to stop a moment to puzzle over markings. If a word has more than one error, the sensible thing is to line it out and write it in correctly above. This is also true of changes in any figure, such as a sum of money. It saves time for both the editor and the compositor. Copy editor's marks are dedicated to speed and convenience. But carried to extremes, they can actually get in the way of efficiency.

Transposition   18. Adjacent elements can be transposed thus:

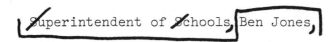

```
Their gear was also stowed away
```

Be sure to shift or insert punctuation marks where necessary:

```
Superintendent of Schools, Ben Jones,
```

Elements which appear on different lines cannot be transposed by this device. They must be lined out and written in. Nor is a compositor likely to understand transposition marks attempting to change elements in a single line which are not adjacent, for example the change from "blue and black" to "black and blue."

Ordinarily, the editor is not allowed to transpose

entire paragraphs by any pencil device. Some desks permit the editor to circle a paragraph and draw a line from the circle to the point at which the paragraph is to be inserted, using an arrow at the end. That sort of thing is a nuisance to the compositor, however, and the customary method of transposing paragraphs is to cut and paste.

Figures and abbreviations 19. A figure to be written out is circled.

20. An abbreviation to be written out is circled, too.

21. Conversely, a word to be abbreviated is circled.

22. A written-out number to be made a figure is also circled. In other words, circling an element means "do the opposite."

L (27) persons appeared at the Community (Bldg), 312 S. Wendworth (Avenue), between 7 and (nine) p. m.

Punctuation Punctuation marks which appear in their proper place ordinarily need not be marked, with one exception:

23. Quotation marks are often bracketed to indicate whether they are opening or closing quotes. (The typewriter does not distinguish them but type does):

Dickens wrote "A Tale of Two Cities."

Punctuation marks can usually be *changed* by printing the correct mark over the incorrect one with a firmly held pencil. Punctuation can ordinarily be *inserted* by drawing in the appropriate mark at the appropriate place.

However, copy editors use special marks for three items of punctuation—the period, the hyphen, and the dash.

24. The period is indicated by drawing at the base of the line a very small "x." (Some desks prefer a dot

with a small circle around it, although this practice is more common to book editing.)

25. A hyphen is indicated by drawing a small "equals" sign at the appropriate place.

26. The dash is drawn to exaggerated length.

27-28. If any doubt could exist as to whether a comma or an apostrophe is intended, they are distinguished by drawing a caret above the comma and an inverted caret below the apostrophe.

Here, then, is the lineup on punctuation:

Opening quote	"	Closing quote	"
Period	x		
Hyphen	=	Dash	—
Comma	⌄	Apostrophe	⌃
Question mark	?	Exclamation point	!
Semicolon	;	Colon	:
Parentheses	( )		

Other devices   29. It is sometimes desirable to be able to say to compositors and proofreaders: "Yes, that's right, believe it or not." Deliberately misspelled words and unusual spelling of names are cases in point. The customary device is to "square" such a word—simply to draw a rectangle around it. Then the operator knows he is to "follow copy." Another trick is to write a circled "ok" or "cq" above the word.

He wrote "Dere Mable"

Where a story has many such words, they need not be handled separately—the page can simply be marked "follow copy." The compositor will set it "as is."

30. Although one underline originally stood for italics and a wavy line was used to indicate boldface, the tendency today is to use a sweeping underline to indicate boldface, even where a firm underline stands for capital letters. (Some desks cling to the wavy line, however.)

"Jones is no communist," he exclaimed.

The abbreviation "bf" (boldface), "ff" (fullface, another term for boldface), and "bfc" for "boldface caps" are also useful in this connection.

31. Anything written in longhand needs special treatment to help distinguish certain troublesome letters. In longhand, the "a" looks much like the "o," the "m" like the "w," etc. It is customary to:

Overscore: ō, m̄, n̄

Underscore: a̲, w̲, u̲

The copyreader's "shorthand" is not an end in itself. The beginner must master it quickly—then use it so automatically that he can devote his full attention to *what* to do, rather than *how* to do it. He should guard against using copy marks for their own sake. Copy marks have one purpose and only one: to make speedy changes in such a way that compositors and proofreaders can perceive instantly what is meant.

Now let's apply these marks to a typical piece of copy. The numbers in the left margin are keyed to the list of marks above:

1, 7   Los Angeles, Calif.--(AP)--A strike of

10   street car and bus operators against the Los

          Angeles Transit Lines began early today when

9   negotiations broke off at 12:30 a. m.

18   Conferences between union representa-

7   tives and federal conciliator Harry Malcolm

19   ended with a union announcement that its ③

26   final proposals had been rejected for the

present.

28   The unions last offer, according to

21   President Donald B. McClurg, was to submit

18, 24   the dispute to an impartial board of arbitration.

17   McClurg, who *heads* is president of the Amal-

27   gamated Association of Street, Electric Rail-

way and Motor Coach Employ*ster*es, said the

14   union was prepared to accept, the results of

23   accept "any results of such arbitration."

6   ] Bowron Makes Plea ④

20   Mayor Bowron, who met earlier with co.

22   and union negotiators in an eleventh-hour

16   plea for postponement *of the* strike, returned late

16   in the evening and remained outside the con-

11   ference rooms until the session ended.

13   He had asked all parties to the dispute

to continue operations during the Shrine

12   convention.

No comment on the breakdown of negotia-

4   tions was immediately forthcoming from LATL

sources.

29   Vice-Pres. Cone T. Bass represented the

2   transit concern in the parley. Before leav-

29   ing the conference room, the vice-president

said:

3, 30   "The company stands ready to resume

talks at any moment."

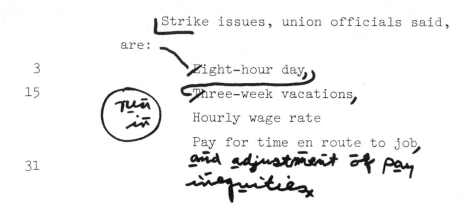

References

References of one kind or another constitute a third set of physical tools. The extent and adequacy of reference books available on the copy desk vary from one desk to another. Some copy desks unfortunately have one dog-eared telephone book and nothing more. Others have a dozen or more reference books on the desk and a comprehensive in-house library to fall back on besides.

A minimum list of references, one which would cope with perhaps nine out of ten of the problems of fact arising during an average day's handling of the news, might consist of the following:

> An unabridged dictionary
> The city directory
> The state "blue book" or handbook
> City and area telephone books
> A good atlas
> City, county, and state maps
> *Who's Who in America*
> *The World Almanac* or other general reference

A more thorough list of references might include these, available either on the desk or in the newspaper library:

ADDITIONAL LANGUAGE AIDS

> *Roget's Thesaurus*
> *Bartlett's Familiar Quotations*
> *Fowler's Dictionary of Modern English Usage*

ADDITIONAL REFERENCES TO PEOPLE

> *Who's Who in the Nation's Capital*
> *International World Who's Who*
> *Who's Who in Australia*
> *Who's Who* (British)
> *Who's Who in Canada*
> *Qui Etes-Vous?* (French)
> *Wer Ist's?* (German)
> *Chi E?* (Italian)
> *Who's Who in Art*
> *Who's Who in Education*
> *Who's Who in Finance, Banking, and Insurance*
> *Who's Who in Jurisprudence*
> *Who's Who in Literature*
> *Who's Who in Music*
> *American Men of Science*
> *Burke's Peerage*
> *Army Register*
> *Navy Register*

ADDITIONAL SOURCES OF FACTS

> *Statistical Abstract of the United States*
> *Congressional Record*
> *Congressional Directory*
> Official publications of state legislature
> Directories and official publications of city and
>   county government
> *The Postal Guide*
> An encyclopedia
> *Year Book of Agriculture*
> *American Labor Year Book*

Ayer's Newspaper Directory
Editor & Publisher International Year Book
Poor's Public Utilities
Moody's Railroads
Lloyd's Register of Shipping
Jane's Fighting Ships
Jane's All the World's Aircraft

But no reference book is any better than the intellect of the person who uses it. Certainly it is among the early duties of the copy-desk apprentice to learn what directories are available and above all *how to use them.* Many times valuable minutes have been lost because someone knew so little about how to use the city directory. It contains more than a mere alphabetical listing of persons and business places in the city. There are tricks to using almost any reference and it is up to the editor to learn them. Even a large dictionary contains vastly more information than the average dictionary user realizes.

The Editor's "Intellectual" Tools

Probably the most important of the copy editor's tools are the *intellectual* ones. No list could possibly include them all. It is assumed these days that a newsman is an educated and literate person capable of putting these tools to work in the interests of producing an accurate, dependable, well-written, grammatically correct, interesting, and soundly wrought newspaper. Beginners sometimes think they should put their college (and especially their journalism-school) training behind them as rapidly as possible when they enter the newsroom. Nothing could be farther from the truth. Making a display of one's erudition is one thing; *using* it and building on it is another.

Here is a tentative list of the intellectual tools the copy desk taps continually:

A thorough knowledge of English grammar, usage, sentence structure, and style

A thorough knowledge of copy-desk routine The beginner usually has to get it for himself on the job, as the routine varies from paper to paper.

Knowledge of how to use the references mentioned above

A thorough knowledge of the community the newspaper serves This, too, the desk man has to construct piece by piece on his own time. Even if the community in which he happens to work is also the one in which he grew up, he'll be amazed at how many things he must learn about it. For instance, he must know the government organization and the full names of its principal personalities, how it works, etc. He must know the city's layout—streets, parks, subdivisions, and all. Where do east and west divide? How do the street numbers work? He must know the city's utilities, its public transportation facilities, and its highway system. He must know the county government, its chief personalities, organization, legislative bodies, etc. He must know something of the school system in the city and how schools are organized in the surrounding area. He must keep brushing up on his knowledge of local personalities—political, business, fraternal, philanthropic, etc. He must know about churches and hospitals and organizations of all kinds.

An alert desk man working in a small or medium-sized city has memorized, for example, that "D.A.R." stands for Daughters of the American Revolution and that the Sons of the Revolution do not like to be confused with the Sons of the American Revolution. He knows that the Rebekahs are related to the Odd Fellows and not the Knights of Pythias, whose auxiliary is the Pythian Sisters. He knows that a Masonic lodge is not likely to be headed by a Noble Grand and that there's no use inquiring what "P.E.O." stands for. This kind of fact he must have at the tips of his fingers.

It isn't necessary to memorize all details, however. A great deal of editing consists of playing hunches. When a list of casualties in an airplane crash comes across the desk, the name of the college president who died will ring a bell in the alert copy editor's head and cause him to do some research, finding out, perhaps, that the man was once assistant pastor of a local church. That sort of thing happens every day. It's based on general awareness and attention to detail.

Newspaper copy is checked carefully, but the idea that "every fact is checked and rechecked and then checked again" is strictly for the publisher's speeches. Few newspapers can afford the time and the personnel to check every fact; they depend on the editor's hunch-playing instincts to spot only the facts that ought to be checked. When a policeman's official report says there was a head-on crash at the intersections of Highways 35 and 14 in Roberts County, the reporter, the city editor, and the copy editor will probably take his word for it that the two cars did indeed crash and that they were pointed at each other when they did so. As a measure of protection, they'll not only say what was said but who said it. There is usually no reason to believe that the policeman would give anything but a true and correct report of what happened, to the best of his knowledge. But the careful editor will make sure that Highways 35 and 14 actually intersect in Roberts County. And he'll be mighty suspicious of the policeman's report if it goes on to say that the chief damage to one car was to the rear bumper and trunk!

Obviously, the editor is especially helpless to check every fact in a report received from one of the wire services. In general, the wire services are extremely careful. Not only have they proved factual on the whole in the past, but they send corrections immediately after errors are found. But even here, an alert editor frequently finds errors and oversights, so he reads telegraph copy carefully, with an eye for slipups and incongruities of all sorts. He cannot afford to assume that "because the AP says it, it's true"—not, at least, in every detail.

The editor with the best hunches is the editor who succeeds. The doubting Thomas who questions every word in the copy or sees a libel lawyer leering at him in every court story will spend so much time on routine checking that he'll never get a chance to edit. The canny hunch player proceeds on the assumption that people are pretty honest and reporters fairly dependable. *But he never relaxes his vigilance for a minute.* A slight incongruity in the circumstances of an accident will leap out of the page at him and he'll do something about it. An irregularity in the spelling of a name will hit him with equal force. He watches the tricky ones—Allegheny, Alleghany, and Allegany, for instance, and Menominee, Menomonee, and Menomonie. He checks Clark and Clarke, Olson and Olsen, Denison and Dennison, and the like.

A broad general awareness and solid educational background   Hunches are based not only on an eye for detail but also on intellectual curiosity and awareness founded on a good education and nurtured on the reading the editor does, what he talks about when he's not on duty, his general attitude toward his own adequacy, and his willingness to build up his own store of information. The editor must be an avid newspaper reader himself. He reads not only to learn techniques—to compare his handling of a story with that of other professionals—but also to keep abreast of current affairs. He reads his own newspaper, the opposition paper, if there is one, metropolitan papers serving his area, and the big, authoritative ones like the New York *Times,* the Washington *Post,* the *Wall Street Journal,* and the *Christian Science Monitor.* He reads the news magazines, too, for deeper insight and clearer perspective on events. And he reads the "think" magazines to broaden the scope of his understanding. Because a big part of his job is to point up what is new over what is essentially background, he obviously must know what *is* new.

Common sense   An even disposition and a sense of the continuity of news are real assets to the copyreader; he is not just a dealer in words and ideas but a dealer with people. He must have respect for the viewpoints and special problems of his coworkers and readers. He must have a feeling for what others can and will read. He must have a sense of balance in all the decisions he makes. Cool judgment is probably the most important intellectual tool of all.

But that is only a beginning. The news editor also

exercises judgment over what his readers shall and shall not read. (Not even the New York *Times* can really live up to its motto: "All the News That's Fit to Print.") He makes decisions about the balance of emphasis in the day's news diet.

Editing Copy

What exactly does editing do to copy? It would be impossible to catalogue every type of correction and adjustment, but in brief, the copyreader does any or all of these things for a news story:

1. He facilitates composing and makeup operations.
2. He regularizes copy to conform to the style of his newspaper.
3. He adjusts story length to space requirements.
4. He detects and corrects errors of fact.
5. He simplifies, clarifies, and corrects language.
6. He clarifies, amplifies, and vivifies meanings.
7. He makes stories objective, fair, and legally safe.
8. He restructures stories extensively where necessary.
9. He alters a story's tone where necessary.
10. He corrects copy in the interest of good taste.

Not all these things need to be done to any one story, but ordinarily any given day on the desk will require the editor to perform them all at one time or another. Any editor must be equipped to perform them when the need arises. The job requires not only that he be able to make such changes but that he be able to tell when they are necessary and when they are not. Let us study separately each of these demands on the editor.

Facilitating Composing and Makeup Operations

After leaving the desk, newspaper copy goes through the hands of half a dozen technicians before it finally appears in the newspaper. The slot man (copy-desk chief) handles it, then possibly the shop foreman, then the compositor, and finally one or two proofreaders. At each of these stages, time is as important as it is on the copy desk or anywhere else in the newsroom. Clean copy saves time; "dirty" copy can cause serious delays. The editor who can make clear, forceful corrections in a hand that is instantly legible is a real asset. Although *what* the editor does with the copy is dictated by other and more complicated considerations, *how* he does it is largely dictated by the thought "Will this be clear to the compositor?" If it is not, the editor can save time by correcting the situation with scissors and paste.

But if he has a *legible hand,* most of his corrections can be made with his pencil. Not all great newsmen have been legible writers. Horace Greeley's copy was all in longhand and it was almost impossible to read. His compositors finally got fed up, so the story goes, and decided on a neat bit of trickery. Taking some of his own copy, they dipped a fly in ink and let it roam across the paper. They then took it to Greeley and asked for a translation. He replied, "The word is 'unconstitutional,' of course, you fools!")

But today an illegible hand is inexcusable. The editor need not be an expert in fine calligraphy; all he need be concerned about is that his copy can be read after he has made his corrections. Precious time is lost whenever the compositor can't understand a correction mark. He takes the copy to his superior, who takes it to the copy-desk chief, who refers it to its perpetrator. Thus the routine of four men may be interrupted. Or the compositor guesses at it and lets it go; the proof desk catches the error (if the copy desk is lucky), the copy and proof are sent to the copy desk for verification, the corrected proof goes to the composing room and must be set and inserted—possibly even after the type of the story has been locked up with all its surrounding type in the page "form." This little circumlocution can upset the routines of many more than four men and waste a corresponding amount of time.

Legible copy doesn't take any more time to write than illegible copy; sometimes it takes less. The first essential is that the copy editor develop handwriting that can be read. Printing is preferable to longhand, and capitals-and-lower-case printing is preferable to all capitals.

One of the main reasons copy should be legible to begin with is the handling it gets before it is set, which smudges the soft-pencil marks. Wherever hot-metal casting machines, such as the Linotype, are used, copy must be folded once—by printers whose fingers may not necessarily be free of ink and graphite —and clamped down to fit the copy holder of the machine. Then, of course, it must be turned. Any-where from eighteen to twenty-one inches of space separate the compositor's eyes and the paper. The light is only fair, and the moving parts of the mech-anism are distracting. Obviously, these are not ideal conditions for reading. It behooves the editor to un-derstand them and be considerate of his colleagues in the composing room.

Making Copy Conform to Style

What does style matter? What difference does it make if "club" is capitalized or not in "Fortnightly club" and "Nebraska Federation of Women's Clubs"? If they are under such pressure, why do newsmen stop to fuss and even argue over some minute style point? The reasons newspapers are careful about style seem to center around two poles: pride in craftsmanship and a feeling that style *does* matter to the reader whether he knows it or not.

The worker with a sense of craftsmanship does not ask whether the results of the care he takes will be immediately apparent to the layman. He simply satis-fies himself that the product is one he can be proud of—and one which other artisans in his own field can appreciate. Certainly some style matters are as imperceptible to the reader as the intricate details that mean sound construction in the work of a cabi-netmaker are apparent to the hasty furniture buyer.

But whether that comparison is valid or not, most newsmen seem to be satisfied that style affects reading at two quite distinct levels—the conscious and the unconscious. The newspaper that is not consistent about the spelling of Yugoslavia (Jugoslavia), Viet-nam (Viet Nam), etc., can expect a loss of confidence on the part of its readers; all but the most careless will consciously notice "Czechoslovakia," "Czecho-Slovakia," and "Czecho-slovakia" used alternatively. And most editors believe an accumulation of small inconsistencies will cause an unconscious loss of con-fidence in their papers. Consequently, most news-papers are fussy about style.

But it's possible to be *too* fussy. Good newspaper style books warn against making a fetish of style. "This style book is not intended to establish a maze of arbitrary rules, but to serve as a guide toward uni-formity," says the foreword to an early edition of the Milwaukee *Journal* Style Book. It goes on, "Although certain preferences can be indicated, often common sense must be the determining factor. In unforeseen cases, where strict adherence to style does not make sense, or causes ambiguity, follow the clear, unmistak-able style that seems necessary. On the whole, how-ever, follow as closely as possible the style set forth in this booklet."

This approach to style advocates a laudable happy medium between rules and common sense. Extreme arbitrariness in style can be a severe handicap. For instance, a certain desk had a sound rule on identify-ing public agencies that have come to be known by their initials. The rule specified that, in the first refer-ence, the agency name should be written out in caps and lower case and followed by the initials in paren-theses, thus:

> A spokesman for the Fed-eral Communications Commis-sion (FCC) said today . . .

All subsequent references would read "FCC" or "the Commission."

This rule yielded to change in specific cases. In time, for example, this desk determined to allow AFL-CIO to stand alone, on the theory that even the most casual reader was probably familiar with the abbreviation. But for some reason the rule was never relaxed on "United Nations (UN)," even after that terminology had appeared on Page One nearly every day for years. When the wire services started calling it "UN" in the first reference, the editors had to insert "United Nations" and put parentheses around the "UN." It led to such confections as this:

> United Nations (UN) Sec-retary General U Thant said today . . .

When such arbitrariness is imposed on the desk, the individual editor usually can do nothing but comply.

The Milwaukee *Journal* rule cited above is more liberal than most. It acknowledges that readability and meaningfulness need not be sacrificed in a slavish devotion to style. There are few rules connected with language that are so perfect, so adaptable to all circumstances, that they may not be broken, at times. With few exceptions, though, style rules make sense. There is a reason behind each. It achieves uniformity, or it is based on some working principle: saving space, for instance, or promoting readability, or both.

Style sheets need revision from time to time, particularly when the nature of the news changes radically. They are often revised not by fiat but by agreement among those who are most concerned with the newspaper's style. In fact, a rather far-reaching change in style has affected American newspapers in the last decade and a half. Fifteen or twenty years ago, style differed persistently from region to region. New England and the Middle-Atlantic states used an "up" style, which means that capitalization was used heavily and abbreviation relatively sparingly. The Midwest was characteristically "down-style" country. But a technological change largely eliminated the differences. The teletypesetter, an attachment to the composing-machine keyboard which operates it automatically by means of punched paper tape, came into widespread use. And the output of the wire-service teletype receiver became the punched paper tape instead of teleprinter copy. The tape can be fed directly to the composing machine, whereas printer copy has to be edited, type marked, and set by hand. This development led to a nationwide regularization of style in wire-service copy. The Associated Press, for example, no longer sent copy in all-capitals, a practice it had followed to permit each copy desk to capitalize according to its own style. It now sent the copy line for line, in capitals and lower case, as it was to appear, and that necessitated a single set of stylistic conventions acceptable to all users of the service. Both AP and UPI adopted similar styles which were neither as "up" as the Eastern nor as "down" as the Midwestern. The only sensible thing for each newspaper to do was to modify its own style throughout to bring it into line with the new wire-service style. The regional patterns thus largely disappeared, even though some of the larger papers, less dependent on the savings that could be realized by the teletypesetter service, retained theirs. The New York *Times,* for example, is just as "up" as ever, and the Milwaukee *Journal* did not abandon its "down-style" tradition until 1970. The Chicago *Sun-Times* and *Daily News* Stylebook reproduced as Appendix A is typical of today's style practices.

Adjusting Story Length to Space Requirements

Flexibility in terms of space is a "must" in newspaper production. This is a cardinal principle in the newsroom and many newspaper habits and customs are based on it. And it is the general news departments that have to be flexible; the space requirements of other departments are fixed. It is a rare day, for example, when an advertisement is changed or abandoned in order to solve some news space problem. It is the news that must be adjusted to the space left after the ads have been planned. So, the first thing a copy-desk chief does each day is to find out the amount of space he will have. Whether an issue will be thirty-six or forty pages is not his decision. Whatever space is allotted to the news departments is his, and only rarely can he get more when news demands exceed the allotted space.

Naturally, no news editor can predict what sort of news day will develop. With a fixed space to work with and constantly changing demands on it, he obviously must have devices of flexibility. By using more stories and letting them run longer, he can fill his space on a dull day. But by far the more recurrent and difficult problem is the opposite. As late-breaking stories press for space, he must be able to shorten other stories to shoehorn in all the significant news.

Because of the demands of timeliness in most news stories, newspapers can rarely solve this problem—as magazines do, for instance—by simply holding out certain features until the next edition. A few stories which do not depend on timeliness for their effectiveness *can* be given this treatment. But most of the material newspapers deal with is "spot" news which must be published while it is still news.

Hence, it is an important skill on the copy desk to be able to reduce a story's length without damaging it seriously from the standpoint of the reader. It is not easy. For this reason a major segment of Chapter 3 is devoted to this phase of editing.

Detecting and Correcting Errors of Fact

If there is one ultimate guiding principle in newspaper work, it is ACCURACY ALWAYS. Nowhere in the newspaper operation is this more important than on the copy desk. The desk provides the last real check on accuracy. Others handle copy after the desk does, but they are not responsible for seeing that the *facts* are accurate—only that the product of their work accurately follows the copy. In fact, if the copy desk performed no other service than to check on facts, it would be worthwhile. Editors know that the reputation of a newspaper hinges on getting the facts right. They know that little errors and big errors alike can lower the newspaper's standing with its

readers. An editor who lets errors of fact slip past him will not be an editor long. This problem is treated more fully in Chapter 3.

Simplifying, Clarifying, and Correcting Language

The extent to which an editor can improve the flow of language in the daily newspaper is limited only by (1) the extent of his own ability to recognize and repair incorrect, confused, and pompous words and sentences, and (2) the time available. Under pressure of deadlines, the copy editor often does not have time to make extensive revisions. He must find ready solutions which can be marked in rapidly with the copy pencil.

The example below—cutlines for two two-column cuts—came across the desk of a medium-sized newspaper at a moment when time was short. It is reproduced here because it is typical of material written under pressure and because it indicates the simple improvements an alert editor can make in seconds.

```
        state                              H. E. Howe Photos

                        top picture,
        A washout of a bridge, xxxxxxxx between Boscobel
and Wauzeka on Highway 60 temporarily stranded nearly
1,000 farmers heading for home when the heavy rains
struck Crawford and Grant counties Saturday night.
        Officials at Lancaster today made a special appeal
to the state highway commission seeking emergency funds
to replace several bridges washed out through south-
western Wisconsin during the storm.
        The lower picture was taken on the Ottmar Boebel
farm in the Maple Ridge area, lashed by tornado -like
winds.
        The guests ripped the roof and barn walls from the
structure but left nearly intact the stock of hay stored
inside.
```

And here is how the story was edited:

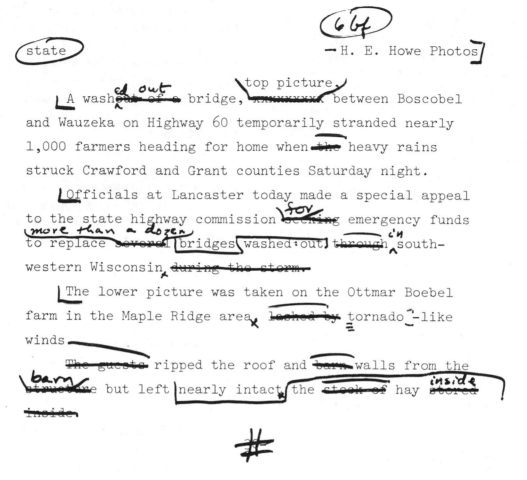

Now let's go back over the edited story to see what was in the editor's mind. For the most part, the corrections are routine, made to improve the language. The editor knew the corrections had not created a masterpiece of prose. But he could feel that in about sixty seconds he had made substantial improvements.

In the first line, the reporter apparently had wanted to get right to the heart of the story with a key word —"washout"—but he had assembled the sentence clumsily. A quick shift in the wording right at the beginning made the sentence "move." In the second paragraph, the editor again eliminated the awkwardness of the original wording with only slight changes. He also substituted the more specific phrase "more than a dozen" (the information was available from the previous day's paper) for the extremely vague "several." He killed the words "in the storm" as superfluous. In the final paragraph, the editor both simplified sentences and eliminated repetitious wording: note the use of both "winds" and "gale," "barn" and "structure." And of course hay in the barn constitutes "a stock" and it is obviously "stored" there.

With a fresh start and a clean page of copy paper, the editor could probably have made these cutlines even better. And he undoubtedly could have made them even more specific: how much hay was in the barn, for instance? But time allowed neither. The editor put a small amount of time to good use, making the story substantially more readable than it was.

Because simplifying, clarifying, and correcting language is such a major part of the copy editor's job, a large section of Chapter 3 is devoted to this subject.

Clarifying, Amplifying, and Vivifying Meaning

Correctness is not enough. Correct language contributes to meaningful communication but does not guarantee it. It is for this reason that *language* problems and *meaning* problems are dealt with separately here. The editor must be so skillful in dealing with language that correctness is second nature to him. The problem of meaning is larger and more difficult. When the editor is in doubt about correctness, he can refer to a set of grammatical rules, but he has no such guide to meaning. Here the editor must concern himself with this recurring question: "Will this language convey meaning to a person of no better than average linguistic skill?" It is not just a question of whether it makes sense to the editor himself; he must consider the reader of lesser reading ability and more limited vocabulary.

Meaningful writing is clear writing founded on clear thinking. Most of the time professional reporters turn out clear, correct, meaningful writing. But not always. That's where the editor comes in. Just as he provides an additional check on the factual correctness of the news story, so he is the final guarantor that the story's larger and smaller meanings will be instantly apparent to the reader. This is an important skill on the copy desk, and a full treatment of the subject is therefore deferred to Chapter 5.

Making Stories Objective, Fair, and Legally Safe

The "watchdog" function of the copy desk is nowhere more apparent than in this part of the editor's job. The editor has two highly specialized responsibilities here.

Most newspaper publishers would concede that the copy desk is worth what it costs if it performs no other function than to keep the paper out of libel suits. This is one of the clearest and most fundamental responsibilities of the copy editor—that he be on the lookout for the kind of accidental defamation that can slip into the paper when reporters are careless ("accidental," because sometimes a newspaper knowingly commits libel as a calculated risk).

The copy editor bears no greater burden than this one. To say that he must be alert is to put it mildly.

A lapse can cause the loss of tens or even hundreds of thousands of dollars to the newspaper. And the editor himself, as we shall see, is not only morally responsible in libel matters as the last person who could have prevented the trouble; he is even legally responsible as a potential respondent in a libel action. Protection against libel requires specialized knowledge of libel law and precedent. It is therefore discussed more fully in Chapter 14.

The editor's responsibility for the content of the material that comes under his pencil does not end with these legal matters. He has a larger responsibility, in a sense, to his larger employer—his reader and the public in general—to see to it that the stories he handles meet his newspaper's and his profession's standards of *objectivity and fair play*. It is a matter of acting in the public interest. The copy editor is in no sense the final arbiter of what is objective and what is fair. He may be overruled in his judgments by his superiors in the newsroom. And he must realize that he himself is subject to prejudices and blind spots.

Not all newspapers are equally devoted to objectivity and fair play. Most of them do, however, abide to the best of their collective abilities by professional standards. In this situation, the individual editor's "pressures" all run in the same direction: his sense of responsibility to himself, his profession, his employer, and the public all conspire to demand of him his utmost skill in making his copy fair and objective.

What constitutes objectivity? Is objectivity enough? What constitutes fairness? Is fairness enough? These issues are discussed more fully in Chapters 3 and 5.

Extensive Restructuring

The copy desk usually enjoys considerable freedom in making broad changes in the nature, structure, and tone of the news it handles, whether local or originating with the wire services. Gross changes are usually performed in consultation with the appropriate department head. But their effectiveness depends on the skill of the individual copy editor.

Extensive restructuring is done to produce the best possible story. Often it means combining related stories. Sometimes it is precisely the reverse, dividing one story into two. Frequently the job is actually performed at the rewrite desk, often at the request of the copy desk. This happens most often when local angles are to be injected into an essentially nonlocal story. The local angle may be spotted in a wire story at the telegraph desk; the story goes to the city desk with the suggestion that local ends be incorporated; the city editor passes it along to a rewrite man who does the job; the finished product goes back through city editor, telegraph editor, and finally to the copy desk.

But more often it is the copy editor who does the job, blending stories together, separating them, cutting them, rewriting parts of them, etc., using all his skill to put the parts back together again in a well-organized, readily understandable whole. The thrust of a story can be changed by the discovery of an angle of local interest. The editor shifts a paragraph or two around, changes a phrase here and there, makes sure that the new shape of the story is coherent and connected and the reader is served by a better story. Changes such as this, while demanding a high order of skill on the part of the editor, may take no more than three to five minutes out of his day. Examples of more complicated restructuring are given in Chapters 3 and 4.

Altering Story Tone

A news story has a "tone quality" that is instantly apparent to the veteran newsman but not so obvious to the beginner. The straight news story has a quality of simplicity and dignity that is not found in the "human-interest short." The interpretive story may adopt a me-to-you tone that is absent in the straight news story. By-line eyewitness pieces accompanying a disaster story sometimes use the first person and are vivid and colorful. Feature stories range from deliberate understatement to tear-jerking pathos, from chatty informality to cool dignity.

The news editor sometimes has to change the tone quality of a story. He may do it in order to make a minor feature more cheerful, to convert an interpretive piece into a straight news story, to tone down overly emotional writing, etc. This is not a frequent assignment and will not be dealt with in detail here. The chief requirement is an "ear" for tone quality and

a sense of consistency. It represents a high order of editorial skill.

Editing in the Interests of Good Taste

The institutional character of the newspaper requires that it conform to mass standards of good taste. The newspaper reaches all literate ages. What is suitable for an adult may not be suitable for a child.

The New York *Times* slogan "All the News That's Fit to Print" conveys the importance that great newspaper places on good taste. The publisher of a smaller paper once said his rule is to "put nothing in the paper that any good mother would hesitate to read aloud to her girls and boys." On the other hand, Charles A. Dana was quoted as saying, "I have always felt that whatever Divine Providence permitted to occur, I was not too proud to print."

Neither of these extreme positions is tenable in the daily newspaper of today. Whether or not distasteful or untasteful news is printed is not a question of taste alone. To suppress a story because it has some unpleasant aspects is to fail to discharge the principal duty of the newspaper. On the other hand, some newspapers which deliberately include material of doubtful character as a lure to readers of similar low taste lay themselves open to censure.

Hence, good newspapers constantly have to balance questions of taste against questions of suppression or partial withholding of the news. The titillating story which has little or no significance can reasonably be kept out of the paper. The story in the mainstream of the news containing unpleasant detail cannot be killed off altogether. Sometimes it is possible to delete those parts of the story which are salacious without failing to tell it in its main outlines. Such decisions must be based on balanced judgment, not on rules about "good taste"; and such judgments must be made by editors. This was clearly pointed up by J. Russell Wiggins, editor of the Washington *Post,* when he said:

Those who get the news have the responsibility to gather all the news. The editors will decide what part of the news cannot, for any reason [of taste], be put into print. They may conclude, in many cases, that the public importance of some news that violates [considerations of taste] is so great that publication is essential nonetheless.

Such decisions are made by the editors. Responsibility to get the news, failure to write it, and failure to print it is not to be shifted to another.[4]

When good taste comes into conflict with the necessity for telling the truth in all its brutal reality —a problem faced by all the news media day in and day out—no textbook maxim is very helpful. Should television have presented hours of film taken shortly after the Nazi crematoria were liberated? In some places the film was shown in prime time. Should television have shown the complete act of assassination when an apparent bystander stepped up and killed the man accused of killing President Kennedy? It couldn't help it—the camera was pointed that way. Was it necessary to use a picture showing the effects of decapitation in order to tell the story of the death of Jayne Mansfield in a highway accident? Some editors used the picture virtually without retouching, others softened the details by means of airbrush techniques, and still others omitted the picture altogether. To determine the bounds of permissible obscenity, the United States Supreme Court uses the idea of a "community standard," yet we know that no clearcut consensus is really possible.

In cases of *Good Taste* v. *Truth,* one is as relative as the other. Yet in each such case, editors have to make decisions with courage and compassion, and every one seems a little harder than the last. These decisions call for more than craftsmanship. The editor is a professional. The profession may not have all the trappings of the familiar learned professions—public responsibility through licensing, *rites de passage* sanctifying exclusive membership, advanced degrees testifying to exclusive access to a scientific or scholarly literature, a code of ethics with enforceable sanctions. Indeed, most of these are inconsistent with freedom of the press. But a news professional has what Rivers and Schramm have called "an individual sense of responsibility," a set of shared aspirations and standards and of commitment to an impersonal goal.[5] The professional has a set of critical standards for his own work and expects that his colleagues apply similar standards in judging him. When his mature judgment fails him, he knows he cannot fall back on some impersonal institution—the paper he works for, the labor union he belongs to, the power structure of the community. He bases his own judgments on his sense of a personal ethic, and he resists and joins others in resisting pressures to do less than that.

---

[4] In the *St. Paul Pioneer-Press and Dispatch Handbook.*

[5] William L. Rivers and Wilbur Schramm, *Responsibility in Mass Communications,* rev. ed. (New York: Harper & Row, 1969), p. 242.

2

The Newsroom and the Newspaper

"Copy readers are sour men with round shoulders. Pedantry has dried their juices; routine has withered their sensitivity. Whereas reporters are skeptical, questing and wise, copy readers have monumental conceits. One of them is that they help reporters." With this bit of sarcasm, John J. Corry, who once edited copy on the national news desk of the New York *Times,* opened a wise essay on the relationship of the copy editor to the news writer. He went on to say:

Everyone knows what copy readers do. They change "which" to "that"; they make Mt. Everest precisely 29,141 feet high; they replace "anxious" with "eager." . . .

But if a desk man is good, really good, he does more: He enters into a partnership with the writer, submerges himself in the story and in effect shares responsibility for it.

The technique is perilous. Deskmen often wrench news out of shape, molding it to a preconceived pattern. Further, deskmen who bleed too much over stories may submerge a writer's news judgment and prose style in their own caprice. But deskmen who do not bleed at all regard a story merely as unmodified prose, something to be stuffed into a column of type. To the reporter, of course, the same story is immediate, prickly with nuance and heavy with significance.

. . . Wise old copy readers . . . ask themselves, What is the intent of the writer? The question has been confined to writers of fiction. But the proliferation of interpretive pieces and the growing notion that soft stories can tell the news . . . make the question pertinent for copy readers, too.

For instance, some of the best stories coming out of the last decade of Southern integration have been soft stories—the bewilderment of an older generation, the menace of a small-town sheriff, the ardor of a civil rights worker. Some of the best foreign news stories have dealt with the minutiae of everyday living. In these stories the partnership between copy reader and reporter is a fragile thing. The intent of the writer can be nullified by ham-handed editing; yet left unattended a reporter's intent may remain obscure.

A copy reader does not conceive this kind of story; he acts as the midwife. And this is the most exacting and hazardous kind of editing. It calls for a coming together with the reporter, who may have written the piece in blood, and a respect for what he is trying to do. The best editing here is the least obtrusive, but it is also the most imaginative. It demands a determined effort to write in the precise word that the reporter sought but failed to find. It demands that the copy reader not interfere with the rhythm of the prose. It demands that the form of the piece, if the writer has a sense of form, be left intact.

.   .   .   .   .

Deskmen and reporters seldom enter into this partnership. Indeed, outside of a few great metropolitan newspapers, copy reading seems to be a dying art. This cannot be disguised by circus makeup and self-conscious attempts at hard-nosed reporting; a badly edited newspaper is a bad newspaper.

It is bad because it has a void where its sense of news should be. It is bad because it confuses mawkish experimentation with creativity. . . . But mostly it is bad because the desks have either surrendered their responsibility or have not learned what that responsibility is. . . .

Undisciplined desk work is pervasive, spilling over into fatuous prose, mishandled news and a generally frightful product. The desk is part of a team; it should help shape, but not to restrain, reporters. . . . But even fine reporters, who write well and understand that news is viable, sometimes forget that news exists in relation to its time and place and to other news.[1]

Chapter 1 concentrated exclusively on the role of the news editor, the related role of the copy editor, and the place they work together—the copy desk. Important as it is, however, the copy desk is part of a larger hierarchical organization. The news editor and his copy editors function at a critical point in the line connecting the event itself with the account of it that appears in the final edition. At this point it seems desirable to discuss other roles and functions in the newspaper and its work-flow system.

---

[1] John J. Corry, "Confessions of an Unrepentant Deskman," *Nieman Reports,* December 1969, pp. 10–11.

Main Departments

Newspaper work divides itself into three basic categories (and in the process into three broad areas for careers in journalism). Each is distinctly different, yet each is wholly dependent on the smooth functioning of the others. These areas of responsibility are usually referred to as "business," "production," and "editorial." Working newsmen are more likely to call them "the front office," "the back shop," and "the newsroom."

Newspaper editing, the chief concern of this book, is actually only one operation among several in the newsroom, but because the copy desk is the crossroads between the editorial and production functions, editors more than any other members of the organization should know how other branches of the newspaper operate in order to do their job with maximum efficiency.

Business Office

The business office is the "counting house" of the newspaper profession. It has the obvious duty of keeping the organization afloat financially, and it operates pretty much like any other business office. Ordinarily, it has four major divisions: an advertising department (which may be broken down into two autonomous departments, classified and display advertising); a circulation department; a promotion department; an accounting or auditing department. Each of these branches is typically headed by a major officer of the business staff. Usually the entire operation is directed by a business manager, to whom each of these department heads is responsible. The publisher himself often acts as business manager, especially on smaller dailies.

Advertising   The advertising department, headed by an advertising manager, ordinarily has four subdivisions:

1. The *local or retail* division consists of a staff of specialists who solicit, lay out, correct, and sometimes "merchandise" local advertising accounts. This is usually the largest of the advertising-department subdivisions and offers the most creative employment in

newspaper advertising for journalism graduates with advertising training.

2. Another group of advertising specialists concerns itself with obtaining and handling *"foreign"* or *"national"* advertising accounts. This division deals with the big advertisers indirectly through advertising agencies, usually with the help of an advertising "representative" in New York.

3. *Classified* advertising, as indicated above, may be handled by a subdivision of the advertising department or by a separate department. Classified has gained steadily in recent years as a source of newspaper revenue and hence is receiving increasing attention among newspaper executives.

4. The advertising department often has a *merchandising* or "service" division, whose purpose is to assist the advertiser in getting the maximum return on his advertising dollar. This is perhaps the most recent and rapidly growing phase of newspaper advertising and is handled by personnel ranging all the way from a part-time troubleshooter to a complex group of researchers ready to provide a potential advertiser with detailed information on the buying habits of the newspaper readers that would affect his particular product.

The advertising manager coordinates all these activities and is ordinarily responsible directly to the business manager—and sometimes directly to the publisher—for their successful operation.

Circulation Circulation is usually headed by a major executive, the circulation manager. Since the newspaper ultimately stands or falls by the number of steady readers, circulation is obviously a major responsibility and a career in itself. The circulation manager may have any or all of these subdivisions under his supervision:

1. *City circulation.* This involves maintaining circulation records for the city of publication; recruiting, supervising, and reimbursing carrier boys; supervising the "district men" who oversee circulation in various areas of the city, taking responsiblity for moving papers to the newsstands, relations with newsstand operators, etc.

2. *Area circulation.* The responsibilities here include dispatching papers destined for the surrounding area by mail and/or by truck if mail service is not rapid enough.

3. *Mailing room.* The circulation manager is also in charge of moving the papers into the appropriate distribution channels as they come to the mailing room from the press room.

4. *Solicitation and promotion.* This involves an office staff in keeping records, notifying subscribers when their subscriptions need renewing, handling complaints, new subscriptions, and renewals over the counter, by mail, etc.

Promotion Promotion, the third major department of the business office, is a relative newcomer. It is essentially the "public-relations" department of the newspaper. Where a separate promotion department exists, it usually is responsible for initiating promotion policies, subject to the approval of the publisher, and it usually coordinates the promotional activities of other departments.

Research Research departments exist on most major newspapers and are of increasing importance to all parts of the newspaper. Sometimes research is a separate department, but more often it is a division of advertising or promotion. Research departments support advertising with market information, editorial departments with analyses of the behavior of readers and their editorial preferences, and circulation and promotion with a wide variety of services, including surveys of public attitudes toward the newspaper and its credibility, analyses of public response to changes in design and format, profiles of reader characteristics, and the like.

Production

What happens in the production department of the newspaper and how it is organized depends in part on the composition and printing methods it uses. For centuries, all newspapers were printed by letterpress: in simple terms, a raised metal or wood surface is inked and then applied to the paper. For many

Plate Making   Curved hot-metal letterpress
plates are shown being trimmed before being
clamped on the press.

Courtesy the Sun-Telegram (San Bernardino, California)
and The Gannetteer

decades, all type was composed or "set" by "hot-metal" methods: a line or a single character is cast from molten type metal in a mold, or "matrix." In recent years, letterpress has been giving way to "off-set" printing, or photolithography, and hot type to "cold type." Offset printing is done from a plate that is not raised but has areas that hold and areas that reject ink. The ink is not impressed directly on the paper but on another surface which in turn makes the impression on paper. "Cold type" refers to any composition method that does not involve casting lines and plates in hot metal and includes film and typewriter systems. Offset printing can be used with either composition method but more often than not is combined with cold-type systems. These matters are discussed in greater detail below and in Chapter 15.

More than 60 per cent of U. S. daily newspapers are produced by offset printing at this writing. How-ever, most newspapers larger than sixty to seventy-five thousand in circulation still use letterpress. Since these papers tend to have more influence, more copy editors, and more professional copy desks in general, letterpress printing systems cannot be ignored.

Production is normally under the supervision of a plant superintendent, who is usually directly responsible to the publisher. Typically, he will have four departments under his control (all under the jurisdiction of different unions): composition, plate making, press, and proofreading. In letterpress shops, plate-making is usually separated into two functions, stereotyping and engraving.

Composition   The composing room is the chief point of contact between editorial and production personnel. It is here that the editor's labors take physical form—his copy is set into type and assembled into pages.

Typesetting processes are more or less automatic. Hot type is set by manually operated or tape-actuated machines like the Linotype, which casts a line of raised type at a time. The lines are assembled into stories, combined with heads set at the same or another machine, and made up into pages by hand, according to instructions from the copy desk. At the same time, another part of the composing room, often called the "ad alley," is setting type for ads, assembling them under the direction of the advertising department, and putting them into the same pages.

In cold-type shops the same jobs are done by other machines, such as self-justifying typewriters or photocomposition machines. Their output is a positive or negative film or print which is assembled into a paste-up of an entire page.

Plate making   Plate making produces a printing surface that will reproduce an entire page. In letterpress printing, the plate is made by the stereotype process. This involves producing a matrix or "mat" of a page and then casting the mat in molten metal into a curved form that can be clamped on a rotary press. The mat is produced by rolling out a reverse impression of the page in papier-mâché.

Offset plates are flexible and hence do not require this intermediate step. The plate is made by a photo-etching process that transforms the surface of the plate into areas that accept ink and areas that reject it. The finished flat plate goes directly to the offset press, where it is bent and clamped on.

Hot-type production systems usually encompass a separate engraving department. Photoengraving is the process by which a picture is etched into a zinc plate. White areas are etched away by an acid bath, leaving only the part that is to print. If the copy is a line drawing, such as the newspaper organization chart shown on page 33, this may be done directly. But when degrees of gray are required, as in photographs, the engraver must "screen" the art, producing dots of varying size which will induce the illusion of shades of gray when the plate is inked and impressed on paper. (See Chapter 9 for more detail.)

Offset plants do not require separate engraving departments. Art is screened, but the result is etched directly on the plate.

Press   The paper is printed in the pressroom. Most small daily papers are run on offset presses. Most larger dailies use rotary, web-perfecting presses: the newspaper is printed on paper fed from huge rolls. In either case, the impression is applied directly or indirectly from the plates made in the plate-making department. A single press prints all pages of the paper; three or four presses may be running the same pages at the same time. They not only print but cut, fold, and trim the papers and deliver them directly to the mailing room.

Proofreading   In a sense, the proof desk lies astride the production, editorial, and advertising departments and is usually responsible to the production superintendent. Its object is to correct all typographical errors. In hot-type systems proof is "pulled" of all material set in the composing room, both ads and editorial matter, by inking the type and taking an impression of it on a simple proof press, and marks correcting the errors are made on the proofs. Proofs are then compared with the copy to make sure that the two conform. Since cold type is composed on paper, the completed job can be read directly. Proofreading is hence a more or less mechanical operation, unlike copyreading (see Chapter 3).

Proofreading is one of the more enduring fixtures in print shops, but some recent developments in production processes may eventually eliminate it. In cathode-ray tube (CRT) composing systems (discussed in Chapter 15), copyreading and proofreading are one step. The user views and corrects copy on the tube; from there, it goes directly through composition and makeup without human intervention. Proofreading is therefore not needed because all the usual sources of human error have been eliminated.

Editorial

The organizational division of the newspaper of primary concern to the copy editor is, of course, the editorial department. Describing a typical editorial department is not easy, since they differ markedly from one newspaper to another. However, it might work something like this:

The editorial department usually has two subdivisions, *news* and *editorial page,* each separately responsible directly to the publisher. The news division is usually under the supervision of a managing or executive editor. The editorial-page crew consists of editorial writers and is directed by a "chief editorial writer," an "editor," an "editor in chief," or sometimes an "editorial-page editor."

The sharp cleavage between the editorial page and the news pages is well founded in newspaper tradition. The idea, of course, is to separate fact from opinion. The newspaper traditionally presents objective fact in its news columns and expresses its opinions on these facts in the editorial columns (or under the signatures of the comment columnists the editor chooses to publish). Hence it is common to put the editor in charge of the editorial page and the managing editor in charge of all news departments—and ne'er the twain shall meet.

However, there are almost as many variations on this theme as there are daily newspapers.[2] Sometimes the "editor" has a chief editorial writer under him on the opinion side of the great divide and a managing editor to supervise news departments. On the very smallest papers, the editor may be his own editorial writer, his own star reporter, and practically everything else.

But returning to our typical example, the managing editor has direct supervision over the "general" news departments and final responsibility over the more or less autonomous sports and society sections. The Sunday department is sometimes under the direction of the managing editor and sometimes under the editor in chief.

The general news department ordinarily comprises at least two subdivisions: the city desk and the telegraph desk. Larger dailies are likely to divide up the labor even more, having separate desks to handle city, telegraph, cable, state, state-capitol, and Washington copy. Typical larger papers have local, telegraph, and

<hr />

[2] For a detailed treatment of how news departments are organized and how copy flows through them, see "The Structure and Layout of Editorial/News Departments," American Newspaper Publishers Association Research Institute Bulletin No. 1008, January 26, 1970. This report covers large and small newspapers in the United States and abroad.

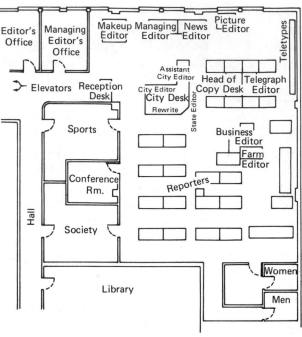

Courtesy the Indianapolis News

Typical Newsroom Floor Plan   The news executives and news editors of the Indianapolis *News* are within copy-passing reach of each other in a large but compact city room.

foreign desks; the New York *Times* has all three plus Albany and Washington desks.

At any rate, the student will understand that an orderly division of labor is necessary in the newsroom and that no two systems will be exactly alike. The typical arrangement in a medium-sized city room is as follows.

The focal point is the city desk, presided over by a city editor who is responsible to the managing editor. Working near him and nominally under his direction are two general news centers besides his own. One is the state desk, headed by a state editor, who directs the work of several score of "country" correspondents in much the same way as the city editor directs the work of a smaller number of reporters. The other is the "universal" copy desk, headed by a news editor who is assisted by several copy editors. A possible third is the Sunday desk, presided over by a Sunday editor who manages a staff of feature writers and

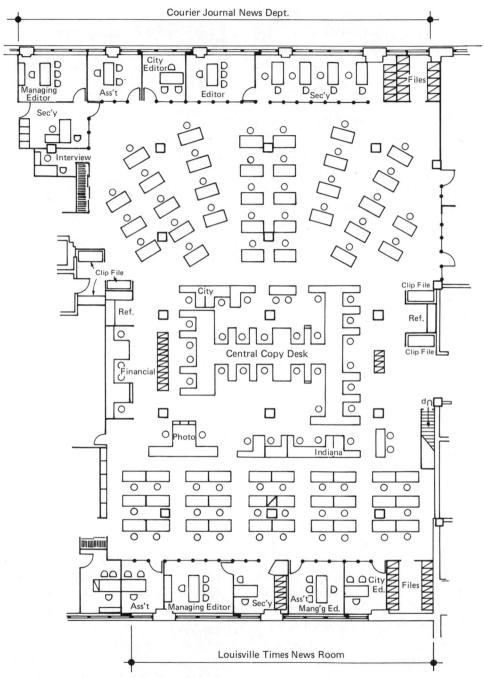

Newsroom of the Louisville Courier-Journal and Times The central copy desk is shared by the staffs of both papers, although each uses the space in its own way. The *Courier-Journal* alone employs twenty-five desk men. Carpeting and other sound-deadening materials make this a quiet place to work, even when the work load is at its peak.

Courtesy ANPA Research Institute and the Louisville Courier-Journal photographers. Copy from city, state, and Sunday desks flows over the universal desk as well as telegraph copy as it comes from teletype machines nearby. That's what makes it universal. Some newspapers have separate copy desks for each, but note that the autonomous departments, sports and society, operate their own copy desks even on newspapers with universal desks. Situations where sports and society copy is run through a single desk along with general news copy are rare.

Still another department in the newsroom may be the "culture" desk, handling music, art, drama, dance, etc. On most small papers, unfortunately, the general reporter who has learned a little artistic jargon writes up cultural events. A medium-sized paper might have one specialist who ranges over all these fields. The largest papers usually employ specialists in each. Just where the arts fit into the organization of the paper necessarily varies widely from place to place. Sometimes they are closely allied to the Sunday department. At any rate, through one channel or another, the staff handling them is ultimately responsible to the managing editor.

Responsibility for pictures also varies widely from city room to city room. In some cases, responsibility for all "art" is taken by a photo or picture desk, answerable directly to the managing editor. This desk is presided over by a picture editor, who is assisted by a corps of local photographers and a special technician or two. The editor is also in charge of the darkroom, where pictures are developed and printed, and for the technical handling of photos as well as seeing that they are taken. Sometimes the city or news editors divide these responsibilities, the city editor making assignments to photographers and deciding how to use their work, the news or telegraph editor handling nonlocal pictures coming in via various syndicated services. (These issues are treated in greater detail on page 41, and in Chapter 9).

Some newspapers, particularly the larger ones, have an additional newsroom operative, the "makeup editor." Makeup is the job of arranging news on the page to achieve a pleasing appearance while at the same time giving each story the "display" it warrants.

Makeup is actually *performed* in the composing room, but it is planned and supervised by the newsroom. On many small-city papers, however, the makeup supervisor is the news editor, who marks up dummies showing where all major stories, at least, are to be placed.

The makeup editor is told how the top news of the day is to be displayed, but he himself works out dummy pages covering details, particularly of inside pages. He also supervises the printers as they carry out his instructions. That is one of the reasons this volume will devote a good deal of space to the "back shop" and to principles of typography (Chapter 8) and makeup (Chapters 10 and 11).

Now it should be clear how the newsroom is arranged in terms of responsibility: reporters are responsible to the city editor; copy editors to the news editor (or where there is no universal desk, to city, telegraph, state, or cable editors); photographers to the photo or city editor; country correspondents to the state editor; foreign correspondents to the cable editor, etc. Each of these editors, in turn, is responsible to the managing editor, who is usually responsible to the publisher.

The publisher, to whom all three major divisions of the newspaper are responsible, is usually the final decision maker for the entire operation. Sometimes he is responsible only to himself, being also owner. But usually he manages the newspaper for a corporation or partnership. Hence, even his decisions may be subject to the approval of a higher authority.

Newsmen are today insisting on a larger voice in controlling the policies of their papers. This is the pervasive theme of *The Chicago Journalism Review* and other publications by and for newspaper people. Some newspapers and newspaper groups are responding, but it remains to be seen what form these developments will eventually take.

Unfortunately, this is not a very sharp or clear picture of the structural organization of the newspaper. If confusion persists, blame it on the healthy lack of uniformity in the way newspapers are organized. The next section may help to clear things up, as it is devoted to functional organization. Its purpose is to show how the various strata of the newspaper staff interact to produce a newspaper day after day.

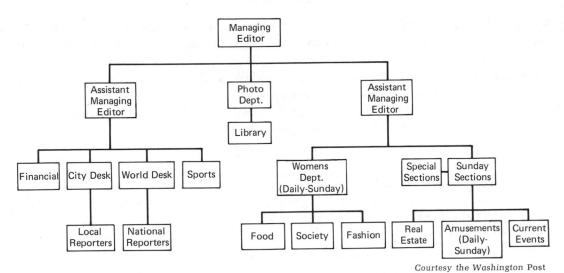

Newsroom Responsibility   How the news departments of the Washington *Post* are organized.

Courtesy the Washington Post

The Flow of News

The complexity and responsibility of the copy desk can be more fully understood by studying the way news copy flows through the orderly channels of the newspaper. News copy originates principally in two places: with the reporters and the wire-service "tickers." All reporting is done at the behest and under the watchful eye of the city editor. Reporters turn their stories over to him and he does some preliminary editing. Is it what he wanted? Does he think the reporter ought to polish up the lead? Develop the story differently? Get more quotes? More details from the morgue? For these or other major changes, back it goes to the reporter. If the city editor thinks it needs just a little checking and polishing, the story moves over to the copy desk.

News Editor

The head of the copy desk is the news editor, the "slot man" who sits inside the U-shaped desk and directs the work of the copy editors ("rim men") who sit on the desk's outer edge. However, the news editor may be enough of an executive to work at a separate desk, making more or less major news decisions sub-

ject to the approval of the managing editor, and supervising a "copy-desk chief" who is in the slot but not empowered to make decisions beyond a rather routine level. This book uses the terms "news editor," "slot man," and "copy-desk chief" interchangeably, but it is worth noting that in some cases these functions are not identical.

The news editor is the first on the copy desk to see a story. If it is a big one, he probably has known it was coming and is prepared for it. If it is routine, he is finding out about it for the first time. He scans the story in a matter of seconds and judges its "worth" in terms of news value. Then he expresses his decision in concrete newspaper terms: he assigns a headline size and style which will convey to the reader an instant impression of the story, and he decides where, in general terms at least, the story will be run: Page One, some special page such as entertainment or financial, or "wild" or "run of paper" inside. Finally, he turns the story over to one of his rim men for the actual editing. The minor story he simply drops into a basket; any rim man can do it. A specialized or particularly important story he turns over directly to the editor best qualified to handle it. (The job of the slot man is discussed more fully in Chapter 12.)

The first thing the copy editor does when he picks up the story is to note any instructions the news editor may have put on the copy. At the very least, there will be headline instructions. He edits the copy, writes a headline, and returns the finished product to another basket for the editor's final perusal. The news editor now satisfies himself that the copy editor has dealt with the story satisfactorily, or he returns it to him with suggestions.

The news editor must also keep track of all the copy that crosses the desk, particularly for makeup purposes. On some desks he does this pretty much by hunch, on others he maintains an elaborate copy-control system: he enters each story on a master list, which includes its length in column inches and the type of headline, and he marks the copy of the story with a "slug" or "guideline" codifying the master-list information.

Composing Room

When the news editor is finished with the copy, he sends it to the composing room, often by pneumatic tube, where it is set in type. First, the "copy cutter," who controls the flow of work to the various typesetting machines, cuts the story into sections known as "takes." By adjusting the length of the takes, he divides the work evenly among the machines. Early in the news day takes can be longer, because there is plenty of time before the first edition goes to press. Later, when deadlines are creeping up, takes are cut shorter so that several machines can be setting a given story at the same time. The copy cutter marks the copy of each take with coded instructions for putting it back into its place in the story, and the code gets "slugged" into type at the beginning of each take. The makeup person can then identify each take in proof and reassemble the story with no trouble and few mistakes. If there is no copy cutter, the copy desk performs this function. Now the story and its headline are set in cold or hot type.

The next process is to make sure that the set type conforms to the copy and is free of error. In hot-metal systems, the type is moved into metal trays called "galleys" and a "galley proof" is pulled and proofread. In cold-type systems, the proofreader checks

roughs. Then he spikes the copy on a hook to be filed away at the end of the day for future reference if necessary.

The marked proof moves back to the composing room so that all lines containing errors can be reset correctly. In hot-metal systems, the compositor sets the correction lines, wraps them in the proof itself, and sends the package back to the galley from which the proof was made. A printer locates the incorrect lines and inserts the corrected lines in their place. In cold-type systems, new lines are composed, then cut and pasted over the faulty lines.

Sometimes a "revise" proof is pulled and sent back to the proof desk to make sure that the correction lines were set and inserted without error. This is routine procedure with legal advertising and other material where special pains must be taken to avoid mistakes. But news routine does not ordinarily allow time for this step.

Page Makeup

Makeup is another way the copy desk gives directions to the composing room. Pages are made up according to "dummies" supplied by the news or other appropriate editor. The page dummy is an example of the interaction of the three major divisions of the newspaper discussed earlier. It originates in the advertising department, where the ads are marked in first. Then it goes to the news editor, who can tell from it how much space is available for news on that page. The news editor then marks in the location of the news stories, at least all the key ones, and finally the dummy goes to the composing room, where it serves as a set of directions on how the page is to be made up. The printer has only to refer to the dummy of a particular page, find the type of the story and head, and assemble it in the form in keeping with the instructions on the dummy.

Where hot-metal methods are still in use, the dummy is next spiked, much as the proof and copy were spiked at the proof desk, and the page form moves from the composing room into the plate-making department. Completed forms are slid onto hand trucks called "turtles" and trundled to the mat roller. The mat roller makes a matrix, or reverse impression, of the type on a sheet of damp, flexible material like papier-mâché. The stereotypers then "pack" the mat by fastening strips of gummed pasteboard to the reverse side of the places where "white space" will ultimately appear. This is done to prevent the weight of the molten metal poured against the mat from forcing it out of shape. Then the mat is dried (moisture in the mat would create dangerous steam under the conditions of extreme heat developed during casting). Finally a curved metal plate is cast from the mat, the plate is cooled and trimmed, and the page is ready for the press.

As we have seen, offset plates are produced by a different plate-making process.

Printing

When all the plates are in place, the press begins to roll, and the original story has now run the full gamut of the production process. Copies of the paper are checked over by the pressmen to make sure that the plates are all printing cleanly, that all the pages are in their proper sequence, that margins are correct, etc. Copies are also hurried to the advertising department and the composing room for final checking.

The copy desk, too, has a chance to check over the first edition and make corrections, even as work progresses on the next edition. Any corrections that must be made are run through the correction process described on page 34. An error in a headline on Page One, for instance, is rushed to the composing room to be reset. The corrected type goes to the page forms to be substituted for the erroneous lines. The page is replated, and finally the press is stopped and the corrected plate substituted.

If the paper issues only one or two daily editions, the heavy part of the day's work is now done. When the editions are many, however, this is only the beginning. (A few newspapers get out only one edition, but most run through three to a dozen in a single news cycle.) At least one representative of the copy desk remains at his post until the last corrected version of the last edition is rolling.

This description of how copy flows necessarily stresses routine. But rarely is a news cycle routine. Each in some way is different from any other. Just how flexible copy flow can be will be seen in Chapter 4.

The Division of Labor in the Newsroom

To understand the structure and functioning of the newsroom it is necessary to see how work is distributed among city, copy, telegraph, state, and photo desks. But the reader is reminded that variation in practices may be substantial from one newsroom to another.

The City Desk

The city desk is responsible for information flowing to the newspaper from all sources (other than the specialized ones handled by the semiautonomous departments such as sports, society, women's, Sunday, etc.) within sharply defined boundaries around the central city. One must expect to find exceptions, of course, where a single paper serves two adjacent cities, for example, or a number of communities (in some cases, the edition and even the nameplate is different for each city or community). However, such exceptions are of little concern at this point.

The city desk is of critical importance to the daily newspaper because of the structure of the typical newspaper's territory. The newspaper is normally in a symbiotic relationship with a city or combination of cities, large or small, and the retail trade area surrounding the city. The city itself is the heart of the territory. It is likely to have the greatest concentration of readers, news sources, and advertisers. For this reason, the newspaper, perhaps even more than its local radio and television competitors, puts its greatest effort into local news. Local advertising revenue accounts for about 85 per cent of all newspaper advertising revenue, and usually the newspaper is the medium the city's people rely on most for information about local issues.[3]

---

[3] Bruce H. Westley and Werner J. Severin, "Some Correlates of Media Credibility," *Journalism Quarterly* 41:325–335 (Summer 1964) finds the newspaper the medium most relied on, especially for local news, but does not find it the most credible to a sample of readers (see pages 320–324).

T-Bar-C Ranch in the Newsroom of the Hartford Times An unusual arrangement of copy-desk space and personnel. It was started by adding a table to the usual C-shaped desk. Then the table sprouted into the shape of a T. Under the bars of the T are the news editor at left and the telegraph editor at right (who needs all that space around him to spread out his wire copy). Pneumatic tubes (not shown) deliver copy from the wire room to the telegraph editor.

The *Times* editors say this arrangement promotes communication among decision makers. The news editor can reach and talk with the telegraph editor on his left, the photo editor on his right, and the slot man in front of him, who in turn can reach and talk to the seven rim men who normally sit across from him.

Note the number and sex of the younger editors.

The city desk is presided over by the city editor, who is in most circumstances the person responsible for local news-gathering operations. He may or may not also be responsible for local photo operations. In general, he keeps a moment-to-moment surveillance over everything going on in the city that has potential value as news. He deploys reporters so that the paper misses as little news as possible, and he sees to it that events are converted into crisp and flowing prose in almost no time at all.

The city editor supervises the entire local reportorial staff (with the exceptions noted above), which may be roughly divided into two classes, "beat" reporters and "general-assignment" reporters. Beat reporters gather news on set, routine rounds ("beats"), which may be established sources such as city hall, police, the county courts, etc., or broad special categories such as business, science, labor, conservation, public welfare, the arts, or education. General-assignment reporters are on call in the newsroom to do whatever job the city editor wants done, from writing obituaries to interviewing celebrities to backgrounding significant news developments. Most newsrooms also have another type of specialist known as the "rewrite

Typical Copy Desk of a Medium-Sized Newspaper The compact, convenient copy desk of the San Bernardino (California) *Sun-Telegram*. The news editor (center) can easily hand stories to six copy editors around the rim. The pneumatic tubes at left carry edited copy to the composing room.

Sun Bernardino (California) Sun-Telegram *photo*
Courtesy The Gannetteer

man"; he writes stories telephoned in by "leg men," who go out after the facts, or from other sources.

Some city desks also act as their own copy desks, with the city editor or assistant city editor in the slot and city-news specialists on the rim. The telegraph desk, too, sometimes has a copy desk of its own.

The Telegraph Desk

Today's newspaper would be an impossibility without the help of worldwide news-gathering agencies. The entire character and worth of the daily newspaper depend heavily on the lightning speed with which news can be transmitted from the farthest outpost of the Old World to the newsroom of the smallest daily in the United States.

Organized, cooperative news gathering among newspapers is little more than a hundred years old.[4] But its origins go back farther than that—to Samuel Topliffe in Boston, for instance. About 1811, Sam started keeping a news ledger. He got the news from "home" by meeting incoming ships in a rowboat, getting the latest intelligence from whatever source, and writing it all down. Boston newspapers and individuals were happy to dig it out of the ledgers.

Or perhaps news-gathering cooperation got its start in the mid-1820's, when a combine of New York dailies began sending a representative to meet ships in the harbor and get the latest world news simultaneously for all its members.

This combine, formalized in about 1848 as an exclusive club called the New York Associated Press, began to put cooperative news gathering on a broad and systematic basis. It brought the news agency through its rowboats-in-the-harbor phase, its carrier-pigeon and pony-express days, to the advent of the telegraph and the cable. It extended news-agency service from its own little inner circle in New York across the nation—and helped assure its future as a nation by providing a channel for the interchange of information.

But it remained for the Western Associated Press, which had its leadership largely in Chicago, to over-

throw the New York group and establish the present-day Associated Press. The Western combination, founded in 1892, revolted when it got tired of being the Eastern group's stepson and handyman. Thus was genuine cooperative news gathering born.

Today there are two full-service news-gathering agencies in the United States, Associated Press, the survivor of the East-West press-association "war" of more than a century ago,[5] and United Press International, the product of a much more recent merger of United Press, founded by and for the Scripps-Howard newspapers, and International News Service, which bore a similar relationship to the Hearst newspapers. Increasingly, however, these two services are meeting competition from a relatively new type of service, typified by the New York *Times* and Los Angeles *Times*-Washington *Post* syndicates, which provide their client newspapers with comprehensive and particularly competent reporting to supplement the fast-breaking "spot" news sent by the traditional wire services. Since the number of wire services has been reduced to two, in fact, major newspapers across the country have been making use of a far wider spectrum of supplementary sources than ever before. Many newspapers take foreign services such as Reuters (British). For a time, more and more newspapers took both AP and UPI, rather than one or the other. But more recently, taking one of the major wire services plus a supplementary service has become the norm.

The AP has two broad systems, its "domestic file" and its "world file." From central headquarters in New York, the domestic file is started on its way across the nation and the world service is fed to clients abroad. The domestic service is based on a "trunk" wire that is the main channel of news to member newspapers and AP bureaus in key cities. The trunk is really four wires: the "A" wire, carrying the main load of general news—about 100,000 words a day; the "B" wire, supplementing the "A" and carrying its overload, if any, but mainly channeling the exchange of regional news; the "Sports" wire,

---

[4] See Victor Rosewater, *History of Cooperative Newsgathering in the United States* (New York: Appleton, 1930).

[5] Consult Peter R. Knights, "The Press Association War of 1866–1867," *Journalism Monographs* No. 6, December 1967.

carrying sports exclusively; the "D" wire, carrying financial matter exclusively.

Most members do not receive these four files, however, but rather a single state or regional wire that is a condensation of all four plus a channel for sending out news of their own localities. This is known as a "split" wire. A circuit serving Wisconsin and Upper Michigan, for instance, is split off from a regional combination out of Chicago so that bureaus in that area can send members news of special regional interest to them. The split wire, which typically carries about 25,000 words in one twelve-hour cycle, is a full service in itself. It carries a condensed version of the general news from the "A," regional news from the "B," sports news, and financial news from the "D," in addition to state news. It is, therefore, usually adequate for papers of up to, say, 20,000 circulation.

But the wire system described here is not a one-way street. The services naturally receive information, not just distribute it. Their headquarters are a clearing house for the exchange of news. For instance, when the French cabinet falls, the story is filed from Paris by cable, international telephone, or by teletype by way of London to New York. New York reworks the story on the world desk and transmits that version to clients all over the world. At the same time, it is edited or rewritten for transmission over the "A" wire—to Indianapolis, let us say. At the same time, an AP staffer covering the Indianapolis 500-mile auto race files his story by telegraph, telephone, or teletype to Chicago. There it is put on the sports wire and moved to New York, where it is funneled to the world desk and transmitted to Paris, among other places.

At the same time, additional services are being transmitted by other means. For instance, AP and UPI each have a separate radio wire. It is filed out of the same offices as the news wire but the news is rewritten for voice before being transmitted to radio members. The wire services also provide an interchange of pictures between members, using separate transmission lines. AP Wirephoto and UPI Unifax transmit pictures by telephone wire, cable, or radio. A photoelectric "scanner" notes changes in light values while the picture revolves on a drum and converts these values into differently pitched sounds. The sounds can be sent over leased telephone wires to a receiver which reproduces the original visual changes in values on a revolving sheet of light-sensitized paper. This in turn is developed by the usual process into a photographic print.

Even newspapers which are not full clients of the picture services can receive in part the benefits of this rapid transmission. Some take a limited service which provides them with only as many pictures from the file as they wish, rather than the full service. Others get the pictures in mat form about a day late. AP Telemats, for instance, makes mats of selected Wirephoto pictures, maps, etc., and sends them by mail to subscribers.

News has an unpleasant way of occurring unexpectedly. And it doesn't wait its turn to move on the wires. This brief overview of the wire-service operation should show that an elaborate system is needed to keep 100,000 words a day flowing evenly on the wires to the newsroom—and in a useful order and content balance. An efficient system is needed in the newsroom, too, to see that the output is handled carefully. This can mean culling a mere 8,000 to 10,000 words out of the 100,000-word output of the trunk wires plus the 25,000 words of the state or "split" wire, and keeping track of stories as they are received. It is not unusual for a single story to come over the wire in anything from two to fifty "takes" separated by minutes or hours and any quantity of other information. Just accounting for it all calls for a certain amount of organization, not to mention putting the stories back together again (see Chapter 3).

This is the job of the telegraph desk. The telegraph desk got its name, of course, in the days when the newspaper received its news by telegraph. At one time, in fact, the Morse operator was a fixture in the newsroom. In more recent times, "telegraph" copy has been moved by teletype. And still more recently, as mentioned on page 19, the teletypewriter has been converted to yield a punched tape that automatically operates a composing machine, instead of teleprinted copy. Though many newspapers which can afford it still use printed wire-service copy and their own tape-punching system, many small newspapers take a limited, regional teletypesetter-tape service. The receiving machine produces both a tape which can directly operate typesetting machines and printed "monitor" copy indicating what is on the tape. Editorial corrections are made by cutting the tape and correcting proof, rather than the usual method of marking copy.

Newspapers differ widely among themselves in handling the telegraph job, as we have seen (page 30). In some newsrooms, the telegraph desk is a separate entity presided over by the telegraph editor and responsible for all wire news except that which has a local "end." But many newsrooms have no telegraph desk as such. In the universal-desk system, the general news desk handles telegraph copy along with local and state news. A telegraph editor, perhaps aided by an assistant telegraph editor, may be responsible for moving wire copy across the universal desk. When there is no telegraph editor, the job is usually part of the duties of the news editor.

The State Desk

City staffs and the wire services provide the great bulk of the day's news. But standing between them, in a sense, is the "state desk," which deserves attention here because its importance seems to be gaining steadily and because it often affords the apprentice editor a unique opportunity.

"State desk" and "state editor" are perhaps the most common designations for the local news operation that extends from the limits of the city of publication to the outer limits of the newspaper's territory. Sometimes its product is called "suburban" copy, sometimes "country" copy, sometimes "county" copy, but in all such cases the operation has the same purpose and fits into the total news function in about the same way.

Individual newspapers differ widely in the way they are organized to handle state news. The newspapers which don't often include news outside their own cities other than occasional "personals" collected and written up by residents of nearby towns (who are given free subscriptions in return) obviously don't need to employ much of a state staff. But the thorough statewide coverage of such newspapers as the Providence *Journal* and the Des Moines *Register* and

Tribune requires maintaining a large full-time staff to give them as thorough coverage of outlying communities as is accorded the cities themselves.

The Syracuse (New York) *Post-Standard* covers a twenty-one-county, 20,000-square-mile area of a million population in six separate regional editions, and sends out many reporters to do it.

The Louisville *Courier-Journal* and *Times,* as the prestige newspapers of an entire state extending from Virginia to Missouri, regionalize their editions differently. Instead of employing staffs and stringers to compete with strictly local newspapers at their own game, they maintain small bureaus at key points to monitor newsworthy events and send reporters from headquarters only on stories of larger significance. Each regional edition contains more or less the same news. However, the news is *played* differently in different regional editions. A story about an event in Paducah, for example, may be put on Page One in the western Kentucky edition and on an inside page in the eastern. But every story that makes these papers makes them for its appeal and significance for Kentucky readers as a whole. One obvious advantage of this system is that it means uniform high quality throughout the paper, something that is not possible when the regional news is relegated to ill-equipped "stringers" (free-lance reporters) and second-string staffers, the better reporters being saved for city and national news.

The Chicago *Tribune,* primarily to meet competition from suburban weeklies, maintains full-time staffs at key suburban points, often using these positions to give experience and seasoning to their newest reporters and editors. These staffs cover spot news on a day-to-day basis for the whole paper and produce a weekly section that circulates only in the suburban area each staff serves.

The Cincinnati *Post & Times-Star* publishes the Kentucky *Post & Times-Star* to serve a large metropolitan area across the Ohio River. The Kentucky *Post* has its own newsroom in Covington with professional staffers and stringers. The paper may be purchased separately or in combination with the parent newspaper, an arrangement similar to that of the *Standard-Times* of New Bedford (Massachusetts) and the *Cape Cod Standard Times* of Hyannis, serving Cape Cod.

Thus the variation from newspaper to newspaper is large in the way the territory outside the central city is covered, but these examples all indicate the importance usually attached to this function. Just as the state staff is often a testing ground for reporters, the state desk is often a testing ground for news executives.

The Photo Desk

There may have been a time when the wordsmith looked down his nose at his fellow newsman who only snapped pictures (and sometimes forgot to supply cutlines to go with them), but that time is gone forever. Now we know that words and pictures can do a better job of telling the day's news than either can do alone. The two can no longer be separated. The "picture page" is gone, for the most part, along with the page of solid, gray print. Whether to meet the competition from television, where the visual and verbal are uniquely fused, or because of what they have learned from *Life, Look,* and the other picture magazines, or because of the development of new capabilities of their own, newspapers are placing more and more importance on enhancing words with pictures. Obviously, someone must integrate words and pictures and seek out new ways of making them work together. This job most often falls on the news editor.

Again, it is hard to find a typical newsroom organization to exemplify the way the photographic staff functions. Some photo operations are part of the advertising department rather than the newsroom, since pictures are as important in advertising as in local news. Some newspapers have a more or less autonomous photo desk headed by a photo editor who directs a staff of photographers, superintends the dark room, and is responsible directly to the managing or executive editor. On others, the photo staff is directed by an assistant city editor and sometimes by an assistant managing editor. In some places, the photography is done by the reporters themselves who are directly under the control of the city desk.

But however the organization is constructed, the news editor is usually involved in making decisions about pictures at several levels. He is informed about what local pictures are coming as well as what local news is coming, and he must take both into account in planning for the use of available space. He is usually also responsible for deciding what nonlocal pictures to use—photos provided by suburban or state staffs and special bureaus, for example, or transmitted over the wire from distant points. He is directly responsible for the way pictures relate to the stories they illustrate and to other art. And he is responsible for their placement in page makeup. Choosing suitable pictures is treated in Chapter 9, and the part played by illustrations in planning page makeup is examined in Chapters 10 and 11.

3

Basic Editing Skills

Chapters 1 and 2 introduced the functions of the copy desk and its milieu. They also introduced the physical and intellectual tools of the news-editing craft—the special language and skills the editor uses to carry out his tasks. It is time to see how these tools work—to develop some understanding of how the manifold problems the editor encounters may be solved with his brain and his copy pencil. The present chapter takes up how the editor reads copy and corrects it to assure that (1) it is grammatically correct, clear in meaning, economical of words, and easy to read; (2) the facts it states are accurate and faithful to the essential truth as it is known; (3) the account of the facts is manifestly objective—or at least as free of bias as human judgment can make it—and as balanced and fair as possible. In addition, this chapter deals with a minor skill—helping the neophyte learn to unscramble and put back together again the running wire story.

Editing for Verbal Clarity and Correctness

Mass media must convey the meaning of complex events to a highly diverse audience. Though the American newspaper does not have a language barrier to cope with, as do Canadian papers, for example, the editor cannot assume that because words are clear to him they are necessarily understandable to every one of his readers. Cultural barriers, for one thing, create wide differences among people in the range and size of their vocabularies and in their abilities to comprehend structural complexity. Newspaper writers and editors have to keep finding new ways of telling the story completely within the linguistic limits of every lettered person—in common words and simple structures.

Most written communications require not only readable writing but impeccably correct writing. Though departures from correct English may in some cases make the going easier for the person of limited linguistic skill, they are an unnecessary annoyance to those who care about the language they use. Correctness must become habitual with the editor, requiring so little conscious attention that he can concentrate his energies on the other part of the job: making the language meaningful and readable. The editor does not have to sacrifice one to achieve the other. Readable, meaningful writing need not be incorrect; correct writing is not necessarily hard to read. The editor strives for both. For instance, when a verb form is incorrect, he substitutes the correct form—and if this makes the sentence harder to read, he finds another way of saying the same thing which is both right and easy to read. Correct writing need not be pompous

writing. In fact, good writing requires that its correctness be inconspicuous.

It is impossible within the scope of this book to include a handbook of rhetoric that will solve all the student's difficulties with grammar, sentence structure, etc. Rather, with an eye on both mechanics and readability, this section will concentrate on the problems of language that seem to give newsmen the most trouble. In Chapter 5, language skills are elaborated, emphasizing the larger problem of meaning.

The example below is a real story that came to the desk of a medium-sized Midwestern newspaper in precisely the form shown. The indicated corrections were made by an editor under genuine newsroom conditions. Editing this story took perhaps fifteen minutes, which is a lot of time to spend on a single inside-page report, especially in smaller newsrooms. However, a careful job was needed, and usually the editor can take at least this much time if the story requires it.

```
       A new three-day-a- week schedule for home delivered
milk will be placed in effect by Plainville dairies the
week of March 4, and a "thrift plan" for daily purchases
will go into effect at the same time be extended to the
entire city.

       Sunday, March 4, will probably xxxxxxxxxxxxxxxx
mark the last Sabbath day delivery inthe city, officials
of the three Plainville dairies agreed.

       Two of the dairies --the Barclay Dairy Co. and thex
Bordon's Kelly-Martin division -- indicated that deliv-
eries will be Monday, Wednesday, and Friday on the West
side of the city, Tuesday, Thursday, and x Saturday on
the East side..

       Plans are still being completed by the xxxxxxxxxxx
Boardman Farm Dairy.

       Officials pointed out that, for the first time,
milkmen will be able to take Sunday off, to spend with
```

their families and that economies of operation by cutting back to a six-day week will be passed onto the x consumers under the "thrift plan."

Under this plan, the first two quarts of home delivered milk purchased in a single daily delivery will be at the regular price -- 19 cents.

But all other quarts bought in the same delivery will be 1 cent less, or 18 cents.

Notices of the new plan were sent out to customers of the Borden Co. on Saturday, with the other two dairies to send out notices soon.

Officials of the Barclay concern said that the new plan has been pending since last September, when negotiations covering the labor angle were completed with the unions concerned. The plan was xxxx scheduled to go into effect December 18, but postponed because xxxxxxxxx xxxxxxxxxx difficulties of plant changes. The new plan involves, most of all, increases in xxxxxxxxxxxxxxxxxx xxxxxxxxxxxxxxxx storage capacity to hold milk the extra day xxxxxxxxx over weekends.

Plainville dairies will put

A new three-day-a-week schedule for home delivered milk will be placed in effect by Plainville dairies the week of March 4 and a "thrift plan" for daily purchases will go into effect at the same time be extended to the entire city, *company* officials said *Sat.*

Sunday, March 4 will probably xxxxxxxxxxxxxxx mark the last Sabbath-day *Sunday* delivery in the city, officials of the three Plainville dairies agreed. *Schedule Set [sub*

Two of the dairies --the Barclay Dairy Co. and then Borden's Kelly-Martin division --indicated that deliveries will be *made* Monday, Wednesday, and Friday on the West

side of the city, [and] Tuesday, Thursday, and ~~a~~ Saturday on
the East side.

Plans are still being completed by the ~~xxxxxxxxxx~~
Boardman Farm Dairy.

Officials *[said the plan will give delivery men]* ~~pointed out that, for the first time,
milkmen will be able to take~~ Sunday off, ~~to spend with
their families and that~~ *[They said the resulting]* economies, ~~of operation by cutting back to a six day week~~ will be passed on to ~~the x~~
consumers under the *[new]* thrift plan.

Under this plan, the first two quarts of home
delivered milk purchased in a single ~~daily~~ delivery will
be at the regular price -- 19 cents.

But ~~all other~~ *[additional]* quarts ~~bought~~ in the same delivery
will be 1 cent less, ~~or 18 cents.~~ *[Notices Sent [sub*

Notices *[on]* ~~of~~ the new plan were sent ~~out~~ to customers
~~of the Borden Co. on~~ *[Borden,]* Saturday, ~~with~~ the other two
dairies ~~to send out notices~~ *[will follow suit]* soon.

Officials ~~of the Barclay concern~~ said ~~that~~ the new
plan has been pending since last September, when ~~nego-~~ *[labor]*
~~tiations covering the labor angle~~ were completed, ~~with
the unions concerned.~~ The plan was ~~xxxx~~ scheduled to go
into effect December 18, but *[was]* postponed because ~~of plant~~ *[changeover]*
~~xxxxxxxxxx~~ difficulties ~~of plant changes.~~ The ~~new plan~~ *[changeover]*
involves ~~most of all,~~ increase*[d]* ~~in xxxxxxxxxxxxxxxxx~~
~~xxxxxxxxxxxxxxxx~~ storage capacity to hold milk, ~~the extra
day xxxxxxxx over weekends.~~ *[Sunday.]*

Following is a complete explanation of the editor's reasoning as he made every correction, as an introduction to problems of simplifying, clarifying, and correcting language. The reader should refer to the original version as he reads the edited one. Perhaps not every editor would agree with all the changes; many undoubtedly could have done a better job.

The lead lacks simplicity and directness. Its sentence structure is difficult, particularly as the vehicle for two rather uncomplicated items of information. Not only is it a compound sentence but its structure forces the voice of both verbs into the passive, a phenomenon that often results when the reporter puts the key words on paper first, then tries to build a sentence around them. The words "a new three-day-a-week schedule" are indeed the key words. But at what cost? Besides requiring the passive voice, the lead demands a labored avoidance of repetition: "will be placed in effect" (both labored and incorrect) and "will go into effect." All this was solved by *putting the logical subject in its logical place*—at the beginning of the sentence. The editor also felt the sentence as it stood called for both attribution and a time "angle," so he slipped them both in inconspicuously at the end.

Paragraph 2 illustrates another awkward effort to avoid repetition. After writing "Sunday, March 4," the writer found himself with the choice of repeating "Sunday" or contriving a synonym ("Sabbath day"). He overlooked another possibility which the editor did not—to use the date only in the first reference. "Officials of" was deleted because it was no longer necessary in view of changes in paragraph 1.

In paragraph 5, the writer again chose a circuitous route. The result is an unnecessarily long and complicated sentence. The editor made two simple sentences of it. Both have the virtues of simplicity and directness. Note that the insertion of "the resulting" was an effective substitute for an entire phrase which amounted to a repetition anyway ("by cutting back to the six-day week"). This, plus general editorial tightening, reduced the total wordage from forty-five to twenty-six.

The next two paragraphs illustrate the role of sentences and paragraphs in relation to meaning. Editors more often divide long sentences and paragraphs into more and shorter ones. In this case, the opposite was done, but for good reason: there is a single unit of thought here, and it can be stated best by wrapping it up in one sentence. Making it two sentences might have improved the readability score, but it wouldn't have helped the reader to grasp its meaning. The change also made possible the deletion of a few now unnecessary words.

But the editor split the very next sentence into two. He felt that two short simple sentences would be clearer and easier to read than the original one sentence. He was chiefly avoiding the afterthought "with" clause, which he considered both awkwardly phrased and not precisely correct. He also added a few touches

designed to improve the flow and naturalness of the wording.

The changes in the last paragraph demonstrate the saving in words that is an important product of careful editing. But the elimination of words for its own sake is not the primary lesson here. Extra words like these actually get in the way of meaning: the simple, direct way is usually the readable and meaningful way. Another improvement in haphazard paragraphing is also shown.

The following example has a rather convincing ring on first reading, but actually it is full of minor confusions:

A new rating plan for young drivers under 25 years and certain reductions of 6 to 11 per cent for adults who drive over 7,500 miles a year were automobile insurance changes announced by the Allstate Insurance Company today.

The plan institutes a sliding rate scale for drivers between the ages of 23 and 25 years to meet the raise in insurance rates for young drivers which went into effect a month ago.

Reductions to adults will apply to bodily injury and property damage rates.

"A new rating plan for young drivers" implies that the insurance company is going to rate young drivers as risks. But the story contains nothing to support that idea; it is about "rates," not "ratings." And why both "young drivers" and "under 25 years"? Isn't everyone under 25 "young"? And shouldn't it read "25 years of age," or just "25"? Why "automobile insurance changes"? Is the insurance going to change? Or just the rate?

Clearly, one of the chief problems in this lead is sentence structure: long, complicated sentences are obstructing the meaning. The main fault seems to lie in the awkward wording "were automobile insurance changes announced by." How can the editor get around that? One possibility would be to take the advice of the King in *Alice's Adventures in Wonderland.* "Begin at the beginning," the King said, gravely, "and go on till you come to the end: then stop." That would mean starting: "The Allstate Insurance Company, a subsidiary of Sears, Roebuck and Company, today announced a new . . . ." The editor supplied the firm's identification because he felt it contributed to the story's total meaning.

But the editor did not have to rewrite the whole lead; a flick or two of the pencil fixed it. Two main things had to be done: He had to withhold some of the detail from the lead in order to reduce it to reasonable and readable length; and he had to repair the structural fault.

> A new auto insurance rate plan for young drivers and certain rate reductions for adults were announced today by the Allstate Insurance Company, a subsidiary of Sears, Roebuck and Company.

Now the lead "reads." The editor worked the deleted details into subsequent paragraphs:

> The plan institutes a sliding rate scale for drivers between the ages of 23 and 25 to meet the increase in insurance rates for young drivers which went into effect a month ago.
> Reductions of 6 to 11 per cent to adults who drive more than 7,500 miles a year will apply to bodily injury and property damage rates.

Now nothing essential has been lost. "Under 25 years" in the original lead was not specific enough, and the ground is covered in paragraph 2 anyway. The details about adult rate reductions need not be in the lead; the editor fitted them nicely into the last paragraph.

Notice that "raise" was changed to "increase." "Raise" may be used as a noun but only to mean "pay raise." Notice, too, that "over" in the lead has become "more than" in the last paragraph. "Over" applies to spatial relationships, not quantitative ones.

The rest of this section will consider more examples of faulty and confused writing and suggest corrections. It will deal first with sentence structure, grammar, and punctuation, then vocabulary and word usage.

Sentence Structure

An early study of readability found that readable writing usually includes a high proportion of *simple sentences*. More recent studies have reached the same conclusion. This does not suggest that editors should reduce every compound or complex sentence to a simple one; it does suggest that simplicity in sentence structure helps convey ideas and information.

Newspaper style in recent years has moved increasingly in the direction of uncluttered writing. Journalism students once were urged to vary their writing by using different grammatical beginnings—a participial phrase this time, an infinitive phrase the next time, and a dependent clause after that. One early textbook used this lead as a commendable example of the substantive-clause beginning: "That the two witnesses to the will of the late **William R. Shields** did not see him sign the document and did not sign in the presence of each other, was developed yesterday afternoon in the suit of Frank W. Shields, his stepson, brought in the probate court to have the will declared void." Perhaps this was sound newspaper writing then, but today it is less acceptable. If what needs to be said is emphasized, lead-sentence structure usually takes care of itself. And it usually comes out simple. But not only leads benefit from simple and direct sentence structure. And we are seeking not only technically simple structure, but simplicity in statement. The editor must be on his guard against confused and complicated sentences anywhere he finds them.

The examples that follow illustrate sentence structures which for one reason or another get in the way of meaning.

> Police today sought two Milwaukeeans who escaped from the Richland county jail Sunday night in a stolen car.

This implies, of course, that they drove the car right out of the jail. The editor changed it to read, "Police today sought two Milwaukeeans who escaped from the Richland county jail Sunday night and got away in a stolen car."

Another tipsy driver who attempted to escape by running across the fields . . .

The previous sentence had referred to a tipsy driver who attempted to escape. But *he* didn't run across fields. The story was corrected to read, "Another tipsy driver who attempted to escape ran across fields. . . ."

Washington—(XP)—The Bureau of Labor Statistics said today that 45,500,000 persons—more than ever before—were employed in non-farm salaried and hourly jobs in mid-September.

This is not incorrect, only confusing. Despite the dashes, the editor felt that there was too much chance that some readers would read it "45,500,000 persons more than ever before." He therefore changed it to read: "The Bureau of Labor Statistics reported today that 45,500,000 persons were employed in non-farm salaried and hourly jobs in mid-September—more than ever before."

MONROE—Junior fair exhibits will be on display at the Green County Fair from July 27 to 30.

What does it mean—that the fair itself will be from July 27 to 30 and the junior fair events at the same time? Or are these the dates of the junior events only? The editor learned that these were the dates of the fair itself and changed the story to read:

> MONROE — The Green County Fair, July 27 to 30, will include a wide range of junior fair events.

One of the wire services committed this one:

It has been pointed out that ships might be one means of smuggling in an atomic bomb to this country and setting it off by remote control.

This sentence contains at least two structural faults. First, the writer separated "in" and "to," for some strange reason. But an even more difficult problem is the faulty parallelism: "ships might be one means of smuggling" but ships cannot be one means of "setting it off." The editor used a minimum of marks to make it read thus:

> It has been pointed out that ships might be one means of smuggling in an atomic bomb to be set off by remote control.

The next example demonstrates the fuzzy thinking that sometimes goes into hasty newspaper writing:

The family reunion of the late Charles Vincent family was held July 30 at the Woodrow Vincent home.

The writer naturally didn't mean to imply that the family was "late," but that's the way it came out. It might be changed to read:

> Descendants of the late Charles Vincent held their family reunion July 30 at the Woodrow Vincent home.

The Hugger-Mugger Sentence

One of journalism's most unfortunate writing habits is illustrated below. What has been called the "hugger-mugger" sentence crowds many facts together without regard for their logical relationships.

Doakes, a Daily News carrier boy when his parents lived at 1705 Jefferson St., is stationed at a base in Okinawa and is a flight leader and assistant operations officer, according to a letter received by his parents.

Notice the juxtaposition of almost wholly unrelated elements—dramatized by the thousands of literal miles that separate 1705 Jefferson St. and a base in Okinawa. The most urgent requirement is to break up an exceedingly long sentence. With one deletion and three short insertions, the editor made it read:

> Doakes was a Daily News carrier boy in 1957 when his parents lived at 1705 Jefferson St. He is now a flight officer and assistant operations officer at a base in Okinawa, according to a letter received recently by his parents.

This change not only made one very long sentence into two much shorter ones but also joined the bits of material about his past and separated it from material about his present activities.

Bad sentences result when unrelated facts are casually juxtaposed. This problem arises often in news writing. One reason is that persons or places need more identification than can be worked into the lead. The tendency is to pounce on the next reference after the lead, whether or not the secondary identification is keyed to the fact the lead tells. For instance, a wire service sent this paragraph:

It was then, continued Jones, an athletic instructor and crack amateur golfer, that "we took her out of the hospital and brought her home to be happy."

A few pages later, the story offered a thoroughly appropriate place to insert the identifying information:

> "I certainly appreciate it," said Jones, "but I can't take money like that. I'm just a working guy but she's had the best medical treatment possible. Sure, it cost money, but we'll get by."
> Jones is an athletic instructor and a crack amateur golfer.

Series

Series often give trouble to newspaper writers. Failure to keep the elements in a series *parallel* is one source of difficulty. For instance, a reporter wrote:

He said he would content himself with committee assignments, some teaching and editing.

Just where does the "some" come in here? Since the man in question was going into semiretirement as a teacher, the word "some" in connection with "teaching" could hardly be omitted. But was he going to do "editing" or "some editing"? If "some" applied to "editing" as well as "teaching," the sentence should have read thus:

He said he would content himself with committee assignments and some teaching and editing.

If the "some" did not apply to "editing," it should have read:

He said he would content himself with committee assignments, editing, and some teaching.

Rearranging word order in series can solve lots of minor problems of this sort. Another reporter wrote this lead:

Northwest Orient Airlines, which will participate in and direct phases of a vital air transport program to the Far East, has put two jet transports on immediate call for government service, it was announced Monday.

The editor considered "participate in and direct phases of" clumsy; he felt that "direct" could be read as either a verb or an adjective in this context. He therefore changed the order (and at the same time substituted a simpler word for a more complex one) thus:

> Northwest Orient Airlines, which will direct and share in phases of a vital air transport program . . .

A wire service sent this one:

The T-men under District Supervisor Boyd M. Martin of the Bureau of Narcotics and local police rounded up 70 persons.

Commas or dashes after "T-men" and "narcotics" would help a little. But switching the series, as in previous examples, would also shift the emphasis from T-men to local police. One solution lies in going to work on the conjunction:

> The T-men under District Supervisor Boyd M. Martin of the Bureau of Narcotics, *aided by* local police, rounded up 70 persons.

Long series should never be allowed to begin a sentence. The lazy reporter's favorite runs something like this:

Henry Jones, president; Albert Brown, vice-president; Andrew Smith, secretary; Rupert Wilson, treasurer, and Egbert Thomas, sergeant-at-arms, are the new officers of William Randolph Post. . . .

It is annoying to the reader to have to wade through a long list of names before he gets any inkling of what happened.

A series should give clear indication of its own beginning and end:

Green County entrants in the State Fair junior dress revue at State Fair Park, West Allis, August 22, will be Donna Olson, daughter of Edmund Olson, Plainville, and Carol Bagby, daughter of Mr. and Mrs. Willis J. Bagby, Mt. Pleasant, Miss Mamie Thomas, county Home Agent, has announced.

Frances Ludwig, daughter of Mr. and Mrs. John Ludwig, Sylvan Township, was named alternate.

Perhaps to the very careful reader, this sentence presents no problems aside from its extreme length. But the editor wanted to separate the one name that clearly belonged outside the list. Otherwise it tends to be read as one more name in the series. As corrected:

> Green County entrants in the State Fair junior dress revue at State Fair Park, West Allis, August 22, will be Donna Olson, daughter of Edmund Olson, Plainville, and Carol Bagby, daughter of Mr. and Mrs. Willis J. Bagby, Mt. Pleasant.
> Miss Mamie Thomas, county Home Agent, also announced that Frances Ludwig, daughter of Mr. and Mrs. John Ludwig, Sylvan Township, was named alternate.

Another editor might have dealt with the problems of length and complexity at the same time, in addition to fixing the series:

Green County entrants in the State Fair junior dress revue have been announced by Miss Mamie Thomas, county Home Agent.

They are . . .

The fair will be held August 22 at State Fair Park, West Allis.

Tight Writing

The desire for economy in words—particularly by the wire services—has produced tight, swiftly paced writing. On the whole, this has proved a boon to newspaper reading. "Tight" writing is characterized by the absence of "breaks" in the flow of simple sentences. Part of the technique is to take identifying phrases which formerly were handled *in apposition* and make them into unofficial titles before the name. The sentence which formerly read:

> O'Rourke testified that he had met Frank Erickson, king of the New York bookies, at the Roney Plaza Hotel, Miami Beach, Fla., in 1967.

is now written:

> O'Rourke testified he had met New York bookie king Frank Erickson at Miami Beach's Roney Plaza Hotel in 1967.

Notice the saving of five words. But more important, notice that five breaks, represented by commas in the first version, have been eliminated.

However, tightening can be overdone, as in the following example. A reporter learns over the telephone that an official is properly identified "Herbert Z. Smith, Executive Director of the Citizens Advisory Committee to the Michigan League of Municipalities." He turns to his typewriter and it comes out "Herbert Z. Smith, Michigan Municipalities League Citizens Advisory Committee Executive Director." The editor should be thankful the reporter didn't make it read "Michigan Municipalities League Citizens Advisory Committee Executive Director Herbert Z. Smith."

Wallace Carroll, editor and publisher of the Winston-Salem (North Carolina) *Journal* and *Sentinel* recently cited the following wire-service lead as an example of "stacked modifiers":

"Teamsters Union President James R. Hoffa's jury-tampering conviction . . . ." It does no good to save a few short words if the result is writing so compressed that even simple words are difficult for the average reader.

Someone once wrote that "the most used unnecessary word in the language is *that.* Inevitably reporters, and even big-shot Washington correspondents, write: 'Mr. Nixon announced that he would call a meeting of the Cabinet tomorrow.' The meaning would be just as clear if *that* were omitted, and it would save Publisher Pennyworth another nickel."

Omitting *that* seems to be dogma on wire-service desks now. But many copy editors on newspapers find themselves putting "thats" back into the copy. "O'Rourke testified *that* he had met . . ." reads better than "O'Rourke testified he had met . . . ." Editors often find themselves putting the innocent little "the" back into wire-service copy, too: "The spokesman would not estimate *the* strength of the North Vietnamese at *the* start of the war or now."

Here is a particularly striking example of "too tight" writing:

WASHINGTON—(XP)—Officials indicated today the nation will meet its draft needs with a slow but sure tightening of regulations the next few weeks and a general overhaul to bring in fresh thousands early next year.

Perhaps even more drastic treatment is indicated, but its readibility can be improved vastly with the addition of just three words:

> WASHINGTON — (XP) — Officials indicated today *that* the nation will meet its draft needs with a slow but sure tightening of regulations *during* the next few weeks and a general overhaul *designed* to bring in fresh thousands early next year.

Agreement in Number

The verb must agree in number with its subject and the pronoun with its antecedent. Words which are actually singular but carry plural implications seem to be particularly troublesome. "Group," "staff," "club," etc., are singular nouns, take singular verbs, and are referred back to as "it," not "they." As elementary as this seems, it is a problem for many reporters. The typical error is this one:

The club will entertain husbands at next month's meeting. They will also elect new officers.

"They," having "club" as its antecedent, must be changed to read "It." Or if that seems awkward, the first sentence can be shifted to the plural: "Club members will entertain . . . ."

Compound subjects take plural verbs.

> Wilson and Jones *are* leaving today to investigate . . .

But it takes a conjunction to combine two or more elements into a compound subject. Words which accompany and modify the subject but are not compounded with it should not be allowed to confuse the question of number.

> Wilson, accompanied by Jones, *is* leaving today to investigate.

A predicate nominative may disagree in number with the subject, but the verb must agree with the subject, not the predicate nominative.

Antiaircraft batteries are the chief cause of casualties, he said.

However, if the correct form seems awkward, the editor might revise the sentence to read:

He called antiaircraft batteries the chief cause of casualties.

Either, neither, and *none* are always singular:

There were five passengers in the Jones car. None *was* injured.

If this seems awkward:

The five passengers in the Jones car were not injured.

Word Usage and Vocabulary

Much of the improvement in the readability of newspaper writing in recent years has been due to a reduction in the incidence of difficult words. Every readability formula lays stress on word simplicity in one way or another. The editor frequently finds it necessary to substitute simpler words for more difficult ones in newspaper copy—and to explain technical terms. Here is a wire-service example:

The prime minister died at his home, Kingsmere, about 20 miles from Ottawa. His physician, Dr. Campbell Laidlaw, said that he died of "hypostatic pneumonia, preceded by an attack of pulmonary edema" . . .

To its credit, the service added: ". . . (accumulation of body fluids)." But that accounted for only part of the reported cause of death. And it's pretty hard going for the general reader.

Much faulty writing for newspapers stems from the reporter's unconscious preference for the pompous. He writes:

Two former Extown men have purchased and assumed operation of a Zeetown drug store.

The editor, preferring plain talk, revises the sentence to read:

> Two former Extown men have bought and are managing a Zeetown drug store.

Another:

The Sherman school is in need of extensive repairs. The Fowler school, located near the north city limits, has facilities for additional pupils which would not necessitate the hiring of an additional teacher.

The reporter's preference for the pompous extends not only to words but also to sentence structure. The editor makes it read:

> The Sherman school *needs* extensive repairs. The Fowler school, *near* the north city limits, has *room* for *more* pupils *without hiring another* teacher.

This time the readable way is also the word-saving way.

Redundancy   Much of the faulty word usage in newspapers has at its source an inexact understanding of words themselves. Redundancies result, for instance, when the writer fails to perceive the scope of a word. The common variety is of this sort:

An evening vesper service will be held . . .

Tonight's meeting will begin at 8 p.m.

The "evening" concept is already present in the word "vesper," and "P.M." is already present in "tonight."

Another reporter wrote:

The building was moved off its foundation by the recent flood and had partially collapsed. It was feared the building would completely collapse.

Collapse and other words (such as *destroy*) imply completeness. A building is not "completely" destroyed by fire: it is either destroyed or it is not. Perhaps it was *damaged.*

A more complicated form of redundancy derives from *contexts,* rather than word meanings. A wire service allowed this sentence:

The two forces going in opposite directions clashed head-on.

The "two forces" were ideological rather than physical, but the redundancy is still there: a "head-on" clash necessarily involves forces going in opposite directions.

"Collided" is a frequently misused word. It implies the impact of two or more objects *in motion.* A train cannot collide with a stalled truck. Similarly, one car cannot "sideswipe" another if both are in motion. They sideswipe *each other.*

A reporter wrote:

Signs . . . will help locate the *site* of the picnic.

He is confusing *site* and *scene.*

Combatting misunderstanding   The alert editor looks not only for *incorrect* word usages; he must also be on guard against combinations of words which *might be misunderstood* by some or most of his readers. For example, this lead sentence is not really incorrect:

> Wisconsin pea growers, already harassed by damaging rains and cool weather, now are having labor troubles, the state employment service said today.

"Labor troubles" is a phrase often used to describe industrial strife. In this case, the "troubles" were due to a *shortage* of labor. The term was unwisely chosen under the circumstances.

Some juxtapositions are humorous, when they are not meant to be. For example, a set of cutlines started with these words:

> Winners take time out to smile at the Dane County Junior Fair . . .

What's so funny about the Dane County Junior Fair?

Transitiveness The *transitiveness* of words gives some writers trouble, too. Most editors will not allow a reporter to write:

He claimed that he had a prior right to the land.

"Claimed" is *transitive* only; one may claim *something* but may not claim that something is the case. In this instance it might be correct to say "He claimed the land" or "He claimed prior rights to the land," but "He claimed *that* . . ." is simply incorrect.

One frequent example of faulty transitiveness (it reflects at the same time the reporter's preference for the pompous word):

The President requested Congress today to give him power to . . .

"Request" is transitive, but "Congress" is its indirect object. Its proper direct object is "power." It would be perfectly correct to say:

The President notified Congress today that he was requesting the power to . . .

But why not use plain talk?

The President *asked* Congress today for power to . . .

Similarly, wire stories frequently carry this erroneous usage:

Jarrett confirmed that . . .

Again, *transitive only.* Inserting one word makes it correct:

Jarrett confirmed *news* that . . .

Other problems Additional word-usage problems are discussed in the following list. It has no pretensions to an encyclopedic compilation. These simply are words that experience has shown are often confused by newspaper writers. Reporters may be forgiven an occasional lapse; editors may not.

ability: *Ability* is the power of applying knowledge; *capacity* is the power of receiving and retaining it.

above: Do not use to mean *more than.*

acquire: He *acquires* material things by his own effort, *attains* a goal or other nonmaterial things, *obtains* material things by effort or deliberate action, *procures* things or services, usually through others. (Why not try *get?*)

administer: Medicine, laws, and oaths are *administered;* blows are *dealt.*

affect: As a verb, *affect* is to influence; to *effect* is to produce or bring to pass; both are transitive. As a noun, *effect* means result; *affect* is a term in psychology meaning emotion.

aggravate: To *aggravate* is to make worse or intensify; to *irritate* is to excite impatience, anger, or displeasure.

aggregate: Don't substitute for *total.*

allege: Do not confuse with *say* or *assert.* An allegation is an assertion without proof but with the implication of willingness to prove. *Alleged crime* is correct but *alleged criminal* is incorrect. He alleges his innocence; he does not allege he is innocent.

allow: Means not to forbid; to *permit* is to grant leave.

allude: Means to make indirect mention; to *refer* is to make direct mention.

alternative(ly): Refers to a choice. *Alternate(ly)* (not the noun) refers to a variation.

amateur: Means nonprofessional; the beginner is a *novice.*

among: Use *among* when more than two is meant; for two, use *between.*

anticipate: To foresee and act or preclude beforehand; to *expect* is to look for with confidence. (He expected rain; he took an umbrella in anticipation of rain.)

anxious: Implies worry, anxiety; *eager* implies anticipation and desire.

appreciate: Do not confuse with *value;* to appreciate is to appraise accurately or value justly.

apprehend: Don't use for *arrest;* don't confuse with *comprehend,* which means to understand fully.

apt: Don't confuse with *likely;* use apt to mean inherent predisposition. *Likely* implies probability.

assert: See *Allege.*

at: Events take place *at* general locations (at the Fairgrounds) but *in* buildings (in the auditorium). They take place *in* large cities but *at* small cities (in Chicago, but at Zion, Ill.).

attain: See *Acquire.*

audience: An audience listens; *spectators* watch.

authentic: Means corresponding to facts; *genuine* means actually proceeding from the reputed source.

avert-avoid: To *avert* is to ward off; to *avoid* is to shun.

balance: Do not use in the sense of *remainder* or *rest.*

ban-bar: These words are not synonymous. The difference is akin to *ban*ishment and *bar*rier.

belittle: To reveal as small *by contrast;* does not mean *deride* or *ridicule.*

beside-besides: *Beside* means by the side of; *besides,* in addition to.

between: See *Among.*

black-blacken: To *black* is to lay on color; eyes and shoes are *blacked.* Reputations are *blackened.*

blond-blonde: *Blond* is masculine, *blonde* feminine.

body: Preferred to *corpse* or *remains. Dead* body is redundant.

brunet-brunette: *Brunet* is masculine; *brunette* feminine.

burglar: A *burglar* breaks into and enters in the night with felonious intent; the same act by day is usually *breaking and entering;* a *thief* takes by stealth, a *robber* by force or threat of force.

capable: Able to do; *susceptible* means admitting influence.

capacity: See *Ability.*

capital-capitol: The *capital* is the city; the *capitol,* the building.

claim: Often misused as an intransitive verb. One may claim a piece of ground but not claim *that* the lot is his.

collide: Both objects must be in motion.

compare to-compare with: Things of the same class are compared *with* each other; things of different classes are compared *to* each other.

compose-comprise-consist: Members *compose* the body, the body *comprises* or *is composed of* or *consists of* its members. *Consists of* takes a noun; *consists in,* a participle.

concert: It takes two or more performers to make a *concert;* one person presents a *recital.*

confess: The accused confesses the crime; he doesn't confess *to* the crime.

consensus: Means in agreement in matters of opinion, testimony, etc. Hence *consensus of opinion* is redundant.

conservative: Do not use in the sense of *moderate* or *safe* in connection with *estimate.*

continual-continuous: A *continual* action recurs or is constantly renewed; a *continuous* action is unbroken from beginning to end.

continue: Continue *on* is redundant when "on" is used in the adverbial sense.

corpse: See *Body.*

couple: Two things or persons that are joined. Takes the singular verb. Do not use when *two* is meant. (See also *Pair.*)

cyclone: A wind, especially a wind storm, that moves circularly; a *tornado* is a cyclonic wind of high velocity usually accompanied by a cone-shaped destructive center; a *hurricane* is a cyclone wind of great force (the term is usually confined to such storms at sea or from the sea); a *squall* is a lesser storm, usually rising suddenly; a *gale* is a strong wind of less than hurricane force; a *gust* is a sudden, brief blast of wind.

damages: When property is damaged, a suit for *damages* may result. What happened to the property is *damage,* never *damages,* no matter how much was done or how many forms it might have taken.

destroy: Destruction is complete; *completely destroyed* is redundant.

die of: One dies *of,* not *from,* a disease or illness; one dies *after,* not *of* or *as a result of* or *from,* an operation.

different from: Never *different than.*

drown: A man *drowns;* if he was *drowned,* call the homicide squad.

during: Implies duration; *in* implies only *within the limits of.* He visited Rome in May; he was in Rome during May.

eager: See *Anxious.*

effect: See *Affect.*

emigrant: The *emigrant* moves out of a country; the *immigrant,* into it.

enormity: Enormity is not the noun form of the adjective *enormous.* Enormous refers to magnitude; enormity to extremity; thus the enormousness of the elephant or the problem, but the enormity of the deed or the crime.

entail: A necessary condition or result is entailed, not *involved.*

evidence: Tends to convince; *testimony* is intended to convince. Do not use *evidence* as a verb in the sense of *to show signs of.* That word is *evince.*

expect: See *Anticipate.*

fail: Do not use in the sense of *did not;* to fail, one must have tried.

farther: Refers to greater distance. *Further* refers to additional time or amount.

feature: A grossly overused word, whether as a verb, noun, or adjective. Avoid.

female: Poor taste when applied to the human race except perhaps in a science story; say *woman.*

fewer: Not as many (items); *less* means not as much (amount, degree, or value).

following: Do not use where *after* is meant.

further: See *Farther.*

genuine: See *Authentic.*

half mast, half staff: An ensign flies at *half mast* at sea; on land, a flag flies at *half staff.*

hanged: Men are *hanged;* things are *hung.*

happen: Things *happen* or *occur* unexpectedly, *take place* by design. See also *Transpire. Happening* should not be used for *event.*

healthful-healthy: *Healthful* means causing health; *healthy,* possessing health.

heart failure-ailment-disease: Heart *failure* (stoppage) accompanies all deaths; for cardiac cases, say *heart disease* or preferably *heart ailment.*

hopefully: Often used incorrectly to mean "it is hoped that . . . ." In "he spoke hopefully of the future," the word is used correctly as an adverb modifying the verb. In "Hopefully the end is in sight," the adverb modifies nothing.

hung: See *Hanged.*

immigrant: See *Emigrant.*

imply: Means to express indirectly, suggest, or hint; to *infer* is to derive by implication.

in: See *At.*

inaugurate: To conduct into office or public use with *formal ceremonies;* otherwise, say *begin* or *start.*

infer: See *Imply.*

inmate: Use for *inhabitant* only in connection with institutions.

involve: One is involved in a situation that is unfortunate but not wrong; one is *implicated* in a crime. See *Entail.*

irritate: See *Aggravate.*

judge-justice: Not interchangeable. A *justice* presides over a justice court, sometimes a police court; members of the U. S. Supreme Court are the *chief justice* and eight *associate justices,* whose title may be shortened to *justice.*

lady: Except on society pages, say *woman;* reserve "lady" for women of genteel birth.

last-latest: Use *last* in the sense of "final"; *latest,* in the sense of "most recent."

lend-loan: Use *lend* as the verb, *loan* as the noun, except that *loaned* is generally preferred to *lent.*

less: See *Fewer.*

liable: Don't confuse with *likely; liable* means answerable for the consequences.

likely: See *Apt* and *Liable.*

locate: Do not use to mean *settle* or *find.* To locate means to determine the place for something.

majority: The leader has a *majority* when he has at least one more than half; he has a *plurality* when he has more than any other but not a majority. The size of a majority is the difference between the leader's vote and all others; the size of a plurality is the difference between the leader's vote and that of his nearest rival. (When you mean *most,* say *most.*)

marriage: The state of matrimony, or the marriage ceremony; the *wedding* is the occasion that surrounds it, the social event.

mentality: Intellectual power. Do not use to mean a system of attitudes, as in "a military mentality."

mutual: Describes a reciprocity between two. Two persons can have a mutual admiration (meaning for each other) but it is incorrect to say they have a mutual admiration *for Jones.* They have a *common* admiration for Jones.

neither-none: *Neither* is correct only when referring to one of two; if there are more than two, write *none.* Both neither and none are singular.

notable-noted-notorious: These are not synonymous. *Notable* means worthy of attention; *noted,* known by common report for something; *notorious,* widely and unfavorably known.

novel: See *Unique.*

novice: See *Amateur.*

nuclear: Refers to a nucleus (as of an atom). More often mispronounced than misspelled "nucular."

oblivious: See *Unconscious.*

obtain: See *Acquire.*

occur: See *Happen.*

odd: See *Peculiar.*

officer: Do not use interchangeably with *policeman.* Some policemen are officers, others are not. Use the appropriate designation of rank, such as *patrolman.*

over: Do not use to mean *more than. Over* means above; *more than* means in excess of.

pair: Like a *couple,* a pair is two persons or animals who are joined, and it is a singular noun. Do not use in place of *two,* as in "a pair of bandits," unless the two are married.

partially-partly: *Partially* is incorrect when a part of a whole is meant; it is correct in the sense of a limited degree. However, *partly* is correct in both senses— and preferable.

past: Applies to all time past; *last* is preferred to past in describing the immediately previous hour, day, week, etc.

peculiar: Do not confuse with *odd.* A peculiar characteristic is one not shared by others. A person cannot be peculiar, but a talent can.

people-persons: Use *people* to refer to populations, races, large groups; *persons,* to refer to individuals.

per: Use Latin with Latin, English with English: *per* annum, *a* year (and why *not* English?).

permit: See *Allow.*

phenomenal: Do not use for remarkable, extraordinary, prodigious. It means known through the senses.

plurality: See *Majority.*

portion: Do not use portion to mean *part.* A portion is a share.

practicable-practical: The practicable course can be brought about; the practical course is adapted to actual conditions.

practically: Don't use for *almost, nearly, virtually.* Practically derives from practical (see above) and is the opposite of *theoretically.*

presently: Does not mean *now* or *for the present* or *at present*; it means *at once* or *immediately.* (Apparently this is a losing battle.)

procure: See *Acquire.*

prone: Means lying face down; *supine* means lying on the back.

proposition: Don't use to mean *proposal.*

proved-proven: Use *proved.*

providing: Don't use for *provided* in this sense: Construction will start soon, provided materials are available.

quite: Incorrect in the sense of fairly or rather ("quite wealthy"). Correct but not recommended in the sense of entirely or thoroughly ("quite finished").

raise: Animals are *raised;* children are *reared.*

recital: See *Concert.*

refer: See *Allude.*

remains: See *Body.*

render: A judgment or lard can be rendered; a song, never.

replica: Only reproductions by the original creator may be called replicas. Any other reproduction is a *copy.*

robber: See *Burglar.*

sanatorium-sanitarium: The *sanatorium* is almost always an institution treating tuberculosis; the *sanitarium* specializes in rest cures.

secure: Means to make fast or to ensure; not synonymous with *obtain.*

sensual-sensuous: Both mean "of the senses"; but sensual conveys the additional implication of undue indulgence in the grosser pleasures.

sewage-sewerage: Sewage goes through the sewerage system.

spectators: See *Audience.*

suffer: Injuries are *received,* preferably, not suffered. (But avoid the devious: say "His wrist was *broken,*" not "He sustained, suffered, or received a broken wrist.")

susceptible: See *Capable.*

sustain: Injuries are *received,* losses are *incurred.* See *Suffer.*

take place: See *Happen.*

testimony: See *Evidence.*

thief: See *Burglar.*

transpire: Means to *leak out.* Do not use for *happen* or *occur.*

trusty: A trusted prisoner who may receive special privileges. A *trustee* holds a public trust, as the trustee of a bank.

unconscious: Don't say unconscious when you mean *oblivious.* Unconscious involves temporary loss of all the senses.

unique: Do not confuse with *novel.* Unique is an absolute; it does not admit of comparison. Hence, do not say very, more, or most unique.

unknown: A person cannot be unknown; he may be *unidentified* or his whereabouts may be unknown. A fire's origin is not unknown but *undetermined.*

verbal: Anything in words; anything spoken is *oral.*

wedding: See *Marriage.*

widow-wife: A man is survived by his wife, not his widow.

youth: Collectively, refers to both sexes (the youth of America); but *a youth* is an adolescent male.

Editing to Save Space

Brevity is not only the soul of wit, it is the heart of readership. (It affects the balance sheet, too: unnecessary words cost as much to set and print as useful words.) Several studies of the relationship between the length of stories—and editorials—and readership have found that, other things being equal, the long story is less likely to be read than the short one. What's more, the fifth paragraph of a five-paragraph story is more likely to be read than the fifth paragraph of a ten-paragraph story.

Length is a more complicated problem for editors than most readers realize. Consider the number of times in a single day the length of a given story might be adjusted. Suppose, for example, that the city editor sends a reporter out on a story which he considers might be worth half a column. He schedules it for that approximate length. But the reporter believes in the story's importance and comes in with notes enough for a column. The city editor advises him to keep it down to about three-fourths of a column. The story is written to that approximate length, but when the city editor sees it, he decides it will have to be cut to the original estimate of about half a column; other and bigger stories have broken since the original assignment and the editor has a better idea now of what space is available. So the copy desk gets instructions to trim the story. But before it is sent to the composing room, the space situation is further tightened, and the news editor decides the story will have to be trimmed even more. When it finally gets into type, it's about a third of a column long.

But that isn't all. In making up an early mail edition, which emphasizes news of the surrounding territory, only the first three paragraphs are used because of tight space and because city news is of less interest to the territory to which the early edition is sent. For the "home" edition, some of the type withheld in the early edition is restored. Thus, the story's length has been revised no less than seven times.

Wire stories are altered in length under even more varied circumstances. The story of an explosion and fire in Muncie, Indiana, would rate two and a half columns in the Muncie paper, but the wire service would probably send only about a third of that for distribution to member newspapers elsewhere in Indiana. Each of these would use as much or as little of the story as news circumstances in each office warranted. And in Chicago, the story would be even further reduced before being put on the "trunk" or main wire for use elsewhere in the United States. And if the California state bureau, being less concerned with the story than the Ohio state bureau, for instance, did not altogether eliminate the trunk-wire story from

the Western file, it would reduce it even further for its members. Each of these, in turn, would adjust the length to suit its own circumstances at the moment. Finally, the world service would probably reduce the story most for its foreign clients, if it sent the story at all. Thus, a story conceivably could be carried at hundreds of different lengths in different newspapers.

Cutting the Straight News Story

Cutting, trimming, boiling, slashing—all terms[1] meaning reducing length, to varying degrees—are important skills in the process of fitting a story into the stream of a day's news events. They are so important that one of the essential characteristics of news-story structure is largely attributable to the need for adaptability in terms of length. Although the "inverted pyramid" structure common to "straight" news writing is also based on the reader's convenience, one of its chief reasons for being is that it lends itself readily to reductions in length.

"Biting off" Many stories arranged in the inverted-pyramid form can readily be reduced by eliminating paragraphs at the bottom. The story below is typical of the sort that can be cut at various points without doing serious damage:

F. T. Carpenter, President of the United Petroleum Gas Company, of Minneapolis, has been named a member of the newly formed Midwestern Emergency Petroleum Fuels Committee by Oscar L. Chapman, Secretary of the Interior.

---

[1] The language used seems to vary from shop to shop. The New York *Times* ranks them, according to Garst and Bernstein's *Headlines and Deadlines* (New York: Columbia University Press, 1940), thus (pp. 53–56): *"Trimming* is a general tightening up of the story, chiefly by eliminating superfluous words and replacing loose phrases with single words that express the thought adequately. . . . *Boiling down* is more drastic and is the process of close paring of all sentences and the sacrifice of minor facts. . . . *Cutting* means the elimination of all but the most important facts, those without which there would be no story or an incomplete one. Often there is nothing left but the bare bones of the story with a shred or two of clothing."

In another shop, "trim" and "slash" are used, the latter, of course, being the more drastic treatment.

W. A. Powers, Minneapolis, manager of supply and transportation of the United Petroleum Gas Company, has been loaned to the emergency office as long as his services are needed, Carpenter said.

Chapman said the committee was formed because "chaotic weather and transportation conditions threaten severe dislocation and spot shortages of various petroleum products in extensive midwestern areas."

The Petroleum Administration for Defense has opened an emergency office in Chicago, Ill.

The entire critical supply situation, Carpenter said, is due to the present chaotic condition resulting from the switchmen's strike.

Boiling   Although chopping away at the end is a perfectly legitimate way of reducing a story's length, it is important to realize that it is only one way. The fact that it is also the easiest way has prompted some bad copy reading. If a copy desk knows no other way to reduce a story's length, or if the routine is so pinched that it allows no time for careful editing, the result can be a final paragraph that goes like this:

> The president said that he had vetoed the bill for four reasons.

Under the heading "The Most Fascinating News Story of the Week," *The New Yorker* frequently dredges up horrible examples of what can happen when stories *not* arranged in inverted pyramid form are hacked off at the bottom:

> CHAMPAIGN, Ill. — (XP) — The little round rings of heavy paper left over when holes are punched in ledger sheets generally are considered useless. But not by Champaign sewer investigators.

Obviously, the straight news story in pyramid form frequently needs a more complicated type of handling. For reasons either of content or structure, it cannot be chopped off. For example:

> MADISON — (Special) — Two new officer candidate programs for college men and graduates have been opened recently by the Marine Corps,

> Maj. Robert S. Hudson of the University of Wisconsin Navy Reserve Officers Training Corps announced Monday.
>
> One program is for college freshmen, sophomores, and juniors, while the other is for seniors and graduates.
>
> An underclassman must:
>
> 1. Be a male citizen of the U.S. and regularly enrolled in the university;
>
> 2. Be over 17 years of age on date of enlistment and under 25 on July 1 of the year his bachelor's degree is granted;
>
> 3. Not be a member of any naval or military organization nor be enrolled in an ROTC advanced corps;
>
> 4. Be in good physical condition and have 20-20 vision.
>
> Admission requirements for seniors and graduates are the same as for underclassmen except that a candidate must be a college graduate or certified senior and cannot be more than 27 years of age on July 1.

Because of its *content,* this story may not be cut substantially. Note that the numbered paragraphs defy cutting: if any of this detail is run, all must be run; if it is not, distortion will result. Note, too, that it is impossible to cut away the last paragraph without serious damage. Since the lead speaks of "two programs," we cannot give essential details on one of them and disregard the other. The editor has no more than three possibilities: to do without the story altogether; to cut it after the second paragraph and exasperate almost every interested reader with his failure to present essential details; or to run it in full.

The editor should not be frightened away from cutting *all* stories that contain numbered paragraphs, however. This device has other uses than to assemble details of precisely uniform value, as in the example above. Reporters often use it as a convenience to clean up minor details. Take a typical school-board story. It might start something like this:

The Extown School Committee voted last night to increase teacher salaries by 5 per cent but postponed action on a proposed addition to the Franklin School.

The pay increase passed by a vote of . . .

Full details on both of these important developments follow. When these have been dealt with, the reporter summarizes all the routine details of the meeting thus:

In other actions, the committee:

ONE. Designated committee secretary Herbert Lapham to represent the group at a meeting to consider the school needs of Oliver Township.

TWO. Voted to reimburse Lapham for expenses of a trip to Lansing on committee business.

THREE. Ordered Lincoln School Principal August Lambrecht to arrange for crossing protection at the intersection of Maple St. and Tower Ave.

FOUR. Audited routine disbursements amounting to $427.31.

FIVE. Decided to postpone the next meeting until February 21.

All of these details may be necessary to complete coverage. But none is essential to the main story. None of them depends for understanding or completeness on the inclusion of any other. All the editor has to do to save space is to make kills based on news values.

Another kind of straight news story defies cutting at the end, despite its traditional inverted-pyramid form, because of its complex internal structure. It sometimes results when the reporter or wire service has done a poor job of assembling the details in descending order of importance. Following is an example, dating from the days before the UP-INS merger, when UP sent all-cap copy.

```
     BELLEVILLE, ILL., OCT. 8--(UP)--THREE MASKED MEN
SEEKING $65,000 IN CASH TORTURED THE 68-YEAR-OLD HEIR TO
A $250,000 ESTATE BY BURNING NEWSPAPERS ON HIS FEET, IT
WAS DISCLOSED TODAY.
     THEY GOT $30 AND TWO WHITE SHIRTS.
     THE INTRUDERS BROKE INTO THE HOME OF GUSTAV A.
BUTKUS ON AN ISOLATED FARM NEAR O'FALLON, ILL., FRIDAY
NIGHT, PISTOL-WHIPPED HIM AND BURNED HIS FEET, ST. CLAIR
COUNTY SHERIFF DEPUTIES REPORTED.
     BUTKUS SUFFERED TWO BROKEN RIBS, A BROKEN LEG, AND
SERIOUS BURNS. POLICE TOOK HIM TO A HOSPITAL, WHICH THEY
REFUSED TO NAME, AND HE WAS REPORTED "DOING WELL."
     THE $65,000 WHICH THE BANDITS SOUGHT WAS THE AMOUNT
OF MONEY REPORTED MISSING FROM THE ESTATE OF BUTKUS'
SECRET WIFE, DEPUTIES ELMER LACQUET, GEORGE BOOS AND
WILLIAM SCHOINDORN REPORTED.
     THE BANDITS USED FISHLINE TO TIE BUTKUS AND MRS.
BERTHA PINGEL, 66, AND HER HUSBAND CHRISTIAN PINGEL, 78,
WHO LIVED WITH BUTKUS. THE PINGELS ARE HIS SISTER AND
```

BROTHER-IN-LAW, WHO ARRIVED FROM GERMANY TWO MONTHS AGO.

THE PINGLES WERE UNHARMED, BUT WERE FORCED TO WATCH THE TORTURE OF BUTKUS. MRS. PINGEL WORKED FREE OF HER BONDS EARLY SATURDAY MORNING AND FREED THE OTHERS.

SHE SAID THE LEADER OF THE GANG WAS A MAN OVER SIX FEET TALL WHO FLOURISHED A LONG-BARRELED PISTOL. ALL WORE HANDKERCHIEFS OVER THEIR FACES.

THE DEPUTIES SAID THE BANDITS APPARENTLY BELIEVED THAT BUTKUS HAD HIDDEN THE $65,000 IN HIS HOME.

MRS. MARY GASS MUELLER BUTKUS DIED JUNE 6, 1949. NO ONE HERE KNEW SHE AND BUTKUS HAD BEEN MARRIED AT COLORADO SPRINGS, COLO., IN 1936. BUTKUS DURING THAT TIME WAS MANAGER OF HER VALUABLE FARM AT O'FALLON.

FOUR DAYS BEFORE SHE DIED, MRS. BUTKUS REVEALED THE MARRIAGE BY FILING A PETITION FOR DIVORCE. SHE CHARGED INTEMPERANCE.

ON THE DAY SHE DIED, SHERIFF'S DEPUTIES WENT TO THE SEPARATE HOMEBUTKUS MAINTAINED ON ANOTHER FARM. THEY MET HIM COMING OUT OF THE DOOR WITH A SMALL BLACK BAG CONTAINING $129,000 IN CASH.

BUTKUS TOLD THE DEPUTIES THAT HE HAD TAKEN THE MONEY FROM HIS WIFE'S SAFE AND WAS ENROUTE TO DEPOSIT IT IN A BANK.

"IT'S TOO MUCH CASH TO BE LEFT LYING AROUND," HE TOLD THEM.

THE MISSING $65,000 WAS REPORTED WHEN AN ACCOUNT-ING WAS MADE OF MRS. BUTKUS' AFFAIRS. HER RECORDS SHOWED THAT $194,000 SHOULD HAVE BEEN IN THE WALL SAFE OF HER HOME.

THE MONEY THAT BUTKUS CARRIED WAS IMPOUNDED AND HIS WIFE'S WILL IS NOW IN LITIGATION.

ET551P

The editor had to reduce this story to a "short" (four or five paragraphs). Suppose he chopped it off after the fifth paragraph. All these references would be unexplained:

"heir to a $250,000 estate. . . ." (Why? When? Why isn't it his outright?)

"on an isolated farm. . . ." (Why? Alone?)

"seeking $65,000 cash. . . ." (Why is the cash on the farm?)

"mission from the estate of Butkus' secret wife. . . ." (Why secret? What's the story?)

The story would have been a fraud on the reader because it would have left too many compelling questions unanswered. There were so many rather spectacular elements to bring into the story at or near the top that the reporter had to delay answering many of these questions.

But something had to be removed to make this story a "short." Supposing the editor took out some angles and played down some others. The "elderly couple" angle, for example, takes a lot of words and isn't essential. However, the "forced to watch the torture" angle is newsworthy in itself. And it answers one of the crucial unanswered questions listed above ("Was he alone?"). If the editor simply said that an elderly couple (not stopping the progress of the story to identify them) who lived with him was forced to watch the torture, he could save a lot of unnecessary detail. (Of course, if the paper had been published anywhere near Belleville, Illinois, the editor would have had to identify the "elderly couple." But if he had been that nearby, he would not have been cutting the story so drastically anyway.)

Now the editor looked at the story the other way around: *what couldn't he do without?* He had to explain why the $65,000 was believed to be in the house, explain how the "secret wife" fit into the picture, and clear up why Butkus was described as an heir. But he could avoid going into unnecessary detail.

Here is how he handled the story. See if he has not preserved all the essentials—answered all the compelling questions—without damaging the story itself.

BELLEVILLE, ILL. ~~OCT. 8~~--(UP)--THREE MASKED MEN SEEKING $65,000 IN CASH TORTURED THE 68-YEAR-OLD HEIR TO A $250,000 ESTATE BY BURNING NEWSPAPERS ON HIS FEET, IT WAS DISCLOSED TODAY.

THEY GOT $30 AND TWO WHITE SHIRTS.

THE INTRUDERS BROKE INTO THE HOME OF GUSTAV A. BUTKUS ON AN ISOLATED FARM NEAR O'FALLON, ILL., FRIDAY NIGHT, PISTOL-WHIPPED HIM, AND BURNED HIS FEET, ST. CLAIR COUNTY SHERIFF'S DEPUTIES REPORTED.

BUTKUS SUFFERED TWO BROKEN RIBS, A BROKEN LEG, AND SERIOUS BURNS. POLICE TOOK HIM TO A HOSPITAL, ~~WHICH THEY REFUSED TO NAME,~~ AND HE WAS REPORTED "DOING WELL."

THE $65,000 WHICH THE BANDITS SOUGHT WAS THE AMOUNT OF MONEY REPORTED MISSING FROM THE ESTATE OF BUTKUS' SECRET WIFE, DEPUTIES ~~ELMER LACQUET, GEORGE BOOS AND WILLIAM SCHOINDORN~~ REPORTED.

An elderly couple

~~THE BANDITS USED FISHLINE TO TIE BUTKUS AND MRS.~~
~~BERTHA PINGEL, 66, AND HER HUSBAND CHRISTIAN PINGEL, 78,~~
WHO LIVED WITH ~~BUTKUS. THE PINGELS ARE HIS SISTER AND~~
~~BROTHER IN LAW, WHO ARRIVED FROM GERMANY TWO MONTHS AGO.~~

~~THE PINGELS WERE UNHARMED, BUT~~ ~~WERE~~ was FORCED TO WATCH
THE TORTURE ~~OF BUTKUS. MRS. PINGEL WORKED FREE OF HER~~
~~BONDS EARLY SATURDAY MORNING AND FREED THE OTHERS.~~

~~SHE SAID THE LEADER OF THE GANG WAS A MAN OVER SIX~~
~~FEET TALL WHO FLOURISHED A LONG-BARRELED PISTOL. ALL~~
~~WORE HANDKERCHIEFS OVER THEIR FACES.~~

THE DEPUTIES SAID THE BANDITS APPARENTLY BELIEVED
THAT BUTKUS HAD HIDDEN THE $65,000 IN HIS HOME.

MRS. MARY GASS MUELLER BUTKUS DIED JUNE 6, 1949.
NO ONE HERE KNEW SHE ~~AND BUTKUS~~ HAD ~~BEEN~~ MARRIED ~~AT~~ the
~~COLORADO SPRINGS, COLO., IN 1936. BUTKUS DURING THAT~~
~~TIME WAS~~ MANAGER OF HER ~~VALUABLE~~ FARM ~~AT O'FALLON.~~

~~FOUR DAYS BEFORE SHE DIED, MRS. BUTKUS REVEALED THE~~
~~MARRIAGE BY FILING A PETITION FOR DIVORCE. SHE CHARGED~~
~~INTEMPERANCE.~~

~~ON THE DAY SHE DIED, SHERIFF'S DEPUTIES WENT TO THE~~
~~SEPARATE HOME BUTKUS MAINTAINED ON ANOTHER FARM. THEY~~
~~MET HIM COMING OUT OF THE DOOR WITH A SMALL BLACK BAG~~
~~CONTAINING $129,000 IN CASH.~~

~~BUTKUS TOLD THE DEPUTIES THAT HE HAD TAKEN THE~~
~~MONEY FROM HIS WIFE'S SAFE AND WAS ENROUTE TO DEPOSIT~~
~~IT IN A BANK.~~

~~"IT'S TOO MUCH CASH TO BE LEFT LYING AROUND," HE~~
~~TOLD THEM.~~

THE MISSING $65,000 WAS REPORTED WHEN AN ACCOUNT-
ING WAS MADE OF MRS. BUTKUS' AFFAIRS. ~~HER RECORDS~~
~~SHOWED THAT $194,000 SHOULD HAVE BEEN IN THE WALL SAFE~~
~~OF HER HOME.~~   #

~~THE MONEY THAT BUTKUS CARRIED WAS IMPOUNDED AND HIS~~

~~WIFE'S WILL IS NOW IN LITIGATION.~~

~~ET551P~~

The sound copy-desk slogan "Do something *for* the story, not just *to* it" is particularly applicable here. Boiling is not done *only* to adjust a story to fit the available space. It is also done in the interest of the reader. The editor is constantly alert for chances to remove wordage which not only doesn't contribute to the story but actually gets in the way of telling it. The fact that the story is shorter when he gets through is a mere by-product. The chief reason for his labor is to make the story better—simpler, more direct, easier to read, easier to understand.

Here is an example of the sort of sentence the copy editor almost automatically prunes:

> It is generally expected that the new barn will have been constructed by the time the fair gets under way this fall.

To serve not only brevity but also clarity, the editor recasts it thus:

> The new barn is expected to be ready for this year's fair.

Thus most judgments on whether a word or phrase stays or goes are based on considerations not only of space but the general well-being of the story. Nevertheless, wholesale cutting simply to fit space is frequently necessary. But even when cutting at the end, the editor should give special attention to the last paragraph of what remains. It should put a finishing touch on the story if possible. This good example of a story ending has been cited by an anonymous writer in *Nieman Reports*[2] from a New York *Times* story on the restoration of the White House:

> William H. Kelley, government project manager, shares the admiration of many of the builders for the carpentry, ma-

sonry and plastering of 1817. However, he observed today that, for all the fine hand work, the building lasted only about 150 years, and he expects the new interior to be standing firm at the end of another 500.

The same author cited the following example of a bad ending—one not blameable on the copy desk but on a bite-off made at the forms as a paper was going to press:

> Then the district attorney asked:
> "Where were you on the night of November 3?"
> The witness hesitated. He coughed nervously.

End of story.

Newsmen are much more concerned with good beginnings than they are with good endings, and that is as it should be; a great many more readers are affected by beginnings, since relatively few who start a story read through to the end.[3] However, a touch of craftsmanship at the end can improve the total impact of a story tremendously for the reader who *does* want all the details.

Trimming Human-Interest Stories

Although doing a careful job of cutting a straight news story is not necessarily easy, it is a lot easier than reducing the length of a couple of other story types. One of these is the human-interest short, the "page brightener," as the wire services call it. These tidbits are usually boiled pretty hard before they even go on the wire, and it is hard to reduce them further without doing violence to the simple story they have to tell. They are not built on the inverted-pyramid principle at all but like a short story, with the climax at the end.

---

[2] "The Shape of the Story," *Nieman Reports,* April 1950, p. 28.

[3] Wilbur Schramm, "Measuring Another Dimension of Newspaper Readership," *Journalism Quarterly* 24:243–306 (December 1947).

Sometimes these yarns are chopped off in makeup by mistake. The results can be disastrous, as *The New Yorker* example cited on page 58 indicates.

The longer human-interest story is almost equally difficult to deal with when it has to be cut. This is the "sidebar" story, which wraps up the human-interest sidelights of a disaster or a war front. Or it might be a story by itself. It resembles the page brightener in structure—its chronological arrangement or some other device builds up to a punch line at the end—and in the fact that it depends on "atmosphere" for its effectiveness.

Obviously, such a story cannot be chopped off at the end unless another punch line appears farther up the story and can be used instead of the one at the end. Sometimes it is possible to move the end punch line farther up the story and remove wordage that way. But whatever is done, the editor must take great care not to damage the principal element that makes the story worth running—its special tone quality.

Here is an example. Note that it has little value of its own but rather depends on the grim war stories that it accompanies. Notice, too, how lacking it is in real news and how much it depends on "atmosphere."

ENROUTE TO THE WAR, July 23-(AP)-Death and dancing--sorrow and laughter. They go side by side in this strange war.

The contrast is poignant. It's like a vivid dream that is't true--yet it is true. It's like a page from the old wars that no one wanted rewritten. The words are being scrawled again in this far part of the world.

Let me take you to two places near an American island air base. American troops left this spot for combat less than four weeks ago. This also is where the jets take for their bombing missions.

First, let's go to a small hotel near the airfield. It's the temporary home ofwives and children of officers of an infantry division, one which has borne the major shock of enemy attacks in the north.

A group of women were seated around a table. They were the wives sweating out the news of their men in combat.

"Bill's got a chance," one of them said. "If anybody gets out, he will."

She was taking about a major general who has been in command of some of the hardest fighting in the war.

He was last seen Friday on a hill overlooking an enemy stronghold rounding up the stragglers and trying to get them back to the American lines.

A dark-haired young woman came into the room. She told the others, "Jim got through. He got back through the lines with some of his men."

One of the women said, "Thank God for that." She was t all, dark and sad eyed.

I don't know who Jim was and it didn't seem right to break in on this little group, clinging together for strength, to ask his name. It was enough that Jim got back.

They tried to be casual and light. But there was an undercurrent of emotion and electric tension. Finally one of the woomen stood up. "I'm going to bed," she said. "Call me if there is any news."

Then another left and the little group began to break up slowly.

A few miles away an air xorc club was bright with lights. An orchestra played sentimental melodies. Couples danced gaily and laughed into each others eyes. At the big bar, fliers and their wives touched glasses and laughed and had a lovely time.

Tomorrow, perhaps, the young men would clibm back into their planes and roar off for another mission over the ocian. But tonight the war was far away and everyone there was having fun.

I don't know which scene was the saddest or if either could mean much to anyone except members of the cast. However, and oold sergeant who was winding up 27 years of amry life stood at the bar looking at the wives and he said:

```
        I run this hotel.  Tomorrow some more of the wives
   are coming down here to stay.  I am going to lock my-
   self in my office, put up an off-limits sign and never
   some out again.  This sort of thing is hard to take."
                                    SM854PCD
```

How could this story possibly be trimmed? In general, it is loosely constructed, but much of the looseness is necessary—essential to the effect it creates. And it was destined for conspicuous treatment below the fold on Page One, with a head designed to point up the special nature of the story. It could not jump to an inside page for obvious reasons.

Let's see how one editor handled this one, and some of the reasoning behind his procedures. His first hunch was that if he could drop the second scene and work on the first, he could just about reduce the story by half. That would preserve the original punch line and help give the story "unity of space." But what would become of the lead? The "death and sorrow"

would still be in the body of the story, but the "dancing and laughter" would be gone. A new lead could be written for the wives' part of the story alone. But the story depends too much on the contrast between the hotel and the bar to justify such a course.

The editor went looking for another bite. The punch line was good, but was there another higher in the story? That "tomorrow, perhaps" paragraph? Structurally, there was some point in returning to the original scene—it provided an epilogue that added to the story, but were those two last paragraphs really necessary? Deleting it saved some real space.

Where could the editor lose some more? Well, here's how he edited the story:

3-30 Tears, Gaiety

```
ENROUTE TO THE WAR, July 25-(AP)-Death and danc-
ing--sorrow and laughter.  They go side by side in this
strange war.

   The contrast is poignant.  It's like a vivid dream
that isn't true--yet it is true.  It's like a page from
the old wars that no one wanted rewritten.  The words
are being scrawled again in this far part of the world.

   Let me take you to two places near an American
island air base.  American troops left this spot for
combat less than four weeks ago.  This also is where the
jets take for their bombing missions.

   First, let's go to a small hotel near the airfield,
It's the temporary home of wives and children of officers
of an infantry division, one which has borne the major
shock of enemy attacks in the north.
```

A group of women were seated around a table. They were the wives sweating out the news of their men in combat.

"Bill's got a chance," one of them said. "If anybody gets out, he will."

She was taking about a major general who has been in command of some of the hardest fighting in the war. He was last seen Friday on a hill overlooking an enemy stronghold, ~~rounding up the stragglers and trying to get them back to the American lines.~~

A dark-haired young woman came into the room. She told the others: "Jim got through. He got back through the lines with some of his men."

One of the women said: "Thank God for that." ~~She was t all, dark and sad eyed.~~

~~I don't know who Jim was and it didn't seem right to break in on this little group, clinging together for strength, to ask his name. It was enough that Jim got back.~~

They tried to be casual and light. But there was an undercurrent of emotion and electric tension. Finally one of the women stood up. "I'm going to bed," she said. "Call me if there is any news."

Then another left and the little group began to break up ~~slowly.~~

A few miles away an air force ~~were~~ club was bright with lights. An orchestra played sentimental melodies. Couples danced gaily and laughed into each other's eyes. ~~At the big bar, fliers and their wives touched glasses and laughed and had a lovely time.~~

Tomorrow, perhaps, the young men would climb back into their planes and roar off for another mission over

the oc&an.   But tonight the war was far away and everyone ~~there~~ was having fun.   #

~~I don't know which scene was the saddest or if~~
~~either could mean much to anyone except members of the~~
~~cast.   However, and oold sergeant who was winding up 27~~
~~years of amry life stood at the bar looking at the wives~~
~~and he said:~~

~~I run this hotel. Tomorrow some more of the wives~~
~~are coming down here to stay. I am going to lock my-~~
~~self in my office, put up an off-limits sign and never~~
~~some out again. This sort of thing is hard to take."~~

SM85lRCD

Now let's look back over the editing job and check the changes. In the first paragraph, two sentences were made one to make the paragraph smoother. The second paragraph was split up mainly to allow a bold-face paragraph to fall at this point. (Notice that the boldface paragraphs are short and, in general, evenly spaced throughout the story. A long boldface para-graph affects readability unfavorably because, in gen-eral, boldface body type is less legible than lightface.) Wordage was deleted in this paragraph, too. Even if the editor didn't have to boil hard, he was wise to trim this section. The reporter oversold here just a little.

In what was originally paragraph 3, the editor cut some more, this time reluctantly. This section was designed to emphasize the proximity of the scene to the fighting. However, something must go, and at-mosphere is not sacrificed elsewhere.

In the old paragraph 4, the 24th Division identi-fication came out. It slowed down the story just a little and the details certainly were not essential to understanding. But the editor didn't get rid of General Dean because the fact that he had been **reported** missing had got a strong play the day before and for several days before that. The story gained in effect by identifying the woman who speaks as his wife. The editor did, however, trim down the material on how Dean was lost. That had been pretty well covered, and

a brief reference should have been enough to recall the general to anyone who was following the news.

The "I don't know who Jim was" paragraph was essentially the wire's explanation to editors that the reporter didn't get the name. It *could* have run, but it wasn't essential.

Now with a hard boiling job on the second scene, the editor snipped it off with a good punch, slightly trimmed down from the original. He reduced a 550-word story to less than 300. It's still a pretty good yarn as these things go. And it served his purpose: it fit in its Page-One spot.

No simple set of rules can be drawn up to help the editor meet all these situations. They are extremely varied. As in other editing tasks, it takes an ear for language and a sense of structure to do a good job. The difficult part is that often a job like this has to be handled in five or ten minutes.

Slashing the Roundup

Editors often encounter still another type of story that is particularly hard to cut. Instead of being built in the traditional inverted-pyramid fashion, like this:

it is constructed more like this:

The "roundup" story often has this structure, particularly if it concludes with a lot of details of almost equal news value. For instance, the state editor concludes a story on local aspects of a regional problem, such as housing or the shortage of doctors, with details from all the communities in the area. Another example is the "holiday activities" roundup; the state editor wraps stories from each community into a single area story. Church festival stories often wind up with a paragraph or two on the plans of each church in the city.

Roundups should run in full if space allows. In all the examples cited, there is a strong reason for carrying the individual community or church details, details which have been gathered at considerable effort and expense. But sometimes, of course, they *must* be cut. Obviously, simply chopping away half or two-thirds of the communities or churches involved is no solution. They are of approximately equal news value, and chopping would leave some of the communities well covered and others not mentioned at all. Under certain circumstances, however, an approximation of that method is possible. For example, if a newspaper is published in several area editions, it might be possible to give the details on individual towns only in the edition which serves those towns. Restructuring a story in this way requires a lot of work and extra "bookkeeping" and is fraught with potentiality for error. But if time allows, it might be the best way to handle the matter.

There is an applicable solution that is more nearly universal, one which both reduces the story in length and avoids hurting the feelings of townsmen and churchmen involved. This calls for getting inside the story and pulling out identical minor details in each segment. Look at the following story:

The solemn 40-day period of Lent, which leads to the joyous celebration of Easter Sunday, will begin tomorrow —Ash Wednesday—and thousands will participate in Lenten religious rites and observances.

Several paragraphs follow on the significance of Lent and Ash Wednesday in the various denominations. This sort of material is germane and hard to cut without doing grave damage to the story as a whole. However, the story continues with a list telling how local churches will celebrate Ash Wednesday:

Ash Wednesday will be observed at St. John's Lutheran Church with a Holy Communion service at 7:45 p.m. The Rev. Paul Ansgar will give the sermon on the topic "The Next 40 Days."

Assisting at the altar with the administration of Communion will be the Rev. Albert Boehm.

At Trinity Episcopal Church, a Holy Communion service will be read at 8 p.m. by Dr. Adelbert Smith, Rector. Dr. Smith will deliver the sermon on "The Story of Lent."

Assisting Dr. Smith in the mass will be the Rev. Roger T. Lindsay, Rector of Our Saviour's Episcopal Church.

St. Paul's Lutheran Church will hold Ash Wednesday services at 7:30 p.m. . . .

Nearly a column of this sort of material follows.

Where the available space precludes so much detail, the editor can set up a system of definitions. In this instance, he might rule that there is room only for the name of the church, the time of the service, and the clergyman in charge. This would omit sermon topics, sermon texts, names of assisting clergymen, etc. Such a system would reduce the material to about half its original length. The important thing is that all the churches get the same treatment. If the sermon topic is omitted in one, it must be omitted in all. Naturally the editor must avoid too rigid an application of his rules. He should not, for instance, omit an important church custom peculiar to one denomination just because similar ground is not covered in the others. And it would be better yet not to run information of this kind as a story. It would be more useful in a well-placed tabulation.

Setting in Smaller Type

Another way of cutting down the space needed to tell a story involves no loss of wordage at all. That is simply to set part of the story in smaller type. Dropping down to 6-point type suggests itself when the material is carried because it has high interest for only a segment of the paper's reading public but lacks *general* news value.

The story above is an example which might lend itself to the 6-point treatment. The details could be set in smaller type at a saving of up to a third of a column of space. The editor could justify his decision on the grounds that members of the individual churches mentioned in the story would be served by inclusion of this material and would be willing to run down through the smaller type to find it. The general reader would get as much of the story as interests him in the first paragraphs.

Editors might well follow this general set of rules for using 6-point:

1. *Use 6-point only where substantial space savings can be realized.*
2. *Don't overdo it.* Legibility drops off sharply and page make-up invariably suffers where 6-point is used.
3. *When in doubt, don't use it.*

Butchering

Every careful newspaper reader has experienced at some time or other the exasperation that results when a story is incomplete. He pursues an interesting angle, rightly and reasonably expecting fuller explanation, clear to the end of the story and finds nothing more. His interest has been aroused but not satisfied.

Sometimes this is the reporter's fault. In striving to find a newsworthy lead, he is sometimes tempted to pick up an angle which he cannot develop in detail. In a story published years ago, for example, a two-column 36-point three-line head proclaimed that Swiss democracy was "more myth than actuality," according to a traveler there. This statement was repeated in the lead, but in the eight paragraphs about a trip to Europe that followed, not one word developed the head and lead.

Even when the fraud is not that gigantic, readers can be cheated when important questions are left unanswered. Therefore the editor must be sure whenever he deletes anything from a story that he is not affecting another part of what remains. Hasty deletions can wreck a good story. The damage is especially devastating when they cut details which broaden out lead materials. Leads built around more than one aspect of the story are particularly tricky. For example, a wire story from Washington carried this lead:

WASHINGTON—(XP)—America's mighty atomic industry this year turned out record-smashing amounts of the stuff that bombs are made of—at the same time giving attention to two new weapon possibilities.

In cutting this story, the editor must be sure he does not prevent both angles from being developed adequately. In this case the story first developed the second angle (weapon possibilities). Then paragraph 2 brought in a third angle which the reporter apparently considered too good to be relegated to a lower position in the story but not related closely enough to the lead material to weave in at the top. Not until paragraph 8 did this sentence occur:

The AEC told Congress that from January through June, the production of uranium-235 and plutonium was at "the highest rate in the history of the project"—exceeding the output for the last entire year.

If lack of space requires heavy-handed editing, something will have to "give" besides this paragraph. It is the only material in the story which supports the facts given top play in the lead, hence probably in the head as well. Even if the third angle has to be removed entirely to make way for adequate development of the first two, the reader will probably be better served.

Another type of story that presents special space-saving problems is essentially chronological except for the lead and is full of detail, much of which is anticipated in the lead. One of this sort started like this:

MADISON, Wis.—Take one man, add three months, 205 hours in the air, an earthquake, a brush with the law, an "arrest," dishonest postal authorities, and winter in South America, and you have the vacation dish of Robert J. Blake, geology graduate student at the University of Wisconsin.

The story went on to some science reporting of the gravity readings Blake was taking during his 40,000 miles of travel and then strung together a series of anecdotes on his adventures. The anecdotes were not bad and couldn't be trimmed much without losing their flavor, so some of them had to go in entirety. But the editor could not just cut out two or three of them and forget the whole thing without doctoring the series in the lead. The reader should not be expected to learn about an earthquake and then never see it mentioned again. If one of the anecdotes falls by the wayside, the angle must be removed from the lead, too. Or the lead must be rewritten to reflect the deletion.

The editor must wield a scalpel, not a butcher knife. In cutting, he must be concerned with the total impact of the story on the reader as well as making sound judgments on what details can be sacrificed. No simple set of rules could ever be adequate to all the space-saving requirements of a busy copy desk. The situations are extremely varied—and there are many more variations than space permits here. But though this list is not exhaustive, here are some points to remember:

1. Do your cutting in such a way as to preserve the essential facts plus just enough detail to answer the reader's most pressing questions.

2. Don't assume that a story can be chopped off anywhere just because it seems to be arranged in inverted-pyramid form.

3. Try to preserve the broad outline of the story where the structure is not the routine inverted-pyramid form.

4. Try to preserve the flavor of the story where it is built around a feature treatment.

5. Read the new version carefully. The process of cutting may have raised new problems. *Read past the cuts to determine whether changes are necessary in what remains*—in antecedents of pronouns, for in-

stance. The new structure may require the insertion of new connective words and phrases. Supply them where they are needed.

6. Remove excess wordage at any time, whether or not you have been given the general instruction to reduce the story in length.

7. Try to preserve or supply an ending which fittingly closes the story.

Editing for Accuracy

The first commandment in the newsroom is ACCURACY ALWAYS. It is also the last. And the copy desk is the last place in the chain of processing for catching mistakes. Accuracy must be uppermost in the mind of the copy editor all the time. There are plenty of valid, ready-made excuses for not getting the news or not getting it first or not getting it in detail: not enough time, money, etc. But there are no excuses for inaccuracy. The newsroom tradition of "getting it first" is perhaps less honored today, when the competition is largely the more flexible and fast-paced media, capable of "scooping" the newspapers every time. But "getting it right" is based on something more fundamental than a competitive position: telling the truth is the newspaper's primary obligation to the reader, if it expects its readers' trust.

The trust of readers is not to be taken for granted. Numerous studies have shown that although people rely on newspapers more than any other medium for general information and even more for local news, they do not necessarily trust the newspaper more.[4] In fact, most studies have shown newspapers trailing television on the score of credibility. The studies do not conclude whether this is because people feel they can "trust their own eyes" or whether they come to place personal trust in the broadcaster on camera; because newspaper news tends to get closer to their own activities and concerns, allowing them more opportunity to check the reported facts against their

[4] *E.g.,* Bruce H. Westley and Werner J. Severin, "Some Correlates of Media Credibility," *Journalism Quarterly* 41:325–335 (Summer 1964). Others are cited in Chapter 13.

own observations; or for some other reason or combination of reasons. They have concluded that the more education a reader has, the higher the status of his occupation, the more urban his residence, the more active he is in the community—the more likely he is to believe the newspaper over television and radio. But the only way to keep winning and maintaining readers' trust is to struggle constantly against all sources of error—even typographical errors—for every error justifies the mistrust of everyone.

Published studies of newspaper accuracy indicate that more errors of fact get past the copy desk than a conscientious news editor should tolerate. The most comprehensive of these studies showed, in fact, that only slightly less than 50 per cent of the stories in three West Coast dailies contained no errors, and that figure excluded typographical errors. Errors in objective details of identification (name, age, street address) were relatively infrequent; errors in the more subjective realms of meaning and interpretation were relatively frequent. Errors increased when the reporter interviewed by telephone instead of face to face. The authors concluded that facts from any source should be considered suspect until verified.[5]

The Straight News Story

The point has already been made that it is not possible to check every fact. The quality that makes it possible for an editor to detect and correct errors is a combination of alertness, skepticism, and a passionate desire for accuracy. He does not have to search reference

---

[5] Fred C. Berry, Jr., "A Study of Accuracy in Local News Stories of Three Dailies," *Journalism Quarterly* 44:482–490 (Autumn 1967). Berry used a method developed by Charnley; consult Mitchell V. Charnley, "Preliminary Notes on a Study of Newspaper Accuracy," *Journalism Quarterly* 13:394–401 (December 1936). See also Charles H. Brown, "Majority of Readers Give Papers an A for Accuracy," *Editor & Publisher,* February 13, 1965, pp. 13, 63; Gary C. Lawrence and David L. Grey, "Subjective Inaccuracies in Local News Reporting," *Journalism Quarterly* 46:753–757 (Winter 1969); Gerald L. Grotta, "Attitudes on Newspaper Accuracy and External Controls," *Journalism Quarterly* 46:757–759 (Winter 1969); William B. Blankenburg, "News Accuracy: Some Findings on the Meaning of Errors," *Journal of Communication* 20:375–386 (December 1970).

books on every point of fact; he does have to have a sixth sense for little inconsistencies that point to a possible error. For example, the editor usually does not wear out a city directory rechecking a list of names the reporter presumably has checked in every possible way unless he is particularly skeptical of the reporter's accuracy. He might, however, question a name which appears to be of Norwegian origin, let us say, and seems to deviate from the typical Norse combination of letters. He checks all of the doubtful ones, in other words. The skill lies in knowing *what to doubt.*

There are no guidebooks to the acquisition of this skill. There are, however, a few tricks that help, one of which has already been suggested. It is to *know the geography of the territory well enough to be able to visualize any place described*—the scene of an accident at a highway intersection, a street to be paved, a flooded river—either in terms of knowledge of the scene or of a map. This ability to visualize a scene is important in checking other errors of fact, as well. The editor does not read about the police account of a shooting in the way his readers do. He reads it carefully for detail. Does the story describe nine shots from a revolver? If so, when did the gunman reload—or was the reporter careless or overzealous?

The editor files away in his head assorted bits of information all his life. He never knows when some piece of trivia may show him the way to an error. Here's the way it works: Reading a story about a regional meeting of the Augustana Lutheran church, an editor encountered a piece of background information which he instantly doubted. The story stated that the denomination in question had 44,000 members. Now the editor happened to know that this faith maintained two colleges, one in Sioux Falls, South Dakota, the other in Rock Island, Illinois. Was it likely, he asked himself, that 44,000 churchmen could shoulder such a burden? The editor referred the story back to the reporter, who went to his notes and found that he had slipped at the typewriter—the figure actually was 444,000. Had the reporter not been at hand, the editor could have checked some suitable reference. Or, since the figure was purely background, he could have removed it from the story.

Another valuable trick is this: *Watch the mathematics.* A Los Angeles newspaper carried this story in the No. 2 spot on its front page:

> The Census Bureau yesterday announced the population of the city of Los Angeles is 1,954,036. The population of Los Angeles County—including the city—is 4,116,901.
>
> The county figure shows the population *has nearly doubled* in the last decade. In 1940, the county population was 2,788,634. The increase of 1,328,258 *is a 47.8% jump.* [Italics supplied.]

It seems inconceivable that an intelligent reporter would equate a 50 per cent increase with doubling the original figure, but there it is. And the editor didn't catch it. The problem of accurately interpreting figures is discussed more fully in Chapter 5.

Finally, the editor can help the cause by keeping attuned to what is *probable* as well as what is *possible.* While reading a story about Senator Blank's attack on the Democratic platform plank on price controls, the editor suspects an error. Senator Blank is not only a Democrat but one who consistently votes with his party. A check proves that Senator Blank was talking about the Republican platform. Many a reporter has written the opposite of what he meant without suspecting it.

It is in spotting errors of this sort that the merely "fussy" copyreader falls down. He is an expert on split infinitives and word usage, but he devotes so much attention to *manner* that he overlooks *matter.* An example is to be found in a story headed "Grateful Family Repays Blood Center." An excerpt follows:

> Monday, grateful members of the family brought some of their friends with them to [the blood center].
>
> The [Jones] family and their friends more than made up for the precious pints of blood [used to save Mr. Jones].
>
> *It was not disclosed what type blood the family had, but it was not believed to be the same as the rare group.* [Italics supplied.]

Without being a medical expert, the editor could certainly act on the *probability* that blood types don't run in families. Had the editor allowed his suspicions to be aroused to that extent, he could have killed the paragraph and done no damage to the story whatever.

When the editor has been alert enough to doubt an inaccurate fact, what can he do to correct it? Some of the solutions have already been suggested in the examples above. To summarize, these are the possibilities:

He can correct the fact himself, if he is certain it is wrong and knows how to make it right. The editor makes many decisions on his own, based on a combination of his own knowledge and the internal evidence in the story. For example, he *knows* that the reporter has simply failed to correct a transposition in his copy in writing "Highway 21"; the story says the accident took place near Willie's Tavern, which is on Highway 12. Fair enough. But making more arbitrary changes on the basis of his own knowledge without going to some more dependable source is fraught with danger. Sometimes it takes a disastrous boner to cure an overconfident editor.

If he is not sure the fact is incorrect, the editor can delete the fact altogether, if it is not essential to telling the story and if he hasn't time to check it. However, if the fact is essential, it must be checked, no matter how much time it takes, against a dependable source.

He can go to the reporter himself, usually the most ready source of correction. If the reporter is in the newsroom, all the editor has to do is refer the story back to him. In some newsrooms, this means sending it "back through channels" (from the rim to the slot to the city editor to the reporter). In others, it is acceptable to go directly to the reporter. The reporter can check his notes or go back to the original source of the information and resolve the editor's doubts.

When the reporter is not in the newsroom and cannot be contacted readily, *the editor has recourse to the reference materials already discussed.* If the fact cannot be found in any ready reference, the copy editor can go to an outside source, provided he can do it by telephone. Otherwise, the story should go back into the hands of the city editor.

In the study of newspaper accuracy cited on page 72, the fewest errors occurred when the source was a handout from a public-relations source. But copy desks can *commit* errors when editors fail to understand the handout. For example, a university public-information office put out a release saying (and the names have been changed), "John Jones, Herbert V. Smith professor of history at the University of Blank, will evaluate the university history department tonight . . . ." The newspaper story came out: "John Jones and Herbert V. Smith, professors of history at the University of Blank, will evaluate . . . ." Professor Jones held a named professorship honoring Professor Smith, and Professor Smith, a very famous historian, had been dead for many years. The paper's credibility suffered badly, especially in the university community where all these facts were well known.

At least one newspaper maintains a continuous surveillance over the accuracy of its staff-produced stories and headlines. As reported in the ANPA Newspaper Information Service Newsletter:

The Bangor (Me.) *Daily News* has a letter-writing program to news sources which they use to narrow the newspaper's credibility gap. The plan works this way: Each day the *News* sends out what they call "accuracy letters" to news sources of a selected number of staff-written stories from that day's paper. The letters enclose a clipping of the news story and ask the source to evaluate the accuracy of the story. Each letter is accompanied by a stamped, self-addressed return envelope.

The responses to the letters are then compiled and circulated among the *Daily News* staffers for discussion and action.

How are the letters received? One superintendent of schools told Mr. John W. Moran, managing editor, in reply to a recent letter: "It is as fine a gesture as I have seen in the areas of personal and public relations."

The paper also attempts to determine the accuracy of its headlines when compared to headlines of similar stories from other newspapers in Maine. Copies of pages containing *News* headlines set alongside headlines from other papers are circulated among the staff for comparison and discussion.

Such concern and constructive effort are all too rare. The importance of the news reader's perception of accuracy should not be underestimated. A study conducted by an unnamed Midwest newspaper has shown that judgments about its fairness and its accuracy are very good predictors of the rating given by the same readers of its overall excellence.[6]

Editing for Objectivity

The whole concept of "news" and the news "story" is undergoing change. The "straight" news story, with its emphasis on objectively reporting today's events ("hard news") and its characteristic structure—the summary lead, the block paragraph, inverted-pyramid style, and careful attribution of facts to their source—is still the standard in many newsrooms. But its adequacy as the sole means of conveying the truth about what is going on in the world has come under attack in recent years. A new, freer news-story form has emerged. It has not by any means replaced the straight news story, but it has gained increasing importance as a means of dealing with issues and trends, rather than events, and in coping with the more complex problems of our times.

The New York *Times* still uses the traditional straight-news format for almost every front-page story; just about every Page-One lead is a summary lead. The same may be said of the Washington *Evening Star,* the St. Louis *Post-Dispatch,* and the Chicago *Tribune,* to name a few. But the *Wall Street Journal,* the *Christian Science Monitor,* the Los Angeles *Times,* the Washington *Post,* the Louisville *Courier-Journal* and *Times, Newsday* (of Hempstead, Long Island), and the Denver *Post,* among others, rely on it much less heavily than they once did, especially in staff-written stories, to convey major local and regional news (except routine local police and court news). And since the newspaper-based news syndicates, notably those of the Los Angeles *Times* and the Washington *Post,* the Chicago *Daily News* and the New York *Times,* offer alternatives to the

---

[6] Reported in Chilton R. Bush, ed., *News Research for Better Newspapers* 1:125–126 (New York: American Newspaper Publishers Association Foundation, 1966).

wire-service file to an increasing number of newspapers across the continent—and these reports, being largely supplemental to the regular wire-service fare, are often of a more interpretive nature—the tendency has clearly been to diffuse this type of journalism rather widely. The wire services carry this kind of story, too, but their stock in trade is, of course, the deadpan report of the very latest developments in the most universally high-interest and high-importance news of the day.

"Interpretive" (or "interpretative") is not an exact descriptive term for this kind of story, but it has come into currency as the handle for a whole series of departures from the straight-news format. Such stories require more editorial skill than straight news does, and for that reason they are dealt with in Chapter 4. In this section, editing straight news stories for objectivity is at point, for much—perhaps most—of what comes under the editor's pencil in the usual North American newsroom is written in detached, objective, straight-news style. Consequently, one of the basic skills of the editor is maintaining and/or bolstering standards of objectivity.

What is the basis for an objective account of the news? A study done for a private contractor some years ago set out to try to specify it.[7] From a series of statements of policy issued by the sponsoring news-handling agency, it attempted to distill what the policies permitted and prohibited in terms that could be reduced to "content analysis" categories describing "objectivity" (although it was more strictly a study of style than of content, as will become clear below). The categories were then applied to various kinds of news accounts in an effort to determine which ones and what percentage fell outside what the policy statements permitted.

Philosophically and emotionally, newspaper objectivity is many things: a state of mind on the reporter's and the editor's part that includes a conscious effort not to prejudge what he sees; not to be influenced by his own personal preconceptions, predilections, allegiances, and biases; not to be swayed by the rhetoric of partisans; always to assume there is "another side" and to make an effort to see to it that the other side has a chance to be heard. Objectivity may also be seen in the light of its effects: the ability of new information to modify the reader's perceptions of the event. But objectivity had to be *manifest* for purposes of the study: the study had to be able to judge what was visible on the surface of the account— the message itself, not the apparent intent of the writer or the message's possible effects—as fully objective or less than that. A crude scale of categories was constructed, ranging from "open advocacy" at one end to a residual category for every statement having no departures from manifest objectivity at the other. The categories were as follows:

Advocacy Statements of advocacy were defined as unattributed statements about what "ought" or "should" be done, statements clearly beyond the limits of the objective news account. Some examples: "The city should take immediate steps to . . ."; "This ought not to happen in civilized society."

Valuation Unattributed statements assigning a "good" or "bad" label to events, persons, or ideas seemed also to be clearly prohibited under the rules of the straight news story. (More difficult to judge were statements about strength and weakness.) Some examples: "attractive candidate," "strong race," "sound idea."

Consequence Unattributed statements about either the causes or effects of events or predicting what will or might happen as a consequence of events, too, appeared to be beyond the pale, but the "rules" were less clear here. The distinction had to be made between the speculative prediction and the reported agenda item. "The House will vote later today" falls in the latter category. But "The coup resulted from failure of the old regime to . . ."; "As a result, the new Parliament will have to consider . . ."; "This latest move will no doubt produce . . ." are consequence statements.

---

[7] The study was conducted at the University of Wisconsin by Malcolm S. MacLean, Jr., John B. Adams, and Bruce H. Westley.

Significance Less clearly outlawed than any of the above types are statements about the relative importance or significance of events. The news media have always arbitrated for their readers on the relative importance of given stories. The most important story gets 96-point headline type and a position at the top of the page, and it is longer than other less important stories. Radio and television sometimes use words to produce the same effect: "At the top of the news today . . ." or "Today's headline story . . ."; "Even more significantly," "Still more important developments came . . . ," etc. These are all significance statements. When such statements become speculation about the effects of the news on the nation, however, they become consequence statements.

Backgrounding Most objective of the categories was the one for statements about previous events that have relevance for today's event. If they are free from speculation about cause and effect and do not assign values to events, persons, or ideas, they fall within the straight-news concept, except that they are statements about events occurring at some time previous to the present news cycle. For example: "He was indicted last May 16 after . . ."; "The case recalled a similar one in 1967 in which . . . ."

What is left is presumably "straight" news: observable events. *Attributed* statements about value or cause and effect are, of course, observable events, as are attributed statements advocating a point of view or course of action.

This system of categories revealed huge differences in the "profiles" of different television commentators and even huge differences between the first part of one commentator's program, which consisted of news, and the last, which was commentary. And it did show up the expected differences between editorials and news stories and between signed and unsigned news stories. Its justification here, however, lies in whether it helped to clarify thinking about the nature of a **manifestly** objective news report and to guide an editor in determining, under a given set of circumstances, whether he needs to do anything and if so, what, in order to attain that goal. Unfortunately, the system did not yield a very reliable measure of mani-

fest objectivity. The policy statements said reporters are permitted to analyze and comment but not to give opinions, for example. But most of the categories may be looked at as different kinds of opinions: an opinion about what should be done, an opinion about who are the good guys, an opinion about why it happened, an opinion about what will happen, an opinion about how important it all is. All the study showed was that the policy on this matter should be clarified: Which opinions are objective analysis and which are biases that should be prohibited from a news report?

The best answer, in terms of the study, is this: The straight news story permits backgrounding and significance statements, is wary of consequence statements, discourages valuation statements, and prohibits advocacy. The interpretive story encourages backgrounding and significance, allows consequence statements when they are well supported by fact, discourages valuation statements of the good-bad variety but permits those of the strong-weak kind when buttressed by fact, frowns on unsupported valuation, and discourages advocacy. It does not permit the reporter full freedom to advocate his own point of view, but it does not prohibit him from assembling a compelling array of fact and qualified judgments leading to the conclusion that "something must be done." (The newspaper, of course, has a right and duty to advocate *its* point of view, but not in its news stories.)

Attribution In this study, attribution proved to be a thorny problem in the same ways it often is on the copy desk. An advocacy statement falls within the rules of manifest objectivity when it is clearly attributed to a specified source. A candidate's statement "This pussyfooting must stop" is an "observable" fact. The problem arises when the attribution is less specific. Reporters have often tried to get around the strictures of objectivity with (1) attribution by passive voice ("it was learned," "it was reported"); (2) attribution by unspecified source ("sources near the President say," "usually reliable sources report," "an unidentified source," "most senators agree"); (3) · attribution by convincing generality ("those who know say," "it was learned from the highest source," "unimpeachable sources confirm," "it can now be reliably reported." Editors sometimes suspect that the unimpeachable sources are the reporters themselves.

In summary, the criterion for attribution is this: *All statements of fact must be attributed to an appropriate source,* except in circumstances where they might have been observed by anyone who happened to be present at the right time and place. Thus an individual's statement of his opinion on a public question becomes an objective fact when the story shows clearly that it is quoting or paraphrasing him and when it repeatedly links what he said with the speaker as the story progresses. It is not necessary to attribute to a specific person the statement that a duplex burned to the ground, because anyone who stayed to the end could have seen that it did. Any casual bystander might have a theory about the *cause* of the fire, based on his observation of it, yet this cannot classify as an objective fact; even if the theory is attributed to someone, the casual observer is not an appropriate or pertinent source of the facts. The opinion of the official whose duty it is to observe the fire and determine its probable cause is an objective fact only if it is attributed to him. After official determination of the cause of the fire, it becomes possible to present it as a fact without attribution, if no doubts have arisen since the official finding.

In editing the straight news story, then, the editor must make sure that statements of fact are properly attributed, that his own biases as well as those of the reporter don't obtrude, and that when two sides of the story are given the treatment does not favor one side over the other. He must have a clear understanding of the forms and traditions of newspaper objectivity and apply it to the copy he edits. Usually he is free to supply missing phrases of attribution, for instance, without consulting his superiors. More drastic decisions, such as excising a statement because he believes it to be inadequately attributed, are sometimes made in consultation with others in the newsroom, rather than on his individual initiative.

Here is a routine example of the way an editor can improve a story from the standpoint of objectivity:

```
      The State will save money if Esperanto is taught at

the University, a small group of World Federalists were

told at their meeting last night.

      Speaker Glenn Tyler pointed out that Esperanto

could be taught by any qualified language instructor to

much larger classes than those for other languages.  A

student would need only one semester of the course to

become proficient in reading and writing.

      A bill now before the Legislature, he said, pro-

vides for the teaching of Esperanto in the University

and nine normal schools.  The bill is now having a

hearing before the Senate Finance Committee.  Tyler

believes the bill will be passed.

      A common language for the entire world, Tyler

added, is the essential thing for successful World

Government.

                         --30--
```

The State will save money if Esperanto is taught at
the University, a small group of United World Federalists was
told at a meeting last night in the Memorial Union.
The Speaker, Glenn Tyler, of Madison, declared that Esperanto, an
international language, could be taught by any qualified language instructor to
much larger classes than those of other languages. A
student would need only one semester of the course, he said, to
become proficient in reading and writing.

A bill now before the Legislature pro-
vides for the teaching of Esperanto in the University
and nine state colleges. Tyler
said he believes the bill will passed.

A common language for the entire world, Tyler
contended, is essential to successful World
Government.

This story illustrates the fact that it is not enough to attribute a statement; it must get *appropriate* attribution. Let's take the corrections one by one:

In the lead, the editor made two important corrections: he filled in the specific names of the institution and the organization. At the same time, he supplied a missing fact and corrected some errors of grammar.

In the second paragraph, he made his first attribution correction: he changed an inappropriate attribution to an appropriate one. A speaker "points out" *facts* or ideas that have general acceptance, not his own opinion, so the editor substituted "declared" for "pointed out." In the second sentence of the same paragraph is an unattributed statement that clearly needs attribution. The attributing phrase in the preceding sentence has no effect on this one. It is not an observable or accepted fact that it takes only a semester to become proficient in Esperanto. So the editor slipped in "he said" at the first logical break in the continuity of the sentence.

In the third paragraph, the first sentence does not require attribution; it is a matter of public record that the bill is before the legislature. The editor removed the phrase because it was repetitious and cluttered the sentence. He deleted the second sentence because it contributed little to the story and contained too vague a time element. In the final sentence of the third paragraph is an example of a fussier sort of attribution than we have encountered before. This statement needs attributing because the report is about *what happened at a meeting, not the subjective states of mind of its participants.* It could be that Tyler will change his mind about all this in a day or so. Saying "he believes" would have been inaccurate. To make the sentence an objective statement of what went on, the editor made it read, "he said he believed."

The final paragraph contains another inappropriate attributing phrase. To say that the speaker "added" this statement to what was previously reported is no grave sin. But it is likely that this addition was in fact a major point in the story; in all likelihood, it was one of his major "contentions."

The editor can frequently improve the news stories he handles by simply attending carefully to the appropriateness of the attributions. He will learn in time that he must attend not only to the word choice but also to the attribution's position in the sentence. With regard to *word choice,* we have seen that each has a more or less special meaning, as in "pointed out." The same is true of "stated," a poor substitute for "said." "Stated" implies that a "statement" has been made. An utterance is not necessarily a statement. "Declared" is a good substitute for "said," if it is not overdone. "Averred" is generally avoided now as too pompous for newspaper use. "Said" itself is the handiest word in the language for attribution. "He said" is so inconspicuous when adroitly inserted as to present no very considerable problem of repetition.

With regard to *position in the sentence,* the importance of the attribution itself—its bearing on the matter of what is said—is the determining factor. This is especially true in leads. "Izvestia, the official government newspaper said today that . . . ." Whatever *Izvestia* has said, it has meaning for American readers because Soviet officialdom said it. Hence, the attribution goes first. In cases where the facts will almost stand alone, the attribution can be tacked on to the end in its least conspicuous form.

Fair play   Fair play and objectivity are closely related but by no means the same thing. What does fairness mean as it applies to the content of newspapers? To whom must we be fair? As we have already seen, there are no simple rules for the editor to follow. One seasoned newsman put it this way: The editor's greatest responsibility is his responsibility to the reader—to see to it that he gets the news. It is not playing fair with him if some special considerations of "fairness" to individuals or segments of the population are allowed to interfere in any way with putting out the news. Is it fair, for example, to the law-abiding mother of a criminal to publish abroad how her son was sent to jail? Maybe not, but it is even more unfair to our readers to deny them access to that news. Is it fair to

a local businessman to publish a story about his minor scrape with the law? It could be argued that it is a first offense, that it could happen to anyone, that his boy at college will suffer the slings and arrows of outrageous fortune if the story becomes known. But if such an arrest is news to anyone, it is news to everyone.

In short, playing fair in the usual sense would mean withholding news. But withholding news, provided that it *is* news and deserves a place in the paper, is unfair to the newspaper reader. Any judgment concerning fair play must take this into consideration. Newsmen agree, however, that when the effect of the story on certain individuals or groups would be dangerously negative, the news should be withheld. They usually withhold the names of juvenile offenders, for example, even when not forced to by state laws. The belief is that the story is small and the potential damage great. If the story is far above the routine level, however, most newsmen agree that it must be printed with full identification of the offender. A capital crime committed by a juvenile is usually handled in the same manner as any other capital crime.

Another example lies in the area of racial identifications. Although practices still vary, especially regionally, the tendency recently has been to avoid stating a newsmaker's race. It might be argued that thus do we withhold a fragment of the news. The rebuttal many newsmen have used is this: The racial tag grew up during a period in which racial differences were important, but for reasons we cannot now take pride in. There was a time when it was deemed necessary to identify the original nationality of an immigrant and the color of a man's skin if it was not white. The manifest unfairness of this sort of tag became apparent to editors and readers alike and it has been dropped where it is not pertinent. That a certain criminal is a Negro is not more pertinent than the fact that his father was born in Georgia, that he was baptized in the Methodist church, or that his hair is curly. It simply has no bearing on the crime. But if he is beaten in a race riot, then obviously his race *is* pertinent, and the editor will see to it that this fact is not withheld.

Newspapers sometimes withhold news in the interest of law enforcement. When publicity would interfere with enforcement efforts, most newspapers are willing to hold up the story. It is a situation subject to abuses and the police are usually expected to show conclusively that a real need exists.

The problems with a "balanced" and "objective" approach to reporting public controversies are illustrated by the findings of a study of fluoridation referenda.[8] Do voters reject fluoridation, even though it is advocated by a large section of the scientific community, out of alienation, ignorance, or apathy? Though the study found some evidence to support the alienation hypothesis (the "no" voters tend to be somewhat more authoritarian than "yes" voters), its major finding was that successful opposition to fluoridation is usually aroused by inducing confusion—making it appear that the scientific community does not agree on fluoridation. The voter readily perceives that he is not capable of judging the pros and cons and tends to take one of two escapes: he does not vote or he votes "no." The appearance of a scientific controversy, of course, is manufactured by the opponents. Instead of mounting fundamentalist arguments against scientific arguments, they create spurious but legitimate-sounding organizations. To oppose the arguments of the National Academy of Sciences, they create the "American Academy of Nutrition." The news report that accepts "both sides" as they are presented thus merely contributes to a confusion which frustrates public decision making.

Other Stories

The rules of objectivity stated here apply to the straight news story. The rules for feature stories and explanatory or interpretive stories that often accompany spot news are just a little more relaxed. The explanatory writer may have a little more leeway because he needs it and because, in theory at least, the reader is told by the by-line that the opinions and interpretations are the writer's. One of the daily decisions of the desk, for example, is whether a wire story needs a by-line. The general rule is that if the story contains substantial elements of interpretation or backgrounding—hence is not thoroughly enough attributed to meet the definition of a straight news story—then a by-line is necessary.

Like so many other aspects of journalism, the theory of objectivity is undergoing change and may one day be abandoned. Not that newsmen are any less devoted to the ideal; rather, they recognize that (1) rules are no guarantee of genuine objectivity and sometimes can be manipulated to pass off a thoroughly dishonest story as lily-white, and (2) rules impose restraints on the news writer that may have been adequate in another day but are inadequate and unreasonable in the atomic age.

The doubts referred to here arise largely over the question of *meaning,* a principal emphasis in news editing. The argument is that the unadorned facts are often inadequate to convey the meaning of the complex events of our time. The writer needs greater freedom than the traditional news-story form allows if he is to convey the full meaning of events. This question need not be debated at length here. The foregoing rules for objectivity in the straight news story are not necessarily the last word on the subject—but *they are the current rules.* Even though the potential newsman will do his craft a service if he questions them and concerns himself with the solutions to the problems they raise, he must expect to abide by them until others take their place.

Handling Wire Copy

More often than not, the universal copy desk is also the telegraph desk. In other words, a general copy desk handles wire-service copy as part of its routine, as Chapter 2 has indicated. This means among other things, that the chief of the copy desk is the chief gate keeper for news of the great world. Under the supervision of the news editor (unless that is his own title, which it often is) or the managing or executive editor, it is his responsibility to decide what wire news

---

[8] Harvey M. Spolsky, "The Fluoridation Controversy: An Alternative Explanation," *Public Opinion Quarterly* 33:241–248 (Summer 1969).

will be carried, at what length, where in the paper, and with what typographical emphasis. It also means that the copy editor will be involved in the process of piecing together the wire news of the day, editing it, and writing heads for it.

How Wire Systems Work

Piecing together wire-service copy requires understanding how wire systems work. The news agency sends a flow of news to many different newspapers having deadlines at differing times of the day. To do its job, it must often split up stories into segments, and it must send corrections, new leads, adds, and inserts in order to keep the news up to the minute.

A single day's file will illustrate how the wire keeps its members up to the minute on stories breaking all over the world. On the left, below, is the actual teletypesetter monitor copy received by afternoon papers in a mid-South region on one November day, showing what was on the teletypesetter tapes. This is prejustified copy; that is, one line of teletype will equal a line of type, but the teletype's ragged right margin will be automatically justified in type per instructions on the tape.

```
Starting PMs Report, A001 Next
```

At about midnight, the afternoon-paper cycle begins. Each item is numbered.

```
A001WX

     czzca oyz

          WX

Haynsworth Bjt 500 two takes
900
```

This is the first story on the A wire. Washington—"WX"—is filing.

This is a "budget" item—one the editors have already been told to expect. It is in two parts, the first of about 500 words; the total is about 900 words. Its "slug" or identification line is "Haynsworth."

```
     By JOHN CHADWICK

     Associated Press Writer

WASHINGTON AP — Presi-

dent Nixon's prestige was on the

line as the Senate neared a vote

today on the Supreme Court

nomination of Judge Clement F.

Haynsworth.

  The Republican President

          *   *   *
```

This is an "overnight," a rewrite from the morning-paper file prepared for early transmission. It can be used as background detail for new developments during the day or can be left as handled here if there are no new developments.

(Omissions of paragraphs of detail are indicated with three spaced asterisks.)

him to disqualify himself and he

had a duty to stay on the cases.

  MORE

  GG-AG108aes Nov. 21

————————

A002WX

    1by1

WASHINGTON Take 2 Hayn-

sworth Bjt A001WX: cases.

 Supporters have denounced

the ethics issue as a smokesc-

reen for those who object to

Haynsworth as a southerner

     *   *   *

cases, "diversity of opinion and

differing viewpoints are whole-

some and vital to the life of the

court."

 AG115aes Nov. 21

————————

A003WX

    zyy

Haynsworth What and Why 190

The first take ends at 1:08 A.M., Eastern Standard Time. There is more to come.

The second item is the second take of the Haynsworth story, the first take of which was No. 001. It "picks up" on the word "cases," the last word in the first take.

This ends the Haynsworth budget item.

The third item sent is an "undated sidebar" on the Haynsworth story. Undated means no "dateline"—no single point of origination. This is slugged "Haynsworth What and Why" and runs about 190 words.

By THE ASSOCIATED PRESS

  The Haynsworth nomination:

What and Why?

  The man: Judge Clement F.

Haynsworth Jr. was nominated

               *   *   *

41-39 against Judge John J.

Parker, who had been selected

by President Herbert Hoover.

  AG118aes Nov. 21

               ————

A004WX

        uiv

Haynsworth Background Bjt

450, 4 Takes Total 1,940

    By BARRY SCHWEID

    Associated Press Writer

  WASHINGTON AP — There

was little reason to suspect, that

sunny day in San Clemente, that

the nomination of Judge Cle-

ment F. Haynsworth Jr. to the

               *   *   *

A second Haynsworth sidebar, this one budgeted, to be sent in four takes.

A007WX

    aee

WASH Haynsworth Back-

ground, A004-006WX, Take 4:   As there is nothing more urgent at this hour, the

confirmation.   four takes move consecutively.

  Vice President Spiro T. Ag-

new moved in to try to hold the

       *   *   *

in the hands of a small group of

senators who remained publicly

uncommitted until the vote it-

self.

  AG153aes Nov. 21   The story is all in at 1:53 A.M.

A010

   czzc

HOLLYWOOD Thomas Col-   The first direct message from AP comes in the form of

umn Adv for today, moved as   a correction in a Bob Thomas column moved two

A137, Nov. 19, in 9th graf, start-   days ahead (an "advance"). It's in the ninth para-

ing the film read it: Wise also   graph.

got 10 per cent of the gross-aft-

er the film turned a profit. The

script, eliminating phrase, in   This means "Go on to the words 'The script,' elimi-

other words, $11,248,100.   nating the phrase 'in other words, $11,248,100.' "

The AP

KC206aes nov 21

————————

A012

　lby1

Telegraph Editors

　The main Apollo 12 budget by
Howard Benedict will be topped
by 10 a.m. EST, with the lead
based on space communications
with the crew.

Another message telling when to expect an update on the Apollo lead, even before it is received.

　No lead is sighted at this time
on a Moon Surprise budget by
Jim Strothman.

Other useful information on what to expect.

　Separates will be provided on
timetable highlights, families,
interview with Apollo program
director.

The AP

KC217aes Nov 21

————————

A013

　zyy

Apollo Bjt 500, Two takes 720

The main moon-landing lead moves next . . .

By HOWARD BENEDICT

AP Aerospace Writer

SPACE CENTER, Houston

AP — Apollo 12's moon voyagers head for home today after
photographing future astronaut
landing sites in the rugged lunar

         *   *   *

A019HO

     qyy

URGENT

Apollo Insert

SPACE CENTER, Apollo Bjt
A013, to cover developments insert after 2nd graf: Clipper.

At 2:23 a.m. EST Apollo 12
changed course slightly to bring
the spacecraft in line for better

         *   *   *

"Attaboy," said Conrad.

At 3:49 p.m.: 3rd graf A013

JJ209acs Nov 21

         ————

. . . and somewhat later an insert to the same story, moved under an "urgent" to give it priority over routine stories. "HO" means "Houston."

Note the pickup in the second paragraph of No. 013 . . .

. . . then, at the end of the insert, another pickup to the main story.

A046

  uivyyx

 SAIGON Vietnam Roundup

a025 sub for last 5 grafs: work-

ing.

 On the battlefields, action

flared anew Thursday and today

     * * *

said one of the homes belonged

to an officer of the national po-

lice.

 zr556aes Nov. 21

Later, a substitute for five paragraphs in a story sent earlier.

No pickup. It ends here.

————————

A063HO

   yyxzyyHO

Apollo Bjt A013 Lead 350

 By HOWARD BENEDICT

  AP Aerospace Writer

SPACE CENTER, Houston

AP — Only hours before start-

ing the long trip home, Apollo

12's orbiting moon voyagers to-

    * * *

A new top on the Apollo budget story . . .

```
Conrad and Bean finished their

second excursion on the moon's

surface.

 Conrad:  9th graf A018 count-

ing previous insert A019HO

 JJ616acs Nov. 21
```

—————

```
A98

Adv Sat Pms Nov. 22

Help for Priests 420

     By DAVE BARKER

   Canadian Press Writer

 MONTREAL AP  —  Many

people go to priests and minis-

ters for help.  What about mem-

bers of the clergy who need help

themselves?

          *   *   *

1 A108WX

       czzcryyr

BULLETIN

Living Costs

 WASHINGTON AP  —  High-

er prices for cars and houses
```

. . . with careful instructions on how to pick up on the previous story.

With all the budgeted stories in and nothing new breaking, there is time to move an advance for Saturday's afternoon papers.

The first "bulletin" moves around 11:00 A.M. Early editions have been closed by this time. As later and final editions near, new stories and new developments must be moved quickly.

were major factors in a four-

   * * *

A109WX

  czzcqyy

URGENT

 WASHINGTON Living Costs

A108WX add: today.

 However, Americans got a

break at the grocery store in

   * * *

A122LAA123

   lbylzyy

Apollo Bjt 2nd Lead A063 320

 By HOWARD BENEDICT

  AP Aerospace Writer

 SPACE CENTER, Houston

 AP — Apollo 12's moon voyag-

ers photographed future Apollo

landing sites for nearly 11 hours

   * * *

smaller antennas were used for

most of the radio conversation.

 There was: 5th graf lead A063

DF1210pes Nov. 21

———

An "add" is moved quickly under an "urgent" priority.

A second new lead moves on the main Apollo story …

… picking up on the previous material.

A128

   lbylryyr

TELEGRAPH EDITORS:

 The following is a hold-for-re-
lease lead for afternoon papers
to the Apollo PMs budget by
Howard Benedict. It past-tenses
the successful firing of the Apollo 12 command ship out of moon
orbit to start the trip back to
earth. It is to be used only after
a bulletin release is moved on
this circuit. This is expected
about 4 p.m. EST, but past experience indicates there may be
a brief delay in confirmation.
Please take every precaution
against premature release.

───────────

HOLD FOR RELEAST

TRANSEARTH   INJECTION

BULLETIN

Apollo Bjt 3rd Lead

   By HOWARD BENEDICT

This message is self-explanatory. An advance is being sent on an expected development in the space flight.

For most afternoon papers it wasn't released in time. However, the morning papers will be ready to snatch at it once it is, assuming that everything went as expected.

Now comes a third new lead . . .

```
   AP Aerospace Writer

SPACE CENTER, Houston

AP — Apollo 12's moon voyag-

ers fired themselves out of lu-

nar orbit today and began the

         *   *   *

hours today photographing fu-

ture Apollo landing sites.

The primary:  4th graf A123.
```

... picking up on the previous one.

```
         ————
```

```
Editors:  End hold-for-release

Apollo blasts out of moon orbit

top to Apollo PMs Bjt by How-

ard Benedict.  Please take every

precaution to guard against pre-

mature release.

The AP
```

AP is taking no chances on premature release!

```
Starting Night Numbers now

A201 is next
```

The night wire opens ...

```
         ————————
```

```
A201

   lbylczzc
```

```
Telegraph Editors

Priorities for Saturday AMs

WASHGINTON  —  Hayn-

sworth decision.

SPACE CENTER  —  Apollo 12

        *   *   *

A203WX

    lbylczzczyy

URGENT

 Telegraph Editors

 WASHINGTON  The  Senate

has started its vote on Hayn-

sworth

 The AP

 JC103pes Nov 21
```

... with a new budget.

Fine. But will it conclude in time for the final edition?

Optional leads   The "optional lead" permits the press association to offer its clients or members an alternative treatment of the same story. The need for an alternate arises frequently with second-day stories. The wire-service editors reason that some news editors, for example those who have no local competition in the opposite cycle, will prefer to handle the story pretty much with a first-day slant: the story is being told locally for the first time in print. But others, especially those with opposition in the other cycle, will prefer a second-day treatment. In such a case, the wire-service sends the story one way and then offers an optional lead which treats the story the other way, picking up on the original story. This makes it unnecessary for the editor to make substantial changes in the story in order to get the treatment he wants. The same device is occasionally used to offer an alternative "straight" or "featurized" treatment at the top of a story or to make available to editors leads stressing different aspects of the same story.

The beginning editor should not regard the system described here as *orders* from the wire services to handle any story in the manner suggested. It is up to the individual member to use the material as he sees fit. The system simply helps the editor solve quickly the problem of keeping the story up to date. The services do, of course, require that they be credited. There is, however, one instance in which the editor must obey a wired instruction. That is the "mandatory kill," which is self-explanatory. An editor's failure to follow through could put the newspaper's wire-service membership in jeopardy.

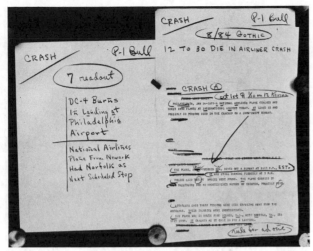

Washington Post *photos*

From Wire Bulletin to Edited Story A
Washington Post editor has begun above the
process of converting the "moving" AP copy
below into a top-of-Page-One story. The story is
firmed up enough in its second lead for an early
edition, so the editor has edited the copy and
written a headline. He can now move the
details in short takes.

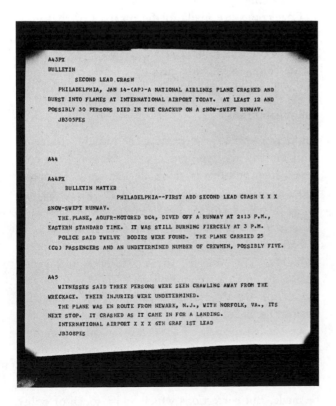

Editing Wire Copy

The task of piecing a wire story together is really quite
simple, as these examples should prove, *when all the
copy is at hand.* It is made more difficult when only
part of it has been received and set in type and the
edition must be put to bed, a problem which is dealt
with in Chapter 4. It is even more complicated when
the editor "compiles" a story—weaves material from
more than one wire service or story into a story of
his own construction. This is described in Chapter 4,
too. But in this case the editor is only doing what the
wire services do every day.

Press-association editors are very skilled at this.
They know how to write the story in the first place so
that new leads can be attached with a minimum of
rewrite. And they know how to wrap into the new
lead the material from the old story which is being
replaced. But careful as they are, they are not infal-
lible. The editor should take the time to make sure
the story makes sense in its final form. He may find
that changes on his own initiative will produce a
smoother story, or that he can clear up confusions and
inconsistencies that crop up in the running story.

Wire editors like to keep inserts to a minimum.
They are sometimes tempted to weave into a new lead
material which is tops in terms of recency alone. In
other words, material which is only new—not also
really important—often is written into new leads and
thus put far higher in the story than it belongs. The
rim man should be able to recognize this situation
and act on it. Here and in everything else he does, his
duty is a broad one: to put the story into the best
possible condition that time allows. He therefore
should not use the wire service's story organization as
a crutch, but make his own decisions as to how the
story can best be told.

Reading Proof

Proofreading as such is a skill essential to successful
operation of a newspaper but, as earlier chapters have
pointed out, it is usually in the province of a proof
desk, ordinarily a part of the mechanical department.

Nevertheless, a section devoted to proofreading is included in this volume for at least two practical reasons. First, some newspapers, usually the very smallest ones, do not separate the proof from the copy function. This means that copyreaders must also perform as proofreaders day in and day out. And more importantly, *some* proofreading is done by most copy editors on newspapers of all sizes. The two chief circumstances requiring the copy editor to read proof are these: (1) The editor often must adjust a proof or a story from an early edition to a new space requirement or to new material. Examples are given in Chapter 4. (2) The editor often helps "read the paper." That is, he proofreads part of an edition after it is rolling as a final check against error.

Proofreading itself—the routine correction of mechanical errors—is not a decision-making task. The proofreader never makes corrections on his own initiative (except, of course, where the proof and copy desks are identical and he is therefore also a copy editor). His duty, basically, is to make sure that the type agrees with the copy. Just the same, it is to the advantage of the newspaper to employ alert, language-adept, libel-conscious proofreaders. Even though it is not their duty to make judgments, they can be very valuable in calling to the attention of the desk mistakes which have survived to the proofroom level.

Routine proofreading is done with the copy at hand but not invariably by checking every word of proof against copy. Straight-news proof is usually read by a single proofreader, who watches for lapses in sense which alert him to the possibility that something has been dropped out: perhaps a line has failed to cast or the compositor has unconsciously skipped a line or part of a line in the copy, or perhaps lines have been lost or transposed in the process of shifting the type. When the proofreader suspects such lapses, he refers to the copy to correct them.

Usually a conscientious proof desk checks all figures against copy as a matter of routine, since figures are especially vulnerable to error and erroneous figures can so often grossly distort the sense of a story. Proof which contains many figures or is otherwise especially subject to error is usually checked by two proofreaders. One reads aloud from the proof and

South Bend (Indiana) Tribune *photo*

Making Proof Corrections   Following the proof at his left, the printer is inserting corrected lines in a galley of type.

marks corrections: the other, the "copy holder," follows the copy.

Corrections are made in the margins of the proof. When space limitations in the margin prevent writing in a full correction, both proof and copy are sent back to the compositor, with the proof marked "see copy" at the appropriate point.

Editing in Proof

Though routine proofreading is largely concerned with making the type agree with the copy, the copy desk often proofreads to make changes of another sort. For instance, when the editor revises a story already in type to incorporate new material, he has to be able to use proof marks as an editing device.

Nevertheless, proof is no place for minor "second thoughts." Time and the stress conditions in the composing room as edition follows edition require that the editor weigh the importance of the correction against its magnitude and the consequent time and labor needed to make it at such a late hour. Changes which correct errors of fact obviously must be made. Corrections which make a substantial contribution to the reader's understanding of the story usually should be made. But corrections which add a touch of polish to the story or substitute a somewhat more felicitous phrase usually must be foregone.

Of course this does not apply when the editor is correcting proof set from teletypesetter tape. In this case he should ideally have the same freedom to exercise judgment as he does in editing copy. Many times he actually does not, especially on small papers that use teletypesetter (TTS) tape heavily and often uncritically, the justification being that proof corrections are too costly. On such papers it is often true that not much editing of any kind is done.

Proof marks have a long history and are more or less constant from one back shop to another. Since many proofreading symbols do not resemble copyreading symbols, everyone on the desk must master proof symbols as a matter of routine.

Generally speaking, there are two ways of marking proof. One of these is the *formal* way, favored in book proofreading. Two marks are made for every correction, one at the point in the proof where the error is, the other in the margin to show what change is to be made. The other method, sometimes called *tracking,* is favored in most newspaper proofrooms. A line is drawn from the error out into the margin, where a proof symbol shows the correction to be made. Because both these systems are useful, they are both shown in the explanation of proof marks which appears on pages 96–97.

A few additional cautions about proofreading:

1. The proof should be clean and clear. If a proof is not well inked, the proofreader is tempted to guess, and guessing can result in failure to detect important errors or correcting lines that don't need it. It takes only a minute or two to get a better proof pulled.

2. A substantial correction in one line—for example, if a whole word or more is deleted or inserted—means that several succeeding lines will have to be reset. It is sometimes possible to avoid this: When a word must be added, another word in the same line or the next may be deleted or shortened to make room; if a word is deleted, another of corresponding length can sometimes be added. Otherwise, resetting will have to be carried to the next paragraph break.

3. Proof marks should follow standard practice and be clear and unmistakable for two reasons: (a)

the correction must pass through several hands; (b) the corrections will probably be made at an advanced stage when time is particularly at a premium.

4. Proof marks should be entered in the margins—never on the printing itself—and invariably beside the offending line, not above it or below it. The importance of this detail may be appreciated by anyone who knows how the compositor makes corrections. He sets them in the order in which he finds them in the margin, and the printer who inserts them works from the proof to the correction line to the galley. If all three are in the same order, his job is made easier.

5. Generally speaking, corrections are made in the left-hand margin for errors occurring in the left half of the column and in the right margin for errors in the right half of the column.

6. When corrections are tracked into the margin, care should be taken to prevent the tracking line from obliterating the wording above or below by drawing it between lines. This is also true when "reading the page," even though the line may have to be drawn across several columns to reach the margin.

7. Confusion can be avoided when more than one error appears in the same line by drawing one tracking line above, another below the line, one to the left, another to the right, etc.

8. When more than one error is found in a single word, it is sound practice to delete the entire word and substitute the complete correct word.

9. It is safer to line out a figure, such as a sum of money, and write the correct figure in the margin than to indicate the correction by means of transposition marks or other symbols.

10. Proofreading requires an eye for type design as well as for other errors. "Wrong fonts" are a frequent source of trouble in newspaper composition. Any proof that contains many of them indicates that a number of "mats" (short for "matrix," the die from which a single character is cast) from some other "magazine" (the storage container for a font, or typestyle) are running through one of the machines, and it is well to let the composing room know about this immediately. A great many more such errors will have to be corrected unless the offending mats are quickly removed.

Formal Proofreader's Marks

Begin paragraph	¶
Change letter	a
Change word	
Delete letter	
Change to capital . . .	cap
Change to lower case . . .	
Change to caps and small caps	
Delete word	
Delete line	
Insert word	the
Insert letter	
Transpose letters	tr
No paragraph	No ¶
Transpose words	tr
Insert space	
Close up—no space . . .	
Close up—less space . . .	
Equalize space	=#
Insert quote	
Insert unquote	
Insert comma	
Insert apostrophe	
Insert period	
Insert other punctuation . .	
Move to left	[
Move to right	]
Move up	⊓
Move down	⊔
Reset to align	
Wrong font	
Transpose lines	tr
Is this what is meant? . .	
See copy	
Ignore mark, leave as is . .	
Reorder lines as indicated . .	tr
Push down workup . . .	
Turn over letter	
Turn over line	⊙
Insert 6-em dash	
Center	⊐⊏
Set roman/Set italics . . .	rom
Set boldface	bf
Insert 3-em dash	
Indent 1 em	⬜
Indent 3 ems	▥

The possibility of erecting a new water pumping station with the state contributing a ~~billion~~ dollars or more was dissclosed today by council President John J. Doe in an interview with a Representative of The Times.

With an an electrically-operated ~~etaoi shrdl etaoin shrdlu shrdlu shru~~ station, city would save at least $100,000 a yar on water costs, Mr. Doe asserted.

Stemming from the same improvement, said Doe was the possibility of a county-wide water system with the city as the nucleus.

The city's chance of getting a new pumping station at half cost revolves around the location of the new Thruway, Doe told the News reporter, adding that state engineers plans are being studied by the council.

"It's coming" Doe cried happily. "Isn't that wonderful news"

Station in Path

Mr. Doe said the original plan indicated the Thruway would run between the Big Rock Ship canal and the Pennsylvania, right-of-way.

said is to build the Thruway east An alternative plan, Mr. Doe of the railway, making it unnecessary to cross the tracks ewst of the station ~~but~~ avoiding replacement of the pumping plant.

that the Thruway, if it uses the ard Roe, district state engineer, "I have been informed by Richsite of the pumping station, can be designed to allow adequate space for a new, smaller station of equal capacity," he said.

LINES TO BE SUNG IN BATH
(From *Quarterly* Sewerage World)
By the Old Hobo
Fourscore and seven years ago,
No one had ever set eyes on
a schmoe.

Tracking

The possibility of erecting a new water pumping station with the state contributing a billion dollars or more was disclosed today by council President John J. Doe in an interview with a Representative of The Times.

With an an electrically-operated etaoi shrdl etaoin shrdlu shrdlu shrr station, city would save at least $100,000 a yar on water costs, Mr. Doe asserted.

Stemming from the same improvement, said Doe was the possibility of a county-wide water system with the city as the nucleus.

The city's chance of getting a new pumping station at half cost revolves around the location of the new Thruway, Doe told the News reporter, adding that state engineers plans are being studied by the council.

"It's coming" Doe cried happily. "Isn't that wonderful news"

Station in Path

Mr. Doe said the original plan indicated the Thruway would run between the Big Rock ship canal and the Pennsylvania right-of-way. said is to build the Thruway east An alternative plan, Mr. Doe of the railway, making it unnecessary to cross the tracks ewst of the station but avoiding replacement of the pumping plant.

that the Thruway, if it uses the ard Roe, district state engineer, "I have been informed by Richsite of the pumping station, can be designed to allow adequate space for a new, smaller station of equal capacity," he said.

LINES TO BE SUNG IN BATH (From *Quarterly* Sewerage World) By the Old Hobo Fourscore and seven years ago, No one had ever set eyes on a schmoe.

The possibility of erecting a new water pumping station with the state contributing a million dollars or more was disclosed today by Council President John J. Doe in an interview with a representative of THE TIMES.

With an electrically-operated station, the city would save at least $100,000 a year on water costs, Mr. Doe asserted. Stemming from the same improvement, Doe said, was the possibility of a county-wide water system with the city as the nucleus.

The city's chance of getting a new pumping station at half cost "revolves around the location of the new Thruway," Doe told the News reporter, adding that state engineers' plans are being studied by the council.

"It's coming!" Doe cried happily. "Isn't that wonderful news?"

Station in Path

Mr. Doe said the original plan indicated the Thruway would run between the Big Rock ship canal and the Pennsylvania right-of-way.

An alternative plan, Mr. Doe said, is to build the Thruway east of the railway, making it unnecessary to cross the tracks west of the station but avoiding replacement of the pumping plant.

"I have been informed by Richard Roe, district state engineer, that the Thruway, if it uses the site of the pumping station, can be designed to allow adequate space for a new, smaller station of equal capacity," he said.

LINES TO BE SUNG IN BATH (From Quarterly *Sewerage World*) **By the Old Hobo**

—

Fourscore and seven years ago, No one had ever set eyes on a schmoe.

4

Some Advanced Editing Skills

Once the editor has learned the basic skills involved in editing copy he is ready for a couple of more demanding jobs. One of these is pushing a developing story through the composing room, perhaps changing it several times for successive editions; it gets pretty complicated when the story is changing frequently and the time is short. The other is putting together a story that combines the best features of two or more versions of the story obtained from more than one source or service, a process called "compiling." Both of these tasks require meticulous attention to detail and at the same time full attention to the content and structure of the whole.

The Developing Story

News is no respecter of the time clock. It happens when it happens, and the entire system of news transmission, handling, and printing is geared to take this unhappy fact into account. As described in Chapter 3, the wire services move very important news instantly and less important news when it can, in any number of takes, with instructions for putting it all together. But the copy editor, too, often has to figure out how to move a story quickly, in pieces, as it breaks, to the composing room, together with instructions for putting it all back together again. In fact it may be necessary to keep several stories moving in this way. Just as the wire-service filing editor's reason for sending news in takes is keeping all subscribers up to the minute on all the important news, so the copy editor's reason for sending copy to composition as it breaks is to cram as much important news into an edition before deadline as possible.

"Bulletining" news is no longer critical in newspaper publication. Radio and to a lesser degree television get the bulletins out first; the newspaper cannot compete for the last-minute flash. What it does best is to amplify, synthesize, and interpret the details behind the bulletins, and that is now what readers expect of it. But instead of making the job of moving a late-breaking story easier for the newspaper, it makes the newspaper's responsibility even greater: readers expect now, more than ever, that the newspaper account will describe a cataclysm in greater detail and fuller perspective than radio and television. A last-minute front-page bulletin telling people what radio and television have been telling them hours earlier is not enough.

Thus the newspaper is faced with extremely contradictory demands: it must publish a coherent account in full detail and with suitable background, and it must do it in spite of rigid deadlines. Therefore every person on a newspaper's staff must be prepared to move quickly and in an orderly way when an important story breaks at an inconvenient time. The editor's job in dealing with last-minute news of any kind—a new story or changes in an old one—is not only to edit it, but to tell the composing room exactly what to do with it, so that it will be set and inserted into the forms speedily and accurately.

The System

A fairly universal marking system has been developed for telling the composing room what to do with copy so that the editor doesn't have to issue instructions personally. Variations of the system are in operation on all copy desks deserving of the name, and they are surprisingly similar. Consequently, the description that follows is typical of all, even if exactly like none.

As noted in Chapter 2, all copy is *slugged* with an identifying code name assigned by the slot man. Each bit of copy relating to a single story—takes, headlines, inserts—gets the same slug. The slug is set in type[1] at the same time as the copy it identifies and moves along with the type it identifies to makeup. When

---

[1] The bar of type is actually the slug, not the code name itself, but the term slug in newspaper jargon has come to mean the name as well.

the type it identifies is put into the forms, the slug is thrown away. Thus slugs are the means for bringing stories and headlines together; the composing room gets its instructions about where to put the completed stories from page *dummies.*

The instructions carried by slugs and dummies are all the composing room needs for the majority of stories it handles in a typical news day. It is when stories already set in type require changes to keep them up to date that the instruction system needs to be extended, to ensure that the composing room will handle the changes accurately and efficiently. Three basic instructions are capable of dealing with just about any change. These are *new lead, add,* and *insert,* and they tell the compositor what to do with copy or type so identified.

A *new lead* is a new top on a story which works in late developments or changes the story's emphasis. It can be of one or more paragraphs, usually is more than one, and never is less than one. It must be written, edited, and marked so that it can pick up on the old story. Otherwise valuable time will be lost in the newsroom reworking details that do not need it and in the composing room trying to figure out where it goes. The first is marked "New lead," the second "Second new lead," etc.

Adds are additional material sent to the composing room as it develops or short takes of a long story broken up to save composition time. They are marked "Add one," "Add two," etc.

Inserts are whole paragraphs of new material that cannot logically be worked into an add or a new lead. They may be inserted into the body of a story or they may replace an outmoded section of a story. Insert copy is marked "Insert A," "Insert B," etc.

Many desks use these additional methods of instruction:

Sub identifies a substitute paragraph.

Add all (sometimes "Add end" or "Add at end") tells the compositor to add the new material to the end of the story as it now stands.

Ten add (sometimes called "A-matter") identifies early details on a story, the top of which is not yet in hand. A lot of detail on a tornado, for example, might be sent out at a time when the facts that will make the top of the story (how extensive, how many casualties, how much damage) are not firm. The first take of such material is marked "10 add," the second, "11 add," the third, "12 add," etc. Then when the top of the story is finally sent, its last take is marked at the end "Pick up 10 add."

Other instructions tell the compositor to handle copy in one "side" fashion or another. The common side devices are the *bulletin precede,* the *follow,* and the *ruled insert,* and copy for them is so marked.

The *bulletin precede* is a boldface paragraph, usually indented, which appears above the story proper and covers last-minute developments. Often it includes later material than the story itself, and it may even contradict the story. The emphasis it receives makes it clear that it takes precedence over the story. Bulletin precedes are used when time is too short to rework a story so as to include just-received changes.

Follows are separate stories, usually rather brief, related to and following the story proper. They usually carry a separate, small head of their own, are set in regular body type, and are separated from the story proper by a short dash.

Ruled inserts lie between these two, both physically and by nature. They are related, short stories which are too good to put at the bottom of the main stories. Ruled inserts are usually set in body type, are usually indented, usually have a head of their own, usually are inserted *within* a paragraph, not between paragraphs, and are separated from the story proper by column-width rules. (Some papers still put the rules all the way around and call these short stories "boxed inserts.")

To show the composing room where new leads pick up on old stories, where inserts are to be made, or what paragraphs a sub subs for, a proof of the story as it was originally set (or, after the first edition comes off the press, the clipped-out story pasted up and marked by page number and slug) accompanies change copy, carefully marked to correspond with the copy. Such a proof is known as a *Cx proof* or an *X-correct.* Besides showing the places where pickups and insertions are to be made, it can also show *kills* and minor corrections

that don't involve a whole paragraph. For instance, the editor would send new copy for a new lead wrapping up the latest and best details on a flood story for the next edition; but all he would have to do in the body of the story to update existing detailed casualty figures is change the figures on the proof.

In hot-metal shops the printer traditionally turns a "pi" line face down at the beginning or end of an incomplete story to mark the spots clearly (see page 108.) The device is known as the *turn rule* (or *turn slug*). But in cold-type operations, such other devices as "more to kum" or "add to kum" sluglines must be used, and indeed are widely used in hot-metal plants, too. When the omission is neither at the beginning nor the end, the printer often stands a line of type or a lead or slug on end, or possibly slips a piece of paper between lines. The up-ended slug or piece of paper is known as a *flag.* The editor marks copy *tr* (for "turn rule") to mean more is coming. Some desks go one step further and tell *for what* the rule is turned: "Tr for add" or "Tr—pick up X-cor," for instance. Thus, when the first take of a story is set, a turn rule is placed at the end to indicate that more is coming, and another is placed at the beginning to stay there until the head goes into place. The last add has a turn rule at the top and an end dash at the bottom. When the missing type is put in place, the printer throws the turn rule or flag away, and the story is ready for the forms.

How the System Works

Now we are ready to look at the system applied to a hypothetical story. Suppose fire breaks out in an apartment house within an hour before the first edition goes to press. Reporters are at the scene. From the look of things, the story is going to be big, but for purposes of the first edition the reporters have only a few of the most obvious facts to telephone to the rewrite desk. The fire is still going strong; the story is, of course, incomplete. But it cannot wait until the last ember is cold: it must be covered in that first edition. With about half an hour to go until press time, the first take comes to the desk and is edited as shown:

~~apartment~~ ~~jones~~

p. 1 (HTK Fire)

stet
caps

Two fire companies were called to the Ainsley Arms
Apartment Hotel shortly before 10 a. m. today ~~and early~~
when fire broke out in the basement, and early
reports indicated that some of the residents were ~~still~~
trapped
in the building.

Fire Chief Kenneth Packland said that residents
~~trapped~~ on upper floors ~~of the building~~ were being removed by aerial ladders. He said that one *un*identified
woman had leaped safely from a third floor window into a
fire department net. He added that every ~~possible~~ effort was being made to remove the occupants ~~who re-~~ *Still*
~~mained~~ in the building.] *Numbers Not Known* [*sub*

It was not known how many had been saved nor how
many remained in the building.

The blaze was being confined to the basement and
ground floor but there was danger, that the fire ,,may *Packland said,,*
get out of hand any minute." He said that the build-
ing's only elevator was out of order and that residents
attempting to reach safety by means of halls and stairs
were turned back by "the terrific heat."

Packland added that thus far there had been no
signs of panic.

(tr)

~~more~~

Because the story is sure to be changing and because it is not possible at this point to determine what
play it will get, it is marked "P1" (page one) and
"HTK," which simply means the head is to come later.

Notice that the copy desk has assigned the slug
"Fire," rejecting the original slug suggested by the
rewrite man. Of course this is a suitable slug only if
the desk is sure that no other fire story in today's
operation is so labeled. In spite of the fact that it is
rather general, this slug has the important advantage
of brevity. It will stay with the story for the rest
of the day, and every piece of copy and art pertaining
to it will be marked "Fire."

In a few minutes, rewrite, with the help of another
reporter digging in the files, has sent over its first add,
and it is marked thus:

~~add apartment~~   ~~jones~~

p.¹ ⟨*add 1 - HTK fire*⟩

]*Houses 125 Persons*[*sub*

⌐The Ainsley Arms, a 45-unit apartment building
housing an estimated 125 persons, is ~~located~~ at 445 W.
Union St. The four-story building was constructed in
1929 at a cost of about $200,000.

⌐Elwood Carrother, 26, a maintenance employee, discovered the blaze in a little-used storage room behind
the building's heating plant system. He reported it to
Manager R. L. Johnson, who called the fire department
at 9:53. Fire Companies 4 and 5 went to the scene.

⌐Capt. Robert Wrendell of Company 4 said the fire
spread rapidly throughout the basement and that the heat
on the first floor was ~~extremely~~ intense.

⟨*fr*⟩

Now, using carbon copies of the first two takes, and
having decided on the play the story is to get in the
first edition, the desk is ready to send out a headline:

p.1 ⟨*HTK Fire*⟩

2-36 Hvy [*Residents Fleeing*
[*Hotel Blaze Here*

Meanwhile, the fire is getting worse. The office is
notified that one person has died and that the blaze is
moving upward through the building. Only minutes
remain before Page One of the first edition must be
plated. What to do with this important last-minute
development? After a hurried conference, it is decided
that the new developments can be handled only in a
bulletin precede. It is edited and marked and the
composing room is notified that it is coming in order
to avoid production delays:

Bulletin Precede — HTK Fire

An unidentified man leaped to his death from the
third story of the Ainsley Arms this morning as flames
spread rapidly to the upper floors. The man, about 45,
died instantly when he landed on the pavement ~~on Union~~
~~st. at the~~ front of the building.

3 em

The "3 em" at the end indicates that a three-em dash is to separate the precede from the story proper.

In the hour before the second-edition deadline, much work remains to be done. The slot man is busy figuring out a new makeup so that he can move the fire story to the top spot. He is conferring on the possibility of getting at least one picture into the second edition. The rim man handling the fire clips the story out of the first edition to use as an X-correct and awaits developments.

The reporter who has been digging into the files on the Ainsley Arms confirms a hunch that there has been a big fire there once before. He writes it up as the first *follow,* often abbreviated *folo* on copy.

Folo — HTK Fire   #5 [Today's Blaze Second in Hotel's 22 Years

Today's Ainsley Arms blaze was the second general
alarm fire in that building's ~~22-year~~ history.

On the morning of July 5, 19 fire broke out in
the rear of a cleaning establishment, ~~that was then~~
~~housed~~ on the first floor of the building. It spread
rapidly up a rear staircase and in five hours did damage
estimated at $15,000, chased more than 100 persons into
the street, ~~in the~~ most of them in their nightclothes,
and caused injury to more than a score of persons. There
were no deaths.

The investigation that followed . . .

Still later, the city hall reporter calls with another side story. This is short, but the news editor considers it worthy of being handled as a ruled insert. This story, as edited, appears as follows:

p.1   Ruled Insert - HTK Fire

~~with apartment fire   smith~~

#5a   Mayor's Family Quit
      Hotel Only Yesterday
                        today's

Mayor Rupert C. Beecall escaped ~~the~~ Ainsley Arms
fire by one day.

Mayor Beecall, who with his wife and two children
lived in the ill-fated apartment house for nearly a year
while their new home was being built, moved the last of
their
~~his~~ belongings from the Ainsley Arms yesterday, he told
a News reporter this morning.   #

This story is slugged to show the handling it is to get, and the place it is to be inserted will be shown approximately on the dummy. The printer is expected to know the paper's policy well enough to take it from there.

Meanwhile, the second lead is taking shape. The desk gets it from rewrite a page at a time but chooses to cut it up into shorter takes in order to reduce the composition time. This copy, as edited, is shown in the three examples which follow:

~~lede apartment   jones~~

p.1   New Lead - HTK Fire

At least two persons were killed and more than 40
others had been rescued this morning as a general alarm
fire raged out of control at the Ainsley Arms Apartment
Hotel, trapping as many as 20 more occupants.

While the rescued streamed down fire department
ladders and leaped into nets, others screamed for help
from windows and the roof. Fire Chief Kenneth Packland
said that every effort is being made to remove the remaining residents.   ] Too Late ?[sub

"I'm afraid it's too late to get them all," he
added ~~ominously.~~

p.1   Add 1- New Lead - HTK Fire

The dead were:

Rex Anderson, 44, a plumber, who leaped to his death from the third floor.

Aimee Angsvold, 59, who died en route to St. Mary's Hospital after being carried from the building. The cause of her death was not known, ~~but bystanders speculated it might have been due to suffocation.~~

Discovered shortly before 10 a. m., the fire swept rapidly upward and by 11:15 had engulfed all but the top floor.]Elevator Quits[*sub*

Escape was cut off almost immediately when the building's lone elevator broke down and intense heat prevented residents from using halls and stairways.

(tr)

~~lede apartment - 2~~

p.1 (Add 2 - New Lead - HTK Fire)

Packland estimated that ~~a total of~~ 40 persons had been rescued, including eight who leaped into fire department nets. The rest climbed or were carried down ladders.

Twelve of the rescued were treated at St. Mary's hospital, a block away. One, Mrs. Edward Smalley, 27, suffered second degree burns. The others received minor burns and cuts or were treated for shock.

All of the city's four fire companies were at the scene. Companies 4 and 5 were joined by Companies 2 and 3 after Chief Packland turned in the general alarm at 11:03 a. m. (tr for K-Cor) ~~pick up~~

Note that these are adds *to the new lead,* not adds to the story proper. They must be so indicated.

Now the desk must take care of pickup. The notation "pick up" at the end of the last take indicates that this is the end of the new lead. The story as pasted up from the first edition appears as follows:

P1 X-Cor
HTK — Fire

BULLETIN

An unidentified man leaped to his death from the third story of the Ainsley Arms this morning as flames spread rapidly to the upper floors. The man, about 45, died instantly when he landed on the pavement in front of the building.

Kill

Kill for New Lead

Two fire companies were called to the Ainsley Arms Apartment Hotel shortly before 10 a.m. today when fire broke out in the basement and early reports indicated that some of the residents were trapped in the building.

Fire Chief Kenneth Packland said that residents on upper floors of the building were being removed by aerial ladders. He said that one unidentified woman had leaped safely from a third floor window into a fire department net.

He added that every effort was being made to remove occupants still in the building.

Numbers Not Known

It was not known how many had been saved nor how many remained in the building.

The blaze was being confined to the basement and ground floor but there was danger, Packland said, that the fire "may get out of hand any minute."

He said that the building's only elevator was out of order and that residents attempting to reach safety by means of halls and stairs were turned back by "the terrific heat."

Packland added that thus far there had been no sign of panic.

Houses 125 Persons

The Ainsley Arms, a 45-unit building housing an estimated 125 persons, is at 445 W. Union St. The four-story building was constructed in 1929 at a cost of about $200,000.

Elwood Carrother, 26, a maintenance employee, discovered the blaze in a little-used storage room behind the building's heating system. He reported it to Manager R. L. Johnson, who called the fire department at 9:53. Fire Companies 4 and 5 went to the scene.

Capt. Robert Wrendell of Company 4 said the fire spread rapidly, throughout the basement and that the heat on the first floor was extremely intense.

The marks in this X-correct show how the editor wants to mesh the old and new parts of the story for the best effect and in order to convey the most information. He chooses a logical pickup point at the end of paragraph 7: everything above that point has been included in the new top; everything below that point, with minor exceptions, is still good. So he kills the first seven paragraphs and makes minor corrections to eliminate duplication and outdated material at the end. Because the X-correct does not involve extensive typesetting, he holds it as long as possible in case more new material should come and have to be added or inserted. None developing, he sends it to the composing room. The changes should be clear to the printers. They have been told to kill the old bulletin precede and top and substitute the new lead and its two adds. Meanwhile, a second-edition headline is being written to take the place of the old one.

Even as it stands, the story is now in excellent shape for the second edition. But the editor leaves it flexible enough and holds onto it long enough so that he can act if something new comes in and has to be worked in. It does, but in this case it is detail, not new top-of-story material. Of four new paragraphs, one must be inserted, since it tells of firemen being overcome and belongs logically with other casualties material. The rest is routine but good detail and can be handled as an *add all.* The edited result is shown as follows:

~~add apartment~~ ~~jones~~

p.1 (Insert A- HTK Fire)

Four firemen had been overcome by heat and smoke.
They were all given emergency treatment at the scene.

(end Insert A)

p.1 (Add A̶l̶l̶ - HTK Fire)

] Building Insured [sub

The building is owned by the Ainsley Corp., of
which Robert R. Etheridge is president and Johnson is
secretary. Johnson said ~~that~~ the building and its
contents were ~~are~~ fully covered by insurance.

As news of the fire spread, thousands of onlookers
~~gathered and~~ milled around the building, shouting advice to occupants still in the building and hampering
firemen. Police Chief J. L. Sullivan ordered 20 additional men to the scene and fire lines were established at a safe distance.

At least six ambulances were transporting the injured to St. Mary's Hospital. They included two police
department emergency vehicles, two fire department
ambulances, and two privately owned ambulances.

~~all for now~~ #

The editor tells the composing room where "Insert A" goes on second-edition proof. (Some desks
receive proofs of everything as a matter of routine.
On others, a note must be sent to the composing room
asking for the proof needed.) It is marked as follows:

X-Cor

P1

▮◧▮◧▮◧▮◧▮◧▮◧▮◧▮◧▮◧▮◧▮
add 1—new lead—HTK FIRE

The dead were:

Rex Anderson, 44, a plumber, who leaped to his death from the third floor.

Aimee Angsvold, 59, who died en route to St. Mary's Hospital after being carried from the building. The cause of her death was not known.

Discovered shortly before 10 a.m., the fire swept rapidly upward and by 11:15 had engulfed all but the top floor.

Insert A

Elevator Quits

Escape was cut off almost immediately when the building's lone elevator broke down and intense heat prevented residents from using halls and stairways.

▮◧▮◧▮◧▮◧▮◧▮◧▮◧▮◧▮◧▮

Incidentally, the subheads have "broken" perfectly. Subheads in old material are often not in the right spots when a new top is added. The editor checks this on the X-correct and if necessary corrects the proof accordingly: he deletes old subheads and writes in new ones.

The resulting second-edition story appears as follows, minus headline and follow:

At least two persons were killed and more than 40 others had been rescued this morning as a general alarm fire raged out of control at the Ainsley Arms Apartment Hotel, trapping as many as 20 more occupants.

While the rescued streamed down fire department ladders or leaped into nets, others screamed for help from windows and the roof. Fire Chief Kenneth Packland said that every effort was being made to remove the remaining residents.

Too Late?

"I'm afraid it's too late to get them all," he added.

The dead were:

Rex Anderson, 44, a plumber, who leaped to his death from the third floor.

Aimee Angsvold, 59, who died en route to St. Mary's Hospi-

tal after being carried from the building. The cause of her death was not known.

Four firemen had been overcome by heat and smoke. They were all given emergency treatment at the scene.

Discovered shortly before 10 a.m., the fire swept rapidly upward and by 11:15 had engulfed all but the top floor.

Elevator Quits

Escape was cut off almost immediately when the building's lone elevator broke down

Mayor's Family Quit Hotel Only Yesterday

Mayor Rupert C. Beecall escaped today's Ainsley Arms fire by one day.

Mayor Beecall, who with his wife and two children lived in the ill-fated apartment house for nearly a year while their new home was being built, moved the last of their belongings from the Ainsley Arms yesterday, he told a News reporter this morning.

and intense heat prevented residents from using halls and stairways.

Packland estimated that 40 persons had been rescued, including eight who leaped into fire department nets. The rest climbed or were carried down ladders.

Twelve of the rescued were treated at St. Mary's Hospital a block away. One, Mrs. Edward Smalley, 27, suffered second degree burns. The others received minor burns and cuts or were treated for shock.

All of the city's four fire companies were at the scene. Companies 4 and 5 were joined by Companies 2 and 3 after Chief Packland turned in the general alarm at 11:03 a.m.

Houses 125 Persons

The Ainsley Arms, a 45-unit building housing an estimated 125 persons, is at 445 W. Union St. The four-story building was constructed in 1929 at a cost of about $200,000.

Elwood Carrother, 26, a maintenance employee, discovered the blaze in a little-used storage room behind the building's heating system. He reported it to Manager R. L. Johnson, who called the fire department at 9:53. Fire Companies 4 and 5 went to the scene.

Capt. Robert Wrendell of Company 4 said the fire spread rapidly.

Building Insured

The building is owned by the Ainsley Corp., of which Robert E. Ethridge is president and Johnson is secretary. Johnson said the building and its contents were fully covered by insurance.

As news of the fire spread, thousands of onlookers milled around the building, shouting advice to the occupants still in the building and hampering firemen. Police Chief J. L. Sullivan ordered 20 additional men to the scene and fire lines were established at a safe distance.

At least six ambulances were transporting the injured to St. Mary's Hospital. They included two police department emergency vehicles, two fire department ambulances, and two privately owned ambulances.

Suppose, as a final blow before the second edition rolls, the editor learns that there has been a third death and that the reporter has all the details. Suppose, too, that the page is made up. With time so short, the news editor writes out the insert paragraph to go with the list of other casualties and takes it himself to the composing room. While the insert is being set, he gets the makeup man to give him a rough "wet" proof of the story as it stands in the forms or as much of it as he needs. He updates the casualty totals in the head and in the lead, and either marks the proof for the insert or simply shows the printer where it goes in the form. The whole change can be managed in a few minutes without holding up the edition.

In so doing, the editor is acting outside the system described here, substituting a certain amount of personal supervision for copy and proof marks. But the system need not be a barrier to meeting emergencies of this nature. Such situations can be met speedily without serious damage to composing-room routine, provided the editor knows the mechanical processes well and is capable of acting swiftly and with initiative.

The story is by no means wrapped up until it is handled in all further editions. But since the main points of the system have been covered, there is no need to go further.

Compiling

One of the most challenging jobs on the desk is "compiling," or assembling from a variety of related materials the best development of a story or cluster of stories. This is no job for a copy butcher or copy fixer; it is more than checking for error and repairing faulty language. It is a *creative* job requiring the editor's sense of news judgment, story pace, and story polish.

Not all desks are in a position to do a lot of creative editing. The smaller and more hard-pressed desks cannot afford to expend care and time on compiling, nor can they afford to pay for the services of a number of wires. But compiling need not be extremely time-consuming. Perhaps it is avoided on some desks that could do more of it. And perhaps it is editor attitudes as much as the clock that stand in the way of it; the copy editor who regards his job as routine can hardly be expected to capitalize on the immense possibilities for improving a story that compiling offers.

But the copy desk that expects truly professional work from its staff gives professional responsibility to everyone capable of handling it. On most of the best desks these days, there are more different versions of the most significant stories than ever before. The reason is that the number of supplementary news services has been growing in recent years. To the New York Times News Service has been added the Los

Angeles Times-Washington Post Service, for example. Some newspapers take both trunk wires (AP and UPI), both of the leading supplementary services, and, perhaps, Reuters and Havas besides. From the point of view of the slot, the best way of dealing with so many sources is to assign trusted editors to stories they really know. This means, among other things, a greater degree of specialization at the desk than ever before. A man who reads *Foreign Affairs* for pleasure is assigned to the latest crisis in the Middle East, while a state-capitol old hand specializes in news from that source and a man who knows Washington works on the tough jobs that come out of the nation's capital. Many good desks still depend on generalists, to be sure, but the increasing complexity of stories, in addition to the greater freedom with which important stories can be treated, increasingly requires the combination of specialization and professional skill.

Making the Decision to Compile

The decision to compile naturally arises only if (1) there are two or more versions of the same story, or (2) there are two or more related stories in the same content area—local, state, and national versions of the same story, for example, or separate stories about closely related developments on two fronts that might be given more meaning treated together. Assuming one of these two circumstances does exist, the editor has to decide whether compiling is necessary and desirable. He asks himself these general questions first: Is the story worth a fussy treatment? Is the time available? Having answered those questions positively, he asks: Can the stories be genuinely improved by compiling, or is there one that is good enough to use by itself?

One of the two following criteria may make the editor decide that one of the stories is more suitable than any of the others or a compiled version:

Angle The editor may deliberately choose a by-line story emphasizing the background of an event over a straight account, a version with a second-day twist over one telling a story for the first time, or a story with a light tone quality over a serious one—or vice versa—depending on his needs. In the first case, he

may feel that spot coverage in other media has been adequate and that the best service he can now perform is interpretive—he can give meaning to the story by relating it to previous events and to other events and trends. If the story has already been told in the previous cycle by a directly competing newspaper, he naturally chooses a story putting the spotlight on new facts and resulting occurrences. If he feels that a light tone is more appropriate than a serious one and he has the choice, he chooses the light story. In all three cases, he chooses the treatment he considers best for the content of the story, his readers, and the competitive situation.

Length and structure The editor may decide simply to use the story that is closest in length to the space he has, or the one that can easily be cut to that length. In this case, he naturally would not use a story that is too long in the first place and also consists primarily of numbered items.

But if no story meets either of these criteria successfully enough to make him choose it over the others, the editor must compare the smaller, internal elements of the stories, no single one of which would be enough to make him choose one story over another.

Leads The editor judges the leads on the basis of their impact on the reader, their success in conveying the essentials of the whole story, and how well they lend themselves to headline treatment. However, all of these attributes must be considered together. Impact, for example, must not be considered alone but with reference to essential accuracy; leads that appeal at first glance may actually be "overselling."

General writing quality Assuming the editor finds one story with a particularly strong lead, he then examines writing quality. It is quite possible for a story to carry an excellent lead and then bog down badly in the quality of the writing that carries the detail. The editor must go far beyond the top to get a picture of the pace and crispness of the writing in the story as a whole. If the writing quality in the story with the good lead doesn't stand up, and it *is* good in another story, the editor is beginning to have a case for compiling.

Early story development An excellent lead is often undermined by the ineffective organization of details high in the story. The editor reads these paragraphs carefully. Do they continue the pace of the beginning? Do they develop the best details in the story beyond those in the lead? Are these details organized and connected with each other logically? Do they logically extend the material in the lead? Do they fill in the holes left by the lead, *i.e.,* do they immediately answer the chief questions raised by the reader?

Detail, fullness, total story organization When a story with a good top falls down later, the difficulty is usually in the matter of fullness of detail. "Fullness" does not merely imply *extent* of detail but the absence of gaps in the story—answers to the most insistent questions the story raises. This fullness, plus the way the details are organized in the main body of the story, is important to the careful editor, since he knows that they are important to the careful reader. Except in the more sensational stories, the hasty readers never get beyond the top.

Having weighed the stories, the editor now has a fairly clear idea of whether he should compile or not. If one story is strong on most of the six counts, he would be wasting his time to compile. But if he sees a good lead in one, good detail in another, and good development in a third, he will obviously serve the total story well by compiling.

It should be noted here that the editor has other methods than compiling or bringing stories together. If one story is decidedly more newsworthy than another but the second is interesting, he can treat the second as a bulletin precede, a ruled insert, or a follow.

How to Compile

Suppose that two wire-service stories are to be combined, one giving an Israeli version of the fighting over the Suez Canal, the other giving the Egyptian version. Perhaps the wire service itself will soon combine these stories, but if the editor cannot wait, he has three options. First, he may treat one as the story and the other as a follow. This is obviously not a good solution; the stories have equal importance and interest and logically belong together.

Second, he may run the first paragraph of one version as the lead ("Israel claimed its jets shot down two Egyptian fighter planes today as . . .") and insert in parentheses the materials from the other source ("In Cairo, Egyptian sources claimed its jets smashed . . ."). But even though this device is easy, most desk men would rather not use it when it means more than one or two short parenthetical inserts in the same story. It has three weaknesses: (1) *The parentheses themselves constitute a barrier.* The reader probably tends to skip enclosed matter unless it is brief. Of all the punctuation marks available, the parenthesis probably has the least instant meaning for the general reader. (2) *It is confusing when the inserted material is long.* If the reader attacks the parenthesized material at all, he can very easily get lost in it and end up with nothing but a muddy, contradictory impression of the facts. (3) *It is not suitable when the inserted material relates to more than one aspect of the story.* Where the material to be inserted touches on more than one aspect of the story, the editor has these choices: he can run one long insert, or he can carry separate inserts in the story at the points where the parenthetical material logically goes. The former method is bad because the insert, being long, damages sound story organization. The latter method is bad because it means the reading process will be disrupted at several points in the story.

Third, the editor may remove datelines, put the main facts from the two stories into a new lead, and weave the details together in the body. This is always the best method of compiling, even though it means time and care. Whenever stories are compiled, several details require attention:

Datelines The problem of datelines arises when the story being compiled originates in more than one place. Imagine that the Israeli version of the story above originated in Tel Aviv and the Egyptian version originated in Cairo. What does the editor do about the dateline? He simply deletes it altogether. That allows him to skip back and forth freely between Tel Aviv and Cairo as long as he makes clear the "where" of the story at every point and the story does not become too confusing. The former problem often can be solved by inserting routine transitional phrases, such as "Meanwhile in Amman . . . ." The latter problem calls for particularly careful attention to story organization.

Credit lines   Removing the dateline, however, creates another problem, if the story is to be credited to a wire service. Wire services are routinely credited in the dateline:

> WASHINGTON — (AP) —
> The Department of Justice to-
> day . . .

The editor cannot simply remove the credit line along with the point of origination, because the newspaper's contract stipulates that the stories the wire service supplies must be credited. Neither is it customary to start the story this way:

(AP)—The Department of Justice announced in Washington . . .

The common method when only one service is affected is to use a credit line, like this

> (By The Associated Press)
> The Department of Justice
> announced in Washington to-
> day . . .

A credit line is also used when a story is compiled from more than one wire service. Putting two ligatures together, thus:

WASHINGTON—(AP)—(UPI)—The department of Justice today . . .

is just not done. Lines crediting an amalgam of wire services vary from one style sheet to another. Three typical ones:

(From Press Dispatches)
(From Chronicle Wire Services)
(From Associated Press, Reuters)

The use of credit lines shown here has no bearing on datelines; whether a dateline is used depends entirely on whether the story originates at one point or more than one.

The time element   Compiling sometimes poses difficulties in handling time, as well as place. Suppose in the example above the Cairo story originated last night and the Tel Aviv story originated this morning. Obviously, the editor must pay careful attention to keeping the two times straight as well as the two places. Usually he says "today" in the lead once and that governs the entire story. Wherever in the story the "today" is inappropriate, the editor must see to it that "last night" is inserted. And when the story shifts back to "today," he must make the shift apparent.

Suppose he is going to compile these two stories:

ERDING AIR BASE, Germany, Dec. 29—(XP)— Four American airmen freed after 40 days of captivity in Communist Hungary were returned by plane to their home base here last night.

Hungary released them at the Austrian frontier yesterday about two hours after the United States government handed over $120,000—described as fines by a Hungarian court which convicted them as border violators.

*   *   *

WASHINGTON, Dec. 29—(XP)—The United States today banned travel in Hungary and ordered the Hungarian consulates in New York and Cleveland to close in retaliation for the detention and fining of four American airmen.

A State Department official said the action was taken shortly after midnight to make sure that the four were safely in American hands . . .

Special attention must be devoted to both the time and place elements:

> (From Press Dispatches)
> Four American airmen freed
> after 40 days of captivity in
> Communist Hungary were re-
> turned to their home bases *in
> Germany last night. Early to-
> day the United States* retali-
> ated by banning travel in Hun-
> gary and closing Hungarian
> consulates in New York and
> Cleveland.
> Hungary released the four
> at the Austrian frontier *yes-
> terday* about two hours after
> . . .

> *In Washington*, a state department official said . . .
> A cheering crowd of relatives and friends greeted the fliers *at Erding Air Base.* . . .

In the absence of a dateline the "where" is inserted in the lead. The two time elements are separately handled in the lead. Time and place are repeated in the body of the story wherever necessary to keep them clear.

Even when the time element doesn't change radically, the editor must be watchful of "when." In a story which involves a chronological sequence of events not necessarily reassembled in chronological order, he must be careful in shifting from one event to another that he does not confuse the order in which the events took place. He often clarifies the time element in this kind of story by means of transitions.

Transitions   It will be recalled that the block paragraph facilitates shifting paragraphs in a news story. But it doesn't always work. When the editor moves paragraphs in one story around or wraps two or more stories into one, he must check the resulting sequence of paragraphs from the standpoint of transitions—the connecting language that helps tie the story together. New ones may need to be added or old ones changed.

Transitions have to do with *time* and *place.* Suppose the editor is compiling two stories describing separate actions on the same battlefront several hours apart. In moving from one action to the other, he will present his reader with an abrupt and confusing change unless he finds some way to tie the two together. He can make the transition smooth and explicable by simply inserting words which make the needed connection in terms of time—"meanwhile," "at the same time," "later," "earlier"—or place—"on the eastern front," "on the Second Division's left," "at the opposite end of the line," etc.

It will be seen in later examples how important to the *flow* of the story transitions can be.

Objectivity   Sometimes the editor is faced with the problem of weaving together the facts from two versions of the same story that are not pitched to the same level of objectivity. One of them may be a straight news story, for instance, while the other is frankly explanatory; one may be fully attributed while the other requires a by-line.

When this difference exists, it is not easy to do a polished compiling job. The story no longer belongs to either writer, so the editor can't credit it with a by-line in order to cover opinion elements. Stripping all the explanatory material out for lack of attribution will probably cut the heart out of the story and raise the question: Why compile at all?

It is possible under these circumstances to come up with an objective story which is straight from beginning to end. It means slipping in a phrase of attribution here and there and cutting out a pure opinion or two, and it's a lot of work. As always, the improvement that compiling will effect must justify the time it consumes.

Delineating the story's scope   A common sort of "wrap" combines stories that have something less obviously in common with each other than stories about a single event. Once in a while the wires seem to be jammed with fire stories, to cite a typical example. First one comes from Pennsylvania, then another from Oklahoma, then another from Idaho. No editor need hang his head in shame if he doesn't see that they all happened in the same twenty-four-hour period, all involved home fires, and all took human life, and he scatters them through the paper. But clearly a better job of telling them can be done if they are all brought together.

There is no very grave problem of scope in this example; these stories all have much in common and are scattered only in terms of geography. The lead writes itself:

Home fires at five widely separated points in the nation brought death to 13 persons last night, nine of them children.

At Erie, Pa., an early morning blaze . . .

The scope of the story is delineated right at the top: "Home fires . . . in the nation . . . ." The reader can assume that the story will not also include floods, famine, and pestilence, nor will it casually wrap in a fire story from Brazil or a hotel fire anywhere. From that point it's largely a matter of pasting the stories up, deleting repetitions, switching datelines into the body, and cleaning up transitions.

It sometimes is useful, however, to treat as one a variety of stories less closely related than this. Sometimes editors like to throw "the elements" into one hopper—all the floods, windstorms, prairie fires, and what have you of the last week or twenty-four hours. This makes the problem of scope a little more complicated. The slot man hands over to the rim man a sheaf of copy which includes a story from Winnipeg telling of increasing flood threats in the valley of the Red River of the North, no deaths; one from Crookston, Minnesota, telling of the flooded Red Lake River, two deaths indirectly; one from New York telling of sudden windstorms that killed thirteen Sunday pleasure seekers in New York and New England; and a windstorm "separate" from Boston covering New England alone. "Why not lead off with the Winnipeg story and wrap in the others?" the news editor suggests. The rim man rejects the idea of telling first one of these stories and then another. He feels that the reader must be able to tell at the outset just how much

ground the story is going to cover, so he must get all of these separate stories into clear focus right at the top—and in such a way that the whole story can be told in the headline as well. The problem, then, is to find a way of making the *scope* of the story clear at the beginning. It involves finding a "peg"—a word or phrase that will tie together all these happenings involving the elements. It is easy when the several element stories actually do turn on one word:

> (By the Associated Press)
> *Rivers* — one frozen, the others flooding — turned an otherwise serene U.S. weather picture today into one of misery and hardship.

But the Winnipeg-Minnesota-New York-New England example doesn't. The editor first considers the peg word "weather" but rejects it on the grounds that floods are not "weather"—or rather that floods are more than weather. What about "the elements"? He rejects that, too, on the grounds that it is too vague. His decision is to say simple "gales and floods," as no one term covers them both adequately. The final story is shown below, with comments on the left pointing out some of the compiling devices used.

The lead combines casualty figures and mentions both gales and floods. Note that it refers to the Red River "system." This is a device to blanket both the floods at Winnipeg (on the Red) and at Crookston (on the Red Lake River, a tributary of the Red).

> (From Press Dispatches)
> At least 15 persons lost their lives as gales lashed New England and New York while flood waters rose again along the rampaging system of the Red River of the North Sunday.

This is from the New York story. It fills out key details of the "gales" part of the story and accounts for thirteen deaths.

> A sudden squall topping off a severe windstorm threw pleasure boaters into choppy seas as New Yorkers and New Englanders took advantage of the year's first real spring Sunday. At least 13 drowned.

A place transition starts the paragraph accounting for the rest of the fifteen deaths.

> At Crookston, Minn., floods which have plagued the city for more than two weeks caused their first fatalities when Mr. and Mrs. Arthur Arsneau, 43 and 34, respectively, were killed in the explosion of

This good little detail about a child logically belongs after the mention of his parents.

The editor begins to break down the casualty figures. The very first words switch us back to the other story without wasted effort.

Best continue with details from New England while he is on the subject.

Here he relates the new casualties to earlier stories.

He switches back to the floods, again using a place transition to make the shift apparent.

More flood detail.

This bit of geographical information, supplied by the editor with the help of an atlas, provides the transition between the Red River and Red Lake River floods and helps return us to further detail from Crookston.

Another transition, turning on "property damage," thus bringing it neatly into the story for the first time.

Now he can clean up the detail on the eastern windstorms.

Finally he pivots on "winds" to swing back for the final cleanup on the Winnipeg floods.

---

their home. The blast was attributed to the rise of the Red Lake River flood waters.

Their bed-ridden son, Milan, 9, was blown out a window but neighbors rescued him.

New England counted three drowned in boat accidents — a father and son on Lake Winnepesaukee at Laconia, N.H., and a fisherman in Manchaug Pond at Sutton, Mass.

At least a dozen others were rescued after their boats overturned in winds up to 65 miles an hour.

The winds swept flames through hundreds of acres of New England woodland.

With 10 deaths previously reported over the weekend in Central and Eastern states, a total of 25 related to weather conditions was reached.

Winnipeg, Man., metropolis of the Canadian interior, was reeling Sunday under the first flood crest of the rampaging Red River of the North and preparing for a second moving up from the North Dakota border.

The Red River had surged over its banks along a 70-mile front. . . .

Aerial surveyors reported that flood conditions were still bad all along the Red Lake River, which pours into the Red at East Grand Forks, Minn.

It was at its worst at Crookston, where the home explosion that took two lives was blamed on rising flood waters. It was followed by fire, which . . .

Property damage, which was estimated in the hundreds of thousands of dollars in Winnipeg, could not be computed in the New England and New York gales. But it was extensive.

Roofs were ripped away, trees were felled, . . .

Winds, which had complicated the flood situation at Winnipeg, died down Sunday. Thousands of flood fighters, weary . . .

This was a thirty-paragraph story and quite a job, all in all. It is not represented here as a masterpiece of story telling but rather to illustrate solutions to the problems of delineating scope in compiled stories where relationships are not too close. It was almost entirely culled from the wire services, which it acknowledges, and the editor wrote only the lead, one other paragraph, and some transitions of a simple word or phrase. The job took about half an hour. A complete rewrite might have been smoother, but it would have taken longer.

It is worthwhile to note here that the scope of a story like this must be indicated in the headline as well as the lead. The headline is therefore reproduced here to show how the editor did it. The banner head:

GALES AND FLOODS TAKE 15 LIVES

First deck:

> East Coast Blow
> Catches Boaters
> Suddenly; 13 Die

Second deck:

> Minnesota Explosion
> Fatal to 2 Blamed
> on Rising Waters

Note that the second and third decks answer the urgent question "Where?" and tell the two main stories.

Developing stories   Another factor common to all roundups concerning the elements complicated this story. The story was developing; it kept building up with new leads and adds every few minutes. Compiling is relatively easy when the stories being combined "lie still." When they keep developing while the compiling is being done or after an early version has been completed, the job can be frustrating.

Once again, *flexibility* comes to the editor's rescue. The flexible editor does not become so enamored of his story treatment that he refuses to work in new details. The editor of the flood-wind story, for example, kept his casualty totals up high in the story where they were easy to get at and then brought them up to date as new figures rolled in. He culled the best new detail from the new leads and wove it into the story where it logically belonged. He did this while the copy was still before him and he continued to do it after the story was in type.

Working in new details is always more difficult when a story has been compiled than when the version of one of the wire services has been used *in toto*. In the latter case, new material is presented to the editor with easy instructions on how to work it into the story. These instructions are of little value when the story is being compiled, especially if the compilation has resulted in a substantial reorganization.

Conflicting facts   When an editor compiles stories he has received from two different sources, he must be aware of the possibility that they may not be in complete factual agreement. Even if he decides to use one story rather than to compile, he still cannot ignore the conflict. Here a parenthetical insert is definitely useful:

> MULDROW, Okla., Nov. 1 — (XP) — An Air Force transport split in midair and crashed in a thunderstorm near here today.
> Army officials at Camp Chaffee, Ark., 18 miles away, said 13 bodies had been recovered.
> (The Amalgamated Press said Trooper Harry Davis of the Oklahoma Highway Patrol put the figure at 12 and that Sheriff Prentice Maddux of Sebastian County, Ark., reported the number as 10.)
> Muldrow is in extreme eastern Oklahoma . . .

The editor has not *resolved* the conflict; he has simply acknowledged it and is showing frankly that his information is not yet firm. He must be willing to sacrifice crispness and neatness to protect himself against inaccuracy.

The most effective combination of two stories may be the simplest combination. The more complicated the job becomes, the less justification for combining the two stories at the copy desk; the job may be one for a rewrite man. The best overall advice might be this: (1) Keep the job simple. (2) Keep the story moving. (3) Watch story organization. (4) Keep an eye on details.

5

Making The News Meaningful

When all is said and done, what competent news editing does is to make the news meaningful for readers. Checking and correcting facts, polishing language, writing headlines, selecting and fitting the news into available space, arraying it in the paper—at all these levels the editor's chief concern is to present as much as possible of significant and interesting news in a form in which it can be read and understood by the majority of readers.

Readability

Meaningful writing is *readable.* It may be helpful in thinking about readability to compare its interrelationships with those involved in an electrical circuit. Amperage—the ease and comprehension with which a reader progresses through a story—varies directly with the voltage behind it—his initial interest in the story—and inversely with the resistance it encounters—unfamiliar words and overly complex sentences. Removing resistances improves his progress. Even when his voltage is high, his amperage increases as the resistances are removed.

The question of readability cannot be divorced from that of *interest,* a complex concept. Interest varies tremendously from reader to reader—and from moment to moment. It cannot be turned on and off. It is not arranged along a single continuum but is rather a bundle of qualities with complicated interrelationships. The reader has many other things to interest him besides a given day's news, even as he is reading it. Poor light, the children scrambling for his attention, the smells of cooking, his thoughts about his job or wife or hobby are all bidding for his attention. The newspaper itself, for that matter, offers lighter fare which requires less effort to absorb than the front page or the editorial page: comics, sports pages, advice to the lovelorn, etc. Ralph Ingersoll has said:

> You can't ask the reader to pass up all these goodies in the back of the paper, and read instead the eight long, dull columns which never seem quite to explain anything to him—which are written as if the reader himself were an expert in foreign and domestic politics and knew all about the machinery and all the leading characters.[1]

It is therefore clear that the important news must be presented palatably to be read: it must be interesting and it must be readable.

Readability Measures

Concern with newspaper readability is fully a century old. It goes back at least to the days of Boss Clark and his superior assemblage of reporters and editors on the old New York *Sun,* when the criteria for readability were summed up in one simple, two-barreled injunction: Use simple words and simple sentences and remember you are writing and editing for people.

Recent scientific research in readability has done no violence to that idea. It has, however, performed an important service in increasing the attention newsmen pay to these doctrines. They know through statistics, for example, that more than a century of compulsory education has not by any means resulted in a wholly literate population. The United States Commissioner of Education reported in 1969 that the country's adult population included at least three million illiterates and that half of the unemployed between the ages of sixteen and twenty-one are what is called "functionally illiterate."[2] Consequently, newsmen know pretty concretely what they are up against in trying to make news readable.

Research has also attempted to define readability by isolating the elements that make writing readable and providing tests to establish roughly, at least, how readable a writer's style is.[3] In scientific research circles, the criteria for readability—or lack of it—are usually grouped in three major stylistic categories. A description of each follows:

Level of word difficulty The difficulty of a word may be assessed by its *frequency* of appearance in the written language. From the standpoint of the editor, a word which appears infrequently in popular writing and everyday conversation will give the general reader more difficulty in comprehending it than the more frequently used word.

Another off-the-cuff test of word difficulty is *degree of structural complexity.* The original Flesch[4] test of word difficulty counted "affixes"—prefixes and suffixes —and showed that words built out of more affixes are on the whole more difficult. Later, Flesch[5] simply counted syllables per word. The theory is that the longer and more complex a word is, the harder it is to grasp *as a word.* "Implementation," for example, is long and cumbersome; it has many affixes; is is also relatively infrequent.

But counting affixes doesn't always work. One of the premises of this test is that the more affixes in a word, the higher the *degree of abstraction.* But the premise behind abstraction is that the more tangible the thing is that the word symbolizes—*i.e.,* the less abstract it is—the greater likelihood the word will convey meaning. And of course many long words are less abstract than many other short words. "Transportation" is in the vocabulary of almost every English-speaking adult, for example, but "ohm" is not.

---

[1] Quoted in Leon Svirsky, ed., *Your Newspaper* (New York: Macmillan, 1947), p. 25.

[2] American Newspaper Publishers Association Newspaper Information Service Newsletter, October 28, 1969.

[3] The Associated Press, United Press International, and some individual newspapers have hired readability experts to ride herd on their staffs and help bring reading difficulty levels down to the point where most subscribers can read and understand their newspapers.

[4] Rudolph Flesch, "The Marks of a Readable Style," Ph.D. dissertation, Columbia University, 1944.

[5] Rudolph Flesch, "A New Readability Yardstick," *Journal of Applied Psychology* 32:221–233 (June 1948).

The four-syllable word is of Latin origin and heavily affixed, but it is not difficult from the point of view of frequency or abstraction. The one-syllable word is not structurally complex, but it is virtually useless in newspaper writing unless it is accompanied by extensive explanation; it is both infrequent and abstract.

Since both "transportation" and "ohm" contradict at least one of the three tests discussed so far, it might be better to assess their difficulty by their *degree of specialization.* Both words convey a wealth of meaning, but only one of them conveys that meaning to the general reader.

Naturally, the editor hasn't the time to apply all these tests to all words scientifically. He hasn't even the time arbitrarily to count affixes or check frequency against an established word-frequency list, such as the one Thorndike[6] developed for studying the difficulty of materials used at various grade-school levels. But the findings of the research are there for his use. With even slight "feel" for word difficulty, the editor can *estimate* pretty accurately a word's frequency and degrees of structural complexity, abstraction, and specialization.

Level of sentence difficulty Readability researchers have been as unanimous about *sentence* difficulty as they have about word difficulty as a basic source of reading difficulty. In general, the research has found that writing in which simple sentences predominate is more readable than writing which includes a high proportion of compound, complex, and compound-complex sentences. Gray and Leary[7] and Dale and Chall,[8] as well as Flesch, include sentence length in their readability formulas. In general, writing can be improved by converting long and difficult sentences into shorter and easier ones—if meaning and "flow" are not damaged in the process.

Degree of conceptual abstraction Short sentences and simple words are no guarantee of readability unless they convey the ideas of the writer lucidly and clearly. Unnecessary conceptual abstraction can arise when an idea was imperfectly conceived in the mind of the writer. But some abstraction is necessary in writing about many political, philosophical, social, artistic, scientific, statistical, or mathematical concepts.

Readability researchers do not agree nearly as unanimously about conceptual abstraction affecting readability as they do about word difficulty and sentence difficulty. It appears that different scientists get at the question in different ways. For example, Lorge apparently ignored the question of conceptual abstraction while being concerned with the degree of abstraction of words. The same is true of Dale and Chall. Gunning[9] suggests the problem in the factor he calls "fog index." However, many researchers do agree that the degree to which abstractions are converted into terms of the reader's own experience determines in large measure the degree to which he absorbs them into his consciousness.

Flesch, and to a lesser degree Gray and Leary, test writing for the personal element by the presence or absence of "personal pronouns," "personal references," and "pronouns" in writing. Flesch's original formula, for instance, measured the number of personal pronouns; his revised formula created two separate measures. One of these retained the word-difficulty and sentence-difficulty factors but used simplified devices for determining them. The other measured a separate "human-interest" factor. This factor was determined by discovering the number of "references to people" and the number of "personal sentences."

In measuring personal pronouns, the readability researchers are getting at the degree to which the abstract is being converted by the writer into the concrete—usually people. The late Walter B. Pitkin advised writers in *The Art of Useful Writing* to *discover* ideas in all their abstractness but to *convert* the abstractions in their writing into terms of "the human struggle." The abstraction "economic depression," for

[6] Edward L. Thorndike, *A Teacher's Word Book of Twenty Thousand Words* (New York: Teachers College, Columbia University, 1931).

[7] William G. Gray and Bernice E. Leary, *What Makes a Book Readable* (Chicago: University of Chicago Press, 1935).

[8] Edgar Dale and Jeanne S. Chall, "A Formula for Predicting Readability," *Educational Research Bulletin* 22:11–20, 28 (January 1948).

[9] Robert Gunning, *The Technique of Clear Writing* (New York: McGraw-Hill, 1952).

example, is more meaningful in terms of the lives of John Smith, unemployed, and his wife Jane.

Context and redundancy   Readability measures based on correlational methods have a major weakness: the formulas invariably deal with "elements" taken out of context. For example, if you applied the Flesch formula to Lincoln's Gettysburg Address and to a scrambled version of the same speech, you would get the same results for both messages. But if you tried to read the scrambled one, you would find the going very difficult. The words are there but not the pattern, the syntax, the familiar ways we have of stringing words together. The same thing would happen if you scrambled together all the *letters* in the Gettysburg Address. A "word" like "xjct" conveys no meaning because it is arranged outside the context of familiar patterns of letters: "t" is often followed by "h" but much less often by "g," for example.

This exercise eliminates the influence of *context* on ease of reading. This is what "information theory" is all about. It tells us that messages tend to contain both *information* and *redundancy,* treating these terms in a special way. Most messages contain both the expected (redundancy) and the unexpected (information). If you have memorized the Gettysburg Address, it would be redundant to you; you wouldn't gain anything by hearing it or reading it another time; you can already anticipate every item in it; it holds no surprises and hence no rewards. A table of random numbers is completely informational; whether you move down, up, across, back, or diagonally, each new item is wholly unpredictable from knowledge of any previous item. A table of random numbers may not tell us something we want to know, but it does tell us pure information. It has no pattern, no syntax; we can have no semantic expectations of it.

The languages we use to convey messages are not like that. According to Shannon,[10] who was the first to bring all these ideas together, all the Western written languages are approximately 50 per cent re-

dundancy and 50 per cent information, with only slight variations from language to language. There appears to be an excellent reason for this. Because the unexpected is information, the unpredictable item in a signal transmitted in a code that has meaning for both sender and receiver carries the most meaning. But in almost all the circumstances in which messages are received or exchanged, there is some "channel noise"—unexpected perturbations (not, in this context, necessarily auditory) of the message, of external origin, not accounted for by the code. Noise tends to reduce the fidelity of the signal and consequently its comprehensibility and meaning. If the "racket" you hear has pattern, is expected, and follows a predictable course, then it interferes less with listening or seeing than if it comes at unexpected times and in unexpected orders. Noise resembles information in that both are at their maximum when they reach randomness.

Thus it follows that redundancy in languages and messages, as it is uniquely defined in information theory, has a real value—it tends to overcome the losses owing to the noise present in most circumstances in which newspapers are read, radio is heard, television is watched, etc. But, on the other hand, it tends to occupy message space that could otherwise be used to convey information.

All this suggests another facet of what has until now been called "readability" and crudely measured by formula. A formula measuring word frequency, for example, is obviously measuring a small part of what is involved in redundancy. Part of the pattern of a language is indeed relative frequencies of elements, whether letters or words. But a much larger part is *sequential order,* which can be measured in the form of sequential probabilities. The formulas leave sequential order out, as we have seen.

One "readability formula" that *does* take it into account and in fact *is* a measure of the redundancy or context value of a passage of prose is known as *cloze procedure.* It tests the probability that a reader will be able to supply missing words in a message from the clues given him by context; usually every fifth word is omitted. The more words a reader can guess correctly, the greater the redundancy of the

---

[10] Claude E. Shannon and Warren Weaver, *The Mathematical Theory of Communication* (Urbana: University of Illinois Press, 1949).

passage *for him.* Wilson Taylor,[11] who invented the procedure, correlated cloze scores with Flesch scores, and the correlations were large enough to suggest that they were measuring the same thing.

But cloze procedure should imply to the thoughtful wordsmith that it is a great deal more than yet another way of telling how easy something is to read. The formulas suggest that maximum readability is what writers should shoot for. But maximum readability in terms of cloze procedure is redundancy—too much readibility at the expense of information. Cloze procedure suggests that writers should seek some kind of *optimal level of redundancy,* a level of readability that is high, but not lacking in ability to carry information. Too little redundancy would be at the expense of information, too, for that would leave the message vulnerable to loss from noise.

In an unpublished study years ago, MacLean and Westley tested this idea by giving two kinds of groups —homemakers' clubs and labor unions, both drawn from equivalent socioeconomic levels—cloze tests on passages from a labor paper and passages from the women's section of the daily newspaper—passages which were equal in difficulty as measured by the Flesch formula. The union members got significantly better scores on the union-paper passages than on the women's-page passages; the homemakers got about the same scores on both. The results seemed to favor information theory at the expense of the Flesch theory: a writer does not help convey meaning by "talking down" to his readers—Flesch's advice in simplified terms—but he increases their comprehension by "talking their language"—more or less Taylor's advice.

But the results of readability research testing word difficulty, sentence difficulty, and abstraction are more direct; they show more concretely what makes writing readable. So far research on information, redundancy, and noise suggests little more than that the communication process is a fascinating business.

The Dale-Chall formula and a simplification of the Flesch formula worked out by Farr, Jenkins, and Paterson[12] are probably the most frequently used readability measures today. Four of the formulas[13] have been further simplified by the availability of scoring diagrams published by Powers and Ross.[14] Danielson and Bryan[15] made a further modification of the Farr-Jenkins-Paterson formula in the process of adapting it to computerization without loss in validity.

Brinton and Danielson[16] put twenty of the separate measures that go into the readability formulas into a factor-analysis scheme that determines the underlying dimensions of what is being measured. Not too surprisingly, of the factors that accounted for the largest part of the variance in the data, one was a word-difficulty factor, having elements such as percentage of easy words and percentage of monosyllabic words, and the other was a sentence-difficulty factor, with elements such as sentence length in words or in syllables.

There is research evidence that careful editing does in fact improve readability and meaning. Razik[17] found that a sample of metropolitan newspaper front pages were significantly more readable than a sample of nonmetropolitan front pages. If it may be assumed that the larger staffs of the larger papers write and

[11] Wilson L. Taylor, " 'Cloze' Procedure: A New Tool for Measuring Readability," *Journalism Quarterly* 30:415–433 (Fall 1953). For a simplified discussion of the whole field, see Chilton R. Bush, ed., *News Research for Better Newspapers* 1:90–95 (New York: American Newspaper Publishers Association Foundation, 1966): "Measures of 'Readability'."

[12] James N. Farr, James J. Jenkins, and Donald E. Paterson, "Simplification of the Flesch Reading Ease Formula," *Journal of Applied Psychology* 35:333–337 (October 1951).

[13] There are more. Klare and Buck found twenty-five methods of measuring the readability of children's materials and fourteen ways of measuring adult materials. See George R. Klare and Byron Buck, *Know Your Reader* (New York: Heritage House, 1954), pp. 100–103.

[14] Richard D. Powers and John E. Ross, "New Diagrams for Calculating Readability Scores Rapidly," *Journalism Quarterly* 36:177–182 (Spring 1959). Based on recalculations given in R. D. Powers, W. A. Sumner, and B. E. Kearl, "A Recalculation of Four Adult Readability Formulas," *Journal of Educational Psychology* 49:99–105 (Spring 1958).

[15] Wayne A. Danielson and Sam Dunn Bryan, "Computer Automation of Two Readability Formulas," *Journalism Quarterly* 40:201–206 (Spring 1963).

[16] James E. Brinton and Wayne A. Danielson, "A Factor Analysis of Language Elements Affecting Readability," *Journalism Quarterly* 35:420–426 (Fall 1958).

[17] Taber A. Razik, "A Study of American Newspaper Readability," *Journal of Communication* 19:317–324 (December 1969).

edit more carefully, this may be taken as evidence that editing produces readability dividends.

Funkhouser[18] has shown that the levels of difficulty used in reporting science to various audiences, from those of *Readers' Digest* at one end to scientific publications at the other, are pretty much as expected when the usual readability measures are used. However, he got the sharpest delineation of this difference by measuring the proportion of "science words" in relation to the proportion of what he calls "activity words." Science words correlated very highly (+ .89) with the percentage of college graduates in the audience for the magazines, while activity words were negatively correlated (— .60) with the same datum —a clear indication that writers and editors of these magazines are taking the interests and linguistic abilities of their audiences into account in the way they present science information.

Another study tested the idea that there is a historic link between "sensationalism" and readability. Stevenson[19] tested the readability of newspapers in two groups which he judged to be "responsive" and "stable" on the basis of a study of their histories at four points in time: 1872 (before the emergence of the "yellow press"), 1895 (in the yellow-press era), 1925, and 1960, the latter two representing points between the yellow-press era and "the present." He expected that, from a standing start in 1872, the responsive papers would show sharp increases in readability up to 1895 but would then decline in readability to a level only slightly more readable than the stable papers, which he expected would show modest but steady increases in readability throughout the period. The data were generally consistent with these expectations except that the stable papers consistently gained in readability between 1872 and 1895 *at a lesser rate* than the responsive papers and that all the papers (with a single exception) showed declines in readability between 1895 and 1925—at the same

rate, on the average. A clear difference persisted to 1960: the "responsives" were consistently higher and the "stables" consistently lower in readability scores.

A study by Carter[20] showed that story structure can influence the reader's comprehension. He presented three groups of readers with three differently structured news stories. All the stories were basically in the inverted-pyramid form, but they varied in the way the aspects of a controversy were presented. The first presented one side of the issue, identifying the source, in the first paragraph, then gave added arguments on the same side in the second, then in the third and fourth paragraphs presented the same material in the same way from the other side. The second story started with a general statement about the controversy, then gave one side and its source followed by supporting arguments, then the other side and its source followed by its supporting arguments. The third story also started with the general statement, then gave both sides without identifying sources, then arguments for one side with the source, then the other side with source.

Reader comprehension of the issues was better for the second and third stories, giving the neutral picture of the controversy first, and was greatest for the third story, which gave a neutral presentation of both sides without identifying the antagonists. This pattern was strongest among persons who said they read newspapers "occasionally." When it came to the supporting arguments, the second story increased comprehension among the occasional newspaper readers but reduced it among readers who said they read newspapers "frequently." We may conclude that structure makes a difference but the ideal structure is not necessarily the same for all classes of readers.

And other evidence shows that the *quality* of a story—the kinds of quality that good editing and proofreading impart—affect the way the message is received. Greenberg and Razinsky[21] produced evi-

[18] G. Ray Funkhouser, "Levels of Science Writing in Public Information Sources," *Journalism Quarterly* 46:721–726 (Winter 1969).

[19] Robert L. Stevenson, "Readability of Conservative and Sensational Papers Since 1872," *Journalism Quarterly* 41:202–206 (Spring 1964).

[20] Richard F. Carter, "Writing Controversial Stories for Comprehension," *Journalism Quarterly* 32:319–328 (Summer 1955). Summarized in Bush, *op. cit.* 1:96–98 (1966).

[21] Bradley S. Greenberg and Edward L. Razinsky, "Some Effects of Variations in Message Quality," *Journalism Quarterly* 43:486–492 (Autumn 1966).

dence that as routine errors were increased experimentally, readers perceived the source as less competent and trustworthy and learned less from the message (but the message was no less persuasive). It must be admitted that the effects were unequivocal only when a very high error density had been reached—48 in a 500-word message. This study was not based on newspaper content, but it is reasonable to suspect that the newspaper reader would be just as likely to be affected by routine errors in the same way. That the problem is not trivial is shown in Blankenburg's[22] survey of the accuracy of 300 stories in two West Coast dailies. Inaccuracies of one kind and another were found in about half the stories. About one-third of the errors were typographic.

Editing for Meaning

An enthusiastic application of readability formulas has not solved all the problems of reaching people with news of complex events. Some news-writing traditions tend to hamper readability. For example:

Inverted-pyramid style This is the traditional structure of most straight news stories. But does it make the news easier to read and understand? It does tend to help the reader to distinguish the more significant parts of the story by putting them at the beginning. Its rationale, of course, is that readers have a limited time to spend on their newspapers and that different readers have different demands for detail in a given story; the reader who wants less detail can leave the story at any point he wishes with the assurance that no more significant details are buried farther down.

Unfortunately, many stories would be better told in the order in which the events took place. The news magazines capitalize on this fact by telling most stories in chronological order. Newspapers can tell *some* of their stories chronologically and some parts

of a story assembled essentially in inverted-pyramid style can use the time sequence.

But most of the time newsmen lay out the facts on the basis of their importance and recency. To make such stories readable requires, among other things, careful transitions between these somewhat arbitrarily assembled facts.

Block paragraphs Although it is no longer the dogma that it once was, news writing in block paragraphs persists. Its theory is that a paragraph must stand as a unit, not dependent for its meaning on what went ahead of it, to enable last-minute changes in space and paragraph order.

Block paragraphs obviously militate against careful transitions. A paragraph that begins "Earlier . . ." may not work in another position in the story. Thus writers and editors are often faced with a choice between an effective transitional phrase and the block paragraph. Most newsmen today would unhesitatingly choose the good transition.

Impersonal tone The traditional separation of news from opinion is largely responsible for the detached, impersonal style characteristic of the straight news story. But whatever its justification, it clearly comes into conflict with one of the best understood principles of readability. From almost the beginning of readability research, it has been clear that, other things being equal, a personalized account is easier to read than a depersonalized account (pages 118–121). Readability research suggests that saying "we" put a man on the moon will make a story more readable and meaningful than the newspaper tradition of saying that it was the country that did it. There have been signs of a relaxation of the impersonal approach, as the discussion at the end of this chapter points out.

Writing as you talk An "easy" solution to the problem of readability has traditionally been to "write as you talk." This is a disarmingly simple panacea. To the extent that it leads reporters and editors away from stilted, legalistic, and technical forms of writing, it is good advice. The reporter who wrote this lead might well have heeded it:

---

[22] William B. Blankenburg, "News Accuracy: Some Findings on the Meaning of Errors," *Journal of Communication* 20:375–386 (December 1970).

The city of Fargo and the Annexation Review Commission were ordered Saturday to file such records of the recent NP industrial area annexation proceedings as affects Common School District No. 126 with the Cass District Court for review.

It's not likely that he would tell the story that way to his wife or his neighbor. But what he might say face-to-face probably would not make a suitable news lead, either. What is said in conversation is based on common backgrounds and common experience, a relatively narrow and unified frame of reference. But reporters and editors must take into account that they are speaking to an "audience" of very diverse backgrounds, and the content of communications must therefore not assume a great deal of commonality. In the example above, the reporter couldn't refer to "that annexation deal on the West Side." Although in conversation this might have been adequate to place the story in his hearers' minds, for many of his readers it wouldn't be enough.

There are other reasons why a conversational approach is inappropriate. The spoken language differs considerably from the written language. Radio newsmen soon found that reading newspapers over the radio didn't work. Material which had been written for the eye was altogether wrong for the ear. They found new techniques to reach their listeners which are quite different from the techniques for reaching readers. It makes sense that the reverse should also be true. Simplicity and directness are valued in both radio and newspaper writing. But devices to attain this goal which work on the radio usually do not work in the newspaper.

Reading for Meaning

In dealing with the meaning of a story, the copy editor is guided by asking two significant general questions: (1) Did the reporter himself understand clearly what he was writing about? (2) Did he tell the story so that the meaning is apparent to his reader?

It is clear that reporters incapable of understanding the materials they work with cannot survive long as reporters. Yet one of the most difficult parts of the editor's job is being unflaggingly alert for indications of a want of understanding on the reporter's part. This is not to imply that newspaper reporters as a lot are mental deficients. But the conditions they work under are unusually demanding, including the pressure of time, the increasing complexity of the facts they deal with, and the fact that they must deal with a wide range of specialized subjects: the day of thoroughgoing specialization in the newsroom is not yet upon us. Consequently, they are bound sometimes to miss the point.

So the editor must read with *skepticism;* the more complex the story, the more intense the skepticism. He must watch each story for *internal evidence* of the reporter's lack of understanding, if any. The editor didn't witness the fire, he didn't study the tax report, he didn't attend the council meeting, so he cannot be expected to know for certain that the reporter misunderstood. But he can learn to recognize signs of inconsistency between parts of the story, signs in the reporter's statements of fact that betray confusion, and signs that the speaker's statements do not square with his past statements or known attitudes.

These are only clues, however, not evidence. Finding such clues, the editor's next duty is to discuss the story with the reporter. Such a conference may lead to the reporter's discussing the story with the news source. At any rate, the editor clearly is not in a position to convert his doubts directly into changes in the copy. The confusions must be painstakingly cleared up at the source.

This sort of copyreading is often done at other levels than the rim. The city editor is the first to subject a story to scrutiny of this kind. The slot may also be a backstop. But the fact that others are concerned with the question of the reporter's understanding does not by any means absolve the copy editor. He is the *last* protector of the full meaning of the story; he cannot depend on others to catch confusions of detail, for instance, because the others are not concerned with detail but rather with the broad outlines of the story.

But perhaps the reporter's original misunderstanding of the news he tells is a smaller part of the problem of meaning than *how he tells it.* The first essential of a meaningful story is, of course, the story's meaningfulness to the writer. He cannot tell it clearly if he doesn't understand it clearly. But his own understanding is no guarantee that he will convey understanding to the reader. The best way the editor can tell whether a story will be clear to the reader is whether he—the editor—grasps the full meaning of it himself. If he doesn't, then the story probably will not be clear to others.

But this test is by no means enough. The editor presumably has a high level of skill in language symbols; if he did not, he would not be trusted to read copy. He also probably has a larger vocabulary and a broader frame of reference than a large segment of the newspaper-reading public. Hence it is not enough that he determine whether the story is clear to him—he must make the difficult judgment as to whether it will be clear to a person of lesser reading competence. There are no formulas for making such a judgment but there are criteria the editor can apply. For instance, he can ask himself: What resources of his own did he tap to achieve understanding of the language or the concept involved? Then: Are these resources likely to reside in the "average" reader? Such resources might include a superior vocabulary, a knowledge of statistics, knowledge of the terms used in courts of law, a smattering of political theory, etc. The general reader cannot be expected to have any of these resources. To be meaningful for him, the story must be told in words he can understand, experiences he has had, and ideas he can grasp.

Verbal Precision and Meaning

Incorrect use of words is one of the most common sources of meaning "leakage" in the newspaper. Examples are found on almost any copy desk on almost any day. This one is typical:

PLAINVILLE—A free smallpox clinic at which children from Plainville and the surrounding area will be given protection from the disease free of charge will be held Tuesday at the Community Building from 9 to 9:30 a.m.

Plainville doctors will administer treatment as well as booster shots for diphtheria and the triple vaccine . . .

Meaning is confused in this example on two levels. The first is simple *inaccuracy*. In paragraph 2, the writer has used the term "administer treatment" incorrectly. The term connotes, if it does not precisely denote, that the doctors will be treating cases of smallpox and other communicable diseases. But this is not the function of the clinic. Many meticulous readers will grasp the truth. But for many others, this wording will produce profound confusion.

The second level of confusion lies in the *vagueness* of the wording: "will be given protection from the disease free of charge"? They were in fact getting "free immunization." "Immunization," it might be argued, is too difficult a word for lead purposes. But in the locale and time of this story, free clinics were familiar; the word could have been assumed to have meaning for almost all readers. Thus the specific word that conveys the meaning is to be preferred to vague words that convey only part of the meaning or possibly a variety of meanings.

Neither the vague nor the patently incorrect usages in this example would be reprehensible in themselves; but here they *reinforce* each other. The vague term "given protection" used in the lead compounds the confusion at the point where the reader encounters the incorrect term "administer treatment."

The edited version read:

> PLAINVILLE — A small-pox clinic at which children from Plainville and the surrounding area will be given free immunization will be held Tuesday at the Community Building from 9 to 9:30 a.m.
>
> Plainville physicians will vaccinate for smallpox and give booster shots for diphtheria and triple vaccine . . .

The editor often can help crystallize meaning by sharpening up the lead. As in the example below, this can mean simply pruning away details which can wait. It came to the desk in this form:

An institute in driver education for high school teachers will be conducted by the Excelsior University Extension Division and School of Education in cooperation with two state agencies.

During the session, August 21 to 26, teachers will be trained in the use of testing devices, educational techniques, and other methods used to increase highway safety. They will also learn . . .

The edited version began:

> An institute in driver education for high school teachers will be held here Aug. 21 to 26.
> The Excelsior University Extension Division and the School of Education will train teachers in . . .

This made the lead clear and crisp and shifted minor details out of major positions.

Technical terms, too, present the editor with a serious problem of meaning. Besides being meaningful to only a limited circle, they have another difficult property—their tendency to be *precise* in meaning. The editor must examine technical terms not only from the standpoint of whether they will convey any meaning at all but also whether "easier" substitute words will convey equally precise meaning. Often the technical term can be used first, then explanatory wording added to make its meaning clear.

Plugging Holes for Meaning

The reporter is presumed to know whether his story is complete. But because he is so close to it and because his time is so short, it often remains for the editor to plug "holes" in the story—any pieces of information that are lacking but are needed to convey full meaning.

Missing facts Watching for missing facts is more or less routine for the copy editor. If an obituary fails to mention funeral arrangements, the editor notices it and checks. If the reporter overlooked that essential part of the story, he digs up the information; if the arrangements have not yet been made, the story is incomplete unless it says so. If a fire story makes no mention of the extent of the damage, again the reporter is queried and the hole is plugged.

Sometimes the reporter is not that easy to reach. Country correspondents, particularly, present this problem. If the missing fact is not worth the time and money involved in a long-distance telephone call, the editor must either "cover up" the missing fact or seek out evidence in the story that will clear it up. For instance, the meaning of part of the detail in the following story was very doubtful indeed:

PLAINVILLE—A Plainville business institution which has been in the same family for an estimated 80 years passed out of existence Monday of this week when Russel B. Wilson of Blue River purchased the Smith and Jones Meat Market and Grocery Store.

*   *   *

The firm Smith and Jones was started by the late Jacob Smith an estimated 80 years ago and he operated the business with several partners until about 50 years ago with John C. Jones they formed a partnership known as Smith and Jones. The business operated under that name for more than the last 50 years.

When Jacob Smith died, his two sons, Herman and Theodore, formed a partnership with John O. Jones and the business was operated by these three men until this week.

The death of John O. Jones, the illness of Theodore Smith, and various other factors helped the two remaining partners in making their decision to sell the business.

This story obviously requires some stringent editing even to make it read. But that won't answer the question: How many John Joneses were there? John O. is mentioned twice and John C. once. Was the last just a typographical error? Or was John O. the heir of John C.? The story is not worth a long-distance telephone call, so the editor reads it a second time for internal evidence—which, unfortunately supports both possibilities. The death of the senior Smith is accounted for and his heirs are named. But John C. Jones's death is not accounted for and his heirs are not specifically named. Maybe it was John O. all along. If the original Smith's sons are still in the business, why is it not logical to expect that the senior Jones's son would be the one who just died? On the other hand, why does the correspondent use the full name three times if there have not been two Joneses?

Couldn't the store have gone through two Joneses in fifty years?

The internal evidence is not conclusive enough in either direction. So the editor pulls out as much of the story as he needs to in order to avoid raising the question at all. He can't kill off all the material about the history of the store, for the lead material requires that he document the "80 years" angle to some degree. If he eliminates that angle altogether, he has only a one-paragraph story left. That's the angle that makes the story. A concluding paragraph like this might be substituted for the three paragraphs above and meet all the requirements:

> The firm was founded by the late Jacob Smith about 80 years ago. The Smith and Jones partnership is approximately 50 years old.

Missing angles Sometimes in confusing facts or misusing words the reporter obscures an important angle to a story. In the example below, both the reporter and the copy desk overlooked the missing angle. It was particularly embarrassing because the competing radio stations didn't miss it—and played it to the hilt:

HARRISBURG, Wis.—A light engined plane, piloted by Hayward Countryman, Adams, crashed on the Roland Henry farm about 5½ miles northwest of here early today after the pilot had bailed out and parachuted to safety.

After circling the Henry farm for nearly 2 hours when he became lost in a fog in this vicinity, the plane became coated with ice, and Countryman reported that he was forced to bail out at about 500 feet.

The plane crashed in a field just northeast of the farm buildings, and landed right side up at about 8 a.m. Slight damage was reported to the landing gear and bottom side of the plane.

Countryman, who received only minor cuts and bruises, was taken to Harrisburg where he was treated by a local physician. Countryman reported that he was traveling from Adams to Milwaukee.

The plane was owned by Co. J of the National Guard unit at Adams.

The editor should have noted that the plane didn't "crash" at all—it came down miraculously all by itself with virtually no damage. The angle, then, could have been pointed up like this:

> HARRISBURG, Wis. — A light plane landed itself on a farm near here early today after the pilot had parachuted to safety.

Missing explanatory material When a daily newspaper in Edmonton, Alberta, ceased publication, the story sent over the wires in the United States contained the usual information: the last issue, publisher's statement about why the paper folded, number of employees, etc.

But there was one thing missing, at least in the opinion of one editor. He knew there was considerable interest in the question of newspaper mortality at that time, especially in his own community, a state capital where competing newspapers had recently consolidated production and business operations while maintaining the papers' separate identities. The unanswered question, he felt, was this: What was left in Edmonton? Did another newspaper survive? He answered the question by going to the latest *Editor & Publisher International Year Book* and wrote the missing explanation into the story. He underwent a little office kidding for being a fussbudget but was vindicated when the New York *Times* queried one of the wire services on the same point half an hour later.

The copy editor is not helpless to provide the explanatory material that the complex news of this day so often requires. He has, in all but the most pinched newsrooms, his newspaper library with its reference materials, a news staff at the beck and call of the city editor, and a telephone at his elbow. The wire services are not only willing but eager to help individual desks clear up factual or explanatory gaps in the news they supply. The newsroom which works in a general atmosphere of "cover it up" and "write around it" not only provides its readers with precious little help in understanding the difficult times in which they are living but demoralizes its reporters and editors, too.

The new emphasis on "explanatory writing," "interpretive reporting," and "backgrounding the news" puts additional responsibility on the desk. Where the straight news story requires the editor to watch for gaps in the facts, the situationer requires the editor to watch for interpretive gaps in the stories he reads—and to fill them when time and facilities permit. The examples above show instances in which the editor was reading not merely for errors of fact but for larger meanings easily overlooked by reporters.

This sort of alertness requires that the editor be able to put himself in the place of the reader, not only the merely curious one for whom the obvious facts are enough, but also the one who is trying to find out something about what it all means. This doesn't call for supplying him with ready-made opinions or necessarily submerging the fact-finding function of the newspaper to its interpretive function. It does call for furnishing the additional facts, where necessary and possible, that reveal relationships between the new facts and what has preceded them, and between new facts and other new facts.

Statistics and Meaning

The problem of dealing with statistical materials has been discussed briefly in Chapter 1, under the heading "Detecting and Correcting Errors of Fact" (page 20). Sometimes errors are made in statistics themselves, sometimes in their interpretation. But they are always tricky and deserve especially close scrutiny at every level of reporting and editing.

In the example on page 73, the reporter mistakenly saw a 50 per cent increase in population as "double" the previous figure. Another oddity of the same sort turned up in a Wisconsin paper:

> Almost half of the students at Excelsior University this summer are actually teachers.
> Nearly one out of every two of these students taught during the past school year, according to the Office of Statis-

tics and Research directed by L. J. Lyons. Most of the lot are high school teachers.
> There are 48 more teachers among the 7,390 students on the campus this year than there were last summer, when total enrollment records were smashed with 8,474 students registered. This year 2,176 of the students are teachers.

The story implies that 2,176 is half of 7,390, and the editor didn't question the inconsistency. If he had, he should have reread the story carefully to see whether his original reading put something into it that wasn't there or overlooked something that was. After that, he could have looked for internal evidence to support one fact or another.

Certainly all these "facts" can't be correct. If the total is right and the number of teachers is right, then the 50 per cent can't be right. Or if the 50 per cent is right, then one or the other of the enrollment figures must be wrong. At several points, enrollment breakdowns provide a check on the total figure. For example:

> The distribution by classes is: freshmen, 133; sophomores, 364; juniors, 685; seniors, 1,091; graduates, 2,874; law and medicine, 360; and specials not working toward a degree, 1883.

That adds up to 7,390, so the total figure apparently is right.

More internal evidence:

> Many of the summer students are returning to the campus this fall. Almost 4,000 were students at the university last semester and 2,221 attended the 1970 summer session.

Students who were in school during the last regular semester could in some cases be doctoral candidates with teaching assistantships, but in general that 4,000 would be almost entirely nonteachers. That being the case, almost all the rest of the summer students would have to be teachers if the 50 per cent figure is right.
More:

> As usual, the College of Letters and Science claims the largest share of students with 2,347. Education is second with 1,400 . . .

Even if all the summer students in the School of Education were teachers, an improbability, the number of teachers not in the School of Education would have to be a highly unlikely two and a half times as many in order to bring the total number of teachers up to at least 3,500, or "almost half" of 7,390. So the 50 per cent figure appears to be the shaky one.

Another possibility, of course, is that the 2,176 figure is not the total teacher figure at all. The first three paragraphs are very confusing on this point. "Nearly one out of two of these students taught during the past school year," says paragraph 2. What is the antecedent of "these"? Does it refer to all students or to those who are "actually teachers"?

What can an editor do about these confusions and discrepancies? It all depends on materials and time available for checking. If the story is office written from a set of statistics, he can check the original source. If it was rewritten from a release, he can check the release. If the story is the release itself, he can check with the office that sent it out—if time and the time of day or night permit. Otherwise, the only thing to do is scuttle the lead angle and find another. A good guess is not good enough where statistics are concerned.

Another source of confusion in telling stories with figures is index numbers. The following dramatic example resulted in outright (though not intended) distortion of an important story. The original error was committed by one of the wire services.

WASHINGTON—(XP)—Retail food prices increased a full 2 per cent in the last two weeks of November, the Bureau of Labor Statistics estimated today.

The increase made a total jump of 2.7 per cent for the month. Farther down the story, this paragraph appeared:

A special survey of 50 foods in seven cities showed the retail food price index on Nov. 28 here stood at 215.7

per cent of the average over the past four years. . . . The index was still under the record 216.8 set in July . . .

Although the story let the reader do his own "ciphering," the implication was clear that the *index* rose from 213.7 to 215.7. The editor in this case was aware that this was not a "2 *per cent* increase." It was actually an increase of *less than 1 per cent* (215.7 is .936 per cent larger than 213.7). But the editor decided that it would be splitting hairs to correct the impression of the story and let it go. He wrote this headline:

Food Prices Jump
2% in Two Weeks

The headline told precisely the story the lead told, so it was accepted without question by the news editor.

But if the editor was vaguely uneasy about a "slight" distortion when he let the story go, his agony must have known no bounds the next day when he picked up the same paper and saw the damage that had been done by his unwillingness to split hairs. Here is the headline he read on Page One:

Food Price Rise in City Under
U.S. Average, Dealers Say

The story began:

> Retail food prices generally haven't increased in Extown as much as the rest of the nation, retail food dealers said Sunday night.
> According to the Bureau of Labor Statistics in Washington, food prices rose a full 2 per cent in the nation during the last two weeks of November and the over-all monthly increase was reported as 2.7 per cent.
> However, several retailers here said Extown food prices have not kept pace with the national trend and they said generally that the jump in prices was about 1.5 per cent in the past month.

This story is an illustration in itself of the careless handling of statistics that often is condoned in otherwise careful newsrooms. How did the reporter arrive at a figure of "1.5 per cent" in telephoning "several" retailers at their homes Sunday night? Were the retailers asked about the very commodities included in the BLS list? Were all the retail outlets in the city adequately sampled?

But the point is that the editor's original carelessness had been compounded and the story was simply false. Actually Extown's price increase was greater than the national average during the month in question, if the 1.5 per cent figure can be accepted. For it seems clear that the retailers were not talking in terms of index numbers based on the four-year average but were answering the question: To what extent have your prices increased during the month of November? If the composite figure of 1.5 per cent is accurate, then Extown's increase was considerably greater than the national average, which was 0.9 per cent. It isn't exactly splitting hairs when a story produces precisely the opposite impression from the truth.

Perhaps more common than the index-numbers confusion is one very much like it involving percentages and percentage points. A typical story goes something like this:

> The Extown Board of Education said today that there are 20 per cent more women enrolled in technical courses this year than five years ago.
> Then the figure was 40 per cent. Today it is 60 per cent.

Now these two statements are contradictory. The increase is one of *twenty percentage points*—but *50 per cent*. The thoughtful reader will see that it is not 20 per cent at all (and he may also lose respect for the paper for its failure to perceive this). For the rapid scanner, the lead amounts to a serious error of fact. To see how serious the error can be, suppose the increase was from 10 to 30 per cent. Here the twenty-percentage-point increase actually *triples* the earlier figure.

The concepts of "average," "mean," and "median" also given trouble to newsmen converting statistical data into a form understandable to the public. Two wire services sent these conflicting versions of the same story:

SERVICE A

WASHINGTON—American families had a median income of $5,700 last year, the Census Bureau reported tonight.

SERVICE B

WASHINGTON—The average family income in the United States last year was $5,700, the Bureau of the Census said today.

The Service A story is the correct version, but many papers chose the Service B story instead, possibly because "median" is not as common a word as "average." One editor, offered this same choice, ran A because he knew B was not strictly correct and because the third paragraph of A contained this explanatory material:

> Median means middle point; half of all other incomes were higher, half lower.

Service B carried an explanation of the figure which was as confusing as its initial statement was inexact.

Some editors might argue that they are concerned with the man on the street, to whom such technical differences are not significant. They put it this way: If we say "average," he knows what we're talking about in a general way—he gets *some* meaning even if it's not quite the precise meaning; if we say "median," he gets no meaning at all. But the editor who chose A pointed out that even though the word "average" is more common than "median," either word will carry the general connotation of "central tendency" to the general reader. But to the more sophisticated reader, the term "average" is clearly wrong.

Editing statistical stories, then, does not mean just checking numbers for accuracy. The editor must often interpret statistics in order to tell the story effectively. Take a business-census story, for example. The reporter in this case found the story to tell and put it this way:

The dollar value of retail business in the state has increased by 200 per cent in the last decade, preliminary results of a business census of the state revealed today.

The editor thought the reporter had passed up other less effective ways of telling the story. Since the story was destined for general news pages, not the financial pages, and since it was meant to be read and understood by persons with no special competence in mathematics, he decided that the lead should make clearer in laymen's terms the extent of the increase. He changed the story to read:

> The dollar value of retail business in the state tripled in the last decade, preliminary results . . .

Both methods of stating the extent of the increase are inexact but essentially accurate. "An increase of 200 per cent" is not a terribly difficult concept for many readers, but it is not as obvious and lacks the supreme simplicity of "tripled." Too few readers appreciate the difference between these statements:

The dollar value of retail business in the state last year was 200 per cent of the figure 10 years ago.

The dollar value of retail business in the state increased by 200 per cent in the last 10 years.

The first, of course, means "twice," the second, "thrice." The simplest expression for the relationship helped tell the story to the nonspecialist reader—and it told it just as well to the specialist.

Restructuring the Story for Meaning

The copy editor is usually empowered to make substantial structural changes in the stories he edits. Depending on their extent and how much they in-

volve the paper's policies, he may make them without consultation with others, or he may consult with his copy-desk chief. The slot, in turn, may consult the city editor. It is an important skill on the copy desk to be able to see how stories can be made more effective—and more meaningful—by restructuring and then to do it without wasting too much time.

In the larger restructuring job, the editor is concerned with the story's total impact on the reader. He may see that restructuring will make that impact greater, or he may wish to restructure to tone it down: deliberately to play down sensational elements in the story which tend, he feels, to get in the way of total meaning, or to get in the way of essential accuracy.

Restructuring takes many forms, depending on the fault in the reporter's work the editor wishes to correct. Did the reporter misjudge the news values involved? Then a new top is indicated. Did he bury some good angle? Then it must be brought up higher in the story. Did he miss an opportunity to assemble a group of related matters in one-two-three order? Putting them in that order may make each of these elements more soundly related to the others and the story as a whole.

The editor looks on all his sources with a critical eye, but especially "handouts" or press releases. Though they are not invariably slanted to put their perpetrators in a good light, it is safe to say that they usually have a broader purpose than simply to tell the story. The best of them will tell it straight, necessitating little restructuring; others need careful reworking to eliminate the influence of the self-interest of the personality or company involved.

The following example is overstated, but it illustrates the problem of getting to the heart of the story, then shifting its elements accordingly:

```
          For immediate release

The Tri-State Telephone Co., which supplies 121

separate communities in Wisconsin, Iowa, and Illinois

with top-grade telephone service, announced today the

completion of a three-year program of improvements which

have provided vastly expanded telephone services to the

three-state area.
```

R. J. Dialtone, president of the far-flung firm, announced today that the tremendous expansion in the company's operations brought about during the three-year period had been a major contribution to tremendous forward strides made in the Middle West by private industry in that time.

He further added that the company's costs have skyrocketed in recent years. Specifically, he said, labor costs have increased 13% in the last two years. Materials costs, following the familiar pattern, have increased 19% in the same period.

Meanwhile, and in spite of mounting costs, Mr. Dialtone declared, the company by a herculean effort has managed to extend its services materially. Specifically, he cited the undeniable fact that the company had installed direct-distance dialing equipment in 17 localities in the last two years and had replaced outmoded central office equipment in 21 other localities.

"Something has got to give," he averred. "The company's financial position will be seriously endangered unless redress is granted."

Accordingly, Mr. Dialtone said, the Tri-State Telephone Co. filed a request with the State Public Service Commission today for an increase in rates.

The increase amounts to approximately 5% on local service and 8% on toll service.

# # #

This handout is obviously designed to emphasize the company's "expansion program" and to deemphasize its request for a rate increase, which is the real point. By cutting and pasting and a judicious use of the copy pencil, the story might be restructured to put the emphasis where it belongs, thus:

Accordingly, ~~Mr. Dialtone said,~~ the Tri-State

today asked

Telephone Co. ~~filed a request with~~ the State Public

Service Commission ~~today~~ for an increase ~~in rates.~~

amounting

~~The increase amounts~~ to approximately 5% on local

service and 8% on toll service.

\# \# \#

The ~~Tri-State Telephone Co.~~ ~~which supplies~~ 121 ~~For immediate release~~

serves

~~separate~~ communities in Wisconsin, Iowa, and Illinois,

~~with top-grade telephone service,~~ ~~announced today the~~

~~completion of a three-year program of improvements which~~

~~have provided vastly expanded telephone services to the~~

~~three state area.~~

R. J. Dialtone, president, ~~of the far-flung firm,~~

~~announced today that the tremendous expansion in the~~

~~company's operations brought about during the three-~~

~~year period had been a major contribution to tremendous~~

~~forward strides made in the Middle West by private in-~~

~~dustry in that time.~~

said

~~He further added that~~ the company's costs have

skyrocketed in recent years. ~~Specifically,~~ he said

labor costs have increased 13% *and* ~~in the last two years~~

Materials costs, ~~following the familiar pattern, have~~

~~increased~~ 19% in the same period.

Despite

~~Meanwhile, and in spite of~~ mounting costs, Mr.

said,

Dialtone ~~declared,~~ the company, ~~by a herculean effort~~

~~has managed to extend its services materially.~~

~~Specifically, he cited the undeniable fact that the~~

~~company~~ had installed direct-distance dialing equip-

ment in 17 localities in the last two years and ~~had~~

replaced outmoded central office equipment in 21 others.

~~localities.~~

⌐"Something has got to give,‿" he ~~averred~~ *said* "‿The company's financial position will be seriously endangered unless redress is granted.‿ #⫿

The beginning editor is inclined to be overwary of handouts or other stories containing favorable mention of commercial interests. But he soon learns to temper his suspicions with a balanced philosophy of his work. His purpose is to tell the news and only the news. Of course he will reject any efforts to point up commercial angles. But just as he will tell the news even though it may have an ill effect on someone—within the boundaries permitted by the laws of libel, of course, including trade libel (see Chapter 14)—so will he tell the news when it may have a favorable effect for someone.

Recasting a story on the basis of news values often means simply giving it a proper *regional* perspective. This often happens to wire stories, and it is not surprising that it should. The wire services pay as much attention as they can to regional needs, as we have seen in Chapter 3. But they must necessarily leave much of the local angling to the newsrooms of the papers they serve. Consequently, when Wisconsin members received the following story, they gave it a stronger regional treatment:

MIAMI, Fla., Feb. 17—(XP)—Police today reported the shooting of a 21 year old unemployed grocery clerk by the proprietor of a liquor store.

Albert E. Marshall of Kenosha, Wis., died an hour after he was wounded early today.

Tom B. Fay, 50, the liquor store owner, told officers Marshall entered his store and said: "Give it to me."

The proprietor replied: "Okay, here it is" and shot him. The holdup man fired at Fay, wounding him in the arm.

No charge was placed against Fay.

Marshall was wanted in Kenosha on warrants charging two robberies last Nov. 16, one in Kenosha County and another in Racine County.

The lazy way would have been simply to set paragraph 2 in boldface. The more careful desk would have recast the whole story with a few pencil marks:

MIAMI, Fla., Feb. 17 — (XP) — Police today reported the fatal shooting of an unemployed grocery clerk from Kenosha, Wis.

Albert E. Marshall, 21, died an hour after he was wounded early today by Tom B. Fay, 50, a liquor store owner.

Fay told officers Marshall entered his store and said: "Give it to me."

The proprietor replied: "Okay, here it is," and shot him. The holdup man fired at Fay, wounding him in the arm.

No charge was placed against Fay.

Marshall was wanted in Kenosha on warrants charging two robberies last November 16, one in Kenosha County and another in Racine County.

This by no means exhausts the possible ways editors can serve meaning by extensive rebuilding. The beginning editor may well be cautioned, however, not to be too bold with the scissors and paste. Extensive restructuring is time-consuming, especially for the novice, and it demands a grasp of not only the full scope of the story but also its details. Many a story has been ruined by inattention to detail in the rebuilding process. Details, perhaps even more than story organization, are the ingredients of meaning. Overlooked or misplaced, they can defeat the editor's purpose.

Combatting Bias

Only a decade or so ago, newsmen agreed that objectivity was the cornerstone of American journalism. Today this proposition is under attack and reexamination. To some critics it is the curse of American journalism, to others a meaningless piece of self-deception, and to still others a worthy but unattainable goal. The student must therefore not expect neat answers to the question "What can be done to copy to make it objective?" And he must bear in mind that what is said about objectivity here may be an amusing anachronism a few years from now.

The basis for objectivity as the solution to a series of contemporary problems in journalism may be traced to the same origins as constitutional protection of a free press. Free spirits like John Milton, protesting an intolerable censorship, argued that the search for truth should be the sole basis for determining what may be said or reported. They contended that only in a free marketplace of ideas, to which every truth seeker should have access, can the truth come to be known. Legitimate authority's only control over the process should be to guarantee that the conditions for a free exchange of information and ideas will be maintained. Each man, "not intending to mislead, but seeking to enlighten others with what his own reason and conscience, however erroneously, have dictated to him as truth, may address himself to the universal reason,"[23] as Lord Erskine put it in his defense of Thomas Paine.

To Paine himself, freedom of the press meant that he could utter and publish his radical views of the crown in particular and governance in general so that his ideas would carry beyond the limits of his own voice. He left England, in fact, when it became clear that such freedom did not really exist there. The fears of the British kings, in repressing his utterances, were confirmed when he came to the Colonies, for his utterances probably helped to bring about the American revolution and influence the content of the first article in the new nation's bill of rights, which established press freedom along with freedom of speech and conscience.

The young nation then was subjected to some of the pains that accompany freedom. The untrammeled press of the new democracy became precisely what the free-marketplace idea had contemplated—untamed

---

[23] *Rex* v. *Paine*, Howell's *State Trials* 22:357 (1792).

and sometimes unreasoning advocacy. The political parties supported organs which poured forth invective against their opponents, and the era came to be known as the era of the scurrilous partisan press. In their zeal, editors often forgot that the point of the free-marketplace principle is to allow truth to surface.

Such a press system required a great deal of the reader, who had to work hard at "getting both sides" and "making up his own mind." The partisan press gave way, in time, to the enterprise press, which had a somewhat different rationale. Instead of being subsidized by the parties to advance a particular point of view, it offered its product to the public for a modest price; the more people willing to pay the price, the more successful it deserved to be. And, not at all incidentally, the more readers it had, the greater its value to the advertiser. Newspapers now competed for readers rather than in a contest of viewpoints.

The clash of ideas was still there in two forms. In keeping with partisan traditions, newspapers at first acknowledged a basic loyalty to a party. But now, rather than serving as a hired advocate giving blind allegiance to the party in return for a subsidy, newspapers became an influence and a force to be reckoned with in party circles. Two critical distinctions in the content of the newspaper were necessary: the distinction between the part of the paper that was privately subsidized and the part that was not, and the distinction between the part of the paper that gave information and the part that gave the paper's own opinions concerning what to believe or what to do about that information.

But how could the reader make the distinctions? How could he tell what was being given him as an unbiased account of what others were saying and what was not? In a series of newswriting conventions, the papers themselves set the standard to tell the facts and only the facts about what others were saying and advocating in the information columns, to reserve the editorial columns for advocacy on behalf of the newspaper itself, and to make degree of objectivity manifest in the way the story was written.

Thus the newspaper became more a common carrier for the ideas of others and less an advocate on its own account. Over the years the party label became less important and more equivocal. Even names were changed, reflecting the trend away from being openly and proudly partisan: the *Independent Republican,* for example, finally became the *Independent.*

At about the same time, the development of the cooperative news-gathering agencies to provide broader coverage of the news of the world at a shared cost may have contributed to the institutionalizing of what was already happening. For them, manifest objectivity was, like honesty, the best policy, because they had to provide news that was acceptable to newspapers of many differing political and ideological persuasions. It appears that the wire services diffused rather than invented the objective news report.

What resulted has been called the "responsible" press. The newspaper was responsible to its own conscience for the opinions it expressed and responsible to the community at large for giving an honest and unbiased (that is to say objective) account of events. The new responsibility was consistent with the newspaper's function as an independent "watchdog" of the processes of government. Its role had changed from being a mouthpiece of a regime or its loyal opposition to an independent check on all branches of government responsible to its readers alone.

The enterprise press was a huge success. From circulations of a few thousand among people already sympathetic to its point of view, the newspaper became a truly mass medium. The process spread over decades, from the dawning of the "penny press" in the 1830's to the "yellow press" beginning in the late nineteenth century when circulations began to soar into the millions. It continues into the present, although other mass media have intervened and circulations have stabilized: it is no longer all things to all people. Its success and its new character as a mass medium has raised a whole new series of problems.

The newspapers that survived the rough-and-tumble search for the mass audience all tended to share one characteristic: they were very large business enterprises, headed not by crotchety editors dedicated to what conscience told them were the most defensible opinions on public issues but by publishers out to make them a financial success. Unbiased, objective reporting helped make that success, so publishers be-

came the stoutest advocates of objective reporting. But people began to wonder whether the publisher could be relied on to permit the truth to be told in every circumstance, including those which threatened the business community that accounted for most of the advertising in the paper. It may be true that the far-sighted publisher who lost the advertising account now and then in order to keep on telling the truth to the extent that competent professionals could discover it was the publisher who tended to be the survivor. Put another way, economic strength provided the firmest basis for dealing with temptation. And economic strength was sometimes purchased through consolidation. In somewhat simplified terms, a responsible press emerged at the price of a competitive press. A single common carrier tended to replace the clash of competitive ideas in the free marketplace.

Another consequence of success was the tendency for the newspaper to become firmly entrenched as part of the Establishment (Horace Greeley never made it, but John S. Knight did). Its publishers were primarily upper-middle class, its reporters drawn from the middle class. Can a newspaper remain unbiased under these circumstances? Politicians have found it easy to call attention to the "one-party press," especially when they seek office for the other party. But they may be missing the mark. At least as persistent as the tendency for newspapers increasingly to prefer the more conservative candidate is the tendency to take no public stand whatever. With it has gone a tendency to offer even on the editorial page a wide choice of advocates—something for everyone instead of (or in addition to) a carefully researched and judiciously reasoned point of view of its own. Thus the mass medium has become ever more the common carrier of the ideas of others and less a trumpeter of its own. In fact, as competition declined, the proprietors of the surviving dailies felt an increased responsibility to be objective: Was it right for them to be advocates at all, since no other advocate was in quite so fortunate a position? Since other voices had been stilled, would it not be fairer for them to be common carriers rather than advocates?

And so objectivity is coming under attack. It is argued that objectivity is a sham, for it yields only the shadow, not the substance, of an unbiased report; it substitutes careful attribution for careful knowledge; objectivity is a human impossibility, in any case: no man can control his biases by an effort of will. It is argued that the traditional objective news report requires the reporter to deal only with the surface of things, that its strictures prevent him from searching out causes, from revealing latent relationships. Its basic problem is, then, that it has failed to bring about the goals of its own creed. Its failure is not, according to its critics, one of conscious or unconscious bias; it is a failure to combat falsity with truth. Under the rules of objective reporting, the reporter, the argument goes, cannot tell what he knows, only what he saw and heard, or a carefully attributed account of what someone else believes he saw and heard. He cannot correct the false impression created by what shows on the surface of events by using his professionally founded ability to go beneath the surface of events. He can quote the senator in what he knows to be a lie but may not say it's a lie and why he knows it is.

But, says the defender of the creed of objectivity, isn't this just another way of saying that the reporter should be an oracle, not a professional observer? That he deserves the right to give his own version of the truth as if it were the truth? Is there really any difference between "depth reporting" and opinion giving? Whatever the merits of this argument, it appears that many an arid tradition in news writing is being observed in the breach, replaced by the force of the work of good reporters who know how to stay within the old rules of the game but who write a much better story when they are freed from the rules. Manifest objectivity is among these rules. So is the who-what-when-where-why lead and the strictly inverted-pyramid structure. These forms are not gone, they are simply being replaced when under the circumstances a better story is possible without them.

The best evidence of this is to be found in the by-lined, staff-written stories in a dozen or so of the best American newspapers. Under his by-line, the reporter who has earned the right is free to conjecture about the facts, not just give them. He does not replace facts with his conjectures about them, he simply adds something to them, a thoughtful idea of what they may add up to or where they are leading us. Instead of winning the credibility of the reader by convincing him that he is giving only the facts, he wins his respect by a spirit of detachment and reason.

What complicates life for the editor is that he can no longer apply such simple rules as careful attribution. Instead he must ask himself whether the nature of the story perhaps does not permit or the writer require that the story be subjected to this type of test. When the reporter is using his skills to observe and evoke events, when he shows that he can translate what he has observed into a full, rounded, human account of some aspect of an event that will evoke the experience for the reader, he can convey a deeper meaning than he ever could by a mere recital of the facts of the case. Then, in fairness to the writer and in responsibility to the reader, the editor must read such copy on its own terms and not in response to the rigid creed of manifest objectivity. He now must substitute wise judgment for a set of unspoken but unambiguous rules. He must still protect the writer from his own folly, but not by insisting that he maintain strict objectivity—not, at least, if doing so will cut the heart out of the story.

Manifest objectivity is not dead. By and large, the wire services for good reason still depend on the hallowed traditions of the straight news story, unbiased in its selection of the facts, objective in its choice of words, detached in its conception of the problem being reported, nonpartisan in every respect, balanced in its treatment of competing ideas. When it makes departures, it gives clear signals that it is doing so. For example, it labels interpretive stories as "situationers" and it uses by-lines on stories which contain any sign of departure from observable facts.

And manifest objectivity is still the order of the day in the routine news story. We may in effect take sides on the issue of poverty; we do not and must not take sides when the news is of pending court cases, of highway accidents, of the day-to-day give-and-take of political campaign oratory, in reports of public meetings, and the like. If the story contains portents of more important issues we can send a reporter out later to find out and tell what it means in a fully rounded, thorough, detailed, dispassionate but not necessarily objective analysis of the problem.

In other words, newspapers no longer are satisfied to confine reports of the human condition to accounts of events. They also do analyses of situations, investigations of problems, studies of issues. The editor has to develop criteria for keeping the reporter within the bounds of analysis. He cannot let him stray into simple opinion. He must still watch for signs of personal bias and deal with it ruthlessly. He must watch for the "company man" who thinks the way to get ahead is to give the story the twist he thinks would please the publisher. He must be more watchful than ever before for the carelessly understood fact, judgment masquerading as fact, shoddy treatment of quotations. And he must judge whether the facts warrant the conclusions reached, whether alternative ex-

planations have been explored, whether the logic used to get from fact to conclusion is defensible, and so on. There have always been "sacred cows" in the newsroom, a source of bias of which any good newsman is properly ashamed, for they are unjustified by any defensible theory of the journalist's public trust: the "business-office must," the publisher's pet peeve, the front-page promotion. But the interpretive news story must not be allowed to become the new sacred cow. When the writer has been given more freedom to wonder, to speculate, to search, to interpret, even to draw conclusions, the editor's function is even more important. Just as the reporter has the freedom to search below the surface of events, the editor must have the freedom to search below the surface of the writer's words. The editor's function is thus increased, not diminished, by this new kind of journalism, and his responsibility to his readers made even heavier.

6

Headline Fundamentals

The construction of headlines is one of the most challenging copy-desk jobs. In summarizing accurately the key facts of a complex story in a limited space, the headline writer must be a consummate artist. This is one genuinely creative skill of the copy editor, and it is becoming more so as headlines increasingly depart from traditional molds and strict rules. The successful editor takes a craftman's pride in his headline. This is true even though his successes are little noticed (except for the occasional self-conscious feature head) and his failures are spread before the public in display type.

The Purpose of Headlines

What are headlines for? What function do they perform? Do we cling to them as a tradition or do they serve a real purpose? Let's examine these questions from the standpoint of the reader.

The first newspaper in the United States had no headlines. In a sense, the nameplate came as close to being a headline as anything else it contained. It read: "PUBLICK OCCURRENCES, Both Forreign and Domestick." At best it was a "label" head. The colonial of that day, if he could read at all, could be counted on to read his little "Publick Occurrences" from the first word to the last. There was little news and any news was eagerly sought. Hence, the reader needed no help in finding what parts of the news interested him.

The same could not be said for today's reader of, let us say, the Milwaukee *Sunday Journal.* It would take him hours, if not days, to read the paper from front to back. Unlike the lady who called the New York *Times,* it never occurs to him to do so. The lady who called the *Times,* the very possibly apocryphal story goes, called to make a minor complaint. During the conversation it turned out that she read the *Times* from beginning to end every day. "Doesn't everyone?" No, dear lady, most of us, not having that kind of time, use the headlines to guide us to stories in which we are interested and to steer us away from stories that are of marginal or no interest to us. This is the *indexing* function of the headline and it suggests the first requirement of a good headline—it should state plainly what the story contains.

But the second principal function of the newspaper headline is even more important: *it must convey accurate information* for the "headline scanner," the person who gets all or most of his information on current affairs from the headlines only. Although we have no way of knowing—yet—just how numerous this breed is, newspaper-readership studies tend to support the notion that they are many indeed.

Thus it is clear that the headline has both of these prime functions:

1. To *index the news* to save the reader's time in finding the parts of the news that interest him most.

2. To *tell the news* to the reader of headlines alone.

The headline has other jobs to perform, too. Among them are these:

3. To convey to the reader the relative *significance* of the news. News significance is expressed in terms of type display—the relative size and weight of headline used—and is decided on by the editor, on the basis of his own expert opinion of a story's value.

4. To convey to the reader the relative *seriousness* of the news. Italics and various decorative typographical devices such as boxes, star dashes, etc., indicate that a story is primarily included for its entertainment value rather than its significance.

5. To make the newspaper *attractive*. The headline in all its various forms is essential to assembling eye-catching, balanced pages.

6. To give the newspaper *character and stability*. The consistent use of familiar headline structures gives the newspaper a relatively familiar and welcome personality.

7. To a far lesser degree to *sell newspapers* on the stands. In the days when several newspapers were competing in one city, front pages were made over several times a day, each with a new banner head, to attract attention. Since newspapers were sold with just the top of the paper showing, the crowd-stopper headline across the top of the page, preferably in red ink, was depended on to sell the paper to a large segment of the potential audience. But with the decline in competition among newspapers in the same cycle and a steady increase in the costs of making over, these practices have pretty much gone the way of the "extra" that newsboys once cried in the streets.

Headline Defined

The term "headline" has pretty much the same meaning from one newspaper to another but is often confused by the public. Any line or collection of lines of display type that precedes a story and summarizes or introduces it can be called a headline. Some people use the term incorrectly to apply only to the "banner line" across the top of Page One. Others incorrectly use it to apply only to the top unit of a series of "decks" in a headline. But all its parts add up to a single headline. A head of two or more decks is still one headline.

The generic term "headline" includes many specialized types, including "jump heads," "kickers," and subheads, all discussed in more detail later in this chapter. But they should not be confused with "cut captions" and "binders." A line or more of type above and directly related to a picture is a cut caption and is not properly called a headline, although under special circumstances a single headline can serve both functions. A "binder" is a display line identifying but not summarizing special material not handled as a news story. Binders are commonly used over full texts of speeches. Thus the binder "Text of the President's State of the Union Message" identifies the material below, but it does not tell what happened, as would a headline which began "President Asks Congress . . . ." Binders are also used over tabular matter accompanying a related news story.

Although headline-writing practices vary from newspaper to newspaper within a small range of differences, newspaper headlines tend to have five obvious distinguishing characteristics.

1. Headlines are sentences, built around action verbs. But

2. They must be adjusted to a predetermined space and typographical style. Hence,

3. They are "skeletonized" to save space. Omitting articles and other unnecessary encumbrances leaves room for more detail in the restricted space headlines are allowed. But more importantly, skeletonizing contributes to a sense of urgency, the rationale being that no words should be wasted in getting the latest intelligence to the readers as quickly as possible. Even though today's increased freedom in shaping and presenting stories has correspondingly given the headline writer greater freedom from strict skeletonization, especially when the feeling tone of the story is relaxed, the basic norm today is still the skeleton form.

4. They use the present tense to convey immediacy and also to save space: usually present-tense forms of verbs are shorter than past.

5. Usually they are set in the style of titles, that is, all principal words are capitalized. Very recently, a trend away from this style has been discernible in some prominent papers: the Louisville *Courier-Journal,* for example, has made the change. It is reasoned that since good headlines should read as good sentences, not good titles, the first word and proper nouns only should be capitalized.

The Head Schedule

Before turning to the creative techniques of headline writing, it will be well to discuss the mechanics of the head schedule, for it is the restricted typographical structure of the headline that governs its construction. For the most part, any newspaper sticks to an established *head schedule,* a sample of all the headlines used on a particular newspaper. It shows the precise forms they must take and it is relatively inflexible.

The news editor increasingly may put together a special headline to meet a special set of circumstances, but he does so with great care. He must make such a headline enough different from the regular ones to give the story the special attention it deserves but he must be sure not to depart so radically from the basic head schedule as to clash with the established character or "personality" of the newspaper. The news editor may also occasionally change to a different headline designation on a story because a good headline will be hard to write if he does not do so. But apart from these occasional exceptions, the head writer has no option to write whatever head gives him the best break. He must somehow tell the story within the precise limits of the headline assigned.

History of Headline Typography

From the typographical standpoint, the headline has an interesting history. With an occasional exception, headlines were essentially labels until intensive and widespread reading of Civil War news forced some changes. Until that time, a single crossline was used to title—or label—a news story. Now, rather than read long dispatches in the pedestrian style of the period, readers demanded news in their headlines. The solution at first was more crossline labels:

LATER FROM CHARLESTON.

★ ★ ★

ARRIVAL OF THE ARAGO.

—

Bombardment of Sumter
Still Progressing.

—

The Capture of Charleston
Problematical.

—

RENEWED REBEL DESERTIONS.

All these decks are still labels; they are not sentences built around verbs. They tend to signify the scope of the story without really telling it. But the seeds of the inverted-pyramid headline, reflecting the inverted-pyramid form of a story, were sown in headlines like this. Probably without realizing it, the printers set their longer crosslines on two lines, centering both, with the bottom one shorter. The top deck, however, was always of one line, centered.

That form persisted until the 1880's, when the "stepped" or "dropline" head first appeared. The circulation war between William Randolph Hearst and Joseph Pulitzer can be credited with the experimentation in headline forms that characterized the Spanish-American War era, during which a quite standard headline form evolved. It consisted of two, three, and even four lines, "stepped" to the right, followed by a series of secondary heads usually taking the form of an inverted-pyramid two- or three-liner, followed by a single crossline or perhaps a stepped two-liner, then another pyramid-style three-liner. To this day the New York *Times* uses a somewhat abridged version of this form on all its major front-page heads:

PRESIDENT URGES AID TO INDUSTRIES HURT BY IMPORTS

Offers Legislation and Says He Favors Continuation of 'Policy of Freer Trade'

TO NAME A STUDY PANEL

Re-examination of Nation's Objectives Sought as Basis for Long-Range Plans

New York Times

There were some variants, notably the full-line top deck and the "hanging-indention" secondary deck. The full-line head is still in daily use on the Washington *Evening Star:*

Hearings Start On Expanding Preschool Aid

Washington Evening Star

The hanging indention is hard to find these days. It was a favorite of the late New York *Herald Tribune* before it modernized its format. With it went a two-line full-line crossline:

Truman, Hopeful to Last, Got Senate to Put Off Anti-Strike Legislation

Raise Was Offered, But No Union Shop

New York Herald Tribune

The hanging indention and the crossline are not altogether dead, however. The *Wall Street Journal,* which is sleek, modern, and low-key, combines them with a flush-left top deck to which is added a "kicker," as seen on the next page.

Stubborn Germs

Increasing Resistance Of Bacteria to Drugs Causes New Concern

Cells Are Found Able to Pass Immunity to One Another; Most Drugs Are Affected

'Like a Science-Fiction Story'

Wall Street Journal

If there is a standard today, it is the flush-left head. And when it carries a second deck, which it often does, the second deck usually is a flush indention (indented at the left, all lines aligning at the left) in smaller type. These are shown in the following illustration:

City Establishes Laboratory to Spot Dutch Elm Blight

Entomologist Also Named By Parks Department in Fight to Save the Trees; Survey to Be Launched

Buffalo Evening News

However, the four-line deck shown here is giving way to three-liners, two-liners, and even one-liners as the trend continues to limit the details covered in the headlines:

Soviets Reject Protests

Call Reaction To Sentences 'Fit of Hysteria'

'One-Vote' Machines Pass Test

OK'd for Friday's Special Election

A decade or so ago, the "kicker" or overline was a daring innovation. Today it is almost as standard as the flush-left head; in fact, some newspapers use it on nearly every major headline. The illustration below is typical of the kicker head in its earliest and simplest form. Note that the kicker is set in italic type and is underscored.

Tonight and Tomorrow

Many Thanksgiving Services Scheduled

The relationship of one deck to another has been freed from traditional constraints, and experimentation with even bolder and more dramatic ways of presenting the news by means of display type is going on constantly. Some idea of the current variations may be seen on page 146.

These headlines reflect only in part the revolution in headline structures; they reflect at least as much changes in approach to makeup, a subject which will be discussed in Chapters 10 and 11. As headlines, they have certain interesting features, all of which are built on a new assumption about the function of the headline: they are meant to be "taken in"—absorbed —not read. When the editors of the old New York *Herald* used twenty-four decks to tell the story of Lincoln's assassination, they must have assumed the reader was going to read them. But evidence that newspaper readers *consult* a headline, rather than read it, before deciding to go down into the 8-point type of the story led to some of the changes apparent in the array of modern headline forms illustrated on page 146. Editors began to try to attract readers to the story. The heavy use of white space, once regarded in the newsroom as sinful, is obviously intended to attract attention to the head and to make its appearance pleasing. Not shown here is another innovation in headline typography: color. Increasingly editors are using a color other than black to draw attention to heads.

Counting the Head

But no matter what form it takes, the headline must still fit the space to which it is assigned. New forms merely add new complications to the process. Constructing headlines that tell the story and also fit the space requires not only patience and flexibility, but the ability to predict whether a given line will "go" (can be fitted into the required space). Consequently, every line must be "counted."

There are no sure-fire or universally accepted counting systems. A head writer can adopt any system that suits him—and works—when applied to a particular head schedule. If he bats about .950 with it, it will serve him well. Some editors write headlines on the typewriter, counting the characters and spaces on the scale below the platen and allowing mentally for fat and thin letters. Most editors prefer to use pencil and paper and a count system that automatically takes differences in the widths of letters into account. A typical system goes like this:

Count all small letters 1 except *l, i, f, t,* which count ½, and *m* and *w,* which count 1½.

Count all capital letters 1½ except *I,* which counts ½, and *M* and *W,* which count 2.

Count all punctuation marks ½ except the dash, question mark, dollar sign, and per cent sign, which count 1.

Count all figures 1.

Count all spaces 1.

Such a system, of course, would apply only to heads set in caps and lower-case letters.

A similar system for all-cap heads would go like this:

Count all letters 1 except *M* and *W,* which count 1½.

Count all punctuation marks ½.

Count all figures 1.

Count all spaces ½.

Hedging the count   Plainly, no system will meet all situations invariably. The same letters in different typefaces differ from each other in relative width. Thus in Erbar, a modern sans-serif type, the *r* occupies relatively less space than the *r* in Bodoni. Consequently, the head writer must adopt "hedging" tactics. In using the caps-and-lower-case count system above, he knows that the presence of a lot of lower-case *r*'s in an Erbar line will make it shorter than his count, since that letter is relatively thinner than others that count 1. He also knows that figures will make a line longer than his estimates, since they are relatively wider than other letters that count 1. He knows, too, that a line that contains many half-count characters may be fatter than his count indicates, since these actually tend to be a little wider than half the width of most 1-unit characters.

In addition, the number of spaces in the line may affect its length. In hot-metal type-casting systems, the compositor generally uses space bands between words in a headline. In order to justify the margins of a line, he can make spaces wider by hand spacing or thinner by using thinner space bands. In cold-type systems, the

Today (Cocoa, Florida)

DR. EGEBERG

EGEBERG'S ADVICE: Penalty's Worse Than the Crime

Nixon: Soften Pot Laws

Bridge to controversy

Conservationists challenge political power
in Washington's 'Three Sisters' confrontation

Christian Science Monitor

Tools of the Trade

Moonbound? Don't Forget Hammer, Brush

Milwaukee Journal

Cincinnati Enquirer

FEAR GENETIC TAMPERING

Harvard Scientists Isolate Gene

Louisville Times

"The list is a bad, bad area for us . . . It's
a real never-never land for regulation."

—an FDA official

"Unfortunately, the definition of 'everybody
knows' (additives are safe) seems to be unclear . . ."

—Medical School official

680 Food Additives Sold Without Tests

Louisville Times

Challenged by criticism
of its facilities and standards,
students and faculty defend . . .

The Law School's Case

A Lovin' Swinger

Sam the kinkajou looks for a new pad

Louisville Times

Ulster hope

Peace prospect survives
—if troops keep lid on

Christian Science Monitor

details differ but the principle is the same. All this means that a space may occupy more or less room than the head writer figured when he counted his spaces 1 or half a unit. Hence, when a line seems slightly long but might go, a large number of spaces may mean it will go, because the compositor can use thins instead of fat space bands; a smaller number of spaces means that it will not.

How much leeway? Given that the headline writer has developed a pretty foolproof count system, how much leeway may he purposefully take in making lines go? He will soon find out that the compositor can go just so far in "squeezing" a long line by reducing the space between words. Beyond a certain point, reduction in word spacing produces a line that is all but unreadable. And because, as the newsroom saying goes, "type is not made of rubber," there is an absolute limit to the number of characters that can be squeezed into a line.

Beyond that, there are various factors governing leeway in head count. First is the form of the head. In the days of stepped and full-line heads, variation from line to line could not be greater than about a unit in a head with a 12-unit maximum or perhaps 1½ units where the maximum was around 20 units, the extent of the allowable variation depending on how particular the newspaper was about the appearance of its headlines. Flush-left heads allow a variation of 2 or more units, depending on where the variation appears. Three units is not too much when it is in the middle line of three and is longer or shorter than the other two. But a variation of even 2 units can be conspicuous in the first or last line of a three-line head.

Headline readability depends in part on even spacing. How much this can be sacrificed in order to shoehorn in a long line or stretch a short one depends on the paper's (and the editor's) standards.

Writing Skills

Writing good headlines is a skill with a very high ceiling. Nobody ever achieves perfection. But more than that, it is a skill basic to communications and as such deserves as careful attention from journalism students who do not plan to enter newspaper work as from those who do. The headline uses a minimum of language symbols to convey a maximum of meaning.

Headline writing does not (or should not) use "a language of its own." Headlines must use language symbols people can understand. The extent to which a headline does seem to have its own language is a measure of its failure as plain, everyday language.

The beginner can profit from understanding this point. He must broaden and deepen his headline vocabulary—but in the words people use and understand. He must pay more attention than ever to both denotations and connotations of words, and examine the words he uses for their exact meaning and for special meanings in the light of their immediate context.

In other words, headline writing imposes a new discipline on the copy editor that can help sharpen his communication skill. And despite its specialized nature, it can help any journalism student improve his general skill as a dealer in words, whether or not he sees the copy desk as his future occupation. In addition, it has many direct applications in such fields as advertising, public relations, trade journals and house publications, magazine editing, etc.

Writing a good headline involves more than simply learning a bag of tricks about the headline count and an accumulating reservoir of trick words that are short. "Flay," "flout," "nab," "hit," "fete," "count," "slap," "peg," "lid," "tiff," "rap," "check," "cite," and the rest are sometimes useful, but they are no substitute for a vocabulary. Some of the basic skills that point to success in head writing are these:

1. *Accurate perception of the story.* Naturally, this is the first on the list. If the head writer cannot see the story clearly and stripped down to its essentials, he will miss the point and the head will probably be misleading. He must be able to recognize what parts of the story are newsworthy, dramatic, significant, and new.

2. *A vocabulary that is both broad and deep.* The

layman's vocabulary is not sufficient to the head writer's task. Constructing sentences within the strictures of the headline requires not just a vocabulary of many words, but knowledge of their precise meanings and connotations and which ones may and may not be used synonymously.

3. *A sharp sense of sentence structure.* Headlines are stripped-down sentences. Sentences take many structures. The head writer depends on flexibility not only in choice of words but in choice of sentence structures (see pages 150–151) so that he can switch word order quickly without damaging meaning.

4. *A keen eye for ambiguity.* The head writer must review his work endlessly to detect ambiguities. He must be able to put himself in the place of many potential readers. What is meaningful and clear to him may not be to others.

Naturally, these are very generalized descriptions of head-writing skills. But before getting into a more specific catalogue of maxims and rules, it will be well to have an example to proceed from. Let's trace the steps one editor took in writing a headline. The story was destined for Page One. It went like this:

> Officials of the city's Department of Social Services disclosed yesterday that they had decided to require narcotics addicts to become affiliated with a rehabilitative program before they will be accepted for welfare assistance.

The slot man had called for a "No. 3" head—two all-cap lines with a maximum count of 16 units each, and three cap-and-lower-case lines in the form of a pyramid with a first-line maximum count of 26.

In headline terms, the story says:

CITY TO REQUIRE ADDICTS
TO SEEK TREATMENT

But this is obviously too long:

$$C \quad I \quad T \quad Y \quad \quad T \quad O \quad \quad R \quad E \quad Q \quad U \quad I \quad R \quad E \quad \quad A \quad D \quad D \quad I \quad C \quad T \quad S$$
$$1\tfrac{1}{2}\,1\,1\,1\,1\,1\,1\,1\,1\,1\,1\,1\tfrac{1}{2}\,1\,1\,1\,1\,1\,1\tfrac{1}{2}\,1\,1\,1 \quad = \quad 20\tfrac{1}{2}$$

"CITY TO REQUIRE," however, falls within the prescribed limits:

C I T Y   T O   R E Q U I R E
A D D I C T S   T O   ? ? ? ?

Obviously, "SEEK TREATMENT" won't fit into the space left. After trying this and that, the head writer goes back to the story and sees that he can change his angle: new restrictions are being placed on addicts who seek support through public welfare. He has a new word that fits about the same space as "REQUIRE":

$$C \quad I \quad T \quad Y \quad \quad T \quad O \quad \quad R \quad E \quad S \quad T \quad R \quad I \quad C \quad T$$
$$1\tfrac{1}{2}\,1\,1\,1\,1\,1\,1\,1\,1\,1\,1\,1\tfrac{1}{2}\,1\,1 \quad = \quad 15$$

Now—what is being restricted?

```
A   I   D     F   O   R     A   D   D   I   C   T   S
1  ½  1  1  1  1  1  1  1  1  1  ½  1  1  1    =    14
```

But now that the top head emphasizes the restriction on aid, what must be dealt with in the second deck? The editor has said neither what kind of aid nor how the aid will be restricted. Soon he has this second deck:

```
W  e  l  f  a  r  e     R  u  l  e     t  o     R  e  q  u  i  r  e
2  1  ½  ½  1  1  1  1  1½ 1  ½  1  1  ½  1  1  1½ 1  1  1  ½  1  1   =   22½
```

A little short. But he has an easy answer for that one:

```
W  e  l  f  a  r  e     R  u  l  e     W  i  l  l     R  e  q  u  i  r  e
2  1  ½  ½  1  1  1  1  1½ 1  ½  1  1  2  ½  ½  ½  11½ 1  1  1  ½  1  1  = 24½
```

The rest goes down without a hitch.

```
P  r  o  o  f     T  h  a  t     t  h  e     R  e  c  i  p  i  e  n  t   =  22½
I  s     S  e  e  k  i  n  g     T  r  e  a  t  m  e  n  t               =  19½
```

An ideal headline for this story. Its meaning is plain to the reader who seeks only the top two lines but even clearer and more detailed for the reader who goes on. And the count worked for the typographical form:

CITY TO RESTRICT
AID FOR ADDICTS

Welfare Rule Will Require
Proof That the Recipient
Is Seeking Treatment

New York Times

Of course, experienced head writers don't write down the count for each character and then add them up, as shown in this illustration. They develop ways of speeding up the process. Some count the characters and then scan the line for characters that count more or less than one, adjusting their count accordingly. Another system is to count each character as one but skip every other half-unit character, or count a unit-and-a-half character as two and skip a corresponding half-unit character.

A Few Tricks

There are more tricks to fitting a headline that tells the story into the available space than can possibly be described here. A few of them will be discussed, however, in the hope that they will put the tyro on the right track toward developing his own tricks.

The top of any headline must be able to stand alone—it must convey meaning without requiring the reader to go on to the second deck. It will not meet good newsroom standards if it depends on the rest of the headline or the lead to make sense. The temptation for the beginner is to write a line at a time. But an acceptable first line will not necessarily allow the whole story to be told in the space that remains. The old-timer would counsel him to *look at the first deck as a whole* and start over.

In the example on pages 148–149, note that the writer had the entire story in mind as he tried the first deck. He therefore composed the entire top deck before counting any one line. Still looking at the *whole deck,* he made the changes that would bring the full story into the space limits. Then he examined the effect and asked himself: Does this give the whole picture? Or are other angles to the story essential to this first telling? This check resulted in another effort that brought the whole story into focus.

Many editors prefer to write the entire headline whole, rather than deck by deck. Some headlines lend themselves to this approach better than others. Here is a typical (and actual) case. The story told of a new outbreak of violence in Belgium as a result of Leopold's efforts to resume the throne. A plan to abdicate in favor of his son developed complications. The head designated by the rim man was to include a flush-left top deck with a maximum line count of 15 units and an indented second deck of two lines with a maximum count of 18. This is the way the head writer put it down the first time:

```
New Belgian
Rioting Threatens
    Hitch Develops
    in Abdication Pact
```

There was no question that this headline told the story. But it was clear without even counting that these original lines wouldn't go. The first line is short (11½ units); the second, long (16). The first line of the second deck could be as short as this one (13½) only if the other (16½) is also short. And not more than two units should separate the paired lines, especially since the head is destined for a conspicuous spot on Page One.

Now to make them line up. The usual first step is to look at the long line: Can it be shortened? And at the short line: Can it be lengthened? For instance, the editor might have made the top deck read:

```
Another Belgian   14½
Riot Threatens    12½
```

This meets the space requirements. But it isn't much of a head. "Rioting" is preferable to "Riot" because the violence was shaping up in several cities, and hence was not *a* riot. "New" is a crisper, more expressive word than "Another." Furthermore, the total picture conveyed in "New Rioting" is more accurate than "Another Riot."

As it happened, the head writer saw another solution. He worked out a different paired-word combination that would use precisely the materials in the originals but with slight differences in form. He changed "New" to "Anew," "Rioting" to "Violence," and he rearranged the word order:

```
Belgian Violence   15
Threatens Anew     15
```

The second deck was adjusted with another head-writer's device—the line switch. It was apparent that the second line was just as much too long as the word "in." Head writers have ways of getting rid of prepositions by revising word order, like this:

```
Abdication Pact   14
Hitch Develops    13½
```

Both of these "tricks" are not so much trickery as two closely related skills. The first is a ready set of *synonyms;* the second and more important is *structural flexibility,* the ability to shift the materials of the story around in various sentence patterns until a combination of words and structure is found which tells the story precisely in the available space. Below is an illustration of the process of combining them at its simplest level. First try:

> Iowa County Fair
> Names Superintendent

This tells it—it's simple and direct—but it doesn't count. The maximum is 21. The first line counts 16; the second, 20. To the veteran head writer, a fast shift in sentence structure will get the desired count. If he were to reason aloud, he'd say: "I can hold that second line—it counts. It can be either a second line, as it is here, in the active voice, or it can be a first line, in the passive voice: 'Superintendent Named.' That means that a preposition must be added to the first line to make *it* count, too. Since a preposition shouldn't end a line (and one doesn't suggest itself anyway), I'll shift to the passive voice, make the second line the first, and pad with the preposition." The result:

> Superintendent Named   19½
> for Iowa County Fair   20

Sometimes a change of word order does not involve a change in sentence structure. Words in a pair or series can usually be shifted to make adjustments in the count:

> Arms Aid Expansion,   19½
> Speedup Indicated   16

That might go, but the spread in count is pretty wide. Switching the paired words produces:

> Arms Aid Speedup,   18
> Expansion Indicated   17½

This cannot be done to any and every pair or series. It is possible only when the two or more words are equals and have no time-sequence relationship. This switch obviously would not work in this head:

> Budget, Zoning
> Meetings Planned

The budget meeting is clearly more important than the zoning meeting. And it would be ridiculous to switch these:

> Boy, 14, Topples
> into River, Drowns

The logical time sequence would be upset.

As he tries out shifts in sentence structure, the beginner will discover that one is not necessarily as good as another, however. One editor came up with this headline after several tries:

> Discrimination Hit   16
> as Stupid in Schools   19

He had wanted to say:

> Discrimination in Schools   23
> Decried as Stupid   16½

Instead of trying to tell that first line in another way, he settled for a new sentence structure. The result was doubtful, to say the least. Examination of the story showed that the speaker was not implying that discrimination is acceptable elsewhere but stupid when practiced in the schools. Yet that is what the head implies. Had the head writer seen a shorter (and for that matter better) synonym for "Discrimination," he might have come up with this vastly superior head:

> Race Bias in Schools   20
> Described as 'Stupid'   19½

Most editors prefer to copyread the story first, *then* write the head. They reason that they are in a better position to tell the story when they have a full grasp of it. Often the head takes shape naturally in the editor's mind as he reads. Sometimes he stops reading to jot down his headline idea, then checks it after reading the rest of the story. Even though the head is ordinarily written largely from the lead, there are obvious risks in writing it from the lead alone, without study of the story as a whole.

A Few Rules

There are lots of "rules" for headline writing. Some are rules indeed, dictated by common sense or by the need for conforming to office style; others are just guides.

Tell the story's essentials Headlines are usually based on the lead. This is not a rule—just logic. With few exceptions—the delayed-punch feature story, for example—the lead of a straight news story summarizes the essential facts. So must the head. The head writer usually finds his best headline material right at the top of the story.

The parts of the lead that lend themselves best to headline treatment are those that *tell the main aspect of the story most fully.* To recognize the main aspect of the story requires that the editor understand the story, which often requires knowing its background. No other part of his job requires more insistently that he read the news—systematically, habitually, and with understanding.

Even when the editor's grasp of the story is less than encyclopedic, he ferrets out the essentials of the story. He examines the lead from the standpoint of structure: What verb carries the freight? What is the kernel of news that verb advances? This helps to strip the lead of nonessentials. When the sentence is complex, the editor seeks out the verb of the *independent* clause. Even after returning from a newless northwoods fishing trip, the veteran can find the heart of a story in the lead by examining its structure.

Second-day stories particularly require the editor to determine their essentials. They are not the same as first-day stories, even if they do deal with the same event. "Two men held up a Sixth National Bank messenger today and . . ." is a first-day story. "Police said today they will question two suspects in last night's daring holdup . . ." is clearly a second-day story. But obvious as it may appear, beginning head writers often fail to isolate *the part of the story that is new.* They will put a head on the second-day story that goes like this:

```
Two Men Hold Up
Bank Messenger
```

when today's story is quite different:

Two Men Face Quiz
After Holdup Here

The first headline is a fraud on the reader; he can't even be sure from it whether a new holdup has been committed.

The story's essentials are not necessarily its bare facts. Frequently it is the *angle* that turns the routine event into news. Divorces provide an almost daily example. The fact might be:

```
Wife Divorces
Henry X. Jones
```

—a fact of passing or no interest. The story in the case usually lies in the *reasons* for the divorce:

Wife Divorces Dentist
for 'Drill-Like' Snore

Inability of beginners to grasp the feature twist of the story has driven more than one exasperated news editor to write *Editor & Publisher* about it. One unhappy slot man told of the treatment accorded this story:

> Two girls, 15 and 16 years old, were arrested in a local department store Saturday for shoplifting. One of them was the daughter of a minister.
> Among the loot was a Bible . . .

The tyro editor, perhaps having just found out that his job wasn't as complicated as he'd thought it might be, wrote:

```
Girls Apprehended
for Shoplifting
```

The boss could hardly be blamed for preferring:

Minister's Daughter
Nabbed Stealing Bible

The process of stripping the story down to its essentials can be illustrated with this typical story:

> The Federal Power Commission has authorized the Northern Natural Gas Co., which serves this city and some 200 others in five states, to put into effect a $5,200,000 rate increase for wholesale natural gas.
>
> The rate increase, which is approximately 3½ cents per thousand cubic feet, is made retroactive to April 27 . . .

What is the headline material here? "Federal Power Commission" is long for headline purposes but can be stripped down to "FPC." However, it may not be necessary to say *who* authorized the price rise. "Northern Natural Gas Co." is long, too, but can be switched to the generic "Natural Gas Firm" or even "Gas Firm." The details about the extent of the firm's territory are sound lead material but strictly a detail as far as the head in concerned. It takes a lot of space to say "$5,200,000 rate increase," too, but the precise extent of the increase is not necessarily required. It is "rate increase" that is essential here. "Wholesale natural gas" is a detail that might add to the head's meaning. The item "3½ cents per thousand cubic feet" is another expression of the extent of the increase; if space permits, it could help give depth to the head, even though it is complicated by the fact that it is a wholesale figure. The "retroactive" angle is clearly a detail.

Here are the essentials, then: "Natural Gas Firm," "Rate Increase," plus a verb. Depending on the count, these materials could be assembled around an active verb—

```
Natural Gas Firm
Wins Rate Increase
```

—or a passive verb—

```
Natural Gas Firm
Granted Rate Hike
```

Being more specific than that presents difficulties.

```
Gas Firm Granted
3½-Cent Rate Hike
```

specifies the extent of the increase but makes the subject ambiguous; "Gas Firm" might mean a firm making or selling gasoline.

Where the head is more than one deck, the first deck is handled as if it were the only one. Then the second deck is used to broaden the meaning expressed in the first. This may mean simply telling the details next most important—or it may mean filling out a point touched on in the top deck. The same examination that ferreted out the *essentials* for the top deck should serve also to find the best *details* for the second deck:

Natural Gas Firm
Wins Rate Increase

FPC Grants Northern
3½ Cents Wholesale

Here specific detail fills out two facts presented in general terms at the top. "FPC" answers the question "Who granted the increase?" "Northern" answers the question "What natural gas firm?" One new piece of information is provided, too—the extent of the increase. It was not essential, comparatively speaking, to the top deck, and it needed room to be qualified properly ("Wholesale").

Get the facts straight Getting at the heart of the story isn't often as simple as in the examples cited above. Complex news of public affairs, for instance, keeps head writers on their toes trying to find ways of telling it in restricted space and understandable terms. The problem will be discussed more fully in the next chapter, but a few examples of inadequate grasp of the essentials of the story follow.

The editor who wrote this head understood the lead, probably, but had forgotten or failed to note a detail farther down in the story:

*Woman Dies in
16-Story Fall from
Medical Arts Building*

A 53-year-old woman leaped or fell to death from a window between the 16th and 17th floors of the Medical Arts Building, Ninth Street and Nicollet Avenue, Saturday afternoon.

On the basis of the lead alone, the head seems plausible enough. But paragraph 3 added this fact:

. . . The body struck the roof of the second floor on an inner court . . .

That means, of course, that it was not a sixteen-story *fall.*

Sometimes the desk man simply reads the story so hastily that he misses a truly essential fact. A student wrote:

```
Airliner
Disappears
in Mid-Ocean
```

when the lead clearly showed that it was the navigator of the airline who disappeared. Another wrote:

```
Assembly Sends
'Home Rule' Gas
Bill to Senate
```

He missed one vital word in the lead: "repealer." The head was directly opposed to the facts.

But more often the trouble is less obvious than this: the editor simply fails to grasp the real significance of the story or perhaps fails to see that a seemingly minor qualification contains an important clue to its full meaning. A student wrote:

```
Democrats Fight
Portal Pay Suits
```

when closer reading would have shown that they had *promised* a fight to *modify pending legislation to outlaw* portal pay suits. Another careless beginner wrote:

```
President Orders
Railway Strikes
Investigation
```

when the facts were that the President had called an investigation of a jurisdictional *dispute* (there had been no strike) affecting employees of a railway-operated *ferry line.*

Another student wrote:

```
Telephone Workers
Set to Strike April 7
```

apparently confusing a strike *vote* with *intention* to strike. The story said that the workers had filed a routine strike notice as a part of bargaining procedure.

Still another student wrote:

```
Senate Ends
Draft System
```

when it should have been clear that the Senate alone had no such power.

Put the key facts at the top   It is not enough to say that the top deck must tell the whole story. The *top* of the top deck should be reserved for the most important parts of the story.

Normal sentence structure will not necessarily put the key facts at the beginning. A headline might logically say:

```
Police Say
Petty Crimes
in City Mount
```

Better headline construction would be:

**Petty Crimes
In City Mount,
Police Report**

This puts the emphasis where it belongs. As we shall see, it is essential to get the attribution into the top deck of the headline. But in cases like this, the attribution is by no means the *news* and therefore doesn't need to go first. It *is* sound to put the attribution right at the top when the attribution has everything to do with the story itself. Note the effect of its position in this case:

```
Moscow Radio Says
German Youth Killed
at West-Zone Rally

German Youth Killed
at West-Zone Rally,
Moscow Radio Says
```

The headline over a straight news story is usually based on the lead, but there are times when the head writer is justified in taking more leeway. When he does so, he must take pains to see that he does not go beyond the story. But the lead paragraph itself, for good reasons, may be lacking in breadth; the larger story may be buried in the specific details. The story below, for example, was written with great care because of the scattered and cautious nature of the facts. It was a second-day story; the opposition had had most of the details in the previous news cycle.

BELGRADE, Yugoslavia — (XP) — Albanian refugees based in Italy are being parachuted into combat against the Soviet-backed Albanian government, Premier Marshal Tito's official newspaper said Saturday.

From abroad came reports, unconfirmed here, that Soviet Russia has sent both jet planes and fresh men to her isolated satellite.

Denouncing "Albanian feudalists and other hotheads" for actions it said might touch off the Balkan powder keg, Tito's newspaper, Borba, declared "armed groups are being parachuted into Albania and they are fighting there."

Yugoslav sources in London declared . . .

It is clear the story hadn't "firmed up" much, even in the second cycle. It is heavily overlaid with careful attribution, for good reasons. The problem in the head is to step back from the accumulation of careful detail and try to tell the larger story. One editor did it this way:

Kremlin Hand Seen in Albanian Fighting

Tito Says Refugees Flown from Italy Could Give Russia Excuse to Attack

Marshal the facts in sentence form The point has already been made that headlines are skeletonized sentences. That means largely dropping out articles, sometimes substituting a comma for "and," and doing without nonessential modifiers, including personal pronouns. But skeletonizing does not mean merely assembling vaguely related words. Headlines are written in sentence form—*and each deck of the head must be a separate sentence.*

Each headline sentence must contain a verb; it is rarely permissible to do without one. But even though the story is written in the past tense, headlines traditionally use the present, with corresponding shifts in related tenses.

Each headline sentence must contain a subject. Some desks allow frequent use of an *understood* subject, even though the reader must get into the story to fill in the gap. For example:

Objects to Use of Highway Fund

Sen. Clem Appleseed of Rockville told the Senate today that he would fight the use of . . .

Other desks avoid this structure, even to the point of outlawing it altogether. Their point is that the head is meaningless without a subject. But some allow the top deck to start with the verb, provided the second deck fills in the missing subject:

Objects to Use of Highway Fund

Sen. Appleseed Vows One-Man Fight

Some desks require that the top deck contain a subject but allow the second deck to do without one, provided its understood subject is identical with the top-deck subject.

Appleseed Vows One-Man Battle

Objects to Tapping Highway Fund

The simple sentence is the most commonly used headline structure and is probably best. Space limits do not often allow room for much more than the usual subject-predicate arrangement. However, other structures are by no means taboo. The skilled head writer often chooses a more complex form deliberately. The compound sentence, for instance, helps point up contrasts:

Council Kills Zoning Plan but Its Ghost Still Walks

The complex sentence allows special angles to come into focus:

Loser on Red China Issue, Russia Stays in UN to Attack U.S.

Sentence form is the unique contribution of the American newspaper to headlines. It has been exported to much of the Western world, especially Canada, Latin America, and Western Europe. British papers still largely use label heads.

Build around a strong verb   Beginners often find it a powerful temptation to dispense with the verb. They begin showing progress when they use not only verbs but strong verbs as the fulcrum of the entire headline. Good head writers choose vigorous, active, positive, colorful verbs. They know that the ideas in the headline are propelled by the verb. All headline words —even the little ones—are selected with care, but the verb is the key to the entire head. A rich vocabulary and an "ear" for words is invaluable.

There are no handy lists of verbs that have "punch." But two verbs—"to be" and "to have"—all but totally lack force. Note the colorlessness of these examples:

Exchange Club Has Meeting

Extown Man Is New Commander of State Vets

Presumably when the reader picks up his paper he asks himself, *"What has happened?"* not *"How are things?"* In general, the head writer prefers to answer the action question with *action* verbs rather than *state-of-being* verbs.

```
    Phone Men Want Verdict
    on State Anti-Strike Law
```

is better written:

Phone Men Ask Verdict on State Anti-Strike Law

To "ask" is to take an affirmative action; "want" describes only a state of being. It is not necessarily news that the telephone workers *want* a verdict. The implication is that they now want it, they have wanted it, and they'll probably go on wanting it. When they *ask* for a verdict, they take an *action* that is part of the day's news.

Generally speaking, headlines demand the *active* voice, rather than the *passive.* This is by no means a rule, however, and the tyro can be led astray by trying to force an active construction on an essentially passive situation. For instance, do not hesitate to write:

Jones Elected Mayor

That's the passive construction. In the active voice it could be said:

```
Voters Choose Jones as Mayor
```

but nothing has been gained by it except awkwardness, while precious space has been lost. Hence, it is preferable not to have hard-and-fast rules about voice. Arbitrary rules in general inhibit good headlines. The happy desk has relatively few rules and depends essentially on the imagination of skilled editors.

It is interesting to note that two common headline injunctions often conflict with each other. Desks which do not allow heads to skip the subject and begin with a verb, as explained above, *cannot enforce a rule against the passive voice.* The best reason for doing without the subject is that the subject itself does not contribute in a major way to the telling of the story:

Slaps Wife, Gets 30 Days

This head tells the story no matter who did the slapping, provided, of course, that he was not a minister, a prize fighter, or a cabinet officer. Supplying a subject adds nothing:

```
Man Slaps Wife, Gets 30 Days
```

It is even a little silly, since presumably the spouse of the wife is a man. It doesn't help, either, to supply a name—Jones, for instance—if it is unknown to the public at large. But if a desk *requires* a subject, the economical way to tell the story is to turn it around into the passive, so that the person important enough to the headline becomes the subject:

```
Wife Slapped . . .
```

It is worth noting that "is" and "are" appear not only as forms of the verb "to be" but also as auxiliaries. In this head—

```
Price Rise Is Cited
at Hearing on Housing
```

—"is" appears not as a form of the verb "to be" but as an auxiliary in a form of the verb "to cite." In this case—

```
Price Rise Puts
Pinch on Workers
Is Complaint
```

—the "is" appears as a form of the verb "to be." But in either case, most head writers prefer to do without the "is" altogether. Some desks taboo its use; others counsel head writers to *avoid* it. Most desks show no enthusiasm for the use of "is" in this sense:

```
Hospital Here
Needs 20 More
Rooms Is View
```

But they usually abhor the substitution of a comma for the "is" in this context even more:

```
Hospital Here
Needs 20 More
Rooms, View
```

Some desks simply allow the "is" to be dropped—

```
20 More Rooms
Is Minimum Need
at Hospital
```

```
20 More Rooms
Minimum Need
at Hospital
```

—but most editors dislike both practices. They prefer to switch to another verb:

20 More Rooms Called Minimum Hospital Need

On papers with a difficult head schedule from the standpoint of count, editors are often allowed to pad heads with "is" and "are" at points where they are not strictly needed.

Don't repeat words; don't use two forms of the same word Headline practice from coast to coast is virtually universal on this point; a key word—a word prominent enough to be noticed in reading—can be used only once in any form in any given head.

```
Two-Alarm Fire
Razes Garage
    Two Firemen Injured
    Fighting Night Fire
    at Pyramid Garage
```

This headline is adequate in every respect except for repetition of words: "two" twice, "garage" twice, "fire" three times.

The no-repeat rule applies to all units of the headline. A word appearing in the banner may not be repeated at any point in a series of decks, not even the last.

As we shall see (pages 182–185), even this rule has its exceptions. In feature heads particularly, words or sounds are sometimes deliberately repeated to produce special effects. And the rule is usually less rigidly applied to prepositions and other "connector" words. Repetitions of minor words may be well spaced but not "stacked"—

```
Senators to Fight
to Keep Price Lid
```

—or repeated too often—

```
City to See Astronaut
in Afternoon Events
    Shepard to Go to Hotel
    First; to Leave for
    Stadium About 2 p.m.
```

And, of course, the rule does not affect:

Crowd Shouts: 'No, No'

Head writers also avoid unconscious alliteration:

```
Churches Join Hands
in Peace Prayer Pact
```

But alliteration may be used deliberately in feature heads to produce an arresting effect.

Avoid structural repetition This rule is neither as universal nor as inflexible as the word-repetition rule. However, most competent desk men try to avoid putting two decks of the head in precisely the same sentence structure:

```
Governor Calls
Special Session
    Legislators Start
    Trek to Capital
```

This one is not too serious—and it is hard to avoid. Some structural repetitions, however, are more conspicuous:

```
Baptists to Hold
Hour of Prayer
    Pastor to Give
    Main Address
```

Put new material into the second deck The temptation for the beginner is simply to say the same thing over again in new words:

```
Students Protest
Increase in Fees
    Complaints Heard at UW
    About Boost in Tuition
```

The only new thing in the second deck is the locale of the story.

Tell the story in specific terms   The head writer may be tempted to write:

Auto Crash	10½
Proves Fatal	12½

but he soon learns that he can say a lot more in the same space:

2 Die as Car	12½
Smacks Tree	12½

Or, with a little more space:

Car Hits Tree;	14
2 Die, 3 Hurt	12½

However, the specific way is not *invariably* the best way. There are times when the head writer can deliberately step back from the details and find better headline material in a more general approach. As we shall see in the next chapter, this technique is more likely to be effective when the story does not involve *events,* as in the present example, so much as *trends.*

Make line and thought break together   Headline space limits put a hardship on copy editors but they should not forget that they also can be a strain to readers. Consider the hasty reader who encounters this headline:

Views Differ
on State Fair
Trade Statute

It happens that the reader has nothing to trade at the state fair, so he skips on to something else. As a result, he misses this story:

> The head of the state's Antitrust Division and representatives of 11 trade organizations differed today on whether the state fair trade law causes higher prices.

This is a dramatic example of the effect of juxtaposed words. The headline writer has this idea to convey—

    State Fair Trade Statute

—and he has to convey it in a headline with a linecount maximum of 12 units. He has to break into the idea somewhere. Let's look at various possibilities.

As it happened, the editor chose the worst possible break:

    -- State Fair
    Trade Statute

"State Fair" by itself is a meaningful combination for most readers. It's part of almost everyone's experience, whether first-hand or vicarious. Having mentally treated this combination as a unit, the reader is hopelessly lost. Only with careful retracing can he pick up the intended meaning. And that won't do. Heads must convey *instant* meaning.

Another:

    ---------------State
    Fair Trade Statute

This is not a bad break from the standpoint of meaning but happens not to work from the standpoint of count. The following break meets both requirements:

    ------ State
    Fair Trade
    Statute ---

but the phrase is in an awkward position. If the head writer understands that he does not have to cling to his original words, he can come up with a better solution:

Fair Trade
Law Debated

or:

Fair Trade
Statute Called
Inflationary

Another example of a bad break:

Bare Plan for
City Spring
Cleanup Drive

So they're going to clean up the city spring?

These examples should make it plain why head writers watch their line breaks carefully. The arrangement of words from line to line has far-reaching influence on conveying the gist of the story. Where the standards are highest, the question gets close attention. Note these five major heads on Page One of a chance-selected issue of the New York *Times:*

**ENEMY STEPS UP
ATTACKS SHARPLY;
OFFENSIVE IS SEEN**

**U.S. PLANS TO SELL
ATOM FUEL PLANTS**

**COMPROMISE PLAN
IS ADOPTED BY U.S.
FOR ARMS PARLEY**

**CATHOLIC PRIESTS
SEEK POLICY ROLE**

**MEMPHIS NEGROES
DISPERSED BY GAS**

Every one of these heads is perfect from the standpoint of line break. And it was no accident. The *Times* desk does not "prefer" to have the ideas and lines break simultaneously—it requires it.

Many other desks are less careful. On some desks, especially those where less time can be spent on headlines, line breaks get attention in direct ratio to the conspicuousness of the heads: perfection is required in the top decks of top-of-Page-One stories, but that's all. Even on some desks with high standards, secondary decks are not expected to break perfectly and some even allow second-deck words to be split between lines.

The line-break rule is the toughest one for beginners. With all the other strains on their facility with language that headlines require, breaking lines right sometimes seems to be too much. Probably it isn't as hard as it seems even to begin with, though, and certainly it becomes easier with practice. But until habits jell, some guidelines are necessary. Here are some "don't's":

1. *Don't break a line inside a verb.* Verbs, even headline verbs, often consist of more than one word. When they do, keep them on one line. Don't say:

```
Legislature Will
Close Books Today
```

Make it read:

Legislature Sets
Adjournment Today

2. *Don't break off a modifier.* Whether it's an adjective-noun, adverb-adjective, or adverb-verb combination, the modifier should not be separated from the word it modifies. Don't say:

```
Start John Doe
Probe in Local
'Morals Case'
```

Here we have two examples of the same thing. "John Doe" modifies "Probe," and "Local" is inseparable from "Morals Case." Say instead:

John Doe Probe
in Morals Case
Launched Here

3. *Don't break a preposition away from the phrase it introduces.*

```
New Hike in
Fees Causes
Student Beef
```

can be made to read:

Fee Increase
Brings Protest
from Students

This rule is sometimes stated: "Don't end a line with a preposition." But when prepositions are united by usage with verbs, the rule breaks down. Note the logic of the position of the word "on" in this headline:

Racers Push On
in Blinding Snow

The rule for prepositional phrases also applies to adverbial clauses.

```
Enemy Halted After
Scoring Brief Gain
```

Most head writers would prefer:

Enemy Stopped Cold
After Brief Advance

In using any of these rules, it is judgment in making exceptions to the rule, not the rule itself, that counts. Many editors, for example, would not object to this head—

Stock Exchange
Prices Fall Off

—despite the fact that "Stock Exchange" modifies "Prices" in this context. The trick is to use the rules to help find good combinations of words.

Punctuating the Headline

Punctuation anywhere in the newspaper requires careful attention. But in the headline it deserves and gets special care. In full sentences, punctuation is a valuable adjunct. But in the skeletonized form of the headline it must carry a far greater share of the job of conveying meaning. Headline punctuation is simple and logical. Since headlines are built in sentences, *they are in general punctuated like sentences.*

Commas   Just as it does in other sentences, the comma has these uses: It separates dependent and independent clauses:

Though Signatures Are Questioned,
More Petitioners Say They Signed

It marks off appositives:

John Jones, 78, Dies Suddenly

It sets off phrases in special circumstances:

In Eastern Iowa, Toll Rises to 10

But it has one special use in headlines that is unlike its use in other sentences: it is often substituted for "and":

County Official Tortured, Shot

Some desks *prefer* the tighter effect that this substitution produces; others rule it out; still others allow the head writer to use either, depending on which gives him the better head.

The comma does not substitute for any other part of speech. It should not be used in place of a verb:

Legislature Nears Adjournment, View

It should not be used in place of a preposition:

John K. Jones Dies, Detroit

Omission or misplacement of a comma can cause confusion anywhere. A classic example of the misplaced comma in the headline is this:

NAM Favors Labor, Blasts Tax Cut Bill

Readers familiar with the viewpoint of the National Association of Manufacturers considered this news indeed—until they figured out the misplaced comma. The head was intended to read:

NAM Favors, Labor Blasts Tax Cut Bill

Periods are used in headlines in all the usual ways except one: they are not used to indicate the ends of sentences, although a few newspapers still use a period at the end of the last of a series of decks. Sentence breaks are indicated with *semicolons* instead, not unlike their customary use in sentences to separate independent clauses:

Gladiolus Show Opens; Thousands Visit Exhibits

Dashes are used on some newspapers to separate independent clauses in subsidiary decks, usually not in the top deck:

Declares Delay Might Hamper President—Training Bill Up in Senate Today

Some less careful desks allow the dash to substitute for an attributing phrase such as "says":

The Worst is Yet to Come—Agnew

The dash also can be handy in creating special effects:

Five Years Ago City Went Wild, But Now—

Weather Outlook
Brighter—Now

Quotation marks are used in headlines much as in other sentences, but most headlines use single quotation marks rather than double ones. They set off words and passages which are directly quoted and have some special piquancy:

Europe at 'Crisis,'
General Testifies

They are also used occasionally to indicate that a word is being used in some special way:

Three More Jailed
in Basketball 'Fix'

And sometimes they are used legitimately to express irony:

Child Movie Fan
'Shoots Up' Store

'Dead' Man Calls Up,
Calls Off Own Funeral

But the ironic use of quotation marks is fraught with potential danger: they can color the news. Except in an occasional feature head, they are best not used at all.

Quotation marks are sometimes used in an effort to make a dangerous headline libel-proof:

```
            Pregnant Woman
            Is Deliberately
               Struck by Truck
```

Pregnant Woman
Is 'Deliberately'
Struck by Truck

Quotes make the second head *seem* more objective than the first by implying that the deliberateness of the act is not proved, only alleged. But it is doubtful whether that would provide much protection in a libel action. (Worse still, trucks cannot act with deliberation; only drivers can.)

Apostrophes are used in the usual ways: to show possessive case and to denote contractions, for instance. The latter is a convenient space-saving device. Many desks allow contractions in headlines that would not be allowed elsewhere. Names beginning with "Mc" or "Mac," for instance, may be shortened with an apostrophe: "M'Carthy," "M'Arthur." But like other headline license, this is subject to severe abuse. Most desks frown on its use in shortening words in general, as in "M'kee" for "Milwaukee."

It is well to avoid stacking apostrophes with other punctuation. The apostrophe with quotation marks can be especially confusing:

Players' "Goodbye, My Fancy"
Starts Tonight in Union Theater

And misplaced apostrophes can be just as obvious as misplaced commas:

High Point
Graduates
Class of '89

Hyphens Desks are not unanimous about using the hyphen. But its presence or absence can make a lot of difference in a headline:

Sheep Killing Dogs
in Roberts County

Now that's interesting; it's usually the other way around. And so it was in this story. The head writer meant:

```
      Sheep-Killing Dogs
      in Roberts County
```

But of course this is a label head. It could read:

```
      Sheep-Killer Dogs
      Plague Farmers
```

The hyphen can be especially useful in headlines in linking together two words which modify a third, helping to determine how to read the combination. Compare:

```
      Across Table Talks
      with Russia Urged
```

with:

Across-Table Talks
with Russia Urged

Colons, too, have special usefulness in the headline. A colon can help save space by allowing the antecedent in a sentence to be shifted into an introductory position. For instance, the head writer wants to say:

```
      'Be There with the Mostest' Men
      Is Red Secret
```

No matter how he tries, this is too long for the head he is writing. So he shifts:

Reds' Secret: 'Be There
with the Mostest' Men

Some desks allow the colon to be used in attribution, as others use the dash:

Agnew: The End
Is Not in Sight

Usually the colon is used when the name of the author of the statement leads off, the dash when it appears at the end.

Question marks come in for some special uses in headlines, too, usually in feature heads:

Annie Oakley? She Had
Nothing on This Coed!

Exclamation points are rarely used in headlines. They are no longer used to give an end-of-the-world emphasis to big stories. Most newspapers prefer to express the magnitude of the story in type size. The exclamation point has an occasional use in feature heads, as shown in the example above.

Headline Capitalization

Schedules calling for all-cap heads use lower-case letters occasionally: MacARTHUR, LaCROSSE, Di-MAGGIO, for instance (instead of MAC ARTHUR, LA CROSSE, etc.). But notwithstanding different practices from one desk to another and the recent trend toward lower-case headlines, headlines generally are capitalized in about the same way titles are capitalized. In caps-and-lower-case schedules, a typical rule goes like this: Capitalize every word *except* articles, prepositions, conjunctions, and parts of verbs other than roots where these words are of four letters or less; treat hyphenated words as two words, capitalizing the word after the hyphen except in Chinese given names, such as Chou En-lai. "Is" and "are" usually are capitalized even when they serve as auxiliaries. And when prepositions are joined to verbs, they are capitalized, as in "Fight On," "Call Up," etc.

On papers which have adopted lower-case headlines, the rules of capitalization are the same as those for straight matter. Some examples are shown on page 146.

Subheads

Subheads are boldface lines of body type inserted in long stories to relieve them of typographical "grayness." They are sometimes centered on the column and sometimes flush left, sometimes in caps and sometimes in caps and lower case. They are usually one line, but some newspapers use two lines.

The same effect—breaking the monotony of a long mass of solid body type—can be achieved with other devices. One is to use a special dash, such as a star dash, followed by a line of boldface, perhaps beginning with a word or two in caps. On special stories, these lines are occasionally led off with initial letters. Some newspapers prefer to break up long stories by boldfacing whole paragraphs, parts of paragraphs, or even parts of sentences. Still others use this device plus traditional subheads.

Handling subheads differs widely from one desk to another; a beginner can tell from a brief study of the subheads in his paper what its policy is. One school of thought holds that the subhead should be written as carefully as the headline—and under the same rules: it should move around a verb and preferably have a subject. Another school of thought says the subhead should be carefully written but in either headline form or as a label, whichever does the better job.

Everyone agrees that the subhead preferably deals with the material in the paragraph that immediately follows. The first school mentioned above insists that the subhead *tell* the content of that paragraph. The second says: Put into the subhead a logical combination of words that points to the material in that paragraph; use the very words in the paragraph wherever possible; use quotation marks (single ones, as in headlines) when the words used are picked from a quotation.

In any case, the subhead is primarily a typographic device. The second school holds that it is so much so that *what* the subhead says is not as important as in a headline and therefore the editor should not waste time fussing over it. The feeling is that subheads are rarely read, anyway; their value is in lightening the appearance of the story, not helping to tell it. Hence, if it comes down to a choice between a subhead just long enough to "let some light" into the column and one which tells precisely what follows in the story, choose the former.

Subheads are usually spaced roughly three paragraphs apart; at least that much space is allowed before the first subhead and after the last. It is wise to plot them through the whole story first before writing them in, to be sure they will be evenly spaced. Most editors avoid inserting subheads too close to a point where the story will shift from two columns to one or will be likely to jump. They also avoid putting them just before or after a boldface paragraph or a ruled insert.

Subheads are called for on most desks only when there is room for at least two. Most editors try to get at least two into the story ahead of the jump and, if possible, to have the jump itself carry at least two.

Jump Heads

The jump head takes many forms, but a given newspaper usually uses only one, which the editor must follow without deviation. Four of the more common types of jump head are shown on page 166.

Perhaps the most common method of all is shown at upper left. Here the jump line gives page and column and at that point one finds either the exact head that appeared over the story on Page One, the same head in smaller type, or the same first deck. An excellent system is that shown in the upper right. Here the entire head is carried over, but it is identified by a key word given in the continuation line and then repeated in a kicker over the head.

Very common is the key-word system shown at lower left. That word, identified in the continuation a fugitive and demanded admittance to the house.

When Mrs. Arnold refused, he threatened to harm the children. She screamed to Nancy and Robert to run away. Snyder, infuriated,

Continued on Page 28, Column 3

CHILD HOSTAGE, 9, IS SLAIN BY FELON

Continued From Page 1

charged through the screen mesh, entered the kitchen, and picked up an eight-inch knife from a table.

At this moment the school bus returning Betty June from the Mahopac School stopped at the door.

Text of Platform Plank

The final compromise was worked out by Assemblyman Paul J. Rogan, Ladysmith, an area advocate, and Greenya, after the governor had proposed to strike

Turn to PLATFORM, page 28, col. 1

Platform

From page 1, column 4

out the area advocacy in the first "compromise" plank.

"The Republican party of Wisconsin believes in the principle of equitable reapportionment. And further believes that persuasive arguments exist in behalf of recognition for area as well as population in the apportionment of legislative districts," the approved plank stated.

Likewise, under the rules as they now stand, voters must check off at least 20 names for Central Committee posts or have their ballots invalidated. Twenty-six are to be elected.

Wheeler's faction has been widely distributing sample bal-

See DEMOS, Page 2, Column 4

DEMOS—*From Page 1*

Roberts Group Files Suit Here

lots with a full slate for all posts. Roberts' group which includes less than a full slate would benefit by "bullet voting" —balloting for less than the full number to be elected.

Miss Bernstein said she did not think there should be a sudent member on the board of trustees, however. "It's good to have a year of perspective."

She said she planned to visit

(See Col. 8, Back Page, This Section)

At 22

(Continued From Page One)

the Poughkeepsie, N.Y., campus often to speak with students, explaining her duties as a graduate student left her schedule more flexible than that of trustees with jobs in industry.

She said she wanted to work with the present student body president, Margaret Beyer, "to see if we can make the trustees accessible to the students."

line, is set in display type and becomes the sole head over the jump. A key-word system that is less common and often a nuisance for the editor and the reader is shown in lower right. Here the first word or two of the headline is the key, but the continuation line doesn't give it; the reader has to remember how the head started out. Needless to say, this system requires extra care in constructing the head in the first place so that the first two words are useful.

There seems to be no single good way to make jump heads do their job: to help the reader find the continuation as quickly and effortlessly as possible. Some newspapers always put all the jumps on the same page, and this helps some. Even better, some put all jumps on the last page of the same section.

The Effect of Headlines

Does all this care with headlines really make any difference? Some years ago, Percy H. Tannenbaum,[1] then of the University of Illinois, constructed three versions of a headline for a fictional story of the trial of a college student for murder on another campus. Using a single version of the text of the story, he made up issues of a campus paper, varying only the headline. One version pointed toward the guilt of the accused, another suggested his innocence, and the third was neutral. Each of 398 student subjects read one paper at his own pace and thoroughness. Later the students were asked to report their belief as to the guilt or innocence of the accused and the depth to which they had read the story. The results are given below:

Effect of Headlines on Judgments of Guilt or Innocence

WORDING OF HEADLINES	PER CENT JUDGING		
	Guilty	*Innocent*	*No Opinion*
"Guilty" headline: Admits Ownership of Frat Murder Weapon	34	16	50
Neutral headline: Approach Final Stage in Frat Murder Trial	26	18	56
"Innocent" headline: Many Had Access to Frat Murder Weapon	22	29	49

It should be emphasized that all subjects read the same story—only the heads they read were different. All three heads were consistent with the facts given in the story and all three were written with manifest objectivity. Yet the data show that the headlines had a significant influence on the way the facts were judged. Further analysis showed that the influence of the headline was least where the story was most thoroughly read. Of those who read thoroughly, 38 per cent gave judgments that agreed with the implication of the headline, but of those who read superficially, 60 per cent gave agreeing judgments. Nevertheless, the danger of "keying" the story with inferential bias is not to be discounted, for many readers, unhappily, are superficial readers.

Experience in head writing will convince the student copy editor that it's possible to say a great deal more in a small space than he at first realizes. But there are times when the problem of telling a complex story in a headline influences how the story shall be played on the page. Horizontal makeup, free-form headlines, and down-style capitalization have made it easier to get a sufficient count to tell a complicated story adequately. The old-time editor decided where the story would go on the page and with what headline, then left it to the rim man to work out how to get the story told. But a bad head can ruin a good story, and a misleading head can influence the perception of the story, as the Tannenbaum study showed. Furthermore, all stories are more complex these days, not just spot news and hard news. Greater subtlety in a story requires greater subtlety in a head. The conscientious editor, then, makes sure that a story gets the play it needs, but he also makes sure the headline form chosen leaves room enough to introduce the story to the reader without sacrificing subtlety or accuracy.

[1] Percy H. Tannenbaum, "The Effect of Headlines on the Interpretation of News Stories," *Journalism Quarterly* 30:189–197 (Spring 1953).

Four Shot to Death, 100 Injured in New North Ireland Riots

Mrs. Gandhi Shifts Cabinet, Shows Power

Los Angeles Times

Effect of Column Width on Unit Count These two headlines, taken from front and inside pages of the Los Angeles *Times,* show what a difference column width makes to the head writer. Both heads are in the same type, but the 13-em column at left permits a maximum count of 17-18; the 9½-em inside-page column width at right has a maximum of 13½ units.

These heads also make the point that a highly condensed display face can be quite legible if properly designed for headline purposes.

Wilcox and Fearn[2] have published a modest study shedding light on this particular problem. To quote them:

The count is most commonly a function of makeup convenience, of typographic aesthetic value and of the need for a uniform system. In assigning count, little attention is given to the communication function.

They said they thought they detected a tendency for editors to favor short-count headlines on aesthetic-typographical grounds. To test the effect of unit count on the accuracy and meaning conveyed by headlines, they conducted an experiment in which they assigned head-count limits on three stories of varying degrees of complexity. They found that *meaning* increased with increased line count, but they found no evidence that *accuracy* decreased with decreased line count. Editing students in eighteen journalism departments across the country served as subjects in the experiment. Even student editors, it appears, were more willing to sacrifice subtlety of meaning than they were willing to sacrifice accuracy. This finding argues well for the profession as a whole.

*   *   *   *   *

These are some of basic problems involved in headline writing. The next chapter continues the discussion and concerns itself with some more specialized head-writing problems.

---

[2] Walter Wilcox and Kathy Fearn, "Headline Count: Should It Be Assigned Arbitrarily for All Stories? Or Vary With the Complexity of the Story?" American Newspaper Publishers Association News Research Bulletin No. 24, October 13, 1966.

7

Polishing the Headline

Good headlines can be turned out only by capable, alert minds. They require an extremely high level of concentration and a considerable measure of creative skill. The following section deals with some elusive matters of discipline that contribute in no small measure to the difference between pedestrian and good headlines.

Self-Disciplinary Practices

Objectivity

Making a headline or any other part of a newspaper objective is an essential aim and perhaps essentially an impossibility. It is compounded as much of the editor's state of mind as of careful attention to the requirements of the craft. It is the editor's duty in writing headlines not only to be as objective as possible—*but to make the objectivity of his headlines manifest to his readers.* And in spite of his own biases and sympathies, the head writer can succeed at it by schooling himself to carry through on five major points.

Attributing facts Objectivity in the headline is largely a matter of distinguishing observable fact from statements that must be attributed to their source. Beginners often feel that they need not be as fussy about attributions in the headline as in the story. However, headlines must be attributed to precisely the same extent as the stories they accompany. Where attribution is only implied in the story, it must be clearly shown in the head. If the story states the precise source, the headline can often merely indicate that there is such a source.

The most obvious type of headline attribution tells plainly *who said it.*

Sadat Raps
U.S. Aid
to Israelis

Specific attribution is feasible only when the individual's name is reasonably well known. Where doubts might exist, further identification of the named person is often called for in the second deck:

Egypt's Premier
Doubts Intent
Is Peaceful

But owing to space limits, the attribution is more often given in general terms:

U.S. Gouged on Tin,
Senators Declare

In this case the lead began:

> The Senate Armed Services
> Subcommittee urged today . . .

It is plain that such a "who said it" must be expressed in general terms.

It is often necessary to show in the head that a statement is an expression of opinion, not a statement of fact, without saying flatly that someone said so. Consider this lead:

> WASHINGTON — A subcommittee of the Senate Labor and Public Welfare Committee has found that self-organization and collective bargaining are steadily losing ground in the Southern textile industry because of employer campaigns . . .

To spell out the "who said it" in a headline for this story would obviously be impossible. And, in a short two-line head, it would squander space to say:

> Senate Group Says

even if that could be said in one line. One editor said it this way:

Union Lag in South
Laid to Employers

The words "laid to" indicate clearly that the employers' blame for "union lag in South"—or the lag itself —is not presented in the story as a fact, only as an opinion. Most head writers prefer to use a nonspecific attribution such as this when it makes room to describe the statement itself more adequately.

Such a head could stand alone. However, when a second deck permits fuller detail, it is often possible to become more specific about who made the statement. In this case, the editor wrote:

Senate Report Accuses Textile
Management of Hampering
Organizing, Bargaining

In other words, he asked himself: What questions are raised by the top deck that need most urgently to be answered in the second deck? One of them was "who says so?" Therefore, he led off the second deck with an enlargement on the original anonymous attribution, even though he felt it was not necessary even at this point to put it in precise detail. About all he did was tell at what level of public or unofficial opinion this idea was expressed.

"Laid to" is only one of many important devices for anonymous attribution in headlines. It will pay to study these other examples carefully:

Vienna Hears
Crisis Looms
in Budapest

'Clean World'
Seen as Goal
of Churches

War Machine Called
Menace to America

South Vietnam Regime
'Corrupt,' UN Told

Democracy Held
Science Bulwark

Closer Ties Urged
on Industry, Labor

Progress Is Cited
in Defense of City

Partition Seen Boon
to Irish Bootlegger

Bond Agreement
Viewed as 'Truce'

New Slash Forecast
in Automobile Steel

Legislature Said
Nearing Finale

Each of these headlines uses a different word to indicate that a view or opinion is being expressed. They do not necessarily seem forced, as special devices in headlines often are. These words are by no means interchangeable. Each contributes something of value to the head besides dealing with attribution.

Some newspapers allow use of quotation marks to indicate attribution, but most editors are wary of that.

The quotes in the following headline, for example, don't really help it from the standpoint of authority:

'Napalm, Firepower
Can Win the War'

Sometimes, however, the *context* of the head allows the quotation marks to serve this purpose:

Bombing's End
'Not in Sight'

Here the implication is clear—the statement is an opinion, not a fact.

The *position* of the attribution in the head is important. Sometimes the attribution deserves first position in the head and should not go anywhere else, as in the "Moscow Radio" example on page 155.

The position of the attribution is largely indicated by the credibility of the statement attributed. Its credibility not only can be based on who said it but also on the relative deviousness of its route to the news columns. When credibility is strong, it is often better to put the attribution last, rather than first:

U.S. Not at War,
President Declares

Even when the source is another newspaper, most editors prefer to say so in the head:

> CHICAGO — (XP) — The Chicago Sun-Times said today it had learned that BCG, a vaccine, has been released by the federal government for general use in preventing tuberculosis.

Because the route of the facts from origin to reader is devious, the headline is made to read:

Vaccine Available
for T.B., Paper Says

The attribution should always go in the top deck when a question of fact is involved. We could not say:

```
Nixon to Blame
for Jobless Increase
        Democrats Say Policies
        Risk Inflation
```

But we can say:

Nixon Gets Blame for Jobless Increase

Democrats Say Policies Pose Risk of Inflation

The first head might be satisfactory if we could depend on all readers of the top deck to read the second, but we can't. Therefore, the top deck must be able to stand alone as a summary of the facts.

The headline must be even more meticulously attributed than the text on a by-line story putting opinions in the lead. As we have seen in previous chapters, the by-line itself is the attribution, as far as the story is concerned. The by-line says in effect: Any opinions expressed here are those of the writer and are not necessarily represented to be objective fact. But the by-line does not give the same protection to the head. It appears below the head and in no sense is a part of it. Especially when straight typographical treatment is accorded the story, it becomes necessary to attribute the head, directly or by inference, to an extent that is not true of the lead. To take a strictly hypothetical example:

BY OLYMPUS NEVERWRONG
(Chief of Bugle Washington Bureau)

(Editor's Note: Mr. Neverwrong has been observing official Washington for more than 20 years. His personal analysis of the confusion there is contained in the dispatch below.)

WASHINGTON (Special) — Official Washington is going around like a chicken with its head cut off . . .

Shall the editor take his cue from the lead?

```
Washington Like
a Chicken With
Its Head Cut Off
```

No, the head has to be attributed in a way that the lead itself is not (though the story *as a whole* is):

Correspondent Sees Confusion Rampant in Nation's Capital

Or the same effect might be created by a kicker:

Neverwrong Writes—

Confusion Rampant in Nation's Capital

The problems this kind of attribution raises are discussed more fully on pages 76–78.

Like all other headline words, these "general attributors" must be watched carefully for misleading connotations. Notice that the same objectivity would not be achieved in the headline above if it were made to read:

```
Newsman Describes
Rampant Confusion
in Nation's Capital
```

Clearly, the implication here is that the confusion exists as a point of fact and the reporter is merely describing it.

Sometimes attribution is not crucial. Take this example:

A high State Department official reported today that the Communist Party had lost a third of its membership in Western Europe — 1,295,000 persons — since World War II. Homer M. Byington, Jr., . . .

Here the lead happens to put the attribution first and in general terms. But the head writer felt the source was so close to being official and what he said was so well substantiated that he could present the story as fact in the top deck. He wrote:

Communist Losses 33% in West Europe

But he also felt that *careful* readers would want to know what the source was, at least in general terms. So he wrote in his second deck:

Falling Off in the Party's Rolls Since '45 Shows Democracy's Renewal, U.S. Aide Says

Attribution is usually not needed at all in either a lead or a headline when the source is official or when the event described could have been observed by anyone who chanced to be at the scene. Hence these heads do not suffer from the absence of attribution:

City Police Seize Cache of Drugs

Thousands of Catholics Join in Peace Prayer

Three Area Men on Casualty List

Fire Levels Hotel Here

Choosing the specific fact Passing up the generalization for the specific fact has its applications in headline objectivity as well as in reporting and editing.

```
House Votes Huge Sum
for Supersonic Plane
```

is one way of telling the story. But how huge is huge? The craftsman prefers:

House Votes a Billion for Supersonic Plane

The idea, of course, is to let the reader decide whether the actual amount is huge, gigantic, immense, less than expected, or trifling.

The head writer can avoid unconscious editorializing in headlines by using specific facts for his headline material. But too much specific detail can obscure meaning in the headline:

```
$1,037,237,329 Voted
for Supersonic Plane
```

Watching the tone quality of words Words both convey meaning and define subjective states. They both denote and connote. One word can color a headline, giving it a meaning far beyond the bounds of the story and the intentions of a careless head writer.

Professionals examine the implications of their headlines minutely. Many innocent-seeming words carry broader or different meaning than their "synonyms." Note the difference between these headlines:

```
Fullbright Replies to Thurmond

Fullbright Answers Thurmond
```

The first is quite uncolored. The second implies a *successful* reply. Yet head writers are tempted to use them interchangeably.

Watching juxtapositions It frequently happens that separate decks of a headline are objective by themselves while the combination of the two is dynamite. The careful head writer not only checks each separately but watches their relationship to each other. Years ago, for example, in a New York election in which Benjamin H. Davis, who had been convicted of conspiracy as a Communist, was his party's candidate for Congress, one desk handled the election-eve headline this way:

Fair Deal Test Expected From New York Vote

Convicted Red Up for Party's Only U.S. Seat

A careful reading would show that the top deck pertained to the total political implication of the election and the second to Davis's race. But many careless readers would be likely to link "Fair Deal Test" and "Convicted Red." The focal point of the confusion probably is the word "Party's," which refers to Communist Party but could easily be read Democratic or Republican in this context.

Watching quotation marks   As we have seen, quotation marks have more than one meaning. They quote, denote special usages of words, and indicate irony. Unless headlines containing quoted words or phrases are carefully constructed, they can be intended to mean one thing but be read to mean another:

```
Sheriff 'Regrets'
Shooting Incident
```

Even if the sheriff was quoted in the story as saying "I regret this unfortunate incident . . . ," many readers might well infer irony from the quotes in the head.

Economy

Headline space is precious. That was especially true when single-column heads anchored the top of every front page and schedules called for many forms of single-column head. To be large enough to occupy top position on the page, they had to be either very short, and therefore hard on the writer, or typographically very condensed, and therefore hard to read. But tight, short, crisp heads are easier for the reader to grasp. The ideal head gets as much information into the limited space as possible, arranged in such a way and using such symbols as to guarantee meaningfulness for most readers.

Today's long-line heads appear at first to be easier to write because of the long count. But the temptation is to squander the space on loosely written heads. The headline writer has more freedom, but he has to learn to use it to produce lean, easy-to-grasp headlines just the same. There is no point in including in a headline *any* symbol—word, abbreviation, figure—which fails to carry meaning for just about everyone. A few specific suggestions follow.

Names   A name becomes a headline word when it becomes a "household word." Until that time, a name cannot stand alone in a headline. Headline names are sometimes made in a matter of days; they can last for generations or drop back into obscurity in a matter of weeks. Half a century after he flew the Atlantic, Lindbergh's name can still be used in a headline without further identification and without qualm. But a former vice-president of the United States might need headline identification over his obituary.

A hypothetical series of headlines will show how a name arises and at the same time will illustrate techniques of identification:

Ex-Soda Jerk Held for Triple Slaying

Ex-Soda Jerk Jones Denies Slaying 3

'Fizzer' Jones Tells of Previous Murders

Jones Murder Trial Opens Tomorrow

Killer Jones Gets Chair

The idea is that with each new mention of the name, it becomes less necessary to link the name with something else that readers will recognize.

The copy editor has to have a pretty clear picture of how well known a name is—not to him and his associates but to the public at large at the time of writing. It is not prominence but newsworthiness that counts. Obviously there is a middle ground where the wisdom of using a name is uncertain. When it is very doubtful, the person can be identified in the first reference ("Scientist Says") and the name can then be supplied in the second deck ("Dr. Schwartzkopf"). If he is a little more prominent than that, he can be referred to as "Scientist Schwartzkopf" or "Schwartzkopf, Noted Scientist." When the name is just about ready to stand alone, he can be called "Schwartzkopf" in the top deck and "Scientist" in the second.

It is just as wrong to *fail* to use a newsworthy name in a head as it is wrong to use an unknown name. This head—

```
Hearing Told Mines Bureau
Failed to Protect Widows
```

—could be greatly improved by saying:

Nader Charges Mines Bureau Failed to Protect Widows

Use first names and nicknames sparingly. Many first names and nicknames are perfectly good headline usage. As of this writing there is only one "Ringo" and only one "Jackie." Everyone knows who "Ike" and JFK were, and nearly everyone has an instant association for "Pat," "Tricia," and "Teddy." There is some danger of flippancy, of course. When the tenor of the story is anywhere from serious to tragic, using nicknames is in doubtful taste.

Nicknames are ordinarily not enclosed in quotation marks when they stand alone in the head; when they appear with the last name, they usually are.

Abbreviations Generally speaking, abbreviations that are allowable in the body of the story are allowable in the headline. Some desks allow "High-way Dept." even though it would be "Highway Department" in the story. But few departures of this sort are ordinarily countenanced. Such abbreviations as AFL-CIO, CBS, UN, FCC, YMCA, etc., would be understandable to just about anyone who reads a newspaper. HCL stood for "high cost of living" in some New York headlines at one time, but not elsewhere. Many desks allow abbreviations of those states which can be expressed in two capital letters alone (N.Y., N.J.), but no others.

Technical and specialized terms Except in an occasional feature head in which a complicated unknown term is used deliberately, specialized terms should be avoided.

```
        Bonn's Ostpolitik:
        Uncertain Infant
```

is specific to everyone acquainted with German, but for most readers, the preferable head would say:

Brandt's New Policy Faces Uncertainty

even if it is less specific.

However, new technical terms can be introduced in headlines where they are adequately explained in the headline itself, as was the case years ago when a now well-known medication first came to attention:

'Cortisone' Offers Relief for Arthritis Sufferers

Tense and Mood

It is not enough to say that headlines tell the story in the present tense. The more precise way of putting it is this: What took place in the last full news cycle is shifted from the past tense to the present.

The use of the present tense to describe a future event is appropriate only when the action is impending and when the time element is stipulated in the same deck. It is incorrect to say:

```
        Brandt Addresses
        Joint Session
```

when the event has not taken place. It is equally unacceptable to say:

```
        Brandt Addresses
        Congress Tuesday
```

because it raises the question: Did he address Congress last Tuesday or will he next Tuesday? It is not incorrect to say:

```
        Brandt to Speak
        to Congress Today
```

but the repetition of "to" makes it clumsy and may be avoided by saying:

Brandt Addresses
Congress Today

The "when" is clearly indicated.

The future tense in all other cases is indicated either by the future tense itself or the infinitive form of the verb:

Thompson Will Go
to Convention

Thompson to Go
to Convention

On most desks these are interchangeable, with the infinitive form preferred.

The past tense is rarely used, and then not usually as the governing verb:

Widows Believed
Mines Bureau,
Nader Team Says

Afternoon papers, particularly, have the problem of tense in *current actions*. If they go to press while an around-the-world flier is making his dash, for instance, the answer is to use the participle:

Briton Crossing Atlantic
on Round-the-World Sail

Verbs with the same word for several forms are tricky. The present passive form of "to pull," for instance, is "pulled," and so is the past perfect:

```
        Marines Pulled
        Back 12 Miles,
        General Reveals
```

Did they retreat or were they ordered back? Even the active and passive can be told in headlines with the same words; two readings of the same head could produce opposite impressions:

```
        President Warned
        of Killings in 1967,
        Probers Disclose
```

The head means to say the President *was warned*. But readers could be excused for reading it that the President *warned* others.

Sometimes confusion arises in verbs and nouns of identical form. An example in a student newspaper read:

Artists Present
Protest Show

This can be read "Artists PRESent ProTEST Show" or, as the head writer had intended, "Artists PreSENT PROtest Show."

Subjunctive mood is often used in headlines when the condition is stated in the story only, not necessarily in the head.

> The Wisconsin Farm Bureau today announced a proposal to take over Cash Crops Cooperative, a 3,500-member commodity bargaining agency to help corn and pea farmers.

The story went on to say that the Farm Bureau "is willing" to take over. The subjunctive is appropriate in a head for this story because of the word "proposal." It is not correct to say:

```
State Farm Bureau
Will Take Over
Cash Crops Co-op
```

because the transaction is conditional on the approval of the co-op. The correct form is:

State Farm Bureau Would Take Over Cash Crops Co-op

"Will" does not mean "is willing." Again, the correct form is:

Dad Would 'Give Away' His Six Children 'Free'

not "Dad Will 'Give Away'." He will give them away *only if* he can find takers.

Tone Quality

The headline should be an accurate, stripped-down statement of what is to follow in the story, not only in content but in tone quality—the tone of voice in which it is told. It is deceiving to the reading public to top a sprightly, tongue-in-cheek, or gagged-up feature story with a deadpan head that merely summarizes the facts; a low-comedy headline should introduce a low-comedy story. And the reverse is perhaps even more true. Feature-head devices on straight news stories not only defraud the reader but give the impression that the paper takes a frivolous attitude towards the important matter under consideration. This must not be taken to mean that important stories should be given dull headlines. A good straight headline requires all the skill that goes into the "page brightener." The difference is that the straight one must not be self-conscious: its job is to call attention to the story, not the head. On most good newspapers, the unity of tone between head and story is extended even to the *form* the headline takes— its typographic presentation—as well as the words it uses. This will be illustrated in Chapter 10.

Padding

Padding the headline means filling it out with words that do not contribute to telling the story. One way has been mentioned—using the valuable space in the second deck to tell in other words what has already been said in the top deck. Other methods include substituting the space-consuming word for the economical one when the line is too short; making a lengthy identification when a shorter one will do; using the most space-devouring verb form, etc. One example should suffice. Compare:

```
City Transportation Firm
Removes Men from Payroll
```

with:

Bus Line Here Lays Off 40 Men; Slump Blamed

The second head is better because it uses its space to tell more of the story.

"Headlinese"

An elaborate langage of headline words has grown up over the years; head writers often have to coin words and force them on the public. But by and large the best word is the word straight out of public speech—not a coined word straight out of other newspaper headlines.

Contrived words cannot be avoided altogether. The trouble is that the head writer often seems to be contriving opportunities to use them, or doesn't bother to reconsider them. "Let's see," he seems to be asking himself, "who slapped whom in this probe?" "Slap," "hit," "score," etc., carry the implication of physical violence. Many good head writers never use them in describing a clash of ideas when a word without connotations of physical violence will go. "Probe" is widely used, but "inquiry" has the same count in caps and lower case and is more accurate.

Ambiguity

Ambiguous headlines are the bane of the copy desk's existence, but careful attention to the following details can help keep them to a minimum.

Context   Because editors have to shift their headline materials around until they find the combination that fits the space, they sometimes fail to notice that a word which was useful in one context is unsound in another. Something like that happened when an editor began to write this head:

```
          Truck Stolen
          With 2,140 Pounds
          of Butter Aboard
```

That was too long, so he switched it to read:

2,140 Pounds
of Butter and
Truck Stolen

He failed to notice that "truck" now could imply vegetables, not vehicle.

The same sort of thing probably caused:

Parks Family in Car
Waiting for a Flat

"Flat" used with "car" naturally means flat tire. But the writer intended to say that a hapless family spent days in the car waiting for an apartment to become available. Another:

Dartmouth Man Feigns
Intelligence in Germany

Head writers capitalize on well-established frames of reference common to a majority of newspaper readers. That helps tell some stories, but common frames of reference can also convey unintended meanings.

Pearson and Allen
Slated to Speak
in North Carolina

Especially since the headline appeared in a newspaper trade journal, it seemed to mean a famous former team of columnists. The Pearson was the late Drew Pearson, all right, but the Allen was George V. Allen, then Assistant Secretary of State.

A student newspaper wanted to say:

```
          One-in-Three Rose Bowl Plan
          Given Chance of Renewal
```

That didn't fit the space, so the head came up:

Rose Bowl Agreement
Given One-in-Three
Chance of Renewal

The juxtaposition of "one-in-three" and "chance" changed the headline's meaning altogether.

Shifting word order can sometimes have ludicrous results:

Jury Studies Auto Accident in Which
Woman Lost Leg for only 15 Minutes

Context can give some remarkable meanings to otherwise innocent words. The newspaper in a college town caught this one and changed it in the second run. It told of awards to three faculty members and another person not currently related to the university. The head said:

3 College Professors, Scholar
Win Year's Guggenheim Awards

Are the professors not scholars? The corrected head said:

3 College Professors, Alumnus Win Year's Guggenheim Awards

Identical nouns, adjectives, and verb forms The following head is decipherable only with careful attention:

Joint Bids to Top Wage Lid Cited

The first four main words may be more than one part of speech. "Joint" is both a noun and an adjective, "bid" is both a noun and a verb, and "top" and "wage" can be noun, verb, or adjective.

That is the problem. The solution is not to do without these words but to use them only in contexts where their intended meanings are unmistakable. Vigilance might have prevented the headline fiasco that occurred above a story about "masked men" who "forced seven persons to lie on the floor" during a jewelry shop holdup. The head began:

Cow 7

Sometimes the implications can be defamatory:

Commander Fixes Legion Convention

The intention was to say he set the date for the convention.

"Kill" can be dangerous, too. The head writer did not intend to accuse the late Senator McCarthy of murder when he wrote:

Pearson Says Sponsors Killed by McCarthy

He simply meant to say that sponsors had been persuaded not to buy the broadcasts of the late Drew Pearson because of accusations by McCarthy.

Overgeneralization The head writer must often generalize when the specific fact cannot be stated within the limits of the headline. But sometimes the result is a genuine overstatement of the story:

Uncle Puts $400 Extra Bite on You

That would have been a good head if the $400 had been a typical individual cost of the defense program this story was interpreting. But it applied only to those having a $5,500 average income; for others the figure ranged above and below $400. For all but a few readers, therefore, the statement in the headline was inaccurate.

Sometimes generalizations are merely funny:

New England Ravaged by Tennis Ball Hail

BOSTON — (XP) — Hail stones as big as *table* tennis balls . . .

Careless word choice can change the meaning of a story entirely. When successful negotiations ended a steel strike, one newspaper spread across the top of its front page:

Steel Strike Broken

Needless to say, breaking a strike and negotiating a settlement are very different things.

Little words   can tamper with meaning, too. The classic example in this case is the accident headline that says:

Mother of 3
Dies in Crash

when in fact she died in a hospital after the accident. Sometimes it can be more complicated than that. Compare these heads:

Catholics Warned
Against Concessions
in Basic Doctrine

Catholics Warned
Against Concessions
to Basic Doctrine

Catholics Warned
Against Concessions
on Basic Doctrine

Each carries a somewhat different meaning. Individual Catholics could not make concessions *in* basic doctrine. Concessions *to* would be all right if there were room to add: "those who would have you change your attitudes toward basic doctrine." The preposition in that last line should convey the idea of "pertaining to." "On" does it with reasonable accuracy.

Stacked modifiers   often promote confusion. For example:

Would Kill Old
Age Lien Law
Repeal Bill

Straining for effect   can produce some comic results:

Say Council
'Digging Own Grave'
Smaller Body Urged

Incongruities   can be embarrassing—

Price Czar Says
All Must Stick
to Ceilings

Senate Supports
Lid on Military

Engineers Hear
Aluminum Talk

Ferry Runs
at Standstill

Road Commission
Drops 'Gravel' Plea
Scratches Condemnation . . .

—especially when the head schedule is all caps and periods are omitted from abbreviations:

**CONGRESS MAY PASS
TOUGH LAW TO DEAL
WITH US HOARDERS**

(U.S.)

**PHILIPPI TO
GET NEW FOE**

(Fraternal Order of Elks!)

The problem of tacking a "switch" onto a phrase rather than a word is common:

Ex-Negro
General
Takes Post

The result, as in this case, can be ludicrous. Of course the head writer meant:

```
Post Taken
by Negro
Ex-General
```

In the same newspaper at about the same time another "relevant" head produced an "Oh, pshaw!" effect:

U of L Refuses
To Give Blacks
Academic Credit

As it turned out, the Black Panthers did not mobilize and storm the administration building when they read this news. Only the headline was guilty of across-the-board discrimination. The story made it clear:

> LOUISVILLE, Ky. (UPI) — The University of Louisville will not give academic credit to five Negro pupils dismissed last spring after a take-over of a campus building.

> The students also were convicted in Police Court and fined and given 30-day jail sentences which have been appealed.

Here is another heartbreaker:

> **Heart Disease Twice
> As Fatal As Cancer**
>
> COLOGNE — Heart and circulatory diseases are the most common causes of death in Germany. Twice as many people die of these diseases every year than of cancer.

Obviousness

The New Yorker magazine is famous for using gems of obviousness as fillers:

Arrival of Baby
Complicates Plans
to Hide Marriage

Roof Leaks Can Be
Detected in Rains

Multiple Births Fast Way
to Rear a Large Family

**Would Raise Farmer's Income
by Letting Him Make More Money**

One of the most painful of all time was recorded by *Time* magazine, which saw it in the old New York *Sun:*

Roosevelt Saw
Death Possible

Fireworks Plant Blast Rocks
Rockland County; Blame Bird
New York Daily News

1 Crow, 1 Shot--2
States Rocked
Seattle Post-Intelligencer

NimrodAims, Fires, CrowTakesOff,
Fireworks Plant Blows Sky-High
Denver Post

HUNTER SHOOTS
AT CROW, BLOWS UP
FIREWORKS PLANT
St. Louis Post-Dispatch

Fireworks Factory
Blown Up by Shot
Fired at a Crow
Philadelphia Bulletin

HUNTER'S POOR AIM
IS A BLAZING SHAME
Indianapolis News

Hunter Bags Fireworks
Plant With Wild Shot
New York World Telegram

Shot at Crow Has 'Atomic' Effect;
Fireworks Blast Alarms 2 States
New York Times

HUNTER'S SHOT AT CROW
SETS OFF ROCKING BLAST
Atlanta Journal

Hunter Fires Shot at Crow,
Fireworks Plant Blows Up
Milwaukee Journal

Something To Crow About

Shot Levels Fireworks Plant
And 'Chases' Hunter Into River
Louisville Courier-Journal

His Shot at Crow Rings the Bell:
Fireworks Plant, 6-Town Alarm
New York Herald Tribune

Hunter Pulls Trigger on Crow
And Sets Off Fireworks Plant

Potshot At Crow
Blows Up Whole
Fireworks Plant
Baltimore Sun

Fireworks
Plant Blasted
Detroit Free Press

When Chain Reaction Starts, Young Man Is So Startled That
He Jumps Into River — Whole Community
Gets Excited.
Kansas City Times

Hunter Eats Crow After Big Bust
New York Post

A Head Writer's Field Day

The Feature Head

On March 5, 1951, a young man out for a walk near the tranquil village of Pearl River, N. Y., leveled his shotgun at a crow on a nearby tree and set off a typical newspaper feature yarn. For whether or not he hit the crow, the young hunter certainly did hit a fireworks plant, and the result was confused with an atomic bomb explosion for fifteen miles around.

Editors across the nation received the story from the wire services and liked it. So, presumably, did their rim editors, who had a chance for a few minutes to put aside the cares of straight, solemn fact telling and let themselves go. The results are shown on this page.

No two of these heads much resemble each other. A few editors considered the story too good for fancy tricks and simply told it as an amazing sequence of events that needed no embellishment. They tended to be on the papers that got the story first. For instance, the New York *Daily News,* famed for its trick-shot headlines, used a head that emphasized the facts. However, the headline of another New York tabloid, the *Post,* a second-cycle paper, gave the story special treatment to help justify its inclusion half a day later.

It is also worth noting that there is no particular correlation between the reputed dignity of the paper and the headline treatment accorded this story. For example, note the light touch used by the New York *Times,* New York *Herald Tribune,* Louisville *Courier-Journal,* and Kansas City *Times.*

The considerable range in treatments accorded this story across the nation serves as an introduction to feature-headline writing. Feature-head writing calls for qualities that probably cannot be taught, certainly not by a textbook. It is a highly personal art that puts a premium on originality. The individual must develop his own bent. If he simply doesn't have one, he should turn his energies to other desk duties; straining hard for effect usually shows. But the only limits on the editor who "has it" will be the extent of his own originality, his ear for language and sense of appropriateness, the leeway his desk allows him, and his ability to accept the judgment of others when they decide the head doesn't "come through."

It may be useful to divide feature heads into two main classes, the teasers and the tellers. *Teasers* never do tell the story; they are designed to excite interest in it and are most appropriate where the story is told chronologically or otherwise builds up to a punch line. Telling such a story in the head spoils the effectiveness of the story itself.

Tellers, on the other hand, convey the meaning of the story at once. They derive their feature twist from some other source than withholding part of the meaning of the story in an effort to entice the reader into pursuing it. They may simply tell it in some striking way or merely in an informal way, contrasting with other headlines only in their less serious tone.

Feature heads can be tested against the criterion "Does it come through," *i.e.,* does it convey its meaning instantly? This does not imply that it has to tell the meaning of the story. But even teasers must hint meaningfully, not merely string meaningless words together in the hope that the reader will be intrigued by the very absence of meaning. The *full* meaning of the head can be postponed until the reader has related the head to the story.

When the feature-head writer begins to gain confidence, he may be subject to either or both of two faults. One is sticking to a "formula": having succeeded once or twice with some particular device, he returns to it again and again. The other is to "slop

over"—consistently to push the story farther than it reasonably goes. This unfortunate development can result from building—and attempting to maintain at all costs—a reputation on the desk as a very funny guy with a feature head.

Sometimes spur-of-the-moment headline ideas can make exceptional once-only use of typographical devices. Several newspapers have, in a puckish mood, created a special version of their own nameplates to illustrate extremely hot weather: limp, sagging, blistering nameplates certainly convey the idea. Then there are such once-only devices as this one:

(✔) Oct. 19: 'Boys Town'

Game With CC Set at Briggs Stadium

Detroit News

However, most feature headlines have to fall back on mere words and punctuation marks. The headlines and stories below illustrate devices that have produced good feature heads. These heads are a part of the schedule and hence of the routine of the newspapers concerned. Often plain puns are used, but more often they are puns wrapped up with other devices. Occasionally they depend on a more subtle play on words:

Driver Surrenders License Piecefully

MILWAUKEE — (XP) — A Milwaukee man, in court on a speeding charge, gave up his driver's license piece by piece in traffic court here Friday.

Kenneth Steinke, 22, was ordered by Judge John Barry to surrender his license. Steinke tore up the license and dropped the pieces on the judge's desk.

Judge Barry suspended the mutilated license for six months and fined Steinke $25.

Officer Sees Through 'Blind Man's' Bluff

CHICAGO — (XP) — Thomas Cohen, 43, Memphis, Tenn., groped along the street Saturday with his tin cup in his hand, tapping the sidewalk with his white cane.

Detective Martin O'Meara saw the "blind man" pause, stoop down, and pick up a cigarette butt. O'Meara took him into custody.

'Joining Army?' Judge Says, 'That's the Ticket'

DES MOINES, Ia. — (XP) — Police gave Thomas Robinson, Runnells, Ia., a ticket Friday for overtime parking.

Robinson later told Municipal Judge Charles S. Cooter that he was taking an Army physical exam when police tagged his car.

"Did you pass?" asked Cooter.

"I sure did," Robinson replied.

"Case dismissed," said the judge.

End rhyme can be effective:

If Tots are Trouble, Then Hers are Double

ONSET, Mass. — (XP) — Mrs. Anita Lopes, 29-year-old mother of 11 children, was advised by doctors Thursday that before the month ends she can expect her sixth set of twins.

And meter can, too, with or without rhyme:

Someone Finally Shut That Icebox Door!

A parenthetical word or phrase can sharpen the play on words:

General Commands 'Lounge Addicts' to Hold (Waist) Lines

Alliteration is overdone, but it can add something provided the headline doesn't depend on it alone:

Sid's Seldom Inn—So She's Seeking Solution

MILWAUKEE — (XP) — Mrs. Mila Ellingsen, 38, sought a divorce Saturday on grounds that her husband, Sidney, 44, refused to do his share of the work in the tavern they own jointly.

The name of the tavern: "Sid's Seldom Inn."

Biblical and literary references can be to the point, if they are familiar and inoffensive:

Ask and It Shall Be Opened Unto Thee

Leo Trainor, 47, of 16 S. Broom St., a frequent "guest" at the Dane County Jail, walked into the courthouse Saturday and asked Superior Judge Roy H. Proctor to give him 10 days in jail as a vagrant.

The judge obliged.

Dialect is perhaps even more risky but its inoffensive use can add a bright touch of color:

Faith and Bejabers, It's Michael Joseph Day!

HOLLYWOOD — (XP) — The wife of singer Dennis Day gave birth Saturday to her third son.

The baby, Michael Joseph, weighed 7 pounds, 12 ounces.

The couple's two other children are Dennis Jr., and Patrick.

Plain talk with a light touch is often preferable to any of the above trick literary devices, however:

No More Snow Seen; Coming Down, That Is

Keep Your Chains On, Folks, More Snow's on the Way

Some New Problems in Headline Writing

We have already seen that new headline forms have yielded both new freedoms and new responsibilities for headline writers. Some of the new forms originated with fresh trends in makeup, discussed at length in Chapters 10 and 11; cleaner and simpler headline forms are consistent with the trends toward horizontal makeup and more white space. But stories are also written in new ways; increased emphasis is being placed on forms other than the straight news story. The effect of these developments on the editing process as a whole is treated in Chapter 5, but two special problems they bring to the head writer deserve special attention here. The first is the "kicker" head, an exemplor of new headline forms. The second is headlines for stories that are not news stories in the usual sense but interpret or comment on the news.

Editorial practice and philosophy vary widely about both, yet both deserve thoughtful consideration.

Kickers

The kicker headline has been with us for many years. At first it was used only occasionally and in highly restricted circumstances; in fact, some editors still believe that it should be used sparingly and only over feature stories. But kickers are being used these days by many papers on every kind of headline, from the "top line" to the single-column "shortie." And the rules for straight news headlines discussed on pages 150–161—concerning the relationship between first and second decks, for example—clearly do not apply.

What should the kicker do? How should it relate to the main head? Because readers don't necessarily read the kicker, nothing essential to the meaning of the headline should be consigned to the kicker. This means above all that essential attributions must not be put there. One might be tempted to say:

```
Operator's View

Mine Regulations
Partly to Blame
for Explosion
```

But we cannot assume that the reader will see the attribution in the kicker, which leaves the first deck a statement of opinion rather than demonstrable fact. Without the kicker, the head should read something like this:

```
Mine Regulations
Called a Factor
in Explosion
```

Now the original kicker may be used to help the head be *more specific* in its attribution:

Operator's View
Mine Regulations Called a Factor in Explosion

The kicker can be used to make the headline more specific in other ways.

Eight Graduate Faculties
at Northernmost Cited

is a complete headline, but it is more specific to say:

Doctoral Programs Surveyed
Eight Graduate Faculties at Northernmost Cited

The kicker can be used simply to add a relevant fact not essential to the main headline, especially if it dramatizes it:

Liner Hits Uncharted Reef
Hundreds of Passengers Are Saved as French Ship Burns in Caribbean

A kicker can, in fact, be used to introduce a theme of the story that cannot be written into the headline itself:

Bumpy Road
Chrysler's Recovery Falls Behind Schedule; New Problems Arise

No Profit Is Seen for 1970; Capital Outlays Are Cut; Minicar Plans Questioned

But Company Is Progressing

Wall Street Journal

Touchy Issue
City's Employees Move to Suburbs

Washington Post

When the head itself is somewhat vague, as on the kind of "situation" story treated more fully on page 80, the kicker can provide a label:

What Apollo is all about
The Most Ambitious Moonwalk

On such stories it is often possible to use an interrogative in the kicker to give a clue to the unanswered questions raised in the article:

New U.S. Assault?
Reds Gird in Laos

What's Deductible?
Death and Divorce Create Common Tax Problems

"Think-Piece" Headlines

This brings us to another relatively new demand on the headline writer: the headline over the "think piece," as newsmen have called it for years, or the "situationer," in wire-service jargon. What is meant, of course, is not the story based on hard facts but the attempt to sum up a situation, dig deeply into a current dilemma, or look ahead to a new problem: an interpretive piece; "soft news" rather than "hard." Such stories have assumed increasing importance in recent decades as newsmen have realized that the newspaper must offer more than last-minute bulletin news, a game at which the newspaper has been a consistent loser to other, more rapid media.

The writer of a think piece has greater freedom than is normally afforded by the spot-news story detailing the latest facts. The head writer has correspondingly more freedom, too. Once again he must give clues to the nature of the story; as the feature headline telegraphs the feature nature of the story, so the headline of an interpretive story should characterize the material under it. That again makes the rules of spot-news head writing inappropriate. The editor has to look at the entire tenor and compass of the interpretive story to determine how he should project it in the headline; the lead usually is not enough.

There are various ways of indicating that a story is not of the spot-news variety. Label heads are often used, or other free forms. Some editors believe the distinction is so important that they assign regular labels to every such story, even using various terms to designate various types: "News Analysis," "Background of the News," "News Interpretation," "Opinion." These labels are conspicuously inserted into the text or the headline—as a kicker, among other possibilities. Some newspapers precede the story with an "Editor's Note" explaining the special nature of the story, particularly when it is in a series.

But even without the aid of such devices, the headline itself can convey the idea. In the following example, the headline is structurally traditional; that is, both the kicker and the main line have verbs. Yet the *language* of the head conveys the idea that this is not a spot-news story:

GIs in an Unhappy Limbo
Morale, War Ebb Together

Washington Post

The same issue of the same newspaper, however, contained other examples that depart from the traditional and adopt labels:

A Mover and Shaker
Vs. the Bureaucracy

Bonn's Ostpolitik: Uncertain Infant

The White House Scorecard

In Vietnam: New Danger
Here and Abroad: Progress

Washington Post

And, in another issue, a combination of the two:

Officially, All Is Well

The Lot of the Soviet Jew

Cambodia: End of Illusion

Hill Outcries Bare Extent of U.S. Involvement

Washington Post

The *Christian Science Monitor* uses both kinds, too:

Congress limbers for health-care debate

New U.S. assault?

Reds gird in Laos

Cable-TV battle shapes in Chicago

Christian Science Monitor

The same is true of the Los Angeles *Times:*

Expected to Dominate in 10 Years

Tide with Navy in Reshaping of Military

but also:

HIT RECORDS

'Jesus Rock'--- Youths' Search or a New Fad?

TROUBLED WATERS

The Tuna Boat Feud---How It All Started

Los Angeles Times

The think-piece headline is set apart from other headlines in both language and form, but the former rather than the latter carries the burden of meaning. The label head is a good structural example of making the language distinctive, but it is the tone quality of the words more than the structure that conveys the significant clues to what is in store for the reader. Even given undistinctive page and typographical treatment, there is no doubt about the nature of a story headed:

Upturns Predicted in Many Areas

Industry Analysts View Economic Picture With Real Optimism

With the exception of the two just cited, all the stories mentioned here had two things in common:

they were staff written and they carried by-lines. The first point simply suggests that ever greater staff time is being devoted to stories of this type by several of the most distinguished newspapers. The second point is more important in this context. The by-line itself is a signal, consistent with the other signals, that this is a special kind of story. While by-lines are often given to straight news stories, to be sure, they are always found above think pieces.

Is it not possible, of course, to set down rules for writing headlines of this kind. Dedicated copy desks are constantly working on new ways of doing the job. The most valuable editors are the ones who are exploring new ways of making the news compelling and interesting. They don't fit the news into the old, familiar formats but are constantly on the lookout for ways of presenting it distinctively. The following full-page illustration from the split page of the *Monitor* shows innovative think-piece treatment.

8

A Smattering of Typography

Because such a large part of the editor's job is paving the way for getting type on paper, he needs to know something about typography. In the first place, he needs to know how type is measured. He should also be able to recognize principal races and families of type. These constitute the twin objectives of this chapter.

Printing from movable type was invented in the fifteenth century, and the invention is usually attributed to Johann Gutenberg of Mainz. Printing had been done for centuries, but movable metal type was the key to the eventual spread of printing. Whereas the existing hand-carved wood blocks broke down after a small number of copies had been made, Gutenberg's original alloy of lead, zinc, and antimony proved capable of lasting through thousands of impressions.

From the fifteenth century through most of the nineteenth, printers assembled type by hand. After various attempts, an automatic typecasting machine was perfected in 1886 by Ottmar Mergenthaler, which cast a solid line of type at a time from a "magazine" of brass matrices assembled by a manually operated keyboard; then it automatically rerouted the matrices back to the magazine to be used again. The Linotype machine increased the amount of type one compositor could set by a factor of seven or eight. In the 1940's, punched tape began to replace the manual operator and started a technological revolution in composition methods that is at white heat as this is written (see Chapter 15).

The Point System

Printers have their own system of measurement, standard throughout the world. For centuries after

Gutenberg, printers were very largely their own type designers and founders, and there was no uniformity in the matter of type size from one shop to another. A *language* of type size arose through the years, including words like "pica," "nonpareil," and "brevier," to indicate approximate sizes. However, it remained for a French printer named Fournier to establish in 1837 the point system, which, with slight modifications, is in use today.

The point, originally a dot the size of a period, or "point," is one seventy-second of an inch. All type sizes are expressed in points and fractions of points. Type-size *names,* which had existed long before the point system was invented, were assigned specific sizes in points. Pica, a type size approximately one-sixth of an inch high, became *12-point* type. Nonpareil, which had been approximately half the size of pica, became *6-point* type. In terms of *space,* 72 points equal one inch, and 12 points equal one pica; the "em" is the square of any size of type.

A piece of type, like any solid, has three dimensions: (1) *height* from top to bottom of the side that prints—the dimension we've been discussing so far; (2) *width* of the side that prints; (3) *depth* from the base to the printing surface. Only two of these dimensions vary. The last named, known as "type-high," is standard in the English-speaking world and Latin America. This dimension measures .918 inches or about eleven-twelfths of an inch.

Measuring Length

The other two dimensions are expressed in points. Type size, for example—not the length of the raised surface that prints but the length of the entire upper surface of the piece of type (in the accompanying diagram, the depth of the letter "H" plus the "shoulder")—is measured in points. If this dimension is 12 points, it is called 12-point type, or pica type. Here are some common measurement problems that may help to clarify "north-south" measurement with the point system:

Suppose you are handling the copy on a story which is to run the exact depth of a two-inch cut. How many lines of 8-point type may you have for the story? If a cutline set in 8-point type on a 9-point slug is meant

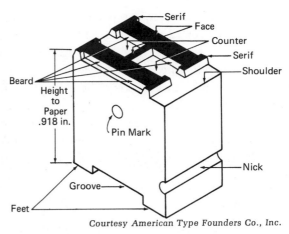

Courtesy American Type Founders Co., Inc.

A Piece of Type

to run alongside a cut that is three inches deep and it runs only twenty lines in type, how many points of spacing will have to be added between lines to make the depth of the type equal the depth of the cut? This is the sort of arithmetic a printer utilizes every hour of the day in performing his duties. And it's handy for the desk man to know, too. Both of them frequently use a "line gauge"—a ruler which is marked off in both inches and picas.

Measuring Width

The width dimension is not usually important in an individual piece of type, since the width of individual characters differs radically even in the same typeface. The capital "W," for instance, is usually several times the width of the small letters "i" or "l."

However, we *are* concerned with the length (or *measure*) of a *line* of type. (How wide is a newspaper column, for instance? All lines in a given column size must obviously be of the same measure). The point system translates to measure by means of that familiar crossword-puzzle standby, the *em.* An em is the square of any size of type, and is so called because the capital letter "M" in any typeface is normally about as wide as it is high, *i.e.,* square. A 12-point letter "M" is therefore both 12 points high and 12 points wide. Ergo, the em of 12-point type is 12 points, the em of 6-point type 6 points. Because the letter "n" is about half the width of the letter "m," half an em is one "en."

The standard measurement of width in printing terms is the *pica* (or 12-point) *em*. Unfortunately, this is often shortened to just "em." When the compositor sends the copy for a headline back to the copy desk with the notation "2 ems too long," he means that the head is 2 *pica* ems too long, or about 24 points too long, even though the line is to be set in 18 or 24 or 30-point type. Thus, even though an em strictly speaking is the square of any type size, the term is frequently used to mean the pica em.

Justification

Justification is the term for "spacing out to fill." Lines are sometimes justified to fit the width of the column by adding space between characters, but more often by adjusting the spacing between words.[1] Hand-set lines had to be filled out by inserting spaces by hand. The Linotype machine justifies lines automatically: between each word it inserts a wedge-shaped "space band"; depending on how high or low it is raised, the space may be made larger or smaller, as needed; because all the space bands in a line are raised simultaneously, all word spaces in a line are equal. In many newspaper shops today, computers do the justifying (see Chapter 15). The kinds of spaces and their nomenclature are shown in the diagram below.

Columns are justified by inserting leading (pronounced "ledding") between lines. Leads are thin strips of type metal or brass, less than type-high so that they won't print, of thicknesses from one to three

points. When the strips are six points thick or more, they are called "slugs."

Races of Type

Texts

Broadly speaking, *black-letter* or *text* typefaces are very black, very ornate, and more or less resemble the work of the monks whose painstaking copying of the scriptures was for centuries almost the only reproduction of written language. Here is a sample:

𝔗𝔥𝔦𝔰 𝔦𝔰 𝔠𝔩𝔬𝔦𝔰𝔱𝔢𝔯 𝔅𝔩𝔞𝔠𝔨 𝔗𝔶𝔭𝔢

Text type (properly but rarely called gothic) was very popular in the Germanic countries and some of their northern European neighbors and in England; the typefaces that Gutenberg designed fall into this race. It is frequently referred to as "old English."

Today, most commercial printing plants keep some text type around for occasional wedding announcements, and it is used often to create a religious atmosphere—even, now and then, in advertising. But despite the significance of black letter in terms of the origins of typography and printing, it is not generally important today in newspaper and book printing.

Gothics

A more descriptive name for this category of typefaces is *block letter*. How the term *gothic* came to be commonly applied in America to block-letter faces is a mystery. In Europe, block letter is known as "sans serif" and "grotesque." Gothics are extremely simple in design, having these virtually universal characteristics: (a) the characters have no serifs and (b) they

---

[1] This has not always been true. Just as manuscript copyists had adjusted the size of individual characters to fill a line, keeping word space constant, Gutenberg cast each character in several widths and used the different-sized characters to produce a justified line.

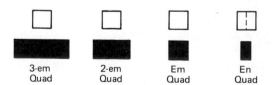

The Language of Spacing

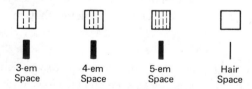

Courtesy American Type Founders Co., Inc.

are drawn to the simple outline of the letter, with each stroke the same width as all others.

This is Folio Medium

A word of explanation: a "serif" is a little finishing stroke on a character; it is a chief characteristic by which one typeface may be distinguished from another. Serifs and other terms used in describing type are shown in the following diagram.

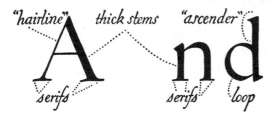

From "On Recognizing the Type Faces" in *MSS by W A D,* reprinted in the *Dolphin,* No. 2, 1935, p. 47. Used by permission of the late W. A. Dwiggins and the Typophiles.

Gothics are unrefined, cold, and emphatic. They are one of the easiest type races to identify. They had great vogue as headline type between the Civil War and the Great Depression and are still widely used; until very recently, the Chicago *Tribune,* for example, had used just about the same gothic banner line since its earliest days.

MODERN SANS SERIFS

Block-letter type has a modern stepchild called *modern sans serif* that is probably the most popular single category of typefaces today for newspaper display heads. Each typefounder and each composing-machine maker has half a dozen versions of them, each with a different name. Some of the common ones are Erbar, Tempo, Kabel, Metro, Futura, Spartan, and 20th Century. These faces have a lot in common with the old block letter. They have no serifs, as the name implies. Although they are not invariably cut so that all strokes are of the same width, they certainly come close to it.

This is a line of Tempo Medium

This is Kabel Black

The modern sans serifs differ from their forerunners, the gothics, in several ways. They simply *look* modern, for one thing. Closer examination will show that the moderns are cut more geometrically. Notice in the example above that the Tempo "o" is a perfect circle. That theme is carried out in the lowercase "e" and "c," and the loops of the "d," "b," and "p," etc.

There is an interesting difference, too, in the way curved strokes are terminated, as in the lower-case "e." Some letters, such as the Kabel capital "K," are formed quite differently from those of the old gothics. Some, like the capital "H," are indistinguishable except to the trained eye of the typographer.

MODERN SQUARE SERIFS

Another offshoot of the gothics is a group of *modern square serifs,* known by such names as Stymie, Memphis, and Karnak. The square serifs have more in common with the modern sans serifs than they have with the old gothics. They, too, are geometrical and streamlined; all the strokes, with very few exceptions, are of the same weight. The basic difference between them is the addition of a rectangular serif, of the same weight as the main strokes of the letter:

This is Stymie Medium

Cursives and Scripts

Cursives and *scripts* arose early in the history of typography. In general, they were designed to emulate handwriting: they are embellished with little strokes that tend to link the characters together. They differ from each other in the *extent* to which the connectors actually link characters:

This is a typical script—Typo Script

This is a typical cursive—Bernhard Cursive

Script letters flow into each other so carefully that the break between letters is not visible to the naked eye. The cursive letter flows only *toward* the succeeding letter. (These should not be confused with italics, which will be discussed later.) Not all the scripts and cursives lean to the right. Some of them lean to the left, resembling backhand writing.

Like black letter, the scripts are relatively little used today. They have virtually no newspaper uses except in advertising and very occasional headlines. Script is sometimes used in wedding announcements and the like where a tone of formality is desired. The cursives have been enjoying quite a vogue lately in commercial printing and advertising, and many new ones have been brought out in recent years for those purposes. They generally convey a personal but informal feeling, in sharp contrast to the romans and italics.

Romans

By far the largest race of typefaces is the *roman,* with its accompanying *italics.* Roman faces represented a revolt from the ugliness and formality of the German-inspired black-letter faces, which moved into Italy during the fifteenth century with the spread of the art of printing. The Italians, having modified the art of their own copyists to a simpler and more classical letter, soon were casting type along the same lines. The first true roman was produced in 1470 by Nicholas Jenson, a Frenchman who had studied with Gutenberg but later established himself in Venice. The face he created is still in use today under the name Cloister Old Style.

Jenson's design has moderate contrast between heavy and light elements (wide strokes and narrow strokes) and has a grace that distinguishes it strikingly from both the black-letter and block-letter faces. It serves as the model for all the roman designs that followed.

OLD STYLES AND MODERNS

Romans in use today fall into two broad categories of design: *old style* and *modern.* The earlier romans, like Jenson's Cloister, were fashioned after the fine manu-

script writing of the day. They reveal in their design that the copyists held their flat-ended pens diagonally to the line, producing a very graceful and relatively irregular character.

The first type designer to break away from the old-style school was John Baskerville, a Briton who took up printing as a hobby at the age of fifty. The new face he designed in 1757 (called Baskerville) featured greater contrast in weight between strokes and sharp, pointed serifs. But it remained for Giambattista Bodoni, an Italian, to gather up the loose ends of the modern trend noticeable in England and France and to create the first real modern—Bodoni. Revived in 1911, it has become by far the most popular roman headline typeface in the United States.

Manuscript writers of Bodoni's day held the flat nibs of their pens precisely horizontal. The effect of this can be seen by comparing the Bodoni (modern) and Garamond (old style) letters below. It is particularly apparent in the "o" and the "a."

These lines are set in Garamond, designed by Jean Jannon in France in 1621, a graceful, elegant example of old style.

These lines are set in Bodoni Bold, a favorite of newspapers; noted for simplicity and precision, it is a true modern.

Careful comparison of these lines of type will reveal the essential differences between modern and old-style romans. All the chief elements of modernism can be seen in the Bodoni example:

Precise uniformity All the heavy elements are of precisely the same weight, all the light elements the same hairlines. The "m" is designed just like the "n";

the loops on the "p," "d," and "b" are exactly the same except for direction. Now note the irregularity of the Garamond, such as the difference in design between the "b" and the "d."

Flat serifs   Whereas the Garamond serifs differ from one letter to another and even within a single letter (note the capital "T"), as they would if made by a pen, Bodoni serifs are simple hairlines for the most part.

Sharp contrasts   Bodoni is characterized by extreme contrast in weight between heavy and light elements. Notice that the Garamond, although no monotone by any means, has relatively little contrast and the lines change in weight gently, gracefully, and naturally, not on the basis of any geometrical plan.

Simplicity   Bodoni's design has a minimum of ornamentation, like all moderns. Garamond, although not heavily ornamented, has its little devices, such as the irregular brackets on the cap "T" and the concave serifs and tops of the vertical strokes of the lower-case "i," "r," "m," and "n." About the only frivolity to be found in Bodoni is the top of the lower-case "t."

Precise alignment   If you draw lines along the bases of the Bodoni lines above, they will show that all the letters line up perfectly except for "descenders," and these line up perfectly with each other. Similarly, alignment is nearly perfect across the tops of the lower-case letters except for "ascenders," and these line up almost perfectly with each other and with the tops of the upper-case letters, with the exception of the lower case "t." Note that the crossbars of "t" and "f" are precisely aligned with the tops of the lower-case letters. Such precision is lacking in the old styles.

It must not be assumed that the moderns have *supplanted* the old-style faces. Old-style versions of Caslon, Garamond, Cloister, and others, although currently out of favor in newspaper headlines and body type, were widely used for those purposes during the 1920's and are still highly popular with advertisers and book designers. This can also be said of Goudy Old Style, although it is of modern American design.

ITALICS

Italics, another broad category of type design, are variations of the romans and modern sans serifs and square serifs. They are grouped here with the romans because the roman variations are more frequently and integrally used than the sans-serif or square-serif variations. They are named for the country of their origin. The Italian scholar, Aldus Manutius, created the first italic type. As a by-product of his lifelong effort to make inexpensive books available to the masses, Manutius designed a sloping typeface said to be modeled after the handwriting of Petrarch. Its characteristics were those of all italics—gracefully designed letters set closely together with a gentle forward slope.

Italics should not be confused with scripts and cursives. Although there is a similarity between the flowing quality of italics and handwriting that produces psychological linking in the perception of the beholder, italics have no connectors and are not linked.

Italics reflect the basic design characteristics of their corresponding romans, while differing from them in detail. This can be seen in the examples below:

This is Palatino

This is Palatino Italic

This is Bodoni Bold

This is Bodoni Bold Italic

This is Karnak Medium

This is Karnak Medium Italic

For example, Palatino and its italics are similar in tone and could be matched up by any layman. But the shapes of the italic lower-case "a" (and the "e," "f,"

Correspondent & Intelligencer. Lithographic Pens

Beethoven Madrigals GREAT Steam Print

Modern ENGLISH Houses

Architectural Drawings HERE in cool GROT

MECHANICAL REPOSITORIES

Scripture Preceptor.

COMMUNIONIST

Ecclesiastical Commissions

HISTORY OF ENGLAND

The recent introduction of the Italian Text, Grand Instrumental Performance

Victorian Decorative Typefaces Type and
typographical devices were ornate in Victorian
times. The faces shown here are typical of the
advertising typography of that time.

Courtesy of Faber & Faber, Ltd., from Nicolette Gray,
XIXth Century Ornamented Types and Title Pages,
pp. 188 & 189

"v," "w," and "y") is noticeably different from its
roman counterparts; looped letters are less rounded;
serifs on lower-case letters are in general longer and
more flowing. The total effect is less angular and more
graceful than the roman.

The designers of newspaper headline schedules
find italics a great boon. It is possible, for example,
to fashion the headlines of a page entirely of the
same typeface, obtaining contrast by using italics.

DECORATIVES

Any typefounder's catalogue will display a variety of
miscellaneous decorative typefaces that might be
classified separately, but have more in common with
romans than any other race. They are specially designed and used to create a particular atmosphere. For
example, Barnum was created to evoke the ornate and
colorful decoration of the circus, Legend to remind
the beholder of Persian characters.

This is Barnum
THIS IS STENCIL
This is Sphinx
This is Cooper Black
This is Legend

The extent to which this sort of thing is carried is illustrated in certain faces imitating typewriter type, which have imperfectly aligned characters or slightly crosshatched letters to produce the effect of the type-writer ribbon.

Traditional designs of type are often embellished with *tooling*. In tooling, part of the face of each letter is cut away according to a standard design. Tooling has the effect of lightening a face while at the same time emphasizing its basic design. It is rarely used in newspaper headlines but is not uncommon in advertising. An odd variety of tooling is the cross-hatching of "typewriter type"; more common are out-line, inline, and shaded. Goudy particularly lends it-self to this treatment:

This is Goudy Hand Tooled
This is Caslon Openface
THIS IS PRISMA

Families of Type Styles

Races of type subdivide into "families" (which in turn are broken down into "series" and finally to "fonts"). A family of type is a group of faces all of which have one basic design in common. The profu-

sion of designs has come about because typefounders frequently redesign many of the common faces and then assign them new names.

Families vary according to *size, style* (old style and modern, roman and italic), *width,* and *weight* or bold-ness. Size and style have already been discussed.

Width is the degree of condensation or extension. Here is the way Folio varies on that score:

This is Folio Medium
This is Folio Medium Condensed
This is Folio Medium Extended

Such terms as "tall" are occasionally used to describe a condensed face, while "wide" and "expanded" are common terms for extended faces.

Weight is usually expressed by the terms "light," "medium," "bold," and "extrabold," although other terms are sometimes used. An extremely bold Bodoni is called "Ultra-Bodoni," for example.

This is Folio Light
This is Folio Medium
This is Folio Bold
This is Folio Extra Bold

Each family consists of a number of *series*. A series consists of all sizes of a given face. Thus Cheltenham Bold Condensed in all available sizes constitutes a series. Cheltenham Bold Condensed Italics in all sizes would constitute another series in the Cheltenham family.

The *font* subdivides the series and consists of a complete assortment of a particular size of a given series and is stored in a single type case. A font of 24-point Cheltenham Bold Condensed consists of all the characters necessary to set material in that size and series. A font of 18-point Optima is shown below.

abcdefghijklmnopqrstuvwxyz
ABCDEFGHIJKLMNOPQRSTUV
WXYZ.,'':;!?-()$1234567890

Principal Families

Some principal families which are useful to know are discussed briefly below to help in recognition. They are shown in display size first, and the text explaining them is then set in 10-point type of the face being discussed.

Baskerville

The quick, brown fox jumps over the lazy dog. 12345678 90 THE QUICK, BROWN FOX JUMPS OVER THE LAZY DOG $%& *The quick, brown fox jumps over the lazy dog.*

This is a so-called transitional face, with characteristics of both old-style and modern faces. Like old styles, it sets compactly and is based on handwriting; as in moderns, letters are in general open, symmetrical, and vertical. Serifs are more delicate than old-style serifs but not as thin as, say, Bodoni's; there is a noticeable but not exaggerated difference between thick and thin strokes; ascenders and descenders are neither especially long nor especially short.

In short, Baskerville is legible, precise, and elegant but has few eccentricities. The loops of "e" and "a" are not as small as old-style loops; "g" and "o" are not quite as open as moderns. "J" descends, "W" has no serif on its middle point, and the tail of "R" is long.

Garamond

The quick, brown fox jumps over the lazy dog. 12345 67890 THE QUICK, BROWN FOX JUMPS OVER THE LAZY DOG $%& *The quick, brown fox jumps over the lazy dog.*

Garamond, a roman old-style, is characterized by irregularity of line. The downstroke of the capital "E" varies in width from top to bottom. The serifs are slightly concave and very delicate. The ascenders are very tall and the descenders very long. The letters are placed quite widely apart. There is an unusually large number of apparently irregular letters. This beautiful face produces a total effect of fragility, grace, and dignity.

Some letters to notice: "c" is very open; "T" brackets are unusually irregular, with the right bracket pointing about straight down, the left bracket turning out to the left; "a" has a very small loop, giving it an unusually tall appearance; "e" is perhaps the most helpful in recognizing this face, with its extremely high crossbar, producing, as in "a," an illusion of tallness; the projection on "g" points straight forward from slightly below the top of the loop.

In case the reader hasn't noticed, the text of this book is set in Lino Garamond #3.

Caslon Bold

The quick, brown fox jumps over the lazy dog. 1234567890 THE QUICK, BROWN FOX JUMPS OVER THE LAZY DOG $%& *The quick, brown fox jumps over the lazy dog.*

Caslon was created by a British engraver named William Caslon in 1722 when British printers tired of the plain Dutch faces then in vogue. The type he designed was more graceful and beautiful than the Dutch faces, and somehow characteristically British. The ascenders are quite tall and the descenders quite short. There is rather striking contrast in the weight of the strokes and the curved strokes are distinctly tapered. The serifs taper sharply.

Key letters: "C" is very closed and the serifs, top and bottom, are carefully matched (a bar on the bottom stroke is unusual); "a" has a rather low loop; tail of "y" is short and its finishing knob curves far back; projection on "g" is shaped like a teardrop and points up; heavy element of "A" is oddly mortised; top and bottom serifs on "E" point far out beyond the rather short middle bar; brackets on "T" are distinctly tapering and not quite a match.

Caslon still enjoys considerable favor as a headline type despite the fact that it loses much of its grace in condensation. Caslon Old Style is widely used in books and magazines and Caslon Bold is still a favorite with advertisers.

Bodoni Bold

The quick, brown fox jumps over the lazy dog. 1234567890 THE QUICK, BROWN FOX JUMPS OVER THE LAZY DOG $%& *The quick, brown fox jumps over the lazy dog.*

The straight hairline serifs, great contrast between strokes, and extreme regularity of the design have already been discussed. This is a very masculine face and even the italics are more masculine than most. Note that "o" really consists of two precisely balanced half-moons connected by hairlines. This structure, typical of the extreme regularity of this face, is carried through all similar shapes, as in "Q," top loop of "g," loops of "a" and "e." With a few exceptions, the serifs are either hairlines or perfect dots connected by hairlines, as in "f" and the projection of "g." The ascenders and descenders are of average length.

Besides being the most popular roman for headline use, Bodoni has some vogue as a magazine body type. It is very popular as an advertising face, as are its more exaggerated versions, such as Ultra-Bodoni.

Bookman

The quick, brown fox jumps over the lazy dog. 1234567890   THE

QUICK, BROWN FOX JUMPS OVER THE LAZY DOG $%& *The quick, brown fox jumps over the lazy dog.*

Bookman was adapted by American typefounders from Scottish origins. It is distinctly a monotone, with very slight variation in the weight of strokes. It is also exceptionally wide, which militates against its use as a headline type (although New York *Times* feature and binder heads use it). There is a hint of old-style backhand in it, notably in "o" and "s." The serifs are short and thick, almost blunt. Although it was first used in printing quality books, it is now more commonly seen in book advertising. It is a simple and honest face which makes up in legibility what it lacks in artistry.

Among the distinctive features are the long teardrop projection on "r," widespread brackets on the "T," slightly backhand "S," and **very** monotone "o," almost a circle but not quite.

America's first great typographer was Theodore Lowe De Vinne. Although he gave his name to a display face which was popular during and after the Spanish-American War, De Vinne's fame rests on his creation of Century in 1895 for the magazine of the same name.

Century is a very regular face which does not fall readily into either the old-style or modern categories. There is perhaps less similarity between members of this family than is usual, making it difficult to recognize. Compare the display type above with the type of this paragraph, which is Century Expanded, and with the next paragraph, which is Century Expanded Bold.

They do have these things in common: they are simply designed, combining regularity typical of the moderns with shaded strokes typical of old style. The contrast in weight is more marked than that of Caslon but somewhat less marked than that of Bodoni. The serifs are long, straight, precise, and regular. The ascenders are rather tall and the descenders rather short. The crossbar of "e" is unusually long.

Century

The quick, brown fox jumps over the lazy dog. 1234567890 THE QUICK, BROWN FOX JUMPS OVER THE LAZY DOG $%& *The quick, brown fox jumps over the lazy dog.*

Cheltenham Bold

The quick, brown fox jumps over the lazy dog. 1234567890 THE QUICK, BROWN FOX JUMPS OVER THE LAZY DOG $%& *The quick, brown fox jumps over the lazy dog.*

Cheltenham, America's second major contribution to typography, was at one time by far the most popular newspaper headline face among the romans and even the gothics. One of the reasons apparently was that it condenses very well, which seemed to please unit-count-conscious newsmen not yet awakened to the value of legibility. The late New York *Sun* went to its grave with headline type almost entirely of Cheltenham Bold and Cheltenham Bold Condensed (in all capitals!). However, the New York *Times* and Chattanooga *Times* still use Cheltenham Bold with italics in all caps to good effect, and the Minneapolis *Star* still uses Cheltenham Bold with italics almost exclusively. The Milwaukee *Journal* uses Cheltenham Medium with italics (and Goudy Bold italics) and wins prizes for typographical excellence.

Cheltenham is rather monotone in design, having only slight contrast between weights. The serifs are exceptionally heavy and blunt. The ascenders are quite tall and the descenders very short. Though all of this generally militates against legibility, it also contributes to the decided masculinity of this face. Cheltenham still has some favor among advertisers who are after an emphatic, down-to-earth appeal.

Among the distinguishing letters are "G," with a "belligerent chin" projection at the base of the lower upward stroke; "A," which has a right-hand stroke projecting beyond the apex; rounded knobs finishing off "c," "s," and "r"; "g," with its lower loop shaped a little like the figure 5; and two versions of "r," one with the projection on a line with the top of the main stroke, the other rising above the line.

Cheltenham Medium and Cheltenham Old Style, although designed very similarly in detail, are quite different in total impact from Cheltenham Bold. These faces, though hardly beautiful, have a good deal of grace, and their italics are quite feminine.

Times Roman

The quick, brown fox jumps over the lazy dog. 1234567890 THE QUICK, BROWN FOX JUMPS OVER THE LAZY DOG. $%& *The quick, brown fox jumps over the lazy dog.*

Times Roman, a face originally designed for the London *Times,* is still used today as newspaper body type and is very popular in book publishing. It is rather a restful face, combining old-style and modern characteristics. Like the old styles, "o," "c," and the looped letters are slightly backhand and not perfectly round. Ascenders are very short, descenders shortish. Serifs are reasonably pronounced and are concave. However, like the moderns, letters are regular, if not geometrical, with rather marked contrast between weights of strokes and similar serifs on each letter.

Some of the distinguishing characteristics of individual Times Roman letters are the high small loop on "e" and the low small loop on "a"; the loop of "P," which is very thick at the top and very thin where it rejoins the stem; the straight, horizontal projection of "g."

The modern sans serifs and square serifs are too numerous to compare at length. Although they resemble each other in the characteristics already mentioned, they differ from each other a great deal in detail. The samples below were chosen to illustrate the extensive choice available in these modern and very popular headline faces.

This is Futura Light

This is Futura Medium

This is Futura Demi Bold

This is Futura Bold

This is an example of Univers 45

This is an example of Univers 47

This is an example of Univers 53

This is an example of Univers 55

This is an example of Univers 57

This is an example of Univers 59

This is Univers 63

This is an example of Univers 65

This is an example of Univers 67

This is Univers 73

This is an example of Univers 75

This is Univers 83

The reader should not be discouraged if he cannot easily identify all of the display type in magazine ads, television visuals, etc. Much of what appears to be display type is actually part of the design of the ad—it is drawn, not set in type. Also, new typefaces appear all the time in response to changing design trends—art nouveau, art deco, pop, op, and the rest. They have their fling and disappear. Sometimes they come back as the taste of a former day is "in" again. Cheltenham, for example, has had a recent revival in advertising where its directness and force is used to convey a sense of urgency.

Special Newspaper Body Typefaces

Up to this point we have been discussing typefaces in general, faces which are used both in display and body sizes. In recent decades, however, a special group of typefaces has been developed especially for newspaper straight matter. Although they are less conspicuous than the headlines, body typefaces exert an important influence on the effectiveness of the newspaper and deserve at least brief study separately.

Like any typefaces, these special body types differ in design and size. But they also differ in a third and highly significant variable—*leading.*

Design

In design, the trend has been steadily in these directions:

Sturdier strokes Modern high-speed presses and the use of dry mats mean that narrow strokes often become obliterated after a few impressions: the type itself takes a beating in the stereotype process; the plate that results takes another beating in the high-speed presses. This virtually rules out Bodoni, for instance, as a daily newspaper body type, and in fact most faces with many hairlines are no longer used as body type.

More openness Because traditional faces frequently have "ink traps"—little corners in which ink-soaked lint can accumulate—the trend has been in the direction of open letters with few sharp angles which eliminate this hazard.

Tall, regular letters Both height and regularity tend to serve legibility,[2] and type designers have increasingly concentrated on these design elements in recent years.

Size

The trend in size has been, in general, in the direction of *larger* faces. Here again, legibility is the spur. Agate

---

[2] See Matthew Luckiesh and Frank K. Moss, *Reading as a Visual Task* (New York: Van Nostrand, 1944).

(5½ point) was the accepted newspaper body-type size for decades during the nineteenth century—and it was set "solid" (no leading between lines) at that. When the more sensational papers began playing with large display sizes, most papers except the New York *Herald* quickly followed suit.

For some years early in the twentieth century, 8-point solid became the custom. Then during World War II, newspapers had to conserve on newsprint, so they narrowed column rules, reduced margins, etc. Many dailies reduced body-type size to 7½-point, 7, and even smaller sizes, with half a point or a point of leading, and realized tremendous gains in space. Since the new faces often possessed greater legibility in design, these reductions in size frequently did not significantly reduce the overall legibility, while economizing on space.

Typographical researchers have established clearly the positive relationship between legibility and the presence of leading between lines (up to a point of diminishing returns). Generally speaking, it can be said that lines of solid 8-point type are less readable than 7½-point lines on 8-point slugs.[3] Much of present-day legibility is due less to larger type than more leading.

The trends in design and size have been set by a number of special "legibility faces" which have been the result of years of research under the direction of the Mergenthaler Linotype Company. Eight-point samples (on 9-point slugs) of some of these faces are shown below:

The quick, brown fox jumps over the lazy dog.
This is Century Expanded No. 8 △ 26, a legibility face.

The quick, brown fox jumps over the lazy dog.
This is Regal No. 1719, a legibility face.

The quick, brown fox jumps over the lazy dog.
This is Ideal No. 1659, a legibility face.

The quick, brown fox jumps over the lazy dog.
This is Times Roman No. 8 △ 584, a legibility face.

The quick, brown fox jumps over the lazy dog.
This is Bell Gothic No. 8 △ 508, a legibility face.

The reader may find it helpful to compare these faces with the other typefaces shown on pages 198–201 for a better understanding of the design features discussed on page 202. And particularly interesting is the comparison between the legibility faces and Weiss Roman, a face which "reads" extremely small in the same size:

The quick, brown fox jumps over the lazy dog.
This is 8-point Weiss Roman.

An additional feature of the legibility faces is their "fitting"—the economy of characters per line. This is particularly important in newspaper body types, of course.

Effect of Type Design

Evidence is accumulating that type design influences the way laymen perceive the meaning of an advertisement or a newspaper story. Wiggins,[4] for example, found that more condensed body typefaces produced faster reading than more extended faces, within a narrow range. But Davenport and Smith[5] failed to find any significant effects on amount read, time spent reading, reading speed, reading accuracy, or comprehension when they varied type height (9 and 7½ points), hyphenation, and justification.

Designers and connoisseurs attribute characteristic feeling tones to type of different styles.[6] Brinton and Blankenburg[7] at Stanford University asked two sets of subjects to judge several typefaces on seven-point

---

[3] Mergenthaler Linotype Co., *The Readability of Type* (New York: Mergenthaler, 1947).

[4] Richard H. Wiggins, "Effects of Three Typographical Variables on Speed of Reading," unpublished Ph.D. dissertation, University of Iowa, 1964.

[5] John Scott Davenport and Stewart A. Smith, "Effects of Hyphenation, Justification and Type Size on Readability," *Journalism Quarterly* 42:382–388 (Summer 1965).

[6] See Clayton Whitehill, *The Moods of Type* (New York: Barnes & Noble, 1947).

[7] Reported in Chilton R. Bush, ed., *News Research for Better Newspapers* 2:67–72 (New York: American Newspaper Publishers Association Foundation, 1967).

Semantic Differential scales, scoring items on paired adjectives such as *strong-weak* or *beautiful-ugly.* The two sets of judges were professionals (printers and commercial artists) and laymen (students). The two groups' judgments of the connotative meanings of typefaces were very similar, although the professionals tended to use more different adjectives to define differences, and laymen tended to approve of Cheltenham and Karnak more than did professionals.

A University of Wisconsin group[8] took this kind of test a step further and used three groups—professionals, semiprofessionals (journalism students), and laymen (other students). To identify the "dimensions of judgment" used by the three groups, the data were analyzed by a rather complex statistical procedure called "factor analysis," which pulls together all the pairs that are correlated with each other and separates them from those which are not. Semantic

Differential scales characteristically fall into three such dimensions, an EVALUATIVE dimension containing such scales as *good-bad* and *beautiful-ugly,* a POTENCY dimension (*strong-weak*), and an ACTIVITY dimension (*active-passive*). The dimensions used by these judges were more similar among the three groups than they were different, although professionals were more likely to use the EVALUATIVE dimension of judgment, semipros the POTENCY dimension, and laymen the ACTIVITY dimension. Not surprisingly, the laymen used a COMPLEXITY dimension less than did pros and semipros.

Editors evidently believe that typographic style relates to special interests. For example, the society and women's pages use what is thought to be a "feminine" kind of type. Haskins and Flynn set out to test ten typefaces for their appropriateness in headlines on pages meant especially for women, again using adjective-pair connotative judgments. The judges were 150 women. The results are given in the following table:

---

[8] Percy H. Tannenbaum, Harvey K. Jacobson, and Eleanor L. Norris, "An Experimental Investigation of Typeface Connotations," *Journalism Quarterly* 41:65–73 (Winter 1964).

How 150 Women Rated 10 Display Faces[9]

FACE	RATED HIGH	RATED LOW
Coronet Light *Home study library can aid grads*	*Feminine, elegant, beautiful, soft, slow, weak, delicate, expensive, exotic, light, shy,* graceful	Interesting (boring), inviting (repelling)
Garamond Italic Home study library can aid grads	*Graceful, loose,* feminine, elegant, beautiful, slow, soft, weak, delicate, ornate, expensive, exotic, light, shy	None

---

[9] The data are drawn from a study by Jack B. Haskins and Lois P. Flynn for the ANPA Research Center and reported in Bush, *op. cit.* 3:1–8 (1968). Highest and lowest ratings among all ten faces are in italics.

Stymie Light **Home study library can aid grads**	Feminine, slow, soft, weak, delicate, light, shy, loose	Graceful (awkward), interesting (boring), ornate (plain), expensive (cheap), inviting (repelling)
Radiant Medium **Home study library can aid grads**	Graceful, elegant, beautiful, expensive, *inviting*	Delicate (rugged)
Caledonia Bold **Home study library can aid grads**	*Interesting,* inviting	Feminine (masculine), slow (fast), soft (loud), weak (strong), delicate (rugged), light (heavy), shy (bold)
Onyx **Home study library can aid grads**	Ornate, exotic	Loose (*tight*), graceful (awkward), elegant (inelegant), beautiful (ugly), soft (loud), interesting (uninteresting), light (heavy), shy (bold)
Bodoni **Home study library can aid grads**	None	Elegant (inelegant), expensive (cheap), exotic (ordinary), loose (tight)
Spartan Medium Italic **Home study library can aid grads**	None	Feminine (masculine), beautiful (ugly), ornate (plain), exotic (ordinary)

Spartan Medium	Inviting	Slow (fast), weak (strong)

Home study library can aid grads

Spartan Black	Interesting	Feminine (*masculine*), graceful (*awkward*), elegant (*inelegant*), beautiful (*ugly*), slow (*fast*), soft (*loud*), weak (*strong*), delicate (*rugged*), ornate (*plain*), expensive (*cheap*), inviting (*repelling*), exotic (*ordinary*), light (*heavy*), shy (*bold*), loose (tight)

Home study library can aid grads

Coronet Light and Garamond Italic were consistently rated highest, but the former showed some negative qualities. Stymie Light was next. Spartan Black was, not surprisingly, the lowest ranked. Bodoni and Spartan Medium, though among the most frequently used typefaces on American front pages, showed few strong "feminine" characteristics.

These studies suggest that questions we have thought to be impenetrable can be investigated, using reasonably rigorous methods.

9

Words and Pictures

Though the competent news editor leaves the technical aspects of photography and other art[1] to his fellow craftsmen, he is involved every day in making decisions about art. He must be able to judge the worth of a piece of art, to act on it in ways that increase its worth, to supply words that help it tell its story, to use it in constructing effective newspaper pages.

The Importance of Art

Pictures help tell the news and today's newspapers are using pictures more than ever before. For several reasons more creative attention is being devoted to how to combine words and pictures into a more telling and effective account of the news. First, new concepts in photography are constantly being applied to photojournalism. Then, the technological revolution keeps turning up better and more economical ways of reproducing pictures in newspapers. Now that a column of pictures probably costs less than a column of type, new newspaper designs and makeup practices assign greater importance to art than ever.

Two nineteenth-century inventions initially made photographic materials available to the newspaper—the camera itself and the etching process that permits reproducing photographs on paper. The camera preceded zinc etching by decades. For nearly half a century, photographs could be reproduced in newspapers or magazines only as woodcuts, and later, copperplate etchings, both made from line drawings. Ironically, some of the finest war coverage by photography, that of Matthew Brady and his small army

_____

[1] "Art" is used here, as it is in most newsrooms, to mean all visual materials—photographs, line drawings, maps, charts—everything visual rather than verbal.

of assistants who roamed the lines during the Civil War, could not be published as photographs in the newspapers.

The first great era of illustrated journalism occurred during the last years of the nineteenth century. During the so-called era of the yellow press, the giants of New York's Park Row made lavish use of line drawings to blow up the Spanish-American war into the most overreported war in history, and they were widely emulated. An example of the kind of emphasis the visual received may be seen in the reproduction of the St. Louis *Post-Dispatch* of that era on pages 228–233. The extremes to which the war news and its visual representation were taken are generally thought to have been a skirmish in the circulation war between William Randolph Hearst and Joseph Pulitzer. Highly visualized war coverage should have been good for the purpose, but it was often fanciful and lent itself to minor hoaxes, such as the serialization of H. G. Wells's *War of the Worlds* in Boston and New York newspapers.[2]

The first zinc-etched, screened half-tone was published in London in 1907. Zinc etching made it possible to reproduce a photograph in all its variation from white through gradations of gray to black, and it enabled photographs to become a part of the newspaper's daily capability.

News editors and publishers were wary of this startling innovation, however, and it took a new kind of newspaper to exploit its potential and explore its dangers. Immediately after World War I, the tabloid picture newspaper burst on the scene, prepared to capitalize fully on the appeal of the vivid photograph. A big and usually sensational picture occupied most of the front page of every issue of Captain Joseph Patterson's New York *Daily News,* and later, Bernarr McFadden's notorious *Daily Graphic.* But the "newsphoto" got both a lease on life and a bad reputation as the *Daily News* recorded scoops like a view of the face of a convicted murderess at the moment of her electrocution and the *Daily Graphic* demon-

strated that pictures could be made to lie by careful retouching.

Early in the 1930's, a new technical capability made spot-news photos all but instantly available to editors everywhere from any point in the world where news was breaking. This was, of course, the system for transmitting pictures by radio. Newsphotos could be scanned photoelectrically, the resulting sound impulses transmitted by wire and wireless, and the original picture restored photoelectrically at the receiving end. The newspaper had an important new means of bringing the news to its readers.

In that same decade, the picture magazine was born, a new protagonist for visual news and a new competitor for the existing media. At the same time, radio was supplanting the newspaper as the medium for getting the news to people first. But photography added a new dimension to the newspaper's ability to compete: the newspaper still was quicker than the magazine and had the advantage over radio of the visual.

Eventually, television became the toughest competitor of all. Of course, it brought both visual and verbal images to people with all the immediacy of radio and graphic power of the newspaper. The newspaper retaliated by adding color to its capabilities in the early days of television, but color television soon overcame any advantage color might have temporarily given the newspaper.

All this is now history, but it helps explain the increasing importance the newspaper assigns the visual dimension. And it helps explain some fairly recent changes in the kinds of pictures newspapers use (see pages 209–213). The importance of art to the contemporary daily newspaper is demonstrated by examining even one issue of one typical newspaper. The Milwaukee *Sunday Journal* published 294 pages on June 14, 1970. Editorial art appeared on 107 pages and ran in at least 10 different widths, ranging from half a column to 7 columns. Some kind of art appeared on *every* page except in a 52-page classified-advertising section. Color was used on 21 pages, 12 of them editorial only, 9 of them advertising only. There were 165 black-and-white halftones, 49 black-and-white line drawings, 22 color halftones, and one

---

[2] See David Y. Hughes, "*The War of the Worlds* in the Yellow Press," *Journalism Quarterly* 43:639–646 (Winter 1966).

color line-and-spot cartoon. Four of the halftones were made from paintings. The black-and-white line cuts included 6 cartoons, 25 sketches and illustrations, strips, weather and other maps, floor plans and other charts, two paintings, and a crossword puzzle.

While those numbers are probably below the *Journal's* Sunday average, the sheer volume and variety of the uses of editorial art point to the importance of art to the newspaper as a whole and the importance to the editor of having some basic skills in knowing what art to use and how. Large metropolitan papers like the *Journal* have many art experts on their advertising and editorial staffs and a large art department serving both. But this does not relieve the general news editor of his responsibility to use art on his pages effectively and with relevance to his news mission. The desk can get help and advice from the specialists, but its decisions are its own.

What Editors Do With Pictures

There has long been a schism between reporters and photographers, a not particularly constructive competition that borders on mutual disgust. But more and more the skills of the photographer and wordsmith are being combined under the hat of one competent newsman, who uses a tape recorder and a camera as well as a note pad and a typewriter. With this sort of change in the wind, it should not be surprising that the way staffs are organized to handle pictures varies greatly from newspaper to newspaper.

The *functions* are pretty much the same everywhere. Someone must go out and take the pictures. Someone must give the photographers their assignments. Someone must develop and print the pictures. Someone must supervise the darkroom. Someone must crop and size the pictures and prepare them for the engraver (or other plate-making step). Someone must write the captions (or cutlines) to go with the picture(s). Someone must decide where the pictures will go in the paper. Someone must oversee all this activity and think about how it might be done more effectively.

But how these functions are organized, how they fit into the chain of command, and who decides what

Photo by John D. Slack
Courtesy Today *(Cocoa, Florida) and* The Gannetteer

An Artful Front Page For *Today* of Cocoa, Florida, the conquest of space is a local story. Here a full-size front-page picture dramatized a lunar space shot. The regular front page was moved to page 3. For experts who deplore reverses (white on blacks and grays), this and other pages shown in this chapter provide an effective rebuttal.

after talking with whom appear to have no consistent pattern in American newspapers. A Master's thesis at Indiana University written by Don Alan Hall[3] set out to discover the pattern—and essentially found that there was none. Less than half a sample of newspapers having 50,000 circulation or more had

---

[3] Rick Friedman, "Study Examines Role of Picture Editor," *Editor & Publisher,* February 15, 1970, p. 32; February 22, pp. 42 and 44.

Courtesy the Telegraph-Herald (Dubuque, Iowa)

Words and Pictures in the Women's Section

A routine department gets nonroutine treatment in the *Telegraph-Herald* of Dubuque, Iowa. At left, a huge reverse — easy to manage with offset — gives impact to the first page of the women's section.

At right, sharp contrast is preserved by the fine screen that offset can handle. The strong angle in the picture at upper right influences the way the whole page is seen and read. The headline is "art," too, and shows another freedom from the typefounder that offset permits.

photo or picture editors. Those that did assigned him immensely varied duties. Whether they had a picture editor on the staff or not bore no relation to the quality and quantity of pictures produced. The study concluded, in fact, that what appeared to make the greatest difference in the quality was the professional competence and attitudes of the photo staff itself and the news executives who made the significant decisions about art.

Photographers go out and take the pictures and come in and develop and print them, usually in the newspaper's own darkroom. Engravers convert the pictures to zinc etchings, printers put them into the page forms. But before and between these steps, one kind of editor or another applies his skills. The photographer goes out under direction from a photo editor, a city editor, a state editor or perhaps an assistant managing editor. Although the photog-

Photos by Fred Comegys
Courtesy the Evening Journal (Wilmington,
North Carolina)

A Prize-Winning Layout This kind of picture editing won for Tom Keane of the *Evening Journal* of Wilmington, North Carolina, an award from *The National Press Photographer* as picture editor of the year.

rapher is, in the best circumstances, encouraged to generate and develop his own ideas for pictures and picture stories, an editor works up photo assignments.

Judging a Picture as Copy

An editor also judges the resulting pictures. While he may do so in consultation with the photographer, the responsibility for choosing the best print to suit his purposes is his. Photos must be judged as both *copy* and *content*. In judging a picture as copy, the editor determines how well it will reproduce. Many things can influence the physical quality of a picture—its copy value—between the snap of the shutter and the picture's appearance on the page. First, there are all

the things the photographer attempts to control: lighting, camera and subject movement, shutter speed, etc. Then things can go wrong in developing and printing—the picture may turn out grainy or not show enough contrast between lights and darks.

Many more possible sources of distortion or deterioration arise in the process of turning the picture from a glossy print into a newspaper plate, especially when letterpress is used. The glossy is converted to a zinc. Both can be scratched in handling. After the zinc goes into the page form a mat is made and cast, which costs some sharpness. As the issue rolls, the picture can lose still more as the high-speed presses wear down the plate and paper lint and ink fill in the etched-out spaces. The picture can be smudged by a dirty tape in the folding process. Some art, for example the mats wire services supply their members by mail, goes from negative to print to mat to cast to mat to plate to press; an already indistinct picture will show little more than a blur after going through all that. When a plastic engraving is used, the plate-making process may be circumvented and the engraved cut fastened directly to the finished page plate. But most letterpress newspapers use zinc engravings, which have to go through the complete stereotype process.

Offset tends to produce a printed picture far closer to the quality of the original glossy print than letterpress. There is no mat-rolling step, for one thing. Because the paper is finer grained, a finer screen is used. Since the plate does not make direct contact with paper, there is almost no deterioration because of wear or ink and lint filling deeply etched surfaces.

In any case, in judging art as copy, the editor needs to know how much loss is likely to occur in processing and printing. What he looks for in a print is sharp focus, good contrast, and uniformity throughout in focus and contrast. But copy should not overwhelm content values. Two of the most famous newsphotos of all time, the execution of a war prisoner and a woman leaping from a blazing hotel, were both badly blurred. Yet editors didn't hesitate to use them, with retouching to overcome some of the worst copy faults. Blurring and other forms of distortion may actually add to the content value of the picture; blurring conveys the sense of motion or great speed, for example.

Eye on the Presidency

He's taking over environmental enforcement

ACTION LINE

Senatorial doves and the war

Courtesy the Telegraph-Herald (Dubuque, Iowa)

Art on the Editorial Page   Art and other
contemporary news-publishing techniques
combine to give this page appeal and ease of
reading. Offset makes it possible; imagination
makes it work.

But more often distortions are copy faults, and the
editor must decide whether, in spite of them, the
picture is too good as content to throw away.

Judging Pictures for Content

Judging pictures for content is subtle art, bringing
into one judgment a series of assumptions about news,
humanity, and aesthetics. Very little sensible advice
can be found in the literature; qualified judges can
reach reasonable levels of agreement, but they find it
difficult to verbalize the process.

Some of the advice that does appear in print is
downright silly, by modern standards. One elderly
textbook suggests that the beginner should judge

content by three exactly equal criteria: news personality, news value, and "the amount of action
portrayed." Applied to one of the greatest newsphotos
of all time, a picture of the dirigible *Hindenberg* in
flames at its mooring tower in Lakehurst, New Jersey,
the score is exactly 66⅔, "since no important persons are shown," which prompts the authors of the
book to warn: "The beginner making use of this
method should therefore realize that a rating of
66⅔ may indicate a picture of major news value.
On the other hand no picture which cannot reach the
60 mark will be worth publication." If the editors of
the Louisville *Courier Journal* and *Times, The Paper*
of Oshkosh, Wisconsin, the *Telegraph-Herald* of
Dubuque, Iowa, *Newsday* of Garden City, Long
Island, and other papers whose photo and news staffs
are leading the way in new directions applied this
test, 90 per cent of their pictures would not pass.

Another book propounded a different way of
guiding the judgments of the neophyte, involving an
understanding of human motives; if you know what
really makes people tick, you can judge how they will
respond to the picture; ergo, you choose the picture
that produces the biggest response. "All news, near or
far, concerns four great elemental themes: *survival,
sex, ambition,* and *escape.* These are the great *motives*
or instincts, which form the pattern of man's existence on this earth. His interest is at once aroused by
anything which invokes them."

Poking fun at early efforts to transform professional hunch and popular psychology into editorial
dicta does not help the neophyte very much in learning to choose pictures, but at least it warns him away
from some of the more obvious pitfalls. There are no
rules; there are very little data on which rules might
be based; the road to wisdom is experience. One of the
reasons there are no eternal truths is the changing
concept of the place of the visual element in the newspaper. If a little hyperbole may be permitted, for
many years three kinds of pictures seemed to get into
the paper regularly: 1) spot news, 2) cheesecake, and
3) three men and a piece of paper. Since the photographer rarely arrived while it was happening, much
spot-news art was reenacted or contrived in one way
or another. Cheesecake was largely supplied by press

Places well remembered

If you happen to be heading for Washington, D.C., this summer, or if you have just visited, these are special scenes to cherish of one of the world's most beautiful national capitals.

Photos by R. Norman Matheny, staff photographer

Washington, D.C., carries both past and present boldly—perhaps because Americans are a people whose present never forgets its past. Above are memorials to the Jima, Lincoln, and Washington, with the Capitol in the background. Lower left, a view of the Capitol rotunda from under "Kerichonria," first King of all Hawaii. And the constant stream of visitors, right.

The last resort of men made desperate

By George Dismaigre

Rebels in Eden: Mass. Political Violence in the United States, by Richard E. Rubenstein. Dupree: Little, Brown. $6.95

This book on violence in the United States does more than merely trace the grammar and appalling events of a country marked by conflict of all kinds. It does more than merely fogrilate the nation for being a violent people with a history of mayhem and lawlessness.

At a time when crime wave are provoking a clamor for "law and order" . . .

. . . From the bookshelf

Reprinted by permission from The Christian Science Monitor. © 1970 The Christian Science Publishing Society. All rights reserved.

Art for Art's Sake These brilliant pictures topped the split page of the *Christian Science Monitor* on the strength of their aesthetic merit rather than their news merit. The remarkable night picture at upper left combines elements rarely put together in a single Washington scene: the Iwo Jima, Lincoln, and Washington monuments and the Capitol dome. The other two are interesting in juxtaposition, both deliberately distorting reality into a circular or "fish-eye" view to convey a special truth about a visit to the capital.

agents and was even more contrived. Three men, etc., is a contrivance for making a picture when nothing visual inheres in the story at all, justified on the ground that if names make news, faces make pictures.

The change discernible in recent years has applied more severe criteria to the first category and has eliminated the other two altogether. In their place are pictures run for sheerly aesthetic reasons or to com-

ment on the human condition. These pictures have to be judged by different criteria altogether.

Spot-news pictures are still the visual life blood of the paper. They still must be judged on the basis of their relation to the story. The closer the relationship, the more likely it is that a picture will be run. The stronger the story, the more likely the picture will be run big, depending in some measure on its characteristics as copy. Not many editors hesitated to run a picture of the shooting of Lee Harvey Oswald by Jack Ruby at the very moment it happened. The picture wasn't just close to the story, it *was* the story.

Size Helps Tell the Story When engineers stopped the flow of Niagara Falls in 1969, the Niagara Falls *Gazette* gave the picture nearly half the front page. It had to be big to convey the enormity of this once-in-history event.

*Photo by Bud Williams
Courtesy the Niagara Falls Gazette and The Gannetteer*

NIAGARA FALLS GAZETTE
Serving the Niagara Frontier for 115 Years

HOME EDITION

Vol. 76—No. 88 Niagara Falls, N.Y. 14302 Thursday, June 12, 1969 40 Pages-3 Sections-10 Cents

LAST OF THE WATER FLOWS OVER AMERICAN FALLS PRIOR TO COMPLETION OF COFFERDAM TODAY

Bared Cataract Exposes Cliff Cracks

Aid to Poor, Surtax Tied

Marines, Foe Clash in DMZ

NLF Seat At Parley Replaced

2nd Body Recovered at Falls Base

ON FALLS FLOOR—Niagara Frontier State Park police struggled over slippery rocks at the base of the American Falls today

Photo by Jon Webb
Courtesy the Louisville Courier-Journal

The Human Condition   None of these photographs is "news," but each is a real eye-stopper. The top picture occupied four wide columns at the top of Page One in the Louisville *Courier-Journal*. The page of pictures below tells us nothing of news but something about man in his world.

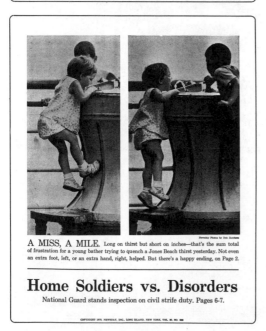

Photos by Don Jacobsen
Reprinted from Newsday, Long Island.
Copyright © 1970, Newsday, Inc.

So the content criterion for spot-news art is how much light it sheds on the story and how much it helps tell it. This is true whether the photographer caught a subject on the run or purposely focused on something that was there all along in order to bring it to public attention. An in-depth story on air pollution will be told more effectively with a picture of belching smoke stacks—even if the reader has seen it many times. A spot-news picture that catches a fleeting one-time-only event contributes to documentation.

It's not being suggested here that all pictures must fit into only one of the three categories—spot news, human condition, and aesthetic—to be any good. The newsphoto that helps tell a great story and at the same time fills the heart with gladness or comments on the human condition is a better picture than one that only helps tell the story. What made the great documentary photography movement that swirled around the Federal Security Agency in the days of the New Deal so startling and fresh was that the photographers knew how to tell the story in terms of its human consequences in films that often were also strikingly beautiful.[4]

Judging a picture for its human-condition or aesthetics elements is, of course, a lot harder than judging it for its spot-news worth. Why should the *Courier-Journal* devote four wide columns to a picture of a bunch of kids whooping it up in the back of a pickup truck (shown at left) or a bevy of high school girls at a cheerleading workshop waving their arms? Why should *Newsday* devote its entire front page to a small girl's effort to get a drink from a water fountain that wasn't built to her specifications (at left)? Even the editors who chose them probably could only answer, "I just liked the picture." But this vagueness should not be confused with lack of a sound policy. These papers—and others—have obviously made it a matter of policy to hire photographers who know how to find pictures such as these and not to run pictures in the two old categories of cheesecake and non-pictures, with results that are happy for their readers

---

[4] See Werner J. Severin, "Cameras With a Purpose: The Photojournalists of the FSA," *Journalism Quarterly* 41:191–200 (Summer 1964).

as well as creatively satisfying for their own staff members.

Mechanics

After deciding to use a piece of art, the editor acts on it in a number of ways. He determines the size and shape it will take, how it will be combined with words to tell its story, and how and where it will be displayed. He expresses these judgments in ways that are fairly uniform from newspaper to newspaper.

Cropping Cropping involves judgments as to what part of a print will be reproduced as a cut, and it should be done in glossy-print stage. The only cropping that can be done to a cast is with a saw, which is likely to leave a ragged edge which prints, especially in a halftone. A glossy proof enables the editor to choose the best part of a picture before the plate is made. The photographer tries to compose his picture well, of course, but often, in his rush, hasn't noticed extraneous elements or bad balance. The editor can correct faults of composition by cutting the picture down for greater emphasis and sharpness to the principal focal point of the picture. He can increase its overall impact by trimming away cluttered foreground material, for example, or excess detail along sides and top that contribute only noise, not information.

Cropping is accomplished simply by drawing lines at the edge of the print itself in wax pencil where the editor wants the picture framed. Glossies must be handled carefully. Instructions marked on the back of a print with a hard pencil or ballpoint pen, for example, can show through and be hard to eliminate in engraving. Some desks prohibit any kind of marks on the backs of prints for this reason.

Cropping is a delicate art that cannot be learned from a book. There are some general principles, but the editor has to treat each picture as a fresh problem and learn from experience. First, he is careful not to trim away *background* that contributes to the scale and sense of the picture. A Kansas wheat-field scene will be flat and featureless if the editor crops away a sky filled with towering thunderheads. Compositional values assume great importance in pictures that con-

vey a mood or a moment, and these are being used more heavily than ever these days.

In cropping, the editor also watches *continuation.* When a gesture is part of the composition, he doesn't cut away a hand or an elbow in order to get closer to an arm or a face.

He watches for *relevance.* There may be four or five people in a picture, but the story may be told more effectively by moving in on the two or three persons whose posture and relationship give the most telling visualization of what is happening. Foreground irrelevancies are especially vulnerable to cropping because they tend to be magnified by being close.

However, too close cropping can cut away meaningful *context* values. A nice example appears on this page, a memorable picture of three astronauts on their return from the first moon landing, as it was reused a year later. The explanation for the way their heads are arranged—the fact that they are looking through the window of a van—is completely cut away.

Some photo editors these days appear to be cropping faces very closely as a policy matter. The trend seems to have gone from busts to heads to faces. The standard portrait years ago was head and shoulders, with lots of unused space around the head. Then it became just the head. Lately some editors are moving in to show just facial features, at the sacrifice of hair and even chins. The effect is often dubious.

Neil, Edward And Mike..Who?

A year after men first left human footprints on the dusty surface of the Moon, the names of the Apollo 11 space explorers have largely faded from the memories of many Cincinnatians and other Americans.

When Neil A. Armstrong stepped off the ladder from the lunar module onto the Moon's surface at 10:56 p. m. July 20, 1969, millions of Americans were watching. They stayed at their television sets for two hours and 21 minutes to watch Armstrong and Col

Neil's Disappointed, Page 6-K

Edward E. Aldrin Jr. walk and work on the Moon and plant an American flag on its surface.

It would seem that the names of Armstrong, Aldrin and Michael Collins, pilot of the command ship, would long remain prominent in the memories

Moonmen In Their Hour Of Glory
. . . from left, Neil Armstrong, Michael Collins and Edwin Aldrin

AP Wirephoto

Poor Cropping Very tight cropping brings up good faces but loses the natural frame that helped explain the composition: the window opening in the van through which the picture was taken.

Good Cropping

The examples of cropping shown on this page illustrate what can be done to enhance a picture. In the river scene, the action is in the distance and a great deal of busy detail clutters the foreground. This material is cropped away, along with unnecessary background, in the interest of producing a picture of highly appropriate shape: the river is long and narrow, and that's the essence of a hydroplane race. The fishtail wake conveys the sense of great speed. Not altogether incidentally, a commercial sign disappears in the cropping, too.

The other picture shows a small girl and her symbolic cowbell at a Louisville Colonels baseball game. With the other face visible but in the background, the sense of being part of a crowd is there. But the out-of-focus faces on the left and part of a face at right just get in the way. The picture is the girl's expression, and cropping brings it out. The location of the main elements in the picture—the face and the cowbell—are carefully placed for balanced composition.

Sizing   Sizing pictures is just what it sounds like—determining the exact size of a cut as it will appear in the paper.

The size and shape of the picture, as cropped, are important to the effect it will have on the reader. It is in part dictated by column width: once it has been decided that the width of a picture will be reduced, say, to two columns (in a 14-pica column with one pica of white space between columns, this means 2 × 14 + 1 or 29 pica ems), its existing proportions determine how deep it will run. If the editor needs just an *estimate* of the depth for purposes of drawing up a dummy, he puts the print down on a page of the newspaper, marks its top and one edge, lays a ruler or "pica pole" diagonally across the print from corner to corner, and marks the point at which this line intersects the nearest column. Then he removes the print and continues the diagonal to the second column away from where the marked edge of the print was. He draws a horizontal line from this intersection across the two columns and the distance between it and where the top of the print was is the approximate proportional depth of the picture (see illustration on this page).

Mat shrinkage can distort the answer slightly, and there are ways of getting a more exact result. It doesn't take a mathematical wizard, after all, to transform width and depth measures from picas to points and compute the result in the formula $w:d::W:D$, where w is measured width, d measured depth, W planned width, and the unknown, D, is estimated depth. There are also elaborate mechanical devices for getting the same answers, for example, a half-circular "slide rule." When pasteups are involved,

Sizing Made Easy   Many editors would regard this picture as too small, considering its copy values; the major figure in it is almost invisible. How much vertical space would it occupy on the page if it were blown up to two, three, or four columns in width?

as they are in offset, the more exact measurements may be necessary.

Mortising   is the term for excising part of a picture and replacing the excision with something else—type or art. Sometimes it involves cutting a rectangular piece away from a corner to make room for the corner of another cut or as a place to put a caption. Or it may involve removing a rectangular area completely surrounded by the cut. This is easy to do in offset; the copy is simply pasted in. It is more complicated in letterpress printing, however, and should not be done without good reason, for it involves actually removing part of a zinc to make room for type.

Retouching   Sometimes an editor may request a picture to be altered in the photographic processing. The darkroom carries out his orders, and he ordinarily must confer with darkroom technicians as to feasibility. Retouching techniques include airbrushing, among others. When the main figure in a cut is surrounded by a background that is too busy or "noisy," it may be possible to soften the background by airbrush methods. If a face is very dark and the surrounding background also very dark, the background can be lightened.

Editors are wary of retouching, especially if it will be visible to any reader, owing to an unsavory history of altering newspaper pictures to change their meaning. But subtle and effective retouching may improve a picture's copy value without necessarily tampering with its content. The same is true of other darkroom skills, such as keying or highlighting (improving contrast) part of a print.

The Picture Page

In the survey of newspaper staff structures reported on pages 209–210, handling the picture page was the most often mentioned duty of the photo editor. The picture page used to be a fairly standardized daily feature appearing in the same position every day, usually the last page or the last page in the first section in full-size papers, and the centerfold in tabloid papers. It was a catch-all and a wastebasket—purely and simply a page of pictures culled from the newsphotos of the day after decisions had been made about pictures elsewhere in the paper. Each picture told its own story. Some were "feature" pictures—a smiling cat was always good—that bore no relation to the news elsewhere in the paper. Others were spot-news pictures illustrating a story running elsewhere in that issue; sometimes the story was keyed "Other pictures on Page 36" and the pictures, "Story on Page 1." Other pictures illustrated a story that ran in yesterday's paper!

The traditional picture page has many weaknesses and appears to be undergoing radical changes which are worthy of note. First, *pictures are considered today as an additional means of telling the news;* it follows that pictures telling the news should be carefully arranged in relation to the words telling the same news. The old picture pages split up story and pictures. There was no sense of enhancing one with the other, no concept that story and picture combinations can in many circumstances tell the story more effectively than either one separately. Since the 1930's, photojournalism magazines had been showing how words and pictures can be combined to give added impact and fidelity to an event or situation. It took the newspapers a couple of decades to catch on.

Perhaps the most striking development in news photography in very recent years is, as we have seen, *the photographer's concern with an aesthetic product and the editor's ability and willingness to treat the photographer's product with respect.* Both photographers and editors are realizing that a picture page offers newspapers an opportunity to convey to the viewer something that is wholly independent of "the news of the day": a moment of reflection on the human comedy or tragedy, a glimpse of something striking, inspiring, beautiful. News photography has always worked at these values, to be sure, but often with pie-in-the-face subtlety: a trick photograph represented the human comedy, a woman falling to her death from a burning hotel represented something striking, cheesecake represented something beautiful.

But there was something cruelly contemptuous of the viewer in this kind of photography, and the effort is successfully being made to upgrade it. Several of the illustrations that accompany this chapter have been chosen to make the point that pictures selected for their aesthetic quality alone can be arrayed on the picture page to good effect. Some of the finest of these examples appeared in a relatively small daily—the *Telegraph-Herald* of Dubuque, Iowa, a 40,000-circulation paper published in a 90,000-population city. A paper doesn't have to have a huge budget or a large staff to realize some of the potential that quality photography and skillful editing can convey. The *Gleaner-Journal* of Henderson, Kentucky, with 9,000 circulation in a 20,000-population city, and the *Bulletin* of Bend, Oregon, produce exceptional art on a day-to-day basis. So did *The Paper* of Oshkosh, Wisconsin, with a staff of four photographers in a city of 50,000, during its short life as a daily newspaper. Not at all incidentally, all of these are offset papers. But simple printing processes don't generate creativity —they merely make it easier to start over again and try something new.

The new picture page, then, offers photographers and editors a chance to work creatively, to pursue aesthetic and human values with skill and dedication. When these goals are served by photographers and editors who understand each other and share these values, the results can be breathtaking.

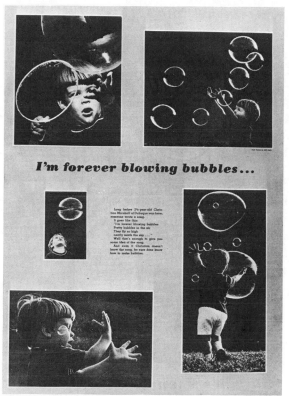

Photo by Bob Coyle

Photo by Bob Coyle

Picture Page—New Style   The editors of the Dubuque *Telegraph-Herald* work for impact on every picture page. Their skill, combined with inspired photography, made the first page shown a thing of joy and wonder. Much of the success of the second page depends on the sequence the editor has chosen. The page is anchored by the large pictures at upper left and lower right, which represent a start and a finish. The action in the first and repose in the second make words unnecessary. On the third page, the silhouette effect is heightened by the black background; the editor obviously knew how to exploit a potentiality of offset.

Courtesy the Telegraph-Herald *(Dubuque, Iowa)*

The size of a picture on the new picture page is governed not only by economics and its news value but also by its characteristics as a picture. The old picture page tended to keep pictures small and crowded together except when a news value dictated otherwise. Part of the reason was surely economic: engraving costs a few decades ago were far higher than composition costs. And perhaps editors used a "something for everyone" rationale. Generally speaking, pictures are still too small, too tight, too closely cropped, too cramped. But in today's offset paper, a page of art is far cheaper to produce than eight columns of type, and editors pay some attention to quality, not just quantity. They still have to worry about the size of their "news hole" and cannot be frivolous about the use of nonpaid space. But they can give a picture the space it needs for its relative impact and information value. Good pictorial display requires (or at the very least is well served by) ample space: space to display the pictures in a way to allow each to "come through" and space between them to allow each to have its own independent place on the page. The point is nicely made in the three pages of pictures reproduced on page 219 from the Dubuque *Telegraph-Herald.* Here the editing is every bit as skillful as the copy. Cropping, sizing—everything as well as the initial photography contributes to an experience for the reader.

Pictures help do the job in all parts of the paper, not just on the general news and sports pages. In recent years many of the best "picture pages" have been the section front pages of Sunday newspapers. The Milwaukee *Journal* runs four-color art on nearly every section front page every Sunday. Four-color spot-news art is really out of the question at present, as it takes too long to process. But there is plenty of time to photograph and process a spread on an historic home for the Home section, to get a quality picture of a work of art for the Fine Arts section, a bit of wilderness in the Outdoor section, etc. The papers that are using art creatively are using it in all parts of the paper to attract attention to all the different features they offer.

The Effects and Influence of Pictures

Unfortunately, very little hard data exists on how people react to pictures—what they see under what circumstances, how they feel about lighting, color, various patterns of words used with visual material. Consequently, most photographers and editors have to fly blind, feeling and guessing their way as they work.

Art and Type

Studies have been conducted to find out how people look at pictures, but so far little effort has been made to find out how readers obtain information from pictures—and how they combine information they get from the picture with the information in words that accompany the picture. Buswell[5] used an eye camera in a study reported in 1935. His evidence suggests that the viewer first *scans* the principal areas of the picture in short, quick bursts, much as he scans a line of print, then returns to certain areas for longer periods. A subject examining an ad with both visual and verbal elements made 40 fixations in all; he moved to the copy block at the 12th, 27th, and 38th fixations, suggesting a sort of information-search process. Bush[6] suggests that the amount of shifting between picture and caption may be a measure of the ambiguity of the picture.

The patterns for arranging words in relation to pictures used to be quite standardized but are less so today. The art would carry a headline across the top (legend) and cutlines below. If there was a related story it would carry its own headline, even if the story ran directly below the picture. As shown in the illustrations in this chapter, the line over the picture is rarely used these days; the caption may run beside the picture or below it; a display line below the picture may take the place of both legend and caption;

[5] Guy T. Buswell, "How Adults Read," *The School Review and Elementary School Journal* 45:Supplement (August 1937).

[6] Chilton R. Bush, ed., *News Research for Better Newspapers* 1:69–70 (New York: American Newspaper Publishers Association Foundation, 1966).

the material below the cut may have both a display line and the usual caption in body type; the caption may begin with a headline-style phrase in all caps; etc. Editors are, in other words, throwing away the old rule book and trying out new ideas.

The omission of the headline or legend over the picture may be at some cost to understanding. Ling,[7] in a Master's thesis done at Stanford under the direction of Wilbur Schramm, reports a study in which the effect of the legend was tested directly. Eight pictures with captions were presented to subjects with and without legends. The legends were written to answer a key question about what was going on in the picture. For example, the legend over a picture showing a woman standing in front of a prison was "Mystery Writer Frees Her," answering the question whether the woman was entering or leaving. Subjects were asked to tell what was in the picture and the answers were scored. In every case, the headed pictures produced significantly higher average scores than the unheaded pictures. (The study did not show, of course, whether the same wording at the beginning of the caption would have produced the same effect.) There is a general lesson about words and pictures in Ling's conclusions. Words can influence what is seen in pictures, much as Tannenbaum found, in the experiment reported in Chapter 6, that headlines influence what is perceived in the story.[8]

There is ample evidence to show that the visual dimension adds information and meaning to the verbal dimension. Anderson[9] has shown that the connotative meanings of statements presented visually (by picture) differ from equivalent statements presented aurally and in print (words). A series of experiments by Kearl, Powers, and their associates[10] has shown that information presented visually through graphs and charts often conveys more understanding than the same information presented verbally. The researchers have also explored the question of what kinds of graphs and charts are most effective. And most important, they found that a "word-picture" combination—for example, a bar graph with a verbal label—is more effective than the picture alone. Severin[11] found the word-picture combination to be more effective than a word-word combination (and more effective than visual and auditory cues presented alone) in producing recognition learning. Swanson,[12] summarizing the evidence from readership studies of 130 daily newspapers, found that visual-pictorial items had the largest readership (viewership) scores among all items. Many other studies with children and adults have reinforced that rather obvious finding. Mehling[13] found that the combination of a newsphoto and cutline was more effective in producing attitude change than was a news-story headline-and-lead combination presenting the same information. Culbertson[14] expected that the greater the *iconicity* of a picture accompanying a verbal message—that is to say, the more the picture resembles the object to which it refers—the more weight it will be given in interpreting the total message—in his study, how pro or how anti a two-sided message was. But interesting as his hypothesis was, the results of the study were inconclusive.

[7] J. Ling, "Degrees of Ambiguity in News Pictures," Master's thesis, Stanford University, 1955. Reported in Bush, *op. cit.* 1:70–72 (1966).

[8] See also Percy H. Tannenbaum and Jean S. Kerrick, "The Influence of Captions on Picture Interpretation," *Journalism Quarterly* 32:177–182 (Spring 1955).

[9] James A. Anderson, "Equivalence of Meaning Among Statements Presented Through Various Media," *A-V Communication Review* 14:499–505 (Winter 1966).

[10] *E.g.*, Hugh M. Culbertson and Richard D. Powers, "A Study of Graph Comprehension," *A-V Communication Review* 7:97–110 (Spring 1959).

[11] Werner J. Severin, "The Effectiveness of Relevant Pictures in Multiple-Channel Communications," *A-V Communication Review* 15:386–401 (Winter 1967).

[12] Charles E. Swanson, "What They Read in 130 Daily Newspapers," *Journalism Quarterly* 32:411–421 (Fall 1955).

[13] Reuben Mehling, "Attitude Changing Effect of News and Photo Combinations," *Journalism Quarterly* 36:189–199 (Spring 1959).

[14] Hugh M. Culbertson, "The Effect of Art Work on Perceived Writer Stand," *Journalism Quarterly* 46:294–301 (Summer 1969).

Color

The newspaper is using color photography, including process color, more and more. Good four-color printing is hard to get on high-speed letterpress equipment. Depending on the quality of the paper and ink used, it tends to transfer onto the page that folds down against it and to show through onto the page behind it. Nevertheless, ROP (run-of-paper) color capability exists for most newspapers printed by letterpress except the smallest. And offset has increased the possibility that even they can include quality color among their assets.

Only a little research has been done on the effects of color in newspaper pictures. The Milwaukee *Journal* research staff[15] has found that ROP color yields increased readership for inside pages with color plates. Scanlon[16] has turned up some fascinating evidence, on the other hand, that a color-television broadcast of a news event may produce some undesirable effects. He had one group of subjects watch unfolding news events on a black-and-white television set while another group watched the same events on a color set. The events were the funeral of a political figure and an important football game. Those who watched the events in black and white wrote longer and more detailed accounts; they referred to many more individual athletes in the football game, for example.

The less eloquent accounts of the color-set watchers may or may not be related to the "color shock" well known to clinical psychologists using the Rorschach test to project personality assessment. Subjects respond to a series of black-and-white ink blots by telling what they see in them. They experience a big response latency when suddenly presented with a blot containing color: they are typically silent for a long period before they resume giving responses, and the responses tend to be more hesitant and fewer in number.

Scanlon also found that the colorcast of the funeral produced more emotional responses than the black-and-white telecast, but the colorcast of the football game did not. We don't know, of course, whether Scanlon's results may be generalized to color and black-and-white photographs in newspapers.

Lighting

Photographers use lighting to produce certain effects, such as "triangle" lighting for portraits and low front lighting to produce a sinister effect. Tannenbaum and Fosdick[17] put these and other hypotheses about lighting to the test in a study which rotated lighting variables and models and asked subjects to evaluate the resulting pictures using the Semantic Differential. Lighting angles appeared to affect the connotative meanings assigned to pictures but almost entirely in the EVALUATIVE dimension. No effects were observed in the POTENCY dimension, contrary to expectations. There was a large interaction between lighting angles and models, which simply says that lighting has different effects on different models. The biggest surprise was that low front lighting produced no consistent variation in the way the pictures were evaluated except that the pictures were judged more *"bad"* under low front conditions than under portrait lighting conditions. Low front lighting had no effect on POTENCY judgments whatever. (Facial expression was uncontrolled in this study and may have contributed to the result in ways we can only speculate about.)

Photographic Bias

Though the camera records "what is there," it is a mistake to imagine that "pictures never lie," or that the camera is an unbiased reporter of what really happened. A picture catches a split second of an event—part, never all, of a reality. And the camera is operated by a human being. As Jacobson[18] has

[15] Personal communication from Newell Meyer.

[16] T. Joseph Scanlon, "Color TV—New Language," *Journalism Quarterly* 44:225–230 (Summer 1967); "Viewer Perceptions on Color, Black and White TV: An Experiment," *Journalism Quarterly* 47:366–368 (Summer 1970).

[17] Percy H. Tannenbaum and James A. Fosdick, "The Effect of Lighting Angle on the Judgment of Photographed Subjects," *A-V Communication Review* 8:253–262 (November-December 1960).

[18] Harvey K. Jacobson, "Objectivity—Photographic Myth?" *National Press Photographer* 25:34–37 (June 1970).

pointed out, "News reporters [with typewriters or with cameras, with words or with pictures] look at ideas and events through their own eyes and their own minds." But they are not propagandists or editorialists on purpose; distortion is usually not a matter of "calculated villainy." "A subtle, and perhaps more frequent, troublemaker is distortion [that results when] media gatekeepers try to cope with a flood of complex data as they process it through an organization. We have a lot to learn about meaningful selection and transmission of data in the 'information explosion'."

Jacobson suggests that the photographer (and, it would seem, the news editor) should realize that what the camera points at is a human judgment and human judgments cannot be freed from bias by an effort of will. Editors should not underestimate the ability of their audiences to spot willful or careless distortion. Both photographers and editors should accept continuing self-examination as healthy.

10

Fundamentals of Makeup

The copy desk has as a part of its day-to-day operation one of the most fascinating and challenging tasks involved in the production of newspapers: assembling and arranging the day's news material on the page. That is what makeup is—the typographical arrangement of the news. Good makeup consists of an *attractive* typographical arrangement which *helps tell* the day's news; the reader should pick up the paper with pleasure, and it should contribute to his perception and understanding of the world about him. Unfortunately, there is a tendency to overlook the news function of makeup and overemphasize the aesthetic. The editor sometimes stops being a keen judge of the news when he makes decisions about makeup. But the editor should bring to makeup both his sense of news and his feeling for attractive format and use them simultaneously. The basic objectives of makeup could be described as:

—helping tell the day's news; smoothing the path of information to the reader; capitalizing on reader habits to help him to find, read, and understand the news with relative ease

—presenting the news in an orderly, meaningful pattern

—expressing through story placement and headline size the relative importance of the news of that day

—making the paper attractive to the reader—an inviting package

The typography and makeup of the newspaper expresses and is in large measure responsible for its "personality." Newspaper personalities range all the way from the raucous to the dull, from the saucy to the staid, from the alarming to the earnest. Some shout, some state firmly, others whisper. Some never use the same Page One makeup twice; others never

224

depart from one basic pattern from day to day and year to year. Because continuity in the personality of a newspaper is important, the desk may not choose any makeup style on any day; it cannot decide on a new typographical "dress" on the instant, for example. Each paper has certain rules of typography and makeup that must be followed. The desk may suggest changes in rules, but final decisions about major changes in the paper's personality obviously rest with higher authority.

The challenge is to make each issue of the paper reflect, both in content and makeup, as accurately as possible the meaning and the coloration of that day's news—within the limits of the paper's personality and rules. Since one news day is never really like any other, that means using the highest possible skill to devise appropriate ways of giving that day's news the presentation that describes it best. The editor can improvise and experiment with new ways of displaying the news as long as he doesn't leave behind the established character of his paper.

The material Chapters 10 and 11 will deal with, then, really breaks down into two broad categories—design and makeup. By design is meant the entire format of the paper, ranging all the way from page size to dashes. By makeup is meant the day-to-day job of putting the paper together under the established design conditions. Overall design decisions are made at the top; only makeup is the job of the working desk man—particularly the man in the slot—but an understanding of design is essential to doing an effective job.

Nothing in actual newspaper practice has changed so much in the last fifteen to twenty years as format and makeup. There appear to be several reasons:

1. *Competition from other media*—particularly television with its multisensory appeal to the public, its relative freedom to explore new forms in the presentation of information, its ability to combine immediacy with visualization—has disrupted established patterns, forcing newsmen's attention on "the package"—the appeal and immediate-reward value of the newspaper. Though the newspaper has clearly survived and has been less affected in many ways than other pretelevision media, notably radio and the mass-circulation magazine, it has been forced to re-examine its strengths and weaknesses, particularly at the point where the reader's critical decision is made: Shall I spend the next half hour reading this printed news package with its promise of information and diversion, or shall I let this other medium tell me and show me what I want to know? Brighter, cleaner, smarter, more attractive, readable, legible, and colorful newspapers have tended to be the result.

2. *New printing processes* and improvements in old processes have given the designers and editors of newspapers a measure of freedom from old constraints, having opened up new possibilities for innovation and posed a challenge for creativity. For example, in offset printing, what can be drawn or pasted in will print. In letterpress printing, only a piece of type-high type metal will print. More attention is given to these developments in Chapter 15.

3. *Continuity with the past has become less important than sharing the excitement of the present and the promise of the future.* Many newspapers still look almost the same as they did sixty years ago. This is not because their editors and executives are too lazy or too ignorant of new developments to modernize. They want to retain a distinctive institutional character, to be perceived as one solid thing in a world of change. But this value has in many cases given way to a desire to move with the times, to use the greater freedom now available to be more responsive to contemporary motivations and values. One of the problems of clinging to the past has been bringing the young into the family of newspaper readers. The age group from twenty-one to thirty is the least well-represented of all adult age groups in the newspaper audience; the teen years are virtually unrepresented.[1] Brighter formats in newspapers developed for the youth culture itself have had an immediate effect on advertising in all the media and some effect (though admittedly not very marked) on the design and makeup of general newspapers.

---

[1] Bruce H. Westley and Werner J. Severin, "A Profile of the Daily Newspaper Non-Reader," *Journalism Quarterly* 41:45–51 (Winter 1964).

4. *Creative, competent editors are getting younger,* and the recency and effect of their exposure to a critical journalism education has told in the newsroom. Though they are not free to try anything they think might be a "kick," their impatience with the drab and the institutional has surely contributed to change.

Evolution of Makeup

Newspapers have always been responsive to changes going on around them, and the evolution of newspaper typography and makeup reflects this sensitivity. Although the differences in newspaper format between Colonial times and the space age are considerable, the change has been gradual and largely dictated by historical factors rather than careful plans. The most sweeping differences came about through wars and technological changes. All too rarely has an effort been made to overhaul the shape and style of the newspaper with the reader's desires and needs in mind; in fact, some modern efforts to do so have failed.

Colonial newspapers, understandably enough, were largely copies of British newspapers of the time. Many of them were attractively printed, but makeup as we know it was not really a consideration. Makeup is largely a matter of placement of headlines and art. The Colonial newspapers had neither in great abundance, consisting almost entirely of body type. "Headings" appeared over major items and an important one usually started in the upper left-hand corner of Page One. But these headings were not headlines in any sense; they were more like the titles of essays. For instance, the *Massachusetts Spy* started its lead story in the March 30, 1775, issue thus:

Political Chronical

For the MASSACHUSETTS SPY: Or

Thomas's Boston Journal

NUMBER VII

To the Inhabitants of the MAS-

SACHUSETTS BAY

My Friends and Countrymen

It introduced a continuation of a Patriot-Loyalist debate. The story was long, so there was no problem of how to make up the front page: it consisted of the heading and four columns of body type.

As we have seen in discussing headlines, this made sense in a day when every newspaper buyer expected to read his little paper from front to back. There was no need to help him find what he wanted to read; he wanted to read it all. So the stories were placed where they fit into the forms. Even the "display" type was really not display type at all. It rarely went above pica in size. The ads, too, were set in small type, but often in limited display style. Body type was small, partly because paper was scarce, with 7-point a common size. No effort was made to show the importance of the story by the size of the headline above it.

This was the essential pattern until the outbreak of the Mexican War, the first event to influence newspaper makeup. Headlines then began to appear over the main story of the day. This became a common practice in 1846 and continued into the gold-rush days of 1849 and later. The headlines consisted of a series of one- and two-line decks, separated by dashes and extending down the column (but never more than one column). Importance was indicated not by type size but by the number of decks. During the late 1850's, several main stories were frequently being given this treatment on Page One—and thus was makeup born.

Meanwhile, the page size had grown tremendously—up to three by five feet!—but later returned to approximately the present full-size format. The Civil War tended to increase the number of headlines on the page somewhat—but it particularly increased the number of decks in a given headline. Headlines usually started at the tops of columns and the story was simply wrapped into adjoining columns with no particular effort to arrange the material in an interesting or attractive way. However, unlike Colonial times, an effort was made to place stories in the paper on the basis of their relative importance.

Late in the century, several events drastically upset the makeup and typographical traditions of newspapers. Press improvements and standardization caused newspaper size to settle down to approximately the present dimensions. The stereotype process freed newspapers from the tyranny of the type-revolving press, which, along with custom and notions of taste, had kept headlines down to one column in width. Newspaper art moved through a series of steps from the painstaking woodcuts of Civil War days to chemically engraved zinc line drawings to photoengraving, which won general acceptance in New York papers in the 1890's. This brought a new element into makeup and news presentation. Especially during the Civil War, woodcut maps and occasional battle scenes had appeared in newspapers, often days after the news they accompanied. But it took a cheaper, faster process to make illustration a regular feature of the newspaper.

Then once again a war forced big changes in makeup practices. The Spanish-American War, which coincided with the circulation war between William Randolph Hearst's *Journal* and Joseph Pulitzer's *World,* produced drastic changes in typography and makeup which started in New York and spread to other parts of the nation rapidly. The changes were largely in type size and measure. But they brought a profound and lasting change in American newspaper format. Where only a few years before the New York *Herald* still clung to the rule that no type above agate could be used anywhere in the paper and no ad or headline could exceed one column in width, the war produced banner headlines across the full width of the paper. They ranged in height up to several inches. Body type was increased from the traditional agate, nonpareil, or minion to the point where the *Journal* carried the lead paragraphs of the story of Dewey's victory at Manila in full seven-column width and 18-point boldface type. (The top banner that day was more than three and a half inches high.)

Although the era of yellow journalism waned soon after the turn of the century and was followed by a period of relative conservatism in makeup, its vestiges remain with us today. The banner head declined in size but remained. The use of photoengraving increased. Aside from the banner, headlines returned largely to one- and two-column width; body type settled back to the single column and modest sizes, but it was more legible and had more leading.

World War I brought a resurgence in sensational typography and makeup but not to the startling degree of the Spanish-American war. By that time editors were accustomed to handling headlines, art, and multicolumn displays. They went all out on the best stories of the war but with a neatness and restraint that distinguished their products from the frantic, end-of-the-world effect that characterized the Spanish war period. Sound rules of makeup had developed during the intervening period—rules which still have a considerable influence on the format of newspapers today. Briefly, they included scaling the size of headlines from large at the top of the paper to small at the bottom, alternating major and minor elements across the page, avoiding accidental "tombstoning," and limiting the number of decks of the headline. Headlines were largely constructed in stepped top decks with inverted pyramids alternating with crosslines in secondary decks.

After World War I came the tabloid, a phenomenon of the 1920's that is still with us. Had the early "tabs" been sound and respectable newspapers, they might have spelled the end of the cumbersome paper of our time. As it turned out, they had only a modest influence on general newspaper practices.

The second major development in this period was the swing to modern typefaces. This brought clean, readable, attractive type into newspapers that had clung for many years to bold and ugly gothics combined with blunt and ugly Cheltenham, although even these had been improvements over the clumsier faces that preceded them.

Finally, there was the beginning of "horizontal" makeup, examined on pages 247–248. It consists in essence of multicolumn headlines and art combined with the trend toward a reduced number of decks.

Technological developments since World War II have largely been responsible for changes in recent years that have produced more variation in newspaper formats than in any other period in history. No longer can it be said that newspapers everywhere look pretty much the same. These technological developments include the following:

Offset printing has worked its way up from the bottom in recent years, being embraced first by small-community newspapers, often weeklies and semiweeklies, then spreading to larger and larger papers,

A Concise History of Makeup   This sequence
of front pages from the St. Louis *Post-Dispatch*
depicts a fairly typical pattern of change in
newspaper format, design, and makeup. In the
1878 issue, news space is smaller than
advertising space. Headlines are labels for
the most part, decks are numerous, and the
headline type, though varied, is small. All news
and news headlines are in single-column
measure. The body type is extremely small.

The differences in the 1898 issue are marked.
The paper's owner-editor-publisher, Joseph
Pulitzer, had helped create a new and more
sensational journalism, reflected in this issue's
makeup. Note the dramatic and unconventional
use of art, the use of wide measure, large type,
and present tense in headlines, wide-measure
columns, large body type with additional
leading. "Fifth Extra" in the ears indicates
that this page was being made over frequently
as the news developed.

Most of the characteristics of the *Post-Dispatch*
"dress" that held fairly constant for more than
forty years were firmly set by 1929 when the
crash was making news. This makeup was quite
typical of the time, although the paper was
ahead of its time in using hanging indentions
in decks. Note the carefully stepped, all-cap
gothic heads, some four lines in length; the
four decks at the top of all major heads; the
combination, typical of the time, of Railroad
Gothic and Cheltenham Bold (with italics),
often highly condensed; the vertical emphasis,
with few heads wider than two columns; the
generally crowded feeling throughout. The body
type is still small but now more extended and
leaded for increased legibility. (Historical note:
Only Charles G. Ross, Chief Washington
Correspondent, rated a by-line this day.)

The fourth and fifth examples depict the radical
changes that were wrought in a recent total
redesign, changing the *Post-Dispatch* from
traditional to contemporary format at one leap.
This included a modern headline typeface
(Bodoni) in place of Cheltenham and Railroad
Gothic; white space instead of column rules;
emphasis on the horizontal, rather than the
vertical; and the use of strong masses throughout the page in place of the top-emphasis
characteristic of the older design. In fact, nearly
all the features of traditional design are
represented in the earlier example and nearly
all the characteristics of contemporary design
are visible in the most recent example,
except fewer, wider columns.

Illustrations courtesy the St. Louis Post-Dispatch

St. Louis Post and Dispatch.

VOL. I.   ST. LOUIS, THURSDAY EVENING, DECEMBER 12, 1878.   NO. 286.

AFTER LOOKING AROUND,

The PEOPLE decide that the Largest Stock, the Latest Styles, the Lowest Prices, the Best Made and Best Fitting Garments are found at

The "Golden Eagle!"

119, 121, 123 FIFTH STREET, AND 508-510 F'

We Manufacture our Goods, and Retail Every arti

DAN'L C. YOUNG

(central circular emblem) **16 Historic POST-DISPATCH Pages**

ARTISTIC POTTERY.

If you wish to see the Finest Display ever made in St. Louis, visit

Miller & Stephenson's

Importers, Wholesale and Retail Dealers in China, Glass, Queensware, Plated Ware and Cutlery,

No. 504 North Fourth Street.

Christmas is Coming

OUR SHAW PATENT

Easy and Reclining Chair

IS THE MOST

APPROPRIATE PRESENT

FOR A

HOLIDAY GIFT!

Don't fail to see them, together with the largest variety ever shown of Patent Rockers, Foot-Rests, Screens, Ottomans, Easels, Parlor, Music and Wall Cabinets; Fancy Desks, Pedestals, Boot-Boxes, Fancy Chairs, Bamboo Rockers, Folding Chairs and Rockers, Smoking Chairs, Fancy and Ornamental Tables, with Onyx, Marquetrie and Rare Marble Tops, in Ebony and Gilt, Walnut, Etc. Every one looking for something useful as well as ornamental will find what they want by calling on

BURRELL, COMSTOCK and CO.

402 and 404 N. Fourth Street.

SIEGEL & BOBB,

HOLIDAY GOODS.

Bronzes, French Flowers, Jardinieres, Card Receivers, Clocks, Statuettes, Busts, Match Boxes, Candelabras, Drop-Lights, German Student Lamps, Porcelain Shades, Crystal Chandeliers, Gilt and Porcelain Chandeliers. We have just received a large invoice of the above articles, purchased for the HOLIDAYS. Examine our stock before buying.

SIEGEL & BOBB,

IMPORTERS AND MANUFACTURERS OF GAS AND COAL OIL FIXTURES.

203 NORTH FIFTH STREET, ST. LOUIS.

KID GLOVES

We received this morning a new lot of our superior

SEAMLESS

Gloves. They excel in shape, fit and quality of the kid. The "Patent Cut" makes them easier to put on and easier to shape to hand. GLOVES SENT BY MAIL when ordered.

H. D. Mann & Co.,

and 419 N. Fourth Street.

WHITE

Wool Blankets, large size,

FIVE DOLLARS,

WORTH $7 00.

BEAVER

CLOAKS made in the BEST manner,

FIVE DOLLARS,

worth $10.

MISSES

BEAVER SHAWLS

Reduced from

$4 50.

H. D. Mann & Co.,

417 AND 419 N. FOURTH ST.

INSURANCE.

Christmas Presents.

SCRUGGS, VANDERVOORT & BARNEY

CONTINUE TO MAKE

Large Daily Additions

To their IMMENSE VARIETY of USEFUL, SENSIBLE and INTRINSICALLY VALUABLE ARTICLES, specially appropriate for

Holiday Presents.

We Present an Assortment of

FINE LACES

At such EXTREME LOW PRICES as to make it VERY DECIDEDLY to the interest of all admirers of these EVER USEFUL as well as RICH AND BEAUTIFUL GOODS to give them a CAREFUL inspection.

Duchesse Lace Scarfs, Barbes, Collars, Sets, Handkerchiefs, Necklaces and Lockets.

Black Thread Laces, Scarfs and Barbs.

Black Guipure Lace Scarfs.

Black and White French Lace Scarfs.

SPECIAL BARGAIN!

LARGE LOT OF

Duchesse Lace Barbe Ends,

Embracing Twelve Different Patterns, at only

$1.00 EACH.

A WONDER IN

Hand - Embroidered

FRENCH

HANDKERCH'EFS

GOODS SELLING BY THE

1,000 Dozens.

1-2 Dozen Very Rich Embroidery on French Russalia only 90c.

1-2 Dozen Very Much Richer Embroidery for only $1.20.

THE RICHNESS AND CHEAPNESS

Of these Goods is Really Astonishing!

421, 423 & 425 NORTH FOURTH ST.

2d EDITION!

5 O'CLOCK

For Additional Telegrams See Fourth Page.

FOREIGN NEWS.

50,000 Russians to Remain in Bulgaria.

No New Treaty to be Effected Between England and Turkey.

King Humbert Looking Around for a New Italian Ministry.

Fenian Prisoners to be Released—Bank of England.

TRAIL OF THE TIDE.

Latest Advices Concerning the Freshets in the East.

Work Almost Entirely Suspended in the Massachusetts Mills.

THE FIRE FIENDS.

VAGARIES OF VICE.

Police Items and General Criminal News Picked Up by Our Reporters.

Four Courts Doings—Warrants Sworn Out This Morning—Cases Disposed of.

STRANGE SUICIDE.

A Man Found Dead in Williams' European Hotel, This Morning.

The Victim John Watkins—Circumstances of the Occurrence.

(COMPLETE MARKET REPORTS.)

LAST EDITION.
5th EXTRA

ST. LOUIS POST-DISPATCH.

THE ONLY ST. LOUIS EVENING PAPER WITH THE ASSOCIATED FRESS DISPATCHES.

CIRCULATION SUNDAY, FEBRUARY 13, 1898. - - - - - - - 115,844.

VOL. 49, NO. 191. WEDNESDAY EVENING—ST. LOUIS—FEBRUARY 16, 1898. PRICE In St. Louis, One Cent. Outside St. Louis, Two Cents.

(COMPLETE MARKET REPORTS.)

LAST EDITION.
5th EXTRA

OVER 250 LIVES LOST ON THE BATTLESHIP MAINE.

The True Story of the Explosion and Its Horrors Told by Sylvester Scovel, Staff Correspondent of the Post-Dispatch.

The Ship Was Lifted Up and a Shower of Human Bodies and Fragments of the Vessel Fell Into the Water.

Agonizing Shrieks of the Wounded Men Filled the Air as Flames Burst From the Ship and She Sank Back Into the Bay.

Capt. Sigsbee Wires Secretary Long That the Explosion Was in the Forward Part of the Ship, Probably in the Magazine, and That He Is Investigating the Cause of the Disaster.

(NOTICE—The Pulitzer Publishing Co. and the Press Publishing Co. will prosecute any newspaper or person violating the copyright by republishing this news without written permission.)

THE CAUSE OF THE EXPLOSION.

Special Cable to the Post-Dispatch.

Copyright by the Press Publishing Company, 1898.

8 p. m.

HAVANA, Feb. 16.—The cause of the explosion is ascribed to bursting boilers and a lamp explosion in the magazine boat Whitehead on board.

The event is deplored and the general hope is expressed that a false construction may not be placed on the event.

HAVANA, Feb. 16.—Passengers on the steamship City of Washington saw the blowing up of the battleship Maine. They heard a shot at 9:25 last night. It might have come from anywhere.

After a ten seconds' interval they felt the City of Washington jump and saw a volcano of fire and showers of boats, bodies, iron and guns.

The explosion raised them up and then they plunged diagonally to the bottom.

Then the Maine settled slowly.

The night was hideous with the cries of men in agony.

"God help us! God help us! Help! Help!" was shrieked from hundreds of throats.

It was very dark. After the first shot the passengers of the City of Washington had time to go to the portholes before the great explosion occurred.

Other witnesses who were looking at the Maine say they first saw flames without noise shooting high from the center of the ship.

Then came the explosion after an interval sufficient to say: "My God, the Maine's blown up!"

All agree that the Maine was raised almost out of the water and then went partially to pieces.

Brass pipe, angle iron, etc., fell in a shower on the decks of the City of Washington, so damaging two of the boats that when they were lowered they were useless.

The City of Washington lay at anchor 300 feet from the Maine.

Out of the dense smoke came anguished cries for help. Simultaneously with the cessation of falling fragments search-lights were thrown on the wreck and its load of agony.

Spanish boats from shore joined those of the Washington alongside at once, but the regular ferryboats passing soon after the explosion didn't stop to offer aid.

The officers of the ship say the explosion was in the central magazine. The theory of the central explosion agrees with the accounts of the spectators on the Washington.

All but the surgeon were talking in the wardroom at the moment of the explosion. Then came the stupendous shock, hurling about articles in all directions.

All knew the warship was gone at the first instant. The common impulse was to lower boats and save life. All the officers below rushed on deck, but could get no further forward than the middle superstructure on deck. All agree that a double explosion occurred from the natural result of an underwater explosion of the magazines. About twenty odd men in the quarter watch were almost all blown into atoms.

The Maine's magazines were reported locked at 8 o'clock, and the keys were hanging in Capt. Sigsbee's cabin.

Captain and officers are very thankful to Spanish officers for their extremely prompt assistance.

Whatever the primary cause of the disaster, it is certain that the Maine's forward magazine exploded and tore more than two hundred sailors above it into shreds.

CONTINUED ON PAGE TWO

TELEGRAMS FROM SURVIVORS TO FRIENDS AT HOME.

Special Cable to the Post-Dispatch.

HAVANA, Feb. 16.—These cablegrams have been sent through to loved ones at home by survivors:

"William Chidweek, New York—Safe; unhurt. JOHN P. CHIDWEEK."

"Blow, La Salle, Ill.—Absolutely unhurt. "GEORGE."

"Mrs. Hannwright, Washington, D. C.—Safe. HANNWRIGHT."

"Col. D. F. Boyd, Baton Rouge, La.—Safe. REX."

"J. H. Mann, Providence, R. I.—O. K. "JOE."

"Gignoux, New York—All right. "E. M. FOWLER."

"Ray, Washington, D. C.—Safe; unhurt." (Not signed.)

"Mrs. W. T. Chiwerius, New Orleans, La.—Safe; unhurt. WAT."

"B. D. Catlin, Gloversville, N. Y.—Safe; unhurt. CATLIN."

"Miss Cecelia Stein, Howardsville, Md.—Safe; unhurt. ALBERT."

"Mrs. Margaret Chidwick, Peterboro, Ontario, Canada—Safe; unhurt. "JOHN P. CHIDWICK."

"George Holden, Burlington, Vt.—Safe. "HAN."

"Katherine Jungf, Naval Hospital, Brooklyn, N. Y.—Safe and unhurt. CARL."

"Kohly, Baltimore, Md.—Arrived well." (Not signed.)

"Col. Wright, Peekskill, N. Y.—Safe; unhurt." (Not signed.)

"A. E. Heneberget, Harrisonburg Va.—Safe; unhurt." (Not signed.)

"Dr. E. H. Geer, Baltimore, Md.—I am safe; tell wife. BLANDIN."

THE NEWS AT MADRID.

Special Cable to the Post-Dispatch.

MADRID, Feb. 16.—The first news received here direct from Havana said the explosion of the Maine was caused by a fire vessel enveloped in flames, which afterward sank.

DE LOME SAILS AWAY.

There Was No Hostile Demonstration Toward Him.

NEW YORK, Feb. 16.—Senor de Lome, former Spanish Minister to Washington, sailed on the steamship Britannic for Liverpool to-day. Complimentary resolutions were presented to him on board by a delegation of Spaniards. There was no hostile demonstration of any kind.

THE WARD LINE'S OFFER.

Steamships Placed at Disposal of the President.

NEW YORK, Feb. 16.—President S. M. Booth of the Ward Line sent telegrams to President McKinley and Secretary Long to-day placing at their disposal the steamship City of Washington, now in the harbor of Havana, and the Vigilance, now en route to Havana, for any purpose and for as long as desired.

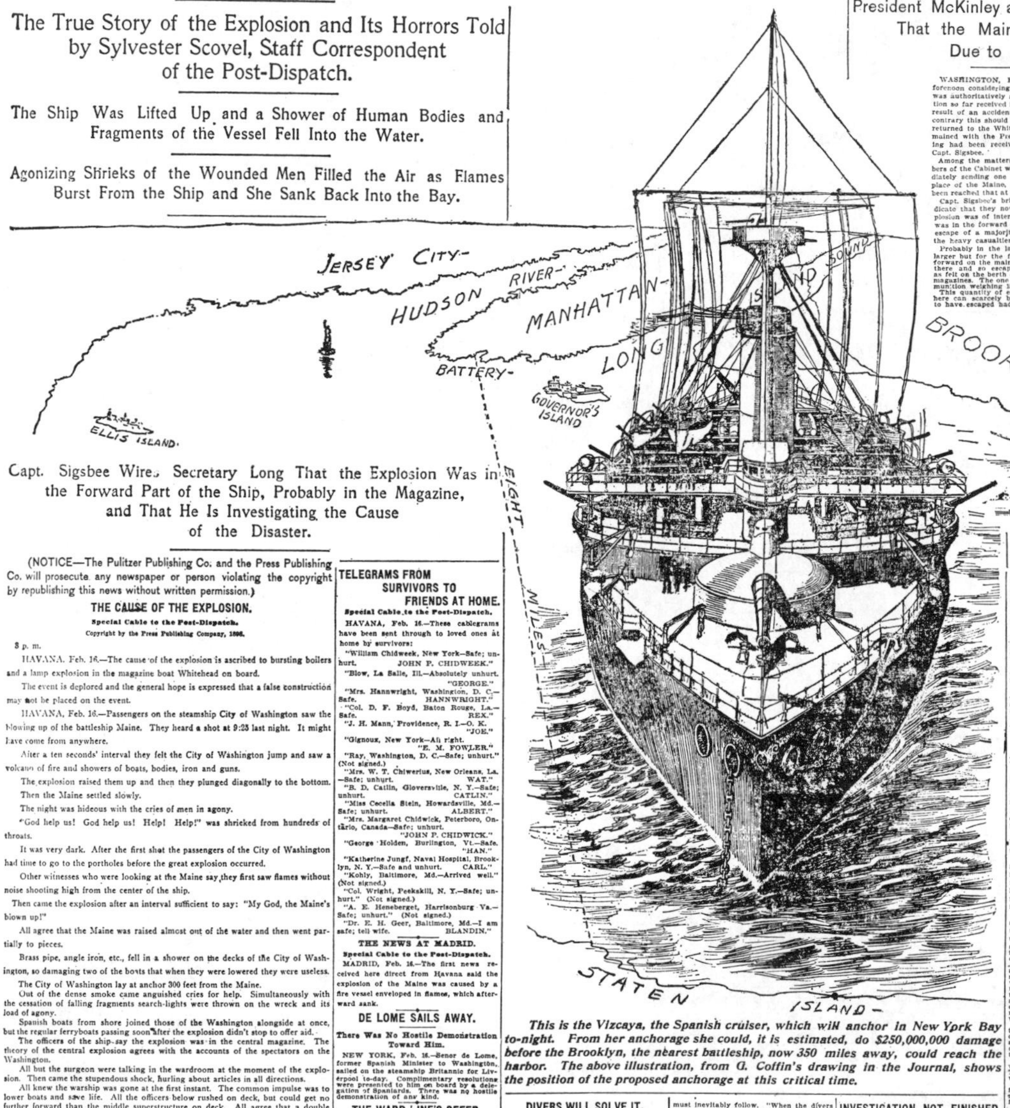

This is the Vizcaya, the Spanish cruiser, which will anchor in New Yprk Bay to-night. From her anchorage she could, it is estimated, do $250,000,000 damage before the Brooklyn, the nearest battleship, now 350 miles away, could reach the harbor. The above illustration, from G. Coffin's drawing in the Journal, shows the position of the proposed anchorage at this critical time.

DIVERS WILL SOLVE IT.

If the Maine Was Torpeded the Fact Will Come Out.

CHICAGO, Feb. 16.—Commander J. E. Montgomery, one of the United States Navy, a commanding officer of a Confederate fleet during the civil war and the man who raised the frigate (afterwards the ram) Merrimac, was very emphatic to-day in declaring the sinking of the battleship Maine in Havana harbor the result of treachery and an act with [illegible] in the world's history. In [illegible] war must inevitably follow. "When the divers go down and examine the hull of the vessel," said Commodore Montgomery, "it will be found that it was stove in by a torpedo exploded under the bow with diabolical intent. To be sure an accident may occur on shipboard—a magazine or a boiler may explode. But consider all the circumstances and you will not entertain the theory of accident."

Commander Montgomery is familiar with Havana harbor. It would be comparatively easy, he says, with small boats or otherwise, to set a torpedo to destroy the American vessel. This is his theory of how the Ma[illegible] wrecked.

INVESTIGATION NOT FINISHED.

Consul General Lee Not Prepared to Make Full Report.

WASHINGTON, Feb. 16.—The following dispatch was received at 11:40 a. m.:

Havana, Feb. 16.—Assistant Secretary of State, Washington: All quiet; great sorrow expressed by authorities. Sigsbee has telegraphed details to Navy Department. Not prepared yet to report cause of explosion.

LEE.

SPAIN IS NOT TO BLAME

President McKinley and Cabinet Conclude That the Maine Disaster Was Due to Accident.

WASHINGTON, Feb. 16.—The Cabinet has been in session all forenoon considering the Maine disaster. At about 1:30 o'clock it was authoritatively stated at the White House that the information so far received indicated that the loss of the Maine was the result of an accident and that in the absence of evidence to the contrary this should be assumed to be the fact. Secretary Long returned to the White House early in the afternoon and remained with the President for some time. Up to 2 o'clock nothing had been received from Havana since the cablegram from Capt. Sigsbee.

Among the matters discussed by the President and the members of the Cabinet was the question of the expediency of immediately sending one or more warships to Havana to take the place of the Maine, and the conclusion is understood to have been reached that at present such a course was not desirable.

Capt. Sigsbee's briefreport, as well as Gen. Lee's dispatch, indicate that they now incline strongly to the belief that the explosion was of internal origin. Both agree that the force of it was in the forward part of the ship and this is borne out by the escape of a majority of the officers, whose quarters are aft, and the heavy casualties among the crew, sleeping forward.

Probably in the latter case the death list would have been even larger but for the fact that the Maine having superstructure forward on the main deck, a portion of the crew were quartered there and so escaped greater part of the force of the explosion as felt on the berth deck below them. The Maine had had three magazines. The one forward was used for the storage of ammunition weighing 15,000 pounds.

This quantity of explosives is so large that the navy officials here can scarcely believe it possible for any man being on board to have escaped had the magazine exploded entirely.

GOVERNMENT WAS WARNED

Report Some Time Ago of a Mine in Havana Harbor.

WASHINGTON, Feb. 16.—At 4 o'clock Secretary Long is up at the Portland awaiting information from Havana. The Secretary thinks that most of the officers of the Maine and perhaps some of the men were ashore on leave and therefore escaped injury.

Secretary Long said that it is inconceivable that the Maine's boilers could have exploded, as the vessel had not had steam up for a fortnight.

This reduces the causes of the explosion to two in number. Either the magazine was touched off or a torpedo or submarine mine exploded under the vessel.

In this connection it is recalled that when the idea of sending a warship to Havana was first broached the Government received a warning that the harbor was filled with submarine mines, connected by wire with Moro Castle.

The tenders Mangrave and Fern have been ordered to Havana.

DE LOME NOTIFIED.

Former Minister Exclaims, "Pray God This Is Not True."

Special to the Post-Dispatch.

NEW YORK, Feb. 16.—Dupuy de Lome, the former Minister of Spain to the United States, was awakened by a reporter of the Post-Dispatch at the Hotel St. Marc at 3 o'clock this morning and informed of the blowing up of the Maine.

Mr. de Lome appeared extremely agitated. He walked up and down the floor for some time before he spoke and then he said:

"This is dreadful; awful! I pray God this news is not true. I pray God Almighty that it is a mistake. Why, I have many dear friends on board the Maine, men that I knew intimately in Washington. I should feel their loss more than would most Americans.

"It cannot be the result of any Spanish agency at all. The Spanish Ministry and the Spanish people have been greatly misunderstood in this country. They all desire peace; they all want peace with America and Americans, not only from motives of policy but because they love America.

"I am forced to say now by this terrible affair what I was precluded from saying before. There is no country in the world that I love as I do America. I love the country and the people, and it is with the keenest regret that I take my leave as the result of this unfortunate letter incident. Nearly all prominent Spaniards and men of influence in my country share my views in regard to America.

"Spain cannot afford to have a war with the United States. If only from motives of policy they are determined not to have any war. There can be no war between this country and Spain. Such a thing is out of the question.

"If the Maine has been blown up in Havana harbor it is the result of an accident. That is absolutely certain. There will be no war."

Mr. De Lome reached the city last night from Washington. He came to close arrangements to sell his household effects before sailing for home this afternoon.

When the news of the blowing up of the Maine first became known here there was great excitement and strong talk. Some believed it a Spanish act and boldly charged De Lome with guilty knowledge of its contemplation. This of course was wild and foolish tal[illegible]

These persons figured it out that the coming of the Vizcaya was part of the scheme. They planned a nice voyage down the bay for De Lome as a guest on the Vizcaya, which these wild talkers were satisfied had been sent here so as to be an asylum for De Lome and the Spanish consul. There is much suppressed excitement th[illegible]out the city.

TODAY'S NEWS TODAY

ST. LOUIS POST-DISPATCH

The Only Evening Newspaper in St. Louis With the Associated Press News Service

FINAL
Stock Market
(Tables in Part III, Pages 35, 36, 37)

VOL. 82. NO. 53.　　　ST. LOUIS, TUESDAY, OCTOBER 29, 1929.—44 PAGES.　　　PRICE 2 CENTS

AIR LINER, 5 ABOARD, IS MISSING IN ROCKIES

Snowstorm Stops Search for Western Express Which Was Due at Albuquerque, N. M. Yesterday

TWO PASSENGERS AND CREW OF THREE

Pilot Who Found Wreck of the T. A. T. City of San Francisco Will Direct Hunt in Same Area.

By the Associated Press.

ALBUQUERQUE, N. M., Oct. 29.—A blinding snowstorm today halted aerial search for the Western Air Express passenger plane missing since yesterday morning in the mountainous New Mexico-Arizona border country with five persons aboard.

Genera Rice, Western Air Express pilot, who located the Transcontinental Air Transport liner, City of San Francisco, which crashed on Mount Taylor early in September with the loss of eight lives, returned late this morning to a snowstorm after flying as far west as Gallup, N. M., without sighting the missing plane.

The heavy snow and poor visibility forced Rice back. Western Air officials said he would not be out again until the storms abated.

Officers of the company held little hope of any successful attempt hunt today on account of the snow and the failure of planes from other sections to reach here due to bad weather.

Regular Service Held Up.

The regular Western Air express service from Los Angeles to Kansas City arrived at Holbrook, Ariz, and was given 6 hours of bad weather conditions there.

But the forestry department also became companies are putting rangers in the field in the vicinity of Mount Sedgewick, a mountain as dangerous as Mount Taylor the air liner, with two passengers and a crew of three, disappeared yesterday morning after passing along the 150-mile stretch of the route between Navajo, Ariz., and Albuquerque. It is thought to have been forced down by bitter water over the Rocky Mountains Sunday, bringing snow and rain which caused Western Air Express to order all planes grounded. The liner came too late to halt the going plane at Kingman, Ariz., where it left at 5:24 a. m. mountain time.

Due in Albuquerque at noon yesterday, the ship was last sighted over Navajo at 10:28 a. m. At Winslow, a few miles east of Navajo, a Santa Fe Railroad lineman said he heard a plane overhead at 11 a. m., but could not see it.

The plane was found from Albuquerque, a suburb of San Francisco.—Kansas City, Mo.

Three On Air Liner.

Those aboard were:

Dr. A. W. Ward, San Francisco, formerly known of general aviation, air agent Government aviation of general authority.

J. E. to Fort Worth, Tex., to fill training department.

W. E. Mers, Mount Vernon, N. Y., on his way home.

C. Dolar, Los Angeles, pilot.

Allen C. Lorric, Burbank, Cal., pilot.

L. Britton, Los Angeles, formerly of Denver, steward.

The wreckage of the company aviator bird has been is to fly over the Navajo Indian reservation, east of the point where the liner was last seen, before being forced to land. On the eastern side of the Navajo reservation and New Mexico boundary they said, they traveled low and numerous emergency places.

Despite hopes that the plane was on some isolated plateau with all the pilots on the elevated big his way to a place where food hope that Dolar had been is to fly over the Navajo headquarters, every effort is being planned to search the territory thoroughly.

T. E. Lesser Wrecked in Region.

No air hunt is to cover in large the territory in which the Transcontinental Air Transports City of San Francisco, was found less than two months ago. Wreckage, but its five passengers and found dead, its five passengers and crew.

'Backward States' Should Stay Out, Let Beneficiaries Frame Tariff, Says Grundy

Under Crossfire of Caraway, Borah and Walsh Lobbyist Deplores "Impertinence" of Senators From Small Commonwealths

By CHARLES G. ROSS,
Chief Washington Correspondent of the Post-Dispatch.

WASHINGTON, Oct. 29.—The "backward states" of the West and South among which he named the State of Senator Caraway and the State of Senator Borah were read out of the Union today by Joseph R. Grundy, master lobbyist for a high protective tariff, in his second appearance before the Senate's lobby investigating committee.

By "backward states" the millionaire president of the Pennsylvania Manufacturers' Association meant those States which have not reached what he considers a proper stage of industrial development.

Replying to angry questions by Chairman Caraway, Walsh and other members of the committee, Grundy suavely declared that whenever a great economic issue, such as the tariff was before the Senate, the representatives of the "backward states" ought to take a back seat and let the matter be settled by the States which had attained a high degree of development under the beneficent protective tariff.

He considered it highly unfortunate that the founding fathers of the nation had permitted each State to have two Senators. He didn't, however, want to criticize them too harshly, for he felt that they had done the best they could in the circumstances.

Suggests a Way Out.

He didn't know just how the blunder of the Constitution makers could be remedied, unless Senator Borah or Idaho, Senator Caraway of Arkansas and the other Senators of the "backward" commonwealths should be guided by a "sense of the proprieties" and let the tariff question be settled by the really great states, such as Pennsylvania.

Meantime, because of the "impertinence" of these Senators—such in his word in reply to a question—the great State of Pennsylvania, with its enormous contribution of taxes as compared with the petty contribution of Idaho, Arkansas and the other benighted states, was being "hamstrung."

It was, as the description may faintly indicate, a stirring session of the committee.

The committee went after the witness rough-shod, and the witness came right back. Senator Walsh, after pointing out that the same degree of industrial development could hardly be expected in the "backward" commonwealths, 750 years old, asked the witness if he didn't want to apologize. Grundy said he would stand by his remarks.

Grundy Stands by His Guns.

The states in his "backward" category, he said, were states that had not taken advantage of the splendid opportunities which the Republican party had given them under the protective tariff. Their upkeep was a drain on the national Treasury. They ought, in fine, to be ashamed of themselves and to keep out of the national legislative picture when matters of grave concern to Pennsylvania were up for consideration. They decidedly should not be raising a "roar" against the protective tariff.

Considering the provocation, the committee held itself in pretty well. Grundy's urbanity and self-assurance were never shaken.

In naming his "backward" states, Grundy flushed Idaho, but not Wyoming. He said he didn't care to tell why he made that distinction.

"Isn't it because I am from Idaho?" asked Senator Borah. "Well, in a way," said Grundy.

So went the examination, hammer and tongs, for more than three hours. When the committee adjourned, Senator Blaine was calling the roll of tariff increases on articles used by the farmer and ironically asking the witness, as the "wet nurse of the Republican party" to come to the rescue. On Blaine's announcement that he had hardly begun his examination, Grundy was told to come back to the stand tomorrow.

Borah Questions Grundy.

Grundy was taken in hand by Senator Borah, whom he had attacked in a prepared statement submitted to the committee last week.

Borah asked what schedules of the tariff bill Grundy was especially interested in. The witness replied he was naturally interested in the woolen schedules, as he had been in the wool manufacturing business all his life. He was concerned also, he said, with advancing the duty on pig iron. Borah brought out that the pig iron duty was increased. Grundy named also the carpet, lace and upholstery schedules.

Borah told him to be continued on Page 2, Column 1.

---

13 LOST WHEN LAKE SHIP SINKS; 68 ARE RESCUED

Captain Goes Down With Steamer Wisconsin in Storm Off Kenosha — Eight of Dead Identified.

ENGINEER FIGHTS OFF RESCUERS

Twenty Men Taken From Two Life Rafts—Some of Survivors Seriously Ill From Exposure.

By the Associated Press.

KENOSHA, Wis., Oct. 29.—Thirteen men went down with the lake steamer Wisconsin, 45-year-old veteran of the Great Lakes, in a storm off Kenosha early today.

More than 40 were saved, many of them maddened and some seriously ill from exposure in the wind-whipped sea. The three passengers aboard were rescued.

Capt Douglas Morrison remained aboard his ship to the last and went down with many of his shipmates. His body was picked up later by Coast Guard crews.

Four hours later a line went from the two life rafts that floated free of the wreck.

Four hours after the Wisconsin went down there were nine known dead, while 64 had been rescued. Four others are missing and are thought to have been drowned. Nineteen are in hospitals and 49 were rescued safely.

Chief Engineer Judas Buschmann, Manitowoc, Wis., clung to a life raft, as the steamer up-ended, rolled over and sank. Rescuers tried to haul him from the water but he fought them off and was used.

For five hours the Coast Guard crews from Racine and Kenosha, and the crew of the tug Chambers Brothers fought 10-foot waves and the driving northerly gale to take off the passengers and crew.

Took to Lifeboats.

Unable to take aboard a line from the rescuers, a 20-man crew set off in five lifeboats and were transferred to the Coast Guard ships.

Twenty men taken from the two life rafts that floated free of the wreck.

Four hours after the Wisconsin went down there were nine known dead, while 64 had been rescued. Four others are missing and are thought to have been drowned. Nineteen are in hospitals and 49 were rescued safely.

Capt. Douglas H. Morrison.
Julius Buschmann, chief engineer.
Joseph Burt, third cook.
"Old Joe", deck hand.
Joseph Jirck, deck hand.
L. H. de Gassogue, deck hand.
Walter Evans, deck hand.
Victor Isbro, deck hand.
One unidentified deck hand.
Carried General Merchandise.

The ship left Chicago at 7:45 o'clock last night, bound for Milwaukee, with a cargo of general merchandise. It was due in Milwaukee at 5 a. m. today. Lake Michigan was kicking high rollers from the east as the Wisconsin put out.

The Wisconsin began taking water a few hours out. At 1 a. m. her wireless reported the going coal into the bilge pumps, but that the steamer was making some progress. The steamer Illinois at that time had gone into the harbor at Racine with a broken rudder chain. She replied the Wisconsin not to attempt to make the regular scheduled stop at Racine because the harbor there was choked with coal boats and craft seeking shelter.

At 3 a. m. the Wisconsin went out an S O S and said it was sinking. At 4:45 a. m. the last word came from the steamer—that she was being abandoned with coast guards taking the Wisconsin's passengers and crew aboard their craft.

Half an hour later the Wisconsin witnessed that water was forcing coal into the bilge pumps, but that the steamer was making some progress. The steamer Illinois at that time had gone into the harbor at Racine with a broken rudder chain. She replied the Wisconsin not to attempt to make the regular scheduled stop at Racine because the harbor there was choked with coal boats and craft seeking shelter.

DR. J. R. STRATON, FUNDAMENTALIST LEADER, DIES

New York Baptist Pastor, Suffering From Nervous Breakdown, Succumbs to Heart Attack.

MANY CLASHES WITH MODERNISTS

He Helped Bryan in Scopes Trial — Had Disputes With Members of His Own Congregation.

By the Associated Press.

CLIFTON SPRINGS, N. Y., Oct. 29.—The Rev. Dr. John Roach Straton, noted militant fundamentalist Baptist preacher, died at a sanitarium here today. He was 54 years old.

Although seriously ill with a nervous breakdown for the last month, death came unexpectedly at 5:50 a. m. after a heart attack. His wife was at his bedside when he died.

He suffered a slight paralytic stroke last April and immediately after went to a sanitarium at Atlanta, Ga., for a rest. He returned to his home a month ago, but soon suffered from a nervous breakdown and entered the sanitarium here.

He was pastor of Calvary Baptist Church in New York, but by his aggressive campaigns against modernism and especially evolution, he gained nation-wide prominence.

Dr. Straton is survived by his widow, Mrs. Georgia Hillyer Straton, and four sons, the Rev. Hillyer H. John Charles, Warren B. and George Douglas.

His Record in Pulpit One of Continual Turmoil.

Dr. Straton was a militant fundamentalist and in recent years had clashed repeatedly with proponents of modernistic teachings. He especially was opposed to the theory of evolution and lent his support to the late William Jennings Bryan at the famous Scopes trial at Dayton, Tenn., in 1925.

His campaign against alleged tendency on the stage date back to 1922 when he engaged in a conflict with William A. Brady, Broadway theatrical producer, on a resolution that the modern stage was a menace to public morals. He opposed the study of Darwinism teachings in the public schools and denounced the Ku Klux Klan doctrines.

Dr. Straton constantly was in conflict with various members of his congregation at Calvary Baptist Church, in New York City, partly through his sermons and because of his other activities. At one time 29 members were suspended because of trouble with their pastor. He also encountered difficulty with the church's board of trustees when he planned a 20-story combination church and hotel on the church site. He blamed "social climbers" for most of his difficulties within the church.

In the last presidential campaign, Dr. Straton was a bitter opponent of Alfred E. Smith, the Democratic nominee. He attacked the former Governor from the pulpit and campaigned against him in the South. A small part of the church's board of trustees held participation in political debates, withdrew from the church and formed a church of their own in Brooklyn.

Dr. Straton had been connected with Calvary Church since 1918. He was born in Evansville, Ind., and was educated in Mercer University and the Southern Baptist Theological Seminary at Louisville, Ky. He also studied at the University of Chicago and the Boston School of Oratory and Expression. He received his doctor of divinity degree at Shurtleff College, Alton, Ill., in 1906.

Continued on Page 2, Column 3.

STOCKS RALLY AFTER DROP OF $10 TO $70; SALES OF 16,410,000 A NEW RECORD

Chrysler Heiress and Fiance

MISS BERNICE CHRYSLER and Edgar W. Garbisch, whose engagement has been announced. Garbisch, a New York cotton broker, was the former West Point and Washington and Jefferson football star.

LOCAL EXCHANGE SLUMPS; 15 ISSUES FALL TO NEW LOW

Trading Is Second Largest in History With Total of 15,629 Shares — Three Bank Stocks Drop.

The continued slump of stock prices during the forenoon on the New York market was reflected on the St. Louis Stock Exchange today when 15 issues fell to new low records for the year, closing from $1 to $15 a share off. In all, 15,629 shares were sold, the second largest day's trading in the exchange's history, the record being 17,342 shares on Nov. 27, last. Three St. Louis bank stocks closed off from 125 to 135 below yesterday.

In explanation, one broker said the decline was caused by liquidation of stocks pledged with banks and brokers as collateral for loan margin loans, brokers having called for cash to meet margin demands.

International Shoe common, also listed on the New York Stock Exchange, fell $1 to a new low of 53½, with 3124 shares sold on the local exchange, of which 1000 were in one block. The preferred reached a new low of 102.

The most active stock was Wagner Electric, with 5720 shares sold, falling to a new low of 25 for the year and closing at 28, or $4 off. Skouras Brothers, with only 10 shares sold, was $15 off with a new low of 10. Missouri Portland closed off $12 off, with a new low of 22.

Other stocks which reached new lows were: Consolidated Lead, 8; Ely-Walker, 28; Hamilton-Brown, 9; Hussa, 3½; Laclede Gas preferred, 95; Laclede Steel, 40; Pickwell Walnut, 15; Rice Stix, 13½; Stix-Baer-Fuller, 26; Southwestern Bell preferred, 113.

Houston Oil was off $7.50 and Century Electric was off $5.50.

Bank stocks with marked decline were First National Bank, which closed 250 off at 510; Mercantile-Commerce, which closed at 290, or 125 off, the high for the day being 325; St. Louis Union Trust, which closed $25 off at 450. Ten shares of Baltimore Bank were sold; 790 shares of Mercantile-Commerce and 75 shares of St. Louis Union Trust Co.

Reported movement in local brokerage offices were again packed to the doors. Many of those who gathered watch the ticker had been sold out.

The market was a topic of conversation wherever business men gathered. Stocks which have marked buried the money in the chicken yard behind a vacant house once occupied by him and his family.

How 50 Leading Stocks Closed Today

By the Associated Press.

NEW YORK, Oct. 29.—Final prices on 50 leading issues traded today on the New York Stock Exchange, together with the net change compared with Monday's closing quotations, are given below. When the market closed the stock ticker was approximately three hours behind in printing transactions:

American Can, $129, off $14.
American & Foreign Power $85, off $22.50.
American Smelting $84, off $4.
American Telephone & Telegraph $204, off $28.
Anaconda Copper $85, off $3.50.
Andre Copper $16, off $5.25.
Atlantic Refining $33, off $5.50.
Baltimore & Ohio $114.50, off $5 cents.
Barnsdall "A" $20.85, off $1.25.
Bethlehem Steel $84 off $10.12.
Briggs Manufacturing $17, off $3.
Canadian Pacific $197, off $11.
Chrysler $32.50, off $4.75.
Columbia Gas & Electric $63, off $15.
Columbia Graph., $19.25, off 75 cents.
Commonwealth & Southern, $12.25, off $2.75.
Consolidated Gas, $91.50, off $5.75.
Erie Railroad, $44.25, off $9.62.
General Electric, $222, off $28.
General Foods, $40, off $5.12.
General Foods, $40, off $5.12.
Gold Dust, $37.50, off $7.12.
Hudson Motors, $42, off $5.25.
Johns-Manville, $115, off $17.
Kennecott, $65.75, off $4.55.
Missouri, Kansas & Texas, $32.12, off $5.25.
Montgomery-Ward, $52.75, off $5.75.
National "Cash Register" A, $70, off $10.
National Dairy products, $48, off $10.50.
New York Central, $169.50, up $2.50.
Packard Motor, $14, off $1.75.
Pan Am. Pet. B, $55, off $11.
Par. Fam. Lasky, $49, off $9.25.
Radio Corp., $38.50, off $1.75.
Sears-Roebuck, $55, off $14.75.
Sinclair Con. Oil, $16, off $2.35.
Stand.-Oil N. J., $57.75, off $7.
Studebaker, $44, off $7.
Texas Corp., $50.75, off $5.25.
Tex. Gulf Sulphur, $50, off $5.75.
Union Carb., $73, up $7.50.
Union Pacific, $208.85, off $26.
United Aircraft, $41, off $16.85.
United Corp, $25.75, off $5.75.
United Gas Imp., $35, off $8.37.
U. S. Steel Shot, $174, off $12.
Vanadium, $52, off $9.12.
Westing, El. & Mfg., $16, off $17.
Woolworth, $75, off $1.

LAST PRICES ARE DOWN; HUNDREDS GO TO NEW LOWS

Bankers, Insurance and Industrial Leaders Put in Orders in Effort to Insure Orderly Market.

CREST OF SELLING SEEMS REACHED

Opening of Market Is Wildest Ever Seen, Blocks of 10,000 and 80,000 Shares Changing Hands.

By the Associated Press.

NEW YORK, Oct. 29.—Powerful buying support, set in motion by New York bankers, today, apparently checked the tremendous flood of liquidation which has been sweeping into the New York security markets for the last week, but not until after another disastrous decline had carried prices of active issues down $10 to $70 a share, and washed away several more billions in quoted values. A brisk rally this afternoon brought about recoveries of $5 to $26 from the low levels in many of the leading stocks, with final quotations generally well above the day's low levels.

Total stock sales set a new high record at 16,410,000 shares, which contrasts with the previous record of 12,894,600 last Thursday and 9,212,800 shares yesterday.

U. S. Steel Declares Extra

Directors of the United States Steel Corporation today declared an extra dividend of $1 on the common stock in addition to the regular quarterly dividend of $1.75.

Trading on the New York curb market also set a new high record with a turnover of 7,096,300 shares, which contrasts with 6,157,900 yesterday and the previous record of more than 6,000,000 last Thursday. Transactions in Chicago curb common alone exceeded 1,000,000 shares.

On the Curb order of the closing prices were: Cities Service, $32.50, off $5; Electric Bond and Share, $59.50, off $25.50; Electric Investors, $55, off $40; Midwest Utilities, $190, off $55; American Superpower, off $19, off $14.12; Associated Gas, $33.12, off $10.85.

It was unofficially reported late this afternoon that the five-hour trading session may be shortened tomorrow in order to permit brokers to catch up with the unprecedented accumulation of work arising out of recent record-breaking markets.

There was no parallel to the panicky conditions of Thursday, and the net losses today were not much more than half as severe as those of yesterday.

The Associated Press average closing price of 50 industrial stocks fell 19.7 points to a new low for the year, 29 railroads stocks declined 3.4 points and 20 utilities fell 22 points to a new low.

Leading New York bankers again met in the offices of J. P. Morgan & Co. early this afternoon, but no official announcement will be forthcoming until late this evening. Spokesman for the bankers stated, however, that orders were being placed by the banking pool to assure an orderly market. The bankers previously had reduced the margin requirements on Street demand loans from 40 to 25 per cent in order to ease the financial burdens of brokers.

Meanwhile, stocks were being bought on the way down by investment, trusts and insurance companies. Albert Conway, superintendent of insurance of the State of New York, was quoted on the floor stating that he had urged insurance companies to invest substantial amounts of their assets in high-grade stocks. A meeting of life insurance company presidents

Continued on Page 2, Column 5.

---

14 PERSONS ON PIKE'S PEAK MAROONED BY SNOWSTORM

Three on Summit and 11 at Timber Line Isolated by Eight-Foot Drifts.

By the Associated Press.

COLORADO SPRINGS, Colo., Oct. 29.—Winter swooped down on this section last night and left 14 persons stranded behind six and eight-foot drifts on Pike's Peak. Three were marooned at the summit and 11 at Glen Cove, near timber line on the auto highway.

Aside from temporary imprisonment in the summit house and at Glencove the 14 will suffer no inconvenience as they are well supplied with food and fuel. Equipment to clear the highways is available at Glen Cove, but the effort will be made to break through the drifts until the storm abates.

OCCASIONAL RAIN TONIGHT, SLIGHTLY COLDER TOMORROW

THE TEMPERATURES.

[temperature table]

Official forecast of St. Louis and vicinity: Unsettled tonight and tomorrow, probably occasional rain; somewhat colder tomorrow.

Missouri: Unsettled tonight and tomorrow, rain probable; somewhat colder in west and north central portions; colder tomorrow in extreme east portion.

Illinois: Rain tonight and tomorrow; not much change in temperature.

Sunset, 5:04; sunrise (tomorrow), 6:27.

LADY ASTOR BEATS MAN TO SEAT IN PARLIAMENT

Arrives at Chair, Heads Foe and Her onds Before Baronet as Sessions Open.

By the Associated Press.

LONDON, Oct. 29.—With unemployment the chief issue facing the second Labor Government of England, Parliament resumed its sessions this morning.

The rush for choice seats in the House of Commons began very early. Some members arrived at 6 a. m. and when the doors opened at 2 o'clock there was a rush and a scramble for the best places.

Lady Astor, who stood at the doors an hour before they were opened, beat out Sir Frederick Hall in a race for the third corner seat above the gangway, reaching it a few seconds before the baronet.

J. H. Thomas, Lord Privy Seal and Minister of Employment, announced he would make a comprehensive statement on unemployment in England next week. Sir James Graham, president of the Board of Trade, told the House, he hoped to make a statement on the hours of the coal miners on Thursday.

The Government is expected to mark time until the return of Prime Minister Ramsay MacDonald, whose place as leader of the party has been temporarily taken by Chancellor of the Exchequer Philip Snowden.

RUSSIA SHOOTS 13 FARM BLOC

BANK AT GORIN, MO., CLOSES

By the Associated Press.

JEFFERSON CITY, Oct. 29.—The Gorin Savings Bank, at Gorin, Scotland County, which had $272,000 total resources, was closed today by its board of directors. No reason was given in the message to the department.

The depository, the sixteenth to close this year, had $10,000 capital, $10,000 surplus, $21,000 loans and $146,000 deposits. The failure is the second at Gorin in five years. The first bank having been closed in 1924. W. H. Ewing is president of the Gorin Savings Bank; L. P. Shidley is cashier.

$47,000 OF NAVY PAYROLL DUG UP IN CHICKEN YARD

Money Had Been Stolen by Lieutenant, Who Surrendered Last Week.

By the Associated Press.

WASHINGTON, Oct. 29.—Navy Department officials announced today they had found $47,000, buried in a chicken yard in southeast Washington by Lieut. Charles Mudd, who disappeared from Charleston, S. C, several weeks ago with a $54,000 payroll.

Mudd walked aboard the receiving ship Seattle in New York last week and surrendered. He turned over $1500 in cash at that time. Officials a little hope of finding the rest of the money.

Mudd told naval officials he had buried the money in the chicken yard behind a vacant house once occupied by him and his family.

ON TODAY'S EDITORIAL PAGE
An Appeal to Reason: *Editorial.*
If Mr. Dulles Just Wasn't Wearing That Hat: *Cartoon.*
Mr. Corsi Fires Back: *Editorial.*

ST. LOUIS POST-DISPATCH

FINAL
★★★
(Closing New York Stock Prices)

Vol. 77. No. 101. (77th Year) ST. LOUIS, TUESDAY, APRIL 12, 1955—44 PAGES PRICE 5 CENTS

STEVENSON CALLS FOR FREE WORLD TO CONDEMN FORCE IN FORMOSA STRAIT

HE ASKS ALLIES, NEUTRALS, REDS ALSO TO ACT ON OFFSHORE ISLES

Appeals for Renunciation by Eisenhower of 'Go-It-Aloneism' Policy — Suggests U.N. Action.

(Text on Page 1B.)

By RAYMOND P. BRANDT
Chief Washington Correspondent of the Post-Dispatch.

WASHINGTON, April 12—Adlai Stevenson, speaking as the titular head of the Democratic party, called last night for a united front with our allies and the uncommitted nations and a renunciation by President Eisenhower of "go-it-aloneism" over Matsu and Quemoy.

The 1952 presidential candidate, in a nation-wide radio broadcast from Chicago, called for a joint declaration by the free nations—and a separate declaration by Soviet Russia if possible—condemning the use of force in the Formosa Strait and agreeing to stand with us against any aggression by the Red Chinese.

Political Expediency.

He charged that the Eisenhower Administration from political expediency had put this country in a position where it faces "another damaging and humiliating defeat or else the hazard of war."

Without naming Senate Minority Leader William F. Knowland of California and Styles Bridges of New Hampshire, chairman of the Senate Republican policy committee, the former Illinois Governor quoted these Republican leaders as saying that unless we support China and Kai-shek we will act in substance to the Communist claim that the United States is a "paper tiger."

Stevenson said he hoped "inflammatory advice in this party and in his administration" would not unbalance the President's consideration of the broader issues in the Far East.

"At this late date," he said, "there may be no wholly satisfactory way of resolving the dilemma we have stumbled into over the offshore islands. But if we learn something from this experience, if we realize at last that we have been pursuing a *clot-cend* policy in Asia through a *steps* we can turn our present difficulties to good account and devise an approach more in keeping with the realities of the A-bomb and the hydrogen age."

Stevenson's solution was for abandonment of "wishful thinking and wishful talking" and the "policy of big words and little deeds."

Open Declaration.

"I would urge our Government," he told his radio audience, "to promptly consult our friends and yes, the uncommitted states too, and as them all to join with us in an open declaration condemning the use of force in the defense of Formosa itself, and agreeing to stand with us in the defense of Formosa against any aggression, pending some final settlement of its status — by independence, neutralization
(Continued on Page 11, Column 3.)

Showers, Cooler

Official forecast for St. Louis and vicinity: Considerable cloudiness tonight and tomorrow with occasional showers or thundershowers ending tomorrow forenoon; cooler tomorrow and tomorrow night; lowest temperature tomorrow morning about 55; highest in low 60s tomorrow afternoon.

TEMPERATURES

DULLES
A DEAD-END KIDDER?

Missouri-Illinois forecasts and weather on other pages: Page 2A, 8A, 9A.
P-D's weather, 24 hours to 10 a.m.: Page 2A.

(Sunset, 6:32 p.m.; sunrise 'to-
row; 5:38 a.m.
(Stage of the Mississippi at St. Louis, 9.9 feet, a fall of 0.5, tee that between 275,000 and above —
Missouri at St. Charles, 12.1 feet, a fall of 0.6.

DULLES SAYS U.S. MOVES ALONG STEVENSON LINES

Except Democrat Would Ignore a Principal Ally, Nationalist China, Secretary Asserts.

WASHINGTON, April 12 (AP) —Secretary of State John Foster Dulles said today Adlai Stevenson's ideas about defending Formosa parallel what the Eisenhower Administration is doing, except that Stevenson would ignore "the loyalty and resources" of a principal ally, Nationalist China.

"Mr. Stevenson seems to assume that that ally can be ignored and rebuffed," Dulles told a press conference in a prepared statement.

Dulles sharply rejected Stevenson contention, in a speech Stevenson broadcast to the nation last night, that America's Formosa policy is based "more on considerations of domestic political expediency than foreign realities."

Dulles denied domestic politics played any part in United States policy toward Formosa. Ke said the policy is based entirely on his and President Eisenhower's judgment of the Far East situation.

Asked about another point *(Continued on Page 4, Column 5.)*

POLICEMAN'S FALL DISLODGES TOY CAR IN BABY'S THROAT

(Picture on page 2A.)

Patrolman Edward Hughes of Webster Groves dislodged an inch-long toy automobile from the throat of 13-month-old Diane Cadenbach yesterday, but he does not recommend the method he used.

When Hughes arrived at the Cadenbach home at 305 Gurrea place, the baby's mother, Mrs. Charles M. Cadenbach, was holding her up side-down up her feet in an effort to dislodge the car.

The baby started to turn blue. Hughes took the child and as he was running across the wet grass of the lawn toward the police car, he slipped and fell. Diane went down with him.

When he got up, still holding the baby, she started to cry—something she had not been able to do w h the toy in her throat. Mrs. C denbach reached in Diane's mouth. The toy automobile was there. The policeman's lucky fall apparently had dislodged it.

BOY, 8, ARRESTED, WAS DRIVING AUTO TO VISIT GRANDMA

NEW YORK, April 12 (AP)—While an astonished policeman held the door, Esperantd Frank Blonde slid from behind the steering wheel of his father's automobile and announced that driving was no problem at all.

"Why, it was simple," he said, calmly overlooking the fact that he had bumped two cars and gouged six red lights in his drive through Brooklyn's Sheepshead Bay section.

When Patrolman Albert Lefane first spotted Frankie's car, it appeared to be going along the street without a driver. Then he noticed the peak of the youngster's cap barely reaching to the window.

The boy told him he was just driving over to see his grandmother. He said he had taken the car keys from his mother's coat pocket. Frank learned to drive by watching his parents. But things were not so simple after that. He was booked as a juvenile delinquent and released in the custody of his mother for a hearing May 17.

LYRIC OF STEPHEN FOSTER EDITED, STATE SPURNS BOOK

ATLANTA, April 12 (AP)—Because a lyric of Stephen Foster was edited, the Georgia State Board of Education refused yesterday to adopt a new music textbook for use in Georgia schools.

The book, "Together We Sing," included several Foster selections.

As Foster wrote it, one line of the old favorite, "Old Folks At Home," begins, "Oh, darkies, how my heart grows weary ..."
In the new book, the line appears "Oh, brothers, how my heart grows weary ..."

Barnyard Zoo of Pigs, Cows, Sheep Proposed for Children

A proposal to establish a children's zoo where St. Louis youngsters could pet lambs and, if bold enough, pick up pigs was disclosed last night by Mayor Raymond R. Tucker.

The Mayor told a fairmers' businessman banquet at Perryville, Mo. that youngsters might be emanating from Forest Park in the near future.

Although he did not elaborate, the Post-Dispatch was told later that the plan to establish a "farm animals" zoo in Forest Park was being indicated hopefully. It might be somewhere between $15,000 and $18,000—
(Continued on Page 5, Column 2.)

U.S. GIVES CITY GO-AHEAD FOR MILL CREEK AREA SLUM PROJECT

Survey Fund of $685,200 Advanced for 460 Acres Bounded by 20th Street, Olive, Grand and Rail Yards.

The Federal Government gave St. Louis the go-ahead signal today for redevelopment of the Mill Creek Valley slum area by advancing $685,200 to finance surveys of the 460 acres bounded by Twentieth street, Grand boulevard, Olive street and the railroad yards.

James W. Follin urban renewal commissioner of the Housing and Home Finance Agency in Washington, notified the St. Louis Land Clearance for Redevelopment Authority that the money, a long-term loan, was being placed in a drawing account to be used as needed.

At the same time, he announced that the Authority already has earmarked $18 413,566 as a capital grant reservation for the project. This is the first step toward underwriting two-thirds of the cost of clearing the area and selling it at reduced price to private redevelopers, a federal contribution that would be called for when all the necessary plans were completed and the city was ready to pay its one-third share.

Room for Expansion.

Redevelopment of the sprawling Mill Creek Valley area will clear large tracts to provide room for industrial and business expansion inside the city. Erection of buildings for St. Louis University as well as apartments may be included.

The surveys to be financed by the federal loan will be conducted by the City Plan Commission and other municipal agencies, with private engineering firms assisting in some phases.

Redevelopment of Mill Creek Valley is visualized as a five-year undertaking—two years for detailed studies required by law, and three years for land acquisition, demolition and construction. It is designated as the city's second urban redevelopment project, the first being the impending rehabilitation of eight and one-half blocks in the Plaza area with a private housing project and a public park.

Some Buildings to Remain.

Twenty times as large as the Plaza district, the Mill Creek Valley project is to be carried out in stages. While many of the dwellings and other buildings in the area are substandard and the district has been officially designated as blighted by the Board of Aldermen, some of the newer structures are sound and will be retained.

A group at St. Louis business men headed by Otto J. Dickmann, Arthur C. Hoehn and Frederic B. Martin last August established the Midtown Industrial Redevelopment Corp. for the purpose of developing a new industrial district in the Mill Creek Valley area. The City Plan Commission has suggested that the section south of Market street, bordering on the railroad tracks be reserved for industry.

The Land Clearance Authority has asked the citizens' committee which is drafting a bond issue program of public improvements to include funds to finance the city's participation in redevelopment of Mill Creek Valley and other areas.

TELLS OF RUSSIAN URANIUM MINING IN CZECH PITS

UNITED NATIONS, N.Y. April 12 (AP)—Russia was reported today to be taking 60 trainloads of uranium ore each week from slave-operated pits in Czechoslovakia.

Josef Koubatsek, 54-year-old Czech told of the operation in an affidavit to United States Authorities in West Germany, which was submitted to the United Nations. The account, which covers Koubatsek's imprisonment as a slave laborer in the Joachimstahler uranium districts from August 1954 until his escape on July 7, 1954, was one of a dozen affidavits for refugees from Czechoslovakia, Poland, Albania and Hungary on forced labor operations.

Tortures, he said, included solitary confinement in dark, narrow dungeons, starvation and beatings. The camps are run under the Communist labor secret police Kubicka said Russians have displayed inspectors and other Czech experts, although their technical attainments are small.

TRAFFIC TIED UP AGAIN BY SPLIT IN BROADWAY LINE

Operations Elsewhere Practically Back to Normal After Zone Fare Confusion.

Traffic again was badly tied up on Broadway downtown during this morning's rush hour, the result of the split in the Broadway street car line and the inability of the company to speed up service in the downtown area.

For a time before 8 a.m. street cars, buses, automobiles and trucks were jammed over a six-block stretch from Cole street on the north to Locust street on the south as street cars of the new North and South Broadway lines turned east off Broadway to make their loops.

Elsewhere on the Public Service Co. system, the company reported bus and street car operations practically back to normal after yesterday's confusion over the new fare system went into operation.

Most Vehicles on Time.

Except for a few isolated delays caused by minor accidents or equipment breakdowns, buses and street cars ran on time, a company spokesman said.

Care of the two Broadway lines ran four minutes late the spokesman said. However, a company supervisor at the scene told a Post-Dispatch reporter that cars were 15 minutes late from 7:15 to 8 a.m.

Yesterday, company supervisors said cars of the Broadway lines were up to 30 minutes late. One extra car was put in service this morning on each of the Broadway lines to help prevent a repetition of yesterday's congestion of passengers in the Franklin-Delmar area.

Traffic policemen went on duty at the central Broadway intersections at 7 a.m. today, half an hour earlier than usual, to police the traffic direction, was on hand to direct operations.

Maj. Cihulka said he would study the situation with a view of proposing a plan to relieve the congestion.

Company Expresses Regret.

The company in a statement expressed regret over yesterday morning's delays on the longer lines.

In anticipating some delays on these lines because of the newness of the plan to our riders, we substantially increased our supervisory and information force," the statement said "We are sorry that delays result.
(Continued on Page 5, Column 2.)

SUSPECT IN BANK THEFT FOUND IN SING SING PRISON

NEW YORK, April 12 (AP)—Police have arrested Edward Schmaier and the last of persons whom they wanted in questions about the $305,000 loot robbery of the Chase Manhattan bank...

CORSI IS NOT QUALIFIED FOR ADMINISTRATIVE JOB, DULLES SAYS

Secretary Had Called Ousted Aid 'Best Qualified Man' in U.S. on Refugee Problems Last December.

By RICHARD DUDMAN
A Washington Correspondent of the Post-Dispatch.

WASHINGTON, April 12—Secretary of State John Foster Dulles said today Edward J. Corsi was not qualified to take an administrative job in the State Department and had said so himself.

Dulles, who called Corsi "best qualified man" in the United States to deal with refugee problems when he named him as his special assistant last December, said at his weekly news conference it was "absolutely not true" that he was compelled to fire Corsi because of attacks by Representative Francis E. Walter (Dem.), of Pennsylvania. Walter has accused Corsi of having associated with Communist front organizations some 20 years ago. Corsi has denied this.

Corsi Offered New Job.

The Secretary dropped Corsi Sunday from the job he had held for 90 days as special assistant on refugee and immigration problems. At the time he let Corsi go, Dulles offered him another job in the department, which Corsi refused.

In a letter to Dulles yesterday, Corsi denounced the administration of the Refugee Relief Act as a "scandalous failure." He said it could not be remedied "until you and the Administration reverse it from the grip of an intolerant minority both in Congress and within the State Department itself, which believes that in this world there is no argument and no inferior race."

Dulles told his press conference, the ousted immigration expert had tried to "get around the law" and become actual administrator of the relief act.

"He indicated to me that he was not interested in and not qualified for administrative work," Dulles said.

Assails Reckless Charges.

As for Corsi's contention that the Administration of the act was a "scandalous failure," Dulles retorted:

"That is typical of the reckless charges which Mr. Corsi does not like when they are directed against him."

Corsi denied immediately after the Dulles press conference that he ever had said he was not interested in or not qualified for administrative work.

"That is just an outright lie," Corsi told the Post-Dispatch.

Summarizing his long career as an administrator, Corsi recalled that, as director of emergency relief for the state of New York during the depression, he directed the work of 18,000 employees and he said one of them was that administration all my life," he said.

Another Disagreement.

The two men today disagreed also about what Dulles said in a conversation they had Friday, when Dulles offered Corsi the substitute job.

Ready to Give Report

DR. THOMAS FRANCIS JR. (left) and DR. JONAS E. SALK shortly before reporting to scientific meeting in Ann Arbor, Mich, today on the Salk poliomyelitis vaccine tests. (Additional pictures in Everyday Magazine.)

Polio Vaccine Program May Start Here Within Two Weeks

Inoculations to Be Given First and Second Graders Free if Parents Request It.

Physicians will begin administering the Salk polio vaccine to pupils in the first and second grade in St. Louis area schools as soon as supplies are received here, possibly in about one to two weeks, the Post-Dispatch was told today.

The vaccine, subject of a favorable report today, will be given free of charge to pupils in three grades if their parents request it. Children in other age groups may receive the paralytic polio preventive from private doctors at a cost expected to be $10 to $15.

Dr. Lloyd L. Tate, director of health and hygiene for the Board of Education, said he expected supplies of the vaccine to be received here within 10 days. This would mean that inoculations could begin by late next week.

Health Officers Target Date.

However, Dr. Elizabeth K. A. Gay, chief of the communicable disease control section of the City Health Division, said there was no indication when the vaccine would arrive here. It was understood that most health authorities were shooting at April 25 as a target date for starting inoculations.

In the city, parents of 22 049 pupils have requested that their children be inoculated, out of a total of 29,666 eligible in the two grades in public, private and parochial schools. The health division will immediately notify physicians here and begin a campaign to get the pupils inoculated as soon as supplies are received.

U.S. HOLDS UP LICENSING OF SALK VACCINE

WASHINGTON, April 12 (AP)—The Department of Health, Education and Welfare put out today—and then corrected—an announcement that the Salk polio vaccine would be formally licensed at 4 p.m. for general use.

The announcement that the Salk vaccine will be licensed at 4 p.m. today was premature," the department said shortly after 2:25 p.m. The original statement came out about noon.

A spokesman for the department said another announcement will be forthcoming later.

In answer to questions he would only say that "technical difficulties" had arisen in making the official evaluation of the product.

Formal licensing requires the signature of Secretary Oveta Culp Hobby. Without her signature the vaccine cannot be sold commercially.

STRONGER COFFEE FOR AMERICANS IS AIM OF GROWERS

SAN JUAN, Puerto Rico, April 12 (AP) — Delegates from 14 Latin American coffee-producing nations were urged yesterday to conduct a promotional drive to sell more coffee for more consumption in the United States and Canada.

Horacio Cintra Leite, president of the Pan-American Coffee Bureau, in a speech to the eighth conference of the Coffee Federation of Central America and Mexico, said "there are many causes for the United States coffee consumption decline." He said one of them was that Americans drink their coffee too weak.

He cited United States Government statistics to show that green coffee imports decreased 12 to 15 per cent in 1954 and per capita consumption by American coffee drinkers decreased 15% per cent.

One remedy is available, he declared—the "Pan-American Coffee Bureau must have for the national stands to educate United States citizens to drink more and stronger coffee."

Coffee Tends in Nicaragua.

Mary from 200 pesons were hauled in tiny two towns north of here for the town's the beckons ... quaking in his Buckleys building on the Bickens — for with Caesar to put in the University of Pittsburgh ... Photographers of ... of ... their ...

Mad Scramble by Reporters For Copies of Vaccine Report

ANN ARBOR, Mich, April 12 — AP News reporters started pulling copies of the report from the press...

SALK POLIO VACCINE FOUND SAFE, EFFECTIVE, POTENT; UP TO 90 PCT. PREVENTIVE

REPORT SAYS INOCULATIONS CAN END YEARLY THREAT TO YOUNG

Discoverer Asserts Substance Could Bring Full Triumph Over Disease, Potentially 100 Pct. Effective.

(Medical Abstract Text on Page 6A.)

ANN ARBOR, Mich., April 12 (AP)—The Salk polio vaccine is up to 80 to 90 per cent effective in preventing paralytic polio in tests last year, Dr. Thomas Francis Jr., of the University of Michigan disclosed today. He analyzed the results of the tests.

The vaccine was found to be up to 80 to 90 per cent effective in preventing paralytic polio in tests last year, Dr. Thomas Francis Jr., of the University of Michigan, disclosed today. He analyzed the results of the tests.

Dr. Jonas E. Salk of Pittsburgh, developer of the vaccine, immediately declared he was sure the vaccine is potentially almost 100 per cent effective and could bring complete triumph over polio.

Dr. Francis's long-awaited official report declared the vaccine had produced an "obvious to successful effect" in preventing bulbar polio, the most dangerous type, among children.

There is no doubt that children now can be vaccinated successfully to end the threat of polio and the anxiety it causes every year, the report said.

Point by point, Dr. Francis detailed the saving of life and limb from the vaccine, made of killed polio virus.

In comparison, of 1,440,000 unvaccinated children in the test program 445 were paralyzed.

Only 113 cases of proved polio among the vaccinated children, many recovering without illness.

But 750 cases of proved polio among the unvaccinated.

Not one child died of polio among vaccinated youngsters, excluding one who died after receiving his second shot of vaccine and undergoing surgery for tonsil removal — a polio epidemic.

Fifteen killed by the disease among about 1,000,000 children unvaccinated.

Dr. Francis reported there was an incredibly low incidence of either minor or severe reactions among the vaccinated, including even minor severe re-actions among the vaccinated children, excluding even minor reactions — skin rashes and feverish feelings—as those getting the real vaccine.

The vaccine is expected to be approved and licensed by the national institutes of health and within a week or two, perhaps, be given to children and permanent women, to forestall polio.

A call to "give the children priority" was sounded by Dr. Dwight H. Murray, chairman of the American Medical Association's board of trustees.

Enough vaccine to inoculate 30,000,000 children with three shots each—a complete course—is expected to come touring from pharmaceutical houses.

Dr. Salk, on the main of new findings, urged that only two shots be given this summer.

This would expand the available supply to make enough available for 45,000,000—about the entire population of children under 10 years of age.

Dr. Salk recommended a booster shot this year for all children who got the actual vaccine last year. Parents of children who participated in the tests may learn from health authorities whether their children received the vaccine or dummy shots.

Spacing of Shots.

Dr. Salk feels that giving two shots spaced two to four weeks apart, followed by a third "booster" shot, should give pupils the trigger of the antibody mechanism to flood the bloodstream with antibodies. Whether his recommendation will be followed remains to be seen.

Dr. Salk said the fact that the three doses were given last year within a period to nine weeks may have explained some of the "lack of protection" against polio in some children last year. Another reason for the lack of complete protection, among vaccinated subjects was that some batches of vaccine used may have contained less of the virus ...
(Continued — Page 7, Column 1.)

On Today's Editorial Page
The Future Of The West End: *Editorial*
Compromise On Laos: *Editorial*

ST. LOUIS POST-DISPATCH

FINAL
★ ★ ★
Stock Market Up
Closing Prices Pages 22D and 23D

VOL. 93 NO. 275 WEDNESDAY, OCTOBER 6, 1971 10c Home Delivery $2.50-a Month

A NEIGHBOR'S WASH was soiled in a fire that burned out a vacant three-story brick building at 5127 Cabanne Avenue yesterday. Arson is suspected. Homes on both sides caught fire, but damage was minor. (Post-Dispatch Photo by James A. Rackwitz)

Parimutuel Betting Loses; Water Bonds Win Easily

Outstate Missourians overcame heavy urban support yesterday and defeated the legalization of parimutuel betting.

However, outstate voters joined metropolitan residents in approving a $150,000,000 state water pollution control bond issue by a wide margin.

Both urban and rural voters joined also in approving three other proposed constitutional amendments put before the state's electorate yesterday.

Metropolitan St. Louis and Kansas City voters approved the proposed amendment to authorize parimutuel betting on horse racing in Missouri by about a 60-to-40 margin. The measure carried in all 28 St. Louis wards and 18 St. Louis County townships. However, outstate voters rejected the plan by a 67 to 33 margin.

The result was a defeat of the plan by a 54 to 46 difference. Final unofficial returns showed 254,239 for and 295,963 against.

The $150,000,000 water pollution control bond issue, on the other hand, swept to an easy victory state-wide by a 3-to-1 margin. Unofficial returns showed 406,476 for and 132,196 against.

Proposition 1, to grant home rule powers to municipalities with 5000 or more population, was approved by urban and rural voters and received a 182,438 plurality. The unofficial vote total state-wide was 350,629 for and 167,745 against. Previously, only communities with 10,000 or more population could adopt home rule charters.

Proposition 2, allowing Greene and Clay Counties to levy a higher property tax than they otherwise would have been permitted to do, passed by a 84,766 margin, 296,352 for and 211,454 against.

Proposition 5, authorizing preferential treatment in hiring practices under the state merit system to all veterans of military service, rather than just those who entered the armed forces from Missouri, passed by a 160,835 margin, 340,708 for and 179,500 against.

All five proposed constitutional amendments carried in every St. Louis ward and St. Louis County township, as they did by comfortable margins in the Jackson County (Kansas City) area.

Gov. Warren E. Hearnes stopped short last night of saying that the massive plurality granted the water bond proposition had convinced him to seek submission to the electorate of his proposed $700,000,000 state transportation bond issue.

However, he did say that the outcome of the water pollution control measure "proves that a bond issue can be passed in Missouri.

"I think it put to rest the feeling that some members of the Legislature had that a bond issue could not be passed in Missouri," the Governor said.

Voting in all areas of the state was exceedingly light, with the exception of St. Louis County.

The parimutuel betting plan drew the most votes, a total of about 550,000—far less than the 700,000 total vote forecast by Secretary of State James C. Kirkpatrick. Even the larger amount he had predicted would be considered a small turnout.

But in St. Louis County, about 146,500 persons cast ballots on the parimutuel betting and water bond proposals. A turnout of about 120,000 had been predicted by local election officials.

The total outstate vote on that measure was 281,752, compared with 268,450 in St. Louis, St. Louis County and Jackson County. These three urban areas make up 47.6 per cent of the state's total population, according to 1970 census figures.

Trends in the election were established early in the vote tabulation and held up throughout the night in one of the fastest vote counts in the state's history.

This was a result, in large measure, of a law enacted in 1969 requiring election judges to turn in their vote tabulations to county clerks and election

TURN TO PAGE 5, COL. 1

All 5 Proposals Carried Here

Every ward and township in St. Louis and St. Louis County produced majorities in favor of all five constitutional amendments in yesterday's special election.

The city and county produced a majority of 49,724 for parimutuel betting, but the amendment lost because of an adverse vote from rural Missouri.

A CLEAN-CUT DECISION: Jim Tom Blair, cochairman of the Missourians for Clean Water Committee, after it was announced that the $150,000,000 water pollution bond issue had carried. (Post-Dispatch Photo)

Jubilant Officials Process Clean-Water Fund Plans

By PATRICK STRICKLER
Of the Post-Dispatch Staff

Missouri's clean water officials lost no time today processing plans to spend part of the $150,000,000 water pollution bond issue approved yesterday in the state-wide election.

"We're starting to work right away today on the 25 applications for money that we have on hand," said Jack K. Smith, executive secretary of the State Water Pollution Board.

"I feel wonderful!" said the state's top clean water official. "Now we can really make some progress in an orderly manner in cleaning up Missouri's water."

The bond issue proposal which appeared in the third position on yesterday's ballot, garnered more approving votes than any of the four other proposals in the election. Only a few outstate counties did not give the bond issue the necessary simple majority of yes votes needed for passage.

The unofficial state-wide tally showed 406,476 Missourians favoring the bond issue, and 132,196 against it. In the St. Louis area, the bond issue was approved by a 5-to-1 margin in both the city and county.

In St. Louis County, the vote was 121,356 for the bond issue, and 25,239 against. City voters approved the proposal 49,034 to 9870, returns showed.

Jackson County (Kansas City) voters also have overwhelming approval to the bond issue. The unofficial count was 44,449 for and 14,323 against.

Most outstate counties joined in approving the bonds. The unofficial returns for outstate Missouri showed 191,637 favoring the proposal and 82,764 against. Fourteen counties failed to come up with the necessary 51 per cent of yes votes needed for approval.

In Jefferson County, the vote was 8819 in favor, or 78 per cent, and 2538 in opposition. Franklin County voters approved the proposal 4311 (77 per cent) to 1319. In St. Charles County, the vote was 7935 (83 per cent) to 1654.

The water pollution bond issue, which had the strong support of Gov. Warren E. Hearnes and leaders of both the Democratic and Republican parties, will generate a total of $600,000,000 in pollution abatement projects in the next seven to 10 years.

The bonds will be sold as needed to match available federal funds for a matching-grant program that enables municipalities to build new or improved sewage treatment facilities with up to 80 per cent fi-

TURN TO PAGE 5, COL. 4

Vote On The Amendments

	AMENDMENT NO. 1 Home rule for charter cities	
Yes 350,629		No 167,745
	AMENDMENT NO. 2 Clay and Green County tax rate	
Yes 296,352		No 211,454
	AMENDMENT NO. 3 $150,000,000 water pollution bonds	
Yes 406,476		No 132,196
	AMENDMENT NO. 4 Legalize parimutuel betting	
Yes 245,239		No 295,963
	AMENDMENT NO. 5 Veterans preference	
Yes 340,708		No 179,500

Vasel Ruling Called Not A Compromise

By ASA E. BRYAN
Of the Post-Dispatch Staff

Members of the St. Louis County Board of Police Commissioners agreed unanimously at the outset of their deliberations that F. J. (Pete) Vasel should be restored to duty, but they were indecisive on the severity of the discipline, Hugh Scott Jr., a board member, told the Post-Dispatch today.

Vasel, who had been a major, was ordered restored to duty at the rank of lieutenant. He has offered to return to work pending the outcome of an appeal to the Circuit Court of the board's action.

His attorney, Merle Silverstein, said he had notified Edwin J. Putzell Jr., the board member who presided at Vasel's hearing, and Superintendent of Police Robert J. di Grazia of Vasel's offer. Putzell left St. Louis today for a trip to Europe.

Board Chairman Norman Parker, who disqualified himself from the Vasel case, said Silverstein was instructed to put the offer in writing. Parker said the board would take up the

TURN TO PAGE 4, COL. 1

U.S. Defeat On School Meal Cut

WASHINGTON, Oct. 6 (AP) — The Nixon Administration conceded defeat today in its effort to hold the line on school lunch money paid states to feed needy children.

The Department of Agriculture said that it would reimburse states at a minimum average of 45 cents a meal to provide free or reduced-price lunches to needy children.

That is a cent less than the 46 cents the Senate called for last week in a resolution aimed at forcing the department to scrap a proposal announced Aug. 13 that would have put the minimum at 35 cents.

Richard E. Lyng, assistant secretary of agriculture, told a press conference that the increase of 10 cents from the original proposal was expected to cost an additional $135,000,000.

That would boost the Government's total 19711-72 school budget to $750,000,000, about 40 per cent more than last year.

Lyng said the cent difference from the Senate version was expected to save the Government about $41,000,000 this school year.

Lyng said the expanded program was expected to help feed 8,000,000 children this year, compared with a peak of 7,300,000 last year.

$480,000 Statue Of Madonna Stolen

ARONA, Italy, Oct. 6 (AP)—A fifteenth century wooden statue of a Madonna with child, valued at $480,000, was stolen last night from the Madonna del Castello Shrine at nearby Invorio Superiore.

Thieves took the 200-pound statute after forcing the shrine door open.

High In 70s

Official forecast for St. Louis and vicinity: Sunny and pleasant this afternoon with the high in the mid 70s; clear and cool tonight with the low 45 to 50 and light northerly winds. Tomorrow sunny and mild with the high 75 to 80. Warmer Friday with the high in the 80s and the low in the 50s; gradually cooling through Sunday with the high around 70 and the low about 45 to 55.

Temperatures	
2 a.m.	55
3 a.m.	53
4 a.m.	53
5 a.m.	54
6 a.m.	51
7 a.m.	50
8 a.m.	52
9 a.m.	57
10 a.m.	61
11 a.m.	65
12 noon	68
1 p.m.	70
2 p.m.	71
3 p.m.	72

Other Weather Information on Page 2A

House Passes Tax Cuts That Favor Individuals

From Post-Dispatch Wire Services

WASHINGTON, Oct. 6 — The House approved today 15.4 billion dollars worth of tax cuts over the next three years for individuals and corporations as part of President Richard M. Nixon's plan to straighten out the American economy.

Passage was by voice vote.

The bill was revised by the House Ways and Means Committee to tilt more heavily toward individual taxpayers than did the form originally proposed by Mr. Nixon.

The Administration accepted the changes and House members approved the measure without further change.

It calls for an increase, effective this taxpaying year, of $25 for each person, to $675, in the personal exemption for individuals on their tax returns. The figure would go to $750 a person next year.

The standard deduction for those not itemizing deductions would go up also to 13 per cent effective this year to a maximum of $1500, compared to 10 per cent last year. This would rise to 20 per cent, to a maximum of $2000 next year. The 7-per-cent automobile excise tax would be wiped out immediately.

For business, the big item is a 7-per-cent tax credit for equipment purchases retroactive to last April 1.

The bill goes to the Senate, where chairman Russell B. Long (Dem.) Louisiana, promised to expedite hearings, which will begin tomorrow.

The bill is expected to reach the Senate floor late in the month, and several Senators have said they would try to increase the tax break for individuals.

Organized labor still is push-

TURN TO PAGE 8, COL. 1

Nixon Speech On Phase 2

WASHINGTON, Oct. 6 (AP) —President Richard M. Nixon will make public Phase 2 of his economic program in a live television-radio address to the nation at 6:30 p.m. (St. Louis time) tomorrow.

Mr. Nixon will speak from his White House office and will speak no longer than half an hour.

Chou Gives Mao Credit For Thaw

Julian Schuman is an American living and working in Peking. He was present when Premier Chou En-lai called in every American working in or visiting China to a meeting in the Great Hall of the People in Peking. His report of the meeting is transmitted by United Press International.

By JULIAN SCHUMAN

PEKING, Oct. 6 (UPI) — Communist Chinese Premier Chou En-lai met with about 60 Americans last night and told them that chairman Mao Tse-tung was responsible for inviting the United States table tennis team to China, an invitation that led to a thaw in Chinese-American relations.

In his two-hour meeting with the Americans, who included Black Panther Party leader Huey P. Newton and former U.S. Department of State officer John Service, Chou limited his discussion to foreign policy and did not refer to the current internal situation in China.

In addition to discussing Mao's role in the Chinese-American thaw, Chou said also:

(1) China agreed with President Richard M. Nixon that the current era was one of negotiations. But he said Chinese leaders believed also that, if necessary, it was an era of armed struggle.

(2) China was willing to negotiate its border dispute with Russia, using the nineteenth century territorial treaties as the basis for talks.

(3) China was keeping an open mind on Mr. Nixon's visit. "It is all right if the talks succeed, and it is all right if the talks fail," he said.

(4) No matter how far nego-

TURN TO PAGE 4, COL. 4

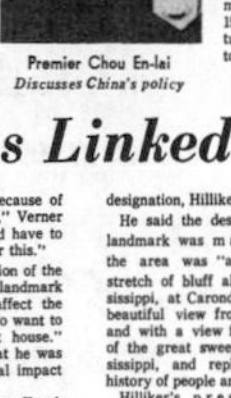

Premier Chou En-lai
Discusses China's policy

Landmark Status Linked To Housing Opposition

By LOUIS J. ROSE
Of the Post-Dispatch Staff

The designation of the river bluff area in South St. Louis as an official landmark was prompted in part by a desire to block construction of a federally assisted apartment building for low- and moderate-income families, an official said today.

Verner T. Burks, an architect and vice chairman of the city Landmarks Commission, said he was opposed to the proposed eight-story apartment at 4718 Broadway and hoped it would not be constructed.

He said that some members of the 12-man commission were hopeful that the commission's action in designating the bluff area as an official landmark would thwart the project.

"We feel this is one area that should be regulated because of its peculiar beauty," Verner said. "I feel we should have to approve any permit for this."

He said the designation of the area as an official landmark "would undoubtedly affect the arguments of those who want to put in the apartment house." But he emphasized that he was not sure what the legal impact would be.

Commission chairman Frank T. Hilliker said the designation was made Monday. The area involved is bounded by South Broadway on the west, the Mississippi River on the east, the north line of Bellerive Park on the south and Mount Pleasant street on the north.

All parcels of land and all buildings within the area were to be considered part of the designation, Hilliker said.

He said the designation as a landmark was made because the area was "an unmatched stretch of bluff along the Mississippi, at Carondelet, giving a beautiful view from the river, and with a view from the bluff of the great sweep of the Mississippi, and replete with the history of people and events."

Hilliker's press statement made no reference to the controversy over the 102-unit apartment building proposed by Laclede Town Co. which manages Laclede Town in Mill Creek Valley.

Opponents of the project argue that it would jeopardize an enclave of luxury and historic homes in the area and could cause severe financial losses for some poperty owners.

They sought unsuccessfully last week to get the City Plan Commission to sponsor a zoning change that would have blocked the apartment complex. The opponents wanted the zoning along a three-block area of South Broadway changed from multiple to two-family.

Plan commission members voted, 6 to 2, in favor of retaining the multiple-family zoning.

A proposed ordinance to change the zoning to two-family was introduced later in the week in the Board of Alderman by Albert (Red) Villa, Democratic alderman from the Eleventh Ward.

Plan Commission members who voted against a zoning change argued that it had been city policy since 1950 to encourage apartment development in the area.

The proposed project would contain efficiency, one and two-bedroom apartments. A petition signed by 2100 persons opposing the development was turned over to city officials earlier this month. Opponents contended that besides destroying the historical atmosphere of the neighborhood, it would cause overcrowding of schools.

News Index
80 PAGES

Editorials — — — — — — — 2E
Everyday Magazine — — 1-12F
Financial — — — — — — 20-23D
Obituaries — — — — — — — 1C
Radio-TV — — — — — — — — 10F
Sports — — — — — — — 16-21A
Want Ads — — — — — — 1-11C

Inmate Charges Price Gouging

JOLIET, Ill., Oct. 6 (AP)—An inmate of the Illinois State Penitentiary in Joliet filed suit in United States District Court yesterday charging that officials increased prices at the prison's commissary in violation of the wage-price freeze.

Robert DeMary asked in the suit that $125,000 in damages be paid because the officials "willfully and maliciously" raised prices at the commissary that sells such items as tooth paste and soap.

reaching the very largest last. Offset is still too slow for the extremely fast runs needed in papers of a quarter of a million circulation and upwards. But offset has its advantages and these have been reflected in a number of changes affecting format and makeup:

1. Offset tends to increase the use of pictures. Art is cheaper and simpler to produce than by the zinc-etch method necessary on letterpress papers.

2. Offset tends to increase typographical variation. Anything that can be cut out and pasted down will reproduce. This invites the use of ornamentation, distinctive type for a particular story, decorative rules to set off large masses of the page or surround small stories.

3. Offset has opened up many kinds of publication never seen before. Underground papers, for example, have sprung up all over the country. They are easy to put together and cheap to print, so new and smaller kinds of audiences may be cultivated. (Is there an audience for a rock-oriented paper on the West Coast? Let's try it. If record-company ads will pay the printing bill, the rest is gravy.) With a huge investment in presses, stereotyping equipment, composing machines, and the whole superstructure of the standard daily paper no longer a necessity, variation and experimentation thrive. The strange new formats and designs cannot help but influence general newspaper practices.

Cold type and other new methods have increased compostion speed. A highly paid and skillful Linotype operator seated at a keyboard can turn out between a column and a column and a half an hour. This has been for more than half a century the limiting factor in newspaper composition, just as the slower speed of a compositor setting a stick of type by hand set limits in the pre-Mergenthaler era. But the teletypesetter, the attachment to the composing-machine keyboard that operates the machine automatically with punched tape, sets lines 50 to 100 per cent faster than a Linotype operator, and cheaper labor can cut the tapes. Teletypesetting also reduces correction costs. The principle of tape-fed composing machines led to other high-speed automatic linecasting machines, whose speed doubled in the absence of the manual operator.

Then the composing-machine makers went to photosetting. Photon, for example, photographs letters selected from a disc which contains all the characters in a given typeface. All sizes are available in one operation by simply changing the focal length—the distance from camera to disc. This system, actuated by tape cut at a typewriter keyboard, is fast and flexible—especially suitable for handling the complex composition requirements of display ads. Meanwhile, typewriter makers came up with systems justifying typewriter lines; they also developed variable-width characters and typefaces that looked more like print. Then the computer makers came up with computerized justification and word division. Some papers have even tried doing without justification altogether.

Where two linecasting-machine companies once offered the only competing ways of composing type—and they were different in only trivial ways—the newspaper-production superintendent today has many basically differing systems of composition to choose from, many of which bypass the hot-type step—that is, they do not require molten type metal. The result has not always been good for aesthetics or legibility, but the combination of cold type and offset has freed the editor from strictures he has had to live with for years. These developments have undoubtedly supported today's tendency to be more experimental and less hidebound in newspaper design and makeup.

Computer editing—a very real and immediate future possibility as this is written—causes newspaper managements to scrutinize all items in the decision process carefully, in order to simulate them accurately in the computer. Its effects on makeup and format are not apparent as yet but will surely be felt.

Closer attention is given to these developments in Chapter 15. The striking fact is that people who enter news editing in this era of revolution in newspaper production will find that their skills and training for today's job probably won't apply for long. Penciling corrections on copy, for example, may well be doomed by technological change. As their skills are outmoded, editors will need to fall back on a sound and basic conception of their roles as decision makers and students of the communication process—and the willingness to seek out and champion new ways of making the process efficient.

Foundations of Good Makeup

The principles of sound news presentation through newspaper format have two chief poles. The first is *typographic*—an attractive combination of readable typefaces in both body and display sizes. The other pertains to *layout*—an attractive arrangement of the materials on the page and throughout the newspaper. The basic materials the editor works with in making decisions about makeup are body type, display type, art, white space, and typographical devices of various sorts. He arranges them with attention to these five main principles: balance, focus, contrast, dynamics, and unity.

Balance

The news editor about to lay out Page One starts with a rectangle of blank paper. Among the things he must decide is how he can array the news materials of that day on that rectangle in a way which will make the page consciously and unconsciously pleasing to the eye. One of his guides in this matter is page balance. Ever since headline and art were combined with body type on Page One, this has been a matter for concern.

There are two kinds of balance—formal and informal. *Formal balance,* or symmetry, was used occasionally in constructing front pages of newspapers. Beginners often take a fancy to formal balance because it is so simple and neat. Most editors, however, stay away from it, for reasons that will be covered shortly.

Formal balance has one simple requirement: everything in the paper that is not positioned squarely along the vertical center line must be duplicated in the same position on the opposite side. If the upper right-hand corner carries an X head with a No. 1 reading out of it into column 8, then the upper left-hand corner must have another X head with a No. 1 reading out of it into column 1. A four-column cut may go in columns 3, 4, 5, and 6, thus balancing itself, but a three-column cut is an impossibility unless it is balanced on the other side of the page by another.

A few newspapers use a semisymmetrical front page. They balance a two-column cut with a two-column typographical display, for instance. And small heads are usually not painstakingly balanced against each other. The New York *Times* sectional front page shown on page 236 illustrates this sort of virtual symmetry. One major head just below the center of the page is not duplicated in the other half of the page. Otherwise the balance is perfect.

Especially when used daily, formally balanced pages have one overpowering fault: they tend to force the news into a formula, rather than letting the makeup adapt to telling the peculiar relationships, values, and relative worth of that day's news. In other words, formal balance tends to make the news fit the pattern of the makeup, rather than making the makeup fit the pattern of the news. There is no more important point about makeup than this: *Whatever its value aesthetically or in other areas, the makeup must help to tell that day's news.* That means it should be flexible enough to express the relative values and interrelationships involved. Formal balance is anything but flexible, and for most editors it is a curiosity; they are concerned with the informal sort.

Shapes and sizes of full-sized newspapers vary a little. But on the whole, they have proportions in common—even in common with the tabloid. The prevailing proportion is approximately the "root 2" proportion, which is in itself a pleasing shape. It is the ratio of 1 to the square root of 2, or 1 to 1.414. The man who draws up a page layout, however, cannot change the dimensions of his page. His problem is to position his materials within it to provide an informal balance which will contribute to the unity and general effectiveness of his page.

Informal balance can be achieved without any special knowledge of proportion. Many makeup men proceed by the "instinct" or "feel" they have for layout. The beginner, however, would do well to analyze balance rather than to proceed by hit or miss. A systematic approach to balance involves halving and quartering the page and noting the desirable relationships among the several parts. The horizontal line

RUTLAND HERALD

Courtesy the Rutland (Vermont) Herald

The New York Times.

© 1951 by The New York Times Company. Reprinted by permission.

THE SUN

Heed Joint Chiefs' Advice, Wedemeyer Tells Congress;
Would Accept Genuine Truce Bid From Reds, He Says

Courtesy the Baltimore Sun

Formal Balance Twenty years ago, many newspapers regularly or frequently laid out front pages strictly symmetrically. The Rutland *Herald* made it a daily practice, and the New York *Times* and Baltimore *Sun* used a variety of symmetrical layouts occasionally. The three examples shown are from the early 1950's.

Virtually no contemporary papers hew to the formal-balance line. The Buffalo *Evening News* (see the "Bancroft *Star*" example on page 261) comes close to the symmetrical every day, but formal balance is for the most part an affectation of the past.

across the center of the page is a real one: it is actually present in the fold of the page. The vertical one is less real but nonetheless useful. These lines create two sets of halves, left and right, top and bottom. Granting that the key focal point is, or was until recently, the upper right-hand corner, is art and type massed about equally in the left and right halves? In the example on this page, a pretty good balance has been achieved. The largest cut plus some sizeable display type in the upper left-hand corner is effectively counterbalanced by the still larger type and two smaller cuts in the right half.

The optimum division of weights between upper and lower halves is normally not really equal. Too many habits of mind and reading dictate that the greater emphasis be at the top. We normally start reading any page of material at the top; "upper" carries a connotation of "superior." But the top half of a newspaper page should not *overpower* the lower half. If it does, balance is not being served. In the example, enough art and display type have been massed below the fold to avoid top-heaviness.

To get at the question of relative weights in the total page, the quarters must also be in a sound relationship to each other. The page in question passes this test well: the four quarters are in reasonable balance. Why?

The elements that contribute to mass in newspaper layout are art and display type. Sometimes art and type combine to create a single emphasis. In other cases, as in the example, they must be considered separately. The greatest single source of mass is the cut in the upper right-hand corner. The upper right is also the chief *focal point;* the large display type in the upper right-hand corner has the greatest attention value. For effective balance, the greater mass below the fold is in the lower left. Thus the superior masses in the upper right and lower left and the inferior masses in upper left and lower right help make this a soundly balanced page.

However, this type of balance is more appropriate for what is here called *modern* than what is called *contemporary* newspaper-page format, a distinction that will be developed shortly. Contemporary front pages tend to be less carefully balanced, quarter by

quarter, and tend even to court greater imbalance deliberately—to the limits of unity (discussed on pages 242–243). They also tend to be more nearly equal in weight between top and bottom than left and right: strong units may appear in the upper right and in the lower left, depending on other factors such as strong typographical displays, unusual shapes, and wide-measure body type to even things out. The value in these practices seems to be surprise and disequilibrium rather than regularity and balance.

Focus

Focus is closely related to balance—and it complicates balance. Reader habit and established newspaper

Courtesy the Toledo Blade

Informal Balance   The quarters of the page are balanced diagonally, and the halves—upper and lower, right and left—are carefully related.

practice for many years all but dictated the position of the chief focal point on the newspaper page. On Page One, the focal point normally was in the upper right-hand corner, not because it belonged there, either for artistic or linguistic reasons, but because it had always been there. But Western languages proceed from left to right and top to bottom. Logically, then, the focal point of a newspaper page should be the upper left.

Artistically, too, when four focal points are located in a rectangle that is higher than it is wide (this is explained more fully below), the one which artistically deserves the greatest emphasis is the one in the upper left, not the upper right. This is where it usually goes in advertising, billboard, magazine-page, and magazine-cover layout, for example. The idea is supported by some research done in the 1930's by Brandt[2] with a grant from Cowles Magazines, Inc. Probably because of the magazine sponsorship, Brandt tested visual explorations of a rectangle that simulated in size and shape the two-page magazine spread (not the upright rectangle of a newspaper page). Using 3,500 adult subjects, he found a consistent tendency for the first fixation to fall above and to the left of center and after that a tendency to move toward the upper left corner past the center point of that quarter. Thereafter, explorations tended to move in a clockwise direction. Subjects spent, on the average, 41 per cent of the time exploring that quarter, 20 per cent in the upper right, 25 per cent in the lower left, 14 per cent in the lower right. Thus the upper half was explored more thoroughly than the lower, and the left half more than the right.

But newspapers have traditionally stressed the upper right of the front page. It evidently started with the emergence of the banner headline, usually assigned to the chief story of the day. Once the reader had chased one line of type across the top of the page from left to right, it seemed logical to have him continue to read down the right-hand column, not skip back to the first column.

───────────

[2] H. F. Brandt, *The Psychology of Seeing* (1934), abstracted in Chilton R. Bush, ed., *News Research for Better Newspapers* 2:102–104 (New York: American Newspaper Publishers Association Foundation, 1967).

Curiously enough, the key spot on *inside pages* has usually been upper *left,* not upper right. Another tradition is in operation here. Advertising customarily

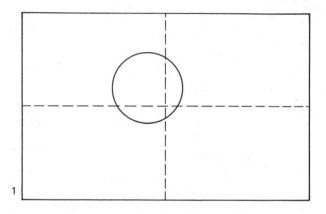

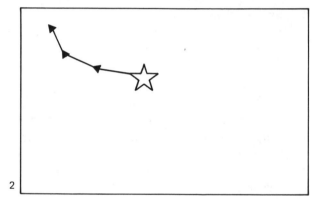

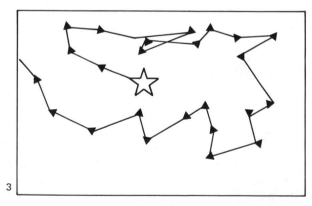

From H. F. Brandt, *The Psychology of Seeing* (1934), abstracted in Chilton R. Bush, ed., *News Research for Better Newspapers* 2:103 (New York: American Newspaper Publishers Association Foundation, 1968).

Visual Focus and Movement   The initial exploratory fixation (1) and subsequent exploratory movements (2), (3), as plotted by Brandt.

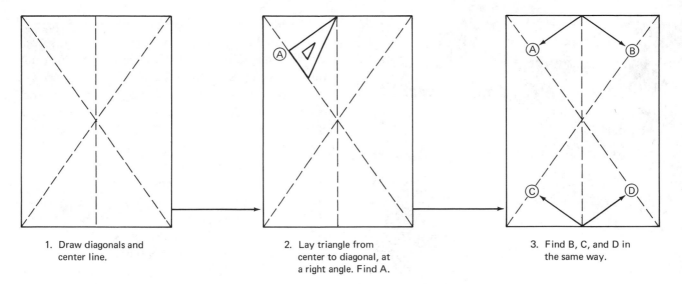

1. Draw diagonals and center line.

2. Lay triangle from center to diagonal, at a right angle. Find A.

3. Find B, C, and D in the same way.

Finding Focal Points in a Rectangle   In planning newspaper pages, these focal points are useful in positioning major elements.

1. Draw diagonals and center line.

2. Lay triangle from center to diagonal, at a right angle. Find A.

3. Find B, C, and D in the same way.

From Grace E. Langdon and Byron C. Jorns, "Proportions for Bulletin and Booklet Layouts and Illustrations," Bulletin 17, Department of Agricultural Journalism, University of Wisconsin, Madison, 1950, p. 21.

has been stacked to the right in the form of a half pyramid with its apex high in column 8. Even when inside-page banners are used, the story cannot read out into column 8, as on Page One, because there is no place for it to go. Presumably the story that is worth a large headline is also worth some length, so the custom has been reversed on inside pages that contain advertising. Whether or not they are topped by banners, their chief focal point is the upper left-hand corner. The inside page which constitutes a first page of a section and/or is a "split" page *and* contains no or little advertising takes on the character of a front page, with emphasis on the upper right.

Thus, each newspaper page has one chief focal point, but like all rectangles, it has some others, too. Langdon and Jorns[3] have shown how they may be found in a rectangle of pleasing proportions. One of

the methods is illustrated on this page. Each point is located very near the center of the four quarters. They are interesting from the standpoint of balance— and for another reason, too. The average newspaper page consists of about 350 square inches of space. In order to interest readers in the page, its immense area must be broken up into segments and each given some attention value. The editor need not be dictated to by these four geometrically derived focal points, but he would be wise to be guided by them. They give him convenient places at or near which he can mass materials to focus interest and break up the potential monotony of the entire area.

This principle is illustrated in the *National Observer* front page reproduced on page 240. Note that each of the four quarters focuses on a piece of art. (Notice, too, that they are balanced in the diagonal fashion described above.) The page shown here is contemporary in many respects, but it adheres to the time-honored methods of balancing elements to give focus to the page.

[3] See Grace E. Langdon and Byron C. Jorns, "Proportions for Bulletin and Booklet Layouts and Illustrations," Bulletin 17, Department of Agricultural Journalism, University of Wisconsin, Madison, 1950.

Focus and Balance   Each quarter of this page has a strong piece of art located near its focal point. Each quarter except the lower right also has one major display-type element. The quarters are balanced diagonally.

Contrast

Working as he does with materials of a very limited range, the news editor must arrange his page carefully to afford as much contrast as possible between and within masses of like materials. Not only does contrast contribute to an attractive page, it is the high road to emphasis. Only by arraying masses in a way that emphasizes the most important elements can makeup give the reader an evaluation of the relative importance of the various stories on the page. Careful attention to the arrangement of contrasting elements in layout not only keeps emphasis on the stronger elements; it also gives more attention value to the weaker elements in the same mass.

We have seen that there are only three essential types of makeup material: type, art, and white space. But they may all be varied in several ways for contrast. In analyzing their contrast values, it may be useful to think in terms of "color"—not chromatic color, but the densities of blacks, whites, and grays that make up a newspaper page. Headlines and art are blacks, grays are body type, and whites are white space. Obviously, massing one color—or element—produces monotony. Juxtaposing them creates contrast.

One of the most effective sources of contrast is in *type size,* especially in the differences in size between display lines and body lines. Another is in *type design:* styles (roman-italic), families (basic designs), and weights (boldface-lightface) may all be juxtaposed for contrast. Even degrees of condensation can be a factor in contrast between display headlines. Varying the *measure* of display or body type or art creates contrast. So does varying the *depth* of headlines.

Two examples of poor contrast are shown on page 241. In both, uncontrasted display-type masses are found in the upper right-hand corner of Page One. The editors probably reasoned that they had several important stories that merited strong treatment in a conspicuous place on the page. To emphasize these stories as they deserved, they used two of the best attention-getting devices available: display type and position at or near the chief focal point on that page. Unfortunately, they overused them. It is axiomatic in layout work of all sorts that *all emphasis is no emphasis, all display is no display.*

Some elements of contrast have been introduced into the individual sublayouts but not enough to prevent them from getting in each other's way. In the top example, only type size contributes to contrast. All the headline faces are of the same family, boldness, and degree of condensation, and all are roman. White space plays an extremely minor role: there is a little between lines and around the short dashes, but the full-line top decks hold it to a minimum, and the stepped and hanging-indention decks let in only a little more. Measure has been varied, but it has not been handled in a way to prevent the characteristic massing of display type.

High Court Backs CBS on Color TV

8-0 Decision Declares Federal Commission Acted Within Rules

Say Broadcasts Not Likely Soon

Court Fight Had Been Started by RCA to Plug a Rival System

W ASHINGTON—(U.P.)— The supreme court today ap-

6 Killed, 7 Injured In Area Crashes

4 Die in One Accident Near Muscoda; 2 Dead In Mishap Near Monroe

S IX persons were killed and seven injured in traffic accidents in the Madison area over the weekend. Four were killed in a crash near Mus-

AIR FORCE INQUIRY IN CRASH OF EIGHT JETS IN INDIANA, 3 PILOTS KILLED

TRUMAN ORDERS U.S. AGENCIES TO HELP 'CHINA LOBBY' INQUIRY; M'ARTHUR SAYS MARSHALL MISSION 'BLUNDERED'

GENERAL CALLS CHARGE HE SOUGHT TO UNIFY FACTIONS A 'PREVARICATION'

CHINESE REDS FALLING BACK FROM THEIR 'IRON TRIANGLE'

ACHESON REPORTS 'HEARSAY' DATA INDICATES SOME ILLEGAL ACTIONS

All Display Is No Display These examples from an earlier era show what a problem it can be for the reader when type is massed with too little contrast. Both papers later changed to contemporary makeup practices that eliminate this sort of typographical hodgepodge.

The lower example introduces some additional elements of contrast but essentially suffers from the same ailments. Art is introduced to separate the two major multiline heads. The effect is spoiled, however, by the condensed boldface-cap lines over the cut. One of the heads is in italics, but much of its effect is lost because it is in all caps, just like the others. Two different families of type are used, but all of the top decks

are condensed or extra condensed, which tends to cut down the effectiveness of the difference. Even less white space is used than in the top example, which at least had some around lower-case display type.

The examples on page 242 illustrate the practice of varying headline depth for contrast. The headlines in the left example show little contrast. The middle headline is indeed double column, the outer ones single column; the stepped lines provide some white space. But contrast could have been improved enormously by varying the depth of the headlines. The middle head could have been dropped back to two lines (and perhaps set in italics), establishing the dominance of the two outer heads without detracting from the attention value of the middle one. A second deck could have been added to each of the outside heads to the same effect.

The example on the right shows strikingly good use of the depth factor. Several different elements contribute to good contrast, including plenty of white space, the box effect created by indenting all lines in the middle story, the two-column measure of the middle story. But the most pronounced is the variation in depth of headlines.

The examples used here are taken from more or less modern but by no means contemporary newspaper formats. As will be seen later, contemporary formats —horizontal makeup in particular—are especially effective in lending contrast to newspaper pages, both front and inside, because they permit the isolation of all headlines from all other headlines. Many of them honor the rule that all display type should be surrounded by body type, art, or margin—never adjacent to other display type—thus assuring full contrast without exception.

Dynamics

The illusion of motion can be effective in advertising layout, where it is possible to break up the angularity of the basic structure by the use of diagonals and curves. Even though the limitations of newspaper makeup do not allow for this sort of thing, efforts have been made to duplicate this function in other ways in page layout. At one time, for example, it was all but axiomatic that minor heads be stepped up the

Effective Contrast in Typographical Display
Two illustrations from the same newspaper
demonstrate how contrast can be obtained
among inside-page headlines. The example at
right shows how type size and style, line length,
rules, and white space can be combined for
contrast. The example at left fails under
similar content circumstances.

columns to direct eye movements toward the focal
point on the page. Efforts like this could not have been
too successful. The "skimmer's eye map" shown on
page 243 indicates how one reader searched one
newspaper page. The path of his eyes was disorderly,
not patterned. Eye-movement studies, although they
are perfectly possible today, have not given us much
help in understanding the dynamics of visual information search. And the "rules" of makeup based on the
presumed behavior of the eyes of readers are not
supported by available data.

There seems to be an independent element in
makeup that can only be described as a dynamic: some
pages "move" in their feeling tone, others are more
static. What makes a page dynamic is not altogether
clear. Generally speaking, newspaper pages of the
nineteenth century were flat and dull until the highly
competitive era of yellow journalism shocked readers
with forceful displays of art, often in unusual shapes
and large sizes, heavy use of multiple-column heads,
large day-to-day differences in typographical arrangement. A similar revolution has happened in recent
years, with horizontal display, great variation in column width, and stories displayed as dramatically on
the lower half of the page as at the top, wide day-to-

day variation in makeup (within limits fixed by basic
format). The result is a dynamic feeling, though nothing really moves except the readers' eyes. Its importance may be understood by comparing print media
with their competitors. Television and film move, and
both of them, plus radio, move through time. The
communicator controls the movement and the rate of
change. In the print media, the communicator offers
choices, but the *receiver* controls the flow of change
from item to item, page to page, section to section.
All the editor can do is to array the choices in a way
to make the reader's progress effortless and at the
same time functional for his information needs and
desires. He cannot really control the process, but he
undoubtedly can influence it. Unfortunately, too little
is known about information-search behavior to set
down prescriptions.

Unity

Newspapers that have been redesigned in recent years
—and examples abound in this chapter—have chosen
a single version of a single family of display type and
stayed with it, at least for all general news pages.
Usually, the type chosen for special pages (such as
editorial) and special sections (such as women's)

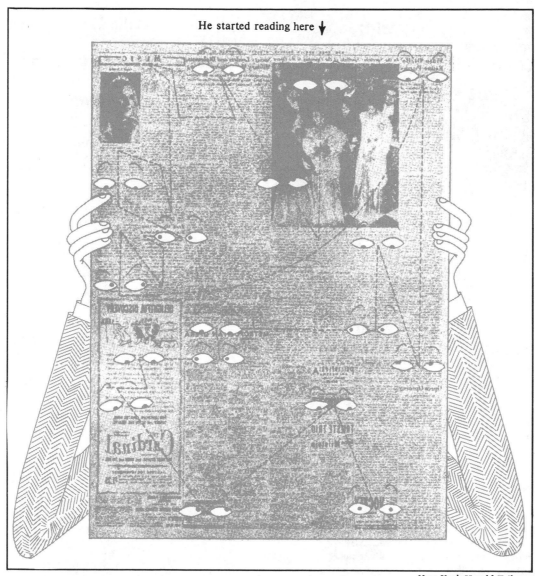

He started reading here ↓

New York Herald Tribune

A Skimmer's Eye Map   The route one pair of
eyes took as it selected the news on a typical
newspaper page.

have used a variant of the same design. This is done
to give a basic unity to entire newspapers, sections,
and pages. Another tendency has been to reduce the
variation in display-type sizes, which also serves unity.

It might appear that contrast and dynamics run
counter to the goal of unity, while balance serves it.
A better way of putting it might be that the goal of
unity sets limits on dynamics, imbalance, and contrast.

Yet it is strikingly true that well-designed contemporary newspapers tend to have greater dynamics and
stronger contrast as well as an established sense of
unity. In any case, the newspaper must be a recog-
nizable entity from day to day, section to section,
page to page, and corner to corner, and it cannot be
if its design and makeup are not consciously pointed
toward that goal.

Courtesy the Washington (D.C.) Evening Star

Courtesy the Knoxville **News-Sentinel**

Contrast and Balance   These two eight-column front pages are more or less made up in the manner known as "contrast and balance." Contrast is carefully worked out at all levels, and each page is also carefully balanced. No single mass of display type is given high focus; no quarter of the page is given greater emphasis than any other quarter; especially in the Washington *Evening Star* example, art is carefully located to produce a balanced effect.

Traditional Systems of Makeup

It has been traditional in textbooks on news editing to sort out various "systems" of makeup and give them labels. The traditional labels, however, do not seem to name the critical factors that differentiate makeup practices today. These are discussed on pages 272–297, but on the chance that some students and their instructors find the traditional scheme useful, a brief treatment is given here.

Formal Balance

Formal and informal balance have been discussed and illustrated on pages 235–237. The essential point is that each element in the makeup that falls on one side of the vertical center line must be duplicated at the same point on the opposite side of the line.

Contrast and Balance

Before the advent of contemporary makeup patterns, this was the most common system. It is characterized

Courtesy the Charlotte *Observer*

Focus Makeup The Charlotte *Observer* consistently arranges its front page around a display headline in the upper right-hand corner —usually the same head in the same position. Great variation occurs from day to day in other parts of the page. The page at right more or less illustrates the principle that other headlines should be arranged to point toward the main focal point of the page: headlines of increasing size are arranged diagonally from the bottom left toward the key focal point at top right. The editors do not slavishly follow this principle, however, as the page at left demonstrates.

by the grouping of major masses of type and art in the four focal areas of the page, usually in the diagonal pattern described earlier—upper right balancing lower left, upper left balancing lower right. The system permits substantial contrast in the weight of each quarter of the page, so long as they balance. Headlines are often stepped diagonally toward the main focal point, but, as we have seen, it is not certain that this actually influences reader response. The Washington *Evening Star* and the Knoxville *News-Sentinel* (illustrated on page 244) are among the newspapers that more or less consistently pattern their makeup along these lines. Obviously, this system is fairly flexible, as traditional systems go.

Focus or Brace

Under this system, one corner, usually the upper right, is sharply emphasized, usually with a strong typographical display. All other elements on the page are subordinated to this one. Usually the next best story gets strong typographical play but not strong position. Other major elements on the page frequently are stepped toward the key focal point to enhance the effect. The strong upper corner may or may not be counterbalanced by a strong lower left-hand corner.

This makeup finds favor with some newspapers because it suits itself to newsstand sale conditions. Note that even when the paper is folded twice, the focal corner attracts as much attention as when the page is opened. Some examples are given on page 245.

Circus

Some editors appear to throw away the rule book and make up the page according to their untamed instincts. Actually, "circus" makeup is usually very carefully planned. The object is to imply that *this* newspaper is so full of so many big stories which the others either don't have or are too squeamish to print that they all have to be shouted about at once. Circus makeup is characterized by immense type masses, large art masses arrayed in unorthodox shapes and positions, headlines in colored ink (usually red), relegation of the nameplate to a minor spot on the page, widely varying headline typefaces with emphasis on the boldest one and little attention to harmony, a lot of multicolumn display, and a spirit of "anything goes except dullness."

Many elements of good makeup contribute to effective circus makeup. Although it is entirely informal, page balance is usually not completely disregarded. Neither is contrast. They simply are achieved in a different way. Effective circus makeup meets the threat of all-display/no-display by introducing such powerful elements of contrast as color.

The Denver *Post* once practiced circus makeup, but it is not used much today, even by the *Post.* Some very contemporaneous designs do borrow some of its vigor and dynamics, however.

Modernism in Makeup and Design

Before turning to the characteristics of contemporary makeup and design, some attention should be paid to the revolution that led to modernism in makeup practices. The principal changes brought about by the modernism revolution included adopting modern typefaces and streamlined headline structure, art in larger sizes and less conventional shapes, and horizontal makeup practices.

Modern Typefaces

The technical distinction between modern and old-style typefaces was discussed in Chapter 8. Although moderns had been around for years, it took some time for newspapers to adopt them. Tradition militated against them, and old makeup methods were not instantly adaptable to them. Modern display type is at its most effective when given modern headline form; the effect of modern forms with old-style types is usually bad. Modern typefaces are clean, sharp, and readable. The modern sans serifs can be condensed readily, the modern romans less readily. But condensation is less important in modern horizontal display.

Modern Headline Forms

The traditional headline form, as we have seen, was many decks of stepped, inverted-pyramid, crossline, hanging-indention, and full-line heads. Stepped and full-line heads especially tyrannized the editor because they are difficult to write. The full-line head, especially in all caps, is also hard to read. And the small amount of white space surrounding the stepped head contributes only a little to legibility.

Modernism ended the tyranny by substituting the flush-left and square-indention heads for the older forms. By their very structure, they are both easier to write and easier to read. The white space to the right of the flush-left and on both sides of the square indention contributes greatly to reading ease. Furthermore, these heads need not be less attractive than the more formal structures. A badly constructed flush-left head may afford little aesthetic pleasure, but a badly constructed stepped head is a real eyesore.

Another important shift in headline structures was the decreased number of decks. Most newspapers of modern design are satisfied with a top deck and one secondary deck, even over top stories. Contemporary forms go even a step further, often eliminating decks altogether and relying on kickers.

The Revolution in Art

When art was introduced into newspapers, many veteran editors looked on it as a sign of depravity. In order to keep the upstart in its place, elaborate rules were built up for its use. For a long time, for instance, no art was allowed to appear in an outside column for reasons of balance. In recent years editors have broken with tradition in a number of ways having to do with the size, shape, and placement of cuts. These matters were treated fully in Chapter 9.

More White Space

Modernists led the way in the judicious use of white space for an attractively streamlined effect. As we have seen, modern headline forms let in more light: flush left and square indention allow more white space around heads; kickers are usually kept short partly for the value of the space this creates. In addition, the trend includes more leading in body and display types alike and more space around rules and boxes.

But the trend does not stop there. Many modernists have effectively substituted white space for rules and dashes, including column rules, cut-off rules, and dashes of all sorts; a few special rules are sometimes reserved for special treatment. This trend has been carried even further in contemporary makeup practice.

Horizontal Makeup

The horizontal theme, one of the key elements in contemporary makeup practice, was a major innovation in modern makeup. The type-revolving press, first used in 1846, enforced vertical display on newspapers. It revolved the actual loose type, not solid plates, which was locked into the forms by means of wedge-shaped column rules, extending from the top of the form to the bottom. Any sort of multiple-column display was thereby ruled out. Although the type-revolving press was replaced by the rotary press not long after the Civil War, multiple-column display was frowned on. Even until the day the Spanish-American War broke out, the New York *Tribune* clung to one column.

But at the same time, the *Journal* and the *World* were vying with each other in the extravagant use of horizontal forms. The *Journal* of April 24, 1898, spread its two banner lines, an inverted pyramid, several paragraphs of summary lead, and a cut a third of a page deep across all seven columns. The space that remained was divided into two-, three-, and four-column displays, body type and all. Another example of makeup practices of that era may be seen in the St. Louis *Post-Dispatch* issue of February 14, 1898, illustrated on page 230.

The sobering-up period that followed the war brought a return to essentially vertical display. The banner head remained and two-column heads became rather common, but the revolution ended there. Tabloids, going their separate way, used horizontal makeup on their smaller pages, but general efforts to brighten up newspaper pages through extensive use of horizontal forms were timid and faltering where they were tried at all. It remained for the editors of the post-World War II era to push horizontal makeup forward until today, when it is in widespread use.

The term itself describes its salient characteristic. The page is broken up into horizontal rather than vertical blocks: stories, pictures, and headlines are proportionally wider than they are long. The elements of horizontal makeup include:

Multicolumn heads   Rather than using single-column heads and long single-column stories, breaking up the page at various levels with occasional two- and three-column heads, editors with the horizontal orientation use striking displays across three, four, five, six, seven, even eight columns at all levels on the page, from an eight-column panel across the top of the paper—perhaps above the nameplate—to a six-column ribbon near the bottom of the page. The single-column head is not ruled out absolutely. It is still used at all levels of the page. But instead of carrying the major share of news, the single-column unit is used sparingly, primarily to break up the horizontal patterns; the wise makeup man realizes that variety in headline length is a valuable source of contrast. The horizontalist is merely making full use of it.

Variation in body-type line length This less conspicuous factor can mean the difference between success and failure in the construction of horizontal pages. Occasional multiple-column headlines do not constitute horizontal display. Whole stories or parts of stories set in wide measure must be used, too. Incidentally, type sizes tend to go up when line length increases.

There appears to be a practical payoff in the wide-measure column, too: it reduces composition costs. A South Dakota State University researcher[4] reported an improvement of 22.7 per cent in cutting TTS tape for a 15-pica measure over 11 picas; twenty-five operators took part in the experiment. However, the wider column does not necessarily reduce reading ease and probably increases it. Wiggins[5] found that reading speed increased with an increase in line length ranging from 10 picas up to 17, then fell off as lines got progressively longer. The typical "wide" newspaper column is usually around 15 picas. (The columns in this book are 19 picas wide.)

Dramatic use of art Generally speaking, horizontal display is more effective when it is carried over into cuts. That means unorthodox shapes, particularly rectangles that are strikingly wider than they are deep. Horizontal display does away with so many of the old rules of makeup, in fact, that it permits editors even to place cuts on the page in unorthodox fashion.

The horizontal mode upsets many of the established rules but it does not ignore the *principles* of good makeup described earlier. It does not substitute something else for contrast, but rather enhances it. It does not ignore balance but achieves it with more striking masses. It capitalizes on motion to a degree that vertical forms cannot. It achieves sharper focus, if anything, by dramatic arrangements.

Horizontal makeup perhaps has done more than any other single factor in the evolution of newspapers to free editors from the heavy hand of custom. Since experimentation has shown that newspaper-page rectangles can be used in vastly more effective ways than traditionalists had imagined, the editor may plan his day's makeup with little or no reference to past structures. It allows the editor to make each day's paper reflect that day's news to a degree not possible when makeup moved within the extremely restricted limits of traditional forms.

At the same time it has promoted readability. Crowding of masses is not a problem in horizontal makeup. Strong elements can be spaced out and isolated from other strong elements. Condensed display type, which is almost always harder to read, carries a smaller part of the headline-information load.

Suggestions for Making Up Modern Front Pages

Now that the main characteristics of modern newspaper makeup have been identified, some rules of thumb can be suggested that may be useful to the beginner.

Alternate major and minor elements along any horizontal line This applies in general to almost any style of makeup but perhaps is less relevant to horizontal. It is a useful guide in front-page and inside-page makeup, and it is just as useful in working with midpage, multicolumn cutoffs as it is at the top.

A major element is a major head, often a one-column head. A minor element is a minor head, a boxed or other specially treated head, or a cut. We are not discussing *weights* here. Both a major head and a cut add weight, but a cut is a minor element. A two-column italic head could have greater mass than a one-column two-deck head, but the former would still be a minor element and the latter a major one. Depth, boldness, and style (roman-italic) play the key roles here.

[4] Larry E. Rolup, "An Analysis of the Production Output Difference Between an 11-Pica and 15-Pica Line Width when Type is Set by the TTS Method," unpublished Masters' thesis, South Dakota State University, 1967. Abstracted in Bush, *op. cit.* 3:19 (1968).

[5] Richard H. Wiggins, "Effects of Three Typographical Variables on Speed of Reading," unpublished Ph.D. dissertation, University of Iowa, 1964.

To take an obvious example, note the "tombstoning" of two similar major heads shown below:

It is corrected by putting a minor element between the two majors:

The same holds true of a four-column layout. Three majors are seen in the illustration below:

When a minor is substituted for the middle one, the effect is strikingly better, whether the minor is a headline, a cut, a box, or anything else that separates the two majors and doesn't overpower them:

Traditionally, the major elements occupy *outside* positions when there are more than two units. But there has long been a tendency to overlook this, particularly when the outside minor is a cut:

Notice the effect when two minor elements are adjacent, in the hypothetical example shown on page 250 ("Pay Boosts OKd for City Employees"), and the ease with which this can be corrected.

Avoid tombstoning Tombstoning results when midpage headlines accidentally land alongside each other —except, of course, when they are lined up under a cutoff rule. The fault lies largely in the fact that the juxtaposition fails to fulfill an understandable pattern such as those discussed above. But tombstoning also

Pay Boosts OKd for City Employes

Index Brings $5-9.50 Hikes

New Annexation Petitions Filed

City employes under civil service, including police and firemen but not school teachers whose pay is determined by the board of education, will receice pay raises of $5 to $9.50 monthly July 1 under authority voted by the city council Thursday night.

It represents the maximum 5-point increase allowable under the city cost-of-living adjustment ordinance, although Personnel Officer Max S. Lindemann informed the council that the national cost of living index figure is 12½ points above the Jan. 1 level.

Need Council Approval

Until last year adjustments were automatic on Jan. 1 and July 1 an-

Statue of Liberty Replica Set Up as Symbol of Boy Scouts' Service

Six speakers dedicated a 15-foot-high replica of the famous Statue of Liberty to Madison Boy Scouts at ceremonies Thursday night on city-owned property off Sherman ave. at E. Gorham st.

Speakers included Marvin B. Rosenberry, former chief justice of the state supreme court; L. J. Marquardt, past president of the Four Lakes council, Boy Scouts of America, which includes Madison; San Orr, president of the Madison Rotary club, which purchased and paid for the erection of the statue; B. L. Gill, chairman of the council's executive board; E. E. Bryant, council president, and Paul Love, executive of Boy Scout Region 7, Chicago.

Represents Slogan

William Spevacek, a member of the executive board, introduced the speakers.

"The statue represents the 1950

University Ave. Project Pushed

U. S. Aid Sought for Improvement

The city council unanimously approved a recommendation by the city plan commission Thursday night to place University ave. on its federal aid urban system and petition for first priority in its improvement.

If the state highway commission approves the petition, Planning Engineer Walter K. Johnson explained, federal aid will pay for 50 per cent of the construction cost and a third of the right-of-way cost in widening the avenue or relocating it from Breese terrace to the city limits.

'Lot-Cutting' Banned

The council also adopted an ordinance prohibiting subdividers to reduce the size of lots to a frontage less than 50 feet and an area below 6,000 square feet. And it tabled, by a 13 to 7 vote, as re-

Alternation   The alternation principle calls for one minor element between majors (above), not two (below).

Pay Boosts OKd for City Employes

Index Brings $5-9.50 Hikes

New Annexation Petitions Filed

City employes under civil service, including police and firemen but not school teachers whose pay is determined by the board of education, will receice pay raises of $5 to $9.50 monthly July 1 under authority voted by the city council Thursday night.

It represents the maximum 5-point increase allowable under the city cost-of-living adjustment ordinance, although Personnel Officer Max S. Lindemann informed the council that the national cost of living index figure is 12½ points above the Jan. 1 level.

Need Council Approval

Until last year adjustments were automatic on Jan. 1 and July 1 an-

Scouts Set Statue Up as Symbol

Six speakers dedicated a 15-foot-high replica of the famous Statue of Liberty to Madison Boy Scouts at ceremonies Thursday night on city-owned property off Sherman ave. at E. Gorham st.

Speakers included Marvin B. Rosenberry, former chief justice of the state supreme court; L. J. Marquardt, past president of the Four Lakes council, Boy Scouts of America, which includes Madison; San Orr, president of the Madison Rotary club, which purchased and paid for the erection of the statue; B. L. Gill, chairman of the council's executive board; E. E. Bryant, council president, and Paul Love, executive of Boy Scout Region 7, Chicago.

Represents Slogan

William Spevacek, a member of

University Ave. Project Pushed

U. S. Aid Sought for Improvement

The city council unanimously approved a recommendation by the city plan commission Thursday night to place University ave. on its federal aid urban system and petition for first priority in its improvement.

If the state highway commission approves the petition, Planning Engineer Walter K. Johnson explained, federal aid will pay for 50 per cent of the construction cost and a third of the right-of-way cost in widening the avenue or relocating it from Breese terrace to the city limits.

'Lot-Cutting' Banned

The council also adopted an ordinance prohibiting subdividers to reduce the size of lots to a frontage less than 50 feet and an area below 6,000 square feet. And it

The investigators said that so far they have found no indication of sabotage.

Appleton, charged that the department's management was poor and its service to the public delayed.

War Casualty List Reunites Mother, Son After 20 Years

Seattle, Wash. — (U.P.) — Because another marine by the same name was killed in combat, marine Pfc. William Harvey Holocker was reunited early today with his mother after nearly 20 years of separation.

Holocker arrived by plane shortly after midnight and saw his mother, Mrs. Anne Deland of Seattle, for the first time since 1932.

Mother and son were so choked up with happiness that neither could say much.

"Finding mother alive was all I ever wanted," Holocker said, "even though I had been told she was dead."

Tears Cloud Eyes

Tears clouded Mrs. Deland's eyes as she clutched the tiny lock

Holockers in the marines with similar first initials. One had been killed in Korea. The other was stationed at Camp LeJeune, N. C.

"So I called North Carolina and it was him — my boy," the mother said joyfully. "He told me that now he had found his mom he was really happy for the first time. 'It's sure wonderful to know you have a mother, alive,' he told me," Mrs. Deland said when she felt more like talking.

During the telephone call. Mrs. Deland learned that the blonde baby had grown into a curly-haired red-topped man.

Holocker was given 12 days' emergency leave to visit his mother.

Chicken Dinner

nock, it may become necessary for government to resort to inducements, or compulsion.

No one will like that much, least of all members of congress. They will be appealing to the voters next year for another term of of-

Madison —(U.P.) - The number of polio cases in Wisconsin reached 20 last week, with seven of them in Milwaukee county, the National Foundation for Infantile Paralysis said today.

The figure is about the same as the 1950 toll for the same period. Nine Wisconsin chapters have received $53,000 from the National Foundation so far this year.

BRITISH G-MAN

car train hit a five-foot section of rail that had been placed across the tracks at 57th and Stewart on Chicago's south side.

The railroad said the train was not damaged, but was delayed about 25 minutes. There were about 200 passengers aboard. None was injured.

in Christmas gift wrappings to a friend as a practical joke.

Hempfner, 22, pleaded guilty to a charge of making explosives with intent to injure. He said he sent the bombs to Charled Clark, Ettrick farmer, "just as a practical joke," before the Christmas holidays last year.

Phone Workers Get Boost

By United Press

Telephone companies across the nation indicated today they would ask rate boosts to offset wage increases granted to their employes.

Northwestern Bell Telephone company officials said they would ask increases for Nebraska, Iowa, the Dakotas and Minnesota if its 17,000 employes accept $3 to $6 a week raises.

At Sioux Falls, S. D., the company said it will ask the state public utilities commission "immediately" to consider increased wages in deciding whether to grant a requested boost.

A company vice president in Iowa said Iowa telephone rates may

Rubbled 'Iron Triangle' Bastion Almost Deserted

By LEROY HANSEN

Chorwon, Korea - (U.P.) - Allied troops found only five Chinese soldiers in this "iron triangle" bastion — massing area for thousands of Communists only weeks ago.

Except for a few hundred white-clad Koreans, the civilians had fled, too, from the rubbled city as the first United Nations troops moved in during a downpour yesterday.

Four shots rang out at their entry. Sgt. 1st class Laverne Klockentager of Ames, Ia., investigated. He reported a few minutes later

taken prisoner. Two other unarmed Chinese were flushed out and taken prisoner.

A fifth Chinese was found lying in a littered home. He died a few minutes later from what appeared to be starvation. The ones taken prisoner looked well fed.

Chorwon, southwest peg of the "iron triangle" where Communists massed their two spring offensives in April and May, lay mostly in ruins.

The city suffered almost fatal damage from the terrific air and artillery bombardment of the past

An Accidental Tombstone

militates against effective contrast. The effect is an undesirable "road" across the page—usually a bumpy one. An example is shown on this page.

Tombstoning can be avoided with attention to detail in making up the page. Alternating major and minor elements across the top of the page, for example, usually means alternating story lengths across a page. A major head is usually followed by a story longer than a minor head's or the depth of a cut. This reduces the chances that midpage heads will accidentally fall side by side.

Otherwise the editor can adjust for tombstoning by substituting a longer or shorter story for one which causes the tombstone, extending a story before jumping it, or rearranging the stories above the tombstone to keep their lengths from clashing.

Follow the step-down principle Basically, the step-down principle says that no head should be lower on the page than one that is smaller, or higher on the page than one that is larger. However, this is not strictly the way it works. Single-column heads should be stepped down in this fashion *with relation to each other.* A small single-column head is not out of place if it rides higher than a larger two-column head. But the two-column head should ride higher than a three-column head if the two-column head uses larger type.

Short heads over short stories are deliberately allowed to ride high on the page when they are given some special typographical treatment—when the head or head-and-story are boxed, when the story is indented on both sides, when the head is given three-quarters-box or some other special treatment, when the story is set off by special decorative rules, or when a combination of these is used. In such cases the story is being treated like a *cut,* not like a story, so it is not subject to the general step-down rule.

Heads that are side by side, as we have seen, *should* be of different sizes. Yet if they are both single-column heads, then the contrast in size should not be too great; contrast can be obtained by other devices, such as roman-italic, white space, and number of lines. Difficulties will be created at other levels on the same page if a small head rides high enough on the page to run alongside a substantially larger one: one or the other is too high or too low to permit careful arrangement of the page at other levels.

Make cuts stand on something or hang from something Generally speaking, cuts should not be thrown into the page like darts into the wall. The page will gain coherence if cuts (and other materials that are treated like cuts in the makeup—boxes, for instance) have something firm to "stand on" or "hang from." They and their cutlines can stand firmly on the bottom of the page. Or they can stand on a cutoff rule separating, for example, a multicolumn head from the material above it. If they don't stand on something, then they should hang from the wing of a multiple-column head, the line that rules off the bottom of a multicolumn typographical display, the rule under a banner, or the dateline cutoff at the top of the page.

Modern forms allow making up good pages without strict adherence to this rule. However, a glance back over the pages already illustrated will give some indication of the almost universal acceptance of this rule. Even most of the horizontal pages follow it rather closely.

Avoid graying out   A page is said to "gray out" if it has large, unbroken masses of "gray space"—body type which is not broken up by at least some headlines. Attention to the focal points will help avoid graying out. Attention to contrast will avoid it, too, because grayness is in a sense a malfunction of contrast. Attention to balance will also help.

Nevertheless, parts of the page seem to have a habit of graying out. The most frequent offender is the bottom third. Here the solution is to go into the lower corners with major multiple-column displays of type, art, or a combination of the two. Another good policy is to have on hand plenty of specially selected "shorties"—short, headed items which can be used to fill out the ends of columns. These help brighten the page in a number of ways but are especially useful in avoiding grayness. A lower corner can gray out despite the presence of one major type display. A cluster of smaller heads will usually repair the damage.

Another danger spot where grayness often occurs is the horizontal fold. A rule of thumb about makeup at the fold says that cuts and headlines should not be placed across it, as they will be obscured when the paper is folded, and bunched and distorted when the paper is unfolded. Current trends have tended to modify the rule, but even the makeup man on a modern page, who doesn't like to be inhibited by arbitrary rules of any sort, would be wise to hold to this much of it: The fold should not be allowed to cut across a *face* in a cut or a *headline*. Usually it is not much trouble to move a head or the face in a cut up or down just enough to clear the fold.

So, when this rule is followed, the middles of pages tend to gray out. The best insurance against grayness

at that point is deep art pushing strong type masses down into the midpage area. When deep art isn't available, a story can be handled in multiple columns for the same effect. The editor who dummies his pages down from the top, without having planned strong headlines around a third of the way from the top, will almost certainly encounter grayness trouble at midpage.

Dummying the Page

Dummying is incidental to making decisions about the news and how page makeup will help tell it, but there are a few tricks to learn about it. A typical dummy sheet is shown below:

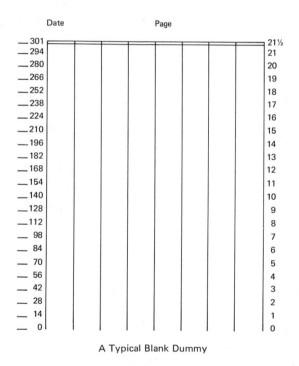

A Typical Blank Dummy

It is a reduced-size version of the page, usually about 8½ inches by 11 inches. This one is conveniently marked off in agate lines on one side, mainly for the benefit of the advertising department, and in column inches on the other. The editor always has plenty of blank dummy sheets at hand. He can use them to sketch out a tentative page, and he might do that several times before a final dummy takes shape.

As we have already seen, when dummies reach the news editor, the space for the ads on inside pages has already been marked in. Dummying isn't a matter of drawing a facsimile of the ultimate page, nor does it merely make timid suggestions to the makeup man. The job is to write down certain precise instructions —and no more—clearly and emphatically, so that the makeup man needs only the dummy to proceed to put the page together. The information he needs includes:

Story and head designation This information is usually written in where the head goes. It includes the head-schedule symbol for the headline and the slug.

Art identification The space occupied by art is usually indicated by crossed lines drawn from corner to corner. The caption, if any, should be identified with a word or two of the head, since there is no appropriate slug, or given a "with" slug: if the related story is "#17 Drown," the caption is marked "#32 with Drown." Wherever a portrait is used, the name line should be indicated on the dummy below the space for the cut with the person's last name.

Rules, dashes, wraps Each era in the evolution of makeup practices has contributed subtle differences in the way format and makeup guide the reader from column to column. In contemporary makeup practice, for example, rules and dashes tend to be minimized and white space substituted for many of them. Hence, wraps are kept simple. If he is to serve effectively as a makeup man, the editor must be sensitive to his paper's practices concerning rules, dashes, and wraps.

Rules, whether horizontal or vertical, are full-length lines; dashes are shorter lines. In the traditional and modern makeup styles, the long or 6-em or "end" dash is used to show that a story is at an end. The short or 3-em or "jim" dash is used as a subdivision between, for example, the main story and the head over a follow. The "dinky" dash, used only

occasionally, is still smaller and subdivides between jim dashes.

Cutoff rules are often used by papers that use no other rules. They show a clean separation between units. If an unrelated story appears under the wing of another, a cutoff is used. If the two stories are related, then probably a jim dash is used, or perhaps a special one such as a star dash (three or more well-spaced asterisks). Cutoffs are also used to carry a separation across more than one column. Hence they are used above and/or below cutlines and cut captions, or to rule off a three-column head from other news matter above it, or to cut off a multiple-column story cleanly at the end.

Generally speaking, a cutoff rule below text matter or its equivalent in white space means either "Go on to the next column to the right" or "This is the end." A rule above and below an insert tells the reader of the main story to skip over the insert. When a paragraph ends at a cutoff rule, that means the story ends. When a rule comes in the middle of a paragraph, the reader is told to go on to the next column. Therefore, the editor must be careful not to end a paragraph accidentally at a rule if he expects readers to go on to the next column.

It helps make the dummy clear to the printer if the editor draws in cutoff rules, dashes, and special devices wherever they are called for. If the editor wants a dash at the end of a story, for example, he should mark a long dash there; he should not draw a line all the way across the column, for the printer could easily interpret that to mean a cutoff rule. A star dash or a wavy rule can also be drawn in. The obvious dashes, such as those between a story and head or between decks of the head, need not be shown.

A story which stays in one column under a one-column head needs no indication as to where it goes. But under any multiple-column head, the printer should be told on the dummy precisely what treatment the editor wants for the story. If the story reads into one column, it can be indicated by an arrow-tipped line pointing into the appropriate column. If the story reads into one column and then wraps into another, the wrap should be indicated with another arrow. Wherever type is to be set other than one column in width, the common method of indicating it is a long looping line crossing back and forth over the column rule to be eliminated.

Jumps   The "jump" is a relatively modern problem for newspapers. Colonial editors didn't have to worry about jumps because they didn't have to worry about makeup. A story ran until it ended. Another story followed at that point. Today, continuation of stories from front to inside pages is an important makeup question; it is also inseparable from problems of news policy. The best stories may be run at full length on Page One, but that often means that good makeup will have to be sacrificed. Or the stories may be kept short in order both to avoid jumping them and to preserve the attractiveness of Page One, but that means readers will be cheated out of good details. Or, as is usually done, a compromise may be made: the stories may be run at full length, with only enough on the front page for good makeup, the rest on an inner page.

Editors have long assumed that the jump produces a substantial falling off in readership. That sounds likely and may be the case. However, the Continuing Study of Newspaper Reading contains some evidence that the drop is not as large as has been assumed. There is evidence, too, that the inside-page head over a jump sometimes attracts attention to a story overlooked on Page One; in fact, the recorded readership of the jumped portion of the story has occasionally exceeded readership of the beginning of the story on the front page. (This could, of course, be merely a reflection on the method of the study.)

A more thorough, more recent, and more careful study performed for the Washington *Post* by a readership-survey organization[6] presents even better evidence on the subject. It showed that losses in readership of a story tend to depend mainly on the reader's interest in the story, not on the inconvenience of jumping. Losses at the jump ranged from none at all to 37 per cent. Such extreme variation suggests that content is the important variable. In some cases

---

[6] Reported in Bush, *op. cit.* 1:82–84 (1966). The study was conducted by Carl J. Nelson Research, Inc., in 1965.

the loss at a jump was less than the loss at a "turn" from one column to the top of the next on the same page. There was some indication, however, that reading fell off more rapidly after the jump than before.

Of course, the wide column typical of contemporary makeup means that more of a front page story can be fitted on a page: the wide column uses up more words per line. Here the problem is more likely to be what to do with short carryovers: they are hard to fit into the contemporary page, and they seem to cheat the reader even more than long jumps because they contain so little that is worth his effort to follow the story inside. The lead story, in modern but not usually contemporary practice, normally reads into the outside column on the right. But when the lead story is long and normal practice means it must be jumped too soon, it can be turned into an inside column, or carry a multiple-column readout headline and be read into the leftwardmost column, which allows turning into adjacent columns to the right.

To indicate a carryover on the dummy, one simply writes "Jump" or "Jp" at the point where the jump occurs. If there is one jump page, that is all that is needed; otherwise the page to which the story carries over is indicated by the page number, circled, or "to p. 37," or the like; the details differ from paper to paper. The way a jump is marked on the jump page depends on the jump-head system used. When there is a head, it is indicated in the usual way with "Jp" or "Jump" or "From p. 1" added.

The completed dummy shown at upper left on page 255 illustrates the chief dummying devices.

A Hypothetical Front Page

Beginners usually make two kinds of error in their approach to dummying. The first is that they work story by story, with the dummy as an end in itself. They must learn to *work with the total news day*. The editor cannot safely decide what to put on inside pages without attention to Page One and the rest of the total space available that day. The story that looks good for page 3 may be needed for Page One, if this turns out to be mild news day. The same thing is true in making up Page One. The editor should make

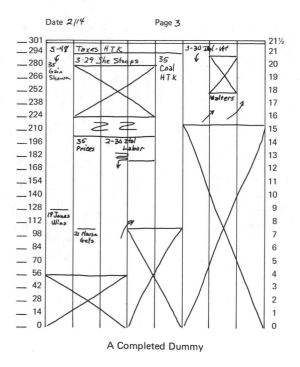

A Completed Dummy

another top-of-Page-One straight story, two strong and three middling stories, and two good features, one better than the other and accompanied by a one-column cut. And suppose he has three-column art accompanying the main story, two-column art with the second story, portrait art with the third, and a two-column feature picture in case it's needed.

Let us assume that the editor is working on a paper that uses modern, not necessarily contemporary, makeup practices. He probably feels that there is so much good art available that the top of the page should support two multiple-column cuts. This conviction is strengthened because two of the cuts are related to the two top stories of the day. Putting them into the page in the conventional way, one cut will fall in columns 2 and 3, the other in 5, 6, and 7, leaving open the column between the two cuts (they should not be juxtaposed in any case) and the two outside columns.

almost no decisions about key spots on the front page until he has a pretty clear general picture of the whole page in relation to the rest of the paper.

The other common fault also has to do with the supremacy of wholes over parts. Beginners tend to work down the page from the top, solving each problem of position and story assignment individually. This is an entirely unsatisfactory attack. The editor must learn to *work with the total page.* That means thinking about the lower part of the page, for instance, while he is dummying key stories into the top. It also means thinking about art and stories together, not as separate problems. The editor who places the art first and then fits the stories into the page around it will have to compromise with the "play" the news deserves. The editor who places the stories first and then tries to fit the art in won't always be able to put it where it will be most telling. The art should be arrayed in the paper on the basis of its relationship to the news. This can be done only if the editor works with both art and news simultaneously.

Suppose the editor is making up Page One and has before him one story worthy of banner treatment, one that would be worth top play on any other day,

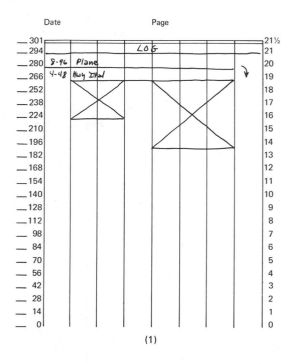

(1)

This looks good. The No. 1 story can read into column 8, the second-best story can carry a second banner reading into column 1, and the third best can be carried into column 4.

But a couple of things are wrong already. In the first place, the No. 1 story is worth more than a column width, and its banner looks top-heavy reading into a single column; it should have at least a two-column readout. To make room for a two-column readout, the second cut will have to be dropped to the bottom of the page or moved to the outside column. If it goes to the bottom, it will no longer appear with its related story. That's bad. Why not move it into columns 1 and 2?

If the editor puts the two-column cut on the outside, the second banner will read into column 3. That's pretty annoying to the reader. And besides, let's say this paper has a rule against it. He could play the No. 2 head across just three columns, reading it into column 3. He could make the head a two-liner to compensate for the resulting loss of emphasis. Then the cut can go under the wing of the head in columns 1 and 2. That will put story and cut together nicely, and the editor gets a dividend: eliminating the second banner means the three-column cut can be moved up next to its related headline:

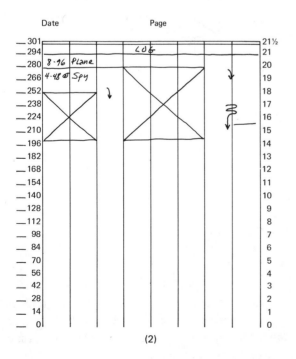

(2)

Now the editor looks at the effect of all this on the page as a whole. Moving these pictures so far to the left has created imbalance at the top of the page. It is so "left-heavy" that it is hard to see how he can compensate for it at the bottom of the page. One attempt is shown below:

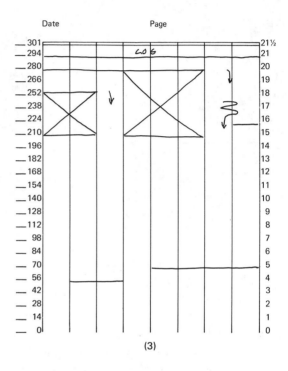

(3)

The editor tentatively spreads the better of the two features across four columns in the lower right spot, the other feature at the bottoms of columns 2 and 3. There are a couple of things wrong with this. The one-column cut will be hard to handle with a four-column spread. It will either have to throw the spread out of balance or be literally thrown out itself. With all the art above, plenty should balance it below the fold. Also, the feature is not worth four columns, but dropping it to three columns will make it insufficient counterbalance for the left emphasis above. Finally, it means that all the wide-measure material is on the right side.

Maybe the editor can use the feature picture down there somewhere. It will have to be on the right side for counterbalancing purposes:

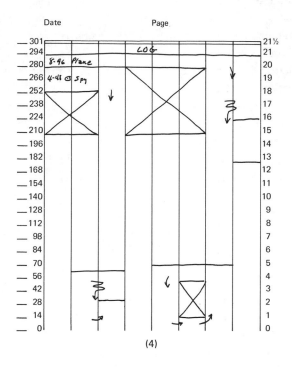

(4)

This solves the balance problem pretty well, although the page is still leaning a little to the left.

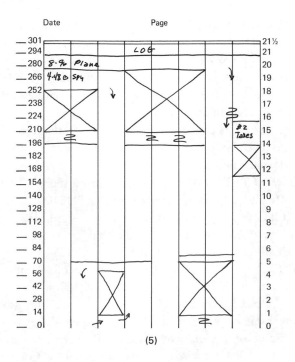

(5)

Another solution would put the No. 3 story in column 8, under the "wing" that will be created when the No. 1 story drops down from two- to one-column treatment. Then the better of the two features could be arrayed across three columns in the lower left and the lesser one in two columns in the lower right. This would mean the extra two-column cut would have to go on an inside page, as shown at lower left.

Once the focal points have been dummied in, the other materials more or less take care of themselves. The five columns of conspicuous space just above the fold under the two cuts provide many possibilities— enough to handle almost any combination of major and minor stories in a normal news day. In this case, the second good feature has been placed under the two-column cut, and the two strong stories are under the three-column art.

The completed dummy is shown below:

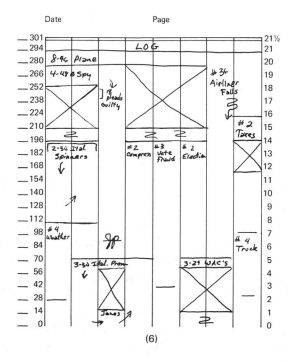

(6)

Note that space is left for short items to fill out the ends of columns but that they are not designated. This can be done at the forms, provided the editor makes sure he has good Page-One shorts in varying lengths and sufficient quantity. Note too that a caption is indicated over the two-column cut at the bottom of the page because there is no other head to tell this story. None is needed for either of the cuts at the top because they run directly under related heads.

The process of dummying this hypothetical front page is described here in such detail to drive home the importance of the two cardinal makeup principles: consider the whole page and the whole news day at once; don't fragment the news and don't fragment the page in order to solve layout problems.

Another principle is this: the editor must keep his makeup flexible. He must not get so enamored of a page that he is unwilling to tear it up and start over again when substantial changes in the news day develop. The editor must have a flexible "makeup" himself. There is no room here for the prima donna. The original page may be a work of art, but if it doesn't tell all the best news—even what came late and upset his calculations—then it isn't a good page, no matter how balanced, contrasted, focused, or beautiful it may be.

Effects and Influence of Makeup

Does page makeup have any actual effect on the way readers perceive their newspapers? Hard-data answers to this question are few. However, a study reported by Click and Stempel[7] at Ohio University in 1967 sheds more direct light on the question than any other to date. It also illustrates that it is perfectly possible to test such questions by empirical methods.

Click and Stempel chose front pages of six newspapers representing various systems of design and makeup such as "balance and contrast" and "horizontal." Though all of them used sans-serif type families in their display heads, four of the faces were judged to be modern and six closer to old-time gothic. (Because a pretest showed that subjects responded

[7] J. W. Click and Guido H. Stempel III, "Reader Response to Newspaper Front-Page Format," *Journal of Typographic Research* 2:147–172 (April 1968).

more to makeup than to typographic variables, papers using other type families were eliminated.) The nameplates of the newspapers were covered with dummy titles (such as the "Cordova *News*"), and the fictitious names were rotated across all the newspapers to eliminate an identity effect. These precautions were taken after subjects on a pretest rated the makeup of the Louisville *Courier-Journal* much more highly when they knew it was that prestigious paper than when they believed it was the front page of a less well-known Ohio newspaper.

The respondents were an unselected sample of college freshmen. They rated the newspapers after a fifteen-second exposure to each front page on a set of polar-adjective scales that had previously been used in studying newspaper images in general. When all the scores were tallied across scales, the differences were rather small. But twelve of the twenty individual scales showed statistically significant differences among newspapers—that is, differences that could not be accounted for by chance.

The meaning of the separate scales can be clarified by looking at what happens to them when the data are subjected to factor analysis. Factor analysis groups together the scales people respond to most similarly. For example, *pleasant-unpleasant, valuable-worthless, important-unimportant, interesting-boring* fall together into what is called an EVALUATIVE factor (see the summary of results in the table on page 259). The actual pages used, with their false nameplates, may be seen on pages 260–261.

The results cannot be said to be perfectly clear-cut. The two most modern (horizontal) pages ranked first and third overall, but they were first and second in the STYLISTIC dimension. One of them ("Bancroft *Times*") came through on the POTENCY and ACTIVITY dimensions as was expected, but the other ("Cordova *Globe*") did not; a more traditional page ranked second on ACTIVITY and POTENCY and inspired the most favorable impression in the EVALUATIVE dimension. However, the most nearly traditional makeup led to the least favorable evaluations in all three of these dimensions.

Some of the individual scale differences are interesting. The most contemporary paper ("Cordova

Globe") was seen as most *pleasant,* most *fresh,* most *easy,* but not most *modern.* A somewhat less contemporary style ("Bancroft *Times"*) was perceived as most *interesting, bold, powerful, loud, active,* and *modern.* The most traditional paper was perceived by this young audience as most *dull, messy, colorless, timid, weak, soft, relaxed, passive,* and *old fashioned.* Yet the two papers most clearly definable as prestige press, even though their identity was concealed, were rated highest on the EVALUATIVE scales overall ("Denton *Record"* and "Denton *Eagle"*).

Although none of the ETHICAL scales produced significant differences, a clear negative correlation between the ranking in the overall ETHICAL dimension on the one hand and the POTENCY and ACTIVITY dimensions on the other is a little disturbing. Since the fifteen-second exposure allowed time for little else than an impression of appearance, it seems that the more vigorous and exciting the paper's first impression the more it is judged to be ethically suspect. When one paper which was low on both dimensions is eliminated, we find a nearly perfect rank-order correlation[8] between *interesting-boring* and *responsible-irresponsible* and between *colorful-colorless* and *fair-unfair;* a like trend occurs in half a dozen other similar comparisons. Rationally, brightness and spirit need not be attained at the cost of truthfulness and responsibility, yet they appear to

---

[8] Spoiled by one tie.

Mean Ratings and Rank Orders by Factors, Judgments of Six Newspapers (after Click and Stempel)

NEWSPAPER (MAKEUP STYLE)	*Mean Rating*	| OVERALL RANK ON FACTORS				
		EVALU-ATIVE	*ETH-ICAL*	*STYL-ISTIC*	*POT-ENCY*	*ACTIV-ITY*
"Bancroft *Times"* (Horizontal)	4.71	3	6	2	1	1
"Denton *Record"* (Brace)	4.71	1	3	3	2	2
"Cordova *Globe"* (Horizontal)	4.65	4	4	1	4	5
"Denton *Eagle"* (Brace)	4.62	2	2	4	4	3
"Cordova *News"* (Contrast and balance)	4.46	5	1	5	5	5
"Bancroft *Star"* (Balance)	3.99	6	5	6	6	6

EVALUATIVE scales: *pleasant-unpleasant,* valuable-worthless,* important-unimportant,* interesting-boring**
ETHICAL scales: *fair-unfair, truthful-untruthful, accurate-inaccurate, unbiased-biased, responsible-irresponsible*
STYLISTIC scales: *exciting-dull,* fresh-stale,* easy-difficult, neat-messy, colorful-colorless**
POTENCY scales: *bold-timid,* powerful-weak,* loud-soft**
ACTIVITY scales: *tense-relaxed, active-passive,* modern-old fashioned**

---

* Differences by papers for these scales are statistically significant.

Horizontal

Brace

Brace

The Six Papers Used in the Click and Stempel Experiment   The front pages, displaying their fictitious nameplates, are identified as to the makeup systems they represent.

CORDOVA NEWS

Contrast and Balance

CORDOVA GLOBE

Horizontal

BANCROFT STAR

Balance

be, at least in the minds of these college freshmen. For many other people, too, vividness = sensationalism = irresponsibility, whether newsmen see it that way or not, just as tabloid size = love-nest murders.

We should bear in mind, of course, that a more representative subject sample, especially including a greater age range, might reveal quite different results. Older people in particular might find the old, comfortable, traditional forms more to their taste.

In an effort to examine some of "the folklore of journalism," Professor Galen Rarick,[9] then of the University of Oregon, tested thirteen hypotheses relating content, structure, format, and typographical variables to readership of newspaper items. The study was done by means of repeated split runs over a thirty-two-day period, allowing for control of content variables.

1. He found no effect on readership of location on left- or right-hand pages and above or below the fold, and little effect if any of location near the front or near the back of the paper.

2. He found no effect on readership of wide-measure *vs.* narrow-measure body type, nor 7-on-8 format (the front page practice of using seven columns in the space normally occupied by eight, spacing widely between columns).

3. A long-line (six columns or more) major head on an inside page produced no more readership for that page than for the same page with no head larger than two columns. The longer heads produced no greater readership for the particular item, either.

4. But location adjacent to related art did appear to increase readership by comparison with location next to an unrelated picture of equivalent size.

5. And the inclusion of thumbnail portrait photographs in a news story did increase the story's readership.

6. "Increasing the size of the headline on a news story increased the readership of that story to a point." The point beyond which no increase was realized was a two-column, two-line head in 36-point type.

---

[9] Galen R. Rarick, "Field Experiments in Newspaper Item Readership," unpublished mimeographed report, 1967. Abstracted in Bush, *op. cit.* 3:13–17 (1968).

7. Incidentally, art increased ad readership and spot color increased it greatly.

No single study ever resolves all doubt, but this one suggests that assumptions about the effects of design and makeup can at least be tested empirically.

Presenting the News Meaningfully

One of the most persistent questions in journalism is one asked by conscientious teachers, actors, orators—anyone who is trying to communicate ideas and information to others. It asks, essentially, *"Are they getting it?"* Faced with the increasing complexity and breadth of the news, editors, writers, and journalism educators are more concerned with the answer to this question than ever before. They want to know whether yesterday's methods are equal to telling tomorrow's news.

Present-day practices require wrapping a lot of different stories into one neat package to toss on the customer's front doorstep. But this process seems sometimes to be far out of line with the news-telling requirements of our time. It is not just that more complicated news is reaching us in greater volume from more news centers more widely spread around the globe than ever before. Events are also harder than ever before to put together logically. What adds up to "a story" in today's world? What are its boundaries when the big story cuts across all the little ones and there are ramifications without end?

Perhaps the whole format of the newspaper needs revision to square it with the demands of today's news. But full discussion of this problem is not in the province of this volume. The purpose in raising the issue here is rather to focus on the importance of meaning, not just in terms of language (Chapter 5) or makeup, but as a whole, within the limits of the present format. What can the editor do to make the total presentation of the day's news as meaningful as possible for as many of his readers as possible?

The devices for presenting the news meaningfully do little more than pick away at the edges of the problem. And some of them do not fall within the copy desk's sphere. Stories which "wrap up" scattered events into a more meaningful whole than is possible within the daily staccato of the datelines often come across the desk. Sometimes some source such as a wire service, for example, will send a background piece relating separate stories from half a dozen European capitals around the larger scheme of European economic union, let us say.

Suppose the editor himself were to rewrite all the news as it reaches him into one big story with each part logically related to the larger story? This would be one way of presenting the news meaningfully. But the newspaper is caught between the speedier media (radio and spot television) on the one hand and the more deliberate media such as the weekly news magazines on the other. Its mission seems to consist in being later but more detailed than radio, and earlier but less contemplative than magazines. If the editor took the time to complete a wrapup every day, it would probably put him too far behind the news itself.

One compromise has already been discussed in Chapter 4 under the heading "Compiling." We have seen that it is possible with the routine tools of the copy desk to enhance the meaning of a few stories by combining them. The undated compilation particularly is an important device; used more widely, it could make newspapers more meaningful than they are now.

Departmentalization

Another frequently advocated way of presenting news meaningfully is departmentalization. This is a broad concept which seems to range all the way from the thoroughgoing variety advocated by Brucker[10] in 1937 to a half-hearted effort to get vaguely related stories somewhere near each other. For Brucker, "tomorrow's newspaper" was to be a full-scale departmentalization job. The news, rather than being scattered where it fits into the paper, was to be carefully assembled on what appeared to be a perfectly logical basis—point of origin: the nation, foreign

countries, etc.—essentially the same arrangement as the one the news magazines are even now finding troublesome and inadequate. Brucker has since had an opportunity to have his own way with a very fine newspaper and seems not to have taken his own advice.

For if it is arbitrary to let the news fall where the makeup allows, it is nearly as arbitrary today to classify the news as "national," "local," "world," etc. A story about mercury levels in the Tennessee River as it flows through Kentucky a few miles above its junction with the Ohio River sounds like a nice local story to Paducah, Kentucky. But the plant that's doing the polluting belongs to a nonresident company incorporated in New Jersey, and the pollution it produces affects the whole Tennessee River watershed, which meanders through five states, and influences a dozen more states downstream. The problems are identified by research done in a dozen universities. Enforcement power lies with both state and federal governments. The basic problem is common to most of the industrialized world. A local story?

Other kinds of departmentalization raise problems, too, including the one that puts the facts on one page, interpretation of the same facts on another, and an institutional opinion of the facts as interpreted on yet another. The sectioning of newspapers, especially Sunday papers, reveals arbitrary editorial assumptions about what interests human beings. One paper puts births, deaths, engagements, weddings, food, fashion, and the arts in one section and sports and business in another. But are men not interested in the arts? Have women no business in business? Is not the logic of separating "business and financial news" from today's economic deliberations in Congress open to serious doubt?

And departmentalized general news doesn't often come off well. The same story can end up on different pages of the newspaper, each department having thought the story belonged on its page. Take a case in point: a newspaper runs two versions of a story relating the prospect of increased natural-gas rates in Michigan. It broke the same day in Detroit and Lansing. In Detroit, one of the wire services got the story from an industry spokesman; in Lansing, an-

---

[10] Herbert Brucker, *The Changing American Newspaper* (New York: Columbia University Press, 1937).

other service got about the same story from the state regulatory department concerned. The two versions of the story probably were distributed to the departments involved on the basis of dateline—the Lansing story to the state-government desk and the Detroit one to the general state desk—and the separate editors made separate decisions to use the story on their own separate pages.

Functional Grouping

Departmentalization of a less sweeping and less arbitrary sort is rather common among carefully edited newspapers. Departmentalization assumes that there are logical departments and that news may be logically assembled in them. *Functional grouping* is quite different. It consists of combining the devices of language and type to assemble related stories near each other and to make the relationship manifest. It juxtaposes elements of the day's news because they are patently related not in some static quality such as point of origin, but in ideas and events that can be better understood when presented in relation to the others.

Functional grouping includes more than mere juxtaposition, however. There are devices for helping to show the relationship of stories whether juxtaposed or not. One of these has been practiced by the New York *Times* consistently for years. The decision that a crisis in the Middle East, say, will be the top story of the day not only determines that it will be placed in the upper right-hand corner of Page One, but that other important stories of an international character will be placed near it. The best national or state story then will lead off the upper left-hand corner, and other stories in that general category will be placed in that part of the page.

But many less rigid newspapers use a variety of ways to point to the relationships among stories. First, they put stories next to related art wherever possible, and the best of them do so in a way to make the relationship clear, as discussed on pages 251–252. Two-column art is placed under the wing of a three-column head, leaving one column of text to start the body of the story and perhaps wrap up under the art. If head, art, cutline, and body type can be put to-

gether into a single rectangle of pleasing shape, all the better still. Nobody has had to shout or point—the connection is obvious. The natural relationship of three-column art to a three-column head puts the head below the cut and cutlines.

Pointing relationships of type to art like this is sensible and seems elementary. But editors often ignore it, satisfying themselves if a story is merely next to its related art. How the reader is supposed to see the relationship is not clear, especially since he is used to seeing unlike and unrelated things next to each other day in and day out. He is more likely to see immediately the connection with a ruled insert in a story announcing "Other pictures on page 3" than the connection between the story and a picture touching it but otherwise giving no clue that it is related in subject matter. Some peculiar typographical devices have been used to try to make such connections, such as an arrow in the middle of a column of type or a hand pointing its finger at a story or cut in an adjacent column. But there are so many ways of making the connection obvious without effort that these things seem contrived.

Related stories can be grouped by makeup alone. If a story goes under the wing of another headline to which it is related, white space or a row of asterisks may be used where the cutoff rule would normally go. A multiple-column head can have two or more stories reading out of it—the head being very carefully written to indicate the common ground covered in the two stories and to tell as much of both as possible—with separate read-out heads at the top of each story to help lead the reader from the main head to the story he wants to read first.

Contemporary makeup practices tend to cancel out some of the typographical methods useful in traditional or modern makeup, but at the same time, its relatively greater freedom permits editors to explore new methods. For example, related stories can be grouped in panels which all share the same length of line, a length different from other panels. And some of the old standby devices are still good today, for example the ruled insert within the column of type devoted to a major story—a useful device when the inserted material is short but worthy of attention.

Nike Site Has S

All will be bustle and activity this week at the old Nike site on the lakefront as final

---
Related story on Page 15, Part 2.
---

preparations are made for Summerfest '70.

The three year old festival,

bearing a greater promise of success than in the two previous years, will open Friday and run through July 26. It will feature national and local entertainers, including classical, rock and jazz musicians and ethnic performers.

The fence surrounding the grounds on N. Harbor Dr. will be covered with gaily colored

Courtesy the Milwaukee Journal

U.S. Has Proof
Red Pilots In Egypt

United Press International

WASHINGTON — The United States said Wednesday it had proof that Russians were flying Soviet-built jet fighters over Egypt and President Nixon ordered intelligence officials to determine if their presence had shifted the arms balance in the Mideast.

State Department spokesman Robert J. McCloskey said the Russian pilots presented a "serious, potentially dangerous" situation and that the

The extent of Soviet involvement in the Mideast is explored by a military expert in an analysis beginning on Page 10A.

Soviet pilots appeared to be strictly defensive — to protect the new SAM3 antiaircraft missile sites which Russia is constructing in Egypt.

Courtesy the Charlotte Observer

PAKISTANI TROOPS OPEN MAJOR DRIVE

New Delhi Says Its Forces Inflict Heavy Losses on Foe in Kashmir Pullback

---

By FOX BUTTERFIELD
Special to The New York Times

NEW DELHI, Dec. 7—In her first major offensive of the four-day-old war, Pakistan began a large-scale tank and infantry attack today against Indian troops guarding a key road in southwestern Kashmir, India reported.

An Indian military spokesman said that Indian troops had

The New York Times received no reports from Pakistan yesterday on military developments there, either from its four correspondents in the country or from news agencies.

fallen back five miles to prepared positions after inflicting what he described as "heavy casualties" on the Pakistanis around the town of Chhamb, near Jammu.

It was with a similar armored thrust at Chhamb that Pakistan began the 22-day war

Three Methods of Connecting Related Stories

Lesser stories may be handled as "follows". This is useful when the related story is substantially less important than the main story.

Most newspapers make regular use of one device or another to let the reader know that one or more stories related to a major front-page item may be found elsewhere in the paper. This is done when the related stories do not justify Page One play—or when

they are so many that they would crowd everything else off the front page. (See illustrations above.)

Sometimes a related story or art that must go inside can be put next to the inside-page carryover of the front-page story. An illustration is given on page 266. Here two stories related to a very long one that started on Page One are next to the jump, one beside it and one below it.

75,000 Swelter at War Protest

Indo-China Troop Pullout Demanded

FROM PAGE 1

members of the American Nazi Party who were accused of disorderly conduct in their harrassment of students.

An e m e r g e n c y supply of water was shipped from nearby Ft. Meyer, Va., and salt tablets were distributed through the crowd.

A LARGE RED sign planted in the middle of the park expressed the primary purpose of the protest.

"We the undersigned," it said in large letters, "protest the invasion of Cambodia and resumption of bombing of North Vietnam and also call for immediate withdrawal of all United States troops from Southeast Asia."

Thousands of signatures were scrawled beneath the letters during the demonstration.

The students began arriving Friday, many f r o m colleges that had been closed by campus protests. Friday night, several thousand gathered at Sylvan Theater, at the foot of the Washington M o n u m e n t, and watched the President's press conference on television. Many shouted their derision as he defended his move into Cambodia.

THE CROWDS on the Ellipse began forming early Saturday as thousands poured into the city. By mid-day, the Ellipse had taken on a Woodstock appearance as the students lounged about in various kinds of dress. The crowd was almost totally young and almost totally white.

Actress Jane Fonda, one of the first speakers, welcomed the crowd with, "Greetings, fellow bums," in reference to Mr. Nixon's characterization of disorderly students.

There were several bizarre scenes. A Negro, Daniel W. Billings Jr., 28, of Cincinnati was roped to a 13-foot cross in front of the speaker's stand.

Military-Conservative Split

242 on UW Faculty Fail to Act on Strike Move

The 242 faculty members who agreed T u e s d a y to strike against the University of Wisconsin failed to take action continuing that strike at a Saturday meeting.

A split between militant faculty members, who wanted the group to reaffirm its decision to be "on strike," and a more conservative faction, who wanted to "go out into the community" without necessarily deserting the classroom, caused a stalemate among the estimated 250 persons present.

THE GROUP, which dwindled to about 75 persons after several hours of haggling, did vote to "organize and go into the community," Prof. Robert Alford, chairman of the Ad Hoc Faculty Committee for Peace, said.

Alford attributed the general confusion and relative chaos which prevailed at the meeting to the general expression of "sentiments" by the f a c u l t y members.

But others felt that the faculty group was "markedly different in character" than the persons who voted last week.

"Many came because the general faculty vote on Friday made what this committee was doing semi-official," one faculty member said.

AN HOUR after the meeting began, faculty members, either disgusted by the conservatives or alienated by the militants, started to leave the meeting, some gathering in small caucuses at the back of the room.

David Siff, assistant professor of English, requested a vote s u p p o r t i n g the four United Front demands, including an end to military research and ROTC on c a m p u s. He also called for a "no confidence in the chancellor (Edwin Young)" resolution but received hostile response to both requests.

The small group remaining at the close of the meeting voted on action centering in 11 committees designed to arouse community support but did not vote to strike the University in order to "shut it down."

The previous statement issued by the ad hoc c o m m i t t e e charged that "President Nixon has created a constitutional, moral, a n d p o l i t i c a l crisis

throughout the country and on university campuses by his disastrous and tragic widening of the war in Southeast Asia.

"THE PRESENT situation on other campuses as well as the present turmoil on our own makes it impossible for us to continue teaching in our classrooms at the University of Wisconsin.

"Our teaching responsibilities, however, extend to the community and to the people of the state of Wisconsin as well as to the students on our campus.

"We intend to continue our teaching function, and thereby serve the students and the people of the state, by leaving our classrooms, and i n s t e a d, by reaching members of the community at their workplaces with our understanding of the nature of this war and what it is doing to American society.

"We regard this effort to reach the citizens of the State of Wisconsin as part of our patriotic duty in this profound national crisis. We call upon all faculty members to join us in this effort."

UW Closure Decision Due; Campus Calm After 6 Days

FROM PAGE 1

ful eye on the Mifflin-Bassett St. area, the center of violence on Thursday and Friday night, but there were no reports of any activity as the night progressed.

However, there were murmurings from area residents who c l a i m e d that police "t r a s h e d" the neighborhood early Saturday morning without provocation.

SEVERAL residents said that police ripped down protective boards that had been erected

$3,000 business loss," a store manager said Saturday. "The place is so full of gas we can't do business."

OTHER RESIDENTS said that police threw tear gas canisters into several homes and refused to allow the persons inside to vacate the gas-filled houses.

Ald. Paul Soglin, Eight Ward, who said Saturday that he witnessed some of the police attacks, said that two persons, one an elderly resident in the 500 block of Mifflin St., were injured during the action.

"Over 20 houses as well as

Ex-Marine Vents Wrath at Cong Flag

W A S H I N G T O N (UPI) — Marty Ratcliffe, an ex-Marine just back from Vietnam, was fighting mad Saturday.

Ahead of him, in the middle of H St., 10 young men were walking toward Lafayette Park, waving Viet Cong flags, and shouting "Ho, Ho, Ho Chi Minh. The NLF (National Liberation Front) is going to win."

"The hell with the NLF," Ratcliffe yelled as he ran up the sidewalk after them. "The hell with the Viet Cong."

Integration by Position The editors have deliberately grouped related stories on the jump page. Two jumps from the front page are positioned next to another story closely related to both.

Most newspapers also try to call attention on the front page to material appearing elsewhere in the paper. At its most routine level, this means listing all the regular features and putting the list in some regular position on the front page—in an "ear" beside the nameplate, in a box in the lower right-hand corner, etc. At least this will tell people who want to consult the television listings where to find them today.

But some editors have gone far beyond the "feature-

finder" device both to promote the best stories and features on inside pages and, in some cases, to group them in some sensible fashion—for example, by subject matter, not by section. A wide range of the nearly limitless possibilities is represented by the illustrations on pages 267–271.

None of these devices really contributes much to solving the big problem of meaning. But they at least show that some editors recognize it and are trying to do something about it.

Indexes and Guides **A.** Many papers still use the routine "ear" index, as does the Washington *Post.* The advantage: the invariable location.

B. Next most common is the routine box at the bottom of the page.

C. In a more elaborate index the *Sunday Oklahoman* calls attention to the best features on inside pages, then lists daily features as usual.

D. When a story is spread out over a series of separate items, the reader can be helped with an at-a-glance box, or "glancer," a single account that connects up the parts and tells him where they may be found.

A

Index

**308 Pages
16 Sections**

Amusements	H 1	Living	G 1
City Life	D 1	Obituaries	D14
Classified	D15	Outdoors	C11
Editorials	B 6	Sports	C 1
Financial	E 1	Style	F 1
Gardens	G 9	Travel	H 9

Courtesy the Washington Post

B

On The Inside

Ann Landers	13A
Bombeck	18B
Bridge Lesson	19B
Classified	9-17B
Comics	18-19B
Death Notices	9B
Editorials	2B
Financial	16-19A
Horoscope	18B
Obituaries	8A
Sports	5-8B
Spotlight	4B
TV Timetable	20A
Theaters	21A
Viewpoint	3B
Women	12-14A

Observer Phone 375-8885

Courtesy the Charlotte Observer

C

Inside Headlines

General News and Business

NIKITA'S 'We Will Bury You' is given a funeral by the State Department. **— Page 14-A.**

BOMBINGS in Italy spread fear, bring on government investigations. **—Page 41-A.**

HELPFUL HINTS on Yule phone calls to Vietnam given by phone company. **—Page 15-A.**

Oklahoma's Orbit

FIRST C5 GALAXY is due at Altus this week. For a preview, see Jim Johnson's report. **—Page 16.**

MISTLETOE, holly and poinsettia are pretty holiday plants, but also can be lethal. **—Page 15.**

Women's Section

TASTY GIFTS from kitchen are always welcome in any home at Christmas season. **—Page 1.**

PUZZLING EYESORE like that awkward fake fireplace can attain a visual illusion of warmth. **—Page 4.**

Inside Features

Country Boy	.........20-A	Public Records	..... 52-A
Discussion Page	.....35-A	Real Estate News	....20-C
Eaker	...............37-A	Today	................20-A
Editorials	.........36-A	Weather Details	......24-A
Obituaries	.... 11, 44-A	Want Ads	235-6722
Oil News	............50-A	Other calls	232-3311
Parr for Course	......37-A		

Courtesy the Sunday Oklahoman (Oklahoma City)

D ## UW Disorder at a Glance

● Police and bands of militant youths, some numbering as many as 2,000, clashed repeatedly during the day Tuesday on the Univerity of Wisconsin campus. The protesters were attempting to enforce a student strike on the campus to demonstrate opposition to U.S. military intervention in Cambodia. **(Story, Page 1).**

● Madison Mayor Dyke had apparently decided late Tuesday not to impose a mandatory c u r f e w on the city. **(Story, Page 1)**

● UW Madison Chancellor H. Edwin Young declared the campus off limits to all but authorized persons. President Fred Harvey Harrington issued a statement vowing to keep c l a s s e s open. **(Story, Page 3)**

Courtesy the Wisconsin State Journal (Madison)

E. The New York *Times*, as a newspaper of record, helps both its readers and researchers who consult it in later years with probably the most detailed summary and index of any American paper.

News *Summary and Index*

WEDNESDAY, APRIL 29, 1970

The Major Events of the Day

International

According to Israeli diplomats in Washington, their Government is convinced Soviet pilots are now participating in the defense of central Egypt against raids by the Israeli Air Force. Israel reported that two of her planes were pursued by eight MIG's on April 18, piloted by Russians. United States officials, it was reported yesterday, are studying their own intelligence reports on this possible development which they believe could have a serious effect on the balance of forces. [Page 1, Column 8.]

In the latest Middle East fighting Israel reported two Soviet-built Sukhoi-7 fighter-bombers had been shot down when the Egyptian Air Force launched a coordinated low-flying attack on Israeli forces in the Sinai Peninsula. Egypt said that all her planes had returned safely from the attack. [9:1.]

The Vatican issued revised rules for mixed marriages between a Roman Catholic and a non-Catholic partner. The norm eliminates the requirement that the non-Catholic promise to raise offspring in the faith, substituting a provision that requires the non-Catholic only be informed of the Catholic's commitment to bring the children up as Roman Catholics. [1:4.]

Communist China expressed support for the declaration adopted at the recent meeting between Prince Norodom Sihanouk, and top Communist officials from North and South Vietnam and Laos. The declaration called for an intensified struggle against the United States and its allies. [4:4-6.]

National

The American Bar Association's Committee on the Federal Judiciary has strongly endorsed Judge Harry A. Blackmun for the Supreme Court. The vote of confidence came on the eve of Senate hearings on his nomination. In contrast to President Nixon's two most recent nominations, no group has emerged to oppose Judge Blackmun. [1:5.]

Supreme Court Justice William O. Douglas, facing possible impeachment, notified a House investigation panel that he has retained a former Federal judge and lawyer, Simon H. Rifkind, to represent him. Justice Douglas also offered the House investigators complete access to his files. [20:4.]

Victims of serious traffic accidents in 1967 recovered only one-fourth of their losses from automobile insurance companies. That is the finding of the first comprehensive study of auto insurance undertaken by the Department of Transportation at the behest of Congress. [1:6-7.]

In the final report of the Democratic party's reform commission, a strong warning was issued that if popular control of the party is not forthcoming, the alternative may be "the antipolitics of the street." Senator George S. McGovern, who headed the 28-member commission, said that the guidelines in the report for the selection of delegates to the party's 1972 convention would be followed by state organizations. [1:2.]

Three operators of an antiwar G.I. coffeehouse were handed sentences of up to six years in prison after their conviction for operating a public nuisance. In addition the coffee-house was fined $10,000. In handing down the sentences, State Circuit Judge E. Harry Agnew said that he could not overlook the influence the defendants could have over so many young people. [1:8.]

Metropolitan

A threatened work stoppage by 20,000 city patrolmen has been postponed until 12:01 A.M. Saturday. The sick-out had originally been planned to start at 12:01 A.M. today to compel the city to give the patrolmen a pay raise of $1,200 a year. The Patrolmen's Benevolent Association contends that its contract mandates the raise because one was given to police sergeants. [1:1.]

A grand jury here indicted two alleged high-ranking Mafia leaders—Aniello Dellacroce of the Carlo Gambino "family," and Angelo Bruno, who is said to be boss of the Philadelphia Mafia. The New York County jury accused the two Mafia leaders and a third man of refusing to answer questions after offered immunity. [1:1.]

The New Jersey Superior Court declared unconstitutional a controversial law authorizing the busing of parochial and private school students at public expense. Judge Joseph A. Stamler ruled that the law violated the United States Constitution's 14th Amendment guaranteeing equal protection of the law to everyone. [1:2.]

National Guard units in New Haven were ordered on stand-by duty for deployment in the event of disorder at a massive rally being organized by the New Haven Black Panther Defense Committee. [1:4-6.]

The Other News

International
Mikoyan recalls the Trotsky-Stalin feud. Page 2
Pnompenh mayor travels with Saigon official. Page 3
U.S. command reports loss of five aircraft. Page 3
Peking hails parley of Indochinese leftists. Page 4
East Germany raises tolls to West Berlin. Page 7
Rhodesian churches defy Government. Page 9
Israel reports downing 2 Egyptian planes. Page 9
Artists still free to criticize in South Vietnam. Page 10
Three friendly neighbors in the Trieste area. Page 13
Soviet scientist supports space cooperation. Page 30

Government and Politics
Democrats press bill on 18-year-old vote. Page 17
Goodell tours Tombs, calls for budget rise. Page 32

General
Three given 6 years in coffee house case. Page 1
National Guard alerted for New Haven duty. Page 1
Sirhan awaits outcome of legal maneuvers. Page 16
Alaska Governor to ask state to build road. Page 18
Food products recalled twice a week. Page 25
Woolworth attacks city's landmark law. Page 27
Black Panther supporters buy guns in Boston. Page 30
Rap Brown given deadline on bail. Page 30
Jury choice begun in Plainfield murder case. Page 32
Police say they seized gun at Panther's home. Page 32
Racial outbreak brings Detroit curfew. Page 32
T.A. is accused of bias by a black patrolman. Page 33
Author in Alioto case silent on sources. Page 35
Ex-employe says Allstate discriminates. Page 37
Exchange accused of bias for banning yarmulke. Page 43
Special press wire rates ended by F.C.C. Page 81
Johnson TV interview abridged at his request. Page 83

Industry and Labor
Printers at Times increase economic pressure. Page 38

Education and Welfare
Educators convince Nixon on budget item. Page 15
Monserrat hopeful on school-aide talks. Page 44

Health and Science
Experts debate advisability of missile systems. Page 14
French implant atom-powered heart pacemaker. Page 50

Amusements and the Arts
Five books on the Mets are reviewed. Page 39
Books on the Mets flood the market. Page 39
Frick Collection quietly turns fifty. Page 47
Hemingway's widow talks of new book. Page 47
Doubts cast on authenticity of a Raphael. Page 47

Fashions and Home
Designers banish knees and taut self-expression. Page 38
Retarded girls learn poise in special class. Page 36
Amusements for children are listed. Page 36

Financial and Business
Nixon adviser sees moderation of inflation. Page 59
Dow continues to fall; closes at 724.33. Page 59
Honeywell meeting adjourned after protest. Page 59
Economic Analysis: Confusion in Wall Street. Page 59
U.S. and Republic Steel profits decline. Page 59
Bethlehem Steel earnings fall in quarter. Page 59
Con Edison shows profit drop in first quarter. Page 59
Banking Committee backs capital-outlay rise. Page 59
American Smelting profit is record for quarter. Page 59
Markets abroad slide; factors are varied. Page 59
House unit cuts fee curbs in mutual fund bill. Page 59

Washington parley on stocks set for today. Page 59
Texaco earnings climb 2.7% in quarter. Page 59
Astronaut Borman to join Eastern Air Lines. Page 59
Norfolk & Western reports drop in income. Page 64

	Page		Page
Advertising News.	70	Grains	69
Amer. Exchange..	68	Market Averages..	65
Bond Sales......	64	Market Place....	60
Business Records.	71	Money	65
Commodities	69	Mutual Funds ..	66
Cotton	69	N.Y. Stock Exch.	60
Dividends	64	Out-of-Town ...	65
Foreign Exchange.	65	Over the Counter.	66

Sports
Angels bring "contending" club to Stadium. Page 52
Indians beat Twins, 3-1, on Horton's double. Page 52
Mets open season with Giants at San Francisco. Page 52
Roche, ailing, loses in tennis at Bournemouth. Page 52
Track freshmen will shift gears at Quantico. Page 52
196 letter men are honored at Columbia. Page 52
N.C.A.A. scores Massachusetts and Villanova. Page 53
Home-court edge goes to the Lakers tonight. Page 53
Nets are talking about title playoff money. Page 53
Reaume tops Updegraff, 1 up, at Pinehurst. Page 53
Met women golfers begin interclub season. Page 53
Admiral's Shield, 20-1, wins Derby Trial. Page 54
Derby jockeys fear My Dad George most. Page 54
Lucky Creed qualifies with 2:01 4-5 mile. Page 54

Man in the News
René Lévesque, leader of Quebec separatists. Page 2

Analysis and Comment
Editorials. Page 40
Letters to the Editor. Page 40
James Reston on Soviet moves in the Mideast. Page 40
C. L. Sulzberger on TV as public opinion-maker. Page 40

Quotation of the Day

"The Christian responsibility to love accepts no barriers and cannot be defined or restricted by legislation." —*Statement by representatives of church groups in Rhodesia, telling the Government they intend to defy a law on race separation.* [9:1.]

F. The *Wall Street Journal* also combines summary and index in its daily "What's News—" at the top of every front page. The right-hand column is devoted to general news briefs. The left-hand column summarizes and indexes the day's inside-page stories.

Courtesy the Wall Street Journal

What's News—

* * *

Business and Finance

EXPRESS MAIL between cities for important documents is being tested by the Post Office. Planners envision charging up to $5 for the premium service, whereby the specially marked mail would be taken quickly to airports, put on commercial flights and then expedited at the destination city. Items mailed at the close of business one day would be guaranteed for delivery by the start of the next business day.

(Story on Page 3)

* * *

Steel-mill employment has held up well in view of the substantial layoffs in other industries. In May, steelmakers employed 405,042 production and maintenance workers, off only 5,755 from the start of the year. But many steelworkers are finding their hours of work cut back, and many summer-replacement jobs aren't being filled this year.

(Story on Page 3)

* * *

An "inflation alert" calling atten-

* * *

World-Wide

AMERICAN FORCES reported killing at least 358 North Vietnamese near Khe Sanh.

U.S. officials termed the fighting the sharpest setback for the enemy in months. They said the action began last Wednesday when apparently inexperienced North Vietnamese troops were caught in the open by rocket-firing U.S. helicopters. B52s followed with saturation raids. In Cambodia, the government sent reinforcements to the seaport of Kompong Som, where enemy forces are said to be massing for a major attack.

Enemy troops also were pressing operations along the single highway linking the seaport with Phnom Penh.

Sen. McGovern charged that President Nixon is determined to keep the Thieu-Ky government in power in Saigon because the Chief Executive believes that "any kind of a government, no matter how tyrannical, would be better than a Communist government." The South Dakota Democrat, in a Metromedia interview, also said he doubts that Hanoi will engage in any significant negotiations in Paris unless the U.S. announces a deadline for total withdrawal.

* * *

Israel will be allowed to buy more U.S. jets if current diplomatic efforts fail, Assistant Secretary of State Joseph Sisco indicated on

G. The Cincinnati *Enquirer* uses pictures to index inside-page items in its huge Sunday edition. That is not unusual, but running the pictorial index across the top of Page One is. The same pictures are repeated in the stories.

One Year After His Historic Moon Landing, Neil Armstrong Is Disappointed Because The Spiritual Message Faded So Quickly. Story Page 6K

The Mill Creek And The Little Miami River—A Contrast Between Life And Death, The Ugly And The Beautiful Are Featured In A Picture Story In The Enquirer Magazine.

What's It Like Being The Mother Of America's Most Politically Active Family? Rose Kennedy Tells Abut It In The First Of A Series. Page 2J.

THE CINCINNATI ENQUIRER

Courtesy the Cincinnati Enquirer

H. The *Christian Science Monitor* also uses pictures to invite readers to look for inside-page stories of special interest. The pictures used as cues are carefully chosen from parts of pictures accompanying the stories inside.

Inside today

U.S. to stand by treaties, Rogers reassures Asians

During his recent visit to Asia, Secretary of State William P. Rogers assured Asian leaders such as President Thieu that United States regional policy would not leave South Vietnam in the lurch.

David K. Willis reports: Page 3

Actor Arkin analyzes his role as director

Old-timey? No, it's actor Alan ("The Russians Are Coming") Arkin directing his first picture. With film critic Louise Sweeney he talked of the difference between being before and behind the camera.

Interview: Page 4

I. Perhaps no other paper has gone quite as far as "Florida's Space-Age Newspaper" to call attention to inside-page features. On this Sunday front page, all the inside sections are identified in color across the top of the page, while the entire wide left-hand column promotes inside stories, grouped by point of origin, and lists daily features at the end.

Sports Highlights

Port Malabar pro Bill Kennedy fires record 66 at Florida Open, 1C.

Tony Jacklin takes four-stroke lead into final round of U.S. Open, 1C. (Complete sports, 1-6C.)

Sunday, June 21, 1970

Florida'

Published by T

DAY

Age Newspaper

any in Brevard County, Florida

Next Space Shot

An Intelsat 3 communications satellite will be launched on a Delta rocket July 15.

TODAY'S Weather

Fair to partly cloudy with widely scattered showers. Low 70-75, high 88-95. Winds variable under 10 mph. (Complete weather Page 2A)

25 Cents

SUNDAY Headlines
Inside TODAY

IN SPACE

Soviet Soyuz 9 cosmonauts, new earth-orbit champs, in excellent health and get heroes' welcome. (15A)

IN THE WORLD

Reds launch strikes in apparent effort to seize routes for troops and supplies into Cambodia. (3A)

While the United States has gained much favorable reaction in Peru for its prompt earthquake aid, Red nations have given nothing but sympathy. (10A)

Prime Minister Edward Heath names 18-member cabinet w i t h Sir Alex Douglas-Home as foreign secretary. (14A)

IN THE NATION

Vice Adm. Hyman Ricko--- sub equipment firm cent "with-   ....revard.
N---

.......ve a wash job to a 151-pound ......nard, that doesn't want one can be hazardous. (1B)

Specials TODAY

THIS IS FATHER'S DAY AND JOHN McAleenan interviews TODAY's Father of the Year . . . and the family of three youngsters, mom and seven dogs who had a hand in writing the winning letter. (1D)

WHATEVER HAPPENED TO LYNDON Baines Johnson? He's pretty much disappeared from public view, apparently writing his memoirs. Other than that and the privileges accorded him as a former President of the United States, it's plain Citizen Johnson now. (1E)

"I'M NOT A ROBOT, YOU KNOW. I mess up just like anyone else. So I have a great night; who's to say there's not some woodchopper somewhere else—right here— who actually IS the world's greatest drummer?" Buddy Rich talking, the greatest — drummer in the world. (Sunrise Magazine.)

Everyday Features

Amy Clark, 1D	Movie Times, 5B
Buddy Martin, 1C	Sports, 1-6C
Business, 14-16C	State News, 6B
Classified, 6-13C	Weather, 2A
Datebook, 2B	Also in Sunrise Magazine
Editorials, 2E	Astrodata
Family, 1-6D	Bridge
HELP!, 1B	Crossword
Homes, 4D	Earl Wilson

Nine Sections

11

Contemporary Trends in Makeup

We have seen that the traditional systems of makeup are inadequate to describe the variation in design, format, and makeup that may be found on newspapers today. Probably the only substitute category system acknowledges three basic makeup patterns: traditional, modern, and contemporary. The *traditional* papers hew to makeup that reflects their past practices, especially on front pages. Yet while carefully maintaining continuity with the past, these papers often turn out on closer inspection to have conceded to some modern practices, such as legibility typefaces to make the body of their papers easier to read.

Modern newspaper makeup generally has adopted even more innovations but have not radically altered their overall design in recent years. They usually retain the eight-column format and follow the kinds of makeup "rules" that are spelled out in Chapter 10. In fact, there appear to be more "modern" newspaper formats at this writing than any other kind.

Contemporary makeup practices are in the development stage at this writing. Some of the characteristics may be noted by examining the changes that have been made when newspapers have been redesigned in recent years. The Louisville *Courier-Journal,* for example, was already "modern" in many respects in the early 1950's, as both front and second front pages show (see page 273). It was using a clean Bodoni Bold and Bodoni Bold Italic for headlines, and it made good use of pictures throughout the page. It was noticeably horizontal in emphasis, even running three wide columns in space normally occupied by four standard columns on the front page. Column rules were eliminated whenever they separated the parts of a story package. Note the absence of other kinds of rules in both stories and pictures on the second front page.

From Modern to Contemporary The Louisville *Courier-Journal* was among the first newspapers to test out some of the attributes of modernism in makeup in the early 1950's. White space was substituted for some column rules, and for its day, pages were relatively horizontal.

Today's *Courier-Journal* is contemporary in nearly every respect, the latest change being from regular headline capitalization to lower case.

Courtesy the Louisville Courier-Journal

On the other hand, the paper is basically in the then-standard format of eight narrow columns separated by rules. The headline forms are essentially traditional, including full-line heads, two-deck major headlines, and standard flush-left subheads in the text. If you moved column 5 over to column 1 and shifted the three left-hand columns one column to the right, the makeup would be pretty much standard for its day. The main focal point of the older *Courier-Journal*'s front page was the upper right, a nearly universal practice at that time. The new one shifts its main point of emphasis for day-to-day dynamics and heightened interest.

Today's *Courier-Journal* has much the same general feeling tone as the older one, but it is far more open, less crowded, more readable, and more legible. It is clearly built on a horizontal principle. The changes probably contributing most to its openness and legibility are the six-column page of 14-pica columns, larger and more legible body type, and increased spacing between lines. Also, the front page has no single-column news headlines and the split page has only one. The same type family is used in all headlines, but it is used dramatically: variation in styles and their location on the page, larger sizes, and longer measure tend to give each day's issue a measure of freshness. The headline forms in no case include second decks, even as "readouts" (a narrower deck reading out from a wider top deck). Consistent use is made of modern headline forms, including many underscored kickers (always in the alternate style— roman if over an italic main head, italic over roman —and invariably letter spaced, for contrast).[1]

Rules are used horizontally but never vertically; six points of white space separate columns. Pictures are used as dramatically as before, but picture interest and reproduction quality have combined to increase their impact and effectiveness. Excellent quality in paper and ink help a picture's reproduction quality and convey a sense of quality in general. Half-column cuts are used but with cutlines set beside rather than

---

[1] Since these examples were selected, the *Courier-Journal* has adopted another contemporary practice. Its headlines are now all in lower-case type, capitalizing only the words that would be capitalized in text.

Courtesy the Cincinnati Enquirer

Revolution in Cincinnati   For more than fifty years, the Cincinnati *Enquirer* looked very much as it did in the 1950's. Then it was totally redesigned for contemporary readers, going in one step from traditional (above) to contemporary (below) makeup practices.

under the picture, which avoids crowding the cut with type and setting a fixed number of lines in short measure.

The Cincinnati *Enquirer* held for nearly a century to its traditional makeup, a classic of its kind—dull, but distinguishable from any other newspaper and an institution in its part of the world, with a vertical head structure of many decks reminiscent of Civil War days. In very striking contrast is today's *Enquirer,* which is contemporary in just about every respect. Its emphasis is horizontal: only one single-column head and six wide columns (13½ picas in this case). It has large, legible body type, varying column widths within a single page, a full pica of white space between columns, no rules at all except to set off an editor's note. Bodoni Bold and Bodoni Bold Italics are used for all heads. Bodoni Bold is even used to set off the promotion for special Sunday-only inside-page features, which is spread across the top of the page above the logotype (nameplate). The head forms are simple: no decks, no kickers—just one simple sentence for each story.

Cuts are used in fairly large sizes, although the art in the upper left could have benefited from enlargement to four columns in the interest of drama and visual detail. Cut lines follow a special design which includes both display and body type.

Two Arizona newspapers, the *Arizona Republic* of Phoenix and the *Arizona Daily Star* of Tucson, are pictured on the next page before and after changeover. The *Republic* actually went through a two-step process, changing first from the standard 8-column format shown to 7½ columns and then to the 6-column, uniform, wide-measure page shown. Except for an all-cap gothic line, the display-type family was not changed, but how it was and now is used is another matter. The two top lines on the older issue are in the old tradition, still honored today by such stalwarts as the Chicago *Tribune.* They gave way on the *Republic* to a multicolumn, high-focus top head. The earlier design was part of the fixed expectations of the readers; the new design allows wide variation in treatment.

Actually, the earlier format is used extremely well in the illustration, in the best tradition of what for a long time was the more or less standard front page. The page has focus, and it is quite well balanced in a wholly informal way. No quarter of the page lacks interest, although the lower left could have used something stronger. Except for the top line, the display type is all of a single family and reasonably readable. The single-column major heads, though legible enough, are extremely short on unit count (about nine units maximum). When heads are adjacent, contrast is excellent (roman *vs.* italics, long measure *vs.* short). The steady progression from large to small heads from top to bottom gives a sense of unity to the whole page.

Yet the new *Republic* is a much more inviting, interesting, and attractive paper. Multiple-column heads, now the rule rather than the exception, increase legibility, simplify typesetting, and give the head writers room to say what the story is about. Two key stories, one in the upper right, the other in the lower left, get still longer headlines to set them apart from the others. Three-column and two-column cuts give strong top emphasis, but the bottom of the new page has much more interest than the earlier page. No news headlines are adjacent to other news headlines.

For what it's worth, the change may be seen as from contrast-and-balance to focus or brace makeup (as described in Chapter 10). But more striking is the change in the general tone of the paper, from closed to open, vertical to horizontal, less readable to more readable.

The *Arizona Daily Star* converted years ago, in keeping with a curious trend of the times, from eight columns to nine. Publishers were trying to get more advertising columns without increasing page size (and without adjusting advertising rates accordingly) and at the same time trying to save paper through mat shrinkage and the narrowing of already minimal margins. (All mats shrink, but some kinds shrink more than others; a narrower newsprint roll can be used to reduce newsprint consumption, a major cost item on newspapers.) It switched in 1969 to six-column format on "outside" pages—that is, front and section front pages. The left-hand column was run to the top of the log and was mainly dedicated to a news summary, leaving five wide columns for the editor to

Reform in Arizona   The changeover in the
Arizona Daily Star of Tucson and the *Arizona
Republic* of Phoenix are discussed in the text.

work with. They are treated in the contemporary manner, more or less, but with clear upper-right focus.

Most of the elements of contemporary page makeup are visible in the Louisville *Courier-Journal* split page shown on this page. Wide columns, horizontal structures, and a few large masses rather than many small ones make every part of the page inviting. The long-line heads over these large masses are in contemporary forms—they are mainly single-line heads with a kicker above or an additional line below. Heads that follow and relate to the top headline or story are in lower-case form. The heads are surrounded by substantial areas of white space to give them greater legibility and separation. Every headline is an island surrounded by either art or body or cutline type, never by other display type. Some contrast is attained in the body of the story with an occasional subhead, an italic cross-reference, as to a related editorial, or the simple "dingbat" of a check mark at the start of paragraphs which have a parallel and sequential relationship to each other. The large gray areas, however, are avoided not so much by such devices as by the careful planning of the page: the stories are broken up into manageable-sized subunits to produce a balanced, focused, contrasting, and unitary page without any large masses of gray.

One consequence of contemporary makeup practices, especially when they include wide-column format, is the necessity (or the opportunity, depending on the editor's view of the matter) of using fewer and larger stories, at least on key pages. This does not rule out good short stories, as the *Courier-Journal* split page shows. But in more traditional makeup, the "shortie" was a necessity on every page; the problem was not what to do with short items but how to lay hands on enough of them. Wire editors would plead with the wire services for more shorties, earlier in the day. The AP Managing Editors organization supported these demands. The amusing human-interest item from the north of Scotland and its ilk became so ubiquitous that their numbers and the space they occupied became a thorn in the sides of conscientious editors. Traditional makeup fostered shorties for several reasons: (1) The editor could dummy in major items without a lot of regard to perfect fit,

filling up columns with short items as they came in. (2) The traditional scaling down of head sizes from largest at the top to smallest at the bottom tended to require extraneous, small, headed items to complete the scheme. (3) Small items were thought necessary to break up gray type areas. None of these reasons applies to contemporary pages such as those illustrated in this chapter. A short item can be chosen and included in a contemporary page on the basis of its merit as a story, not as decoration or filler.

The necessity for longer stories at the same time is consistent with an even more significant trend in the content and mission of the daily newspaper. In-depth reporting and interpretation require space for realization, and thus the requirements of makeup and content are mutually supportive. The *Courier-Journal* split

Contemporary Makeup on a Second Front Page
This first page of the second section of the *Courier-Journal* of Louisville has many of the characteristics of contemporary design, format, and makeup.

Day-to-Day Variation in Contemporary Format
These three front pages of the *Southern Illinoisan,* a Lindsay-Schaub newspaper serving Carbondale, Herrin, and Murphysboro, illustrate the day-to-day makeup changes that are possible without affecting day-to-day continuity in the paper's general appearance. All three are built around large cuts, giving two of the three pages upper left-hand emphasis, one upper right. The differences in makeup all the way down the pages reflect differing news days. Note the different ways connections between related stories are made apparent. While the format is still eight columns with column rules, the head forms and general horizontal emphasis make this a contemporary-looking paper.

Courtesy the Southern Illinoisan

Contemporary Trends in the Swedish Press

Many contemporary trends in newspaper design and makeup are more or less worldwide. The front pages of *Dagens Nyheter* of Stockholm, *Dala-Demokraten* of Falun, and *Arbetet* of Malmö illustrate their application in Sweden. The first two papers hew to the eight-column tradition, but the third radically mixes line lengths. All three use variants of Bodoni, the headline face currently so popular with American editors. Note the upper-left emphasis in *Dagens Nyheter;* dramatic use of a five-column line drawing with unconventional placement of cutlines; kickers and other contemporary headline forms; lower-case headlines; picture placement on the outside margins. *Arbetet* is, by comparison, splashy, a smorgasbord promising interesting reading on inside pages, with heavy use and uncon-

ventional location of art. *Dala-Demokraten* is somewhat less contemporary and more sedate in tone.

The editorial page of *Sydsvenska Dagbladet* of Malmö and the sports page of *Vestmanlands Läns Tidning* illustrate contemporary makeup practices on inside pages; note modern display faces in both. The dignified but attractive layout of the editorial page shows numerous conventions familiar to American readers: wide-measure leaders, extra white space in place of column rules, line drawings, a lively cartoon panel. The sports page is clearly horizontal, focuses on a reverse (in Ultra Bodoni) in the upper right with a large cut, locates art dynamically. Yet many traditional and modern conventions of makeup are also carefully satisfied.

page is evidence of this. The two related stories at the top, developing local and national aspects of the long-term problem of mercury pollution in streams, are meritorious not because of their immediacy but because of the complexity of the problem and its importance to the region. Such a story deserves extended and unified treatment, and it gets it here without having to continue to another page or to another day.

The possibility of jumping a long story adds flexibility to a page. But jumps are usually made from the front page only, not from section front pages. This does make it harder to make up a page such as this one, by comparison with the first news page. However, this paper has a "slop" page (or "slopover" or "junk" page) that is used on occasion to carry a jump from the split page. This cannot be done when the jump page appears in the first section, as it sometimes does. Some tabloids are not so squeamish. Where the back page is in effect a section front page—usually the "first" sports page—editors have invented a new track event: the "backward jump" carries stories over from the last page to earlier pages in the same section. The fans do not seem to have been asked what they think of this.

Format Changes

As we have seen, newspapers went from six wide columns and less in the eighteenth century (wide by comparison; 13 pica ems was the standard thirty-five years ago) to seven and eight and finally, in many cases, nine ever narrower columns in the mid-twentieth century. In the last two decades, the trend has gone the other way, under the leadership of the *Wall Street Journal,* the Louisville *Courier-Journal* and *Times,* and the *Christian Science Monitor.* At present, American newspapers vary in format enormously, and this once again urges the idea that learning the rules of makeup is less important than learning the principles. And because of trends toward experimentation and individualism, further modification in formats and perhaps even greater variability from paper to paper can be expected as more rules are broken and principles stretched.

As this is written, half a dozen fairly common newspaper-format situations prevail. The standard eight-column format is still in widespread use, although, of course, special variants are more often than not found in the front page and/or editorial page and often on section front pages, especially the departmental ones and especially in Sunday papers. When the Los Angeles *Times* was redesigned in the late 1950's, for example, it changed to six-column front and split pages but kept its basic eight-column format inside. Perhaps even more common is the front-page format of one wide column and five, six, or seven columns of regular width (regular, these days, usually meaning 11 pica ems). Some of these front pages substitute white space for column rule, follow a horizontal design, and use other contemporary devices, but more often they simply show the one change in the left-hand column.

Some illustrations of variants in the structure of front pages are given on pages 281–283. Each presents a distinct set of problems in makeup. In many cases the problem largely solves itself: the wide left-hand column is often used for standard material and the editor has to worry about making up only the columns that remain. The front page of the *Christian Science Monitor* used to illustrate "modular" makeup on page 286 shows a left-hand column, which, though not wider than the others, is set off from top to bottom and leaves a four-column panel to be made up as a distinct frame. The basic structure of the paper is five 15½-em columns throughout, but the editors change the pattern to fit the need every day. In the present illustration, note the variation in this respect on the front page.

As this is written, only a few newspapers have followed the lead of the *Wall Street Journal* and Louisville *Courier-Journal* in changing to six-column format throughout. It is not an easy change to make, mainly because national advertising is designed for the narrower column. This may mean making a gift of the white space that fills out a two-column ad in what used to be a three-column space. Newspaper managements hesitate to increase advertising rates even when ads get improved display. There are many mechanical complications in changing over, too, including redesigning sports box scores, etc.

Courtesy the Minneapolis Tribune

Courtesy El Mundo (San Juan, Puerto Rico)

Courtesy the Lexington Leader

Courtesy Today (Cocoa, Florida) and The Gannetteer

Typical Variations in Front-Page Format All of these pages set aside a wide left-hand column. For the Minneapolis *Tribune* and *El Mundo* of San Juan, Puerto Rico, it is two columns wide (these might be called "six-and-two" pages). The Lexington *Leader* and *Today* of Cocoa, Florida, are in the seven-and-a-half-column tradition.

Four Modern Seven-and-a-Half-Column Pages

The Pensacola *Journal* uses distinctive material in the wide left column to frame a six-column format made up in an essentially horizontal way, but with numerous single-column heads. An interesting touch is the policy of centering all headlines, a rarely encountered practice that lends distinction to the page.

The Rochester *Democrat and Chronicle* sets off the wide first column, too, but allows a dramatic picture to occupy the entire top of the page. The remaining six columns are laid out in a strongly horizontal fashion, with single-column elements for occasional contrast.

Inside-Page Makeup

The way makeup styles translate to inside pages is shown on page 284. All three pages have a similar amount of space for news in roughly similar form—the ads are pyramided to the right, leaving a triangle encompassing about half the page. The *traditional* Chattanooga *Times* uses its space in much the same way it handles a corner of the front page. Two single-column heads dominate, anchoring the cut between them. The single two-column head is carefully put

in subordinate position. This is a well-handled inside page in the traditional style.

The same may be said of the *modern* Los Angeles *Times* page. But here a cut at the upper left dominates the page and most of the heads are two columns wide, with only one major single-column head. Notice that this paper follows the common practice of wide columns on the front page but narrow columns on the inside pages.

The *contemporary* Louisville *Times* page is also dominated by a cut—of three wide columns. Above

Courtesy The Gannetteer

The Hartford *Times* and the Yonkers *Herald Statesman* both also use wide left-hand columns distinctively, the former to promote inside-page features, the latter to do the same but also to give special treatment to a reader-service feature. On both pages, this leaves six columns

with very wide bands of white space between them. Of course there is nothing in this arrangement to prevent editors from setting one or more stories in two-column measure, using a larger body type, as the *Times* does to display a copyrighted story reporting a sample-survey study commissioned by the paper.

the fold are only two heads—also three columns wide. Even the standing head is in two-column width. Both dominant heads are in italics of nearly the same size and family, but contrasting boldness.

Thus it can be said that general systems of makeup are applied to both front and inside pages. Section front pages often differ strikingly in makeup from the news pages of the paper. The contrast is especially apparent in the papers of traditional makeup which present bright, modern, attractive section front pages using altogether different materials. Thus it might be

said that the traditional papers' tendency to emphasize continuity with the past comes at the cost of section-to-section continuity. Some illustrations of section front pages are shown on page 285.

The horizontal structure, in use for more than two decades, has been especially helpful in solving the long-standing problem of what to do with small and awkwardly arranged "holes" in inside pages. A story of suitable length may be arranged in any number of columns to fill them, headed with a single-line headline of type size appropriate to the story's length over

Inside-Page Makeup in Traditional, Modern, and Contemporary Format   These pages show how three newspapers that more or less fit the three categories handle inside pages with approximately the same kind and amount of space.

Courtesy the Washington Post

Courtesy the Baltimore Sun

Three Sprightly Section Front Pages Even in papers that have not changed their front pages much in recent years, the section front pages in both daily and Sunday issues allow for wider variation in design, format, and makeup and greater freedom for the editors than do the regular news pages. Indicative of the creativity of editors when given the opportunity to exercise it are these Sunday sectional front pages from the Washington *Post,* the *Sun* of Baltimore, and the Cincinnati *Enquirer.*

Courtesy the Cincinnati Enquirer

Modular Makeup   Almost without exception, these pages from the *Christian Science Monitor* are made up in modular style (whether or not the editors themselves call it that): every unit is assembled in a single rectangle. This is not easy to do on inside pages with ads, but the editors do not try to handle all pages in the modular fashion.

the tops of all the open columns. Sometimes this can be done at the forms. The story is split up and shoehorned into the holes; a two-line head of two-column width may be butted to make a single-line four-column head.

Modular Makeup

Some newspapers of contemporary format make use of a device called "modular" makeup to give the newspaper page a clear and carefully shaped construction. All the elements on the page are grouped in clearly rectangular form to echo the larger rec-

tangle of the page itself. Within each rectangle—ideally—is one item or one set of related items.

The front page and two inside pages of the *Christian Science Monitor* shown on this page illustrate the point. Each page is a structure of rectangles of varying shapes. The front page is basically composed of four—the elongated vertical rectangle at the left and three others laid out horizontally from top to bottom. The result is a pleasing and coherent whole. In terms of content, the page is composed of six rectangles, the long vertical one at the left, a short vertical and a horizontal at the top and at the bottom, and a horizontal one in between, all of aesthetic proportions. The point is best illustrated by the middle rectangle of the three main ones at the right. Its headline, art, and text are carefully combined into a single pleasing shape. The unity of the whole is thus enhanced and the relationship among these elements is made clear.

The contemporaneity of this design is all but exceptionless. The highly legible headline and body type, the wide columns and their arrangement, including the variation in column width between the top rectangle and the two below it, the headline forms and lower-case style, and the extra-wide bands of white space between columns and above and below heads and art all are contemporary features. The unconventional combination of data chart and pictorial visualization at midpage bespeaks the spirit of innovation of the developing contemporary tradition. Not least, though least apparent to most observers, is the excellent quality of ink and paper, yielding very sharp black-white contrasts which are both aesthetically pleasing and a major factor in legibility.

Photo by Ralph Eugene Meatyard

They Try Harder   The "underground" or "New Left" press may prove to be an influence on the "straight" press in a number of ways— makeup, photography, style, and a certain irreverence toward old ways of doing things. Many of these papers seem to be indifferent toward craftsmanship, but others aren't, including the *blue-tail fly*, a student paper.

Tabloid Makeup

Until just after World War I, newspaper size had been quite standard for many decades. Then there appeared a truly revolutionary format—the tabloid paper. Tabloids existed in the United States before 1919 and were a going concern in England as early as 1903, but the New York *Daily News* and the New York *Graphic* were the two papers that developed and exploited the full tabloid pattern—small size, lots of art, and a love-nest murder every day or so. Because of this unsavory early history, the aura of journalistic rascality still clings to the tabloid, and very few "respectable" papers use this format.

The tabloid size lends itself particularly to the needs of the commuter who takes public transportation; it is compact and convenient to handle in a confined space. Hence the tabloid is largely an urban phenomenon, although there are many exceptions to this. The greatest tabloid success in recent years is a *sub*urban phenomenon—the excellent *Newsday* of Long Island, where the requirements of the commuter are still relevant. (Interestingly enough, the late founder of the new tabloid success was a daughter of the founder of the first tabloid success. But any qualitative relationship between the two papers ends right there.)

The importance of tabloid makeup is greater than the relative incidence of tabloid newspapers, however. Regular newspapers are increasingly putting in tab size *part* of what they offer: the pullout magazine, television section, etc. Some papers, including the Chicago *Defender,* are tabloid during the week but full size on Sunday (a legacy of the Boston Hearst papers). Editors are having to learn to shift from full-size pages to tabloid and back again—and how to handle magazine format as well.

Many tabloids (the *Defender,* for example) still reflect the basic formula of the *Daily News* and the *Graphic.* The front page features one large type mass, usually a very boldface gothic in all caps, and one large piece of art—or an art layout—with almost no text. The news pages start with key spreads on pages 2 and 3, which together have about the same amount of space as the conventional front page but present different makeup problems because they are nevertheless two half-size pages and cannot be treated as a

The Telegraph-Herald

DIGEST

Hal Reynolds

Hal Reynolds, chairman of the City Housing Authority, warns those attending yesterday's meeting not to get their hopes for special housing needs too high .... **Page 14.**

★ ★ ★

The Dubuque Metropolitan Crime Commission discusses an "Operation Crossroads" proposal for two hours last night before tabling the resolution until a special meeting next Monday .... **Page 11.**

The city fire department hopes to move into its new headquarters sometime next week .... **Page 14.**

The opening of the World Youth Assembly at U.N. headquarters is enlivened by a Puerto Rican factional fight, Soviet attempts to bar Nationalist Chinese, South Koreans and South Vietnamese, and a Yippie threat to wreck everything. .... **Page 2.**

A pioneer in the use of methadone for treatment of heroin addicts say there are unreasonable and unworkable provisions in the proposed federal regulations governing community methadone programs. .... **Page 19.**

U.S. Air Force planes have flown more than 120 bombing sorties against targets in Cambodia since American troops were withdrawn back into South Vietnam last week. .... **Page 2.**

The House moves today toward its first encounter with curbs on presidential action in Cambodia—an issue that tied up the Senate for almost two months. .... **Page 2.**

With signs pointing toward creation of two new agencies, the White House unveils today a plan for reorganizing the federal government's environmental protection program... **Page 20.**

The Boeing Company has won a major defense contract to test a new airborne warning system, giving a big boost to the ailing aerospace giant and to the depressed Seattle area. .... **Page 2.**

★ ★ ★

Will speed up Viet pullout

WASHINGTON (AP) — Secretary of Defense Melvin R. Laird today announced a speed-up in the withdrawal of U.S. troops from Vietnam.

Laird told a news conference that more than 50,000 American servicemen will be withdrawn by Oct. 15.

He said U.S. forces in Vietnam will go below the 384,000 troop ceiling projected by President Nixon for mid-October.

"We will be at that troop ceiling on Oct. 15," the defense secretary said.

Where to find it . . .

Classified	24-27
Comics	18
Editorial	4
Markets	22
News of Record	24
Obituaries	22
Sports	15-17
Dr. Steincrohn	24
Weather	22
Women's News	7-9

Weather . . .

Fair

Farm subsidy lid voted

Story: PAGE 28

The Telegraph-Herald

DUBUQUE, IOWA, and EAST DUBUQUE, ILLINOIS

134th Year, No. 162 — THURSDAY, JULY 9, 1970 — 28 PAGES — 4 SECTIONS — 10c

Associated Press

New base

Barbed wire rings the new Fire Support Base Bravo in Vietnam which the First Air Cavalry Division set up as they returned from service in Cambodia.

U.S. general is missing

SAIGON (AP) — Maj. Gen. George W. Casey, Commander of the U.S. 1st Air Cavalry Division, and six other Americans have been missing in Casey's helicopter since Tuesday morning, the U.S. Command announced today.

The announcement gave no indication whether enemy action was believed responsible for the disappearance of the big UH1 Huey helicopter.

The command said the helicopter was last heard from at 10:10 a.m. Tuesday, and an extensive search has failed to locate the craft or any of its occupants.

Casey was en route to visit wounded members of his division, but the command, for security reasons, refused to reveal the area where his aircraft was believed down.

The command said those aboard the helicopter with the general were his aide, Capt. John A. Hottell III of Saint Bethlehem, Tenn.; 1st Lt. William F. Michael, Monroe, Wash., the pilot; Sgt. Maj. Kenneth W. Cooper, Colorado Springs, Colo., command sergeant major of the 1st Air Cavalry; Spec. 4 William L Christienson, St. Paul, Minn., the door gunner; Spec. 4 Ronald F. Fuller, Providence, R.I., the crew chief; and Spec. 4 Vernon K. Smolik, Garfield Heights, Ohio, a stenographer.

Gen. Casey, 48, of North Scituate, Mass., was on his second tour in Vietnam and commanded one of the best known American units here. He was graduated from West Point in 1945.

His wife, Elaine Morton Casey, and their five children live in North Scituate.

Six American generals have been killed in action in the Vietnam war and several have been wounded. Two of the generals were killed earlier this year.

No major fighting was reported today in Vietnam or Cambodia.

GEN. GEORGE CASEY

1st Cavalry Commander

Who's liable for rock fest damage?

MADISON (AP) — Are local governments financially responsible for damage to persons and property at rock festivals?

Atty. Gen. Robert Warren said he is not certain and has asked his staff to check out the possibility that the state's mob damage statute could be used by victims of the more violent aspects of the large music fests.

The law provides that a person who is injured or has property destroyed by mob violence may recover damages from the county or, if the damage occurs in an urban area, from the city. In addition, the law allows an injured person to hold the mayor or county sheriff liable for the injury if the official knew of the situation and took no action to stop it.

The confusion enters because of a recent Wisconsin Supreme Court decision which calls the legality of the statute into question because participants in rock festivals may themselves contribute to the very situation that results in their injury.

Warren, who said the festivals are characterized by "wholesale rape, extortion, violence, shooting, stabbing, promiscuous sex, nudity and excessive drinking," observed in an interview Wednesday that participants may, in effect, be responsible for their own plight.

Robert Warren

Asked if the music fans might be prohibited from collecting damages because of their own participation in the event, Warren said the principle of "estoppel" would probably enter the case. Estoppel holds that a person cannot claim another is responsible for an injury if it was caused by a prior negligent act of his own.

Warren has described the festival-goers as a "locust plague" who behave like "lemmings as they participate in the rape of the environment."

He stopped short of calling the recent Iola affair a riot.

That festival erupted into gunfire after a motorcycle group was hired to supervise "security operations." Several persons were injured.

A state representative from the Iola area Francis Byers, R-Marion, said the event left the town "looking like a World War II battlefield."

Other state and local officials have called for an investigation and legislation to prevent a recurrence of the events.

The court decision, which concerns the position of insurance companies which must pay riot claims, noted that the logic behind the mob damage statute was that increased taxes because of damage claims would make citizens and government more "diligent" in attempts to prevent riots.

Although it did not invalidate the statute, the Supreme Court said such laws may be unreasonable in an era of "confrontation politics" when riots occur spontaneously and authorities are largely helpless in preventing their outbreak.

Without showing that authorities were in some way negligent, the court held they may not be automatically held liable for damages.

The Supreme Court decision was rendered last winter on an appeal from Milwaukee County.

The case of a rock festival may be somewhat different, however, in that it is not usually a spontaneous occurrence and authorities are aware of plans long before the event actually materializes.

Clarke-Loras Singers place high at festival

The 48-member Clarke-Loras Singers, directed by John A. Lease of the Clarke College music faculty, have captured a first place and a second place award in the International Music Festival currently being held in Llangollen, North Wales.

The Music Festival's office told the Telegraph-Herald that the Dubuque group today won first place over 15 other groups in the "youth choir" division. Second place went to a Czech choir and third place to an English group.

"Youth choir" competition is for groups of less than 50 members age 16 to 25. The Clarke-Loras group has 48 members.

On Wednesday, Festival officials said, the Clarke-Loras Singers placed second in the folk song competition in a field of 23 entrants. The group sang two songs in each contest.

The Clarke segment of the choir was to compete in the female choir division contest this afternoon. On Friday, Festival officials said, the group will compete in the mixed choir division.

The Clarke-Loras Singers have been on a nine-country concert tour of Europe since June 11.

Viet battle toll lowest in 3½ years

SAIGON (AP) — Sixty-one Americans were killed in action in the Vietnam war last week, the lowest total in 3½ years, the U.S. Command announced today. Another 463 Americans were wounded.

The weekly casualty report closed out a six-month period during which the total of U.S. combat deaths were the lowest since the last half of 1966, when the American buildup was in full swing.

South Vietnamese combat deaths last week exceeded those of the United States for the 60th consecutive week, and their six month total was the highest of the war for the Saigon government's forces.

The government said 371 South Vietnamese troops were killed and 1,027 wounded last week.

The allied commands claimed their forces killed 1,395 Viet Cong and North Vietnamese.

The American death toll was the lowest since the week ending Dec. 3, 1966, when 44 American deaths in action were recorded.

'Red Chinese key to future of Indochina'

TOKYO (AP — Communist China is the "key to the future of Indochina," Secretary of State William P. Rogers said today, and if Peking would "talk sensibly" about a settlement for the war, the Nixon administration thinks it "could work out a peaceful settlement very quickly."

Rogers also said in a television interview with NHK, the Japan Broadcasting Corp., that the U.S. military presence in Asia would be unnecessary if "Communist China would ever stop its belligerent attitude toward its neighbors."

Rogers did not indicate whether Washington has made any approaches to the Chinese concerning Indochina.

But he did say: "we have done everything we can to improve our relations with China. They have given some indication they might like to improve relations, but so far the progress has been very slow."

The secretary of state said he believes Thailand, Laos, Cambodia and South Vietnam, "cooperating and working together with other Asian nations, will be able to maintain their independence.

"And we think, too," he went on, "that Cambodia-- because of its feeling of nationalism, because it has been invaded by the North Vietnamese--has a good chance of retaining a non-Communist government."

Asked how the withdrawal of 150,000 U.S. troops from South Vietnam by next May would affect the security of that part of Southeast Asia, Rogers said the South Vietnamese government now has about 1,034,000 troops, "well armed, well equipped, well trained, and we think that those troops, together with our air power and the remaining American troops and the troops from Thailand and South Korea, will be able to maintain the security of South Vietnam."

In a speech earlier today, Rogers said the United States will not allow differences with Japan in the commercial field to cause a rupture between the two countries.

"Japan has to play a part in the security of this part of the world," he told the U.S. Embassy staff. "Japan is in a position in the years ahead to play an important part in security, not only here, but in the world generally.

"The fact that we have had a breakdown in textile negotiations will not affect the reversion of Okinawa to Japan."

Rogers discussed Japanese-American disputes over trade with Prime Minister Eisaku Sato and other Japanese officials Wednesday. He said the United States is going to compete from time to time with Japan because both nations are great industrial powers.

Associated Press

Woe is me!!

Wags, the pet of the H.E. Peterson family of Oklahoma City, looks properly dejected as she takes it easy with a broken leg. Her mournful look seems to say it's far from a dog's life.

Courtesy the Telegraph-Herald (Dubuque, Iowa)

The Telegraph-Herald DIGEST

Colt .45's are state champions

Story: PAGE 8

* * *

Antonio de Oliveira Salazar

Antonio de Oliveira Salazar, premier and dictator of Portugal for 36 years, died at his home in Lisbon today after a long illness... Page 3.

Jordan accepts the U.S. Middle East proposal but says it can't leash the Palestinian guerrillas. Israel delays its decision. ...Page 2.

The West German and Soviet foreign ministers open talks to complete a nonaggression pact which the Bonn government hopes will open the way to better relations with Eastern Europe. ....Page 2.

U.S. B52s bomb at six points along the Cambodian and Laotian borders amid reports of new enemy buildups. ....Page 2.

The House may decide today whether to junk its ancient rule permitting members to vote secretly on many major issues. ....Page 3.

An election-year spending controversy between the White House and Congress is likely to flare again as the Senate considers a $4.4 billion education appropriation bill. ....Page 3.

The Nixon administration's bid to halt the arms race and a U.S. admiral's warning of growing Soviet naval power have refueled the heated Senate debate over the nation's defense budget. Page 2.

Sen. Strom Thurmond appears headed for a reconciliation with President Nixon following a feud over proposed administration desegregation programs for the South. ....Page 2.

Before the Penn Central reorganized under the Bankruptcy Act, the Department of Transportation told Congress such a move could lead to government subsidy or takeover of the nation's railroads. ....Page 3.

President Nixon plans two meetings today with top advisers, one on cutting defense costs and the other for an "overview of the economy." ....Page 2.

Where to find it...

Classified	13-15
Comics	11
Editorial	4
Markets	12
News of Record	5
Obituaries	12
Sports	6-7
Dr. Steincrohn	5
Weather	12
Women's News	9-10

Weather...

Fair

'We don't want them here'

By JACK BRIMEYER
T-H Staff Writer

A small girl sat sobbing in the back seat of the family auto.

Her father, with a haggard, expressionless face and a minimum of conversation, packed family possessions on a pickup truck.

None of the Clarence Schmitt family was interested in talking. They just wanted to get out. To leave the farm they had known for years. Leave it in hands of people who would use it for a rock festival next weekend.

A long-haired youth came out the back door, burdened by several kitchen chairs. He was followed by another. And another. They seemed to understand. No talk.

Down the blacktop road came more cars. Each filled with curious persons gawking at these strange people from Chicago.

Two youths had stationed themselves at the end of the lane "to keep the tourists moving."

"They don't seem to want us here," said one as he plopped down on a stuffless chair retrieved from a junk heap.

This was part of the scene Sunday as the small community of Wadena in Fayette County reacted to the news that 40,000 persons

Personal Report

would convene there Friday for three days of rock music.

The Schmitt farm was purchased last week by the Wadena Development Co. which is leasing it to Sound Storm Enterprises Inc., for the festival.

The firms—both based in Chicago—have some mutual stockholders and officers.

Schmitt claimed the development firm told him they wanted the 220 acres for a resort area and horse ranch.

Sound Storm verified that and said it would be used for those purposes...after the fest.

Talk tends to be pretty cheap around Wadena, but topics were routine: the county fair, the weather, crops, gossip.

They've been furnished with a new topic and if the fest can't be legally stopped, then surely it can be talked to death.

"We don't think much of it," says a farmer whose land borders the Schmitt farm. A group of neighbors is gathered on his front lawn, watching the cars pass.

There is some talk of getting out the shotguns. One fellow suggests piling hay in the road. No one listens. They all talk.

They can't tell you why they are against the rock fest. They're just against it. Like communism.

They are shown a newspaper article in which the promoters detail plans for the fest. They sit quiet for a minute and then one pipes up: "They are a bunch of liars."

The rest of the groups nods agreement.

They are asked how they know the promoters are liars. "We just know," answers one who just appointed himself spokesman.

In Wadena, the mayor, Leallen Knox, ambles across his living room and dumps his plump body on the end of a piano bench.

He is worried about the safety of 231 Wadena residents.

"Speaking for myself," he said, "I want to see it stopped. You dump 50,000 people in here, what are you going to do with them, just plain speaking?"

"The promoters seem perfectly sincere and it appears that it will go through. There's no use fighting and antagonizing them; that's the thing we don't want."

He doesn't yet know what will happen but he said he will stay in Wadena the weekend though others have said they would pack and move out until it's over.

Outside, down the street a bit, some people sit on the sidewalk chatting about the fest. The talk is the same. "We just don't want them here."

Some more cars drive by, headed toward the festival site where four stakes mark the perimeter of the 150 by 75-foot stage.

Some young workers sweep out sheds, readying them for festival headquarters. Others are building toilets. One group has a tent already set up—their quarters until the rock fest ends at sundown next Sunday.

They feel the animosity around them.

Says one, girl turning bacon on a griddle, "They don't understand that we want to be left alone as much as they do."

* * * * * * * * *

County officials bid to stop rock fest

By JOHN MC CORMICK
T-H Staff Writer

WEST UNION, Ia. — The Fayette County Courthouse Supervisors' room was packed today as two sides squared off to determine whether a rock festival can be held here this weekend.

Promoters of the rock festival, slated for 220 acres near Wadena, told county officials, "We want to cooperate. If we all work together, we can get ready for this."

Murry Moorhatch, security consultant for Sound Storm Enterprises, Inc., of Chicago, continued, "We feel we have the best possible plans and facilities" for the three day event that opens Friday.

Supervisors and other officials called the special meeting to consider what methods, if any, can be implemented to stop the fest.

Petitions circulating in the county appealed to the supervisors and other elected officials of the county and state to "do everything within their power to prevent the establishment of a Rock and Roll Resort" in the county.

The petitions said the festival "would destroy the use and enjoyment of our property and will promote crime and law enforcement problems with which our County is not equipped to cope."

Fayette County District Attorney Walter Saur said he is running an investigation of Sound Storm.

"We don't want to be unfair," he said, "but we can't help but be concerned since no one spoke with us. This thing is being foisted upon us."

He said the promoters have to show "that this could be controlled" adding that he is interested in the "general safety and welfare of the people living here and those coming here."

Saur has been in contact with the State Attorney General's office where an official said possibilities are being explored but that this is "strictly a county matter."

County officials have requested and received a copy of the appeal for injunction used in Jo Daviess County, Ill., to bar the rock fest from that area.

Fayette County supervisor, John D. Fay, said this morning that "We are doing everything we can" to stop the event.

"Why pull an underhanded deal? Why not stay in Chicago? That may be the way they do it in Chicago, but that's not the way they do it in Fayette County," he said.

The festival is expected to attract some 40,000 rock fans. Moorhatch said that 150 acres of the farm site would be devoted to parking.

One person who refused to sign the petition is Ray Herwig who runs Wadena's only store.

He said this morning, referring to some of the young people working on the fest, "They haven't said a word in my store that couldn't be repeated from a pulpit.

"They've been extra good to me. They're clean and they pay cash.

"But," he added, "I may have to eat a lot of crow when this is over."

The Telegraph-Herald

DUBUQUE, IOWA, and EAST DUBUQUE, ILLINOIS

134th Year, No. 176 | 16 PAGES | MONDAY, JULY 27, 1970 | 2 SECTIONS | 10c

Staff Photo

Double delight Shelly and Sherry Ellingson flank their bermuda-decked dad as they all await the result of the judging in the 27th annual Twin-O-Rama in Cassville, Wis. yesterday. Over 2,000 attended the unique outing which saw 275 twins compete. (Picture page: PAGE 16.)

Church aboard Julie N.

The excursion boat Julie N. Dubuque was the site of religious services Sunday as about 150 members of St. John's Episcopal Church, 1410 Main St., attended the church's annual Sunday School picnic aboard the boat.

The Rev. Franklin Klohn conducted a prayer service on board shortly after the boat began its five-hour journey downriver and back about 9 a.m.

Rev. Klohn said he had planned the event with the help of the boat's captain, who is a member of the congregation.

Clock fund short

The move-the-clock campaign hasn't raised the necessary sum, but proponents are going ahead with recommendations to the City Council tonight that bids be sought to put it on the pedestrianway.

This morning the clock fund stood at $21,600, a bit more than a third of the amount estimated to do all that is necessary to complete the project.

Four four-digit contributions from local business and industry account for most of the total collected to date.

Individual contributions total $5,600. A six-hour telethon last night raised $1,600, not an encouraging sum.

City Manager Gilbert Chavenelle is still solid in his stand that city treasury money not be used to support the project, said urban renewal project engineer Robert Urell this morning.

The council supports that stand.

The clock-moving is ineligible for federal urban renewal financing.

The problem is time. Engineers say the clock-removal should start no later than Aug. 13 in order to coordinate smoothly with the rest of pedestrianway construction.

If the clock was removed after that date, costs would escalate substantially because of increased contractor liability for pedestrianway paving, trees and other architectural features, said Urell.

Urell mentioned one route the council might pursue: Advertise for bids on the project in hopes that all the money will be raised, and, if so, let the contract.

The council session starts at 7:30 p.m. and the clock's public hearing comes near the end of a relatively short, routine agenda. The hearing should start about 8 p.m.

Cablevision 10 will broadcast the meeting.

Modernization will precede cutbacks

SEOUL (AP) — The United States has agreed that the modernization of South Korea's armed forces will precede any withdrawal of American troops, Defense Minister Jung Nae-hiuk said today in a report on his meetings in Honolulu last week with Deputy Defense Secretary David Packard.

Jung told the National Assembly's foreign affairs and defense committees that Packard and his aides agreed to postpone talks on the U.S. troop cutback until the two governments agree on plans for the modernization of Korean forces.

Jung said Korean and American military leaders would meet in Seoul this week to discuss detailed programs to modernize South Korea's 600,000-man forces.

Jung denied reports that the United States intends to put into effect its plan to withdraw 20,000 of its 62,000-man force stationed in Korea with or without Korea's consent.

The United States also agreed at Honolulu to provide the South Korean Air Force with a squadron of S2 reconnaissance planes shortly, he said.

In Washington, the Defense Department declined immediate comment on Jung's report.

Last Thursday, Pentagon officials said the United States had agreed to help stabilize the air defense of South Korea, but they indicated that would occur during a reduction in U.S. ground forces.

Black militant party chief killed

HOUSTON, Tex. (AP) — Two police officers, perched atop St. John's Baptist church, returned fire from black militants Sunday night, they said, killing one Negro and wounding two Negroes and a white man. A bystander was hit by a militant's bullet, authorities charged later.

The intelligence officers had been posted on the churchtop in a predominantly Negro neighborhood to observe a rally staged nearby by People's Party II, a black group. Killed in the gunfire was Carl Hampton, 21, the party chairman.

Police said that in all about 100 shots were fired and that the exchange of gunfire ended quickly. They said that after the shooting about 30 armed blacks stalked the streets brandishing shotguns and rifles and warning police to stay away.

Before order was finally restored, police said a battery of helmeted officers charged a concentration of 150 to 200 blacks, striking them with rifle butts and making about 75 arrests.

The rally was an impromptu affair hastily assembled to protest the arrest of two Negro youths earlier in the day.

After the trouble was put down police raided the three-story brick building housing headquarters of People's Party II and confiscated what they called a large quantity of rifles, shotguns, pistols and ammunition. Officers did not immediately issue a count of the weapons.

An official police statement said two officers encountered Herbert Joseph Gerac, 19, armed with a pistol, and a 15-year-old carrying a shotgun in the middle of the street in front of People's Party II headquarters about 6 p.m.

Police said the youths pointed their weapons at the officers. They said Gerac broke and ran into the rear door of St. John's and pointed his pistol again.

Police said they could not shoot for fear of hitting two women. Three men church members wrestled the pistol from Gerac, charged later with carrying a pistol and assault. The younger one was turned over the juvenile authorities.

The rally of about 150 persons followed the incident by several hours. O.J. Norris, chief of police intelligence, said the rally had broke up when someone in the street saw the officers and ran into People's Party II headquarters.

Norris said a group of armed men then moved back onto the street.

"One shot at us," said Norris. "We didn't return the fire then. Two Negro males ran across the street and began shooting at us again. We shot them. Four more armed men came down the street shooting at the church roof. We hit one and the rest ran back into the headquarters building. Then we were being sniped at from all around and we returned the fire."

Authorities sent 125 to 150 men into the area in what Police Chief H.B. Short said was a preplanned response to possible mass disturbances.

Officers said literature of the militant Black Panthers was found in the headquarters. The 15-year-old arrested earlier with the shotgun said 40 to 45 men, mostly young, lived in the party headquarters.

"We were shooting to kill," said Norris. "They were shooting to kill me and I sure wasn't going to shoot for their legs. This isn't a cowboy movie where you shoot to wound them."

Mark Hapler, speaking for Mayor Louie Welch, who is in Europe, said the mayor "was pleased with the restraint the police exercised over the past two weeks while being goaded into this type situation."

Contemporary, Modular, Offset The Dubuque *Telegraph-Herald* is setting a blazing pace among offset dailies with pages as bright and modern as these—inside and out—day after day. The same front page is shown before and after a page-size change that reduced the size by half a column. Modular makeup is carried out even on the inside news pages.

When Will These "Trees" Be Removed?

These hulks of trees continue to "stand" on the Southside in the vicinity of Washington pk. and Dr. Martin Luther King dr. The trees were destroyed during a recent storm and have not been taken away as of today. Residents of the neighborhood are upset. Trees which suffered similar damage have already been removed from white neighborhoods. Now the Southsiders wonder: Does the color of one's skin play a part in tree removal these days?

HANK AARON, (R) is seen here holding the Baseball Commissioner's balloting. Aaron received the award from Commissioner Bowie Kuhn Award given to the player receiving the most votes in the All-Star (in rear) at a luncheon yesterday. (UPI)

Courtesy the Chicago Daily Defender

Two Styles of Tabloid Makeup The Chicago *Defender* more or less follows "traditional" tabloid makeup, with eye-filling type on the front page promising a lot of exciting news inside (but note that the pictures relate to a local civic-betterment issue). The back page is in effect a sports-section front page.

unit. Inside pages continue to convey the sense that every story is a stop-press exclusive. The two-page-spread picture layout is maintained. The small-size page limits the number of positions that are open enough for effective display of art, so the one "double truck" in the paper (that is, the two-page spread in the middle of the paper that is one sheet, allowing margins to be omitted) is especially appropriate as a picture page.

But quite a few tabloids have moved away from this traditional standard makeup to experiment, for exam-

ple, with various ways of using the front page to direct attention to what is inside. Some start a major story on the front and continue it inside, using most of the front-page space to promote other inside-page stories, sometimes keying one of them with a front-page picture. Some summarize all the principal inside-page stories, making the front page more or less a sampler. Some start more than one story on the front but set aside space for an index to inside-page features.

And some tabloids, including the exemplary *Newsday,* do very different things on the front page on

Newsday/ THE LONG ISLAND NEWSPAPER — 5 CENTS SATURDAY JUNE 20, 1970

$20 Million Federal Grant To Help Modernize LIRR

The sum made available to the Metropolitan Transportation Authority will cover two-thirds of the cost of 120 new Budd cars that the railroad has ordered. The grant will free state funds for other improvements. Page 3.

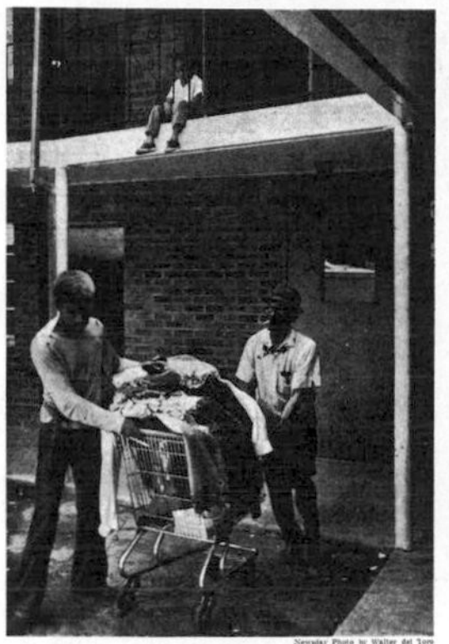

Newsday Photo by Walter del Toro

Moving Day At the Motel

Eight welfare families that had been housed in a Manhasset motel found new quarters yesterday, with six of the families moving into Mitchel Gardens. At left, belongings are carted from the North Shore Motor Lodge, and below, a child takes clothes into her new home. (Story, other photos on Page 5.)

Newsday Photo by Dick Yarwood

COPYRIGHT 1970, NEWSDAY, INC., LONG ISLAND, NEW YORK. VOL. 30, NO. 247

UPI Telephoto

Long-Haired Youths at Ottawa News Conference Where Easing of Drug Penalties Was Urged

Canada Urged to Abolish Jail Terms for Drug Use

Ottawa (UPI)—A government-appointed commission recommended yesterday sweeping changes in Canada's drug laws that would eliminate jail sentences for the possession and use of drugs ranging from marijuana to the psychedelics and heroin.

The government immediately announced that it was considering the elimination of jail terms for possession of marijuana, but balked at easing the penalties for the use or possession of "hard" drugs.

The Le Dain Commission on nonmedical uses of drugs released its recommendations yesterday following speculation that its report would deal only with marijuana. But the report of the five-man commission covered the whole spectrum of narcotics and cannabis drugs.

Health Minister John Munro said that the government supported only the recommendation of lenient penalties for possession, insofar as it applied to marijuana and the other cannabis drugs such as hashish. Munro said that the government did not support the commission's recommendation for low penalties for all drug possession.

The commission was formed a year ago to advise the government on drug policy while more detailed studies were under way. Its power is limited to making recommendations to the government. The commission said that laws against marijuana and other forms of cannabis should be less severe and should be enforced through Canada's food and drug act rather than the narcotics control act, which now carries penalties up to life imprisonment for pushers.

While recommending continued prosecution of persons trafficking in drugs, the commission urged abolition of jail sentences for "users" of the "psychotropic" or mind-altering drugs: The whole range from tranquilizers pep pills, marijuana and hashish, to heroin and opiates. A maximum fine of $100 was suggested as an alternative punishment.

"There is universal agreement," the commission report said, "that cannabis is not a narcotic and should not be classified legally with the opiate narcotics."

The commission, headed by York University Law School Dean Gerald Le Dain, was unanimous on all points except the recommendation of reduced penalties for possession. Commissioner Marie-Andree Bertrand, a criminology professor at the University of Montreal, called for aboltion of all penalties for possession of marijuana and hashish.

"While we feel that the offense of simple possession should be retained on the statute book, pending further investigation and analysis, which we hope to carry out in the ensuing year, its impact of the individual should be reduced as much as possible," the report said.

The Royal Canadian Mounted Police, which makes most of the drug arrests, would not comment on the commission's action.

Dr. J. Robinson Unwin, director of the adolescent department at the Allan Memorial Institute in Montreal, which works with drug-troubled teenagers, said that he "utterly agrees" with the commission recommendations. "It was the most sensible thing the government could have done," he said.

Commented a 19-year-old Montreal college student: "That's groovy, man. But what will we do with all the American kids who will want to move here now?"

Mental Hospital Aide Seized

Hauppauge—A 51-year-old attendan at Suffolk Psychiatric Hospital was arrested yesterday on a charge of having sold drugs to a former mental patient who died Wednesday of an overdose of barbiturates.

Detectives identified the suspect as Mrs. Dorothy L. Miller of 9 Cedar St., Selden, a psychiatric aide at the hospital, a state institution for Suffolk residents, located at Central Islip State Hospital. Police said that they seized at her home more than 14,000 barbiturates in pill and capsule form, and two additional kilograms of barbiturates plus several hypodermics and needles.

Police said that Mrs. Miller met Mrs. Louise S. Johansen, 47, of 9 Edgewood Ave., Port Jefferson, while Mrs. Johansen was a patient at the hospital last year. Police said that Mrs. Miller had access to Mrs. Johansen's records and sold drugs to Mrs. Johansen.

Mrs. Johansen was pronounced dead at her home of an overdose of barbiturates at 1 PM Wednesday. The Suffolk medical examiner, Dr. Sidney Weinberg, said yesterday that the official cause of death would be pending until toxological tests were completed.

Mrs. Miller was arrested in Central Islip and charged with fourth-degree selling of drugs, a felony. Police refused to say where the drugs were obtained.

Dr. James Brice, the director of Suffolk Psychiatric Hospital, said that Mrs. Johansen was admitted to the hospital Dec. 2, 1969, and was released Dec. 24. She was discharged from the hospital's care Jan. 6, 1970. Brice said that Mrs. Miller worked in a team with a doctor and a social worker from 4 to 9 PM and then, until midnight, made certain that patients received proper medical care. Brice had no comment on Mrs. Miller's arrest.

Mrs. Miller was arraigned before District Judge Alexander Kramer. She was held in $5,000 bail and scheduled to return Tuesday with an attorney.

Suffolk police arrested two other drug suspects John DiMartino, 21, of 175 W. 19th St., Deer Park, a musician, was arrested and charged with sale of hashish. Also arrested was Gary Lukowicz, 22, of 48 Kilburn Ave., Huntington, a clamdigger, who was charged with sale of marijuana. Both were arraigned before Kramer and held in $250 bail for examination July 9.

2

BEHIND THE NEWS

Here are the special sections—and their highlights, features and insights—in the pages of Newsday today.

SPORTS—Pages 16-23

OPEN SOUNDOFF: Dave Hill, battling for the lead in the U.S. Open golf tournament, labels the course "farm land."

READY TO CONCEDE: Battista's rivals figure he's a cinch to win his third Newsday Eastern Open bowling crown tonight.

WEEKEND WITH NEWSDAY—Pages 1W-44W

SPEAKING OF YOSSARIAN: The role of the reluctant hero of "Catch-22" seems ready-made for Alan Arkin, a Yossarian type.

RADICAL RADICALIZED: A Long Islander, who served 20 months for refusing the draft, describes his imprisonment.

VIEWPOINTS—Pages 1A-3A

UNIQUE? Not the U.S., Flora Lewis says, in a look at the problems of education vs. freedom vs. tranquility.

HAWK TALK: I. F. Stone levels a blast at the seven dovish senators who endorsed aiding Israel with more jets.

BUSINESS—Page 28-Back Page

SICK ECONOMY: Economist finds that the administration is trying aspirin where stronger medicine is needed.

Altshul	3A	News Calendar	15
Art Topics	28N	Obituaries	26
Business Page	28-32	Burton On Books	23W
Classified	14A-43A	On the Isle	42W
Comics	40W, 41W	Oppenheimer	31W
Editorial	1A	Radio	42W
Gelmis	33W	Resort & Travel	15-19W
Genauer	27W	Sports	16-23
Horoscope	40W	Stock Market	30-31
Kitman	39W	Television	42W, 43W
Lewis	2A	Thimmesch	2A
Moses	2A	Viewpoints	1A
Movies	36W, 37W	Weekender Puzzle	29W

Total Pages Today—120

THE WEATHER

Sunny today; high in 70s. Clear tonight; low in 50s. Partly cloudy tomorrow; high in 70s. Precipitation probability 10% today, near zero tonight, 10% tomorrow. Sun sets 8:31 PM today, rises 5:25 AM tomorrow. (Tide tables in Sports Section.)

Newsday

Anthony E. Insolia, Day Managing Editor; Arthur G. Perfall, Night Managing Editor; Lou Schwartz, Assistant Managing Editor; Richard W. Estrin, Executive News Editor; Paul Back, Art Director; David G. Gelman, National Editor; Mel Opotowsky, Suffolk Editor; Joseph C. Koenenn, Nassau Editor; Stanley Asimov, Assistant to the Publisher; David Targe, Advertising Director; John J. Mullen, Circulation Manager; Frank M. Farrell, Business Manager; James Genovese, Production Manager; David R. George, Promotion Manager.

Nassau Telephone: 741-1234. Suffolk Telephones: 588-2121, 665-2161, 368-0210, 643-8183, 727-2228. New York City Telephone: 291-0330.

Second class postage paid at Garden City, N.Y. Published each weekday afternoon by Newsday, Inc., 550 Stewart Ave., Garden City, N.Y. 11530, and Union Ave., Ronkonkoma, N.Y. 11779. Subscription rates: 5¢ a copy. By carrier 30¢ weekly. By mail postpaid in United States $15.00 per year in advance.

Newsday

Long Island's *Newsday* is the epitome of contemporary makeup practice in tabloid format. Although front-page emphasis varies greatly from day to day, these pages are fairly typical. Notice the horizontal and even modular structure of the first two news pages.

different days—a strong head and related art on a single top story one day, a large-type summary of an especially good interpretive story on another, a spread of feature photos on another, and so on. *Newsday*'s last page is invariably reserved for business news, not sports, for many of its potential 2.5 million readers commute to businesses in Manhattan.

Variation in inside-page makeup ranges on tabloids nearly as widely as it does on full-size papers. The two examples shown are representative: the *Defender* inside pages are standard urban tabloid; *Newsday*'s are distinctly contemporary, using simple headline forms in largely horizontal array.

Summary

The following table summarizes ideally the main points that distinguish traditional, modern, and contemporary design, format, and makeup characteristics. No newspaper is likely to fall in the same column in every characteristic.

Contemporary and Offset The front and second front pages of *The Paper* of Oshkosh, Wisconsin, are contemporary in every respect, including lower-case headlines, a rarity elsewhere. The art is of especially high quality (the photograph in the upper left of the front page was in brilliant color). *The Paper*, founded in 1967, had the advantage of starting with, not converting to, new technology. Unfortunately, it has ceased publication as a daily.

Courtesy The Paper (Oshkosh, Wisconsin)

	TRADITIONAL	MODERN	CONTEMPORARY
Format	Column rules with little shoulder. Traditional rules and dashes throughout.	Column rules with wider shoulders or white space between columns. Some rules and dashes.	White space instead of column rules and all other rules and dashes with few exceptions.
	Column widths fixed, usually quite narrow.	Some variation in column widths; many two-column leads to separate heads; basic column widths often extremely narrow.	Basic column width wide, often varied to produce special displays.
	Margins usually narrow.	Margins often narrow.	Margins often wide.
Design	Headlines tend to fill out column, leaving little or no white space around them.	Headlines run to modern forms, such as flush left, allowing some white space.	Headlines designed to permit as much white space as possible.
	Limited range of headline forms; usually traditional faces; frequent multiple decks.	Fairly wide range of headline forms, from modified traditional to contemporary; modern faces.	Fairly limited range of simple headline forms; contemporary design.
	Fairly wide range of type families in headlines, many of traditional design.	Headline faces limited to one or two families, usually of modern design.	All headlines usually from a single family of modern design.
	Body type usually small and without much leading (with exceptions). Old-style faces preferred (with exceptions).	Body type usually large, more heavily leaded, and varied in size (larger when set in two-column measure).	Body type usually large legibility face of modern design and very heavily leaded, larger still when set in extra-wide measure.
Makeup	Chiefly single-column heads; two and three-column heads for variation. Vertical effect.	Deliberate mixture of single- and multiple-column heads; page still anchored to one- and two-column major heads. Neither distinctly horizontal nor vertical effect.	Mostly multicolumn heads with a few singles. Essentially horizontal effect.
	Limited day-to-day variation in makeup patterns.	Wide day-to-day variation in makeup patterns.	Editors try to make each day's front page like no other.

TRADITIONAL	MODERN	CONTEMPORARY
Main emphasis at top of page. Feature and minor stories below fold. Lead story usually upper right.	Emphasis spread among chief focal points on page. Main emphasis less clearly at top; usually upper right but sometimes upper left.	Emphasis almost anywhere on the page. Upper left preferred to upper right.
Balance assured across top of page; top overbalances lower half.	Balance assured throughout page by attention to relative weights at focal points.	Some deliberate imbalance within clearly understood limits.
Inside pages made up in same patterns and with same materials as front pages.	Inside pages often very different from front pages in makeup and even in design.	Inside pages often include special materials but carry out same patterns as front pages.
Art used sparingly, in moderate size and traditional position, usually not in outside columns.	Art used lavishly and in widely varying sizes but placed for balance. Some freedom in style and location of cutlines.	Art used lavishly for dramatic effect in widely varying sizes and locations on the page. Cutlines often treated unconventionally.
Carefully prescribed captions and cutlines. Column is basic unit manipulated in makeup.	Makeup distributes masses, with some attention to their shape.	Story or story-and-art unit is basic element; much attention given to its shape.
Deliberate tombstoning and other makeup practices often produce cluttered effect, especially at top of page.	Tombstoning avoided and other measures taken to separate major heads.	Every headline separate from every other headline.

Three Front Pages of "Traditional" Design

The Chattanooga *Times,* which bears a close resemblance to its nephew, the New York *Times,* has moderated its traditional design slightly over the years. But it still retains its own special headline typefaces and is essentially vertical in structure — although more multicolumn heads and larger pictures are now in regular use.

The *Sun* of Baltimore also uses traditional display faces. It is anchored at midpage and above to single-column heads, but it uses large cuts high and low on the page, carefully respecting informal balance.

The New York *Times* is also vertical in emphasis and clings to its traditional headline forms, even the multiple-deck pattern at the top of the page. But the lower half of the page is more open and horizontal.

Three Front Pages of "Modern" Design   All three of these pages are basically modern. They use a major one-column head with a deck to anchor the top of the page; they follow the standard rules of makeup, the Knoxville *News-Sentinel* somewhat more so than the others; heads are carefully patterned under the cuts. But the student should be able to spot several contemporary themes here, as well.

Courtesy the Louisville Times

Courtesy the State Journal (Frankfort, Kentucky)

Two Front Pages of "Contemporary" Design

The Louisville *Times* is characteristically horizontal, with single-column heads the exception. Note the "human-condition" art and the way it is placed on the page. Note, too, the six-column format, which is carried out throughout the paper (except for classified-ad pages). Every issue, though using the same basic elements, is different in striking ways from every other.

The *State Journal* of Frankfort, Kentucky, an offset paper serving a city of less than 25,000 persons, is strikingly contemporary in design. Although the format is eight columns, it is always open, horizontal, and modular in part. It uses pictures in dramatic sizes and locations (without sacrificing balance) and has exceptional day-to-day variation in makeup patterns.

12

Newsflow Management

The copy editor is part of a stream of decision making that begins when the reporter decides what parts of the story to include and what parts to exclude, and ends with the reader deciding what parts of the paper he'll read and what parts he'll skim. Between the poles stands the copy desk and its manager—the news editor or assistant managing editor or slot man or copy-desk chief—who makes the critical judgments at the critical juncture in the flow chart—the juncture between editorial and production decision making. The desk's manager is the last institutional gatekeeper and has final responsibility for everything in the news sections of the paper. The reader, of course, must take it from there.

The slot man is, in a very real sense, a production manager. It is his duty to coordinate most of the separate operations that contribute to the manufacture of the product. It is a mass-produced product, but its ingredients vary from day to day and even from hour to hour. The news editor has a fixed space, more or less, at the start of each day, but he has no certain conception of the nature or shape of the materials that will become available to fill it. He knows that there are reporters on duty that day, like all other days. But he has no way of knowing for sure the volume or importance of the news they will turn up. He knows that the wire services send approximately the same wordage day after day, but he can't predict the worth or variety of the material they will transmit.

Every news day, therefore, is unpredictable. But the news editor must, come what may, convert it into one of the most predictable things in American life today—a newspaper which will be delivered at the subscriber's door or at a given newsstand at just about the same moment today as every other day. And he must do this with the joint efforts of several crews of fallible human beings, all of whom must work together unerringly, at high speed, and so steadily that their time is neither wasted nor squeezed too hard.

The Problem

If merely filling the space with available materials were the crux of the problem, however, the job would be relatively simple. But the space must be filled with the *latest and best* materials, arranged to give some clue to their relative importance and recency. How does the news editor perform this daily minor miracle without succumbing to drugs or madness? It helps to look at the problem as two major contradictions.

Space vs. Materials

The amount of space devoted to news in a specific issue of a newspaper is not decided ordinarily on the basis of how much news needs to be told. Unfortunately, the mechanical and financial exigencies of newspaper production usually dictate the amount of "news hole" and the shape it will take. The business office gets first crack at the total amount of space and may use it as much as it needs for the amount of advertising sold for display in that particular issue; the news editor must adjust his space requirements accordingly. In fact, he usually cannot participate even in the decision about what pages will be allotted to news and what to such other departments as sports, society, women's section, etc. This decision, too, is made at a higher level.

Ordinarily, the news editor is simply presented with dummies of the pages it is his duty to fill. His first working premise is that he has precisely this space and no more to work with. This is a generalization, of course, to which exceptions are sometimes made. If he is convinced he can't turn out a good paper in the space set, he may take the matter across channels to the business office and fight for extra or less news space. But he cannot depend on this working. He may or may not get his way, and if he tries too often, he'll be fired.

And occasionally the news editor is presented by the business office with a sudden change in the space available, even after he has started moving copy. Sometimes the advertising department makes an honest mistake. If it is discovered early enough, the news editor can make his adjustments with ease; if it is very late in the news day, the discovery can be just short of disastrous. Or the classified-advertising space allotments estimated at the beginning of the news day may change. Classified deadlines are usually later than display-ad deadlines, with the result that the final space they occupy may turn out to be anywhere from one to half a dozen columns more or less than the business-office estimate. This can have the harrowing effect of changing the news space by half a page or more at the eleventh hour. The editor has to be flexible enough to meet such a contingency.

Advance planning of the broad categories of news is possible to a limited extent. But the news editor is at the mercy of late news breaks at every stage in the creation of today's newspaper. The wire services send budgets at the start of each news cycle indicating what major stories to expect; the city editor plans the use of his reporters in advance, and he can gauge fairly well the length that *predictable* stories will run. But neither the wire services nor the city editor can allot space in advance for the unpredictable events that are the lifeblood of news and newsmen.

Time vs. Materials

The amount of time available to the desk is, like space, relatively fixed. Like all other parts of the newsroom, the desk works against deadlines. But the problem of time from the desk's standpoint is more complex than from the standpoint of the reporter. The reporter has only a few (usually only *one*) story to write by his deadline; the desk has all news copy to edit, mark, and get to the composing room. Hence, the desk depends on a steady flow of work to operate efficiently, not a "run and wait" schedule. The desk which operates from one crisis to another, interspersed with periods of idleness, can hardly be expected to do good work. Neither can the desk that has to do all its work ten minutes before deadline. It is up to the news editor to put the desk on the calm, even schedule that is the first requisite of careful editing.

Production, too, depends for its efficiency on the man in the slot. The composing-room superintendent cannot keep work flowing smoothly through his machines if the work does not flow smoothly to him. Pages cannot be made up when type is missing. The plate-making operation will break down altogether if it all must be done at the last minute. Whether or not the presses roll on time is therefore largely the responsibility of the news editor.

The deadlines the news editor must meet are of a particularly inexorable sort. The newspaper's edition times tie into a complex system of distribution, and if deadlines are not met, the whole network is thrown out of phase. But the editor is in a position to decide not to meet a deadline. He bases his decision on the worth of the story balanced against the probable cost in overtime and unsold papers and the ability of his editorial and production staffs to handle the delay. For example, if a major public disturbance breaks out shortly before the final edition is to roll, the news editor, perhaps in consultation with the managing editor, may decide to hold the "final" until the disturbance has been thoroughly covered. An early edition might be held for a late-breaking story which would have its greatest value in that edition. A "first-run town," let us say—one of those served by the first mail edition—is the scene of an important story. The story may be good enough for all editions but it will be worth most in its own region. If the delay means missing distribution connections, the editor can let the first run go on time, meanwhile pushing the late story through as rapidly as possible; Page One is made over as soon as the story is set, and the press is stopped momentarily and the new page substituted. In this way the first run is printed on schedule, yet most of the first-run papers contain the new story.

On all hot-type letterpress papers—which include most of the larger newspapers—all the news editor's timing decisions are largely influenced by one particular production bottleneck—the stereotype operation. It is not possible to stereotype a lot of pages at one time, except in plants where the plate-making process has been completely or partially automated. The orderly construction of the newspaper therefore requires that completed pages move through the stereo department in a steady flow over a period of several hours. Consequently, in order to prevent a bottleneck, the news editor must release his inside pages for plating early, and long before those—such as Page One—which plate up late.

Material destined for pages that may be plated early must be chosen at a time when the news editor is in no position to know what the total news picture is going to be for that day. On a dull day, he may find himself with several Page One stories frozen on an inside page. And the material must not be subject to change as the news day progresses; if compelling late developments should come along on a story already plated, the editor must (a) replate that page (which would upset the plant routine unnecessarily and increase costs), (b) carry the new material elsewhere in the paper (which would confuse the reader), or (c) do without the later developments (which would deprive the reader).

Preliminaries

A good news editor does not actually break down his job as we have done here, solving the time and space aspects of the problem separately; he works on them simultaneously, throughout the news day. The early steps he can take to lighten his burden later in the day are:

Measuring Available Space

Subject to the possible shifts mentioned above, the available news space may be determined from the dummies supplied to the desk with the ads drawn in. By merely totting up the space left over, the editor can get a more or less exact picture of the space he will need to fill. If the dummies are not available, he can measure up the page forms, after the ads are in place.

The editor also notes the *shapes* the space takes. Although Page One will take the same shape every day— varied only by the quirks of Page One "musts" not under the editor's control—inside pages vary from day to day in the proportion of space available for news. "Open" pages (having lots of room above the ads) can carry multiple-column cuts, for instance.

Large newspapers often keep track of all copy with an elaborate copy-control system so that the desk has an instant view at any time in the day about how much more copy will be needed to fill. Small newspapers often do without such a careful system, the editor relying on hunch, past experience, and frequent checks with the composing room to accomplish the same end. But even the hunch player needs to know at the start whether this Tuesday paper is larger or smaller than the usual Tuesday paper at this time of year.

Gauging the Probable News Day

As we have already suggested, it is not possible to predict what sort of news day lies ahead every time. However, the news editor has ways of guessing whether he can expect a heavier- or lighter-than-average news day in terms of volume of local and nonlocal copy.

The city desk, of course, can give the best rough estimate of the local situation. But the slot man has nobody to consult on the wire-service potentialities. He depends on other ways of estimating the wire-service volume. For instance, each wire service informs editors about what predictable news it will be sending in an advance "budget"—a preliminary statement of stories that are upcoming that day. Then they keep informing editors throughout the day of stories not predicted in the budget but which will move soon. By following these clues, the news editor can do some planning even before he sees many of the stories.

But there are subtler hints than this. A slow day can be predicted by an astute editor on the basis of the sort of material that is being sent. If the wire service sends minor features at a time that good new tops on overnight stories are ordinarily rolling, the editor can presume that—for a while, at least—things will be slow. If, on the other hand, the service is sending good news stories at a time when it is usually sending "advances" for the next day's paper, it can be presumed that the day will be a heavy one.

Another way of judging the news day is to watch the "splits"—those times when the wire service switches from sending national copy from a central point to sending regional or state copy from another point. If they occur at the usual times, then the news day appears to be normal; if they don't, it is probably abnormal in one way or another.

Checking Everything Already in Type

For various reasons, the editor may find that a lot of material is already in type as his day begins. Material already in type falls into these categories:

Overset is type which simply didn't get into the edition it was intended for, for one reason or another. It is usually assembled in galleys in the composing room and not killed except on orders from the newsroom. The usual procedure is to get a proof of all the overset. Some of it can be salvaged with a few minor proof corrections and used either as second-day or "time copy." Pressure on the news hole, however, may dictate that almost all overset be killed, even if resources have been wasted in setting it; today's news will probably contain something better.

Early copy has been sent to the composing room and set the day before or earlier still for use today. It is sound to move some inside-page material the day before to help take the pressure off the composing room or the desk. On afternoon papers, much can actually be done at the end of the previous day, after the last edition has rolled, to ease this pressure. On morning papers it is more likely that this chore will be done early in the news day. In any case, the news editor will need proofs of this material or just notes identifying all these stories and indicating the amount of space they will fill.

Time copy and filler is material deliberately backlogged to give the editors and makeup men some flexibility. The two terms are not synonymous. "Filler" is time copy consisting of short paragraphs, usually without a headline of any sort. "Time copy" is the term for the entire range of material of this type, from fillers to long story-and-picture features. Filler and time copy are available by mail from the wire services and from other sources.

One of the most important early steps in the news editor's job is to make certain that plenty of material of this type is available—and in variety. He must make sure that he has plenty of filler, plenty of time shorties, plenty of longer features, and plenty of "plug art," in a wide range of sizes. Plug art consists of cuts that are virtually as timeless as time copy and used in much the same way, either to fill a hole or to plug a spot for a picture the editor knows is coming later in the day. It has a use on early inside pages, too. The editor can't wait for good local art or timely spot pictures from such sources as AP Wirephoto for this kind of page. The page has to go, and it will be a better page with some sort of art. Plug art is not necessarily poor art. It simply does not depend on timeliness for its effectiveness.

Much time copy and plug art is set and never used, but it is better to have too much than too little. It takes the desperation out of having to fill holes, and it can always be replaced in later editions with live news. More flexible makeup practices have made it easier in recent years to avoid wasting space with time copy and filler.

Feature material like the comics, puzzles, clothing patterns, etc., which occupy all too much precious space the editor could use for more serious material, usually go into regular feature pages typically handled so automatically that the news editor is not required to check on them except in an emergency. However, the comic strips and other features, including staff-originated material, which are regularly carried on certain news pages must be checked at the beginning of the day and usually must be deducted in computing available space.

Moving Copy

With these preliminaries out of the way, the editor is ready to start the orderly procession of news copy. Early in the day, he is:

—watching and maintaining a flow of work through the desk and composing room

—keeping a check on the volume of copy moved

—steadily moving along plenty of good inside-page material not subject to change and guarding against the possibility that in moving too much of it he is crowding out better material which he has not yet even seen

—moving plenty of shorts, both for the inside pages and for Page One

—watching for material for special pages, such as financial or entertainment

—dummying inside pages. Copy and dummies go to the composing room as soon as they are finished in order to get early pages into the forms (or pasteups).

—substituting plugs, if he is handling an early edition, on inside pages for material ultimately destined for them that is delayed for one reason or another

—holding back on key stories for Page One and other good positions in the paper, sketching out possible layouts long before dummies are required. Sometimes a Page One story can move early, marked HTK, if necessary, in order to postpone the decision as to the play it will get. This is especially desirable if the story is longer than usual. Any takes that can be moved in advance should be to avoid rushing the composing room later. If the story is developing, some of these takes may be superseded by adds reflecting later developments. The news editor simply has to use his judgment whether to risk this or not.

—watching the balance of the news for that day. Owing to the wide range of appeal a daily paper must have, the editor tries to balance the "light" against the "heavy," especially on Page One. So he particularly watches for features, local or otherwise, which will take the curse of extreme solemnity off the paper's offerings. Of course he won't use a weak feature in place of a solid news story just for the sake of balance. But the better-balanced offering is the better offering, provided the editor doesn't have to strain to achieve it.

This summary, though by no means complete, gives some idea of the range of the news editor's duties in moving copy during the early and middle portions of the day. Unless these early stages proceed without delay and confusion, the editor cannot devote enough of his attention during the later stages to the material for the "showy" pages, including Page One. As we have seen, the editor does much of the spadework on these pages in the earlier phases. But usually the conscientious editor avoids making final decisions on them too early in the day, for it is here that he gets his last chance to meet his ultimate objective—getting the most of the latest and best into the paper.

As deadlines on early editions approach, the editor begins to feel the pinch of a special copy-control problem: when to stop moving the short takes of stories that are breaking late and save them for later editions. It is at this stage that the desk can suffer a bad case of the jitters if the editor's planning has been inadequate. Holding back too long on too much material can result in unnecessary last-minute pressure on both the composing room and the desk, producing serious errors and frayed tempers.

The news editor needs time before deadline for another important job—supervising makeup on the key pages. Large papers sometimes leave this job to a makeup editor who spends most of his time in the composing room but works closely with the copy-desk chief. On smaller papers, the news editor usually is his own makeup editor. That means that he not only dummies all the pages but is also responsible for "steering them in"—seeing to it that the printers actually put them together as he planned and helping the printers to meet last-minute emergencies. This is a closer supervision, on the whole, than the editor exercises over the makeup of lesser inside pages, and it is performed right at the composing "stones" (now almost always made of steel, not stone), the surfaces on which the pages are physically assembled. The news editor watches every step in the makeup or offset pasteup. The importance of two points already raised in earlier chapters can be seen here: the editor should know something about type and be able to read type upside down and backwards; he should have a good personal relationship with the men in the shop. They are working at top speed and the tension is high.

Among the things the editor does as the pages are being made up are:

—checking to see that major stories have been set and are going into the pages as planned

—choosing shorts for Page One, assuming he has not done this during dummying

—checking all stories labeled "must" to make sure they are not inadvertently left out

—helping the printer guard against makeup errors or misinterpretation of his dummies. Makeup errors include failure to get a changing or sectional story into the paper with all its new tops, ads, and inserts in the proper order, the omission of rules, dashes, or slugs, errors in jumps, etc.

—adjusting story length where necessary. The exigencies of makeup often force last-minute bite-offs. The editor must be at hand to decide what paragraphs a story can lose without too great damage. Some papers allow the printers to do this, with results that are often disastrous.

—reading headlines—at least the bigger ones—in type as an additional check against conspicuous errors

—deciding what stories must be withheld, if he has not estimated space and type correctly. Minor wire stories are usually the first to go. The editor may have anticipated this possibility and marked some stories "optional." In general, all local material should be used if possible. It has been gathered and written at greater expense and has a more certain audience. But any of it that would be nearly or just as good tomorrow as today may be held back. An advance, for instance, on an event taking place on Friday is usually as good in the Tuesday paper as in the Monday paper.

"Reading the Paper"

After the first edition has begun to roll, the desk checks rush copies of the paper for errors. This job is called "reading the paper"; suddenly the copyreader becomes a proofreader. As in so many practices discussed here, different desks have different procedures in correcting the first run. On the New York *Times,* for instance, each copy editor is responsible for checking over all the stories he has handled. On other papers, each copy editor is responsible for reading an assigned segment. The *extent* of the correcting at this stage varies from desk to desk, too. Some desks will be satisfied to check headlines on Page One. Others will correct every typographical or other error on Page One and all the conspicuous errors (in headlines, cut captions, etc.) on the inside pages. Still others are able to give the entire news space a thorough reading.

How extensive the corrections can be is determined in large measure by mechanical limitations. If the composing room is setting copy for a second edition due shortly, it may not be able to spare enough men to manage all the corrections the desk would like to make.

Here are some other things reading the paper can accomplish:

1. The news editor can double-check the fine points of his page makeup. Some things can easily elude him in makeup or pasteup. It is often only after the paper has begun to run that he can catch such mistakes as faulty column rules, inappropriate dashes, wrong materials used in a box, etc.

2. The jumps may be checked. This involves making sure that the jump "reads"—that lines have not been lost or disarranged—and checking the continuation lines, both "continued on" and "continued from."

3. The desk can watch for unfortunate juxtapositions in the page. If a filler about the national birth rate directly follows a wedding story, for instance, a change now can spare the paper and the wedding principals embarrassment. Some desks are careful to check adjoining headlines to avoid similarities in wording and structure.

4. The desk can check against the possibility of lost stories. Sometimes a list of key inside-page stories is kept to provide a check. Often the city desk will check all of its stories with a view to tracing any that might be missing. Such a check by the state desk is common, too. When there are several regional editions, a careful check must be made of the stories that have been shifted between editions.

5. The news editor is now in a position to check his bite-offs—the cuts he ordered while the pages were being made up. If they are unsatisfactory, he can make the page over in some way to restore the missing paragraphs or insert a transitional sentence to smooth over a rough spot caused by a cut.

6. The entire paper can be checked for the ever-present possibility that a story or picture carries a head or caption intended for another.

Page corrections are made in the manner of proof corrections. A line is drawn from the error to the margin and the correction noted. Gross errors are often corrected right at the forms under the direction of the news editor.

How important does a correction have to be to warrant a page makeover? Editors in general like to correct all errors within the capabilities of the mechanical department. This is a good rule of thumb, for if more are ordered, the preparation of the next edition is jeopardized. Practices vary from place to place. A routine typographical error, the only one on a page which will be replated in the next edition anyway, can usually wait. Any conspicuous error, even though not disastrous, is worth fixing at once. This does not necessarily mean stopping the press and waiting until the correction can be processed, but it does mean getting the correction made and the new plate on the press as soon as it can be made. Errors which will cause acute embarrassment to the paper or its readers usually require stopping the press and waiting for the new plate. Errors of such magnitude that they hold the threat of libel may call for not only the stopping the press but recalling all copies of the run.

Handling Editions

Newspapers differ a great deal in the number and types of editions they produce in a day. The smaller papers usually have only one. But even many in the small-to-medium class, not to mention the large ones, have anywhere from two to half a dozen editions for the copy desk to worry about. Meeting a series of editions compounds the necessity of being able to adjust routine to new and difficult fast-developing stories. Planning the different editions for each news cycle is therefore a subject for forethought.

Why should there be more than one edition? The answers are closely related to one central consideratiton: competition. First, a newspaper may produce a series of editions *to meet the special news needs of certain areas* in its territory. The paper that is best for the city of publication may not be best for outlying territories, and vice versa. So a series of "state" or "area" editions may be made over from the "city" edition to put the emphasis on the news needs of the area to which they are sent. They carry different materials and display them differently for maximum effectiveness in the disparate locales.

A newspaper may produce a series of editions *to meet competition for street sales.* Usually this applies only in the largest cities and in cities where competition between newspapers is brisk. In New York, for instance, afternoon editions are issued from midmorning to late afternoon, and morning papers start early the previous evening. A paper may issue as many as eight separate afternoon editions as a matter of routine, each designed to attract customers at the newsstands by appearing to be later than the previous edition and later and better than other papers on the same newsstand. Street editions in the larger cities are often specially timed to meet major population movements. New York morning tabloids have a heavy sale among homeward-bound theatergoers, for instance, and Detroit papers adjust their editions to shift changes in the automobile plants.

Besides essentially street-sale and area editions, newspapers usually issue at least one edition especially designed *for home delivery in the city of origin.* Home editions are often strikingly different from street editions, for instance, being designed for the armchair reader rather than the man on the street. They are often more sedate in appearance and emphasize completeness rather than lateness.

Finally, daily editions of many newspapers are designed *to attract a particular kind of reader* by coming out at the precise moment when a type of news he fancies is just in—and complete. For instance, the Wall Street final, carrying complete closing stock quotations and financial news, "hits the street" just as the financial district is closing for the day. The summer sports finals are rolled just in time to include complete coverage of the afternoon ball games.

Newspapers nowadays rarely issue "extra" editions, whose purpose was *to capitalize on a story of superlative importance* whenever it occurred. Radio competition was largely responsible for the demise of the extra as such, but the word hangs on. Some papers like to attach the word to regular editions which are topped by some better-than-usual story.

Copy Control and Makeover

Problems in meeting editions can be summarized under two chief headings: copy control and page makeover. Each edition, as we have seen, has its special content or content emphasis. Certain stories are especially dedicated to certain editions, either meaning that they run in those editions alone or that they run in one position in one edition and a different position in another edition. The desk therefore must operate some sort of copy-control system to be sure that (1) the appropriate stories are in type at the right time, and (2) they actually get into the appropriate spot in the appropriate edition and are thereafter killed or shifted according to plan.

Production of a series of editions involves page makeover, but the number of pages made over and the extent of the changes varies considerably. It is possible to label as a second edition a paper which is identical with the first except for a couple of minor changes on Page One. More often, however, anywhere from two to half a dozen pages are made over from one edition to the next.

Thus the desk must not only send appropriate copy to the composing room, it must also give the composing room precise instructions about substituting new material for old material. And it must do all this at the appropriate time. A skilled "floor man" can make over a page with remarkable speed, but the copy desk should allow him enough time by doing its own part of the job thoroughly and in plenty of time. This usually means that the slot man must make most of his decisions about the second edition shortly after the first edition has been wrapped up. It also usually means that he must move the copy destined for the second edition during the lull between the time the last story for the first edition is sent to the composing room and the time the first edition is being checked for error; or earlier still; or shortly after the first edition is corrected. The second edition won't be ready to roll until pages are made up and pages can't be made up until the type that goes into them is in hand.

Instructions are usually outlined on two written forms: a "kill sheet" and a dummy for the new page. The kill sheet is a copy of the page as it appeared in the earlier edition, marked by the copy desk to show what material will remain and what is to be pulled out to make room for new material. The dummy shows how new and old material are to be arranged for the new edition. Workable practices for marking kill sheets and makeover dummies can be devised by anyone who has clearly in mind what must be done. Stories and art which are to be killed (or at least removed from this page) are often marked on the kill sheet with a solid black, vertical line. Items to be retained are marked with a small black circle.

The same page after the changes have been made:

Courtesy the Wisconsin State Journal (Madison)

If only a few changes are necessary, the makeover dummy may show them only and not the elements which are not to be shifted in any way.

Edition changes are rarely justified when they are based on content changes inside the paper only. If an edition is designed for some special reader group, it can best be served at both levels, inside and out front. This applies not only to editions designed to meet regional demands but also to the Wall Street final, a racing extra, etc. The regional edition will be different from other regional editions in both state-page and front-page content and emphasis. In the Wall Street final, it is standard practice to put some sort of summarizing information on Page One, with full detail inside. Page One traditionally carries, at a minimum, a nontechnical "news-page" summary of the day's market news, while the financial pages carry a fuller treatment in story form and a table of all closing quotations; a sports final might carry a

Courtesy the Wisconsin State Journal (Madison)

The Same Inside Page in Three Editions

This split page is a state page in the first two editions and a city page in the final. Thus the first changes relatively little, while the second is largely killed.

Courtesy the Wisconsin State Journal *(Madison)*

baseball roundup or at least all scores on Page One, with full details on the sports pages.

For this reason, almost any edition change involves some sort of Page One makeover and at least one inside-page makeover. Sometimes a number of inside pages are involved. The three inside pages shown on page 307 illustrate what can happen to a state page in two regional and one in-city editions. The material that is of considerable interest in the outlying territory but of substantially lesser significance in the city is replaced with material geared to city readers. It becomes, in the later edition, essentially a city page, rather than a state page.

The first of these editions goes to the most distant cities in the territory. Although the page is largely unchanged from the first to the second edition, both being noncity editions, notice how the emphasis is shifted. The Grantsburg story tops the first edition because Grantsburg is a "first-edition town." The story is not killed in the second edition but shifted to give it a different news value. A late story from a second-edition town takes its place. There are only three kills: two minor stories from first-edition towns and the coupon, which was pulled out to make room for news.

The changes from second to final editions are much more extensive. More of the state material could be retained were there not so much good city news to take its place. As it turns out, only four stories go through all three editions.

Makeover often involves page changes, too. In the first two editions, this page was the first in the second section. But as a city page, it has been shifted into another position in the final. This is a routine change and has obvious reasons; it belongs with state news in the first two editions, and as the best state page gets the most conspicuous state location; it belongs with city news in the third edition and as the best city page gets the best city position.

But even though most edition changes necessarily involve making over more than one page, they should not involve more pages than the size of the production crew or the plate-making bottleneck allows. The desk should plan the first edition carefully enough to confine major changes in other editions to the mini-

mum number of pages. In the illustration above, for example, only two pages needed to be made over to get in all the changes the desk wanted; material subject to change was planned for them and them only, not scattered throughout the paper. Makeover can be justified only when it affects a minimum number of inside pages.

Regionalizing the News

As the newspaper has come to be related more to a region than to the city of publication, its whole task has changed, and with it, the kinds of editions. The pattern especially on evening papers of a series of "late city" editions for street sales, characteristic of many metropolitan papers about thirty years ago, has gone the way of the street-sales extra. Some regular dayside editions, especially racing finals and a late Wall Street edition containing closing stock quotations, survive in some circumstances. But today the editioning of newspapers is much more often based not on the demands of special readers in the city but on the requirements of many people in a large geographical region. These regions often have peculiar shapes and often cross state lines. The Louisville *Courier-Journal,* for example, serves the information needs of people who live in a region bounded by Missouri on the west and Virginia on the east and includes a substantial part of Indiana. It manages to do it with a concept, a system of staffing, and a series of editions both interesting and expensive.

In concept, the *Courier-Journal* is different from most newspapers. It does not rely on the bane of most state editors, the "stringer." Stringers are reporters who are paid for their "string"—by the column inch of published output. They are either competent reporters or editors of other newspapers in the region or nonprofessionals. The professionals save the best material for their own papers. The nonprofessionals often don't know a good story when they see it. In their attempts to "localize" their regional editions, therefore, state editors often carry trivia they wouldn't dream of putting in their own home editions.

The *Courier-Journal*'s policy has been to run only news of genuinely regional interest and, except for the Indiana edition, to carry most of the best of it in all editions. This means paying a small staff of good re-porters in the regions concerned and a staff of general-ists who can go out on special stories and pictures. It also requires top-level management to make it all work out every day of the week, and close coordina-tion with the circulation departments to get all the papers to right areas at the right times.

Editioning, then, involves largely the location of the story in the paper and not whether it runs at all. Few stories run in one regional edition only. Many run in all editions. Some run in more than one regional edition but in different locations: what is on Page One in an edition for one area is carried on the split page of another; less important news is on the split page of the area edition but on the slop page of others. So at least three pages have to be made over to make the system work—front, split, and slop. Two house staffs are actually involved in editioning—a large Kentucky staff and a smaller Indiana staff. The edi-tions are West, East, and Mid-Kentucky, Louisville area, and Indiana.

On pages 310–311 are three front pages of the *Courier-Journal* and four of the five split pages that are the key to the paper's success. Only the art and two stories are retained on the front pages of all editions, "U. S. Force" in the upper left and "Nixons Welcome" at the bottom. "Newport Bingo" is front-page news out in the state but not in the city or out of state. In the city edition, it is replaced on the front page by a national story and is run inside: it is deleted from the Indiana edition. A Louisville story with a regional aspect replaces a Kentucky-edition national story in the city and Indiana editions.

Much more extensive makeover is required on the split page. Nothing in the Indiana edition runs on other split pages. "UK Press Freedom" runs in all Kentucky editions in the same spot, except the city edition in which it is shifted inside. "Newport Bingo" goes from Page One in state editions to the split page in the seven-star (city) edition. A Bowling Green story is on the split page only in the edition serving its area; in others it runs inside and is left out of the edition that reaches the opposite end of the state.

The reader can imagine the impositions this system forces on the copy desk: careful attention to traffic from edition to edition; extra head writing to accom-modate the changes from place to place; close atten-tion to variance in length as a story is shifted; a lot of professional dedication to bring to such widely separated areas the best combination of stories to serve their purposes. The quality of service does not vary from edition to edition; the best is not reserved for the large urban readership and whatever will do in a hurry palmed off on outstate readers. Every story is as carefully staffed with highly qualified professionals as the most complex central-city series. This kind of excellent service is not typical of newspapers gen-erally, but it gives them all something to aim at.

Meeting Emergencies

Emergencies of an almost limitless variety can disrupt the orderly routine of newspaper production. When a New England hurricane flooded out the Providence *Journal* and *Bulletin,* it was equal to the situation, managing to publish in the plant of a Boston paper without missing an edition. When a sleet storm com-pletely disrupted electric power for days, the LaMoure, North Dakota, *Chronicle* got out on time by hooking a gasoline engine to the press. Physical emergencies like those evoke ingenious adaptive behavior, but they are rare, unlike day-to-day *news* emergencies, which present themselves frequently and demand rapid, flexible, cool-headed reactions of the copy desk.

It would be impossible, of course, to catalogue every imaginable news emergency and how to deal with it. If it were possible, there would be no real emergencies left. But news emergencies in general may be discussed with a view to meeting them.

Some "emergencies," if that isn't pushing the word too far, are more or less predictable. When the gov-ernor is at death's door, certain advance steps may be taken to make it easier to meet the "emergency" of an announcement of his death half an hour before the final edition rolls. Standing obituary copy can be set in type. Then one take of new material can be pushed through in a few minutes to pick up on it. A rather full coverage of such an event is possible, in fact, if a lot of sidebar material is gotten up in advance and

One Day: Three Front Pages, Four Split Pages
The five-star (mid-Kentucky), seven-star (city final), and West editions, showing changes in an ordinary news day.

pushed into an inside page after the word comes. It is even possible to get up a complete page of such material, plus carryover from the main story, which can be all plated up before the word comes, ready to replace an existing page.

The emergency when a supremely important story breaks unexpectedly is quite different and a good deal more difficult to handle, depending on the amount of time available. Newsmen well remember, for example, the attempt to assassinate President Truman at about 2:15 P.M., Eastern Standard Time, a very unfortunate hour from the standpoint of afternoon-paper deadlines, especially in the eastern part of the country. With as little as half an hour remaining before the last regular edition, many editors had to make over Page One and at least one inside page in order to "get covered" on one of the biggest stories of the year.

Worse yet, the story was very slow to "firm up." Subsequent events proved that this was indeed an attempt on the President's life, but at the time it was by no means clear. Consequently, the wire services were careful not to push the story beyond the known facts, which were few and scattered. Not until the third lead, sent an hour after the event, did the AP dare to move even assassination-attempt *speculation* to the top of the story. In 1963, the assassination of President Kennedy posed a similar problem for afternoon papers. The event was of far greater significance, since the assassination attempt was successful. But this was not known at once.

No wire service and no newspaper wants to be in the position of publishing as fact a major story that proves to be something else (witness the embarrassment over the premature publication of Dewey's Presidential-election "victory" in 1948 and the "false armistice" near the end of World War I). Stories about events like the Truman or Kennedy assassination attempts call for caution at the same time they call for fast, decisive action. Sometimes it is possible to hold the play down in earlier editions and wait to go "all out" until the story becomes firm. Such treatment is often forced on the desk by the time limits anyway.

Incidentally, wire-service practices are designed to help news editors face emergencies of this kind. For instance, in the Truman attempted-assassination story, AP editors recognized that most news editors would be sending the story to their composing rooms in very short takes. Hence, it was sent in takes averaging only five lines in length, with wide spacing between them. The wire services also help the editor anticipate emergencies by sending advances whenever possible, allowing the story to be set in type hours in advance and even put into the forms. This practice sometimes reduces the emergency to simply deciding when the story will be released.

Suppose that the first word of a major, unexpected story comes along when two editions remain. The choice need not be between full coverage and no coverage. Certainly in the second of the two editions the story can probably be treated as fully and played as strongly as it warrants. To get the story into the earlier edition, the editor can simply pull one story out of Page One, move it to an inside page, and substitute for it a short version of the new story, perhaps with some decorative typographical treatment to give it attention value. Some papers label such stories, in heavy type above the headline, "Latest," "Bulletin," or perhaps "Extra." Another possibility is to pull out a cut rather than another story. This has one big advantage: nothing need be done on any inside page to accommodate the change. The resulting makeup problems can usually be solved by treating the story in such emphatic bulletin fashion that its typographical effect is much the same as the cut's. The story can be indented, set in boldface, and perhaps heavily leaded.

Because both these treatments are emphatic and obvious, they help deflect the inevitable reader question: If the story is so big, why isn't it up in the banner? The answer to the question is twofold: (1) it's too late to make over the page; (2) the story is still too short for a banner head. The editor's bulletin treatment in effect acknowledges the reader's question, saying, "This just came in, and believe us, it's hot. Sorry we haven't more detail; we don't want to raise your expectations with a banner head." The reader would have a right to feel cheated if a banner appeared over a story only a few inches long. It is unsound to raise his expectations without the means for satisfying them. The bulletin treatment implies from the start that the story is new and incomplete.

When it comes time to move the story into the top spot where it belongs, new problems present themselves. First, the editor must not do this before the fullness and certainty of the story justify it. Assuming that the passage of time *has* yielded a firmer story, the editor may be tempted to move the new story into the top spot, then shift the old banner story into the second spot, the second into the third, etc. This would satisfy his desire to be consistent about news judgments. But it would foist an all but impossible task on both the production department and the copy desk itself. Clearly, there is time neither to rewrite all the heads on Page One or to set them. The new top story must go into the top spot with as few changes as possible in the rest of Page One. Simply pushing the former top story inside is almost always out of the question: the story that was the best in the paper an hour ago can hardly lead off page 17 now. The top story must be shifted to another high Page One spot, and other adjustments will have to be made to make the page indicate the relative merits of all the stories it presents. In general, the short time available places these limits on the editor's judgments:

1. He will have to drop something out of the paper altogether to make room for the new material. It can hardly be a front-page story, so he must remove an inside-page story that either can be tossed out or held for another day. This makes room for something coming off Page One, which in turn makes room for the new story after a minimum number of shifts on Page One.

2. Changes must involve a minimum number of pages, a minimum number of headlines, and a minimum number of columns. Printers can make changes more rapidly if they don't have to justify a lot of columns at the last minute.

3. The changes should be made simultaneously by the desk, the compositors, and the makeup men, rather than successively. Sound editorial management can make this possible. The editor should decide and alert his production crew soon after the break comes about what pages will be involved in the changes; then, as soon as possible, he should give the composing room instructions about what is going to happen to old material. At the same time, he should move the story into type in short takes. It doesn't require much imagination to see that the changes will be made much more slowly if each step is completed before the next begins—editing, followed by composition, followed by proofreading and correction of galleys, then Page One makeover, then inside-page makeover.

It may be necessary to "railroad" unchecked copy to the compositor if running the story through the usual proofreading procedure will mean missing an edition. The editor can be forgiven, perhaps, for considering it more important to be covered on the story than to have it letter perfect. Besides, corrections can always be made after the first plate is made and a new plate put on the press in a few minutes.

Perhaps it is emergencies of this sort that illustrate best a point emphasized earlier in this book. The news editor needs to know a lot more about newspapering than what goes on in the newsroom; he must work so closely with the production departments that he must know their part of the job thoroughly, as well.

13

News Judgment

Deciding the selection and play of the news is perhaps the heaviest responsibility of the copy desk. In almost everything else he does, the editor acts primarily as a technician responsible to a set of technical standards. As gate keeper of the flow of ideas and information to his readers, he has a higher responsibility, a responsibility not only to the specific aims of his own newspaper, not only to the standards of the editor's craft, but to the public his newspaper serves.

A mere technical competence in the selection and play of the news is enough in some newsrooms. A slavish devotion to the attitudes of the owners may once have been a chief ingredient of success in others. But fortunately, in most newsrooms the editor has a higher and more severe taskmaster: the information requirements of the reading public. To serve it well with the ideas and information that are the ingredients of the democratic process is the real vocation of the news editor.

Where Decisions Are Made

Newspapers differ extensively in the point at which major news decisions are made. On many smaller ones, all decisions except a few "close ones" are made right on the desk by the man in the slot. On others, the news editor functions apart from the desk as the chief news decision maker. Often the managing editor leaves routine matters to the news editor but decides the top play each day. Some metropolitan newspapers arrive at major news judgments during a Page One conference of a number of top editors. In still other newsrooms, at least some of the decisions are handed down for all the resident editors by wire from the highest echelons of the chain ownership. However, it is perhaps typical that someone along the news stream, usually at the desk itself, is responsible for making most of the decisions about what news gets into the paper, in what detail, and with what prominence and position. He will here be referred to as the news editor.

The news editor is the next-to-last, and in a sense the most critical, decision maker in a chain of decisions between an event or situation and the reader's opportunity to know of the event or learn of the situation.[1] As a gate keeper, the editor makes a binary decision—go, no go—on each story, paragraph, quote, or word of explanation; he starts with hundreds of thousands of words and has to reduce them to fit his space budget by a process of considered elimination. What is available to him is the product of a series of decisions made earlier—by wire-service filing editors, say, who also have to sift from a glut of information just enough to fit the limits of the day's file. Before him, editors have made assignments, reporters have chosen to go to source A but not source B, sources have decided whether to talk or not, photographers have chosen to frame a picture a certain way and not other ways.[2] Another series of decisions determines the final decision in the process of bringing information to reader and reader to information, that of the reader himself to attend or not attend to the information. The media reader-viewer-listener makes decisions

about how to use his time; if he chooses to use some of it seeking information in the media, which medium? Within the medium what segment (a news report or other program on television? which section of the newspaper?), and within the segment what items?

How Decisions Are Made

The conjunction of a piece of information and an information seeker is not fortuitous but is the joint product of two very complex processes, the choice behaviors of the reader and the editor. How and what the reader (information seeker) chooses from among the myriad pieces of information available to him is a systematic behavior that is little understood but can be determined. Naturally, his choice behavior is related to how and what the editor chooses from among the glut of information available to *him;* indeed, the reader's choice process and the editor's selection behavior are in some degree interdependent. As a professional, the news editor is interested in these processes. Knowing more about them won't resolve his own decision problems directly, but it's part of the professional, reliable knowledge he needs to avoid making faulty assumptions. The research literature tells something about both processes, if only enough to show that they are more complicated than we thought.

A study of twenty-eight dailies receiving both the AP and UPI files showed that the telegraph editors ranked "interesting leads," "conciseness," and "completeness in detail" in that order as criteria in deciding what version of a story to use. "Background" and "personal appeal" were ranked less high.[3]

In a study of twenty metropolitan dailies, Stempel[4] found that the filing behavior of the wire services had less to do with telegraph editors' choice of wire news than the production schedule of the newspapers. Early closing times for inside and front pages, for example, limited the choices of the gate keeper and affected the

[1] For discussions of the chain of decision processes, consult Scott M. Cutlip, "The Content and Flow of AP News—from Trunk to TTS to Reader," *Journalism Quarterly* 31:436–460 (Fall 1954). See also Robert L. Jones, Verling C. Troldahl, and J. K. Hvistendahl, "News Selection Patterns from a State TTS-Wire," *Journalism Quarterly* 38:303–312 (Summer 1961).

[2] The gate-keeper idea originated in a study done by a group of social scientists headed by Kurt Lewin at the University of Iowa concerning the meat-buying behavior of housewives. It simply identified the food chain as a series of gates manned by gate keepers making binary choices. See "Channels of Group Life," *Human Relations* 1:143–153 (1947). David Manning White picked up Lewin's hint that such processes might apply to the flow of news and studied the choice behavior of one telegraph editor and the reasons he gave for his choices. See "The 'Gate-Keeper': A Case Study in the Selection of News," *Journalism Quarterly* 27:383–390 (Fall 1950). The same editor's decisions were reexamined seventeen years later: see Paul B. Snyder, " 'Mr. Gates' Revisited: A 1966 version of the 1949 Case Study," *Journalism Quarterly* 44:419–427 (Autumn 1967).

[3] B. H. Liebes, "Decision-Making by Telegraph Editors—AP or UPI?" *Journalism Quarterly* 43:434–442 (Autumn 1966).

[4] Guido H. Stempel III, "How Newspapers Use the Associated Press Afternoon A-Wire," *Journalism Quarterly* 41:380–384 (Summer 1964).

kind of news that got into the paper. Westley reported a similar conclusion in an unpublished study of the influence, if any, of personal values on the selections news editors made from the wire—did the editor tend to overchoose news in the value categories which ranked high in his personal value hierarchy? It turned out that his choices were largely dictated by what wire material was in hand when the pages closed; little variation could be accounted for by personal values.

There is some evidence that editors agree about what is news, and more than one explanation for it. Gold and Simmons[5] reported that twenty-four evening papers in Iowa that subscribed only to a particular regional wire service used anywhere from 5 per cent to nearly 70 per cent of the file. However, the papers were so similar in their rank ordering of types of stories that the "coefficient of concordance" worked out to .915 (perfect agreement in ranks would have been 1.0). Gold and Simmons were not sure whether to attribute this to uncritical acceptance of what the wire sent or shared standards of judgment, but preferred the former explanation. So did Gieber[6] in a more intensive study of sixteen Wisconsin telegraph editors. Hardt and White[7] reported that six North Dakota afternoon papers seem to repeat a great deal of the news carried by a metropolitan morning paper that circulates throughout the state (the Minneapolis *Tribune*) but show considerable independence in the way they play the news. These two studies sprang from one by Breed[8] in which he interpreted interview data obtained from editors to mean that they were influenced by larger papers in the way they played the news. Breed never seemed to understand that this probably cannot be true. The wire services give a

summary of the play in a few leading papers late in the cycle, but far too late to influence the play of that day's news by others.

On the other hand, there is evidence that editors make unique choices of news. Stempel[9] found only 31 per cent agreement among six editors using the Michigan TTS wire. Deutschmann[10] found wide variation in the use of items from eleven categories in a study of the newspapers of three large cities. In a later study of twenty-five afternoon dailies of more than 100,000 circulation using both wire services, Stempel[11] found that only thirty-two of 156 national stories were used by at least five of the twenty-five papers. Finding that these editors' judgments were not unidimensional, Stempel sought out a multidimensional explanation for the editors' preferences. He subjected the data to a procedure known as Guttman scaling, which determines whether a single dimension of judgment accounts for most of the decisions made—in this case, the editors' decisions to use particular stories. Stempel's data were clearly not unidimensional, so he used another procedure called factor analysis to determine whether a number of different dimensions could be found which would account for the editors' decisions. In effect he was testing two common hypotheses about the nature of news. The first more or less says that "news is news" and competent editors should agree in judging it. If this were the basis for the judgments in his data, he should get a unidimensional solution; in other words, the stories being judged should fall along a single dimension from least newsworthy to most. But that hypothesis had to be rejected: that was not the way his editors were judging the news.

The other popular hypothesis about the nature of news is that stories have characteristics that contribute

[5] David Gold and Jerry L. Simmons, "News Selection Patterns Among Iowa Dailies," *Public Opinion Quarterly* 29:425–430 (Fall 1965). The data were taken from a University of Iowa Ph.D. dissertation by Jeff Clark.

[6] Walter Gieber, "Across the Desk: A Study of 16 Telegraph Editors," *Journalism Quarterly* 33:423–432 (Fall 1956).

[7] Hanno Hardt and Michael White, "Front Page News Similarities in A.M. and P.M. Papers," *Journalism Quarterly* 43:552–554 (Autumn 1966).

[8] Warren Breed, "Newspaper Opinion Leaders and Processes of Standardization," *Journalism Quarterly* 32:277–284, 328 (Summer 1955).

[9] Guido H. Stempel III, "Uniformity of Wire Content of Six Michigan Dailies," *Journalism Quarterly* 36:45–48 (Winter 1959).

[10] Paul J. Deutschmann, "News Page Content of Twelve Metropolitan Dailies," mimeographed report, Communications Research Center, Michigan State University, 1959.

[11] Guido H. Stempel III, "An Empirical Exploration of the Nature of News," in *Paul J. Deutschmann Memorial Papers in Mass Communications Research* (Cincinnati: Scripps-Howard Research, 1963), pp. 19–23.

to their newsworthiness. Some common ones cited in the textbooks are proximity, timeliness, prominence, human interest, etc. If these are the criteria editors use, editors should tend to agree that a given story has more human-interest value than another, and this would mean that high human-interest stories should rank similarly, or should be correlated with each other. Factor analysis simply identifies the items that are highly correlated with each other. These factors may then be seen as the dimensions of judgment being used by the news editor in making their decisions.

Actually Stempel's twenty-two news items did yield six rather clear factors but these were in some cases hard to identify by looking at the items that fell into each factor. The first factor looked like a combination of suspense and conflict, which might be labeled "sensationalism." These items concerned a threatening flood, a grenade explosion in a post office, the possibility that Russian planes were flying over Alaska, and the like. A second factor appeared to be a concentration of public affairs information items. A third looked like human interest, since it largely contained items about newsworthy persons and emotional events in the lives of plain people. The other three factors could not be readily explained. Thus it appears that news judgment is a multidimensional process, not a unidimensional one, but that we cannot account for more than a small part of what kinds of dimensions are involved. Conventional concepts in any case help only a little to explain what is going on.

Criteria for Choosing News

Several factors, including page deadlines and edition times, limit the editor's freedom of choice. The information is not there all at once. Wire news moves throughout the day, and local news flows to the desk in much the same way. How, then, can an editor choose wisely among the pieces of information he does have at hand at a given time and be sure that what he chooses will serve the information requirements of his audience? All he has to do is be sure it is (1) interesting for most people most of the time but at the same time (2) an authentic reflection of the condition the world is in and how it is changing; (3) meaningful to

all segments of the reading audience; (4) in a form that inspires confidence in the medium; (5) the very information that individuals and communities need to solve their problems. This is a ridiculously large order, but it forms a rough outline for the more realistic discussion that follows. In choosing stories, the editor is concerned with factors of human interest, with the authenticity and accuracy and meaning of all the news of a given day, with the credibility of his medium, and with the social relevance of the news and his own responsibility in presenting it.

Human interest (or, "All they want to do is sell papers.") "Human interest" is both an old-time catchphrase of the newsroom and an empirically testable theory of how people are motivated to select and respond to information in the mass media. Reading, viewing, listening—attending to news—is a motivated behavior. The editor cannot reach people with information that is not interesting enough to cause them to read it. Without understanding something about the information-search motivation and behavior of people in the audience, the editor cannot hope to understand much about the consequences of his choices.

Researchers have tried to determine scientifically what the old concept of "human interest" means to readers and newsmen. Lynch and others[12] asked subjects to respond on adjective-pair scales to the concept "the human quality in the news" and found that they judged the concept principally in a PERSONALISM dimension (*intimate, sympathetic, personal*), an INFORMATIVE dimension (*informative, valuable*), a DIFFICULTY dimension (*easy, light, simple, shallow*), and a RESTRAINT dimension (*cautious, restrained*). It would, of course, be more valuable to know how people judge the merits of stories that editors select for human-interest values.

Editors have to be concerned with how interest is distributed in the heterogeneous population they serve. Many media are "particularistic," but the newspaper is not one of them. To be sure, the *Wall Street Journal* is

---

[12] Mervin D. Lynch, Brian D. Kent, and Richard P. Carlson, "The Meaning of Human Interest: Four Dimensions of Judgment," *Journalism Quarterly* 44:673–678 (Winter 1967).

more particularistic than most. It can select its news on the basis of what it knows about the characteristics of its special audience and what interests tend to go with these characteristics. But the general news media, including the general-circulation daily, are "universalistic" in all respects but one, the economic-geographic. That is to say, the newspaper's audience is homogeneous only with respect to the economy and geography of the area the newspaper serves. In all other respects it is forced to be all things to all people. The economics of daily-newspaper publishing is bound up in the capacity to reach the entire literate population of Red-Eye, Utah, or whatever community it serves. American newspapers have not been a stratified social phenomenon, although to some degree they are elsewhere in the world. In Great Britain the reader can choose the brash afternoon papers or the stately morning papers. He also has a choice between essentially provincial papers and national papers, between Labor-oriented and Tory-oriented papers, and this is generally true of Western Europe. But the newspapers of North America are not stratified, even politically. Our newspapers strive to be truly universalistic.

This could imply a "least-common-denominator" view of the newspaper audience: the news editor's decisions should be guided by the basic interests shared by people of all strata. There is some merit in this view, but it can lead to excessive preoccupation with human but very trivial news. A better guiding principle is to consult the variability of the audience and then see how many interests can be served. Newsmen can ask what the community *needs* in the way of information, not alone what the man on the street is *interested* in, and offer the community a set of choices, knowing that the needs of informal neighborhood influentials may be different from those who make decisions for the local financial community, and that these will differ from the information needs of young housewives, etc.

But at the same time, newsmen need to know more about the *way* people seek information in the media and in their exchanges of information with others. They also need to know what *motivates* information-seeking behavior, which has been defined as "a persistent tendency to place a positive value on informa-

tion that is potentially relevant to the individual's orientation to his surroundings."[13]

Schramm[14] has proposed two basic motivations for information seeking, an "immediate-reward" motivation to acquire information which provides immediate gratification (as viewing a beautiful scene), and a "delayed-reward" motivation for information which provides gratification when it is used later. For most users of the term "information seeking," the latter is the more significant motivation. Rees[15] found that persons who scored high on "need for achievement" also tended to choose delayed-reward magazine content, although this was not generally true of television content. Her findings may provide a significant clue to media differences. Television content runs so strongly to the immediate-reward category that individual differences in information seeking from television are of little predictive value. The print media tend to offer content more balanced between immediate and delayed reward. In testing for the effects of format variables on people's choices in print media, Powers and Kearl[16] found that their effects were trivial by comparison with the influence of interest in the subject matter offered.

Buss[17] related curiosity, need for cognition (need to know), and anxiety to various patterns of media use. The "curiosity" measure correlated to a modest degree with "willingness" to use movies, radio, and television, but the measure used is one of what is called "reactive" curiosity, or a seeking of *stimulus variability*, not a search for reliable information. Need for cognition correlated quite strongly with willingness to use magazines, but the relationship to newspaper willingness was very slight. Anxiety was expected to suppress curi-

[13] Bruce H. Westley and Lionel C. Barrow, Jr., "An Investigation of News-Seeking Behavior," *Journalism Quarterly* 36:431–438 (Autumn 1969).

[14] Wilbur Schramm, "The Nature of News," *Journalism Quarterly* 26:259–269 (September 1949).

[15] Matilda B. Rees, "Achievement Motivation and Content Preferences," *Journalism Quarterly* 44:688–692 (Winter 1967).

[16] Richard D. Powers and Bryant E. Kearl, "Readability and Display as Readership Predictors," *Journalism Quarterly* 45:117–118 (Spring 1968).

[17] Linda J. Buss, "Motivational Variables and Information Seeking in the Mass Media," *Journalism Quarterly* 44:131–133 (Spring 1967).

osity; the relationship, however, was essentially zero, as was the relationship between anxiety and television use.

Interest in news is obviously a multifaceted phenomenon. But is there a pattern, a persistent structure, in the way people's interests are developed and persist? Philip Anast[18] classified 130 hypothetical news items into sixteen standard categories (foreign, crime, sports) and got preference data by having respondents place the items on a seven-point scale indicating interest in reading them. The four factors that emerged included a classic immediate-reward factor (mishaps, crime, disaster, human interest) and a delayed-reward factor (economic, political, foreign, welfare-education), a vicarious-experience factor (entertainment, society), and a personal well-being factor (health and scientific, with welfare-education getting a strong secondary loading). Anast's rather discouraging finding was that people who were most interested in what he called controversy (or delayed-reward news) tended to be more critical of the performance of the press than those who were more interested in other classes of news. And this relationship was not an artifact of education; it held across all educational levels.

A somewhat similar analysis was carried out by Stempel.[19] Unlike Anast, Stempel found within the delayed-reward category a rather clear division of interests into economics, national politics, and public health and welfare. He also got two immediate-reward factors, one including items that emphasize people in ordinary life ("School Board Hires Nine Teachers"), the other emphasizing people in conflict or suspenseful situations.

Studies such as these provide some clues as to how editors categorize and compartmentalize the news in choosing it and how readers categorize and compartmentalize news in selecting what the news editors provide them. The question naturally arises whether news editors and readers perceive the news in similar ways, and whether newsmen can predict how readers will judge (use) the news they provide. The evidence on this question is not very clear. Atwood[20] got newsmen and subscribers to sort stories as they believed a news editor would and as they believed a subscriber would. The correlations were quite high. Significantly, though, the desk men were less able to anticipate subscriber preferences than were other staff members!

Authenticity (or, "It's only a newspaper story.")   As a responsible gate keeper, the editor must be concerned with the authenticity of the stories that come over his desk. There have been numerous newspaper hoaxes in history and no doubt there will continue to be. Wisconsin newspapers at one time sought protection of the law to punish persons who phone in false information. There had been a rash of telephoned engagement and wedding announcements designed to embarrass or malign the individuals named.

Sometimes editors place such blind faith in the wire services that they accept whatever the services send. The filing editors, aware of this, often send messages emphasizing a story's tentativeness or uncertain parentage. Yet sometimes they, too, are taken in. The writer once spotted two kidnapping stories within the space of a month which looked spurious and turned out to be. Other newspapers and radio stations rushed these stories to their audiences without a second glance. Sometimes it's possible to check out the dubious aspects of a story or have the wire service check. If not, it is better to wait and be sure than to run the risk of misinforming readers.

False information widely disseminated has been known to cause panic when it contains the elements of terror. For example, "sex maniac," "mad bomber," and "Boston strangler" scares can induce a fear that even the fullest and most responsible reporting cannot allay. Sometimes the reporting actually contributes to the panic. In the case of the dramatization of *The War*

[18] Philip Anast, "Attitude Toward the Press as a Function of Interests," *Journalism Quarterly* 38:376–380 (Summer 1961). The factor names are Westley's, who feels entitled to suggest them since this work was done under his direction. Anast's purpose was to identify a cluster of controversial items, for which the second factor became the ideal choice.

[19] Guido H. Stempel III, "A Factor Analytic Study of Reader Interest in News," *Journalism Quarterly* 44:326–330 (Summer 1967).

[20] L. Erwin Atwood, "How Newsmen and Readers Perceive Each Others' Story Preferences," *Journalism Quarterly* 47:296–302 (Summer 1970).

of the Worlds on radio in 1938, everything was done to make clear that what was "happening" was indeed a dramatization, but panic ensued anyway.[21] In the case of "the phantom anaesthetist," the local newspaper appears to have been a genuine contributor to what social psychologists have called a case of pure collective hysteria.[22]

This case deserves detailed attention. A woman asked a neighbor to call the police and tell them that she and her daughter had been gassed by a prowler. The next day the local paper gave front-page play to "ANAESTHETIC PROWLER ON THE LOOSE." That day, another resident reported that the night before the original incident he had been ill and had checked whether he had left gas on. At about the same time, a third resident reported a similar attack of illness. The latter two incidents were attributed originally to prosaic causes; an anaesthetic was not suspected until the paper reported the first incident. No new incident occurred on the two successive days; neither did the paper publish on those days. The next day there were two "cases," the day after that, three, and then none—no paper that day, either. There were four, five, and seven on successive days. In every case, the symptoms were real and in some cases physical, but in every case seen by physicians they were diagnosed as hysteria. The "gas" was very strong and easy for the victims to describe—but they all described it differently. All the victims recovered quickly and fully.

In retrospect, the police acted as hysterically as the victims and, since many editors consider anything police say or do as fact, the newspaper continued to give credence to the anaesthetist. With few exceptions, the victims did not know each other, so it appears probable that the news stories were responsible for the original diffusion of the panic. A second-day headline read "MAD ANAESTHETIST STRIKES AGAIN," and even when there was no new "attack,"

the paper ran a story that almost pleaded for more panic:

> Mattoon's "mad anaesthetist" apparently took a respite from his maniacal forays Thursday night, and while many terror stricken people were somewhat relieved, they were inclined to hold their breath and wonder when and where he might strike next.

Three metropolitan papers circulating in the area joined the chase after the panic was more than a week old but quickly made up for lost time with even more lugubrious phrasing:

> Groggy as Londoners under protracted aerial blitzing, this town's bewildered citizens reeled today under the repeated attacks of a mad anaesthetist who has spread a deadly nerve gas into 13 homes and knocked out 27 victims.

Only one of the three papers exhibited any skepticism; none of them interviewed a physician until the panic was two weeks old.

The incident illustrates that even professional newsmen can be victimized by public hysteria, despite their professional skepticism and presumed reverence for hard fact. Here there were no hard facts except the hysteria itself; the professionals became the agents of hysteria as well as its victims.[23]

Credibility (or, "They never seem to get it right.") At stake in the judgments news editors make is the trust readers are willing to assign to the judges. This is a game the newspaper can't win every time. The news media are constantly being criticized and the criticism is often politically inspired. One politician struck a chord in many liberal breasts by repeating the phrase "one-party press." There was merit in this accusation, especially as the reference was to the candidates

---

[21] Hadley Cantril, *The Invasion from Mars* (Princeton, N. J.: Princeton University Press, 1940).

[22] The fullest account is Donald M. Johnson, "The Phantom Anaesthetist of Mattoon: A Field Study of Mass Hysteria," *Journal of Abnormal and Social Psychology* 17:221–235 (1943).

[23] A follow-up study twenty-three years later found that most of the older residents of Mattoon remembered the "mad gasser" and only about one-fourth of them accepted the "mass hysteria" explanation. See Rita James Simon and James Lumpp, "Mattoon, Illinois, Revisited: The Scene of the Phantom Anesthetist," *Journalism Quarterly* 44:734–737 (Winter 1967).

supported by newspapers on their editorial pages. Another politician at another time made political hay with the conservatives by damning the Eastern knee-jerk liberal press, with pointed reference to some of the most carefully edited and statesmanlike newspapers in the land. However, between the time of the first accusation and the second, there appear to have been no substantial changes in the degree or direction of the partisanship of the American press.

But the credibility of the paper is nevertheless a trust that is fragile and very much at stake in news decisions. People do not necessarily trust the newspaper, and to a dismaying degree they tend to place more trust in television than in newspapers.[24] Perhaps the fact that television news is personalized by the presence of the respected newsman on camera has something to do with television's greater credibility in the view of many watchers. A large study carried out in Wisconsin, however, shows that a person who has attended college, lives in an urban area, has a high-status occupation such as one of the professions and whose father also was in a high-status occupation, and regards himself as middle class is likely to trust the newspaper more than television. On the other hand, the "ideal type" of television truster is a woman of low income and education whose status is as low as or lower than her father's status and who regards herself as "working class."[25] Rural people are especially distrustful of the newspaper, and of all employment categories, rural workers are least likely to be regular newspaper readers. The nonreader tends to be low in education, isolated both physically and in the sense of not having frequent association with other persons, low in income, low in occupational status, and likely to regard himself as "working class."[26]

Carter and Greenberg[27] have shown that the Roper question is biased in favor of television, and that when people are asked to choose the medium they would find most believable in the case of conflicting reports, the answer depends largely on which medium is most used. Those who rely mainly on newspapers choose newspapers on this question and vice versa.

Jacobson[28] found that what has been thought of as credibility is really a two-factor attribute, on the basis of a factor analysis of adjective-pair responses to each of the media as sources of news. *Authenticity* was made up of trust, accuracy, expertise, and openmindedness. *Objectivity* clustered together biased-unbiased and impersonal-personal scales.

Sargent[29] reported a study in which college-student subjects were asked to judge newspaper messages on eleven-item adjective-pair scales. The messages were attributed to both personal and impersonal sources (*e.g.,* Reston in the New York *Times vs.* the *Times*). Stories attributed to personal sources were assigned higher values, especially on the evaluative scales *accurate, sincere, responsible,* and *impartial.*

General distrust of the media and of the information about government that people learn from the media is a widespread phenomenon, and there is some indication that it is increasing.[30] In an effort to determine the criteria of judgment people use in assessing the information media, Tannenbaum and McLeod[31] have shown that a general EVALUATIVE dimension is the largest factor in judging all media. That is, people evaluate media mostly in a good-bad

[24] Elmo Roper and Associates, *The Public's Attitude Toward Television and Other Media* (New York: Television Information Office, 1964).

[25] Bruce H. Westley and Werner J. Severin, "Some Correlates of Media Credibility," *Journalism Quarterly* 41:325–335 (Summer 1964). See also Bradley S. Greenberg, "Media Use and Believability: Some Multiple Correlates," *Journalism Quarterly* 43:665–670 (Winter 1966).

[26] Bruce H. Westley and Werner J. Severin, "A Profile of the Daily Newspaper Non-Reader," *Journalism Quarterly* 41:45–50, 156 (Winter 1964).

[27] Richard F. Carter and Bradley S. Greenberg, "Newspaper or Television: Which Do You Believe?" *Journalism Quarterly* 42:29–34 (Winter 1965).

[28] Harvey K. Jacobson, "Mass Media Believability: A Study of Receiver Judgments," *Journalism Quarterly* 46:20–28 (Spring 1969).

[29] Leslie W. Sargent, "Communicator Image and News Reception," *Journalism Quarterly* 42:35–42 (Winter 1965). However, the subject's agreement or disagreement with the positions taken in the messages had a far larger effect on the ratings assigned than did media differences or personalization.

[30] Robert L. Bishop and Sue A. Schultz, "The Credibility Gap: Is It Widening?" *Journalism Quarterly* 44:740–741 (Winter 1967).

[31] Percy H. Tannenbaum and Jack M. McLeod, "Public Images of Mass Media Institutions," in *Paul J. Deutschmann Memorial Papers . . .,* pp. 51–60.

(*pleasant-unpleasant, valuable-worthless*) way. And, as in most studies measuring connotative meanings, they also judge them along a POTENCY dimension (*bold-timid*) and an ACTIVITY dimension (*active-passive, tense-relaxed*). But there are two other dimensions that are unique to media studies, an ETHICAL dimension (*fair-unfair, truthful-untruthful, accurate-inaccurate, unbiased-biased*) and what Tannenbaum and McLeod call a STYLISTIC dimension (*exciting-dull, fresh-stale*). But though all the media are judged on the EVALUATIVE dimension, the print media far more than the electronic media are judged along the ETHICAL dimension. It is safe to say that people judge newspapers with their ethical performance in mind more harshly than radio and television.

The newspaper industry has shown increasing concern over "the credibility gap" in recent years. The Associated Press Managing Editors Association[32] set out to determine the reasons for it. They asked a series of questions of two groups, twenty-five editors and twenty-eight public officials and other community leaders. Because the samples were so small, the results are little more than suggestive. The community leaders in many cases saw the problems differently than the editors did. Among the possible reasons for the credibility gap, the public rated these higher:

MAJOR CAUSE OF PUBLIC DISTRUST	EDITORS %	LEADERS %
Sensationalism—too little serious news	4	75
Commercialism—more concerned with profits than professionalism	4	22
Failure to print corrections	23	40
Defensiveness—newspaper sensitivity to criticism	11	49
Aggressiveness of reporters and photographers	4	33
Anonymity—too much use of unnamed sources	12	36
Class bias—slighting and misrepresenting minorities	5	15
Venality—too easily influenced by pressure groups	5	33
Deadline pressures, emphasis on latest news	29	41

Reasons for the credibility gap seen as major more often by newsmen than community leaders:

MAJOR CAUSE OF PUBLIC DISTRUST	EDITORS %	LEADERS %
Inaccuracy—routine errors and typos	56	10
Public frustration—press is blamed when problems mount	54	24
Public ignorance of how news is processed	29	10
Competition for professional talent	33	15

Though newsmen and community leaders rated a few items similarly, the gap is visible here; it would surely be far wider if "the public" and not its acknowledged leaders were asked these same questions. According to a study by Donohew,[33] publishers and community leaders tend to see things eye-to-eye. He found that the influence groups of publishers—that is to say, persons publishers named as influential on them—were in large measure merchants and pro-

fessional men: about one-fourth were merchants and about one-third were professionals. This understandable stratification may be one cause of alienation.

Universality of meanings (or, "It's all so *irrelevant*.") As a universalistic medium, the newspaper has a re-

[32] *Editor & Publisher,* August 30, 1969, pp. 12, 13.
[33] Lewis Donohew, "Publishers and Their Influence Groups," *Journalism Quarterly* 42:112–113 (Winter 1965).

sponsibility to reach and serve the information needs of all segments of society. But it has been apparent for some time that large segments of society are not reached effectively and that their hostility toward the establishment bias of the newspapers seems to be increasing. The renewed vigor of the black press and the emergence of an underground press may be seen as a consequence.

Newspapers are finding it increasingly difficult to reach people in the central-city black ghetto, the very heart of their circulation area. Newsboys are harder to find, and route men are, too. At least a few newspaper circulation managers are advising publishers to forget the core as a circulation base. But some newspaper managements are renewing their efforts to reach the black population. *Tuesday*, a black-oriented weekly supplement, is distributed by many newspapers in their central-city areas only. A black-oriented comic strip became available in 1969. And a rundown of Brotherhood Week awards from the National Conference of Christians and Jews indicates that many newspapers are giving high priority to depth reports of problems relating to intergroup relations. For example, the following were cited:

—the Milwaukee *Journal* for a series of feature stories on the life styles and achievements of the black community
—two Charlotte *Observer* reporters for a similar series
—the *Long Island Press* for a series of personality close-ups from "Black Long Island"
—editorials in the *Arkansas Gazette* for endorsement of civil rights causes
—*The Paper*, late of Oshkosh, Wisconsin, for a photo story of the friendship between two boys, one black, one white.

And there were many more. However, with the growth of alienation in contemporary society, the question arises as to how the alienated can be reached by media and whether they respond to information and other mass-media content in unique ways. Do the alienated seek immediate-reward gratifications only and avoid information that contributes to the search for consensus? McLeod, Ward, and Tancill[34] found that adults who scored high on an alienation scale were no more likely than others to spend excessive time with the media, as an "escape" hypothesis would suggest. As usual, education showed a positive relationship with time spent with print media and a negative relationship to radio and television time. The alienated were less likely to give "informational" reasons for their mass-media preferences and more likely to give "vicarious" reasons, just the opposite of the highly educated respondents. The expected preference of the alienated for "sensational" content was not found.

Sometimes alienation takes the form of protest, and sometimes protest arises over differences in news judgments. About two hundred young people, for example, demonstrated against the Vancouver *Sun* and the Vancouver *Province* for their disregard of a story about a youth killed by Berkeley police. In fact, press coverage of this story was a frequent cause of anger against the establishment press.[35] To the protesters the coverage was poor, a direct result of the tendency of the newspaper to get the story first from the police, since every paper has a police beat, and the tendency not to get the story from the "other side" at all, when the other side is demonstrators. A further indication of the estrangement between youth and the press is seen in the report of a conference of editors and publishers of the "straight press" on the one hand and college editors on the other. *Editor & Publisher*, the industry spokesman, headed its story "Loud Voices from Bearded Faces."[36]

Editors have tried for years to reach young people through special sections devoted to their interests. One features syndicate asks in its promotional advertising: "Who looks like Brigitte Bardot, thinks like Ralph Nader, and writes like a hip Ann Landers?" Their youth advice columnist, of course. Little wonder that the special sections have met with only partial success. Several studies have shown that they claim little attention of upper teens. Radio has been the primary medium for the teen market. Television viewing is at

[34] Jack McLeod, Scott Ward, and Karen Tancill, "Alienation and Uses of the Mass Media," *Public Opinion Quarterly* 29: 583–594 (Winter 1965–1966).
[35] *Editor & Publisher*, June 7, 1969, p. 15.
[36] *Editor & Publisher*, February 22, 1969, p. 13.

an all-time low in those years. Newspaper reading of general news by teen-agers is about half that of adults.[37] But newspapers keep trying.

There is evidence of alienation in the newsrooms themselves. As this is written, "countermedia" publications have been springing up all over the country, some inside the industry, some outside, some left-oriented, some right-oriented. The inside papers, led by the lively *Chicago Journalism Review,* are mainly devoted to telling each other the stories they feel they are prevented from telling the public and to complaining of the lack of diligence, to put it mildly, on the part of news executives to tell the news without fear or favor. They complain of timidity, bias, repression, and a general management commitment to establishment values and methods. They call for "an end to the lie of objectivity." Some are obviously the work of professionals, others are barely literate.[38]

Community involvement (or, "What do they care about us?") The interdependent relationship between the newspaper and the community it serves is the central fact of a newspaper's existence. The economic foundation of the newspaper is the retail market of the city. With more than 85 per cent of its advertising revenue from local sources, the newspaper has just about lost the battle for national advertising revenue to television and other national media. (It is not losing national advertising, but its *share* of advertising budgets is not increasing as budgets increase.) But in local advertising it is stronger than ever.

In the usual city surrounded by suburbs which in turn are surrounded by open country, the patterns of relationship between newspaper circulation and degree of urbanism are simple and clear. Saturation is at its highest in the city itself and thins out with distance from its core. But, as we have seen, this relationship is today at its weakest in the very center; concentrated

there are the development of urban blight and the people least likely to be part of the newspaper audience. In fact, the changing patterns of urban, suburban, and interurban life have exerted pressure on the central-city daily. James Force[39] found in a study of the fifteen largest metropolitan areas between 1946 and 1961 a persistent trend toward fewer central-city dailies and more suburban dailies, a large net gain in suburban daily circulation (not, however, as huge as suburban population growth), and a substantial loss in central-city circulation while total central-city population showed a substantial increase. A similar study of twenty-one metropolitan areas between 1950 and 1968 showed that the same trends were accelerated in the 1960–1968 period.[40]

In "interurbia," where numerous cities make up an urban-industrial complex, the reader's choice of newspapers is closely related to where he works or shops or used to live or visits friends; but there is no such relationship with the television station he views.[41]

So the newspaper depends on the community. And the community, although it has other information sources, may depend in some measure on the quality of its newspaper. The factual basis for such a relationship is not easy to establish, but a study of six counties in Kansas by Brandner and Sistrunk[42] suggests that the quality of education reporting in a community may be related to the proportion of high-school graduates that go to college. The six counties were selected because they were atypical in the relationship between median family income and college attendance: three were low in college attendance and low in income; three were high in college attendance and low in

[37] "A Profile of the Teenage Reader," in Chilton R. Bush, ed., *News Research for Better Newspapers* 3:61–75 (New York: American Newspaper Publishers Association Foundation, 1968).

[38] See Spyridon Granitsas in *Editor & Publisher,* August 1, 1970, pp. 17, 34.

[39] James Force, "The Daily Press in Suburbia: Trends in 15 Metropolitan Areas," *Journalism Quarterly* 39:457–464 (Autumn 1962).

[40] Kenneth R. Byerly, "Metropolitan and Community Daily Newspapers: A Comparison of Their Number, Circulation and Trends for 1950, 1960 and 1968 in the Nation's 21 Most Populous Metropolitan Areas" (Chapel Hill: School of Journalism, University of North Carolina, 1968, mimeo.).

[41] Leo Bogart and Frank E. Orenstein, "Mass Media and Community Identity in an Interurban Setting," *Journalism Quarterly* 42:179–188 (Spring 1965).

[42] Lowell Brandner and Joan Sistrunk, "The Newspaper: Molder or Mirror of Community Values?" *Journalism Quarterly* 43:497–504 (Winter 1966).

income. Distances to colleges were reasonably similar. An examination of their newspapers showed that in the three high college-attendance counties, the education reporting was extensive and serious. In the low college-attendance counties, the newspapers covered school activities almost entirely on their sports pages. While other explanations are possible, the authors believe this is evidence that the newspaper can mold local opinion, not merely mirror it.

There has been a tendency in recent years to minimize the mass media as a source of influence.[43] A series of studies by the Bureau of Applied Social Research at Columbia University on the way people make up their minds during an election campaign[44] and about consumer goods[45] and the way physicians decide to adopt new drugs[46] tended to show that *interpersonal* influences were more effective than mass-media influences. People with whom the decision maker had frequent contacts seemed to be the chief source of influence and they, of course, were not usually "community leaders" but more often persons on the same socioeconomic level. Massive campaigns to establish or change people's opinions often failed.[47] It was argued that attitudes are embedded in strong predispositions and complex cognitive patterns and that isolated facts from impersonal media were not enough to produce change.

The "two-step flow" hypothesis was advanced, which says that information reaches decision makers through influentials. But this does not appear to be the case where major news stories are concerned.[48] Most readers learn about news events directly from the mass media or turn to the media immediately when they first hear of events from other sources. But even though they may get news *information* from the media, the *opinions* they hold on them seem to be influenced more by the opinions of their reference groups than the ready-made opinions of the information media.[49]

Nevertheless, Douglas, Westley, and Chaffee[50] have shown that when a community does not have clearly formulated attitudes toward a social issue, an information campaign can both increase the level of knowledge within the community and bring about attitude change toward the issue. The process is aided by interpersonal communication, to be sure. In some measure, this study supports the idea that the mass media outside a social system are the source of new information that propels change, while interpersonal communication adjusts attitudes and values (and dictates whether to accept or ignore or alter the new information) to the prevailing consensus within the community. The latter process appears to bring about change while in fact it is resisting change. The former is the true agent of change, but it lacks the appearance because change is not really accepted until it has been tested and modified in the crucible of discussion.

All this may seem to be a little remote from the decision processes on the copy desk, but it seems reasonable to assume that those decisions are still important to the community. The newpaper and the community are bound together in a process of facing

[43] Joseph T. Klapper, *The Effects of Mass Communication* (New York: The Free Press, 1960).

[44] Paul F. Lazarsfeld, Bernard Berelson, and Helen Gaudet, *The People's Choice* (New York: Columbia University Press, 1944); Bernard R. Berelson, Paul F. Lazarsfeld, and William N. McFee, *Voting* (Chicago: University of Chicago Press, 1954).

[45] Elihu Katz and Paul F. Lazarsfeld, *Personal Influence* (Glencoe, Ill.: The Free Press, 1955).

[46] Herbert Menzel and Elihu Katz, "Social Relations and Innovation in the Medical Profession: The Epistemology of a New Drug," *Public Opinion Quarterly* 19:337–352 (1955–1956).

[47] *E.g.,* Shirley N. Star and Helen MacGill Hughes, "A Report on an Education Campaign: The Cincinnati Plan for the United Nations," *American Journal of Sociology* 55:389–400 (1950).

[48] See, for example, Paul J. Deutschmann and Wayne A. Danielson, "Diffusion of Knowledge of the Major News Story," *Journalism Quarterly* 37:345–355 (Summer 1960).

[49] The very significant finding that information givers and information seekers tend to be the same people has made the whole two-step-flow idea just about untenable, although the finding is consistent with the reference-group hypothesis. See Verling C. Troldahl and Robert Van Dam, "Face to Face Communication About Major Topics in the News," *Public Opinion Quarterly* 29:626–634 (Winter 1965–1966).

[50] Dorothy Douglas, Bruce H. Westley, and Steven H. Chaffee, "An Information Campaign That Changed Community Attitudes," *Journalism Quarterly* 47:479–487, 492 (Autumn 1970).

change and acting deliberately—not always rationally—to diffuse information and act on it in the interest of survival and a better life. Toward these ends, newspaper managements often deliberately involve their communities in discussing the service the newspaper renders and how it might be improved. Press councils are springing up here and there across the country. These are community organizations that meet regularly with officials of the media to discuss topics of mutual concern. Their "paramount concern is newspaper content and, more specifically, the reasons for selection of news and information appearing in the newspaper."[51] That should be reason enough to give careful thought to news judgment. The community cares.

[51] Kenneth Starck, "What Community Press Councils Talk About," *Journalism Quarterly* 47:20–26 (Spring 1970).

14

The News Editor and the Law

The newspaper has two chief lines of defense against the ever-present danger that what it prints will involve it in expensive legal difficulties. The first is the general, necessarily incomplete, knowledge of publication law which the newspaper has a right to expect of everyone who handles the news. The second is the thorough knowledge commanded by the newspaper's attorneys. These roles are supplementary but very different. The former can be called *preventive,* the latter *corrective.* To oversimplify, the newsman's duty is to *keep* the paper out of court; the lawyer's is to *get* the paper out of court—with its shirt.

Editors often ask the newspaper's counsel to play a preventive role, as well, by consulting him before a story is run rather than waiting for a libel suit to be filed. But the fact that many newspapers now employ counsel on a consulting basis should not lull the working newsman into a relaxed attitude toward the potentiality for legal trouble in the news matter he handles. After all, the lawyer does not sit at the copy desk or proof desk to review all material going into the paper. He can only be consulted when there is *reason to fear* the consequences of a publication. Only the alert newsman whose knowledge of the law is sufficient to allow him to make successful guesses about the extent and nature of the danger can guarantee with reasonable certainty that dangerous material will be brought to the attention of legal counsel—or excised on the grounds of its obvious danger.

While it is the duty of all newsmen to be fairly expert on libel and other legal matters, it is particularly important for the copy editor. He will not, of course, have to defend the newspaper against a suit if and when one is brought, but he should test every piece of copy he sees for its potential danger. Neither must he be equipped to make final judgments. They will be made at higher levels, perhaps in the office of the publisher, who holds the ultimate responsibility, legal and otherwise, for what the paper prints. *But the publisher cannot make such decisions unless he is presented with them.* He can't review every story before publication, either. The way the editor functions in behalf of his paper in legal matters is to sense danger, exercise his knowledge of the law to test whether the danger is real, and, if so, call the danger to the attention of his superiors for their final decision. Then, if they wish, they may consult counsel before making it.

Libel and the News

Freedom of the press is a civil liberty guaranteed by the First Amendment to the Constitution. Libel is a *tort*—a legal "wrong" against any person. Libel law can be viewed as a means by which the people guarantee that the civil liberty of freedom of the press is not converted into license by those who exercise it. It limits freedom of expression in much the same way that laws against obscenity limit freedom of expression. But it need not be viewed as a civil right *in conflict* with another civil right. It can be argued that the one tends to make the other workable. Ideally, libel law can be said to be in the interests of the press and the public if for no other reason than in helping guarantee public support for the preservation of freedom of the press. Publishers properly keep an eye on developments in the law of libel to guard against the possibility that it might swing from a proper limitation to an unreasonable restraint on freedom of expression. But those who cry "Press freedom!" at every adverse decision cannot properly be defended as guardians of our civil liberties.

Thus, it is not only in its self-interest that the newspaper rejects the simple proposition that it shall avoid legal trouble by not defaming anyone. Such an easy way out would also almost certainly guarantee the newspaper's extinction. In simplest terms, defamation means hurting reputations, and telling the news is impossible without hurting reputations. The newspaper has not only the right but the concomitant duty to publish the news as it finds it, exercising

reasonable discretion in order to minimize the chances of wronging an individual member of society.

The resulting day-to-day decisions are rarely easy. There are no simple "right" and "wrong" answers, because there is no "law"; the fifty states and the District of Columbia all have laws relating to libel but none has a single comprehensive statement that editors can refer to when they are in doubt. *Courts* decide libel cases, usually with, sometimes without, benefit of jury. Their decisions are based on "the merits of the case," as judged in the light of the facts and the findings of other courts before them.

The accumulation of decisions that gives the courts "precedent" for their decisions can be said to be based on general public sentiment—to have a *social* origin, in other words. Partly because of its social origin, libel law refuses to "sit still"; it is an extremely dynamic branch of the law. Changes in public attitudes toward personal traits, for example, may wreak their ultimate changes in what happens in a libel case. For example, the appellation "syndicalist" has been held libelous *per se* (explained on pages 331–332). Though syndicalism is still a crime, it is hard to imagine a libel suit being brought today on the basis of such an outmoded word. Conversely, in recent years courts have held that the appellation "communist" is libelous *per se,* though it was once not a nasty word at all.

Furthermore, the courts and the legislatures can and do change the law. A famous decision in 1964 and its aftermath have produced far-reaching changes in the law of defamation and has created some ambiguities which cases before courts at this writing may help resolve. This situation illustrates an important point about the editor's understanding of the law. It is not enough to learn what journalism and law textbooks say about it; he must pay attention to ongoing developments. It may be years before the implications of a new rule of law are fully explored by the case-law process.

The editor's surveillance is further complicated by the fact that published words can have consequences unfavorable to the newspaper whether or not a court decides a libel has been committed. Obviously, the newspaper suffers when it commits a libel, is successfully sued, and pays damages. But a successfully defended suit is also costly, for the newspaper suffers legal expenses in the process and often a marked loss of prestige as well. No matter what the court decides, there seems to be a tendency on the part of the public to view a libel struggle between an individual and a powerful, established newspaper in simple David-and-Goliath terms. The financial loss in cases settled out of court is just as hard to bear as if the cases had been settled under public scrutiny.

The mere *threat* of libel can have an adverse effect, too. In one instance, an important news source who was a powerful political figure and leading attorney of his community considered that he had been damaged by a publication which was merely careless and may have been defamatory. He "disciplined" the newspaper for a time by "clamming up" as a news source. No newspaper can call itself really "free" if it is not free from pressure of this sort.

Incidentally, the editor has a personal and highly practical stake in helping keep libel out of the stories he handles: he himself may be a respondent in a libel action, among many individuals. The publisher is, of course, always ultimately responsible for whatever his paper carries, and he is usually sued. But the person who gave out the story may also be made a respondent. Anyone on the staff who had a hand in the story may be named, too, provided he exercised some sort of judgment (compositors, for instance, have been declared not personally responsible). When reporters and editors are named in the initial specifications, however, they are often dropped as respondents before the case actually comes to trial.

It is of particular interest to the copy desk that the headline may be the basis for a libel suit, even when the accompanying story contains nothing defamatory. This is a clearly established principle. It is no defense that the damage done in the headline is somehow undone in the story. Perhaps the headline's greater conspicuousness and greater potential for ambiguity suggests that it should deserve even closer attention than the story itself.

How can the newspaper avoid getting into trouble with the law? A tentative answer will serve to introduce a brief discussion of the legal problems involved: Ask first whether material is libelous. Then ask whether suit is likely to be brought. Then ask whether suit is likely to be successful—can the newspaper expect to present a good defense? Finally, ask how important the story is. Ask not only *how much is risked* but also *for what purpose.*

This ushers in a final preliminary point. It is that newspapers often knowingly commit libel. This is not necessarily due to callousness, a devotion to "sensationalism," or a craven desire to peddle lots of papers on the streets. It is most often due to a high sense of responsibility, tempered by the paper's natural concern with its own solvency. In its simplest terms, the decision is between publishing the facts at the risk of incurring loss through libel and withholding the facts at the risk of denying the public part of the intelligence it has a right to.

What is Libel?

Perhaps the most frequently quoted definition of libel is that of the Illinois Criminal Code:

A malicious defamation, expressed either by printing or by signs, pictures or the like tending to blacken the memory of one who is dead or to impeach the honesty, integrity, virtue or reputation or publish the natural defects of one who is alive, and thereby to expose him to public hatred, contempt, ridicule or financial injury.

While this is a very careful definition, worked out in the course of centuries of legal decisions, it does not answer all questions about the nature of libel. It can, however, provide some important clues.

Defamation

The important first noun is *"defamation."* Defaming has been defined by an Iowa court as "taking from another his reputation." This provides the first clue to an important point that will be enlarged on below: that defamation depends not so much on what has been said as on *what people think* as a result of what has been said, or, more realistically, what a court judges to be the effect on people's minds of what has been said.

This definiton of defamation makes no mention of how or through what channels a person might have been defamed—*libel* or *slander.* Briefly put, slander is oral (spoken) defamation and libel is published or printed defamation. Since the spoken word preceded the printed word, slander is the parent of libel. Their differences, which are many, center around the fact that slander, by its nature, reaches few persons whereas libel reaches many. (Defamation by radio is treated more as libel in some states and slander in others.[1])

Now notice that the definition qualifies the noun "defamation" with the adjective *"malicious."* The concept of malice in the law of defamation has always been slippery, but it is critical in determining the defenses that may be used when a libel suit is brought, and it bears on the kind and amount of damages that the court may award. This is the issue that has come into question in case law since the 1964 Supreme Court decision in *New York Times Co.* v. *Sullivan.* This case has assumed such importance to the whole fabric of the law of libel that it will be treated in considerable detail on pages 339–341.

Another important word in the definition is *"tending."* This reminds us that it is not always necessary to show that the publication actually caused people to change their attitudes. Witnesses are sometimes paraded to the stand to testify to the effect of the words on them. But what the court has to decide from their testimony is not what the total actual damage was, but whether or not the words used tend to "impeach the honesty," etc., of the injured party.

The word "tending" also raises (and begs) this type of question: How many people and what sort of

people must be influenced in their attitudes toward the defamed person if the offense is to be defined as a libel? But the question is not legitimate. A jury determines whether the "natural tendency" of the words is to cause others to think less of the person libeled. *How many* people rarely has much bearing, because, for instance, the disapprobation of many distant persons may be less damaging than the disapprobation of a few nearby. *What sort* of person doesn't apply, either, since, for example, some people might think more highly than before of a minister accused in a newspaper story of leading a ghetto demonstration. Further, it is fruitless to argue that intelligent people will react one way and less intelligent people in another.

A publication is libelous of any person if its natural effect is to make those who read it think less of that person—and "those who read it" can be taken to mean "a substantial number of right-thinking people." However, this definition is perhaps inadequate if libel does not cause a person to be less highly regarded in the community but rather to be "shunned." A story saying or implying a man has a social disease can cause him to be both shunned and looked down upon. A story saying a man has a highly contagious disease may only cause him to be shunned. Such publications have been found libelous.

It is useful to focus on the idea of "tendency" and "effect" for another reason. It helps make clear why the dictionary is no authority in determining whether or not a word is libelous. It does not matter what it says about the meaning of a word; it is for the jury to decide how the word would be construed by those who read it at the time and place and under the circumstances of publication.

The final *"or"* in the definition is also important, for it makes clear that the injury must not necessarily be translatable into financial terms. Financial injury not accompanied by loss of esteem usually is not libel, however; loss of esteem not accompanied by financial injury may be libel.

"Public" indicates that ordinarily one may not be "privately" libeled; the injury must arise out of the effect the words may be expected to have on others, not their effect on the person libeled.

---

[1] For a detailed treatment of this subject, see Harold L. Nelson and Dwight L. Teeter, Jr., *Law of Mass Communications: Freedom and Control of Print and Broadcast Media* (Mineola, N.Y.: The Foundation Press, Inc., 1969), pp. 66–73. See also George Van Os, "Defamation by Broadcast: A Lively Dispute," *Houston Law Review* 2:238–250 (Fall 1964), reprinted in David G. Clark and Earl R. Hutchison, eds., *Mass Media and the Law: Freedom and Restraint* (New York: Wiley-Interscience, 1970), pp. 249–265.

Civil and Criminal Libel

"Civil" libel has been mentioned above and involves an important distinction. Defamation through printing, etc., can be said to have two major kinds of effect with which the law is concerned. One is to cause injury to an individual member of society. The other is to cause injury to society as a whole. The first is *civil* libel; the law allows the injured party to go to court and obtain redress for his injury. Like all civil actions, the matter is between the first party and the second, with the public only providing the means, through the courts, of refereeing the contest. In a *criminal-libel* action the public, having been wronged, acts directly through the courts to exact punishment.

It follows that the kinds of defamation that might result in injury to the public on the one hand and to individuals on the other are quite different. Without examining these differences in detail, it can be said that defamations which have a tendency to cause a breach of the peace fall into the criminal category, while those which tend to cause injury or suffering to an individual constitute civil libel.

Criminal libel has a more interesting past than present. The trial of John Peter Zenger, for example, an important symbol in the struggle for freedom of the press, was a criminal libel action. Today criminal libel actions are rare.[2] In the rare cases where it is invoked, it is the tendency of the words to incite a breach of the peace, not merely the injury to reputation, that is involved.[3] Also, when a publication defames a dead person, action is possible only through criminal libel; it has been held that the reputation dies with the person, which means that no civil action is possible. The defamation does not extend to his descendants, for instance, since it is his memory that has been blackened, not their reputations. Likewise, a member of an organization cannot obtain redress when that organization is ridiculed or falsely accused except in the rare case where he can show that he himself has somehow been identified. However, criminal action is possible in such a case, although such actions are rarely brought.[4] Malice is not assumed in criminal libel and must be shown.

Because almost all libel actions against newspapers are civil actions, the remainder of this section will be confined to that subject. Henceforth the word "libel" will be used to mean "civil libel" unless criminal libel is specified. The injured party is always referred to as "person," "individual," etc., but corporations and partnerships are treated as persons under the law and thus may be injured by a libelous publication.

It now becomes necessary to make another distinction in "types" of libel. In past decisions, courts have held certain words to be libelous *per se*—in and of themselves whenever applied to any person. However, the libelous potential of publications is not limited to such words. Others which may be innocent in themselves can prove to be dangerous in certain contexts. These are known as libels *per quod*. The precise legal distinction is not crystal clear, but for our purposes it need not be. The editor needs only to know that he must look beyond the mere word in assessing the libel hazard. It is not libelous to say of a married woman that she gave birth to an eight-pound boy but to say falsely that she did in the second month after marriage is another matter. In the days when newspapers carried hotel guest lists and the reporter wrote the intrinsically innocent words "Mr. and Mrs." when it

---

[2] Reported cases of criminal libel held closely to about a hundred per decade for the thirty years preceding World War I, then fell sharply to around ten or fifteen per decade. Consult John D. Stevens, Robert L. Bailey, Judith F. Krueger, and John M. Mollwitz, "Criminal Libel as Seditious Libel, 1916–65," *Journalism Quarterly* 43:110–113 (Spring 1966). The indication is that criminal libel as a basis for preventing both breaches of the peace and false and malicious criticism of public officials (sedition) has largely disappeared from the courts. In the *Garrison* v. *Louisiana* case, the Supreme Court overturned a conviction which had been upheld by the Louisiana Supreme Court against a district attorney who charged that certain judges were lazy and inattentive to their duties; a Kentucky sedition statute was outlawed by the Supreme Court.

[3] Consult Nelson and Teeter, *op. cit.,* pp. 279–280.

[4] Nelson and Teeter (*op. cit.,* pp. 280 ff.) cite the 1952 case in which a group libel statute was upheld by the U. S. Supreme Court in a 5–4 decision (*Beauharnais* v. *Illinois*). The majority held that the court could not prevent a state from making it unlawful to publish anything "which portrays depravity, criminality, unchastity, or lack of virtue of a class of citizens . . . or exposes the citizens of any race, color, creed or religion to contempt, derision, or obloquy or which is productive of breach of the peace or riots." The minority termed it "state censorship" and "a startling and frightening doctrine."

should have been only "Mr.," his newspaper found itself with a libel suit on its hands.

The distinction under discussion has another important aspect when and if the case comes to court. Because libel *per se* is obviously defamatory, it is not necessary for the plaintiff to show that in some specific way he has in fact suffered as a result of the publication. Libel *per quod,* on the other hand, requires proof that special damages were suffered.

It must be clear that both "publication" and "defamation" must be present to make a libel. There is a third such essential element, however: *"identification"*: the person suing for libel must have been identified in the publication as the person involved. From the standpoint of the copy desk, devices for concealing the actual name, age, and street address don't often work; it is not necessary in a suit to show that *all* readers would be able to identify the person or that a majority would or that a lot of people would. The disapprobation of the few who could identify the person might be as damaging as if the name itself were used.

Identification need not even be by words, for that matter. It has been established that a picture can identify a person as positively as his name. This underscores the importance of precision in carrying out the routines of newsroom and composing room. Many libel cases arise simply out of misidentification: if A's picture is used where B's was intended, the potential for a libel suit is obvious. We might be on perfectly safe ground in describing B's alleged crimes and running B's picture, but we defame A if his picture— no matter how inadvertently—appears instead.

It is up to the plaintiff to show that he (or the corporation or partnership) was the one injured by the publication. It is not enough that he show that a group of persons was injured and that he is a member of that group. The courts ruled as long ago as 1815 that criticism of a group does not of itself constitute a criticism of an individual member of that group. The only danger of libel in an attack upon a group is the possibility that a court will determine that the injurious language clearly pertained to *every* member of the group and hence to the individual. In general, the smaller the group the greater likelihood of such a finding.

The importance of identification in libel makes it clear why *full* identification is the only safe practice in stories containing any defamatory material. The chances are that there are many John Joneses. The field is narrowed immensely when his age is given. When his address is given too, the newspaper virtually guarantees that no other John Jones can consider that he has been identified. This is true, of course, only when the name, age, and address are correct.

Only rarely is there a question about whether a defamation has been published or not. In instances where a libelous statement is discovered and corrected after the edition is on the press, a reasonable effort to track down and destroy the offending copies might become grounds for alleging that there has been no publication in fact. Such acts also constitute evidence of good faith, which, as we shall see, can mitigate the consequences of libel.

One further point must be raised about the word "defamation." A publication is not a libel when its natural effect is to have people think only a little less of a person. Publications can range from the mildly disparaging to words causing almost everyone to shun the person for life. But disparagement is not defamation. A publication must, as stated in the Illinois definition, inspire "hatred, contempt, [or] ridicule" in order to be libelous.

The concluding words in the Illinois definition given above contain an aspect of libel often overlooked. "Financial injury" means just that. To call into question the professional qualifications of lawyers, ministers, teachers, architects, engineers, and the like may damage their earning power and provoke prompt reprisal in the form of a libel suit. Professional disparagement that results in financial injury need not also have the effect of exposing the individual to hatred, contempt, or ridicule. It is enough that he has been damaged in his profession. A person injured in the pursuit of his occupation, whatever it may be, can be awarded heavy special damages. Corporations, too, have a right to protect their good name against false and defamatory publications.

Lest this recital of what constitutes libel appear to imply that almost nothing the newspaper says is really safe, let us turn briefly to what is *not* libel. The point has already been made that mere disparagement does not constitute libel. A publication which causes a person anguish but does not affect his reputation is not a libel. A publication is not libelous merely because it causes financial injury.

Defenses

In determining what is libelous, we have been talking about the *offense* alone. If no offense exists, then the case must be dismissed. Once it is clear that a publicatiton is a libelous offense, its perpetrators do not necessarily have to pay. They may be able to defend themselves.

A comprehensive list of all the complete defenses in libel could include as many as nine. Four of these can be disposed of in a hurry. As with other torts, libel has a *statute of limitations.* This means that if suit is not brought within a stated time after the commission of the libel, there is no recourse to law. The length of time varies from one state to another. The second is the *absolute privilege* that protects judges, witnesses, legislators, etc., against actions for defamation as *participants* in public and official proceedings, but has no bearing on *reports* of these proceedings. The third simply says that a *libel action may not be brought a second time* after having been settled once. The fourth says that *an action may not be brought where the injured person has accepted or agreed to an out-of-court settlement* for the same libel. These do not pertain to the language of the publication and are included here only to complete the record.

Three complete defenses against the libel hazard make it possible for newspapers to publish the great volume of defamatory material that they must. These are *truth, statutory privilege,* and *fair comment or criticism.* All three are well established as complete, though qualified, defenses, and collectively are as important to freedom of the press as the First Amendment itself.

First, it may be wise to make a distinction between the two concepts "complete-incomplete" and "qualified-unqualified." If a *complete* defense is established, no damages of any sort may be recovered; the defendant need not establish any other defense. Truth, fair comment, and privilege are all complete defenses.

They are all *qualified* defenses in some states and some are qualified in other states. For instance, some states, as we shall see, qualify truth as a defense with the stipulation that the truth must be for good motives and justifiable ends. In these states, truth is a complete, though qualified, defense.

Two of the three most significant defenses in a libel action are closely affected by the *Times* v. *Sullivan* interpretation of what constitutes an actionable published defamation. All three—truth, fair comment or criticism, and statutory privilege—can in most circumstances be overthrown by a showing that the publication was actuated by *malice.* The *Times* rule, in giving a closer definition to malice, has clarified the question of truth as a defense where some part of the facts presented are shown to be false. The closer definition of malice also affects the amount and kind of damages that the courts are likely to award. Finally, the new rule has had some influence on the burden of proof in establishing actual malice (*i.e.,* is it necessary for the defense to establish or the prosecution to disprove actual malice?).

In fact, under the new rule, one of the three defenses—fair comment or criticism—is open to serious question as a distinct defense. And there is a further complication: *Times* v. *Sullivan* itself speaks only of public officials and what they may expect when they seek redress in the civil courts; subsequent cases appear to be widening the application of the *Times* rule from persons whose performance in their role is subject to public criticism to issues of general public concern.

Because these questions are not well established at present, the defenses will first be presented as they were understood in the decades before 1964; only then will the influence of *Times* v. *Sullivan* and subsequent cases be discussed.[5]

Truth

Truth is a defense in civil libel well established in Anglo-Saxon law. We have come a long way, how-

[5] For a useful discussion of *Times* v. *Sullivan* and subsequent cases, see John Alkazin, "The Defamation of a Public Official," *University of San Francisco Law Review* 1:358–368 (April 1967). This article also appears in Clark and Hutchison, *op. cit.,* 236–248.

ever, from the days when it was generally held that "the greater the truth the greater the libel." The rationale of truth as a defense might be seen in this light: If the press is to perform its function in a democratic society it must be free to publish the truth even though it may sometimes hurt. If published truth causes public injury, as when it tends to incite to riot, then it has no justification; the state may even proscribe it as a matter of criminal law. If the truth tends to cause injury to private individuals, it may be justifiably published only if there is good reason to believe the public will thereby be served—hence the common qualification that truth is a defense only when published *for good motives and justifiable ends.*

About half the states accept truth as a defense qualified this way or in similar language such as "good faith," "proper occasion," or "justifiable purpose." The others treat truth as an unqualified defense in civil libel. After all, qualification does not add greatly to the difficulty of the defense. When a story has been judged in the usual way for its news value, it is not ordinarily hard to show that the motives were good. If the story is one which would ordinarily be laid before the public as a matter of public interest, then it is not hard to show that the ends are justifiable.

The defense of truth means that words which are true may safely be published without fear of retribution even though they may be defamatory. However, several very important limitations on this defense must be observed.

1. *The burden of proof is on the defendant.* The newsman must ask himself not only whether the words are true but whether he can *prove* they are true. It is not up to the plaintiff to prove that the story is untrue; it is up to the defendant publisher to show that it is true. This immediately involves the rules of evidence and the whole question of what the courts regard as proof of the fact, too broad a subject for this summary handling of the libel hazard. All that can be done here is to underline, overline, box, check, and asterisk this important fact: No matter how sure the reporter is that his facts are correct, both in detail and in substance, his certainty is no measure of safety

unless it can be transformed into the kind of proof that a court will accept. The reporter's good faith in the matter, his *belief* that the facts are right, has no bearing on truth as a defense. (N.B.: This generalization has particularly been affected by the *Times* rule.)

2. *Facts, as journalism defines facts, do not qualify as truth as the law defines truth.* To justify a publication on the ground that it is true, it is necessary to show that the facts themselves are true. Accuracy is not enough. If an informant tells a reporter that another person has committed a crime, the reporter satisfies the journalistic definition of fact if he writes that the informant said it (or that it was said). In defending a libel suit, however, he must be able to prove that the accused person did in fact commit the crime.

3. *The justification must be as broad as and specific to the charge.* If a person is labeled a "notorious criminal" it is not sufficient to show that he was once convicted of some petty crime. If a story accuses a person of embezzlement, it is not enough to show that he "diverted funds," which may be a lesser crime, and it is not enough to show that he has been guilty of other crimes than embezzlement, even though they may be equally serious. The newspaper must be prepared to prove embezzlement.

Truth is perhaps the most powerful defense in libel. Applications of the New York *Times* rule since 1964 have given newsmen much more protection from libel suits under the truth defense than they have ever enjoyed before. When stories about public officials or public personages have an underlying justification in terms of public interest, they must no longer be correct in scrupulous particulars. The rule protects the publisher of a defamatory falsehood from a libel judgment unless it can be shown that the publisher knew that what he published was false *or* that he published it with reckless disregard of whether it was false or not.

Statutory Privilege

A second complete, though again qualified, defense is statutory privilege, sometimes called *qualified privilege* to distinguish it from the absolute privilege attaching to judges, etc., described earlier. It is called statutory privilege because in most states it has been established by statute. The rationale of privilege is also based in the First Amendment and considerations of the public interest. The courts and statutes have protected the right to publish facts about the public business which it is in the interest of the public to know, even though they may be damaging to the reputation of an individual. It would be contrary to the public interest if sources of information and ideas were so hedged around by fear of reprisal that large parts of the public business were kept out of the public prints.

As a consequence, newspapers and other purveyors of information are protected in spreading public affairs on the record—to the extent, at least, that public and official proceedings may be fairly and truly reported without fear of libel. It is clearly defamatory of a person to report that he has been charged with a heinous crime. It becomes possible to report such a fact because it is part of the procedure of a democratic society to try him for the crime publicly and officially. The right to publish the fact is therefore immune to libel. Reporting the charge is safeguarded as long as the charge is official and part of a public record or proceeding—whether or not it subsequently proves to be true. This does not extend the right of saying that a person is *guilty* of the crime before a court has so determined, and it does not give newsmen the right to speculate on his guilt or innocence or to publish information lacking such authority which would tend to imply his guilt or innocence.

Since statutory privilege is often part of the written law, it is possible to examine a typical definition. The New York law, for example, defines it in the following terms:

An action, civil or criminal, cannot be maintained against a reporter, editor, publisher or proprietor of a newspaper for publication therein of a fair and true report of any judicial, legislative or other public and official proceeding; or for any heading of the report which is a fair and true head note of the article published. This section does not apply to a libel contained in any other matter added by any person concerned in the publication, or in the report of anything said or done at the time and place of the judicial, legislative or other public and official proceeding which was not a part thereof.

In one important respect this definition is not typical. Most states qualify their definition of privilege with such language as "for good motives and justifiable ends." Thus in most states, proof of actual malice is enough to nullify the defense of privilege. All the other important things to remember about privilege are contained in the New York definition:

1. *"A fair and true report."* This language makes it clear that newsmen must be vigilant even when reporting privileged proceedings. One of the most dangerous sources of libel is reporters and editors going beyond the factual reporting which is essential if the immunities of privilege are to be enjoyed, especially in reporting court trials that command widespread interest.

2. *"Any judicial, legislative or other public and official proceeding."* This phrase is extremely important because it establishes quite clearly the limits of the defense of privilege. The "and" is especially significant, as it indicates that it is not enough that a proceeding be official nor is it enough that it be public; it must be both. Legislative committee hearings, for instance, are official and ordinarily public. However, executive sessions of such committees are official but not public and hence do not carry immunity. A public meeting, even if it is sponsored by some public or semipublic agency, is only public and not also official, hence, not privileged. A few states have extended privilege to meetings which are public, though not official. This is far from being a generally accepted principle, however.

Some documents fall into the shadowy area between public and not public, official and nonofficial. The police "blotter" is one. The blotter is the running record of the department's activities, usually kept by a desk sergeant. It is often his source of specific information in supplying news to reporters. Some states have, by statute, declared the blotter to be public and official and hence privileged. In a greater number of states, either it has been ruled not privileged or no clear statute or court ruling has appeared.

It must not be assumed that *any* legislative or

judicial *document* is privileged. Certain court records and proceedings are official but not public:

a. *Grand jury proceedings* are secret and may not be reported. The indictment or failure to indict which results from these proceedings is privileged and may be reported. A report of a grand jury proceeding subjects the publisher not only to loss of privilege should libel be involved but also to citation for contempt.

b. Most *juvenile court proceedings* are secret. Publication of them is not privileged and may also cause citation for contempt.

c. When, due to the nature of the testimony, a judge "clears the court"—orders the public from the courtroom—the press is similarly excluded and may not report the proceedings. Both contempt and loss of privilege are again at stake. However, the judge may permit some court officer to report the essence of the testimony, and his words may safely be quoted as a fair and true account.

d. Certain *pleadings* are not privileged until they become part of the record of a trial. In general, these are pleadings which are entered before trial commences. The most dangerous example is divorce pleadings. When suit is filed for divorce, attorneys for both parties file pleadings which contain the grounds for divorce and answers thereto. Such material tempts the reporter because it often contains sensational disclosures. When a case actually reaches open court, pleadings become a part of the record of the court and public. Then and only then are these documents privileged. In the frequent instances where the action is dropped or is settled "in chambers," the pleadings are sealed and never do become a public record, hence are not privileged at any time.

3. *"Does not apply to a libel contained in any other matter."* It is the proceeding itself that is privileged; events which occur at the same time and place as the proceeding are not immune. The reporter is safe in supplying details not part of the proceedings as long as the details cannot be construed as commenting on the defendant's guilt or innocence. "The defendant visibly paled at the mention of the knife"; "the witness wrung his hands fearfully"—such comments are obviously not a part of the record (the court reporter does not record changes in skin tint or motor activity) and are not privileged.

Matter which has been stricken from the record is treated by the court as though it hadn't happened. Consequently, the stricken testimony, however accurate, is not protected, even when the fact that it was stricken is also duly reported.

Comments by officials *about* public and official proceedings are not part of the proceedings and are not privileged. In order to get a better picture of the background of an arrest or civil or criminal court case, the reporter frequently seeks information from persons able to supply it—policemen, prosecuting attorneys, court officials—but he writes such matter into his story at the risk of libel. Privilege attaches to any legal arrest, whether or not there is a warrant, in spite of the fact that any arrest discredits the person arrested. But statements about the facts leading to the arrest made by the arresting officer or the desk sergeant or the district attorney are not privileged. Should the arrested person later be freed, he may sue for libel; if he does and nonprivileged matter is the basis for the suit, the newspaper must resort to some other defense than privilege.

Obviously, statements not a part of the proceedings which are not potentially libelous do not destroy the privilege that attaches to the proceeding.

Fair Comment or Criticism

The third complete defense in libel is *fair comment* or *criticism*. Like truth and privilege it is qualified, largely by the presence or absence of malice (it is this defense that has been most directly affected by the *Times* rule). Along with truth and privilege, fair comment protects the publisher in the exercise of his editorial vigilance over public affairs against the crippling prospect of libel suits. It is not, however, a right reserved to publishers of the written word and broadcasters of the spoken word, but to all citizens, who are within their rights in criticizing public officials and others who seek public approval so long as the criticisms are fair and reasonable and not malicious.

There is an interesting contrast between fair comment and privilege. Privilege is a defense; an unequivocal defamation may be defended on grounds of privilege. The establishment of fair comment, on the other hand, means that there has been no libel. In effect it says: These unkind words have been directed against the individual's professional *work,* not against his person; hence the individual has not been defamed at all.

To avail itself of the defense of fair comment, the newspaper must be able to show that the criticism has been of the individual *in his capacity as* a public official or public figure, not defamatory of the person. It is reasonably safe to condemn the acts of a public official in vigorous terms, but it is unsafe to imply that his imperfections as a public official carry over into his private life or arise out of a general want of integrity or morality. This distinction is important to the *rationale* of fair comment, which makes it possible for the public and its agents in the press to criticize the public personage's performance as such but not to defame his character.

What makes a person a public personage? In general, it can be said that those who invite public approbation for their acts are the very ones who must accept disapprobation of the same acts. Among the persons and institutions falling into this category are:

—officials of government, whether elective or appointive, and candidates for public office

—administrators of justice, including the judiciary and court officers

—institutions, both public and private, if their function is a matter of public concern, and the officers and employees of such institutions (universities, hospitals, churches, etc.)

—anyone who in cultural or entertainment pursuits appeals to public acceptance (authors, artists, actors, singers, etc.)

It is for the jury to decide whether a person falls into this category.

In appraising privilege and fair comment a difficult distinction arises between fact and opinion. Statements of fact in many circumstances are defensible on the grounds of fair comment. It is often up to the court to decide which is which. In general, the acts of a judge or legislator during an official proceeding may

be described factually (without actual malice) under the protection of privilege; his acts may be appraised (without actual malice) under the protection of fair comment. Of course nothing resembling privilege obtains with the theater, but the play, actors, director, scene designer, etc., may be criticized (without actual malice) with the protection of fair comment, provided the criticism is fair and provided it is stated *as an opinion.*

Following is a checklist of elements that must be present in utterances in order to be protected by the defense of fair comment. It may be useful in assessing the libel hazard in, say, a theater or literary column.

1. Fair comment applies only where the subject of criticism is a matter of public interest or concern; it deals only with matters that invite public attention and tend to seek public approval.

2. The comment must be an intellectual appraisal or evaluation (not, for instance, the pretext for a personal attack).

3. It must be stated as opinion.

4. It must be an honest opinion.

5. It must have a basis in fact.

6. It must be free from the imputation of corrupt or sordid motives.

7. It must be free of actual malice.

Nothing in the list limits the notion of fairness to temperate wording, giving "both sides," freedom from bias, or providing a means of rebuttal. The wording may be vigorous, the ideas opinionated, the bias obvious—and the defense of fair comment still appropriate. In a celebrated Iowa case, for example, a newspaper had commented on a vaudeville troupe in these terms:

> Effie is an old jade of 50 summers, Jessie a frisky filly of 40, and Addie, the flower of the family, a capering monstrosity of 35 . . . long skinny arms . . . talons . . . strange creatures with painted faces and hideous mien. Effie is spavined, Addie is stringhalt, and Jessie has calves as classic in their outlines as the curves of a broom handle.

This language, caustic and intemperate as it may seem, was held to constitute a fair comment. Had it been shown that the publication was actuated by malice, of course, fair comment as a defense would have been defeated. But ridicule, sarcasm, and invective do not overthrow the defense of fair comment, if the jury decides that actual malice is not present. (If the language tends to incite to violence, there is a possibility, of course, of a criminal-libel action.)

Perhaps the most important single thing to watch for in testing the prospects of defending a story, editorial, or column as fair comment is its imputations. Questioning the motives of the performer or public servant can overthrow the defense.

A second key check is in the relationship of the opinion to the facts. Gross deviation from the facts can wreck the defense of fair comment; minor deviations from the facts are acceptable. The jury must examine the criticism in its entirety and determine whether the facts are susceptible of the opinions expressed. If a story falsely accuses a public official of complicity in some illegal act, he may sue successfully despite the fact that he happens to be a public official. The defense of privilege does not apply if the facts are inaccurate; opinions relating to a public official's public capacity lose the protection of fair comment when they are grossly at variance with the facts. Thus it would be extremely risky to comment adversely on the qualifications of a public official because he filed a public report late when in fact the report was filed on time. The fact that the publisher, reporter, or editor believed the facts to be true does not excuse defamation. Again the defendant must prove the truth of the facts forming the basis of the opinion if he is to avail himself of the defense of fair comment.

It is almost needless at this point to say that the *Times* rule has altered this issue profoundly. It was once argued that truth was the appropriate defense in cases involving defamatory facts and fair comment the appropriate defense where judgments or inferences were involved. The line between fact and comment has always been hard to draw, but as Nelson and Teeter point out, the *Times* rule may make such a distinction unnecessary.[6]

Perhaps the greatest difficulty in predicting the libel hazard in fair-comment cases arises in the twilight zone between those acts which are clearly of a public nature and those that tend to reflect on the individual as an individual. For instance, may a newspaper safely comment on the habitual drinking of a public official? Such conduct might be said to disqualify him for high office, even though its effects may not clearly be seen in his public acts. Or it might be said to be a private matter bearing only on the individual's personal reputation.

Other Complete Defenses

The two complete defenses that remain to be discussed are less securely anchored in law. *Consent* or authorization, in its simplest aspects, is rather obvious. If a person reads and approves a story about himself before publication and then after publication brings suit for libel, the newspaper has but to prove that consent to publication was obtained. A libel has been committed but the defense is complete; no damages may be assessed. "Consent does not include an assent obtained by fraud or duress or from . . . [an] incompetent person. . . . [It] may be express or implied. If express, it may be written or oral."[7]

Express consent is rarely granted; or perhaps those foolish enough to grant consent to a damaging story are rarely foolish enough to sue. Implied consent is not clearly established in law. When a person has availed himself of an opportunity to reply before publication to a defamatory charge, courts have held that he has thereby given his consent to the publication implicitly. Such a defense holds, of course, only when the individual has not demanded or indicated his wish that the story be withheld.

The complete defense of *self-defense* is also in a formative stage. Courts have held that a newspaper has a right to strike back against someone who has begun a controversy against it. The newspaper

. . . may not only block or parry the blow—that is, deny the charges—but may also use reasonable affirmative force—as, for example, by publishing statements exposing what it believes to be infirmities or misconduct of the

[6] Nelson and Teeter, *op. cit.,* pp. 148–149.

[7] Harold L. Cross, "Current Libel Trends," *Nieman Reports,* January 1951, pp. 1, 7–11.

plaintiff, though such statements be libelous and turn out to be false, provided they were made in good faith, on reasonable grounds, and without actual malice.[8]

Thus, even when libelous statements cannot be defended on the grounds that they are true, privileged, or constitute fair comment, it may be possible to defend them on the grounds of self-defense.

The Times Rule

From the foregoing discussion it should be plain that there have been rather clear-cut ways for the news editor to test the libel hazard in a particular story. He first asks whether the elements of libel are all present: Is the material defamatory, does it identify the person defamed, and was it (or will it be) published? If the answer to all these questions is "Yes," then he asks whether there is a genuine risk that it cannot be defended. Can he establish the essential *truth* of the defamatory material? Is the defamatory material protected by *statutory privilege*? Is the person defamed a public official or a person whose acts are on other grounds subject to *fair comment* or criticism? Only one defense need be established, but the burden of establishing it is obviously on the defense. The last step is to ask: Is it possible for the plaintiff to overthrow the defense by proving actual malice? To do so the plaintiff must assume the burden of proof.

What *Times* v. *Sullivan* appears to have done is to redefine "actual malice," making the whole question of liability for libel turn on whether in publishing information or opinion defamatory of someone the defendant was either aware that it was false or showed "reckless disregard of whether it was false or not." The plaintiff still assumes the burden of proof. Such a formula obviously gives the press a kind of judicial benefit of the doubt, because knowing falsehood or reckless disregard for truth is difficult to prove.

The case arose when the New York *Times* carried a paid advertisement signed by sixty-four prominent personages pleading for fair treatment for Negroes in the South. The ad cited recent instances of unfair treatment in Montgomery, Alabama, and decried the performance of the city's police. Suit was brought by the Montgomery Commissioner of Public Affairs

against the newspaper and four Negro clergymen who were among the signers of the ad. Although he had not been named in the ad, the commissioner argued that he had been identified in that everyone knew he was the person responsible for the performance of the city's police. Some of the facts in the ad were erroneous. The defense disputed neither this nor that the paper's Advertising Acceptability Department had not checked the text for errors (it felt it had no need for questioning the truthfulness of such a distinguished array of signers). The Alabama Supreme Court upheld a $500,000 award to the plaintiff but was overruled by the United States Supreme Court.

It is the language of Mr. Justice Brennan's majority decision that has had such a profound influence on United States libel law. Referring only to the defamation of the public official, Justice Brennan wrote that the First Amendment

. . . requires, we think, a federal rule that prohibits a public official from recovering damages for a defamatory falsehood relating to his official conduct unless he proves that the statement was made with "actual malice"—that is, with knowledge that it was false or with reckless disregard for whether it was false or not.

The Supreme Court in *Times* v. *Sullivan* indicated that First Amendment interests in full and free discussion were more important than the libel laws and judicial precedents of a state jurisdiction. One outcome of this decision should be that variations in libel laws of the states will be reduced.

Various judicial tests of good motives as a condition of truth as a defense have been accepted in various jurisdictions and at various times. Actual malice has been defined in terms of intent ("intent to do harm"), personal motive ("hatred"), dishonesty (the words are not the writer's honest opinion; the writer had no reason to believe his words were true), recklessness, vehement language (from which bad motives may be inferred), and unfairness ("a reasonable man would not regard the language to be fair").[9] All suffer from a degree of vagueness and were difficult to prove or disprove in a court of law. The *Times* rule, at least, has the virtue of clarity, even if it makes actual malice

[8] *Ibid.*, p. 10.

[9] Nelson and Teeter, *op. cit.*, p. 148.

even more difficult to prove. The *Times* rule turns not on what is in the heart of the publisher of a false defamation or what his intent was or what the extravagance of his language might imply, but instead turns on his *ethical performance* as a truth seeker and teller. It underscores the first principal of journalism: Guard truth.

As we have seen, the *Times* rule was initially applied to the case of a public official seeking redress in a civil court. But subsequent cases have shown that the rule is more widely applicable. For example, the Alaska Supreme Court applied the rule to the defense of fair comment in determining that there was no actual malice involved when a newspaper, in dropping a widely syndicated column, called the column "garbage" and the columnist "a garbage man."[10] It was also applied in the case of a nationally known scientist who sued a newspaper for falsely stating that he had been cited for contempt of Congress. Even though he was not a public official in any sense, the court declared the scientist was "projecting himself into the arena of public controversy" and therefore "should have no greater remedy than should his counterpart in public office."[11] Thus it would appear that the *Times* rule is being applied as widely as the defense of fair comment.

In a case of trade libel, a New York newspaper reported in its financial section that a film-processing company was in financial difficulties. The company sued for $5 million, alleging that the story was misleading and contained false information. A New York Supreme Court ruling[12] invoked *Times* v. *Sullivan*, saying that there had been no showing that the writer "entertained serious doubts as to the truth of his publication," and commenting on the tendency of the old rule to induce an undesirable self-censorship. The case involved a broad public interest in public companies and trade in their securities in the stock market. The court said the ordinary buyer of stocks had as much right to information as "the rich and institutional purchaser" and it was up to newspapers to be responsive to such a broad public interest. They might not if they had to defend the truth of every factual item they report.[13]

The Supreme Court even applied the *Times* rule in a case involving a complaint that the report of a play in a news magazine invaded privacy by suggesting that the facts given in the play accurately portrayed events in the real incident. It ruled that there was enough public interest in the play and the real-life story it retold to warrant sending the case back to a lower court to determine whether the magazine had shown reckless disregard for the truth in representing that the play was a reenactment of the event.[14]

The new rule does not by any means give blanket license to the publisher to defame public officials or public personages. When a national magazine accused a college football coach of revealing secrets to a rival coach, the Supreme Court examined the evidence of the magazine's efforts to verify the facts and found "an extreme departure from the standards of investigation and reporting."[15] The court disagreed on this "extreme departure" test, but the case makes it clear that shoddy work by reporters and editors can still get newspapers into trouble with the law of libel.

Since the *Times* rule has been enunciated, the Supreme Court has attempted to define "reckless disregard," saying:

There must be sufficient evidence to permit the conclusion that the defendant in fact entertained serious doubts as to the truth of his publication. Publishing with such doubts shows reckless disregard for truth or falsity and demonstrates actual malice.

But at the same time, it emphasized that recklessness itself can also be a basis for reckless disregard, as "when a publisher's allegations are so inherently improbable that only a reckless man would put them in circulation" or "where there are obvious reasons to

---

[10] *Ibid.*, pp. 148–149 (*Pearson* v. *Fairbanks Publishing Company*).

[11] *Ibid.*, pp. 94–95 (*Pauling* v. *Globe-Democrat Publishing Co.*).

[12] This is not an appellate court. At this writing, the case had not been reviewed.

[13] *Editor & Publisher*, January 24, 1970, p. 18.

[14] Nelson and Teeter, *op. cit.*, pp. 100*ff.* (*Time, Inc.* v. *Hill*).

[15] *Curtis Publishing Co.* v. *Butts*.

doubt the veracity of the informant or the accuracy of his reports."[16] Nelson and Teeter advise that reporters and editors should apply two tests here: (1) source credibility (Would a reasonable man believe such a source?) and (2) verification (Were reasonable steps taken to ensure credibility?)[17]

The newsman is now in a position to reduce the test for libel from the longer series of questions propounded on page 339 to something simpler: Is it true? If false, was a sufficient effort made to assure its truth? Before *Times* v. *Sullivan*, he could safely publish if the story was true *and* his motives were good. Since 1964—or until some new doctrine or clarification emerges—he can safely publish even if he is not certain the story is false, provided a serious effort has been made to determine truth of falsity. Before 1964, the publisher had to be prepared to prove truth—the burden was his. Since 1964, the plaintiff has had to be willing to shoulder the burden of showing that the publisher was heedless of truth. But the only way to assure that the plaintiff will not succeed lies in the newsman's ethical concern and performance as guardians of truth.

Damages

Damages enter the picture after it has been shown that a libel has been committed and is indefensible. Three distinct types of damages are recognized in libel cases:

Compensatory (or general) damages are allowed to the injured person by the court to compensate him for nonpecuniary losses he has suffered as a result of the publication. The idea is to "make the plaintiff whole"—to restore him to the condition he enjoyed before being injured. He is not required to prove that he has suffered injury; he is presumed to have suffered as a result of an indefensible libel. Such sufferings include injury to reputation, loss of physical and mental

well-being, or injury to business or professional standing.

Although, as we have pointed out above, the court is not interested in the effect of the defamation on the person libeled but rather in its effect on others, the plaintiff can introduce evidence of his injuries in an effort to increase the amount of the general damages. Correspondingly, the defense cannot defend the case on the ground that there was no suffering but can introduce evidence to that effect in an effort to reduce the general damages.

Special damages, on the other hand, are those awarded for pecuniary losses actually resulting from the publication. Their extent and kind are not presumed and must be based on evidence. The plaintiff can recover special damages in addition to compensatory damages. He need not prove special damages in order to recover compensatory damages.

Punitive (or exemplary) damages provide one of the rare instances in which punishment is meted out for a civil offense. If actual malice is found, the court may award punitive damages in addition to either or both of the other two types. Such an award is set as an example to others who might similarly err.

These are the basic kinds of damages courts award, but in special circumstances there arises a fourth—*nominal* damages—traditionally amounting to six cents. When the court feels that an indefensible libel has been committed but that no injury has been done to merit awarding the other three kinds of damages, then it may award nominal damages.

Mitigation of Damages

The plaintiff must prove actual malice, and he may do so by introducing direct evidence or by inference. Malice may be inferred from a refusal on the part of the newspaper to publish a retraction or by repetition of the story or its damaging parts. It is thus possible to talk about *partial defense,* in contrast with the *complete* defenses described above. Partial defenses do not prove that a libel was defensible, but they can be introduced to *mitigate* or reduce damages.

Partial defenses are of two kinds, those which show

---

[16] Nelson and Teeter, *op. cit.,* p. 105 (*St. Amant* v. *Thompson*).

[17] *Loc. cit.*

affirmatively that the publisher held goodwill toward the plaintiff and those showing that the publication was made in good faith. In both, the most important single act on the newspaper's part is the publication of a retraction. Such a publication, made promptly and without reservation, especially if given equal prominence with the defamatory matter, clearly shows good faith and tends to indicate an absence of ill will.

Other ways the newspaper can defend itself against the charge of malice include being prepared to show that:

—the story came from some usually reliable source, such as a wire service

—the newspaper investigated carefully and thoroughly

—other newspapers carried the story or a similar one

—the story was "common knowledge" before it was published

—the general conduct of the plaintiff had made it easy to believe that the story was true

Perhaps the reader is already familiar with the newsroom adage that any newspaper that hasn't at least one libel suit pending isn't worth much. Lest he interpret this to mean that there is something honorable or enviable about libel, the novice will do well to see the adage in this light: While it is true that vigorous, fighting newspapers are more likely to get into libel difficulties than their more placid and less effectual opposite numbers, even they prefer to calculate their risks. An alert copy desk can serve by preventing the unintentional, "noncalculated" story from wreaking unnecessary and costly consequences.

Other Legal Restrictions

Besides civil and criminal libel, the laws of the nation and the several states (and sometimes of lesser levels of government) impose additional restraints on publication. Federal law prohibits the dissemination through the mails of obscene matter and information about lotteries. Laws of the various states prohibit publishing information about gambling, the name of

a woman who may have been raped, and advocacy of anarchism and other "isms." Most states have laws prohibiting the publication of false or misleading advertisements, advertisements for narcotic drugs, and advertisements which fail to meet minimum standards of taste and morality. A few cities have ordinances similarly limiting what may be published in newspapers. The courts are empowered to hold newspapers in contempt for publishing information forbidden by the courts, for statements which are deemed by the court to reflect adversely on its dignity, and for certain acts of the newspaper's representatives in the courtroom.

In addition, newspapers are limited in what they may publish by two important civil rights, the right of privacy and the right of the creative individual to the fruits of his own work (copyright). The federal courts and approximately two-thirds of the states have recognized the common-law right of *privacy,* a newer tort than libel but in some ways related to it. It involves such matters as (1) physically trespassing or intruding into a person's personal sphere; (2) putting a person into an embarrassing "false light"; (3) making unauthorized use of a person's name or picture for advertising purposes. Newspapers and magazines are often involved in the second and third of these causes for action. Publications may not safely use a person's name or picture in an advertisement or newsphoto without that person's written consent. Editors must watch out for pictures used in a misleading way. For example, written permission should be obtained before using a picture of a happily married couple to illustrate an article on divorce.

Copyright, on the other hand, is much more clearly established, both in common law and in the statutes. Certain newspapers are copyrighted daily and other newspapers copy from them at the risk of litigation. The right extends to the words used, however, and not the facts conveyed. Consequently copyright law does not prevent one newspaper from stealing a story from another, provided it rewrites it.

Each of these restrictive areas is a large subject. Because only one has a common, direct bearing on the copy desk, only it will be discussed here in detail. (Those who wish to learn more about privacy and copyright will find them treated fully in Nelson and Teeter.[18])

Postal Regulations and Lottery

The one remaining legal area in which the copy desk can play an important sentinel role is the threat to the newspaper's valuable second-class mailing privileges that lies in publishing wittingly or unwittingly any matter which gives publicity to lotteries. The assumption is that the federal government, in its responsibility for delivering mail of all kinds, cannot be powerless to control the nature of the material it handles; it is therefore empowered to exclude from the mails whatever materials are deemed to be contrary to the public interest.

The present regulation, as revised in 1909, prohibits the publication of information about any scheme offering prizes depending in whole or in part on chance. Over the years there has been established for the copy desk a simple test of any such scheme. To be a lottery for purposes of the postal regulations, a scheme must (1) offer a *prize,* (2) require *consideration,* and (3) select the winner(s) on some basis of *chance.*

A news story mentioning a lottery (whether by name or not) is just as dangerous as an advertisement. It is subject to action by the post-office department whether it describes the event before or after it occurs. A prize may be anything of value, not necessarily money. The consideration may be money or anything else of obvious value, even an expenditure of time or effort conditional to participation. When money is paid for a commodity or service, such as a newspaper subscription or admission to an entertainment, but such purchase is a condition of participation, it constitutes consideration.

Thus it is clear that "turkey raffles," drawings for automobiles, bingo games, keno games, door prizes, and the like are lotteries, and stories before or after the event can be the basis for criminal penalties plus the loss of mailing privileges. It therefore behooves the copyreader to watch for mentions of lottery in the most innocent-appearing stories. Often they are

disguised, not necessarily deliberately. More often than not the promotion is nonprofit, designed to aid some worthy cause or organization, which makes the story *seem* all the less hazardous. Copy desks are often lulled to sleep because so many stories dealing with lotteries are published without consequences. The individual postmaster is assigned a sort of primary responsibility for seeing to it that nothing unfit enters the mails at his post office. Some are less vigilant than others. The threat is ever present, however.

Usually there is nothing much at stake but mailing rights in publishing material about a lottery. Of course, no newsman likes to have anyone else tell him what should or should not go into his story. But rarely is an important story very much affected by the lottery limitation. The regulation itself gives the newspaper an easy "out" when a charitable organization must be denied publicity for a lottery: the paper need only quote the regulation to pacify the publicity chairman.

One example of the effect of postal regulations on the news has resulted in an interpretation of the regulations which is still in effect as of this writing and is highly significant. In 1947, a typical "drawing" was held in Ahoskie, North Carolina, as part of a civic promotion sponsored by a local service group. When the winning ticket was drawn, its holder turned out to be a Negro. The event had been considered "all white." A deputation went to the Negro and attempted to give back his money. He declared he'd settle for the Cadillac. When the dance-band vocalist who had drawn the number protested, the story came to the attention of newsmen.

It was quite a story and a great many newspapers across the nation used it, despite the fact that it could not be told without reference to the lottery. Among them was the late St. Louis *Star-Times.* The St. Louis postmaster subsequently ruled that the paper should have been barred from the mails. When the *Star-Times* appealed to the post-office department, the department solicitor issued an interpretation in these words: "I have concluded that despite the literal wording of the law it was not intended to exclude from the mails publications of such items . . . which have a news value in their own right and in which

---

[18] *Ibid.,* pp. 155–232.

the lottery element is *only incidental to a newsworthy event.*" (Italics supplied.)

There the matter stands. It is still rather ambiguous. The interpretation is still just that, not law. It does appear, however, that newspapers may now safely include in a story material about a lottery provided the story cannot really be told or told fully without reference to the lottery. It is perhaps prudent not to regard a turkey raffle as incidental to a picnic, but it does appear to be safe to tell the whole story when the "lucky winner" dies of a heart attack on learning that he has won the turkey.

Pretrial Publicity

The First Amendment guarantees the press the right to publish and, inferentially, the public the right to know the facts, but the Supreme Court has overthrown convictions on the ground that excessive or prejudiced publicity given cases before trial has denied defendants their rights under the Sixth Amendment. The Sixth Amendment guarantees the defendant the right to a public trial before an impartial jury. To preserve this guarantee, the court may take steps to allow veniremen to be challenged, in the selection of a jury, if they are suspected of prejudice. It may also instruct juries to ignore inadmissible evidence from any source, including news stories appearing before they were impanelled, and it is empowered to protect the jury from information it should not consider while the case is being tried; it can warn the jury against discussing such information in the jury room. But is it realistic to expect a juror to strip his mind of prejudicial thoughts or facts by an effort of will? The bar and bench—and a substantial segment of the press as well —agree that it is not, and that the court's powers here are insufficient to assure impartiality. They have sought agreement on ways of actually curtailing the dissemination of pretrial information that would be inadmissible in court and could influence the outcome of the case. Sometimes prejudicial pretrial information has so saturated a community that only a change of venue (shifting the trial to another jurisdiction) will prove effective. But when the case gets nationwide publicity, as it did in the Dr. Sam Sheppard and Billy Sol Estes cases, a change of venue is pointless.

We do not know very much about the effects of various types of information on jurors or what countervailing effect the court's instructions might have. Wilcox[19] has summarized the issues and reviewed the available studies from both a legal and a behavioral-science point of view. Kalven and Zeisel's study[20] of the jury process is the best source from the legal side. The clearest evidence on the effects of pretrial publicity has been produced by Tans and Chaffee,[21] who found that such inadmissible information as a previous conviction or a confession do influence potential jurors to believe in the guilt of the accused; they also found similar effects for the admissible information of arrest and accusation. Wilcox and McCombs[22] got similar results, except on the latter point.

Everything that *is* known indicates that pretrial information can be prejudicial. Consequently, in many states bench, bar, and press have made earnest efforts to work out guidelines for the behavior of all these groups to assure that the public will get a full account of cases without jeopardizing justice. In many newsrooms, such guidelines are the policy of the paper. In others, where they have not been developed or are not yet in effect, typical ones are nevertheless a useful reference tool for the conscientious editor.

As this is written, the bar of Kentucky, but not yet its bench and press, has approved a set of guidelines. At least some Kentucky newspapers, the Louisville *Courier-Journal* and *Times* among them, have adopted them as the best available set. The guidelines first state some general principles:

—the press's right to print the truth
—the right of the parties to a fair and impartial trial
—the shared responsibility of lawyers and journalists to prevent the pressure of publicity from influencing the trial

[19] Walter Wilcox, "The Press, the Jury and the Behavioral Sciences," *Journalism Monographs* No. 9, October 1968.

[20] Harry Kalven, Jr., and Hans Zeisel, *The American Jury* (Boston: Little, Brown, 1966).

[21] Mary Dee Tans and Steven H. Chaffee, "Pretrial Publicity and Juror Prejudice," *Journalism Quarterly* 43:647–654 (Winter 1966).

[22] Wilcox, *op. cit.*, pp. 21–22.

—the judge's responsibility to preserve order in the court

—the importance of objectivity and accuracy in reporting

—the presumption of innocence

—the public's right to know how justice is being administered

—the impropriety of a lawyer's using the media to influence the case in his favor

The guidelines then state that "proper journalistic and legal training should include instruction in the meaning of constitutional rights to a fair trial, freedom of the press, and the role of both journalist and lawyer in guarding these rights."[23] They go on to detail some journalistic do's and don'ts:

1. It is appropriate to make public the following information concerning the defendant:

(a) The defendant's name, age, residence, employment, marital status, and similar background information. There should be no restraint on biographical facts other than accuracy, good taste and judgment.

(b) The substance or text of the charge, such as complaint, indictment, information or, where appropriate, the identity of the complaining party.

(c) The identity of the investigating and arresting agency and the length of the investigation.

(d) The circumstances immediately surrounding an arrest, including the time and place of arrest, resistance, pursuit, possession and use of weapons, and a description of items seized at the time of arrest.

2. The release of certain types of information by law enforcement personnel, the bench and bar and the publication thereof by news media generally tends to create dangers of prejudice without serving a significant law enforcement or public interest function. Therefore, all concerned should be aware of the dangers of prejudice in making pretrial public disclosures of the following:

(a) Opinions about a defendant's character, his guilt or innocence.

(b) Admissions, confessions or the contents of a statement or alibis attributable to a defendant.

(c) References to the results of investigative pro-

cedures, such as fingerprints, polygraph examinations, ballistic tests, or laboratory tests.

(d) Statements concerning the credibility or anticipated testimony of prospective witnesses.

(e) Opinions concerning evidence or argument in the case, whether or not it is anticipated that such evidence or argument will be used at trial.

Exceptions may be in order if information to the public is essential to the apprehension of a suspect, or where other public interests will be served.

3. Prior criminal charges and convictions are matters of public record and are available to the news media through police agencies or court clerks. Law enforcement agencies should make such information available to the news media after a legitimate inquiry. The public disclosure of this information by the news media may be highly prejudicial without any significant addition to the public's need to be informed. The publication of such information should be carefully reviewed.

4. Law enforcement and court personnel should not prevent the photographing of defendants when they are in public places outside the courtroom. They should not encourage pictures or televising nor should they pose the defendant.

5. Photographs of a suspect may be released by law enforcement personnel provided a valid law enforcement function is served thereby. It is proper to disclose such information as may be necessary to enlist public assistance in apprehending fugitives from justice. Such disclosure may include photographs as well as records of prior arrests and convictions.

6. The news media are free to report what occurs in the course of the judicial proceeding itself. (The bench should utilize available measures, such as cautionary instructions, sequestration of the jury and the holding of hearings on evidence after the empaneling of the jury, to insure that the jury's deliberations are based upon evidence presented to them in court.)

7. It is improper for members of the (bench)-bar-news media or law enforcement agencies to make available to the public any statement or information for the purpose of influencing the outcome of a criminal trial.

8. Sensationalism should be avoided by all persons and agencies connected with the trial or reporting of a criminal case.

The Kentucky guidelines also include a section on reporting civil procedures, including the following:

---

[23] The full text is given in *The Kentucky Press*, July 1970, pp. 5–7.

8. FAIR TRIAL: Litigants in civil causes, including causes having special news value because of public interest in the subject matter, are as much entitled to a fair trial by an unbiased jury as is a criminal defendant. Jurors summoned to decide questions of civil liability or damages should be free from public clamor and special influences. News media should be wary of contrived information, the effect of which would be to influence potential jurors as to liability or amount of damage awards. The media acknowledge that the pretrial reporting of civil cases may involve the same risks to the administration of justice as the pretrial reporting of criminal cases. Pretrial coverage of civil cases should be balanced to minimize this risk.

Newsmen should use care in reporting portions of jury trials which take place in the temporary absence of the jury. To publicize the court's rulings as to evidentiary matters may cause jury prejudice.

· · · · ·

12. INCOMPLETE REPORTING: Civil suits have two sides. It is unfair to report only a portion of the facts presented at a trial, as though they were the only facts. Trials proceed without regard to deadline. Reporting of only one aspect of a case to meet a deadline may give the public a distorted view. Good coverage requires that the news media follow up in a subsequent report with the other side of the story. Incomplete reporting of civil trials or reporting only those cases on which the newsman has had a helpful tip can give a distorted picture of courthouse news.

The proposed Kentucky guidelines also include sections on access to public records and reporting juvenile court proceedings.

The editor plays a watchdog role here, as he does in protecting the paper against libel. He questions a point and the point is discussed and in some cases referred to the paper's legal counsel. Close attention to guidelines will be expected on any newspaper which through its professional associations has in effect promised to abide by them. On newspapers that haven't, the news editor still has an obligation to his professional conscience not to ignore the rights of defendants and litigants.

15

What's In Store

In 1955, the newspaper business seemed to be the victim of television competition and its own conservatism:

> . . . it seems to me that the daily newspaper is in a very threatened position. Let me overstate the case a bit. The steady decline in number of publishing units has been arrested—momentarily to be sure—but the decline has been steady for a long time. Circulations are up, yes—but they are not at the moment keeping pace with population growth. And for many years now, profits have been falling even though general economic conditions have been favorable enough to keep volume on the rise. This is not a healthy condition but I do not see how it could be otherwise in an industry seemingly married "until death do us part" to a hopelessly outmoded technology. So far the industry has reacted by such shortsighted expedients as TTS and mat shrinkage. These may keep it afloat for a long time. But in the long haul I'm not betting too heavily on Mr. Gutenberg and Mr. Mergenthaler in a tag match with modern electronics.
>
> There is something unhealthy about an industry that can do nothing in the face of a serious problem except curtail, shore up outmoded machines, squeeze its advertisers with a little narrower column and a little more shrinkage—that has nothing to speak of to spend on research.[1]

From that time to this, a remarkable revolution has occurred—much of it in the last five years—in the technology of newspapering. Its effects seem so far reaching and its course so complicated that it is difficult to conceive what newspaper desk work will be like in the future—even the immediate future. Since it is not possible to determine just how a plethora of inventions and applications of new technologies will be combined into a new system for producing news-

---

[1] Bruce H. Westley, "Journalism and the Social Need," *Journalism Quarterly* 32:474–475 (Fall 1955).

347

papers, this concluding chapter has to settle for a look at what is happening now and some guarded speculation about how these new developments will affect the traditional functions of the copy desk.

There has been much hand-wringing by some newsmen to the effect that machines are going to take over their jobs. It is true that computers are faster readers, have better memories, and can make decisions more quickly on the basis of more information than the news editor. In fact, computers can do routine writing more quickly and just as badly as writers who write routinely. It is no trick to program computers to output routine obituaries, for example, from a coded input of details supplied by the mortuary. By deliberately inducing variations in story and sentence structure and in vocabulary, the program can produce about what rewrite men produce with the same materials. What the reporter can do unthinkingly the unthinking computer can do as well.

But computers cannot take the place of a man who knows how to exercise judgment about what news is most important and most interesting and how to improve the structure and flow of a story. Computers can indeed be programed to select and play today's news on the basis of how a particular newspaper treated similar news in the past. But while computers can *simulate* what editors do, there is little doubt that an editor's spontaneous judgment is a better selector of the news of a given day than is an approximation of what he did in the past.

What computers can do and are doing is to implement human judgments with vastly increased speed. For example, the editor of the future, working at an electronic console, will make his own decision about play of the news on Page One; the computer will get the type set and in the page in less time and with less error than has ever been possible without it.

Recent Technological Innovations

In the last few years, the newspaper back shop has been converted from a system not much different from the one Johann Gutenberg perfected to one relying heavily on modern electronics. There was a long lag between what the technicians knew could be done to speed up and reduce the costs of newspaper production and the sudden burst of activity at the end of the 1960's which realized many of their ideas. Publishers were suddenly presented with a dozen ways of doing practically everything, and tremendous energy and competitive fervor is still being expended on technology. Changes that have already been made are more profound than the widely spaced innovations of the distant past: rotary presses, web-perfecting paper, automatic assembly and casting, halftone engraving, wired transmission of photographs, etc. The changes of the past few years have involved transmission of information, composition, makeup, plate making, printing, and editorial decision making. Some current developments on all these fronts will be described briefly.

News Transmission

For decades, the wire services depended on the teletype (an improvement over hand-key telegraphy, after all) to transmit news to client newspapers. The system yielded all-caps copy that had to be marked for capitals as well as edited, and it produced the 25,000 words a day adequate for most small and medium-sized dailies. If a newspaper wanted to publish a full report of the stock market, for example, it needed another wire to receive the material, and the cost of composition and correction was astronomic.

Teletype uses coded, punched tape which transmits impulses over telephone wire. As we have seen, it was discovered that a similar tape on the receiving end could replace an operator's hands in hot-type machine composition, with resulting savings in time and correction costs. Then linecasting-machine speed was increased nearly twofold, saving even more time and linecasting costs. The tendency was, to be sure, to rely more on the filing editor and less on the local editor to judge the news. But editors learned to read tape and thus to trim stories before they were set and to copy edit after composition (in proof), rather than before. These changes largely affected the smaller papers at first; the savings involved were not sufficient to justify these methods in large newsrooms, except where there were no editorial judgments to make, as with stock

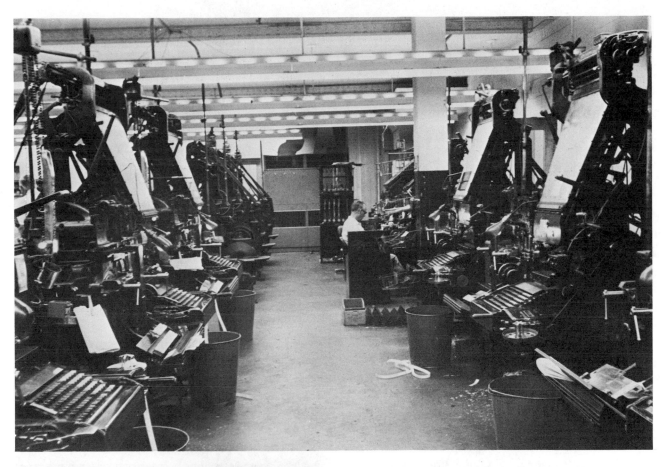

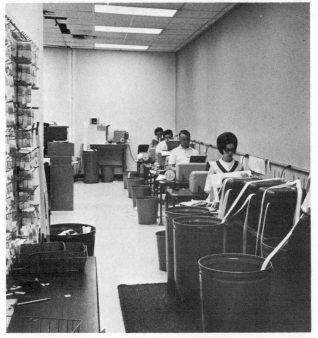

No Hands A. In the composing room of the Pensacola (Florida) *Journal*, composing machines operate automatically using automatically justified perforated tape. A single operator is seen setting corrections by hand.

Pensacola (Florida) Journal *photos*
Courtesy The Gannetteer

B. The tape is cut by operators working at typewriter keyboards.

quotations, sports box scores, and other routine but costly composition.

Now the telephone companies are working on the concept of the "Central News Bank" to be maintained by the wire services. As it is, they point out, the wire services send perhaps 50,000 words to a newspaper, which on the average prints about 15 per cent of them. Selection is slow and painful; stories pile up on the news desk awaiting handling; the system described in Chapter 3 for putting it all together is laborious. The telephone companies suggest instead that the wire service should file stories and pictures in a data bank at a central point. The editor would simply dial the computer to get a listing of available stories and visual material—or he could be fed an updated budget periodically on a cathode-ray tube (CRT) or high-speed page printer in the newsroom. The editor would then call up only the copy he wanted and then edit as usual—or he could receive it as a computer tape or paper tape that would go directly to composing machines. But, say the telephone companies, more likely the editor would receive, edit, and transmit material to composition directly on the console of a sophisticated control system such as a CRT unit. (The potential role of CRT units is discussed more fully later.) Thus the proposed system is an information-retrieval system similar to the ones being developed for libraries and newspaper morgues.

Composition

Far more important than teletypesetting's immediate effect on the balance sheet was the breakthrough it effected in automating composition. Linecasting machines assemble lines of matrices the width of a column, justify them automatically, cast them into a solid line of type, and redistribute the matrices into the channels of the magazine from which they were drawn. One operator at one $7,500 to $15,000 machine can set a column of type and correct it in about an hour. Such speed helped make the present-day newspaper possible, but it was still too slow for an industry competing with instantaneous electronic media. And rising labor costs were making it prohibitive.

The emergence of photo-offset printing led to a search for cold-type composition methods to replace the hot-type linecasting systems in use since before the turn of the century. As it was, type was set and proofed, and the proof was pasted up for the camera. Some sort of shortcut seemed possible. At first it appeared to be the typewriter. Of course there were disadvantages. Typewriter type was poorly designed and relatively illegible, partly because all typewriter characters were of exactly the same width—the small "i" and the capital "W" occupied the same amount of space on the line. Furthermore, typewriter lines had to be respaced to justify them. So the typewriter makers improved the design of their typefaces and devised variable-width characters. Then they made justification possible in a single step. The trend toward adoption of offset in the smaller papers continued, and the first round in the equipment revolution was assured. By 1969, 80 per cent of nondaily newspapers and nearly 500 of the roughly 1,750 daily newspapers had converted from letterpress to offset and in most instances from hot-type systems to cold. Offset was still not practicable for large dailies—those of roughly 100,000 circulation or more—because of its slower speeds, higher plate-making and paper costs, and greater paper waste. Furthermore, it was a long time before offset quality equaled the quality of the best letterpress printing.

But the revolution in composition had its effect on the larger papers as well. Some simply used tape-cutting and justifying machines and retrained their linecasting-machine operators to the typewriter keyboard. Others installed computers to output justified and hyphenated punched paper from continuous unjustified tape, probably the most widespread truly automated process in use on metropolitan newspapers today.

The new photocomposition systems such as Photon have a number of advantages over hot-metal linecasting systems, particularly in speed and flexibility. The operator of a linecasting machine works with one magazine at a time. Each magazine contains one set of mats—one family of type in one size. In display sizes, each mat has only one die; in smaller sizes, each mat has room for two dies and thus can

A Phototypesetter This high-speed unit will produce camera-ready text from either justified or unjustified tape at a rate of twenty-five to thirty lines a minute for any measure up to 33 picas. When it is fed with unjustified tape, it automatically justifies and hyphenates. Changes in type font and size can be made in less than a minute.

Courtesy the Compugraphic Corporation

readily be changed from a roman to an italic or a lightface to a boldface in the same size—but that's all. To change to another size in the same face or to another face requires changing to another magazine.

Photocomposition systems such as Photon can make instant changes from size to size and family to family from information keyboarded into a tape input along with the text itself. They operate from rapidly revolving discs which are also capable of moving forward and backward at great speed. Each disc contains a large number of fonts of different typefaces. The forward-and-back motion shortens and lengthens the focal length to produce differences in size. Lines are assembled by photographing letters one at a time at the flash of a stroboscopic light. All instructions to the machine about typeface and size, measure, form (justified, flush left, centered, etc.) as well as text are keyboarded into a single tape input.

The output is either a positive black-on-clear or black-on-white plastic which is then cut and assembled into ads or whole pages. These pasteups are then ready for offset plate making. In hot-type systems, photocomposed material is photoengraved and put into page forms for stereotyping. The advantages of photocomposition to hot-type systems are thus at their greatest for complicated composition, as in grocery ads, and least for straight matter, as in the body of a news story. For this reason, many hot-type newspapers use photocomposition for display advertising only.

Photocomposition has been a great source of savings in the composing room, and without any sacrifice in quality. In fact, substantial improvements in quality are possible. Furthermore, the pasteup process by which phototype is assembled—and this is true in both offset and letterpress systems—yields far greater flexibility in makeup. To run a line of hot type at an angle across a column or page or copy block is a terribly painstaking and costly luxury. The spacing has to be done by hand and sometimes even requires pouring hot metal into the angular spaces. But phototype film can be pasted down at whatever angle is desired and that's all there is to it.

At least six different photocomposition systems are in widespread use. Some manufacturers have developed a wide variety of models differing in their range of type sizes and speed. Some offer separate machines for body sizes (such as 5–24 point) and for display sizes (30–120 point). Some are especially versatile in ad composition and others especially rapid for straight matter. Some photocomposition systems can set straight matter from a direct input of prejustified paper tape provided by the wire services, or from computer-justified magnetic tape.

Both of the two major electronic media giants, CBS and NBC, have entered the newspaper composition competition. RCA produces through what it calls Videocomp full pages in reduced size ready for camera enlargement. Videocomp codes copy for typeface, size, and format and reads the code into a computer. The copy is then keyboarded into the computer, which outputs justified and hyphenated tape. A tube scanner reads line drawings onto tape from 35-millimeter film, yielding a hard-copy output on high-resolution photo paper or a film positive which can be put directly on offset masters suitable for short runs or on 35-millimeter tape for storage. Full-size halftones are stripped into blown-up pages per programmed instructions as to location.

Many larger papers have adopted photocomposition systems for display advertising and have stayed with tape-fed hot-metal systems for straight matter and classified ads. Smaller papers which have converted to offset use self-justifying typewriter for straight matter, and assemble display heads for ads and news stories using simple headline composition systems. Some find that cheaper photocomposition systems pay in composing display ads.

The special problem of classified-ad composition, storage, and manipulation has produced several special photocomposition systems for use with large and small ad sections. Individual classified ads are small revenue producers, and they require a great deal of handling: each has its own number of insertions, classification, etc. They used to be manipulated by a printed code that told what classification they belonged to and what days they ran. Human operators shifted them, set them into the forms, and pulled them out by hand. Now a single special computer sets them, classifies them, corrects them—and even checks the credit rating of the advertiser and bills him.

Electronic Editing

A cathode-ray-tube (CRT) editing console consists of a display terminal much like a small television picture tube and an attached keyboard. CRT units are already in use on a few newspapers but thus far only for specific chores. Several newspapers use them to handle classified ads in combination with computers, as described on page 352. The operator takes the ad over the telephone, keyboards it into the display terminal, reads it back, corrects it, codes it, and reads it into computer tape for later classification and composition.

But it is the CRT's potential as an aid to news editing that has spurred manufacturers on to testing it and debugging it for use on copy desks. As this is written, no system is yet past the test stage. But what CRT will be able to do for the editor is to read continuous tape, including wire-service tape, into the unit's memory, then call it up, ten or a dozen lines at a time, and allow the editor to correct it either with a light pencil or respacing and rekeyboarding. Then it reads the edited matter back into the computer for automatic justification and composition by whatever composition system is in use. In an ideal combination with computers and electronic composition systems, the CRT output would go directly to the page for which it is intended, untouched by human hands. News selection and judgment, headline decisions and headline copy, and makeup could all be handled at the same terminal.

In its present form, CRT has some disadvantages, not the least of which is that its image on the screen is peculiarly hard on eyes and nerves. But even its most enthusiastic proponents don't assume that editors will spend their working days staring at a restless tube image. What will probably happen is that the editor will work with hard copy, as he does now, leaving it to nonprofessional employees to make the actual corrections and give the actual instructions at the terminal console. Such details remain to be worked out.

But CRT has great advantages, as well. CRT printers can set type at 1,000 words a minute, and a laser-beam system is expected to increase that speed. CRT units are expected to be especially useful in handling editions rapidly, including highly localized editions, since they can transfer stories from place to place at hitherto unknown speeds and without fear of human error. In combination with the new hardened-plastic lightweight plate described on page 354, they can be expected to revolutionize the production processes of even the largest newspapers now wedded to letterpress.

The Research Center of the American Newspaper Publishers Association has produced a computer program that will edit a story to any desired length. Teletypesetter tape is read into the computer in justified or unjustified form. The program breaks the story into segments and "evaluates" the importance of each part. The segments are rank-ordered according to importance and the story is stored until it is needed. The editor determines the story length he desires, and he types in this information. The output is the most important parts of the story on justified tape of the required length to the nearest complete sentence. The key to the system is in the rules of computer logic that shape the program. Unsound logic will produce bad computer judgments. At this time, details are largely unavailable on how the program determines the importance of the segments without benefit of human judgment and how the discrete sentences that make up the story are rearranged—if they are—into a coherent sequence.

Plate Making

Stereotyping (described in Chapter 2) has been the standard plate-making system for high-speed web-fed rotary presses—the only kind of presses that have had the speed and durability to produce large-circulation newspapers with many pages. Units can be added to increase the number of pages being run.

The process of producing an offset plate starts with a pasteup which is put on a board in front of a camera which exposes a sheet of page-size film to the pasteup. The negative is positioned on a light table and "light leaks" around the cuts and display type are painted out. The negative is then exposed under an extremely bright light to a light-sensitive aluminum plate. This is treated with an albumen solution to make the surfaces which are to print water repellent. The plate is flexible and light and can be locked directly onto the offset press. Only the water-repellent parts of the plate pick up ink, which is transferred to a blanket, which in turn lays an image down on the paper. This printing process is correctly termed *photolithography* and popularly called *offset;* sometimes these words are combined into terms like "photo-offset." Photolithography describes the plate-making process, which involves the use of light. Offset describes the printing process.[2]

Whereas stereotype plates are heavy and require extremely heavy presses to rotate them at high speeds, the lightweight offset plate allows the presses to be lighter. Stereotype plates are nevertheless somewhat cheaper to produce, and rotary presses are in general capable of higher speeds than offset presses. The combination of greater speed, lower paper and ink costs, and ease in adding printing units makes the stereotype/letterpress system the preferred one for large-circulation papers.

Lightweight plastic letterpress plates point the way to the future for larger papers. One such plate, pioneered by the South Bend *Tribune,* is capable of 350,000 impressions at more than 50,000 an hour. Because it requires less impression (pressure) than a metal plate, ink consumption and wear are reduced. Such plates also mean lighter, faster presses in the future of letterpress newspapers: high-volume presses using plastic plates can be tied into cold-type composing systems. A photographic negative is made from a pasteup, as in offset, or from phototypesetter film. Unexposed areas are etched away and a relief plate of transparent plastic is produced and then

---

[2] In printing terminology, an offset occurs any time an impression is made from something other than a plate—when wet ink on one page transfers to another, for example, producing a reverse image unintentionally, or when a plate makes an ink impression on the tympan or undersurface, the tympan transferring the impression unintentionally to the back side of subsequent sheets.

put through a hardening process. Being flexible, the plate is simply mounted on a curved metal saddle and attached to the press. It is claimed for the plastic plate that it produces a cleaner image and wears better than the type-metal plate.

Electrostatic printing, or xerography, is used for reproducing magazine mailing labels and the codes on checks, as well as in office copying machines. In electrostatic printing, a metallic powder adheres to an electrostatically charged area of a specially treated plate. It has been part of the dreams of newspaper-plant superintendents for years, but the prospects for an electrostatic high-speed web-fed press are fairly dim as this is written. Electrostatic printing *is* used on the newspaper, however, for speedy production of multiple proofs of photocomposed ads, as well, of course, as for routine office copying.

Satelliting

The *Wall Street Journal* has for years published simultaneously in satellite plants at as many as six locations around the nation. Copy is edited at a central point and transmitted by tape. Makeup instructions are transmitted by facsimile. Computers and long-distance communications technology now allow newspapers and other publications to be printed from facsimile pages produced centrally. This could make some newspapers truly national. But since most newspapers depend on the local market as their economic base and are concurrently locally slanted, satelliting may well become primarily important in freeing downtown newspapers from the problem which is becoming nearly insuperable in such cities as Chicago —simply moving newspapers out of the central city to its environs after they have been run. The Chicago *Daily News* and *Sun-Times* carefully located their plant in the heart of the city beside the Chicago River so that ships of seagoing size could bring newsprint directly to the presses. But traffic conditions in that location now make it all but impossible to move the completed papers fast enough at rush hours to newsstands and distributors in the city and suburbs. Some newspapers are experimenting with helicopter delivery, but satelliting could solve the traffic problem for many others.

Blue Sky

Satelliting, of course, could change the whole structure of newspapers. But the possibility of combining satellite systems, information retrieval, and electrostatic printing conjures up a whole new concept: an electronically delivered newspaper. Little of the old newsroom would remain, and the whole apparatus of reproducing newspapers at a central point would disappear.

Electronic information retrieval is not a pipe dream. The United States Department of Commerce uses it to send selected published materials to those who want them. The customer files a card giving his mailing address and indicates categories of items in his field of interest. New publications are coded in the same categories. Whenever something is published in a category the customer has checked, it is automatically copied, labeled, and sent to him. This is called IRAD (Information Retrieval Advance Designation).

Libraries use IR (Information on Request), a system that prints out and delivers to the user a list of everything that falls within a requested set of identifying and limiting categories. The New York *Times* has announced that it will offer to anyone willing to pay for the service a computerized IR system on the order of an "instant electronic Library of Congress" tapping its own morgue and library sources as well. The National Aeronautics and Space Administration has a system that uses CRT consoles to display a particular class of information drawn from a data bank that is continuously updated and corrected. These are the screens that NASA staff members are seen monitoring in television coverage of the Houston space center during a launch. Whenever hard copy is needed, a printout is delivered by pneumatic tube to the station calling for it.

IBM has a service it calls CIS (Current Information Selection). A user supplies information categories and the CIS files them on the basis of key words. It then runs a weekly check of user key words against new information, which has been similarly keyworded. A list of the new items in the categories the user is interested in is sent to him, and he returns a card with the items he wants punched out. Back come microfiche cards containing the items he wants, each card containing ninety-eight pages of copy. Needless to say, the user needs a microfiche reader to complete the system.

Information Retrieval in the Newsroom

Retrieval was well advanced when ANPA RI, the research arm of the American newspaper industry, asked scientists at the Massachusetts Institute of Technology how some of its well-developed IR engineering could be adapted to the newspaper. This led to project INTREX, which applied retrieval principles first to the newspaper morgue. This involves inputting full texts, automatically indexing the content, and recalling them to on-line remote-access points. Such a system can be made compatible with computer time-sharing systems and hence does not require an in-house computer. Thirty accessors can use the computer simultaneously. The user can call up all stories falling within a given field or category by first typing in the category names, then learning how many items are involved, then placing restrictions on the categories, such as only those items under a given by-line. The corresponding stories can then be printed out. The input can be the same punched paper tape that activates typesetting machines. Two kinds of classification are carried out. The inputter adds identifying information to the tape such as a news category, edition, headline, dateline, etc. All words in the first paragraph and all capitalized words are input automatically. The identifying "phrases" are then decomposed into separate words, which are "stemmed" by lopping off prefixes and endings and listed as an index. Matching stems are fed in at the retrieval phase.[3]

Personalized News Retrieval

Under the current system, delivery is still the worst bottleneck. The newsboy at the end of the line is the costliest and least efficient part of the system; getting bundles of papers to the newsboy by truck is nearly as wasteful of time and money. Then, too, the editor has to struggle to give the reader something he can't get

---

[3] American Newspaper Publishers Association Research Institute Bulletin No. 97, December 1968.

A

Courier-News *(Plainfield, New Jersey) photos*
Courtesy The Gannetteer

Old Hands, New Tricks A. When the *Courier-News* of Plainfield, New Jersey, converted to automatic tape-fed linecasting in 1966, fingers accustomed to the Linotype keyboard (above) were retrained for the typewriter keyboard used in cutting teletypesetter tape (below) at a local adult school. The retraining program was arranged by the paper and the union. Production was begun at about 250 lines an hour, but within a year, most of the operators were cutting 600 lines an hour.

B. This man, who once spent his day at a linecasting machine, now supervises a battery of sophisticated automatic composing machines like this tape-fed Intertype.

B

effortlessly from the electronic media. He tries to make the paper's content closer to the particular interests of the reader by producing costly special sections and zoned editions. To be sure, the great flexibility of CRT editing and high-speed composition can make editions a lot easier to handle than they now are. But consider the possibilities of combining the information-retrieval principle with an electrostatic printout from a receiver in the home. Instead of the editor calling up the stories or information he wants from a central data bank, the reader may some day be able to call up from the newspaper's data bank the paper he wants.

Computer companies already have the know-how to produce a new kind of newspaper, a personalized periodical. Each copy would be tailor-made to the subscriber's advance instructions. No attempt would be made to deliver all the news to all the readers as we do now. Two practical methods already exist for delivering such a newspaper, and the third one, the electronic printing press, may soon be within reach.[4]

Hence an inquiry system of dissemination bypassing the six o'clock news and the afternoon newspaper on the doorstep is now possible. A user of printed media now reads when and what he wants from an available store of information, but he wastes time turning pages and searching columns. And he is at the mercy of the clock if he wants to find out what a network news team thinks happened today. He also must wait interminably for the items he is interested in while other messages he doesn't want go by. With electronic news retrieval, the user dials for the information he wants when he wants it. Like the patron of the revolutionized data-accessing library, he asks his home information-retrieval system to print out what he wants to see or read, or display it on a screen. Housewives could dial the ads they wanted to see and get copies of the ones they wanted to take to the store. The receiver could tie in with other data banks for encyclopedia-type information, for example, or school courses, or with the local library's retrieval system.

Many barriers prevent an immediate linking of elements into a successful home-delivery system. As is often the case, the hardware (machinery) comes first and the software (ideas and systems for use) comes slowly. For example, the hardware was ready for home-delivered facsimile newspapers in the late 1930's and early 1940's; radio station WQXR was delivering "fax" newspapers to its parent New York *Times* on a demonstration basis at that time. Yet that proved to be the end of the road for the facsimile newspaper: the electronic giants were turning their creative energies to developing and marketing a new plaything they were calling "television." Facsimile continued to be used for other things, but delivering newspapers to the home was not one of them.

Conclusion

The 1955 prognostications quoted at the beginning of the chapter have been nullified by events. The daily newspaper *was* threatened by a cumbersome technology, but it has since embraced the electronics revolution. It has already enlarged its capacity to compete with other media, and more spectacular gains are in the offing. It *did* expend little on research and development, but that is no longer the case, either. In one five-year period in the late 1960's, it was estimated that American newspapers spent in excess of half a billion dollars on plant expansion and modernization. The industry now maintains its own research and development establishments, including a research center concerning itself with news research alone.

There are other signs of health not visible in 1955. Daily newspaper circulation is more than keeping pace with population growth; newspaper advertising is increasing at a rate considerably in excess of growth in gross national product; newspaper employment is increasing at a rate far greater than total employment.[5]

Technological change will undoubtedly make today's skills irrelevant and this book outmoded before

---

[4] Thomas N. Billings, "The Information Business—1985," *Seminar*, September 1968, pp. 15–18.

[5] As of 1968. See "Trends in the Daily Newspaper Business," American Newspaper Publishers Association report, 1968.

too long. These changes may not necessarily be good for readers or editors. Those already in effect were undoubtedly delayed for many years because their effects on labor were feared by the industry's unions—to the point where rising labor costs were threatening the very existence of the industry in an increasingly competitive world—and history will probably repeat itself. But the industry has learned to a degree that necessary changes in technology can be achieved without attacking unions and employees head on. In many cases, agreements were patiently developed that called for retraining men in new skills. The International Typographical Union maintains a retraining center for the purpose. A man who learned the Linotype keyboard in his youth is now retrained on the typewriter keyboard in the interest of reducing the cost of linecasting.

The newsman who has a healthy skepticism about the part computers play in dehumanizing life will quite understandably worry about what will become of his ability to make news judgments in computerized newspaper technology. But he must learn to distinguish between a professional concern with change and a nonprofessional concern with his own skills and prerogatives. The professional's contribution is not a unique skill but a unique concern and responsibility for a function; the copy pencil is not the only way news can be edited. His concern with the impact of technology should center on ways of making it help him provide reliable and unbiased news.

Appendix A
CHICAGO SUN-TIMES AND DAILY NEWS STYLEBOOK[1]

This stylebook is designed to set forth for The Chicago Sun-Times and The Chicago Daily News certain rules governing capitalization, abbreviations, punctuation, spelling, etc. In general these rules should be followed.

But there is not one single rule in this stylebook that cannot be broken at times, if common sense so dictates.

RESPONSIBILITY FOR STYLE

The editorial copy desk is responsible for marking copy to conform with stylebook rules. The proofroom and composing room should follow copy, but each is responsible for calling attention of the appropriate editor to obvious violations of rules.

Since this stylebook makes no attempt to cover every possible contingency, questions of style may arise in which common sense might produce variable answers. In such an event, staff members should seek a ruling from the head of the editorial copy desk. Together with the managing editor, the head of the editorial copy desk will decide such unanswered style problems.

ADVERTISING COPY

The rules set forth in the stylebook do not apply to paid advertisements.

GOOD TASTE

The newspaper does not (except in unusual instances):

(1) Use the name of a rape victim.

(2) Use the name of a child whose parents may be involved in scandalous conduct or scandalous litigation.

(3) Use the name of a juvenile involved in a misdemeanor. When juveniles are involved in felonious crimes —shootings, stabbings, armed robbery, etc.—that are given prominent display, the disclosure of their names should be considered an integral part of the story. While it is our desire to protect juveniles, it is also our duty to our readers to inform them fully about the identity of criminals, young or old, in major stories.

[1] Copyright 1969 Field Enterprises, Inc. Reprinted by permission. Ellipses replace strictly local material.

(4) Involve innocent members (adult or minor) of a person's family, merely because that person figures in a crime story or in an episode of a scandalous nature.

(5) Resurrect a person's past unless it is germane to an important current story.

(6) Engage in any form of race or religious labeling, except where such identification is necessary to accurate understanding of the story.

LANGUAGE

The best news writing is that which most directly reflects the speech, idiom and vocabulary of the people involved in the story. This means that in our writing we should try for the vigor and brevity which are more characteristic of the way people talk than of the way they write. Individuals do not communicate with each other in complex and heavily structured sentences; newspapers should take their cue from this fact and communicate with their readers in the way that its readers communicate with each other.

On occasion, this will mean that we will be using language (including profanity) which in the past may have been considered taboo. It is the responsibility of both the writer and the editor to judge the appropriateness of the language to the story. If the language is not appropriate or obviously intended to shock, rather than inform, it should be deleted, whatever its nature or no matter how innocuous it might be. If the language is appropriate in its particular context, it should be allowed to stand.

Finally, we should remember that no guidelines can substitute for good writing and forceful expression. A newspaper with a staff that knows how to reach these goals will be the newspaper that is best read, best remembered and most successful.

SIMULTANEOUS REBUTTAL

Any person or organization whose reputation is attacked is entitled to simultaneous rebuttal.

In all controversial stories—labor, politics, scandal, etc.—both sides must be presented simultaneously, if at all possible. When not possible, the story is to say so— that spokesmen were unavailable or declined to comment.

In short, the newspaper must be fair to all persons at all times.

THE ANONYMOUS QUOTE

The anonymous quote, especially in stories involving controversial issues, is to be avoided except in rare cases when the reasons for concealing the identity of a source is manifestly clear to the reader. The newspapers cannot serve as a platform for persons unwilling to accept personal responsibility for their statements. Neither can we tax the credibility of the newspaper by carrying quotations without attribution.

1   CAPITALIZATION

1.1   CAPITALIZE title preceding a name: Sec. of State Johnson Q. Jones, Agriculture Sec. Richard A. Smith. LOWER CASE a title standing alone or following a name: the mayor; Herman Fox Quill, governor of New York. EXCEPTION: Capitalize all references to the President of the United States: President Bemisdarfer, President-elect John F. Johnson, the President, the Chief Executive and the Presidency (of the United States). Note: In all secondary references to the incumbent President and all living former Presidents use Mr. (See 2.25)

1.2   CAPITALIZE government titles when used with a name: Queen Elizabeth II, Prime Minister Harold Wilson, etc. LOWER CASE when standing alone or following a name: the queen, the prime minister.

1.3   CAPITALIZE Pope in all usage: pontiff is lower case. (See 6.7, 6.9)

1.4   CAPITALIZE foreign religious leader titles such as Imam, Patriarch, etc., but LOWER CASE standing alone or following a name. EXCEPTIONS: Pope and Dalai Lama are capitalized in all usage.

1.5   CAPITALIZE titles of authority before a name but LOWER CASE when standing alone or following a name: Ambassador John Jones; Jones, ambassador; the ambassador. Corporate and union officials' titles are lower case even before the name.

1.6   Long titles should follow a name: John Jones, executive director of the commercial department of Blank & Co. (See 2.21)

1.7   LOWER CASE occupational or "false" titles such as day laborer John Jones, rookie left-handed pitcher Bill Wills, defense attorney John Jones. Note that in private practice "attorney" is not abbreviated. (See 2.21)

1.8   CAPITALIZE Union, Republic, Colonies in historical references to the United States, Republic of Korea, French Fifth Republic.

1.9   CAPITALIZE U.S. Congress, Senate, House, Cabinet; all references to [general assemblies or] legislatures when preceded by name of state; [a named, specific city's] City Council; all references to major divisions of the United Nations (in second references to UN General Assembly and Security Council make it Assembly and Council); principal legislative bodies of all nations (see 7.1); cabinet-level departments in foreign governments: Foreign Office, Health Ministry.

The building is the Capitol (Washington . . . only); the city is the capital.

Do not capitalize "congress" when it is used as a synonym for convention.

1.10 CAPITALIZE full names of committees of legislative bodies only: Senate Judiciary Committee, House Ways and Means Committee; City Council Finance Committee. In subcommittee names, capitalize only the name of the parent committee: Judiciary subcommittee on refugees. LOWER CASE committee and subcommittee in all cases when standing alone. (See 7.3)

1.11 CAPITALIZE full titles: Interstate Commerce Commission, Internal Revenue Service, International Atomic Energy Agency, etc. LOWER CASE commission, service, authority, etc., standing alone. (See 7.3)

1.12 CAPITALIZE Supreme Court, Juvenile Court, U.S. Court of Appeals, Appellate Court, etc. Specify which U.S. court, such as District, Patent, Tax, etc. Make it Juvenile Court Judge John Jones. A federal court is lower case. (See 7.7)

1.13 CAPITALIZE Social Security Administration, Social Security Act, Social Security standing alone, Selective Service System, Selective Service.

1.14 CAPITALIZE U.S. armed forces: Army, Air Force, Navy, Marine Corps, Coast Guard, National Guard but LOWER CASE all foreign ones except Royal Air Force, Royal Canadian Air Force, French Foreign Legion.

1.15 CAPITALIZE Swiss Guard, Evzone, Bengal Lancer, Coastguardsman, National Guardsman, etc. LOWER CASE soldier, sailor, guardsman, marine (when referring to an individual in the corps; when the term is applied to a unit or an action by the service it should be Marine offensive, Marine appropriation), but upper case Marine used as an adjective.

1.16 CAPITALIZE Joint Chiefs of Staff but LOWER CASE chiefs of staff and joint chiefs.

1.17 CAPITALIZE holidays, historic events, ecclesiastical feasts, fast days, special events, hurricanes, typhoons, etc.: Arbor Day, Christmas (never Xmas), Good Friday, Passover (or Feast of the Passover), Memorial Day (not Decoration Day), Mother's Day, Purim, Fourth of July (July Fourth, the Fourth), Maundy Thursday, Hanukkah, Holy Week, Lent, Rosh Hashanah, Shabuoth, Sukkoth, Tishah Be'av, Yom Kippur, Yule (avoid the word if possible), Apple Week, National Safety Week, Hurricane Hazel, Typhoon Tilda, Battle of the Bulge, Battle of Bataan, New Year's (Day, Eve), but LOWER CASE: What will the new year bring? At the start of the new year, etc.

1.18 CAPITALIZE Antarctica, Arctic Circle, Antarctic, Arctic.

1.19 CAPITALIZE specific and descriptive regions: Middle West, Midwest, Middle East, Mideast, Far West, the South, the East, the East Coast, North Pole, Old World, Orient, Corn Belt, . . . Near North Side, . . . South Side, . . . Great Lakes, South Seas, . . . but make it southern Illinois, western Pennsylvania. An exception is Southern California. An individual is a Northerner, a Southern farmer, an Easterner.

1.20 CAPITALIZE ideological or political areas: East-West, West Berlin, East Germany. Make it Iron Curtain, Bamboo Curtain, but free world. LOWER CASE mere direction: The wind was from the west. (See 1.34)

1.21 CAPITALIZE political parties and members: Democratic Party, a Democrat, Republican Party, a Republican, Socialist, Independent (when that is the name of the party), Nationalist, Communist, Congress (India), Viet Cong (treat as plural), etc. LOWER CASE when referring to abstract principles or forms of government: democratic, republican, communism, socialism, radicalism, etc. Make it left-wing party, left-winger, the left wing.

CAPITALIZE Red when used as political, geographical, military, descriptive, etc.; Algerian Liberation Front, Alliance for Progress.

LOWER CASE nationalist in referring to a partisan of a country; allies (except when specifically referring to the Allies of World War II).

1.22 CAPITALIZE names of fraternal organizations: B'nai B'rith, Ancient Free and Accepted Masons (AF&AM), Knights of Columbus (K. of C. as a departure from 2.1 because one word—"of"—is spelled out.) (See 2.7, 2.8) LOWER CASE women's auxiliary.

1.23 CAPITALIZE Deity and He, His, Him, denoting the Deity but not who, whose, whom. CAPITALIZE Talmud, Koran, Bible and all names and books of the Bible, confessions of faith and their adherents. (See Section VI)

CAPITALIZE Satan, Hades, but not devil.

1.24   CAPITALIZE Civil War, War Between the States, Korean War, American Revolution (the Revolution), World War I, World War II, Vietnam War, etc.

CAPITALIZE names of races: Caucasian, Mongolian, Negro, Indian, etc. LOWER CASE black, white, red, yellow. Do NOT use "colored" for Negro except in the National Assn. for the Advancement of Colored People. (See preface on Good Taste)

1.25   CAPITALIZE a common noun as part of a formal name: The Sun-Times and Daily News Building (note that all words are spelled out and there is no abbreviation or hyphenation of the name except in Sun-Times), Wrigley Building (building is never abbreviated in body type), Sherman House, Woods Theater, Executive Mansion [federal and specific state], County Building, City Hall [specific city's], Statehouse [specific state's], and specific names of specific rooms in hotels or other concerns, as, the Red Room, the Grand Ballroom, the Wedgwood Room, the Normandie Room, etc., Hoover Dam, Illinois River, Red River Valley, Kane County Courthouse (but the dam, the river, the valley, the courthouse). In plural usage, make it the Illinois and Mississippi rivers. Make it Western Av. Methodist Church, the Fourth Presbyterian Church, Niles Twp. High School, U. of C. Fieldhouse.

1.26   CAPITALIZE species of livestock, animals, fowl, etc., but LOWER CASE noun: Airedale, terrier; Percheron, horse; Hereford, whiteface, etc.

1.27   CAPITALIZE names of flowers: Peace rose, etc. If Latin generic names are used, CAPITALIZE the genus (camellia, Thea japonica).

1.28   CAPITALIZE trade names and trademark names when they are used, but try to use generic terms if the meaning is not impaired. (Electra, Astrojet, but Boeing 707 jet, Pan Am Clipper).

·   ·   ·   ·   ·

1.29   Some proper names have acquired independent common meaning and are not capitalized. They include paris green, diesel, dutch door, brussels sprouts, etc. Check the dictionary.

1.30   CAPITALIZE the principal words of titles of books, plays, hymns, poems, songs, etc., lower casing all articles, conjunctions and one-syllable prepositions of four letters or less unless they are the first words of title. Place all in quotation marks: "The Courtship of Miles Standish." (See 3.23)

1.31   CAPITALIZE the first word of a quotation mak-

ing a complete sentence after a comma or colon: Franklin said, "A penny saved is a penny earned."

1.32   CAPITALIZE names of organizations, expositions, etc.: Boy Scouts, Red Cross, World's Fair, Illinois State Fair, Expo 67, but LOWER CASE scout or fair standing alone.

1.33   Capitalization of names should follow the use or preference of the person. In general, foreign articles are lower case when used with a forename, initials or title. Make it President Charles de Gaulle, de Gaulle.

In Chinese hyphenized names note the lower casing: Mao Tse-tung.

In Anglicized versions the article usually is capitalized: Fiorello La Guardia.

It is Irenee du Pont but Samuel F. Du Pont (his usage). (See 5.12)

1.34   CAPITALIZE fanciful appellations: Hoosier State, Iron Curtain, Bamboo Curtain, Leatherneck, Project Mercury, Berlin Wall, Operation Deep Freeze (Deepfreeze, one word, is a trademark). (See 1.20)

1.35   CAPITALIZE decorations, awards, etc.: Medal of Honor, Purple Heart, Nobel Peace Prize, Pulitzer Prize, Pulitzer Prize-winning.

1.36   CAPITALIZE names of schools and colleges within a university: Medill School of Journalism, Harvard Law School. LOWER CASE departments: department of history, political science department.

1.37   CAPITALIZE U.S. Weather Bureau, Chicago Weather Bureau (but the weather bureau), Chicago Board of Education, School Board (but the board). Capitalize high school and grade school when preceded by a specific name. (See 7.2)

·   ·   ·   ·   ·

1.39   CAPITALIZE all references to the Earth as a planet in this Spage Age. The matter one plants flowers in is earth.

1.40   CAPITALIZE identifying noun before a number as in Room 465, Local 2168, Legion Post 4827.

2   ABBREVIATIONS

2.1   First mention of organizations, firms, agencies, groups, etc., should be spelled out. Exceptions: AFL-CIO, FBI, NATO, SEATO, YMCA, . . . PTA, etc. When spelling out can make a sentence too long or cumbersome, then abbreviate and spell out in later reference.

2.2 ABBREVIATE time zones, airplane designations, ship's distress call, military terms, etc.: EDT, CST, MIG-21, B-60, F-4, absent without official leave (AWOL), SOS (but Mayday), USS Iowa, SS Brasil.

2.3 ABBREVIATE business firms (but see 5.12): Warner Bros.; Brown Implement Co.; Amalgamated Leather, Ltd. Omit "Inc." after a company name if the title of company is clear without it. (Note that it's the Metropolitan Opera Company, Little Company of Mary Hospital.)

2.4 ABBREVIATE and capitalize street designations (see 2.5): St., Av., Blvd., Pkwy., Ct., Pl., Rd., Ter., Dr., Hwy. (when it's a street name: Northwest Hwy.), but OMIT such designations except where needed to distinguish between thoroughfares. Use abbreviations (and capitalize) for North, East, South, West, before EVERY street. If a direction word is part of the street's name, it should be written out: N. Lincoln Park West, E. South Water, South Chicago Av. In adjectival use make it the Whipple St. residents....

2.5 SPELL OUT and capitalize when a street is part of a business, political or social center; State Street, Wall Street, Fifth Avenue, Madison Avenue, Logan Square, Fleet Street, La Salle Street, 10 Downing Street. (See 4.30)

2.6 ABBREVIATE federal highways: U.S. 66, but make it Illinois 83, Indiana 29, Interstate 90, Stevenson Expressway.

2.7 Lower-case abbreviations usually take periods: c.o.d., f.o.b., a.m., p.m., m.p.h. Make it 35-mm. (film), 105-mm. (armament). (See 1.22)

2.8 When an abbreviation consists solely of capitals or caps with the ampersand, omit periods: UN, DP, GI, OK, GOP, GM&O, B&O, AF&AM. If one or more words in the abbreviation are spelled out, use periods: U. of C., U. of I. (See 1.22)

2.9 Periods are always used with abbreviations of geographical names or names of persons: N.Y., F.D.R., G.B.S. (except that in headlines periods may be omitted from names for space reasons).

2.10 ABBREVIATE versus as vs. (with period).

2.11 ABBREVIATE states that follow cities (towns, villages, etc.), air bases, Indian agencies, national parks. Spell out names of states following a county: Cass County, Indiana, but Champaign County (Illinois) coroner.

2.12 Spell out Alaska, Hawaii, Iowa, Ohio and Utah. ABBREVIATE other states:

Ala.	Ind.	Mont.	Pa.
Ariz.	Kan.	Neb.	R.I.
Ark.	Ky.	Nev.	S.C.
Calif.	La.	N.C.	S.D.
Colo.	Mass.	N.D.	Tenn.
Conn.	Md.	N.H.	Tex.
Del.	Me.	N.J.	Va.
Fla.	Mich.	N.M.	Vt.
Ga.	Minn.	N.Y.	Wash.
Ida.	Miss.	Okla.	Wis.
Ill.	Mo.	Ore.	W.Va.
			Wyo.

In adjectival usage of states make it: An Ottawa (Ill.) contractor.

2.13 Omit the state or country after these cities only:

Domestic

Atlanta	Houston	Oklahoma City
Baltimore	Indianapolis	Omaha
Boston	Iowa City	Philadelphia
Buffalo	Los Angeles	Pittsburgh
Cheyenne	Louisville	Reno
Cincinnati	Memphis	St. Louis
Cleveland	Miami	St. Paul
Dallas	Miami Beach	Salt Lake City
Denver	Milwaukee	San Diego
Des Moines	Minneapolis	San Francisco
Detroit	New Orleans	Seattle
Honolulu	New York	Washington

Foreign

Algiers	Havana	Prague
Amsterdam	Guatemala City	Quebec
Antwerp	Jerusalem	Rio de Janeiro
Athens	Leningrad	Rome
Belgrade	London	Rotterdam
Berlin	Madrid	Saigon
Bonn	Manila	San Salvador
Bombay	Mexico City	Seoul
Brussels	Montreal	Singapore
Bucharest	Moscow	Stockholm
Budapest	Naples	Tel Aviv
Buenos Aires	New Delhi	The Hague
Calcutta	Oslo	Tokyo
Cape Town	Panama City	Toronto
Copenhagen	Paris	Vancouver
Dublin	Peking	Vienna
		Warsaw

But omit the country in any dateline where the name of the country is in the first sentence.

. . . . .

2.15 Do NOT abbreviate fort, mount, point, park or port in names of cities or Army posts: Fort Knox, Mount Vernon, Port Washington, Highland Park, Point Pleasant, EXCEPT in headlines when necessary.

2.16   ABBREVIATE St., Ste. as in St. Louis, Sault Ste. Marie, St. Lawrence (except Saint John, New Brunswick). Abbreviate Mt. in usage for mountains, as Mt. Everest.

2.17   All states are spelled out standing alone: He went to Oregon at the turn of the century.

2.18   SPELL OUT always the names of Canadian provinces and Puerto Rico. ABBREVIATE only U.S.S.R. and U.A.R. of foreign countries. (Egypt is not the name of the latter.)

2.19   ABBREVIATE United States and United Nations in titles: U.S. Jaycees, UN Educational, Scientific and Cultural Organization (UNESCO).

  SPELL OUT United States when used as a noun. U.S. may be used as a noun in texts or direct quotations. Make it UN in secondary reference.

2.20   ABBREVIATE and capitalize religious, fraternal, scholastic or honorary degrees, etc., but lower case when spelled out: B.A., bachelor of arts, PhD (no periods, no space).

2.21   ABBREVIATE titles of officials preceding a name (see 1.6, 1.7; see Sec. 6 for ecclesiastical titles; see 2.31 for military titles), as:

Sen.	Mr.	Mlle.
Rep.	Mrs.	Prof.
Gov.	Dr.	Sec.-Gen.
Lt. Gov.	Mme.	State's Atty.
Comdr.	M.	Supt.
Ald.		

2.22   SPELL OUT plural forms. Thus, Senators Paul H. Harrison (D-Ill.) and Bourke Bemisdarfer (R-Iowa); Representatives Charles A. Johnson (R-Ind.) and F. Edward Jones (D-La.). Aldermen so-and-so. (See 3.20)

2.23   SPELL OUT captain in nonofficial uses, such as sports.

2.24   SPELL OUT governor in nonpolitical uses, as Governor John Smith of the Federal Reserve System.

2.25   Mr. is used only with Mrs., with secondary references to U.S. Presidents (see 1.1), with clerical titles (see Sec. 6) and in secondary references in obituaries.

2.26   Avoid Dr. as an academic title, reserving it for men of the cloth with doctoral degrees and MDs, dentists and veterinarians.

2.27   ABBREVIATE names of political parties after names of members of Congress as: Sen. Everett M. Daffron (R-Ill.), Rep. Marguerite S. Jones (R-Ill.). For members of the [state] General Assembly indicate the legislator's city: Rep. Paul Smith (D-Vienna), avoiding the use of numerical designations of districts. . . .

2.28   Do NOT abbreviate President, vice president, detective, expressway, points of the compass (except in street addresses; see 1.19, 1.20), department, postmaster general.

2.29   ABBREVIATE most months when used with dates: Oct. 12, 1942; but spell out otherwise as October, 1960 (see 4.12). Do not abbreviate March, April, May, June or July. Thus, June 29, 1913. (In tabular or financial matter the latter may be abbreviated as Mar, Apr, Jun, Jul and spell out May.)

2.30   The women's auxiliaries of the military services, the abbreviations for which have become well-recognized words and are pronounced as such, are abbreviated Spars, Wacs, Waves, Wrens. The same applies to Amvets. In the same manner, spell it Scuba when referring to skindivers who use self-contained underwater breathing apparatus. (Please keep in mind the fact that Scuba divers use compressed air rather than pure oxygen.)

2.31   ABBREVIATE military titles:

Army

General	Gen.
Lieutenant General	Lt. Gen.
Major General	Maj. Gen.
Brigadier General	Brig. Gen.
Colonel	Col.
Lieutenant Colonel	Lt. Col.
Major	Maj.
Captain	Capt.
Lieutenant	Lt.
Chief Warrant Officer	CWO
Warrant Officer	WO
Sergeant Major	Sgt. Maj.
Specialist Nine	Specialist 9
Master Sergeant	M. Sgt.
First Sergeant	1st Sgt.
Specialist Eight	Specialist 8
Platoon Sergeant	Platoon Sgt.
Sergeant First Class	Sgt. 1/c
Specialist Seven	Specialist 7
Staff Sergeant	Staff Sgt.
Specialist Six	Specialist 6
Sergeant	Sgt.
Specialist Five	Specialist 5
Corporal	Cpl.
Specialist Four	Specialist 4
Private First Class	Pfc.
Private	Pvt.
Recruit	None

Navy, Coast Guard

Fleet Admiral	Fleet Adm.
Admiral	Adm.
Vice Admiral	Vice Adm.
Rear Admiral	Rear Adm.
Commodore	None
Captain	Capt.
Commander	Comdr.
Lieutenant Commander	Lt. Comdr.
Lieutenant	Lt.
Lieutenant Junior Grade	Lt. (j.g.)
Ensign	None
Commissioned Warrant Officer	None
Warrant Officer	WO
Master Chief Petty Officer	None
Senior Chief Petty Officer	None
Chief Petty Officer	None
Seaman	None
Seaman Apprentice	None
Seaman Recruit	None

Marine Corps

Commissioned officers are abbreviated the same as Army, warrant officers the same as Navy. Noncommissioned designations are the same as Army except specialist and:

Master Gunnery Sergeant	
	Master Gunnery Sgt.
Gunnery Sergeant	Gunnery Sgt.
Lance Corporal	Lance Cpl.

Air Force

Air Force commissioned officers are abbreviated the same as Army. Noncommissioned designations include:

Chief Master Sergeant	Chief M. Sgt.
Senior Master Sergeant	Senior M. Sgt.
Technical Sergeant	T. Sgt.
Staff Sergeant	S. Sgt.
Sergeant	Sgt.
Airman First Class	Airman 1/c
Airman	None
Airman Basic	None

The Air Force also may designate certain other descriptions as radarman, navigator, etc., but such designations are not abbreviated.

The Navy has numerous ratings, such as machinist, torpedoman, etc., and they are not abbreviated.

The Army, Coast Guard and Marine Corps also may describe personnel by specific duty in addition to rank.

3   PUNCTUATION

Punctuation in printing serves the same purpose as voice inflection in speaking. Proper phrasing avoids ambiguity, ensures clarity and lessens the need for punctuation.

The Period

3.1   The period is used after a declarative or imperative sentence: The facing is Vermont marble. Shut the door.

3.2   The period is used in a rhetorical question sometimes in the form of a suggestion: Why don't we go.

3.3   The period is used in summary form: 1. Korean War. 2. Domestic policy. A. Punctuate properly. B. Write simply.

3.4   The period is used in ellipses: The combine . . . was secure. (Note three dots—and only three—are used within a sentence. Period and three leaders are used between sentences.)

The Comma

3.5   The comma separates words or figures:

What the solution is, is a question.
June 29, 1913.   November, 1963, was the month.   1,234,567.
The comma serves in a series:
The woman was short, slender, well-dressed and old.
x, y and z   1, 2 and 3

3.6   The comma is used to set off attribution. The work, he said, is exacting.

3.7   The comma is omitted before Roman numerals, Jr., Sr., Inc., the ampersand, dash, in street addresses, telephone numbers and serial numbers: Louis XVI, John Jones Jr., Brink's Inc., Smith & Co., 321-3000, 12345 Oak St., A1234567. (See 4.28)

The Semicolon

3.8   The semicolon separates phrases containing commas to avoid confusion, and separates statements of contrast and statements too closely related:

The draperies, which were ornate, displeased me; the walls, light blue, were pleasing.
The party consisted of B. M. Jordon; R. J. Kelly, his secretary; Mrs. Jordan; Martha Brown, her nurse; and three servants.

The Apostrophe

3.9   The apostrophe indicates the possessive case of nouns, omission of figures and contractions.

Usually the possessive of a singular noun not ending in "s" is formed by adding the apostrophe and "s"; of a plural noun by adding the "s" and then the apostrophe: boys' wear.

The apostrophe is used in the possessive "es": Joneses' house.

The "s" is dropped and only the apostrophe used in "for conscience' sake" or in a sibilant double or triple "s" as "Moses' tablet."

3.10   The apostrophe is used in contractions: I've, isn't (but "s" should be used as a contraction for "is," not "has": He's ready to go. She has gone.) and in omission of figures: '90, '90s, class of '31.

3.11   The apostrophe should follow the style of the official name of group, institution, locality, etc.: Actors' Equity Assn., Court of St. James's.

The Colon

3.12   The colon precedes the final clause summarizing prior matter; introduces listings, statements and texts; marks discontinuity, and takes the place of an implied "for instance": The question came up: What does he want to do? (Note that first word following colon is capitalized only if it begins a complete sentence.)

States and funds allotted were: Alabama $6,000; Arizona $4,000. (See 4.22)

3.13   The colon is used in clock time: 1:55 p.m. (See 4.33)

3.14   The colon is used in Biblical and legal citations: 1 John 3:4-8. Illinois Statutes 3:245-260. (See 4.5)

The Exclamation Point

3.15   The exclamation point is used to indicate surprise, appeal, incredibility or other strong emotion: How wonderful! What! He yelled, "Come here!"

The Question Mark

3.16   The question mark follows a direct question, marks a gap or uncertainty and in the latter use is enclosed in parentheses:

What happened to Jones? It was April (?) that I saw him.

Parentheses

3.17   Parentheses set off material, such as nicknames or identification; or an element of a sentence; or insertion of identifying material: Harold (Red) Grange, the Galloping Ghost. But when a nickname is used alone with

a surname, it takes no punctuation: Babe Ruth. (See 3.26)

3.18   If identifying material is used within quoted matter, set it off with parentheses: "That proposal," he said, "and one by (Prime Minister Harold) Jones are being studied."

3.19   Where location identification is needed: The Ottawa (Ill.) contractor.

3.20   Parentheses are used around political-geographical designations: Ald. Leon M. Brown (5th), Sen. Theodore F. White (D-R.I.) and Rep. Charles A. Green (R-Ind.) were invited. (See 2.22, 2.27)

3.21   Parentheses set off figures or letters in a series: The water is (1) tepid, (2) muddy from silt, (3) unpalatable and (4) unfit to drink. The order of importance will be (a) general acceptance, (b) costs and (c) opposition.

3.22   Where part of a sentence is parenthetical and the punctuation mark comes at the end of the sentence it goes outside: He habitually uses two words incorrectly (bring and take).

Ordinarily the mark goes inside: (The foregoing was taken from the essay.)

Several paragraphs of parenthetical matter start with the opening mark on each paragraph and the final paragraph is ended with a closing parenthesis with the punctuation inside.

Quotation Marks

3.23   Quotation marks enclose direct quotations; phrases in ironical uses; new slang expressions; misnomers; titles of books, plays, motion pictures, songs, operas, paintings, poems, lectures or speeches when the full title is used.

3.24   Do not use quotation marks around musical works that are identified simply by number, form, etc. Thus it's Beethoven's Symphony No. 6. If the identifying name is used, however, enclose it in quotes: "Pastoral."

The forms of musical compositions, when not part of a formal title, are never capitalized.

3.25   Omit quotation marks with names of animals, characters in plays and books, fire engines, homes, newspapers, magazines, almanacs, dictionaries, encyclopedias, gazetteers, TV programs and transportation vehicles of all kinds.

3.26   Use quotation marks instead of parentheses around nicknames apart from the name: Grange, who weighed 198, was called "Red." (See 3.17)

3.27 The comma and period are placed inside the quotation marks. Other punctuation is placed according to construction: Why call it a "gentlemen's agreement"?

3.28 The sequence in multiple quotations: "The question is 'Does his position violate the "gentlemen's 'post-haste' agreement" so eloquently described by my colleague as "tommyrot"?'"

The Dash

3.29 The dash indicates a sudden change. Examples:

He contended—no one denied it—that he had priority.
If that man should gain control—God forbid!—our troubles will have only begun.
The monarch—shall we call him a knave or a fool?—approved it.

3.30 The dash is used [in a dateline] after the logotype and before the first word of a story: IRON CITY, Mich. (UPI)—Mayor, etc.

The Hyphen

3.31 The hyphen is one of the least correctly used and most abused marks. It is used properly to form compound words, to divide words in composition, in figures, in some abbreviations, and to separate double vowels.

A basic rule is that the hyphen should be used when it increases clarity, but its overuse should be avoided. Make it: anti-bias, anti-humor, build-up, pro-power, super-bomb, super-blast.

Generally, Webster's Unabridged is our guide except when a combined form makes the word too long to be easily read, beclouds the meaning or makes pronunciation difficult.

3.32 Adjectival usage must be clear.

The 6-foot man eating shark was killed (the man was).
The 6-foot man-eating shark was killed (the shark was).

3.33 Suspensive hyphenation: The A- and H-bombs were exploded.

3.34 In prefixes ending in a vowel and followed by the same vowel, the hyphen is used: pre-empt, re-elect, pre-election, co-operate, semi-independent, etc.

3.35 Spell it co-ed.

3.36 Never use the hyphen with adverbs ending in "ly" such as badly damaged, fully informed, newly chosen, etc.

3.37 The hyphen also serves to distinguish meaning of similarly spelled words: recover, re-cover, overall (garment), over-all (entire); resent, re-sent.

3.38 The hyphen separates a prefix from a proper noun and words describing combined nationalities: pre-Raphaelites, un-American, Polish-American group, etc.

3.39 The prefix "ex" is hyphenated: ex-champion.

3.40 The hyphen has been abandoned in weekend, year-end, worldwide, nationwide, etc.

3.41 Do not hyphenate proper names in adjectival usage such as Latin American.

3.42 Hyphenate compound modifiers. The union won a 10-cent-an-hour raise. But the raise amounted to 10 cents an hour.

3.43 Here's how we handle some of the more commonly used hyphenated words or words one might be tempted to hyphenate:

able-bodied	empty-handed
about-face	empty-headed
baby-sitter, baby-sit	fade-out
bas-relief	fair-minded
best-selling	far-flung
bird's-eye	far-gone
box-office (adj) box office (n)	fire-eater
	first-nighter
broad-minded	flare-out
brush-off	flare-up
bull's-eye	flatfoot, but flat-footed
by-product	follow-up (adj, n)
call-up	foul-up
carry-over	free-lance (v, adj) free lance (n) free-lancer
cave-in	
clear-cut	globe-trotter (but Globetrotters)
cliff-hanger	
close-up (n) closeup (adj)	grown-up
cold-blooded	
corn-fed	hara-kiri
court-martial, courts-martial	hard-boiled
cover-up	helter-skelter
cross-examine	hocus-pocus
cross-fire (v) cross fire (n)	home-building
cross-section (v, adj) cross section (n)	honky-tonk
cross-purpose	knee-deep
cure-all	knee-high
deadend (v, adj) dead end (n)	law-abiding
deaf-mute	lean-to
die-hard (adj) diehard (n)	like-minded
dog-eared	long-standing
double-check (v) double check (n)	man-made
double-cross (v) double cross (n) double-crosser	man-of-war (warship)
	middle-aged (adj) middle age (n)
double-talk	mix-up
dropout	money-maker
dry-dock (v) dry dock (n)	mop-up
	muscle-bound

nose-dive (v) nose dive (n)

old-fashioned

open-minded

pain-killer

papier-mache

part-time

pell-mell

penny-pinch (ing), penny
  pincher

pigeon-toe (d)

plug-ugly

point-blank

poker-faced, but poker face

post-mortem (adv) Seven
  cases were examined post-
  mortem. All other uses
  postmortem

pot-shoot (er)

purse-string (adj) purse
  string (n)

push-button (adj) but push
  button (n)

push-up

red-handed

red-hot (adj, n)

right-hand man

right-of-way

roly-poly

runner-up

send-off

set-to (n)

shake-up

shirt-sleeved

short-circuit (v), short-
  circuiter, but short circuit
  (n)

short-haired

sight-seeing, but sightseer

stand-up

strong-arm (adj)

takeoff

take-over

teeter-totter

tie-up

tip-off

top-heavy

top-notch (adj) topnotch (n)

vote-getting, vote getter

walk-up

war-horse

warm-up

whistle-stop

window-shop (v)

witch-hunt

worn-out

4   NUMERALS

4.1   The basic rule is to spell out numbers below 10 and to use figures for those above nine. (But it's the Ten Commandments, the Big Ten, the Northwestern eleven.)

4.2   Write 2d, 3d (not 2nd, 3rd), 22d, 43d, etc.

4.3   Regardless of any other rules, sentences should not begin with numerals; if necessary to start with a number, spell it out: Fifth Army headquarters announced, etc.; but the 5th Army headquarters, etc.

4.4 Ages: John Jones, 6. The 2-month-old child. The Kentucky Derby is a race for 3-year-olds. All ages should be in numerals, including such ages as those of contracts (a 5-week-old agreement. But it's five-week vacation.

4.5 Bible References: 2 Corinthians 4:3. (See 3.14)

4.6 Birthdays: A party was given on her 7th birthday.

4.7 Caliber: 6-inch guns; six 6-inch guns; .38-caliber revolver, etc.

4.8 Centuries: The 9th Century, the 12th Century Crusades, etc.

4.9 Combinations and Series: When the 10-or-above rule dictates that any number in a series be a numeral,

make all numbers in the series numerals. The week's casualties included 24 killed, 175 wounded and 5 missing in action.

4.10 Compound Modifiers: A 2-by-4 board, etc.

4.11 Dates: July 5, 1960, but the Fourth of July or July Fourth. (See 2.28)

4.12 Decimals: 3.2 beer; he batted .333.

4.13 Dimensions: The box was 2 feet wide, 3 feet long, 4 feet deep. But not in distances below 10: His home was four miles away.

4.14 Documents and Papers: Sec. 5, Art. 6. Page 1. Chapter 3. Column 4, etc. (But follow basic style in referring to amendments to the Constitution: Fifth Amendment, 14th Amendment, etc.)

4.15 Election Returns and Votes: Johnson 9, Smith 5. The subcommittee vote was 4 to 3. By a 3-to-3 vote, the subcommittee, etc.

4.16 Fractions: Spell out when used alone; five-eighths, one-fourth. Use figures for all numbers with fractions: 5½, 10¼, etc.

4.17 Height: 5 feet 9 inches (no comma); 5-foot-9-inch as a modifier.

4.18 Latitude and Longitude: 7:48 east; 52°35′5″N, etc.

4.19 Measures: 4 pints 7 ounces (no comma); 3 tablespoons, 6 cups, etc.

4.20 Military: 1st Army, 2d Fleet, 3d Air Force, 4th Corps, 5th Division, etc. 2d Lt. John Jones, 1st Lt. James Brown.

4.21 Missiles: Atlas 2, Titan 3C.

4.22 Money: 5 cents, $2, $3.98, $1,000, $2 million, $4 billion (carry decimalization to one place: $4.4 million, but if an exact amount is given, make it $4,451,342). Same rule applies to nonmonetary numbers. But in a casual reference, spell it out: He risked a million in the deal.

4.23 Music: Op. 2, Op. 103; Hungarian Rhapsody No. 5. (See 3.24)

4.24 Number or When Number Is Understood: Engine Co. 5; No. 8 on the Hit Parade; Chicago's No. 1 public enemy.

4.25 Odds: 3-to-1 favorite; he is giving 7 points, etc.

4.26 Percentages: The stock pays 5 per cent; one-tenth of 1 per cent, three-tenths of 1 per cent, etc. (The symbol % is used only in tabular matter and headlines.) All percentages are in numerals but the hyphen is used only when the use is adjectival: An increase of 5 per cent, but a 5-per cent increase.

4.27 Political Division: 1st Congressional District, 3d Senatorial District, 2d Ward, 4th Precinct, etc.

4.28 Roman Numerals: Use for personal sequence, Pope, war, royalty, act, yacht and horse: John Jones IV, Pope John XXIII, World War II, King George V, Act II, Shamrock IX, Hanover II, etc., but Queen Elizabeth 2 (the ship). (See 3.7)

4.29 Scores: Northwestern 9, Illinois 6; Northwestern won 9-6.

4.30 Sentences: In prison sentences, it's one-year sentence, sentenced to three to four years (but 8 to 12 years, because the 10-or-over rule makes 12 a numeral). Note that hyphens are not used in these terms because the use is not adjectival. But it's three-to-four-year sentence and 8-to-12-year sentence.

4.31 Streets and Numbers: 9 E. 9th; 1234 N. State, etc.

4.32 Temperatures: 2 above zero; 4 below zero (use the form —4 only in tabulations or headlines and layouts).

4.33 Time: 1:55 p.m., 5 a.m.; he won the race in 4:05:16; the running time was 4 hours 9 minutes 16.2 seconds (no commas), etc. (See 3.13)

4.34 Weight: 3 pounds 6 ounces (no commas), etc.

4.35 Spell out indefinite numbers: twenty-odd, between ten thousand and twenty thousand.

4.36 Spell out two-story house, four-mile walk, fifth-grader, etc.

4.37 Plurals of numbers take no apostrophe before the "s": 6s and 7s, 1920s, '30s.

5 SPELLING

5.1 The first preference in spelling is the short version in Webster's New International Dictionary with exception as given in this section; the U.S. Postal Guide; and Webster's Dictionary of Geographic Names.

5.2 Conforming to the agreed spellings of the wire services, we shall use these place names:

Algiers	Bayreuth
Antioch	Beirut
Antwerp	Belgrade
Archangel	Bern
Athens	Brunswick
Baghdad	Bucharest
Bangkok	Cameroun
Basel	Cape Town
Castel Gandolfo	Mukden
Coblenz	Munich
Cologne	Naples
Copenhagen	North Cape
Corfu	Nuernberg
Corinth	Peking
Dunkerque	Pescadores Is.
Florence	Prague
Formosa Strait	Rhodes
Frankfurt	Romania
Genoa	Rome
Goteborg	Saint John, New Brunswick
Gulf of Riga	St. John's, Newfoundland
The Hague	Salonika
Hamelin	Sofia
Hannover	Taipei
Hong Kong	Tehran
Jakarta	Thailand
Katmandu	Tiflis
Kingstown	Turin
Kurile	Valetta
Leghorn	Mt. Vesuvius
Lisbon	Vietnam
Macao	Warsaw
Malagasy	Wiesbaden
Marseille	Zuider Zee
Mt. Sinai	

5.3 It's Vietnam the country, Vietminh the political party and Vietnamese the citizen.

5.4 Where old and new names are used, or where quoted material uses a different form, one is enclosed in parentheses: Taiwan (Formosa); Gdansk (Danzig), etc.

5.5 In Chinese names, the name after the hyphen is lower case: Chiang Kai-shek, Mao Tse-tung. It is Peking People's Daily, People's Republic. By contrast, Korean names usually are three words, all capped, with no hyphens: Chung Hee Park, Kim Il Sung.

Spanish names often have two surnames, the first being the family name of the father, the second that of the mother. Because of this, it is wrong, and nearly always insulting, to use only the mother's family name in second references. Rafael Trujillo Molina, for example, may be called Trujillo Molina or Trujillo in second references, but not Molina alone. One can't go wrong in using both, although the best rule is to use the individual's preference. Adolfo Lopez Mateos, for example, prefers to use both Lopez and Mateos, but Fidel Castro Ruz rarely uses Ruz in second references.

5.6 A consonant after a vowel and ending a final accented syllable is doubled: corral, corralled; transfer, transferred; canal, canalled.

5.7 A final consonant is not doubled when the accent in

the word falls on an earlier syllable: total, totaled; kidnap, kidnaped; channel, channeled; cancel, canceled.

5.8 It is drunken driving.

5.9 It is GI and GIs for persons, GI's and GIs' for possessive.

5.10 Be sure of words ending in ise, ize, yse.

5.11 Some preferred spellings, a few of which are at variance with the dictionary:

adviser
accommodate
acknowledgment
aide (in reference to a person)
airline
allegeable, manageable
alleging, managing
anti-bias
anti-tumor
arbor, ardor, armor
Asian flu
auto; not "automobile"
auto maker, steel maker, but shoemaker
ax

baby-sit
baby-sitter
baby-sitting
baritone
B B gun (no hyphen)
blond (all usage)
boy friend
brunet (all usage)
build-up
buses (vehicles)
businessman, cameraman, newsman

cab, cello, copter, phone (no apostrophe)
cabdriver, cabbie
caddie, caddying
caliber, fiber, theater
cancel, cancelable; cancellation, canceled, cancelling
canvas (fabric)
canvass (solicit)
capital (city); capitol (building, but see 1.9)
catalog, demagog, dialog, epilog, prolog, synagog (no "ue")
catarrh, catarrhal
catsup
cattleman, lumberman, newspaperman
cave-in
cease-fire (n, adj)

chaperon (v, n; masc. and fem.)
chauffeur
cigaret, etiquet, omelet, quartet, but silhouette
clique, plaque (no "c" before "q")
clue
coastguardsman, national guardsman
co-captain, co-chairman, cohost, co-worker, co-pilot
coeducation, but co-ed
coexist
combat, combating, combated
confidant (n; masc. and fem.)
connoisseur
controller
cooky
court-martial (pl. courts-martial)
cross-country, cross-examine

dietitian
disk (disc in zoological sense)
doubleheader
drought
drugstore
duffel
dumfound

employe
embarrass
enclose, enclosure
endorse
ensure (see "insure")
esthetic
eyewitness

fallout
fieldhouse
firsthand, secondhand
flier (aviator); flyer (train)
fulfill
furor

gaiety, gaily
gibe (taunt), jibe (harmonize)
girl friend
good-by

good will (n) good-will (adj)
grandchild, grandson, grandfather, etc.
gray (but Greyhound buses)
great-aunt, great-grandfather, great-great-grandparent, etc.
guerrilla (warfare), gorilla (in zoo)
halfway, midway
hara-kiri
harass
head-on (adj); but the train hit head on.
hemorrhage
hitchhiker
high-rise (all uses)
holdup (n), hold up (v)
homemade, homemaker, homeowner
homestretch, backstretch
home town
hydroelectric
impostor
impresario
interstate, intrastate
insure (See Webster's on "ensure" difference)
ionosphere
isotope
jibe (harmonize), gibe (taunt)
judgment
jujitsu
jukebox
jury room
kegler (bowler)
khaki
kidnaped, kidnaper, kidnaping
lakefront
lambaste, lambasting
left-wing (adj), left-winger (n), left wing (n)
liaison
likable, livable, lovable, etc.
liquefy, stupefy, rarefy
machinegun (v, n, & adj)
marshal (v and n), marshaled, marshaling
miniskirt
molotov cocktail
naphtha
non-co-operation
old-timer
obbligato
one-man, one-vote (adj), one man, one vote (other)

overall, over-all (see 3.38)
paraffin
per cent
percentage
permissible
phony; phonies (pl.)
phosphorous (adj), phosphorus (n)
post office
programmed, programming
propeller

quarterback, fullback

restaurant, restaurateurs
rumba, rumbaed

saber, scepter, sepulcher, etc.
salable, sizable, usable
sanitarium, sanatorium
school board
schoolboy, schoolbook, schoolteacher
sirup
sitdown
skeptical
skillful
skindiver, skindiving
spacecraft, spaceman, spaceship, spacewalk but space flight, space guns, space suit
sportcaster, sportswriter, sports editor
stanch (v)
staunch (adj)
strong-arm
submachinegun
subpena, subpenaed, subpenaing
sulphur
swastika

takeoff (n), take off (v)
teen-aged, teen-ager
thunder shower
thunderstorm

ukulele
under way

vacuum
vice admiral, vice chairman, vice president (but vice-presidential)

wash 'n' wear
weekend
weird
wheel chair
whisky, whiskies
wiretapping

X-ray (v, n & adj)

• • • • •

5.13   Some of the general rules for prefixes and suffixes (don't hesitate to refer to the dictionary):

all (prefix) hyphenated: All-Star

ante, anti (prefix) solid: antebellum, antiaircraft—except in proper noun usage such as anti-American, etc. (but anti-espionage, anti-riot, anti-government, anti-recession, anti-secrecy)

bi (prefix) solid: biennial, bifocal

co (prefix) solid: coequal, coeducation (but many exceptions)

counter (prefix) solid: counterfoil, etc.

down (prefix and suffix) solid: downstroke, touchdown

electro (prefix) solid: electrolysis

ex (prefix) hyphenated: ex-champion

extra (prefix) solid: extraterritorial

fold (suffix) solid: twofold

goer (suffix) solid: churchgoer

in (prefix) solid: insufferable; (suffix) hyphenated: stand-in

infra (prefix) solid: infrared

inter (prefix) solid: interstate

intra (prefix) solid: intrastate, intramural

mid (prefix) solid: midafternoon, midday, midyear, etc.

mini (prefix) solid: miniskirt

multi (prefix) solid: multimillion, multicolored (but multi-ton)

non (prefix) solid: nonpartisan, nonsupport

over (prefix and suffix) solid: overcome, overall (see 3.37), pushover

post (prefix) solid: postwar (but for post-mortem see 3.43)

pre (prefix) solid: predetermine, predawn (but pre-empt, pre-election, etc. See 3.34)

self (prefix) hyphenated: self-defense

semi (prefix) solid: semiannual

sub (prefix) solid: subfreezing

super (prefix) solid: superabundance, superman

trans (prefix) solid: transcontinental, transoceanic (but hyphenated with proper noun: trans-Atlantic, trans-Canadian, etc.)

tri (prefix) solid: trifocal

ultra (prefix) solid: ultraviolet

un (prefix) solid: unshaved, unnecessary (but hyphenated with proper noun: un-American)

under (prefix) solid: underground, underdog

uni (prefix) solid: unicolor

wide (suffix) solid: worldwide, nationwide

yard (suffix): shipyard, stockyards (but Union Stock Yards, Stock Yard Inn), back yard (n), back-yard (adj), front yard (n), front-yard (adj)

6   RELIGION

6.1   There is only one way to refer to religious denominations and members and officials of them—the correct way. While general usage and correct titles of [most] faiths are listed in this section, many are not. In case of doubt, consult authoritative sources.

6.2   Members of the National Council of the Churches of Christ in the U.S.A. (official title, which may be reduced to the National Council of Churches):

African Methodist Episcopal Church
African Methodist Episcopal Zion Church
American Baptist Convention
Antiochian Orthodox Archdiocese of Toledo and Dependencies
Armenian Church Diocese of America
Christian Methodist Episcopal Church
Church of the Brethren
Church of the New Jerusalem
Exarchate of the Russian Orthodox Church in North and South America
Friends United Meeting
Greek Orthodox Archdiocese of North and South America
Hungarian Reformed Church in America
International Convention of Christian Churches (Disciples of Christ)
Lutheran Church in America
Moravian Church in America
National Baptist Convention, U.S.A., Inc.
National Baptist Convention of America
Philadelphia Yearly Meeting of the Religious Society of Friends
Polish National Catholic Church of America
Presbyterian Church in the U.S.
Progressive National Baptist Convention, Inc.
Protestant Episcopal Church
Reformed Church in America
Romanian Orthodox Episcopate of America
Russian Orthodox Greek Catholic Church of America
Serbian Eastern Orthodox Church
Seventh Day Baptist General Conference
Syrian Antiochian Orthodox Church
Syrian Orthodox Church of Antioch
Ukrainian Orthodox Church of America
United Church of Christ
United Methodist Church
United Presbyterian Church in the U.S.A.

6.3   Other communions include:

Roman Catholic Church
Church of Jesus Christ of Latter-day Saints (Mormon)
The First Church of Christ, Scientist
Seventh-day Adventists
Church of Christ
Jehovah's Witnesses
American Lutheran Church
Lutheran Church-Missouri Synod

6.4   Jewish groups are:

Union of American Hebrew Congregations (Reform)
United Synagog of America (Conservative)
Union of Orthodox Jewish Congregations (Orthodox)
Rabbinical groups:

Central Conference of American Rabbis (Reform)
Rabbinical Assembly of America (Conservative)
Rabbinical Council of America (Orthodox)
Union of Orthodox Rabbis (Orthodox)

The Synagog Council of America represents both congregational and rabbinical groups of Orthodox, Reform and Conservative Judaism.

6.5 Capitalize the word "church" when part of a title or when used to designate a religious body as a whole: First Presbyterian Church, the United Methodist Church, the Roman Catholic Church (but, a Roman Catholic church, a Lutheran church, the church).

6.6 Terminology of Jewish groups should be followed in naming the place of worship as a temple or a synagog.

6.7 Capitalize: High Church, Low Church, Holy Land, Holy See, Pope. (See 1.3)

6.8 Capitalize: Bible, Holy Bible, Biblical Scripture, Scripture, Holy Writ, Word of God, Gospel, Testament, Old Testament, Beatitudes, Ten Commandments, Lord's Prayer. Lower-case "bible" when used in nonreligious sense as: the bible of the sports world.

6.9 Lower case: heaven, papal, pontifical, pontiff, blessed sacrament, holy communion, benediction, apostle, mass, requiem mass. (See 1.3, 6.7)

6.10 In general, in writing of clergymen, follow this form:

The Rev. John Jones, but Mr. Jones. Do not use Rev. without first name or initials.

Make it the Rev. Dr. John Jones, Dr. Jones if the degree is held.

6.11 Roman Catholic Usage:

The Rev. John Smith, Father Smith.
The Rt. Rev. Msgr. John Jones, the Very Rev. Msgr. John Jones; Msgr. Jones in second references in both cases.
The Most Rev. John Jones, Bishop of the Denver Roman Catholic diocese; Bishop Jones.
Albert Cardinal Smith, archbishop of the Roman Catholic archdiocese of Chicago; Cardinal Smith.

A mass is offered, celebrated, read or said—never held. High mass is sung, a low mass is said. The rosary is recited or said—never read.

It's Rota; Sacred College of Cardinals.

6.12 Episcopal Usage: A deacon or priest is referred to as the Rev. John Jones; Mr. Jones in a secondary reference. If a priest and he prefers to be called Father Jones (which is usual designation in High Church), that is permissible.

A dean is the Very Rev. John Jones, Mr. Jones, or Dean Jones.

A bishop is the Rt. Rev. John Jones, Bishop Jones.

6.13 Jewish Usage: Rabbi James Wise, Rabbi Wise, Dr. James Wise (where degree is held).

Do not refer to a rabbi as "Rev."

For spelling of Jewish holidays see 1.17.

6.14 Christian Science Usage:

Practitioner, Lecturer, Reader. Do not use "Rev." in any form.
Reader John Holmes of the First Church.
The Mother Church (Boston church only).

6.15 Methodist Usage: Bishop Charles W. Brashares, head of the Chicago area of the United Methodist Church (never Rt. Rev. or Most Rev., because there are no prelates in the Methodist Church). Pastors follow the Rev. John Jones form.

6.16 Latter-day Saints (Mormon) Usage:

President David O. McKay, President McKay.
Elder Harold B. Lee, Elder Lee.
Presiding Bishop Le Grand Richards, Bishop Richards.

6.17 It is incorrect to apply the term "church" to any Baptist unit except a local church. The organization of Southern Baptists is the Southern Baptist Convention. Other faiths have diocese, archdiocese, area, synod, presbytery, etc. Use the correct designation.

7 GOVERNMENT

7.1 Legislative Bodies: Capitalize names of legislative bodies and distinguishing substitutes for such names and terms for secondary references:

City Council (the Council—both only in reference to [a specific city's]).
County Board (the board).
Illinois General Assembly (the General Assembly, the Legislature).
Illinois House (the House).
Illinois Senate (the Senate; 3d Senatorial District, but senatorial).
U.S. Congress (Congress; 5th Congressional District, but congressional).
U.S. House of Representatives (the House).
U.S. Senate (the Senate).

In foreign legislative bodies, capitalize the name but lower case the parenthetical translation: Bundestag (parliament), but West German parliament, Chamber of Deputies (the chamber), Cortes, Diet, House of Commons (Commons).

7.2   Boards and Bureaus:

Illinois Parole and Pardon Board (but the board).
U.S. Weather Bureau (but the weather bureau).
Chicago Board of Health (but the board).
Chicago Board of Education (School Board, the board).

7.3 Committees and Commissions: House Ways and Means Committee (the Ways and Means Committee in a secondary reference; but the committee).

Illinois Commerce Commission (but the commission).

7.4 Departments: Capitalize State Department, Chicago Police Department (but the police department); Chicago Fire Department (but the fire department), Cook County Health Department, Illinois Revenue Department, etc.

7.5 Embassies, Legations, Consulates: The British Embassy (the embassy), the French Legation (the legation), the Swedish Consulate General (the consulate).

7.6 Legislative Areas: 2d Congressional District (the 2d District in second reference; but the district).

5th Ward (the 5th Ward committeeman, but ward, the ward committeeman, etc.).

·   ·   ·   ·   ·

8   TRANSPORTATION

8.1 Airlines: Note variations in form and spelling:

Air Canada
Air France
Alitalia

American Airlines
Braniff International Airways
British Overseas Airways (BOAC)
Canadian Pacific Airlines
Continental Airlines
Delta Air Lines
Eastern Air Lines
El-Al Israel Airlines
Icelandic Airlines
Japan Air Lines
KLM (Royal Dutch Airlines)
Lufthansa German Airlines
Mexicana de Aviacion, S.A. (CMA)
Northwest [Orient] Airlines
Ozark Air Lines
Pan American-Grace Airways
Pan American World Airways (PAA)
Royal Dutch Airlines (KLM)
Sabena Belgian World Airlines
Scandinavian Airlines System
Swissair
Trans World Airlines
United Air Lines
Western Air Lines

The lines in whose names the air lines is two words are: Delta, Eastern, Japan, Ozark, United and Western.

8.2 Railroads: Consult the Official Guide of the Railways for spellings, some of which are:

Chicago & North Western Ry. (C&NW).
Gulf, Mobile & Ohio R.R. (GM&O)
Illinois Central R.R. (the IC).
Penn Central
Santa Fe Ry.
The Rock Island Lines

·   ·   ·   ·   ·

Appendix B
A GLOSSARY OF
NEWSPAPER TERMS

ABC Audit Bureau of Circulations, an organization which compiles statistics on circulation.

ad Abbreviation for advertisement. Usually refers to display advertising.

ad alley Section of production department devoted to composing advertisements.

add (1) Copy to be added to a story already written. (2) Copy mark on such matter, as "add 1 fire."

ad side Same as *ad alley;*[1] sometimes used to refer to advertising department.

advance (1) A preliminary story concerning a future event. (2) A story written in the past tense about an impending event and held for release the moment the event takes place.

advertising cutoff A special rule used to separate advertisements from news matter and from each other. (See also *cutoff rule.*)

agate Type 5½ points in depth, the smallest ordinarily used in newspapers.

agate line The common unit of advertising depth (14 to the inch).

alive Copy or type still usable.

alley Section of a print shop devoted to a particular task. (See *ad alley.*)

all in hand When all copy has been sent to the composing room it is said to be all in hand. (See also *wrap up* and *put to bed.*)

all up Means the copy is all in type.

A.M. A morning paper.

A-matter Material to be set in advance of the main body of the story, often *under-dash* matter. Some use the *ten-add* device.

angle (1) A slant or special aspect of a story. (2) The aspect emphasized in a story.

ANPA American Newspaper Publishers' Association.

---

[1] All italicized words in the body of this glossary may be found as boldface entries.

AP   Associated Press.

APME   Associated Press Managing Editors' Association.

art   A general term for all newspaper illustrations.

ASNE   American Society of Newspaper Editors.

assignment   A reporter's task, usually temporary. (Compare *beat*; see also *general-assignment reporter.*)

assignment book   The city editor's record of assignments given out to reporters.

astonisher   Slang for exclamation point.

back room   The production department, especially of a small newspaper.

back shop   Same as *back room* but often used on larger newspapers as well.

bad break   Term used by printers and makeup editors for difficulties in *breaking* a story from one column to another or one page to another, as when the break comes at the end of a paragraph (giving the reader the impression the story ends there) or when the first line in a column is very short. (See also *widow.*)

bank   (1) A part of a headline (also called a *deck*); usually used to designate a secondary part of a headline. (2) A table in the composing room, usually sloped, used to store type temporarily before it goes into a page form. Often designated by the section of the paper for which it is destined, as "news bank," "sports bank," "ad bank," etc.

banner, banner line   A large headline of one or more lines extending across a page or almost the full width of a page. Also called *line, ribbon, streamer.*

bastard type   Type that does not conform to the standard point system.

beat   (1) A reporter's regular run, as police beat, city-hall beat, etc. (Distinguish from *assignment.*) (2) An exclusive story; *scoop.*

Ben Day   A special engraving process using various patterns to obtain shading effects in line engravings.

binder   A small *banner* head across an inside page usually used with the full text of a speech or an especially long story or to tie in several related stories. (See also *blanket head.*)

bite off   To remove paragraphs at the end of a story in making up the page in order to fit the space. What has been removed is known as the "bite-off."

black-letter type   See *text type.*

blanket head   A headline topping all columns occupied by a certain story (see *binder*) or department (see *logotype*). It may blanket cuts, statistical summaries, etc., as well as news matter.

bleed   A cut bleeds when it runs to the edge of a sheet. (Sometimes used loosely in newspaper makeup to indicate a cut which runs to the edge of an outside column.)

blind ad   A classified ad which does not reveal the identity of the advertiser.

blind interview   An interview story in which the identity of the interviewed person is not revealed. He is often called "a usually well-informed source," "a highly placed official," "a source close to . . .," etc.

block-letter type   See *gothic type.*

blotter   See *police blotter.*

blow up   To enlarge any printed or engraved matter. Such an enlargement is a "blowup."

body type   The type in which most of the newspaper is set; usually 7- or 8-point type. The term "body matter" is sometimes used to indicate that which is to be set in body type. (Distinguish from *display type.*)

boil   To reduce the length of a story, usually by small excisions of "fat," or excess wordage. (Compare *cut.*)

boiler plate   News material, ordinarily *time copy,* in stereotype form and used as *filler* by small newspapers.

boldface   Type which is darker or heavier. Abbreviated "B.F.," "BF," "Bf," "bf." (See also *fullface.*)

book   (1) A page of copy with attached carbons. (2) One average-length *take*—300 to 400 words. (3) A handful of copy on the same story from various sources.

border   Strips of type metal used to form a *box* around a story, head, or ad.

box   An enclosure of rules or border used to give a headline or story prominent display. The so-enclosed head or story is called a "box head" or "box story."

boxall   Copy mark meaning "Enclose several units (head, story, and picture, for example) in a single box."

break   (1) The point at which a story turns from one page to another or, especially, from one column to another (see also *bad break, breakover, jump, wrap*). (2) The point at which a story happens or becomes available for use in the newspaper.

breakover Also called "carryover." (1) To carry a story from one page to another. (2) The portion of a story carried over to an inside page. The page on which breakovers are concentrated is sometimes called the "breakover page." (See also *jump*.)

brightener Short for "page brightener." (1) A brief, amusing feature story. (2) The headline over such a story.

bromide A trite or hackneyed expression.

budget A wire-service or other statement of the day's stories in hand.

bug (1) A typographical device inserted in heads and ads for emphasis or to break up areas of white space (see *dingbat*). (2) A telegrapher's key. (3) The union label of the International Typographical Union.

bulldog The earliest edition of a paper. In the case of Sunday papers, it is often printed several days ahead of its publication date.

bulletin (1) A short lead of important or last-minute news. When it pertains to a story already received, it is usually set in boldface type at the head of the previous story and called a "bulletin precede." (2) The first news transmitted by a press association pertaining to a new and important news event or new devlopment in a running story. A bulletin ranks below a *flash*.

bureau A subsidiary news-gathering force operated by newspapers and press associations at important news centers such as Washington.

business-office must A "must" story ordered by the business office, such as a Page-One box devoted to a promotion.

by-line The reporter's signature carried at the top of a story.

C. & l.c. Copy mark meaning *"caps* and *lower case."*

C. & s.c. Copy mark meaning *"caps* and *small caps."* Rarely used in newspapers.

cablese The skeletonized and telescoped language used in transmitting news by cable to reduce transmission cost.

California case The standard arrangement of letters in each font of hand-set type.

camera-ready copy Copy that is ready for photoengraving or photolithography.

canned copy Publicity material sent to newspapers.

caps Capital letters. (See also *upper case*.)

caption The headline appearing over a piece of art. (Distinguish from *cutline*.)

carryover Same as *breakover*.

case The type container, holding a single *font* of type. "Learning the case" means learning to set type by hand.

casting box Device used to cast papier-mâché matrices into type-high plates.

center To set a short line of type so that an equal amount of space appears to left and right of it.

CGO *Slug* meaning "can go over" marking material which can be held up for use in the next day's issue if necessary.

chalk plate A plate used in making engravings.

challenge To refer a story of doubtful authenticity to the desk chief.

chapel The union organization within a particular shop.

chase The rectangular metal frame into which hot type, engravings, etc., are fitted to make a page form. (Distinguish from *form*.)

check up To verify a story.

cheesecake Leg art.

circus makeup Unorthodox makeup using heavy display type, multiple-column heads, much art, and sometimes color. Traditional rules of makeup are deliberately broken to create a calculatedly frantic effect.

city desk The nerve center of the city room, presided over by the city editor.

city editor The executive editor in charge of the collection and writing (and often the editing) of city news.

city room The place in which the news organization functions.

clean copy Copy requiring few corrections.

clean proof Proof requiring few corrections. (See *galley proof*.)

clean tape Tape for the operation of automatic composition machines that has been corrected.

Cleantape Trade name for a system of tape-operated composition.

clip (1) Abbreviation for "clipping." (2) Editorials and other matter reprinted from other publications.

clipsheet A sheet, usually printed, containing publicity material or news matter. Publicity offices and wire services send out clipsheets.

cold type Composition system that does not use hot-metal linecasting.

color (1) To color a story is to introduce elements of bias. (2) To give a story color is to brighten up the writing with human-interest material. Such a story can be called a "color story."

column (1) Vertical area in a newspaper page, usually 10½ to 13 ems in width. Abbreviated "col." (2) The more or less regular output of a columnist.

column inch The standard unit of advertising space used by smaller newspapers. It is one column wide and one inch deep.

column rule Thin line (usually 1 point or ½ point wide on a 6-point slug) running from top to bottom of the newspaper page between two columns.

composing room Section of the production department devoted to hand and machine composition of news and ads. (Sometimes loosely used to cover the entire *back shop.*)

compositor Worker who sets type by hand or machine.

condensed type Type designed to be narrower than the standard face: the opposite of *extended type.* Extremely narrow versions are called "extra-condensed."

copy Term applied to all manuscript or typescript material.

copy boy The errand boy of the city room.

copy cutter Composing room employee who controls the flow of copy to the compositors; he cuts copy into *takes* of appropriate size, depending on the current necessity for speed, in order to maintain a steady work load on each machine. Also supervises reassembly of type into original story form.

copy desk The desk, often horseshoe shaped, at which copy is edited. On smaller newspapers, frequently all copy is edited at a single *universal desk.* Larger papers usually have several separate copy desks: *cable desk, city desk,* telegraph desk, etc. (See also *rim* and *slot.*)

copy editor Same as *copyreader.*

copy fitting Accommodating copy to space; for example, determining the size of type that will make a given amount of copy fit a predetermined space.

copy holder Proofreader's assistant who holds the copy and reads aloud from it while the proofreader is correcting the proof (or the proofreader may read aloud).

copyreader A newsroom employee who puts copy into final shape before it is sent to the composing room. He corrects language errors, checks for consistency and accuracy, and writes headlines.

copy writer Employee of the advertising department of a newspaper, commercial organization, or especially an advertising agency who prepares advertising copy.

correspondent A reporter who submits out-of-town stories to the newspaper. He may be a "staff correspondent," in which case he is usually a full-time employee, or he may be "on *string,*" hence paid on the basis of the quantity of copy accepted by the newspaper. He may or may not be a full-time member of a *bureau.*

country copy Copy submitted by *correspondents,* usually *stringers,* who cover suburban or rural areas.

cover To get all available news about an event. A reporter "covers a story" when he gets the facts and either writes the story or telephones the facts to a rewrite man. He "covers a beat" by contacting a specific area of news sources daily. Coverage in this sense usually involves the reporter's presence at the scene of the event.

coverage (1) The extent and thoroughness of the newspaper's reporting. (2) The extent and thoroughness of its circulation.

cq Proof mark meaning "correct."

credit line A line acknowledging the source of a story or cut. (Examples: "By the Associated Press," "Arthur M. Vinje Photo.")

crop To cut away portions of a picture to give it the desired size, emphasis and/or composition.

crossline A one-line head which is part of a headline of several decks. It is either centered or full-line.

crusade A newspaper campaign advocating a specific reform.

CRT editing system A system of editing using a cathode-ray tube and a computer or memory bank and producing paper or electronic tape as input for composing machines, among other capabilities.

cub A beginning reporter.

cursive type One of the basic races of type, characterized by connecting flowing lines similar to handwriting.

cut (1) As a noun, any photograph, illustration, diagram—any "art"—used or being prepared for use in a newspaper. (2) As a verb, to reduce the length of a story by cutting out large parts of it, often at the end. (Compare *boil.*)

cutline(s)   Explanatory matter appearing below a cut. The *caption* is the headline over a cut. (Note: In some newspaper offices the two definitions are reversed.)

cutoff rule   A line placed horizontally across one or more columns to separate units such as boxes, cuts, multicolumn heads, etc., from the rest of the page. Their purpose is to guide the reader and avoid confusion. (See also *advertising cutoff.*)

cylinder press   A press commonly used by very small newspapers which prints on separately fed sheets of paper on a revolving cylinder usually coordinated with a shuttling flat bed on which the page forms are clamped.

dateline   (1) The line giving the point of origin and (not always) date of transmission of a story of other than local origin. Usually includes the *ligature* of the wire service which transmitted it: "MADISON, Wis., Sept. 24—(AP)—" The state or country is usually omitted when it is well known. (Compare *undated story.*) (2) The line at the top of Page One giving the date and place the newspaper is published.

dash   (1) A short horizontal line of varying length used to separate parts of a headline, headline from story, or story from other stories. It may also consist of a row of stars, a curved line, etc. The length usually has specific meaning. (See *dinky dash, end dash, jim dash.* Distinguish from *cutoff rule.*) (2) A punctuation mark.

dayside   The part of the news organization that works days. (See also *lobster trick, nightside.*)

dead   News matter which has been *killed*, hence cannot be used in the newspaper. The term applies to both type and copy and includes material which has already been run.

dead bank   A bank in the composing room where *dead* type is assembled.

deadline   The last moment at which copy may be accepted in order to meet a particular edition.

dead stone   Same as *dead bank.*

deck   A part of a headline; sometimes used to refer only to a secondary part of a headline. Usually synonymous with *bank.*

desk   A copy desk.

desk chief   Executive employee supervising a particular copy desk. (See also *slot man.*)

desk editor   A minor executive supervising a group of reporters and/or copyreaders.

devil   A printer's apprentice or helper.

dingbat   Generally, any typographical ornament.

dinky dash   The shortest dash, sometimes only one em in length, used to separate subdivisions of a story within sections separated by a *jim dash.*

display ad   Advertising matter other than classified.

display type   Type larger or heavier than that normally used as the *body type* of a story or an ad.

distribution   (1) The act of putting type back into the *case.* (2) The mechanism on a *Linotype* machine which automatically returns mats to their appropriate channel in the *magazine.* (3) The function carriers perform for subscribers.

district man   (1) A reporter assigned to a particular district of a city, usually a *leg man.* (2) A man who supervises carriers in a specific district.

dog watch   Same as *lobster trick.*

dope   More or less private advance information, often based on gossip and rumor.

dope story   An interpretive article as distinguished from a straight story. Also called a "background" story or *think piece.* Usually written under a *by-line.*

doublet   Term applied to a place where an error appears twice by accident. Also called a "doubleton."

double truck   A two-page editorial or advertising layout made up as one, hence eliminating the *gutter.*

down style   A newspaper style calling for a minimum of capitalization.

DPR, NPR   Telegraph terminology meaning "day press rate" and "night press rate."

drop, drop head, dropline head   A type of headline in which each line is stepped to the right:

THIS, THEN, IS
　　WHAT IS KNOWN
　　　　AS A DROP HEAD

dummy   A diagram or *layout* of a newspaper or magazine page showing the position of each ad, story, head, and cut. The dummy may be full size or reduced.

dupe   Abbreviation for "duplicate." (1) If two stories giving the same facts inadvertently are printed in the same issue, one is a dupe. (2) The carbon copy of a story.

ear   A little box appearing on either side of the Page-One *logotype* generally carrying such information as the weather report, the newspaper's slogan, etc.

edition   Each separate *run* of a newspaper. A newspaper may have several editions, as state edition, early-*mail edition,* market-final edition, etc.

editorialize   To express opinion in a news story or headline.

electrostatic printing   A printing process in which a metallic powder adheres to an electrostatically charged area of a specially treated plate.

electrotype   A copper-plated duplicate of type or art, usually mounted on a wooden base.

em   The square of any given size of type (the letter M in standard type is usually as high as it is wide). The term is most frequently used as an abbreviation to indicate a standard measure of width, the *pica em.* (Distinguish from *quad.*)

en   Half an em.

end dash   A dash indicating the end of a story. It is usually about 6 ems in length. Also called a "6-em dash." (Compare with *dinky dash, jim dash.*)

etaoin shrdlu   A *pi line* frequently used by compositors because it's quick. (The first two vertical rows on a Linotype keyboard appear in that order from top to bottom.) (Compare *flag.*)

exclusive   An exclusive story; *scoop* or *beat.*

extended type   Type designed to be wider than the standard face.

extra   An edition run off in addition to regular editions to cover some important news event. Extras are rare today due to radio-news competition.

face   (1) The characteristic design of type: Cheltenham, Bodoni, Goudy, etc., are names of typefaces. (2) The printing surface of a piece of type.

fake   A falsified story.

family   All type of any one design, including all styles, widths, and sizes.

fat   (1) Used to describe any line, especially a headline, when it contains too many letters to be set in the allowed space. (2) Used to describe extended type.

feature   (1) To give prominent display to a story or to play up a particular angle of a story. (2) A story which is interesting and usually timely but not strictly news. (3) Syndicated matter such as comics, humor panels, columns, etc.

feature finder   An index.

file   (1) To transmit a story by telegraph, teletype, or cable. (2) One day's output by a press association. (3) A collection of back issues.

filler   Short items of *time copy* which can be used to fill out small *holes* in inside pages.

first-day story   A story published for the first time; a story dealing with something that has just happened. (Distinguish from *follow-up* or *second-day story.*)

flag   (1) The *nameplate* or *logotype* at the top of Page One. In some shops it means the *masthead.* (2) A *lead, slug,* or piece of paper inserted in a column of type indicating to the printer that some correction must be made at that point. (Compare *pi line; turn rule.*)

flash   The first brief information of a very important story. The press associations use the terms only for news of extreme moment. Hence, the flash outranks the *bulletin.*

flat-bed press   Any press that prints from type held horizontally on a flat surface. Often used synonymously with *cylinder press.*

flimsy   (1) Thin paper used to make carbon copies. (2) The carbon copy itself.

floor man   A printer who makes up pages at the *stones,* as distinct from a *compositor,* who sets type.

flush   Means "even with the column margin" on either left or right. Thus a "flush-left head" is one which is set even with the margin on the left. "Flush left and right" is a term sometimes used to designate a *full line.* "Flush and indent" is a direction to the compositor to make the first line flush and succeeding lines indented (usually one em.) (See also *hanging indention.*)

fold   The point at which a paper is folded, especially the horizontal fold across the front page.

folio   A page or page number.

follow   (1) A *sidebar,* often separated from the main story by a *jim dash* and (usually) carrying a small head of its own. Abbreviated "folo." (Distinguish from *add.*) (2) A *second-day* or *follow-up* story.

follow-up   (1) As a noun, *a second-day* story. (2) As a verb, to get new information on yesterday's story.

follow copy   (1) On copy, a direction to the compositor to set the type exactly as written, despite seeming errors. (2) On proof, especially proof containing many errors, a direction to the compositor to correct the proof as the copy was written; avoids a lot of proof marking.

font (1) A complete assortment of type of a given design, style, and size. (2) Occasionally, the *case* in which a font of type is stored.

foot slug The slug, usually 12 or 18 points wide, used at the bottom of a column as a buffer between type and *chase*.

form A complete page of type within a *chase*.

format The size, shape, and style of a page, section, or book.

four-color printing A photoengraving process whereby color is reproduced by a set of four separate plates, one each for yellow, blue, red, and black.

fourth estate Traditional name for the press.

front office (1) The business office. (2) Sometimes, especially on small newspapers, all white-collar departments, as distinguished from all production departments.

fudge A detachable part of a page plate which may be chiseled or replaced by another to make possible the last-minute news. Often used in carrying last-minute sports developments. Also called a "fudge box."

fullface An almost obsolete term for *boldface*. Abbreviated "ff."

full line A line of type *flush* to both right and left.

future A note about a story that can be expected to develop later. Such notes are usually kept in a "future book," which may also serve as the *assignment book*.

FYI "For your information."

galley (1) A shallow, three-sided metal tray in which type is placed after being set. (2) A rough measurement of length equivalent to a galley: about 20 inches.

galley proof A proof of a galley of type.

general-assignment reporter A reporter not assigned to a *beat* or to a particular story but available to the city editor for whatever *assignments* turn up.

ghost A ghost writer—one who writes stories for another's signature.

glancer Slang for an at-a-glance feature which sums up a story or series of related stories or the main stories of the day.

glossy Short for "glossy print," a shiny-finished photographic print favored by photoengravers.

goodnight The closing of a news department after a final edition. To "get goodnight" is to be released from duty.

gothic type One of the basic races of type, characterized by no serifs and strokes of equal weight.

grapevine Miscellaneous *time copy* already in type.

graveyard shift Same as *lobster trick*.

green proof Uncorrected *proof*.

gray out A page grays out in a particular area when that area consists largely or entirely of body type, producing a gray and uninteresting appearance.

guide, guideline The identifying *slug* placed at the beginning of every piece of copy.

gutter The margin between facing pages.

hairline A very thin *rule*.

halftone A screened photoengraving. A picture is photographed through a screen and etched onto a metal plate in such a way that small dots of varying size produce a printed effect of lights and shadows.

handout A press release supplied by a publicity agent.

handstuck Set by hand. (See also *stick*.)

hanging indention A headline or part of a headline set "*flush* and indent." Its first line is a full line and the rest are indented, usually one em. The last line may or may not be flush to the right. (See also *square indention*.)

hard news News based on hard facts that are new. (Compare *soft news*.)

head rule The line running horizontally across the top of the page. It separates the columns from the dateline, page number, etc.

head schedule A record of the typefaces and positioning of all headlines used in a particular newspaper, usually specifying the unit count for each. Sometimes abbreviated "hed sked."

head slug A *slug*, usually 6 points deep, separating the first line of a news column from the *head rule*.

hell box Box or other receptacle into which discarded type is thrown.

hold, hold for release "Delay publication until further orders."

hold the paper, hold the press An instruction to hold up an edition in order to include some news of superlative importance. More frequently used on movie sets than in newspaper offices.

hole (1) The space available for news after ads and *musts* are in. Sometimes called "news hole." (2) Any vacant space in a page *form* or a page *dummy*.

hot type Type cast from molten metal. The *Linotype* and *Monotype* systems, for example, cast hot type. (Compare *cold type*.)

hook A spindle used to hold copy or proof. (See also *spike*.)

human-interest story A pleasant little news oddity, usually brief.

HTK Copy mark meaning "head to come"; indicates that the headline will be written and sent to the composing room later.

imposing stone Full title of *stone*.

indent (1) As a verb, to make indentation, *i.e.,* to leave space at either end of a line. (2) As a noun (pronounced "INdent"), an indented story or an indented portion of a story. Thus, a "boldface indent" is a story set in boldface type and indented on both sides.

index A guide to the news and/or features to be found on the inside pages, usually placed on the front page.

insert Later information to be put into the body of a story already sent to the composing room. The first is usually marked at the top of the copy "Insert A," the second "Insert B," etc. (Distinguish from *add, ruled insert*.)

intaglio printing Printing process differing from letterpress and photolithography in that it prints from ink in a depressed surface rather than on a raised surface. (See also *rotogravure*.)

Intertype Trade name for a typesetting machine similar to the *Linotype*.

inverted pyramid (1) The standard straight news story form, with the facts in descending order of importance. (2) A headline form, especially for secondary decks. The first line is usually set full line and the others are centered, each shorter than the one above. Now fairly archaic.

issue One day's newspaper. It may consist of several *editions*.

italics Italic type: characters slant to the right. Abbreviated when marking copy "itals." or "ital."

ITU International Typographical Union.

jim dash A short dash, usually about 3 ems in length, used between decks of a headline, between a story and its *follow*, etc. Sometimes called a "short dash" or a "3-em dash." (Compare *dinky dash, end dash*.)

job An order for commercial printing.

job press Any press devoted to commercial printing.

jump The continuation of a story from one page to another (but not from one column to another on the same page). Such a story is called a "jump story." The portion on the first page ends with a "jump line" ("Continued on Page 6"; "See FIRE, Page 3"), and the portion carried inside begins with a "jump head" and a "jump line" ("Continued from Page 1"). (See also *breakover, carryover;* distinguish from *turn, wrap*.)

Justape Brand name for a computer system for justifying lines before automatic typesetting.

justify To space out a column or line of type to appropriate length. Thin *leads* are inserted between lines to bring all columns to an equal length in order that the page may be locked up. A line of type is justified by adjusting word spacing.

kicker A line just above and part of a headline, often underlined, identifying the story briefly or pointing up an interesting sidelight. Also called "overline."

kill To eliminate all or part of a story, whether in copy or type. A story is killed by *spiking;* type is killed by throwing it into the *hell box*.

label head A dull, lifeless headline, usually lacking a verb. (Distinguish from *standing head*.)

late watch Same as *lobster trick*.

layout (1) A combination of stories, pictures, diagrams, etc., about a single subject. (2) Arrangement of pictures or other art work from which a single *cut* is made. (3) *Dummy*.

layout man (1) An artist who prepares special arrangements of pictures and type for advertising and news displays. (2) A composing-room employee who designates the form and sizes in which advertising type is to be set.

lead (pronounced "led") A thin strip of metal of varying length and from 1 to 4 points in thickness used for additional space between lines of type. For example, a *lead* (leed) may be "leaded (ledded) out" to produce more white space and hence greater contrast. (See also *justify;* distinguish from *slug.*)

lead (pronounced "leed")   (1) The first paragraph (or paragraphs) of a news story (compare *top*). (2) A tip which may lead to a story.

leaders (pronounced "leeders")   A row of dots, often used in tabular material, to guide the reader's eye.

lead (or **lede**) **to come**   Copy mark indicating that the lead will be sent to the composing room later. This is often done with a running story in order to save many revisions of the lead as the story develops.

leg man   A reporter who works "the street," gathering facts which he telephones to the *rewrite man.*

letterpress printing   Printing process in which ink is applied to paper by means of a raised surface. The original printing process.

letter space   To insert thin spaces between letters in a line of type.

library   Same as *morgue.*

lift   (1) To carry type forward from one edition to the next. (2) To steal another reporter's story.

ligature   (1) A group of letters formed as one character. The common ones are ff, fi, fl, ffl and ffi. (2) The letters designating a wire service—AP, UPI, etc.

linage, lineage   The number of agate lines of advertising printed in a specific period.

line   (1) Same as *banner* or *top line.* (2) Short for *agate line.*

line cut   An unscreened engraving which prints only black and white. Also called a "line engraving." (Distinguish from *halftone.*)

line gauge   The printer's ruler, marked off in picas and inches, and often nonpareils and/or agates, too.

Linotype   Abbreviated "Lino." (1) Trade name for a typesetting machine which sets a line of type at a time. (2) Generically, all typesetting machines of that kind (spelled with a lower-case "l").

live type   Type which may still be used.

lobster trick   The skeleton staff which takes over after the last edition of a morning paper has gone to press. Also called "lobster shift," "dog watch," and "late watch."

local   A local news story, usually a *personal.*

localize   To play up a local *angle* in a telegraph story.

lock up   To *justify* the columns and tighten the *quoins* on a page *form* before it goes to the *pressroom.* The process is called "lockup."

log   (1) Short for *logotype.* (2) A city editor's *assignment book.*

logotype   A word or words cast on one line of type. Often used to refer to the *nameplate* of a newspaper, which is usually cast as a logotype, and to section headings such as "Capital Times Sports." (Distinguish from *ligature.*)

lower-case letters   Small letters; so called because in early type cases they were in the lower, nearer section. Abbreviated "l.c." in marking copy for composition.

Ludlow   Trade name of a typesetting machine which casts display-size slugs from hand-set matrices up to 144 points in size. Used in setting headlines and display advertising.

magazine   The part of an automatic typesetting machine which stores the matrices while not in use.

mail edition   An edition, usually an early one, distributed principally by mail to out-of-town subscribers.

makeover   The process of making a new *stereotype plate* for a newspaper page to add late stories, bring existing stories up to date, make *must* corrections, etc. Page One and often other pages are made over for each new edition. Also called *replate.*

makeready   The process of preparing a page *form* or *stereotype plate* (depending on the type of press) for the press *run.* It consists of making adjustments in the height of the type or the plate and in the *tympan* to assure even printing and the proper placement of the printing on the sheet.

make up   To arrange pictures and news matter in a page for maximum effectiveness. The noun "makeup" refers to the effect produced. It is usually supervised by a "makeup editor" who directs the work of production-department employees called "makeup men."

makeup rule   A flat piece of steel used by printers in inserting or lifting a line out of a galley or form, to scrape edges of type, to make type stand on its feet, and in many other tasks. Virtually the badge of the trade.

mandatory kill   A message used by press services to make certain that an erroneous or libelous story already sent is eliminated by member or client newspapers.

markets   Term for the section of the paper devoted to news of securities, grain, livestock, etc.

masthead   (1) Statement of name of paper, its ownership, place of publication, subscription rates, etc., usually appearing on the editorial page. (2) Incorrectly used as synonym for *nameplate*.

matrix   Plural: "matrices." Abbreviated "mat." (1) The papier-mâché impression of an entire page from which *stereotype plates* are cast or of a single cut or ad. (2) The little brass mold from which a single letter is cast.

mat roller   The machine which makes a page matrix (mat) for casting plates.

measure   Printer's term meaning "length of line."

Media Records, Inc.   A national organization which reports facts about newspaper advertising.

mill   Slang for "typewriter."

milline rate   A unit for measuring the advertising rate of a publication in relation to circulation—specifically, the cost of one agate line per thousand readers.

minion   Seven-point type.

Monotype   Trade name of a typesetting machine which casts a single letter at a time in justified lines. (*Linotype* and *Intertype* machines cast a line at a time.)

more   Copy mark at the end of a page to indicate that the story does not end here—more is coming.

morgue   The newspaper's repository for clippings, cuts, mats, photographs, and all kinds of reference material.

mortise   To excise an area from an engraving in order to insert another engraving, type, or other matter.

must   A copy mark, usually ordered by an executive, meaning that the copy must run that day without fail, as *business-office must*.

nameplate   The newspaper's name in large type at the top of the front page. (Compare *logotype;* distinguish from *masthead*.)

NANA   North American Newspaper Alliance, a news syndicate.

national advertising   Advertising of trademarked products which are or could be sold throughout the nation.

NEA   (1) National Editorial Association, an organization of weekly and small daily newspaper editors. (2) Newspaper Enterprise Association, a general feature service.

new lead   A lead paragraph or several paragraphs, usually based on new material, to be substituted for the top of the story already received or in type. Also called "new top."

news hole   See *hole*.

nightside   The night shift of either a morning or afternoon newspaper. (Compare *dayside, lobster trick*.)

nonpareil   Six-point type.

obituary   A biography of a dead person, abbreviated "obit." "Canned obits" are obituaries prepared in advance of the person's death and filed in the *morgue*.

off its feet   Describes type that does not stand straight up and thus makes only a partial impression of each line or character.

offset   (1) Photolithographic printing, so called because of the nature of the process (see *photolithography*). (2) The effect obtained when the back side of a printed sheet carries an accidental impression.

OCR   Optical Character Recognition; involves electronic scanning and identification of characters at high speeds, producing input for any purpose, including composition.

outline cut   A halftone in which the background has been cut away.

overline   Same as *kicker*.

overset   Type which has been set but cannot be used due to lack of space. Similarly, an edition is "underset" when the quantity of news in type is insufficient to fill the available space.

pad   To make a story or headline longer by using more words than are necessary.

page brightener   See *brightener*.

page proof   The proof of an entire page, usually pulled to catch such errors as unmatched stories and heads or cuts and captions, gross headline errors, and other makeup errors.

paste down   A method of composing display type for photolithography. The compositor simply chooses the letters from an adhesive-backed alphabet and pastes them down.

pasteup   The process in offset printing of making up a page for the camera—pasting in proofs of heads, body type, and line drawings.

patent, patent insides   Same as *readyprint*.

perforator Any machine that perforates tape for automatic typesetting.

personal A short news item, usually of one paragraph, about routine comings and goings of residents of the community. Often called a *local.*

photocomposition Any system that composes type photographically.

photolithography A printing process wherein ink is applied to paper not directly from type but from a rubber roller that has taken the impression from the plate.

pi Hopelessly jumbled type.

pica (1) Twelve points. (2) Twelve-point type.

pica em Twelve points by twelve points; a basic unit of length and of area.

pick up To add material already set. Such material is called "pickup." A "pickup line" gives directions as to the point in the new material at which the old is to be added.

pi line A machine-set line which has been filled out with random letters; or a type-high blank *slug* used at the top or bottom of a take to indicate that there is more to come on that story. (See also *etaoin shrdlu;* compare *flag, turn rule.*)

pix Short for "pictures."

planer Wooden block struck by printers with a mallet to level a form while it is being locked up.

plate The single piece of metal or plastic from which a page is printed—directly, in letterpress; indirectly, in offset.

platen press A small job press which works with an open-and-shut motion, pressing an inked flat form against a platen carrying a flat sheet of paper.

play The position and typographical treatment—*i.e.,* emphasis—given a story. A story can be given "heavy" or "big" play, "light" or "little" play, can be "played up" or "played down."

P.M. An afternoon (evening) newspaper.

point (1) The unit of measurement in which type sizes are designated—approximately one seventy-second of an inch. (2) A term for the period.

police blotter The record of the day's events kept in all police stations, usually available to police reporters.

policy story A story which reflects the newspaper's stand on an issue.

pony service An abbreviated wire news service, usually delivered by telephone or commercial telegraph to smaller newspapers. Also called the "pony wire."

precede New developments on a story from a different point of origin. (See also *bulletin.*)

predate An edition issued before its announced time of publication. (See also *bulldog.*)

preferred position Advertising-department term referring to a special arrangement under which, for an established increase in rate, the advertiser is assured the position in the paper he desires. Otherwise the advertiser must take his chances as to where the ad will run. (See *run of paper.*)

press agent A person hired by an institution, business establishment, or individual to obtain favorable publicity in the press.

proof An inked impression of type or of an engraving taken before it actually runs in the newspaper in order to correct errors.

proof press The press used to take *proofs.* The process is known as "pulling" a proof.

proofreader Composing-room employee who reads proof for typographical errors and to see that it conforms to copy.

public relations The science and art of attitude control. A public-relations man seeks to create public favor for his employer not only by pushing his employer's product effectively, but also by advising his employer on policies affecting public attitudes; hence, a broader field than *press agentry.*

puff A personal publicity story or other favorable personal mention.

pullout A newspaper section designed to be easily separated from the rest of the paper.

put to bed Close and ready for the press all pages of an edition.

Q and A Copy in question-and-answer form, such as verbatim testimony.

quad A large blank character used for spacing in lines of type. An em quad is a blank character as wide as it is high. An en quad is half as wide as it is high.

query (1) Brief summary of a story sent to the newspaper by a correspondent, usually including estimated length. The executive editor replies by stating the number of words desired. (2) Press-association term for a question asked by a member newspaper or subscriber.

quoin   One of a pair of wedge-shaped metal locks used to hold a page form together so that it can be lifted and carried. Quoins are tightened in the process of *lockup* with a "quoin key."

railroad   To rush copy to the composing room without close editing or proofreading; an emergency measure.

readout   A headline or deck subordinate to a streamer or a multiple-column news display head which is directly followed by the story.

readyprint   Newsprint with one or more inside pages already printed with features and ads. Also called "patent."

register   Correct placement of printing on the sheet. In color printing, register means the correct placement of each plate so that the colors mesh properly. (See *four-color printing*.)

release   (1) To permit publication of a story at a specified date and/or hour (see *hold for release*). (2) The order on the copy setting forth the release time. (3) A common term for a publicity handout. (4) A statement by a photographed person authorizing use of the photograph.

replate   To recast a page of type in order to insert later information or make corrections between editions. (See also *makeover*.)

reprint   Material carried from late editions of one day's paper to the early editions of the next, sometimes so labeled.

retail advertising   Advertising designed to sell goods locally at retail.

revise   A second proof made after the first has been corrected to check for possible errors in the corrections.

rewrite   (1) To write a story again to improve it. (2) To revise a story already carried in another newspaper. (3) To write a story from facts given by another reporter, usually a *leg man*. The reporter who rewrites is the "rewrite man"; he often works at the "rewrite desk."

ribbon   Same as *banner*.

rim   The outer edge of the copy desk around which *copyreaders* sit, as opposed to the *slot* or inner edge presided over by the executive in charge of the desk.

ring   To circle a copy correction.

roller   Cylindrical, revolving press attachment which spreads ink over the plate before each impression.

roman type   (1) One of the basic races of type, characterized by serifs and strokes of unequal weight. (2) Upright type, as distinguished from italics. Abbreviated in marking copy "rom."

rotary press   A *web-fed letterpress* press that prints from rotating curved plates.

rotogravure   An *intaglio* printing process in which copy is chemically etched out on a copper roller. Abbreviated "roto" or "gravure."

routing   (pronounced like "out," not "oot")   Removing metal from blank areas in a casting or cut which might otherwise print or smudge. This is done either by hand or with a power router.

rule   A type-high metal strip that prints as a line or lines. (See also *advertising cutoff, column rule, cutoff rule, head rule, makeup rule, turn rule;* distinguish from *dash*.)

ruled insert   A short story related to another larger story and inserted between rules within the body of the main story.

run   (1) Another term for a reporter's regular *beat*. (2) A press run; *edition*. (3) To print a story.

run in   Copy mark directing the compositor to incorporate two or more paragraphs into one or to convert tabular matter into paragraph form.

running story   (1) Same as *sectional story*. (2) A story which develops over a period of several days or more.

run of paper   (1) Advertising which does not rate *preferred position*, hence may be placed anywhere in the paper that is convenient to the makeup man. Abbreviated ROP. (Compare *wild*.) (2) Run-of-paper color is the capability of using color on any page.

runover   Same as *breakover*.

sacred cow   A subject or personality that always receives favorable news treatment in a given newspaper.

SAP   "Soon as possible." In wire-service messages it has even taken the form "SAPPEST"—"even sooner than possible."

Scan-a-Graver   Trade name for a machine that produces halftones electronically on a plastic plate.

schedule   Abbreviated "sked." (1) The city editor's record of assignments. (2) The copy editor's record of stories handled. (See also *head schedule*.)

scoop   An exclusive story.

second-day story   A story covering new developments on a story printed in a previous news cycle. (See also *follow-up.*)

second front page   The first page of the second section when it carries entirely or largely news matter. (Compare *split page.*)

sectional story   A story received on the news wire in several segments and/or sent to the composing room in several *takes.*

see copy   Copy or proof mark telling the composing room to correct a story as it was shown in the copy.

send down, send out   To send a story from the copy desk to the composing room.

separate   A story played separately from a related one.

series   (1) All sizes of a single face of type. (2) Several related stories, usually under a *by-line,* run on successive days.

set and hold   Copy mark meaning "Set in type and hold for release."

shank   The main body or stem of a piece of type.

shirttail   Slang for *follow.*

short   A minor, brief story.

short dash   Same as *jim dash.*

shoulder   The space on a piece of type between the bottom of the character and the edge of the *slug* or *shank* on which it is cast.

side, sidebar   A story connected with another more important story and usually run beside the main story or beside its carryover. Sometimes also called a *with story.*

sidelight   A story run in connection with a major event which gathers together odds and ends of information pertaining to it, including color and personalities.

signature   The name of the advertiser as displayed in the ad. Often shortened to "sig cut."

sizing   The process of determining the size of a cut.

skeletonize   To reduce copy to bare essentials by eliminating articles, etc.—for headline purposes or to reduce cable tolls.

skyline   Term sometimes used for a *banner* head that runs above the *nameplate.*

slant   (1) To manipulate facts unobjectively. (2) To emphasize a certain aspect of a story.

slot   The inner edge of the horseshoe-shaped copy desk. (Compare *rim.*)

slot man   The head of the copy desk, so-called because he sits in the *slot.*

slug, slugline   (1) A story's identifying mark; may be either the briefest possible statement of the nature of the story, as "hotel fire," or the first line or first few words of the headline; usually includes the headline designation, as "#2 HOTEL FIRE." May be used as a verb. Also called *guide, guideline.* (2) A Linotype line. (3) A piece of line-spacing material thicker than a *lead,* usually 6 points. (See also *head slug* and *foot slug.*)

small caps   Small capital letters, as opposed to full-size capitals. Rarely used in newspaper printing. Abbreviated "s.c." in marking copy.

soc, sox   Society.

soft news   Usually interpretive pieces and situationers that contribute more perspective than new facts. (Compare *hard news.*)

solid   Unleaded type; *e.g.,* 9-point type on a 9-point slug.

space bands   Thin wedge-shaped devices used on line-casting machines to provide spacing between words and at the same time *justify* lines.

space grabber   Slang for *press agent.*

spike   A spindle on which discarded copy is placed. Hence, to spike a story means to discard it.

split   A change in transmission point in a regional wire; as, the first state split.

split page   The first page of the second section, whether or not it carries news matter. (Compare *second front page.*)

spot news   News obtained at the scene of the event, hence fresh, live news. Usually used to refer to unexpected events.

spread   (1) A story and its related *with* stories and art given prominent display. (2) Any big *layout,* especially an elaborate pictorial layout.

square indention   The form taken by a secondary deck when all lines are set flush to an indentation. (Compare *hanging indention.*)

squib   A short item.

standard type   Type of standard width. (Compare *condensed* and *extended type.*)

standing Any matter which is retained in type from one edition to the next.

standing heads Heads, usually label heads, which are kept standing in type and used again and again, such as *town lines* used in *country copy.*

state editor Editor who supervises staff men or *correspondents* covering the surrounding area. He may also supervise an independent state copy desk.

stereotype (1) To convert the flat newspaper page into a semicylindrical metal *plate* to fit a rotary press; a "mat" of the page is made and then cast. (2) Same as *bromide.*

stet Copy or proof mark meaning "Let it stand." Used to indicate that a correction is in error and the copy should run as originally written or set.

stick (1) A metal tray used to hold type while it is being set by hand; also called a "composing stick." (2) A rough unit of length: a stick is about two inches of type or about 100 to 150 words; also called a "stickful."

stone Steel- or marble-topped table on which page forms are made up.

straight news A factual recital of news without coloring, embellishment, or interpretation.

streamer Same as *banner.*

string (1) Newspaper clippings pasted together end to end or pasted into a book. (2) A single reporter's total output in a given period.

stringer A reporter who is on *string* or "on space," *i.e.,* paid by the inch.

style sheet A compilation of typographical, spelling, capitalization, grammar and other rules of uniformity and good taste applying to a particular publication.

sub A copy mark telling the editor or the compositor to substitute a piece of copy for another already received, as "sub for second add—fire."

subhead A short head, usually of one line, usually set in boldface body type, serving to break up the monotony of a solid column of small type; usually written about the part of the story directly below it.

suburban copy News copy covering outlying territory. Not essentially different from *country copy.*

symposium interview An interview story involving more than one interviewee, whether interviewed in a group or separately, on a particular topic.

syndicate An organization which buys and sells feature material of all kinds. It may or may not be connected with a newspaper, chain of newspapers, or wire service. (Not a proper term for "wire service.")

tabloid A newspaper of small page size, usually five columns wide and sixteen to eighteen inches deep.

take A short section of copy not a complete story in itself. A *running* or *sectional story* usually goes to the composing room in takes; the copy cutter may break it up into even smaller takes.

tear sheet A full newspaper page torn from the paper and mailed to the advertiser as partial proof of insertion.

telegraph editor The executive in charge of handling telegraph or wire news as distinguished from local news. He may also supervise the newspaper's own foreign and domestic correspondents. On larger papers his duties may be divided among a state editor, a cable editor, and a telegraph editor. On smaller papers he edits all wire copy himself.

teletype The automatic printer used to receive wire news.

Teletypesetter The brand name, often used generically, as in this book, for a system of automatic linecasting. It includes a perforator which cuts paper tape and an attachment to the keyboard of the linecasting machine which operates the machine automatically from the perforated tape.

ten-add A device allowing the desk to send extensive details of the story before the *top* is sent. The first *take* is marked "ten-add," the second "eleven-add," etc. (See also *A-matter, under-dash matter.*)

text type One of the basic races of type, characterized by its blackness, ornateness, and resemblance to medieval manuscript writing.

think piece A background or opinion article.

30 Copy mark meaning "the end," often written at the end of a piece of copy; slash marks (////) or a cross-hatch (#) are more common. In some offices "30" means only the end of the day's work or the end of a news cycle.

ticker Slang for *teletype.*

tie-back The part of a story which connects it with some previous event.

tie-in The part of a story which connects it with some other, perhaps more important, story. Local *angles* are often dug up to tie in with some national news event.

tight   Generally: too full, overcrowded. Applies to lines of type, pages, sections, entire editions.

time copy   Copy which is relatively timeless. It may be used any time within a reasonable period; hence it is usually backlogged to fill *holes* in a "loose" paper. The term applies whether it is in copy or type.

tip   A bit of information which leads to a story, whether it originates with the news staff or elsewhere.

toenails   Slang for "parentheses."

tombstone   To place side by side two or more headlines similar in typeface, type size, and depth.

top   The opening paragraphs of a story; press associations especially use it in such orders as "hold for new top." (Compare *lead.*)

top deck   The first and most important part of a headline.

top line   The top *banner* when there is more than one.

town line   A standing head used on the state or suburban page to indicate the point of origin of the news carried below it.

tr   (1) Proof mark meaning "transpose." (2) The copy mark for *turn rule.*

trim   Same as *boil.*

turn, turn column   A column out of which a story may be *wrapped* without the necessity for a jump head, *i.e.,* a column on a page that has one to the right of it. Even the right-hand column on Page One is a turn column on papers which allow a story to wrap into the first column on the second page without a jump head.

turn rule   A rule or type-high slug turned upside down in a galley to indicate that an addition or change must be made at that point before the type goes into the forms. When marking copy for composition, it is abbreviated "tr." (Compare *flag; pi line.*)

turn story   A story begun in one column and continued in the next. (See also *wrap.*)

turtle   A metal truck used to transfer a page *form* from the *stone* to the *mat roller.*

tympan   The surface which backs up the paper while the printing impression is being made.

typeface   See *face.*

type-high   The height of type—.918 inches—hence, anything that will show in print: a type-high rule, slug, etc. Anything less than type-high will show in print as *white space.*

typo   (1) Slang for "typographical error." (2) Slang for a member of the *ITU.*

undated story   Story which originates in several places at once, such as a weather roundup, and hence either carries no *dateline* or substitutes a *credit line,* such as "By the Associated Press," for the dateline.

under-dash matter   Prepared, detailed material which can be added to today's story; a "canned *obit,*" for example, can be added to the brief announcement of a death to flesh out the story. Such material usually is separated from today's story by a *dinky dash.*

underlines   Sometimes used synonymously with *cutlines.* (See also *caption.*)

Unifax   The *UPI* system of transmitting photographs by wire.

universal desk   A copy desk at which all copy, except for such specialized copy as sports and society, is handled.

UPI   United Press International.

upper case   Capital letters. (See also *caps;* compare *lower case.*)

up style   A newspaper style calling for much capitalization.

urgent   Wire-service designation for material of several paragraphs, whether a whole story, a *new lead,* or an *add,* with priority just below that of *bulletin.*

wash drawing   A brushwork illustration. Besides black and white it has varying shades of gray. *Halftones,* not *line cuts,* are made from them.

web or **web-fed press**   A press that prints on continuous paper rolls.

white space   Blank space in ads, heads, etc., left open for attention value.

widow   Printer's term for a short word or part of a word standing alone on the last line of a paragraph of body type, especially when it occurs as a *bad break.*

wild   A story that is wild may go on any inside page. (Compare *run of paper.*)

Wirephoto   The telephonic photo-transmission system operated by the Associated Press.

with story   A *side* story on a bigger story; provides an at-a-glance summary of the bigger story or tells another closely related story.

workup A printing error caused when spacing material or the blank ends of linotype slugs work up to type-high and thus print unintentionally.

wrap To continue a story from one column to the next (always to the right). (Compare *break, breakover, jump.* See also *turn.*)

wrap in To fuse details from one story into another.

wrap up In general: finish. An edition is wrapped up when all copy has gone from the copy desk to the composing room. A story is wrapped up when all the facts are in.

wrong font Type of one size or style appearing erroneously with type of another size of style. Proof mark is "wf."

X-correct A proof of a story accompanying change copy marked to show the composing room where and how the change copy is to be treated.

Xerography Electrostatic printing.

Index